Paris

"All you've got to do is decide to go
and the hardest part is over.

So go!"

TONY WHEELER, COFOUNDER — LONELY PLANET

CATHERINE LE NEVEZ, JEAN-BERNARD CARILLET,
CHRISTOPHER PITTS, NICOLA WILLIAMS

Contents

COVID-19

We have re-checked every business in this book before publication to ensure that it is still open after the COVID-19 outbreak. However, the economic and social impacts of COVID-19 will continue to be felt long after the outbreak has been contained, and many businesses, services and events referenced in this guide may experience ongoing restrictions. Some businesses may be temporarily closed, have changed their opening hours and services, or require bookings; some unfortunately could have closed permanently. We suggest you check with venues before visiting for the latest information.

Île de la Cité (p195)
Art nouveau metro sign

Les Halles (p121)
A traditional brasserie near Tour St-Jacques

Montmartre
& Northern Paris
p132

Champs-Élysées &
Grands Boulevards
p92

Louvre &
Les Halles
p106

Le Marais,
Ménilmontant
& Belleville
p154

Eiffel Tower
& Western Paris
p80

St-Germain
& Les Invalides
p222

The Islands
p194

Latin
Quarter
p205

Bastille &
Eastern Paris
p180

Montparnasse
& Southern Paris
p246

Right: rue de
l'Abreuvoir in
Montmartre
(p132)

CATARINA BELOVA/SHUTTERSTOCK ©

WELCOME TO
Paris

Paris' grandeur is inspiring, but what I love most about the city is its intimacy. Its quartiers (quarters) are like a patchwork of villages, and while it's one of the world's major metropolises – with all of the culture and facilities that go with that – there's a real sense of community at the local shops, markets and cafes that hasn't changed since my childhood. Yet because every little 'village' has its own evolving character, I'm constantly discovering and rediscovering hidden corners of the city.

By Catherine Le Nevez, Writer
For more about our writers, see p416.

Paris' Top Experiences

ICONIC MONUMENTS

Paris' streetscapes – lamplit bridges, awning-shaded cafe terraces filled with wicker chairs, and broad boulevards lined with cream-coloured Haussmannian apartment buildings – are emblematic. More recent structures like the Louvre's glittering pyramid and the Fondation Louis Vuitton's glass sails have meshed into the architectural fabric of the city, while famous monuments such as its arch and tower have become synonymous with Paris.

Above: Pont Alexandre III (p97)

Eiffel Tower

Although no one could imagine Paris today without its signature spire (pictured right), Gustave Eiffel only constructed this graceful 320m-high tower – then the world's tallest – as a temporary exhibit for the 1889 Exposition Universelle (World Fair). Its popularity saw it become the defining fixture of the city's skyline. p82

Arc de Triomphe

Paris' magnificent, intricately sculpted triumphal arch (pictured above), completed in 1836 to commemorate Napoléon's 1805 victory at Austerlitz, guards the Champs-Élysées. Some of the best vistas in Paris radiate from the top. p94

Hôtel des Invalides

Louis XIV built the Hôtel des Invalides (pictured above) in the 1670s to house 4000 *invalides* (disabled war veterans). In the Cour d'Honneur, the Musée de l'Armée showcases French military history. Napoléon is laid to rest in the golden-dome-topped Église du Dôme. p231

2 ARTISTIC TREASURES

With an illustrious artistic pedigree – Renoir, Picasso, Monet, Manet, Dalí and Van Gogh are but a few of the masters who have lived and worked here over the years – Paris is one of the world's great art repositories. In addition to world-famous national museums, scores of smaller establishments feature every imaginable genre, diverse venues mount major exhibitions through to offbeat installations, and the city is filled with vibrant street art.

Musée du Louvre

The *Mona Lisa* and *Venus de Milo* are among the priceless treasures housed inside the fortress turned royal palace turned France's first national museum, the labyrinthine Musée du Louvre (pictured below). One of the best ways to discover its incomparable artworks and artefacts is by following thematic trails, from the 'Art of Eating' to 'Love in the Louvre'. p108

Musée Rodin

At the lovely Musée Rodin, Auguste Rodin's former workshop and showroom is filled with sculptural masterpieces such as *The Kiss*, while its rambling sculpture garden is a romantic setting to contemplate works like *The Thinker* (pictured above). p230

Musée d'Orsay

Within grand former railway station Gare d'Orsay, richly coloured walls at the Musée d'Orsay (pictured above left) make this national museum's impressionist and post-impressionist canvases appear as if they're hung in an intimate home. p224

CULINARY EXPLOITS

France pioneered what is still the most influential
style of cooking in the Western world and Paris is
its showcase *par excellence*. Here, the food and the
dining experience are considered inseparable and
whether you're in a charming neighbourhood bistro, an
elegant brasserie or a once-in-a-lifetime haute cuisine
restaurant, you'll find that places pride themselves on
the preparation and presentation of quality produce. Do
as Parisians do and savour every moment.

Bistros

Tucked in Paris' back-streets, you'll find exciting neobistros where creative young chefs forge their reputations coexisting alongside timeless bistros honouring classic cookery techniques such as La Tour de Montlhéry – Chez Denise. p125

Brasseries

Grand brasseries are a hallmark of Paris' dining scene. Seafood is typically a speciality. Montparnasse has a splendid line-up along bd du Montparnasse, such as art deco showpiece Le Dôme (pictured above left), renowned for its shellfish platters. p255

Gastronomic Extravaganzas

Paris has a galaxy of Michelin-starred restaurants helmed by legendary chefs. Restaurant Guy Savoy, ensconced in the neoclassical former mint, the Monnaie de Paris, is one of the finest. p238

Above: Jellied tomatoes served at Restaurant Guy Savoy (p238)

LA GRANDE EPICER

4. SPECIALISED SHOPPING

What really sets shopping in Paris apart is the city's incredible array of specialist shops. Candles from the world's oldest candle maker, paints developed with celebrated artists at venerable art-supply shops, beautiful fragrances from small perfumeries, statement-making homewares from up-and-coming local artisans and, this being Paris, a cornucopia of fine food and wine shops are just some of the treats in store.

Gourmet Goods

Patisseries with jewel-like tarts and cakes, *fromageries* filled with aromatic cheeses, chocolatiers displaying stunning seasonal creations, caves stocked high with wine bottles: Paris is an epicurean's delight. Whet your appetite at the magnificent food emporium La Grande Épicerie de Paris (pictured left). p245

Below: Shop window in Le Marais (p177)

Antiques

Shop for a piece of Parisian history at the city's antique dealers. An incredible array of sellers display furniture, *objets d'art,* furnishings, prints, paintings and countless other items at the vast flea market in northern Paris, the Marché aux Puces de St-Ouen (pictured above). p152

Fashion

Options to make over your wardrobe are limitless at Haut Marais emerging designer boutiques, Triangle d'Or *haute couture* flagships and wonderful vintage boutiques. For inspiration, reserve ahead for fashion shows at *grand magasin* (department store) Galeries Lafayette (pictured left), topped by a century-old stained-glass dome. p104

5 GREEN ESCAPES

While Paris is Europe's most densely populated capital, there are numerous opportunities to escape the urban environment and unwind in the fresh air. Paris is graced with beautiful parks, gardens, squares and sprawling lawns such as the Champ de Mars at the foot of the Eiffel Tower. Either side of the city are its *poumons* (lungs), the rambling forests of the western Bois de Boulogne and eastern Bois de Vincennes.

Jardin du Luxembourg

At Paris' most popular inner-city oasis (pictured below), children's activities span modern playgrounds and nostalgic attractions, including puppet shows, pony rides and wooden sailboats to prod on its octagonal pond. p228

BENSLIMAN HASSAN/SHUTTERSTOCK ©

Promenade Plantée

The world's first elevated park, the Coulée Verte René-Dumont, better known as the Promenade Plantée (pictured above), runs 1.5km atop a disused 19th-century railway viaduct. p182

Jardin des Tuileries

Part of the *axe historique* (historic axis) through central Paris, adjacent to the Louvre, these symmetrical formal gardens (pictured right) were designed by André Le Nôtre in the 17th century. p118

6 WATERWAY EXPLORATIONS

RUDY BALASKO/SHUTTERSTOCK©

Flanked by quintessentially Parisian landmarks, Paris' most beautiful 'boulevard' of all, the Seine (pictured above), flows through the city's heart and around its islands. The river's Unesco World Heritage–listed riverbanks, islands and 37 bridges are perfect for promenading, particularly along the reclaimed car-free stretches on both the Left and Right Banks. Linked to the Seine is the city's network of canals. Waterside entertainment options abound, including summertime the beaches, Paris Plages.

The Seine

Taking to the Seine on a river cruise is an idyllic way to sightsee. A handy alternative to traditional trips is the hop-on, hop-off Batobus. p334

Canal St-Martin

Bordered by shaded tow-paths and criss-crossed by iron footbridges, the charming, 4.5km-long Canal St-Martin has swing bridges that pivot 90 degrees when boats, pass through the canal's double locks. p31

Parc de la Villette

Northeast of Canal St-Martin and Bassin de la Villette, the Canal de l'Ourcq and Canal St-Denis intersect at futuristic park/cultural precinct Parc de la Villette. p136

7 ARCHITECTURAL WORSHIP

The city's revered French Gothic masterpiece, Cathédrale Notre Dame de Paris, dating from the 12th century, miraculously survived a devastating 2019 fire and rebuilding works are continuing apace to restore it to its former glory. Until Notre Dame reopens in 2024, there are scores of other magnificent churches that can be visited all over the city, where you can admire art, artefacts, and religious relics and take in ethereal music performances.

BOTOND HORVATH/SHUTTERSTOCK ©

SERGEY DZYUBA/SHUTTERSTOCK ©

Sacré-Cœur

Staircased, ivy-clad streets slink up the hill of the fabled artists' neighbourhood of Montmartre where a funicular glides up to the dove-white domes of Basilique du Sacré-Cœur (pictured above). p134

Sainte-Chapelle

Classical concerts provide the perfect opportunity to truly appreciate the beauty of Paris' oldest stained glass at the gem-like Gothic holy chapel Sainte-Chapelle (pictured top left), consecrated in 1248. p200

Église St-Eustache

Architecturally magnificent, Église St-Eustache (pictured above right), completed in 1632, is also musically outstanding, with one of France's largest organs, featuring 101 stops and 8000 pipes. p119

8 LITERARY ENCOUNTERS

Maison de Victor Hugo

Visit the recently renovated home of *Les Misérables* and *The Hunchback of Notre-Dame* novelist Victor Hugo (pictured left), overlooking one of Paris' prettiest squares, the place des Vosges. p160

Maison de Balzac

Honoré de Balzac's residence and writing studio, the Maison de Balzac, where he worked on the *Comédie Humaine,* is a charming property close to the Eiffel Tower in the neighbourhood of Passy. p86

Shakespeare & Company

Latin Quarter bookshop and writers' hub Shakespeare & Company (pictured below left) has an esteemed pedigree and is a magical place to browse the shelves or attend a reading. p219

Over the centuries, Paris has nurtured countless French authors and expat writers who have lived and written in the city. Paris' literary heritage is palpable at atmospheric bookshops and *bouquiniste* (secondhand bookseller) stalls lining the Seine, and at literary bars once frequented by luminaries. Today, you can follow in their footsteps on walking tours, pay your respects at cemeteries, and learn about their legacies at their former homes turned museums.

What's New

A host of new developments are underway in the French capital, from inspired culinary and fashion directions through to major museum openings and reopenings, and grand-scale infrastructure projects as the city prepares to host the 2024 Summer Olympics and Summer Paralympics.

Olympic Overhaul

While art nouveau gallery the Grand Palais readies itself to host Olympic events, a temporary Grand Palais is taking over next to the Eiffel Tower on the Parc du Champ de Mars. And the children's science museum, Palais de la Découverte, relocates to the Parc André Citroën.

Landmark Palace

For the first time, the monumental Louis XV–built palace Hôtel de la Marine (p96), spectacularly set on Paris' place de la Concorde and most recently used as the French navy's HQ, opened to the public in 2021. Guided tours illuminate its extraordinary life story.

Parisian History

Paris' history museum, the Musée Carnavalet (p161) – set in a pair of remarkable *hôtels particuliers* (private mansions), the 1560-built Hôtel Carnavalet and 1688-built Hôtel Le Peletier de St-Fargeau – reopened in 2021 following four years of renovations and expansion.

Medieval Heritage

The national museum of the Middle Ages, the Musée National du Moyen Âge (p208), incorporating both the 15th-century mansion Hôtel de Cluny and the *frigidarium* (cold room) of a Roman-era bathhouse, was set to reopen after renovations in early 2022.

LOCAL KNOWLEDGE

WHAT'S HAPPENING IN PARIS

By Catherine Le Nevez, Lonely Planet writer

Paris has had some tumultuous times recently, not least Notre Dame's 2019 fire and COVID-19 pandemic, but there are plenty of exciting developments happening here.

Vibrant street art continues to breathe life into the historic cityscapes; new and rejuvenated museums are opening their doors; expanding transport networks, along with vastly improved cycling infrastructure and pedestrianised areas, are seeing a dramatic reduction in pollution; and parks continue to open in innovative spaces, such as additional sections of the former Petite Ceinture steam-train railway line that once encircled the city, now forming a biodiverse green corridor.

Best of all, Parisians are coming up with creative solutions to live more sustainably, from urban farming (including on the city's rooftops) and zero-waste dining to fashion upcycling and salvaged fabrics being used to produce ingeniously original pieces. Paris today has the palpable energy of a city on the move.

WWI Remembrance

On the outside western wall of Cimetière du Père Lachaise (p157), the Monument aux Morts Parisiens de la Première Guerre Mondiale was unveiled on the 2018 centenary of the armistice marking the end of WWI.

WWII Liberation

On 25 August 2019, the 75th anniversary of the 1944 Liberation of Paris, freeing the city from Nazi Occupation, the Musée de la Libération de Paris (p249) opened across from Les Catacombes, commemorating instrumental figures, including French Resistance leader Jean Moulin.

Contemporary Art

Paris' circular former grain market and stock exchange, the Bourse de Commerce, is the setting for the Collection Pinault – Paris (p120), the private contemporary-art collection of François Pinault, with a destination restaurant by celebrated chef Michel Bras.

Fêted Food Hall

A galaxy of Michelin-starred chefs, including Thierry Marx, Olivier Bellin and Anne-Sophie Pic, set up in the open-air Left Bank 'mini-district' Beaupassage (p236) in 2018, followed by more openings in 2019, including a bar-restaurant in a former church.

Franco-Asian Flavours

Paris is getting its spice on: red-hot new Franco-Asian neobistros fusing both Asian and French flavours in contemporary bistro dishes include Double Dragon (p168), Cheval d'Or (p145) and Maison (p170), the 'home' of talk-of-the-town chef Sota Atsumi.

Eco-Responsible Kitchens

Prioritising the planet through ethical sourcing and elimination of food waste is big right now in Paris. Pioneering restaurants include For the Love of Food (p164), Fief (p169), Les Résistants (p145) and L'Avant-Poste (p140).

FAST FACTS

Food trend: Small, tapas-style sharing plates accompanied by superb wines at *caves à manger* all over the city

Hectolitres of wine consumed in Paris each year: 5.23 million (1.9 million bottles per day)

Distance travelled by the Eiffel Tower's lifts each year: 103,000km

Pop: 2.2 million

PARIS　　LONDON　　ROME

≈ 2235 people per sq km

Sustainable Fashion

Fashion is also increasingly eco-conscious. Brands like Sézane (p131) are blazing the trail, and the city has set a target date of 2024 to become the world's first sustainable fashion capital.

Rooftop Views

Sublime views now extend from a slew of new rooftop bars, providing unique perspectives of the city.

Need to Know

For more information, see Survival Guide (p329)

Currency
Euro (€)

Language
French

Visas
Not required for citizens of the EU or Schengen countries. Other nationals need ETIAS preauthorisation; some require a Schengen visa.

Money
ATMs widely available. Visa and MasterCard accepted in most hotels, shops and restaurants; fewer accept American Express.

Mobile Phones
Check with your provider about roaming costs before you leave home, or ensure your phone's unlocked to use a French SIM card (available cheaply in Paris).

Time
Central European Time (GMT/UTC plus one hour)

Tourist Information
Paris Convention & Visitors Bureau (Paris Office de Tourisme; Map p386; ☑01 49 52 42 63; www.parisinfo.com; 29 rue de Rivoli, 4e; ☺10am-6pm; ☎; ⓂHôtel de Ville) Paris' main tourist office is at the Hôtel de Ville. It sells tickets for tours and several attractions, plus museum and transport passes.

Daily Costs

Budget:
Less than €100
→ Dorm bed: €25–50
→ Espresso/glass of wine/ *demi* (half-pint of beer)/ cocktail: from €2/3.50/3.50/9
→ Metro ticket: €1.90
→ Baguette sandwich: €4.50–6.50
→ Frequent free concerts and events

Midrange: €100–250
→ Double room: €120–250
→ Two-course meal: €20–40
→ Admission to museums: free to around €15
→ Admission to clubs: free to around €20

Top end:
More than €250
→ Double room at historic luxury hotel: from €250
→ Gastronomic-restaurant lunch/dinner *menu:* from €50/80
→ Private two-hour city tour: from €150
→ Premium ticket to opera/ballet performance: from €160

Advance Planning

Two months before Book accommodation, organise opera, ballet or cabaret tickets, check events calendars for festivals, and make reservations for high-end/popular restaurants.

Two weeks before Sign up for a local-led tour and start narrowing down your choices of museums, pre-purchasing tickets online where possible to minimise ticket queues.

Two days before Check the weather forecast and pack your comfiest shoes to walk Paris' streets.

Useful Websites

Lonely Planet (lonelyplanet. com/paris) Destination information, hotel reviews, traveller forum and more.

Paris Info (www.parisinfo.com) Comprehensive tourist authority website.

Sortiraparis (www.sortiraparis. com) Up-to-date calendar listing what's on around town.

Secrets of Paris (www.secrets ofparis.com) Online resources and more.

HiP Paris (www.hipparis.com) Not only vacation rentals ('Haven in Paris') but articles and reviews by expat locals, too.

WHEN TO GO

Spring and autumn are ideal. Summer is the main tourist season, but many places close during August. Sights are quieter and prices lower in winter.

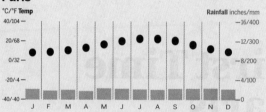

Arriving in Paris

Charles de Gaulle Airport
Trains (RER), buses and night buses to the city centre €6 to €18; taxis €50 to €55 (15% higher evenings and Sundays).

Orly Airport Trains (Orlyval then RER), buses and night buses to the city centre €9.50 to €12.10; T7 tram to Villejuif–Louis Aragon then metro to centre (€3.80); taxis €30 to €35 (15% higher evenings and Sundays).

Beauvais Airport Buses (€17) to Porte Maillot then metro (€1.90); taxis during the day/night around €170/210 (likely more than the cost of your flight!).

Gare du Nord train station
Within central Paris; served by metro (€1.90).

For much more on **arrival** see p330

Getting Around

Walking is a pleasure in Paris, and the city also has one of the most efficient and inexpensive public-transport systems in the world.

Metro & RER The fastest way to get around. Metros run from about 5.30am and finish around 1.15am (around 2.15am on Friday and Saturday nights), depending on the line, with all-night services under consideration. RER commuter trains operate from around 5.30am to 1.20am daily.

Bicycle Virtually free pick-up, drop-off Vélib' bikes have docking stations across the city; electric bikes are also available.

Bus Good for parents with prams and people with limited mobility.

Boat The Batobus is a handy hop-on, hop-off service stopping at nine key destinations along the Seine.

For much more on **getting around** see p332

Sleeping

As one of the world's most visited cities, Paris has plenty of accommodation across all budgets but it often books up in advance, especially during peak times (April to October, as well as public and school holidays). Advance reservations are essential at these times, and recommended year-round.

Although accommodation outside of central Paris can be marginally cheaper, travel time and costs mean that staying in one of Paris' *arrondissements* is more atmospheric and better value.

Useful Websites

Lonely Planet (lonelyplanet. com/france/paris/hotels) Reviews of Lonely Planet's top choices.

Paris Attitude (www.paris attitude.com) Thousands of apartment rentals, professional service, reasonable fees.

Haven In (www.havenin.com) Charming Parisian apartments for rent.

For much more on **sleeping** see p278

ARRONDISSEMENTS

Within the bd Périphérique ring road, Paris is divided into 20 *arrondissements* (city districts), which spiral clockwise like a snail shell from the centre. *Arrondissement* numbers (1er, 2e etc) form an integral part of all Parisian addresses. Each *arrondissement* has its own personality, but it's the *quartiers* (quarters, ie neighbourhoods), which often overlap *arrondissement* boundaries, that give Paris its village atmosphere.

First Time Paris

For more information, see Survival Guide (p329)

Checklist

➡ Check passport validity and visa requirements

➡ Arrange travel insurance

➡ Confirm airline baggage restrictions

➡ Book accommodation well ahead

➡ Make reservations for popular and/or high-end restaurants

➡ Buy tickets online for the Louvre, Eiffel Tower etc

➡ Organise international roaming on your phone if needed (and be sure to check roaming charges)

What to Pack

➡ Comfortable shoes – Paris is best explored on foot

➡ Phrasebook – the more French you attempt, the more rewarding your visit will be

➡ Travel plug (adapter)

➡ Corkscrew (corked wine bottles are the norm); pack it in your checked baggage for flights

➡ Umbrella – for the unpredictable weather

Top Tips for Your Trip

➡ An unforgettable introduction to the city is a river cruise (or hop-on, hop-off Batobus trip) along the Seine, floating past quintessentially Parisian landmarks like the Eiffel Tower, Musée d'Orsay and the Louvre.

➡ The metro is inexpensive, efficient and easy to use. Cycling is a scenic alternative.

➡ Pre-book attractions online wherever possible to avoid standing in long ticket queues.

➡ Brush up on at least a few basic French phrases. Interacting with locals in French (even if only a little) is not only respectful but will make your time in the city infinitely more rewarding.

➡ Above all, don't try to cram too much into your schedule. Allow time to soak up the atmosphere of Paris' neighbourhoods – lingering over a coffee on a cafe terrace and exploring the backstreets are as much a part of the Parisian experience as visiting major sights.

What to Wear

As the cradle of *haute couture* (high fashion), Paris is chic: don your smarter threads (and accessories such as scarves). You'll also stand out less as a tourist and therefore be less of a target for pickpockets. Dress up rather than down for the 'nicer' restaurants, clubs and bars – no jeans, shorts or trainers/sneakers. Bring sturdy shoes whatever the season – cobbled streets aren't kind on high heels or thin soles. Dress respectfully when visiting religious sites.

Be Forewarned

In general, Paris is a safe city. Most areas are well lit and in most areas there's generally no reason not to use the metro late at night, including for women travelling alone. Pickpocketing is typically the biggest concern. Always be alert, ensure you don't carry more money than you need, and keep valuables such as credit cards and passports secure and out of sight.

Money

Visa and MasterCard are the most widely used credit cards; American Express is typically only accepted by upmarket establishments such as international chain hotels, luxury boutiques and department stores. Chip-and-pin is the norm for card transactions. Ask your bank for advice before you leave. ATMs (*points d'argent* or *distributeurs automatiques de billets*) are everywhere. You can change cash at some banks, post offices and money-exchange offices. Many shops don't accept €100 bills or higher.

Taxes & Refunds

Prices displayed in shops etc invariably include France's TVA (*taxe sur la valeur ajoutée;* value-added tax).

Non-EU residents can often claim a refund of TVA paid on goods.

Tipping

Taxis Taxi drivers expect small tips of around 5% of the fare, though the usual procedure is to round up to the nearest €1 regardless of the fare.

Restaurants French law requires that restaurant, cafe and hotel bills include a service charge (typically 15%). Many people leave a few extra euros for good service.

Bars and cafes Not necessary at the bar. If drinks are brought to your table, tip as you would in a restaurant.

Hotels Bellhops usually expect €1 to €2 per bag; it's rarely necessary to tip the concierge, cleaners or front-desk staff.

Language

1 **What are the opening hours?**
Quelles sont les heures d'ouverture?
kel son lay zer doo·vair·tewr

French business hours are governed by a maze of regulations, so it's a good idea to check before you make plans.

2 **I'd like the set menu, please.**
Je voudrais le menu, s'il vous plait.
zher voo·dray ler mer·new seel voo play

The best-value dining in France is the two- or three-course meal at a fixed price. Most restaurants have one on the chalkboard.

3 **Which wine would you recommend?**
Quel vin vous conseillez?
kel vun voo kon·say·yay

Who better to ask for advice on wine than the French?

4 **Can I address you with 'tu'?**
Est-ce que je peux vous tutoyer?
es ker zher per voo tew·twa·yay

Before you start addressing someone with the informal 'you' form, it's polite to ask permission first.

5 **Do you have plans for tonight/tomorrow?**
Vous avez prévu quelque chose ce soir/demain?
voo za·vay pray·vew kel·ker shoz ser swar/der·mun

To arrange to meet up without sounding pushy, ask friends if they're available rather than inviting them directly.

See Language (p345) for more information.

Etiquette

Overall, communication tends to be formal and reserved, but this shouldn't be mistaken for unfriendliness.

Greetings Always greet/farewell anyone you interact with, such as shopkeepers, with *'Bonjour (bonsoir* at night)/*Au revoir'*.

Shops Particularly in smaller upmarket boutiques, staff may not appreciate your touching the merchandise until you have been invited to do so, nor taking photographs.

Speech Parisians don't speak loudly – modulate your voice to a similarly low pitch.

Terms of address *Tu* and *vous* both mean 'you', but *tu* is only used with people you know very well, children or animals. Use *vous* until you're invited to use *tu.*

Conversation topics Discussing financial affairs (eg salaries or spending outlays) is generally taboo in public.

Waitstaff Never use *'garçon'* (literally 'boy') to summon a waiter, rather 'Monsieur' or 'Madame'.

Perfect Days

Day One

Louvre & Les Halles (p106)

Start with a stroll through the elegant **Jardin des Tuileries**, stopping to view Monet's enormous *Water Lilies* at the **Musée de l'Orangerie** and/or photography exhibits at the **Jeu de Paume**.

> **Lunch** Savour French bistro fare at Chez La Vieille (p123).

Louvre & Les Halles (p106)

IM Pei's glass pyramid is your compass point to enter the labyrinthine **Louvre**. Visiting this monumental museum could easily consume a full day, but once you've had your fill, browse the colonnaded arcades of the exquisite **Jardin du Palais Royal**, and visit the beautiful church **Église St-Eustache**. Tap into the soul of the former Les Halles wholesale markets along backstreet legacies like the old oyster market, **rue Montorgueil**. Linger for a drink on **rue Montmartre**, then head to the late-opening **Centre Pompidou** for modern and contemporary art and amazing rooftop views.

> **Dinner** Frenchie (p126) offers walk-in wine-bar dining.

Le Marais, Ménilmontant & Belleville (p154)

There's a wealth to see in Le Marais by day (**Musée National Picasso**, **Musée Carnavalet**, **Maison de Victor Hugo**, **Musée des Arts et Métiers**...), but the neighbourhood really comes into its own at night, with a cornucopia of hip bars and clubs.

Day Two

Champs-Élysées & Grands Boulevards (p92)

Climb the mighty **Arc de Triomphe** for a pinch-yourself Parisian panorama. Stroll Paris' most glamorous avenue, the **Champs-Élysées**, and flex your credit card in the **Triangle d'Or**, **Galeries Lafayette** or **place de la Madeleine** before going behind the scenes of Paris' opulent opera house, the **Palais Garnier**.

> **Lunch** Café Jacques (p91): casual yet classy, with ringside tower views.

Eiffel Tower & Western Paris (p80)

Check out global indigenous art at the **Musée du Quai Branly**. This cultural neighbourhood is also home to the world's largest Monet collection at the **Musée Marmottan Monet**, contemporary installations at the **Palais de Tokyo** and Asian treasures at the **Musée Guimet**. Sunset is the best time to ascend the **Eiffel Tower**, to experience both dizzying views during daylight hours, and glittering *la ville lumière* (City of Light) by night.

> **Dinner** Traditional French bistro fare at Firmin Le Barbier (p89).

Montparnasse & Southern Paris (p246)

Detour for a drink at a historic Montparnasse brasserie like **Le Select** or continue down the Seine to party at **Les Docks** or aboard floating nightclubs moored near France's national library, the **Bibliothèque Nationale de France**.

Latin Quarter (p211)

SERGEY RYBIN/SHUTTERSTOCK ©

Canal St-Martin (p146)

BRUNO DE HOGUES/GETTY IMAGES ©

Day Three

The Islands (p194)

 Start your day on the Île de la Cité, the site of Notre Dame. The cathedral was ravaged by fire in 2019; rebuilding works are expected to take several years. For beautiful stained glass, don't miss the island's **Sainte-Chapelle**. Cross the **Pont St-Louis** to buy a **Berthillon** ice cream before browsing the Île St-Louis' enchanting boutiques.

> **Lunch** Deliciously Parisian hang-out Café Saint Régis (p202).

St-Germain & Les Invalides (p222)

Swoon over impressionist masterpieces in the magnificent **Musée d'Orsay**, scout out the backstreet boutiques and storied shops of St-Germain, sip coffee on the terrace of literary cafes like **Les Deux Magots** and laze in the lovely **Jardin du Luxembourg**, the city's most popular park.

> **Dinner** French classics in art nouveau jewel Bouillon Racine (p236).

Latin Quarter (p205)

 Scour the shelves of late-night bookshops like the legendary **Shakespeare & Company**, then join Parisian students and academics in the Latin Quarter's bars, cafes and pubs on **rue Mouffetard** or hit a jazz club like **Café Universel**.

Day Four

Montmartre & Northern Paris (p132)

Montmartre's slinking streets and steep staircases lined with crooked ivy-clad buildings are enchanting places to meander, especially in the early morning when tourists are few. Head to the hilltop **Sacré-Cœur** basilica, then brush up on the area's fabled history at the **Musée de Montmartre**.

> **Lunch** Gourmet sandwiches and pastries at Pain Pain (p144).

Montmartre & Northern Paris (p132)

 Stroll the shaded towpaths of cafe-lined **Canal St-Martin**, and visit the futuristic **Parc de la Villette**, the kid-friendly **Cité des Sciences** museum and the instrument-filled Musée de la Musique, within the **Cité de la Musique**. Sailing schedules permitting, hop on a **canal cruise** to Bastille.

> **Dinner** Brilliant French cooking at Le Bistrot Paul Bert (p186).

Bastille & Eastern Paris (p180)

The Bastille neighbourhood calls for a cafe crawl: classics include the cherry-red **Le Pure Café** and absinthe specialist **La Fée Verte**. Salsa your socks off at the 1936 dance hall **Le Balajo** on nightlife strip **rue de Lappe** or catch electro, funk and hip-hop at **Badaboum**.

Month By Month

Januarye

The frosty first month of the year isn't the most festive in Paris, but cocktails – as well as the winter *soldes* (sales) – brighten the mood.

🍷 Paris Cocktail Week

Participating cocktail bars all over the city create signature cocktails for late January's Paris Cocktail Week (www.pariscocktail week.fr). There are also workshops, guest bartenders, masterclasses and food pairings.

🎆 Chinese New Year

Paris' largest lantern-lit festivities and dragon parades take place in the city's main Chinatown in the 13e in late January or early February. Parades are also held at other locations including Le Marais.

February

Festivities still aren't in full swing in February, but couples descend on France's romantic capital for Valentine's Day, when virtually all restaurants offer special menus.

🍴 Salon International de l'Agriculture

At this appetising nine-day international agricultural fair (www.salon-agriculture.com), produce and animals from all over France are turned into delectable fare at the Parc des Expositions at Porte de Versailles, 15e.

March

Blooms appear in Paris' parks and gardens, leaves start greening the city's avenues and festivities begin to flourish.

☆ Printemps du Cinéma

Selected cinemas across Paris offer filmgoers a unique entry fee of €4 per session over three days, typically in late March (www.feteducinema.com).

☆ Banlieues Bleues

Big-name acts perform during the Suburban Blues (www.banlieuesbleues.org) jazz, blues and R&B festival at venues in Paris' northern suburbs.

April

Sinatra sang about April in Paris, and the month sees the city's 'charm of spring' in full swing, with chestnut trees blossoming and cafe terraces coming into their own.

🎆 Foire du Trône

Dating back over a millennium, from the year 957, this huge ride-filled funfair (www.foiredutrone.com) is held on the Pelouse de Reuilly of the Bois de Vincennes from around late March to late May.

🏃 Marathon de Paris

On your marks...the Paris Marathon (www.schneider electricparismarathon. com), held on a Sunday in early April, starts on av des

Champs-Élysées, 8e, and loops through the city, finishing on av Foch, 16e, attracting some 60,000 runners from around 145 countries.

🍷 Paris Beer Festival

Craft beer's popularity in Paris peaks during the Paris Beer Festival (www.paris beerweek.fr), held from late April to early May, when events take place across the city's bars, pubs, breweries, specialist beer shops and other venues.

May

The temperate month of May has more public holidays than any other in France. Watch out for widespread closures, particularly on May Day (1 May).

🎆 La Nuit Européenne des Musées

Key museums across Paris stay open until midnight for the European Museums Night (www.nuitdesmusees. culturecommunication. gouv.fr), on one Saturday in mid-May, with free entry; there are also guided tours, workshops and entertainment.

👁 Portes Ouvertes des Ateliers d'Artistes de Belleville

More than 200 painters, sculptors and other artists at over 100 Belleville studios open their doors to visitors across four days (Friday to Monday) in mid-May (www.ateliers-artistes-belleville.fr).

🏃 French Open

The glitzy Internationaux de France de Tennis Grand Slam (www.rolandgarros. com) hits up from late May to early June at Stade Roland Garros in the Bois de Boulogne.

June

Paris is positively jumping in June, thanks to warm temperatures, a host of outdoor events and long daylight hours, with twilight lingering until late.

☆ Fête de la Musique

This national music festival (www.fetede lamusique.culture communication.gouv.fr) welcomes in summer on the solstice (21 June) with free live performances of jazz, reggae, classical and more at bars and makeshift stages all over the city.

🎆 Marche des Fiertés (Pride)

Late June's colourful Saturday-afternoon Marche des Fiertés (www.inter-lgbt. org) celebrates LGBTIQ+ pride with a march that incorporates over-the-top floats and outrageous costumes, and crosses Paris via Le Marais.

☆ La Goutte d'Or en Fête

Raï, reggae and rap feature at this two-day music festival (www.gouttedorenfete. wordpress.com) on square Léon in the 18e's Goutte d'Or neighbourhood.

July

During the Parisian summer, 'beaches' – complete with sunbeds, umbrellas, atomisers, lounge chairs and palm trees – line the banks of the Seine, while shoppers hit the summer _soldes_ (sales).

☆ Paris Jazz Festival

Jazz concerts swing every Saturday and Sunday afternoon in the Bois de Vincennes' Parc Floral de Paris during the Paris Jazz Festival (www.festivals duparcfloral.paris).

🎆 Paris Plages

From early July to early September, 'Paris Beaches' set up along Paris' riverbanks in two main zones: the Parc Rives de Seine and the Bassin de la Villette (with swimming pools in the canal).

🎆 Bastille Day

The capital celebrates France's national day on 14 July with a morning military parade along av des Champs-Élysées and a fly-past of fighter aircraft and helicopters. _Feux d'artifice_ (fireworks) light up the sky above the Champ de Mars by night.

🏃 Tour de France

The last of the 21 stages of this legendary, 3500km-long cycling event (www. letour.com) finishes with a dash up av des Champs-Élysées on the third or fourth Sunday of July.

Top: Paris Plages (p27)
Bottom: Entrance to Rock en Seine (left)

August

Parisians desert the city in droves during the summer swelter when, despite an influx of tourists, many restaurants and shops shut. It's a prime time to cycle, with far less traffic on the roads.

☆ Rock en Seine

Headlining acts rock the Domaine National de St-Cloud, on the city's southwestern edge, at this popular three-day music festival (www.rockenseine.com).

September

Tourists leave and Parisians come home: *la rentrée* marks residents' return to work and study after the summer break. Cultural life shifts into top gear and the weather is often at its blue-skied best.

☆ Jazz à la Villette

This prestigious jazz festival (www.jazzalavillette. com), held from late August to early September, has sessions in Parc de la Villette, at the Cité de la Musique and at surrounding venues.

✸ Festival d'Automne

The long-running Autumn Festival of arts (www. festival-automne.com), from mid-September to around early January, incorporates painting, music, dance and theatre at venues throughout the city.

☆ Techno Parade

On one Saturday in September, floats carrying musicians and DJs pump up the volume as they travel through the city's streets during the Techno Parade (www.technoparade.fr).

◉ Journées Européennes du Patrimoine

The third weekend in September sees Paris open the doors of otherwise off-limits buildings – embassies, government ministries and so forth – during European Heritage Days (www.journeesdupatrimoine.culturecommunication.gouv.fr).

❄ Journée Sans Voiture

This annual car-free day on a Sunday typically in September sees pedestrians and cyclists reclaiming Paris' streets from mid-morning to early evening.

October

October heralds an autumnal kaleidoscope in the city's parks and gardens, along with bright, crisp days, cool, clear nights and excellent cultural offerings.

❄ Nuit Blanche

From sundown on the first Saturday of October until sunrise, museums stay open (for free), along with bars and clubs, for one event-packed 'White Night' (ie 'All-Nighter').

❄ Fête des Vendanges de Montmartre

This five-day festival (www.fetedesvendanges demontmartre.com), held over the second weekend in October, celebrates Montmartre's grape harvest

> **WINTER ICE SKATING**
>
> Come winter, ice-skating rinks pop up across the city, including in some truly picturesque spots, such as Galeries Lafayette's panoramic rooftop. Skating is usually free, with a charge for skate hire. Venues change from year to year; check www.parisinfo.com.

with costumes, concerts, food events and a parade.

☆ Pitchfork Music Festival Paris

The Grande Halle at the Parc de la Villette is the centrepiece for this three-day fest (www.pitchfork musicfestival.fr) of pop, rock, indie, hip-hop and urban music in late October/early November.

✕ Salon du Chocolat

Chocaholics won't want to miss this five-day chocolate festival's tastings, workshops, demonstrations and more at Paris Expo Porte de Versailles, 15e (www.salon-du-chocolat.com). There are special activities for kids.

November

Dark, chilly days and long, cold nights see Parisians take refuge indoors: the opera and ballet seasons are going strong and there are plenty of cosy bistros and bars.

❄ Illuminations de Noël

From mid-November to early January, festive lights sparkle along the av des Champs-Élysées, rue du Faubourg St-Honoré and av Montaigne, in the 8e, among other locations, while department stores including Galeries Lafay-

ette and Le Printemps have enchanting window displays.

🍷 Beaujolais Nouveau

At midnight on the third Thursday (ie Wednesday night) in November – as soon as French law permits – the opening of the first bottles of cherry-bright, six-week-old Beaujolais Nouveau is celebrated in Paris wine bars, with more celebrations on the Thursday itself.

December

Twinkling fairy lights, brightly decorated Christmas trees and shop windows, and outdoor ice-skating rinks make December a magical month to be in the City of Light.

❄ Le Festival du Merveilleux

Filled with fairground attractions of yesteryear, the private museum Musée des Arts Forains (www.arts-forains.com), in the 12e, opens from late December to early January with delightful rides, attractions and festive shows.

❄ New Year's Eve

The Eiffel Tower, 7e, and av des Champs-Élysées, 8e, are the ultimate Parisian hotspots for welcoming in the New Year.

With Kids

Parisians adore les enfants (children) and the city's residential density means you'll find playground equipment in parks and squares throughout the city. Families have an overwhelming choice of creative, educational, culinary and 'pure old-fashioned fun' things to see, do and experience. Plan ahead to get the best out of kid-friendly Paris.

Sailboats in Jardin du Luxembourg (p228)

Science Museums

Cité des Sciences

If you have time for just one museum, make it this one (p136). Book interactive Cité des Enfants sessions (for children aged two to 12) in advance to avoid disappointment.

Musée des Arts et Métiers

Crammed with instruments and machines, Europe's oldest science and technology museum (p161) is fascinating. Activity- and experiment-driven workshops are top-notch.

Galerie des Enfants

Natural-history museum (p209) for six- to 12-year-olds within the Jardin des Plantes.

Art Attack

Centre Pompidou

Modern-art hub (p116) with great exhibitions, art workshops (for kids aged three to 12) and teen events in Studio 13/16.

Musée en Herbe

Thoughtful art museum (p120) for children with an excellent bookshop and art workshops for kids aged two to 12.

Palais de Tokyo

Palais de Tokyo (p85) offers interactive installations, art workshops (for kids five to 10 years old) and storytelling sessions (for tz hree- to five-year-olds) as well as family activities for everyone.

Treasure Hunts with THATMuse

All ages will get a burst of art adrenaline with a THATMuse (p337) treasure hunt at the Louvre or Musée d'Orsay. Play alone or in teams.

Hands-On Activities

Crafty Happenings at the Musée du Quai Branly – Jacques Chirac

Mask making, boomerang hurling and experimenting with traditional instruments…the ateliers (for three-year-olds to teenagers) at this Seine-side museum (p84), devoted to African, Asian and Oceanic art and culture, are diverse and creative.

Music at Philharmonie de Paris

Concerts, shows and instrument workshops are part of the world-music repertoire at the city's cutting-edge philharmonic hall (p150) in Parc de la Villette.

Bag Painting with Kasia Dietz

Design and paint a reversible, hand-printed canvas tote with Paris-based New Yorker **Kasia Dietz** (www.kasiadietzworkshops.com; workshops €115-150; ☺ by reservation) during a half-day bag-painting workshop – ideal for fashion-conscious teens (and parents).

Model Building

Workshops at Cité de l'Architecture et du Patrimoine (p85) see kids (aged four to 16 years) build art deco houses, châteaux and towers in miniature form.

Nature-Themed Workshops

Children's workshops (€15.50; English available) at the **Musée de la Chasse et de la Nature** (www.chassenature.org; ☺11am-6pm Tue-Sun; Ⓜ Rambuteau).

Parks & Outdoor Capers

Sailing Boats in Jardin du Luxembourg

Playgrounds, puppet shows, pony rides, chess and an old-fashioned carousel: this legendary park (p228) has pandered to children for generations. But it's the vintage toy sailing boats that are the real heart-stealers.

Jardin des Tuileries

These elegant gardens (p118) stage kids' activities and a summer amusement park.

Parc Floral de Paris

Easily the best playground (p184) for kids eight years and older: outdoor concerts, puppet shows, giant climbing webs, 30m-high slides and a zip line, among other high-energy-burning attractions.

Jardin d'Acclimatation

At this enormous green area (p88) with cycling paths, forest, lakes and ponds in the Bois de Boulogne, renting a pedalo or rowing boat is a warm-weather treat (bring a picnic), while recent years have seen a slew of attractions added to its amusement park.

Locks on Canal St-Martin

Watching canal boats navigate the **locks** (Map p137; 10e; Ⓜ République, Jaurès, Jacques Bonsergent) is fun, fascinating and free. Lunch waterside with a croque monsieur from Fric-Frac (p143).

Boat Trips on the Seine

Every kid loves a voyage down the Seine with Bateaux-Mouches (p336) or Bateaux Parisiens (p336). But there is something extra special about the one-hour 'Paris Mystery' tours designed especially for children by Vedettes de Paris (p336).

Riverside Play

Giant board games, a climbing wall, a 20m-long blackboard to chalk on, tepees and events 'n' shows galore line Parc Rives de Seine (p233).

Puppet Shows

Parisians have entertained their children with puppet shows for centuries. Pick a fine day and head to parks such as the Jardin du Luxembourg (p228) or Parc Monceau (p137).

Animal Mad

Equestrian Shows at Versailles

Be mesmerised by world-class equestrian shows (p267). Show tickets and training sessions include a stable visit.

Sharks at Aquarium de Paris Cinéaqua

Centrally located Cinéaqua (p88) has a shark tank and 500-plus fish species, and screens ocean-themed films.

NEED TO KNOW

Babysitting Hotels can often organise sitters for guests.

Equipment Rent strollers, scooters, car seats, travel beds and more while in Paris from companies such as Kidelio (www.kidelio.com).

Paris Mômes (www.parismomes.fr) Parisian kid culture (up to 12 years); print off playful kids' guides for major art exhibitions before leaving home.

Former enclosure at Ménagerie du Jardin des Plantes

Ménagerie du Jardin des Plantes

The collection of animals (p209) in Jardin des Plantes includes snow panthers and pandas; combine with the neighbouring natural-history museum (p209), particularly its Grande Galerie de l'Évolution.

Parc Zoologique de Paris

Observe lions, cougars, white rhinos and a whole gaggle of other beasties at this state-of-the-art zoo (p184) in Bois de Vincennes.

Theme Parks

Disneyland Resort Paris

A magnet for families, this park (p263) 32km east of Paris incorporates both Disneyland itself and the cinema-themed Walt Disney Studios Park.

Parc Astérix

Shuttle buses run from central Paris to this summer-opening **theme park** (☑09 86 86 86 87; www.parcasterix.fr; A1 motorway btwn exits 7 & 8, Plailly; adult/child €51/43, shuttle bus from Paris adult/child return €20/16; ◷10am-10pm mid-Jul–Aug, 10am-6pm daily Apr & Jun–mid-Jul, shorter hours May, Sep, Oct & Dec), 35km north of the city, which covers prehistory through to the 19th century with its six 'worlds', adrenaline-pumping attractions and shows for all ages.

Screen Entertainment

Digital Exhibitions

Gaîté Lyrique (Map p386; ☑01 53 01 51 51; www.gaite-lyrique.net; 3bis rue Papin, 3e; variable; ◷2-9pm Tue-Sat, noon-6pm Sun; Ⓜ Réaumur–Sébastopol) features digital-driven exhibitions, video games for older children and teens, laptops to use in the digitally connected cafe and a library with desks shaped like ducks for kids under five to sit at and draw while older siblings geek.

Special-Effect Movies

Cité des Sciences (p136) boasts two special-effect cinemas: **Géode** with 3D movies, and **Cinéma Louis-Lumière** screening animation and short films. Top it off with a cinematic trip through the solar system in the planetarium).

Behind-the-Scenes Tour at Le Grand Rex

Whizz-bang special effects stun during behind-the-scenes tours at this iconic 1930s cinema (p130). Stand behind the big screen and muck around in a recording studio.

Art Illuminations at Atelier des Lumières

Artworks projected on this former foundry's bare walls (p163) dazzle kids and adults alike.

Easy Eating

Pink Flamingo Pizza Picnic

Where else are you sent away with a pink balloon when you order? Kids adore take-away pizza from Pink Flamingo (p144) on Canal St-Martin.

Park Pavilion

On Sundays, cool bar-restaurant Le Pavillon Puebla (p148) in the Parc des Buttes Chaumont has children's activities and shared pizzas.

Games Galore

Healthy salads with board games on the side are the order of the day at Soul Kitchen (p142).

Above: Jardin des Plantes
Right: Parc Astérix

Cafe Fun

At Le Square Trousseau (p187), kids are given chalk to get creative on the pavement out front, and can head to the playground in the park opposite.

Train Depot Dining

In a former railway depot, La Felicità (p252) has old railway carriages, regular activities for kids, and pizza, pasta and gelato galore.

Multicourse Dining

Bustronome

Kids can play 'I spy' spotting Parisian landmarks while dining on multicourse *menus* cooked in the purpose-built galley of this glass-roofed bus (p90).

Le Train Bleu

Train-obsessed kids will also love the multicourse *menus* at this magnificent railway-station restaurant (p189) inside Gare de Lyon.

Bouillon Racine

A dazzling introduction to French cuisine (p236) and art nouveau architecture.

Firmin Le Barbier

Budding chefs can see how it's done in this cosy open-kitchen bistro (p89) near the Eiffel Tower.

Arnaud Nicolas

Junior gourmands can dig into the three-course kids' *menus* at this charcuterie boutique and restaurant (p89).

Rainy-Day Ideas

Cirque d'Hiver Bouglione

Clowns, trapeze artists and acrobats have entertained children of all ages at the city's

winter circus (Map p386; 01 47 00 28 81; www.cirquedhiver.com; 110 rue Amelot, 11e; tickets from €27; Oct-Mar; Filles du Calvaire) since 1852. The season runs October to March; performances last around 2½ hours.

Musée des Arts Forains

Check for seasonal events at this nostalgic fairground museum, such as its Christmas season during Le Festival du Merveilleux (p29).

Musée des Égouts de Paris

Romping through sewerage tunnels, learning what happens when you flush a loo in Paris and spotting rats is all part of the kid-cool experience at this quirky **museum** (Map p406; 01 53 68 27 81; place de la Résistance, 7e; adult/child €4.40/3.60; 11am-5pm Mon-Wed, Sat & Sun; Alma Marceau, RER Pont de l'Alma).

Les Catacombes

Teens generally get a kick out of Paris' most macabre sight (p248), but be warned: this skull-packed underground cemetery is not for the faint-hearted.

An Afternoon at the Theatre

Paris' diverse theatre scene stages bags of *spectacles* (shows), *théâtre classique* (classical theatre) and other performances for kids, some in English; weekly entertainment mag *L'Officiel des Spectacles* (www.offi.fr) lists what's on.

Musée de la Magie

This **museum** (Map p386; 01 42 72 13 26; www.museedelamagie.com; 11 rue St-Paul, 4e; adult/child €14/10; 2-7pm Wed, Sat & Sun, plus school holidays; Sully–Morland, St-Paul) is pure magic!

Creative Endeavours

Crafting workshops at Seize (p179) will fire up kids' creativity.

Like a Local

Paris is among the world's most visited cities, but it's not an urban resort. The city has the highest population density of any European capital, and its parks, cafes and restaurants are its communal backyards, living rooms and dining rooms, while neighbourhood shops and markets are cornerstones of local life.

e terrace in Montmartre (p148)

Dining Like a Local

Parisians are obsessed with talking about, shopping for, preparing and above all eating food. Quality trumps quantity, which is reflected in the small, specialist gourmet food shops thriving all over the city.

Sunday (and often Saturday) brunch has become a highlight of the weekend's social calendar from around noon to 4pm. Be sure to book for popular venues.

Another shift towards informal dining is the profusion of casual wine bars where, rather than ordering full *menus* (two- or three-course set menus), locals gather to share small tapas-style plates over *un verre* ('a glass').

Drinking Like a Local

Given Paris' high concentration of city dwellers, most bars and cafes close around 2am due to noise restrictions, and nightclubs in the inner city are few. Cocktail bars continually shake up Paris' drinking scene, though, with a slew of specialists across the city. Craft beer also stakes its claim in this wine-drinking city, with numerous Parisian breweries in fully fledged operation. Paris Cocktail Week (p26) and Paris Beer Festival (p27) are now fixtures on the city's calendar.

And while the image of Parisians sipping *un café* on a wicker-chair-lined cafe terrace is timeless, recent years have seen a dramatic improvement in the quality of the coffee. Led by pioneers like Belleville Brûlerie and Coutume, a new wave of Parisian roasteries sees hip Parisians attending cupping sessions and buying beans to brew up at home.

In summer, ephemeral bars, often with pop-up restaurants, food trucks, DJs and live music, open in unique spaces such as railway-station yards, rooftops, courtyards, parks and along the riverfront. Check www.parisinfo.com for the year's locations.

Conversing Like a Local

Food and drink aside, conversations between locals often revolve around philosophy, art, and sports such as rugby, football (soccer), cycling and tennis. Talking about money (salaries or spending outlays, for example) in public is generally taboo.

Dressing Like a Local

It's nearly impossible to overdress in this fashion-conscious city. Parisians have a finely tuned sense of aesthetics, and take meticulous care in their presentation. Parisians favour style over fashion, mixing basics from chain stores like H&M with designer pieces, vintage and flea-market finds, and statement-making accessories.

Hanging Out Like a Local

Parisians generally work to live rather than the other way round. Thanks to the much-debated 35-hour standard working week, long annual leave and a lot of public holidays, Parisians aren't driven to make and spend money 24/7/365. Instead, leisure activities factor highly in Parisians' *joie de vivre* (spirited enjoyment of life), along with the company of friends and family (children are treated like little adults and welcomed with open arms just about everywhere).

Cinemas, theatres and concert venues, as well as art exhibitions, festivals and special events, draw huge local crowds.

Sunday is the main day of rest, when most workplaces (including the majority of shops outside the ZTI tourist zones) close and locals head to museums, parks and *jardins partagés* (community gardens); visit www.paris.fr for a list (and map) of gardens that are open to the public.

Year-round, you'll find locals kicking back all along the banks of the Seine but never more so than on warm summer evenings with a picnic and bottle of wine.

NEED TO KNOW

Metro Parisians from all walks of life – from students to celebrity chefs – use the metro. Get a Navigo pass to save money and zip through the turnstiles.

Vélib' bikes Virtually free Vélib' bikes are hugely popular – Parisians flit all over the city on two wheels.

Meeting the Locals

The best way to get a feel for local life is to head to areas where Parisians work, live and play away from the busy tourist sights. Great neighbourhoods to start exploring:

➡ Bastille (4e, 11e and 12e)

➡ Belleville (20e)

➡ Butte aux Cailles (13e)

➡ Canal St-Martin (10e)

➡ Château d'Eau (especially on and around rue du Château d'Eau, 10e)

➡ Clichy-Batignolles (17e)

➡ Faidherbe (particularly on and around rue de Charonne, 11e)

➡ Latin Quarter (5e)

➡ Ménilmontant (20e)

➡ Sentier (2e)

➡ South Pigalle (aka SoPi, 9e)

Local-led tours and activities are also a fantastic opportunity to get an insider's perspective of the city:

➡ Parisien d'un Jour – Paris Greeters (p337) Led by volunteers.

➡ Ça Se Visite (p336) Discover the city's northeastern neighbourhoods.

➡ Localers (p337) Insider and themed city walks.

➡ Meeting the French (p337) Behind-the-scenes tours and activities, such as dinner with a Parisian family.

Navigation

Street numbers notated *bis* (twice), *ter* (thrice) or *quater* (four times) are similar to the English a, b etc. If you're entering an apartment building, you'll generally need the alphanumeric *digicode* (entry code) to open the door. Once inside, apartments are usually unmarked, without any apartment numbers or even occupants' names. To know which door to knock on, you're likely to be given cryptic directions like *cinquième étage, premier à gauche* (5th floor, first on the left) or *troisième étage, droite droite* (3rd floor, turn right twice). In all buildings, the 1st floor is the floor above the *rez-de-chaussée* (RdC; ground floor).

For Free

Paris might be home to haute couture, haute cuisine and historic luxury hotels, but if you're still waiting for your lottery numbers to come up, don't despair. There are a wealth of ways to soak up the French capital without spending a centime (or scarcely any, at least).

CATHERINE LE NEVEZ/LONELY PLANET ©

Pavillon de l'Arsenal (p161)

Free Museums

On the first Sunday of the month, national museums and a handful of monuments are free (some during certain months only).

EU citizens under 26 get free entry to national museums and monuments.

At any time you can visit the permanent collections of Paris' *musées municipaux* (www.paris.fr/musees) for free (some only when temporary exhibitions aren't taking place).

Temporary exhibitions at both national and city museums always incur a separate admission fee. Some museums have reduced entry at various times of the day or week.

Year-round freebies include Paris' fascinating town-planning and architectural centre, the Pavillon de l'Arsenal (p161), and the Nouveau Musée du Parfum (p98).

The Musée du Louvre (p108) is free from 6pm to 9.45pm on the first Saturday of the month.

Museums and monuments offering free admission on the first Sunday of the month include the following.

Arc de Triomphe (p94) November to March

Basilique de St-Denis (p139) November to March

Château de Versailles (p264) November to March

Cité de l'Architecture et du Patrimoine (p85)

Conciergerie (p201) November to March

Musée de la Chasse et de la Nature (p31)

Musée de l'Histoire de l'Immigration (p184)

Musée de l'Orangerie (p118)

Musée des Arts et Métiers (p161) Also free every Friday from 6pm

Musée des Impressionnismes Giverny (p276)

Musée d'Orsay (p224)

Musée du Quai Branly (p84)

Musée Guimet des Arts Asiatiques (p87)

Musée National d'Art Moderne (p116) Within the Centre Pompidou

Musée National du Moyen Âge (p208) Watch for renovation closures

Musée National Eugène Delacroix (p232)

Musée National Gustave Moreau (p98)

Musée National Picasso (p160)

Musée Rodin (p230) October to March

Above: Panthéon (p207)

Left: Château de Versailles (p264)

Panthéon (p207) November to March

Sainte-Chapelle (p200) November to March

Free Churches

Some of the city's most magnificent buildings are its churches and other places of worship. Not only exceptional architecturally and historically, they contain exquisite art, artefacts and other priceless treasures. Best of all, entry to general areas within them is, in most cases, free.

Do respect the fact that although many of Paris' places of worship are also major tourist attractions, Parisians come here to pray and celebrate significant events on religious calendars as part of their daily lives. Keep noise to a minimum, obey photography rules (check signs), dress appropriately and try to avoid key times (eg Mass) if you're sightseeing only.

Free Cemeteries

Paris' celebrity-filled cemeteries, including the three largest – Père Lachaise (p157), Cimetière de Montmartre (p138) and Cimetière du Montparnasse (p249) – are free to wander.

Free Entertainment

Music

Concerts, DJ sets and recitals regularly take place for free (or for the cost of a drink) at venues throughout the city.

Busking musicians and performers entertain crowds on Paris' streets and squares and even aboard the metro.

Literary Events

This literary-minded city is an inspired place to catch a reading, author signing or writing workshop. English-language bookshops such as Shakespeare & Company (p219) and Abbey Bookshop (p221) host literary events throughout the year and can point you towards others.

NEED TO KNOW

➡ Paris has hundreds of free wi-fi points at popular locations, including parks, libraries, local town halls and tourist hot spots. Locations are mapped at www.paris.fr.

➡ Consider investing in a transport or museum pass.

➡ Theatre tickets are sold for half price on the day of performance.

➡ Paris' parks are perfect for picnics made from market fare.

Festivals

Loads of Paris' festivals and events are free, such as the summertime Paris Plages (p27) riverside beaches.

Getting Around

Walking

Paris is an eminently walkable city, with beautiful parks and gardens, awe-inspiring architecture, and markets and shops (well, window-shopping never goes out of style) to check out along the way.

For a free walking tour (donations encouraged), contact Parisien d'un Jour – Paris Greeters (p337) in advance for a personalised excursion led by a resident volunteer.

Cycling (Almost Free)

If you'd rather free-wheel around Paris, the Vélib' (p341) system costs next to nothing for a day's subscription, and the first 30 minutes of each bike rental is free.

Buses (Cheap as Chips)

Instead of taking a bus tour, simply hop on a local bus. Particularly scenic routes include lines 21 and 27 (Opéra–Panthéon), line 29 (Opéra–Gare de Lyon), line 47 (Centre Pompidou–Gobelins), line 63 (Musée d'Orsay–Trocadéro), line 73 (Concorde–La Défense) and line 82 (Montparnasse–Eiffel Tower). Time it to avoid peak commuting hours, when buses are packed sardine-can-style.

Under the Radar Paris

Paris' magic lies in the unexpected: hidden parks, small, specialised museums and galleries, and other tucked-away treasures. Discovering the secret side of Paris helps counterbalance tourism pressures, and rewards visitors with less crowded, more local experiences and a richer appreciation of this multifaceted city.

Parc des Buttes Chaumont (p138)

Tourism and Overtourism in Paris

Prior to the onset of the COVID-19 pandemic that upended travel worldwide, tourist numbers were surging in the French capital, with more than 52 million overnight visitors in 2019 alone. While Paris didn't experience a tourism backlash from residents in the way that cities such as Amsterdam, Barcelona and Venice did, high visitor counts nonetheless affected the city's star attractions (such as the Musée du Louvre, where staff went on strike in 2019 to protest against overcrowding), as well as its social fabric (including the rise of home-sharing platforms like Airbnb leading to a shortage of affordable residential apartments).

Solutions to overtourism are being implemented as a result. Pre-pandemic, many top sights – such as the Eiffel Tower and the Louvre – had already introduced compulsory time-slotted tickets to help manage numbers; many more sights implemented them under COVID-19 health measures. City authorities outlined restrictions for tourist buses to combat noise, congestion and pollution and, in 2021, won a court challenge to legalise rules restricting the use of properties for short-term holiday rentals. These rules make registration mandatory for all properties, cap primary-residence rentals at 120 nights per year, and require second-home owners to change the registered use, as well as purchase a commercial property of an equal or larger size and convert it into housing. The city's eco-initiatives also make it more sustainable and enjoyable for both residents and visitors.

Travellers in Paris can help reduce overtourism by planning a trip outside the peak summer tourist season, visiting popular sights at quieter times (listed by many places on their websites), seeking out alternatives to the top attractions, and setting out to parts of the city that fly under the tourism radar.

Less-Visited Sights

Paris is spoilt for choice with museums that in any other city would be headliners but here often lose out on the limelight to the top-billing institutions.

Wonderful lower-key alternatives to the Musée d'Orsay for impressionist and post-impressionist art include the Musée de l'Orangerie (p118), home to Monet's enormous *Water Lilies,* and the enchanting Musée Marmottan Monet (p86), in the duc de Valmy's former hunting lodge, with the world's largest Monet collection. Paintings by Monet and others are also displayed at the Petit Palais' Musée des Beaux-Arts de la Ville de Paris (p97), alongside medieval and Renaissance *objets d'art.*

If you're interested in romantic art, instead of viewing Eugène Delacroix' works at the Musée du Louvre, try the lovely Musée National Eugène Delacroix (p232), and his frescoes at colonnaded church Église St-Sulpice (p232). In a garden-set mansion, the Musée de la Vie Romantique (p138) is a delightful ode to the era.

In lieu of checking out modern and contemporary art at the Centre Pompidou (closing for an estimated four years of renovations from late 2023), consider smaller venues like the city-run Musée d'Art Moderne de la Ville de Paris (p85); or focus on a specific artist at venues such as Dalí Paris (p139), featuring more than 300 works by the surrealist; or Giacometti's sculptures, paintings and drawings at the Institut Giacometti (p250). Digital art is projected at the Atelier des Lumières (p163). Paris is also a fabulous canvas for colourful graffiti and street art, showcased at the Galerie Itinerrance (p251), which can advise on street-art walking tours.

There are a wealth of other museum options in every genre all across the city.

Paris' parks and gardens offer wonderful slices of local life and plenty of fresh air. Beyond the well-known Jardin des Tuileries and Jardin du Luxembourg are gems like the Parc des Buttes Chaumont (p138), Parc Montsouris (p253), Parc Monceau (p137) and Parc de Belleville (p170), with elevated city views. Parc André Citroën (p250) is home to the helium-filled sightseeing Ballon de Paris (p250), which monitors Paris' air quality and provides aerial views of the city.

For more Parisian panoramas, consider swapping the Arc de Triomphe for its counterpart, the modern Grande Arche de la Défense (p91), just west in the city's high-rise business district of La Défense.

Less-Explored Neighbourhoods

Vibrant neighbourhoods give an insight into the non-touristy side of Paris. Just east of Montmartre in the 18e, Château Rouge (named for a since-demolished 17th-century red-brick mansion) and La Goutte d'Or ('Drop of Gold', for the wine produced here until the 19th century) plunge visitors into *petite Afrique à Paris* ('little Africa in Paris'), a multisensory swirl of street-market stalls, independent shops and creative endeavours. The **Institut des Cultures d'Islam** (ICIC Léon; 01 53 09 99 84; www.institut-cultures-islam.org; 19 rue Léon, 18e; 11am-7pm Tue-Thu, Sat & Sun, 4-8pm Fri; Château Rouge) FREE is here and arranges walking tours. Dig deeper into the area at Little Africa Paris (www.littleafrica.fr). You can learn more about Black history across the city with tours offered by Entrée to Black Paris (entreetoblackparis.com).

Paris is also home to three Chinatowns, in the 13e, 20e and 3e; a 'Little Tokyo' area in the 2e; and 'Little India' in the 10e, among other multicultural hubs. Numerous little-touristed village-like quarters are tucked all over the city.

For more local-led tours and off-the-beaten-track neighbourhoods, see Paris Like a Local (p36).

NEED TO KNOW

Grand Paris Paris spreads much further than its 20 central *arrondissements*. The outer suburbs are becoming increasingly integrated, including a dramatically expanding metro network, as part of the Grand Paris (Greater Paris) plan (p304).

More information Uncover more of unexpected Paris on the tourist office website: www.parisinfo.com (search for Paris Inattendu).

Musée du Quai Branly – Jacques Chirac (p84)

Museums & Galleries

If there's one thing that rivals Parisians' obsession with food, it's their love of art. Hundreds of museums pepper the city, and whether you prefer classicism, impressionism or detailed exhibits of French military history, you can always be sure to find something new just around the corner.

Paris Museum Pass

If you think you'll be visiting more than two or three museums or monuments while in Paris, the single most important investment you can make is the Paris Museum Pass (www.parismuseumpass.com; two/four/six days €48/62/74). The pass is valid for entry to over 50 venues in and around the city, including the Louvre, Centre Pompidou, Musée d'Orsay and Musée Rodin (but not the Eiffel Tower), the châteaux at Versailles and Fontainebleau and the Basilique de St-Denis.

One of the best features of the pass is that you can bypass the long ticket queues at major attractions (though not the security queues). But be warned: the pass is valid for a certain number of days, not hours, so if you activate a two-day pass late Friday afternoon, for instance, you will only be able to use it for a full day on Saturday. Also keep in mind that most museums are closed on either Monday or Tuesday, so think twice before you activate a pass on a Sunday.

The Paris Museum Pass is available online as well as at participating museums, tourist desks at the airports, branches of the Paris Convention & Visitors Bureau, and other locations listed on the website. EU citizens under 26 years and children under 18 years get free entry to national museums and monuments, so *don't* buy this pass if you belong to one of those categories.

Performances

Many museums host excellent musical concerts and performances, with schedules that generally run from September to early June. Some of the top venues:

Musée du Louvre (p108) Hosts lunchtime and evening classical concerts throughout the week.

Musée d'Orsay (p224) Concerts at 12.30pm Tuesdays mid-October to early June, plus various evening classical performances.

Musée du Quai Branly – Jacques Chirac (p84) Folk performances of theatre, dance and music from around the world.

Centre Pompidou (p116) Film screenings and avant-garde dance and music performances.

Children's Workshops

If you have kids in tow, check out the day's ateliers. Although these are usually in French, most activities involve hands-on creation, so children should enjoy themselves despite any language barrier. At major museums, it's best to sign up in advance.

PLAN YOUR TRIP MUSEUMS & GALLERIES

NEED TO KNOW

➡ City museums (eg Petit Palais, Musée Cognacq-Jay) are free; many other museums have one free day per month.

➡ Temporary exhibits almost always have a separate admission fee.

➡ Check if you qualify for a reduced-price ticket *(tarif réduit):* students, seniors and children generally get discounts or free admission with valid ID.

Dining

Although there are plenty of tourist cafeterias to be found in Paris, the dining options in museums are generally pretty good – some are destinations in themselves. Even if you're not out sightseeing, consider a meal at one of the following:

Les Ombres (p90) and **Café Jacques** (p91) These two dining options at the Musée du Quai Branly have ringside seats for the Eiffel Tower.

Les Grands Verres (p86) Sustainably themed restaurant at the Palais du Tokyo.

Le Restaurant (p225) and **Café Campana** (p225) Within the Musée d'Orsay; the former was the art nouveau railway station's showpiece restaurant.

Musée Jacquemart-André (p137) Lunch or tea in the sumptuous dining room of a 19th-century mansion.

Collection Pinault – Paris (p120) A restaurant by renowned chef Michel Bras complements the exhibitions at the Bourse de Commerce.

Public Art

Museums and galleries are not the sole repositories of art in Paris. Indeed, art is all around you, including *murs végétaux* (vertical gardens adorning apartment buildings), and street art ranging from small murals to artworks covering entire high-rises to Invader tags (tiled Space Invaders–inspired creations) marking street corners. Enjoying art in Paris is simply a matter of keeping your eyes open.

Big-name installations have become destinations in their own right. Niki de Saint Phalle and Jean Tinguely's playful *Stravinsky Fountain* – a collection of 16 colourful animated sculptures based on the composer's oeuvre – is located next to the Centre Pompidou. Daniel Buren's zebra-striped columns of varying heights at the Palais Royal is another

---

TIPS FOR AVOIDING MUSEUM FATIGUE

➡ Wear comfortable shoes and make use of the cloakrooms.

➡ Drink plenty of water.

➡ Sit down as often as you can; standing still and walking slowly promote tiredness.

➡ Reflecting on the material and forming associations with it causes information to move from your short- to long-term memory; your experiences will thus amount to more than a series of visual 'bites'. Using an audioguide is a good way to provide context.

➡ Studies suggest that museum-goers spend no more than 10 seconds viewing an exhibit and another 10 seconds reading the label as they try to take in as much as they can. To avoid this, choose a particular period or section to focus on, or join a guided tour of the highlights.

---

beloved Paris fixture; the installation was originally greeted with derision but has since become an integral part of the historic site. Both the Jardin des Tuileries and the Jardin du Luxembourg are dotted with dozens of sculptures that date from the 19th and early 20th centuries; the Jardin des Tuileries also contains an area with more contemporary works from the likes of Roy Lichtenstein and Magdalena Abakanowicz.

One of the best areas to go hunting for contemporary public art – and architecture – is out in the business district of La Défense, where you'll find dozens of works by well-known artists such as Miró, Calder and Belmondo. Metro stations, too, often contain some iconic or unusual additions, from Hector Guimard's signature art nouveau entrances to the crown-shaped cupolas at the Palais Royal.

Opening Hours

Most museums are closed on Monday or Tuesday – it's vital that you verify opening days before drawing up your day's schedule.

General opening hours are from 10am to 6pm, though all museums shut their gates between 30 minutes and an hour before their actual closing times. Thus, if a museum is listed as closing at 6pm, make sure you arrive before 5pm.

Major museums are often open one or two nights a week, which is an excellent time to visit as there are fewer visitors.

Tickets

Consider booking online to avoid queues where possible (eg for the Louvre, Musée d'Orsay, Centre Pompidou); print tickets before you go if necessary. In some cases you can download the tickets onto a smart-phone, but check beforehand. Also ensure you can download more than one ticket onto your phone if need be.

If you can't book online, look for automated machines at museum entrances, which generally have shorter queues. Note that credit cards without an embedded smart chip (and some non-European chip-enabled cards) won't work in these machines.

Museums & Galleries by Neighbourhood

Eiffel Tower & Western Paris (p85) Paris' largest concentration of museums, from the Quai Branly to Musée Marmottan Monet.

Champs-Élysées & Grands Boulevards (p96) Musée des Beaux-Arts de la Ville de Paris, Musée National Gustave Moreau and more.

Louvre & Les Halles (p108) The Louvre, Centre Pompidou, Musée de l'Orangerie and others.

Montmartre & Northern Paris (p137) Musée Jacquemart-André, Cité des Sciences, Le 104 and others.

Le Marais, Ménilmontant & Belleville (p160) Musée National Picasso, Mémorial de la Shoah, Lafayette Anticipations and L'Atelier des Lumières, among others.

Bastille & Eastern Paris (p182) Cinémathèque Française and others.

Latin Quarter (p208) Musée National du Moyen Âge, Muséum National d'Histoire Naturelle and Institut du Monde Arabe.

St-Germain & Les Invalides (p232) Musée d'Orsay, Musée Rodin and more.

Montparnasse & Southern Paris (p249) Fondation Cartier and others.

Lonely Planet's Top Choices

Musée du Louvre (p108) The one museum you just can't miss.

Musée d'Orsay (p224) Monet, Van Gogh and company.

Centre Pompidou (p116) One of the top modern-art museums in Europe.

Musée Rodin (p230) Superb collection of Rodin's master-pieces in an intimate setting.

Musée National Picasso (p160) An incomparable over-view of Picasso's work and life.

Best Modern Art Museums & Installations

Centre Pompidou (p116) Huge selection of modern art and big-name temporary exhibits.

Palais de Tokyo (p85) Interac-tive contemporary-art exhibi-tions and installations against a stark concrete-and-steel backdrop.

Jeu de Paume (p118) Exhibi-tions of contemporary photogra-phy in the Jardin des Tuileries.

Atelier des Lumières (p163) A former foundry houses Paris' first digital-art museum.

Fondation Louis Vuitton (p88) Striking glass building staging modern-art exhibitions.

Pinault Collection (p120) Major contemporary-art museum that opened in 2021.

Best Unsung Museums

Cité de l'Architecture et du Patrimoine (p85) Standout museum devoted to French architecture and heritage.

Musée Jacquemart-André (p137) Gorgeous 19th-century home hung with canvases by Rembrandt, Botticelli and Titian.

Musée des Beaux-Arts de la Ville de Paris (p97) Fine arts inside the Petit Palais.

Musée de la Vie Romantique (p138) Dedicated to the work of two romantic creators.

Musée Nissim de Camondo (p138) Eighteenth-century *objets d'art* inside a lavish mansion.

Musée Cognacq-Jay (p161) Treasure trove of artwork and *objets d'art*.

Best History Museums

Musée de l'Armée (p231) Within the monumental Hôtel des Invalides complex, com-memorating French military history.

Musée de Montmartre (p137) Relive the days of Toulouse-Lautrec and Maurice Utrillo.

Mémorial de la Shoah (p156) Moving Holocaust museum and documentation centre.

Musée du 11 Conti (p232) In the 18th-century royal mint, Monnaie de Paris.

Best Museums for Non-European Art

Musée du Quai Branly – Jacques Chirac (p84) Overview of indigenous art from around the world.

Musée Guimet des Arts Asia-tiques (p87) France's foremost Asian art museum.

Musée du Louvre (p108) Meso-potamian, Egyptian and Islamic artefacts.

Institut du Monde Arabe (p208) Art and artisanship from the Middle East and North Africa.

Best Small Museums

Musée de l'Orangerie (p118) For Monet's sublime *Water Lilies* series.

Musée Maillol (p235) Splendid museum focusing on the work of sculptor Aristide Maillol.

Cinémathèque Française (p182) Props, early equipment and short clips bring cinematic history to life.

Musée Marmottan Monet (p86) The world's largest Monet collection.

Best Science Museums

Cité des Sciences (p136) Excel-lent science-related exhibits and attractions for all ages.

Muséum National d'Histoire Naturelle (p209) Dinosaur skel-etons, taxidermic elephants and excellent temporary exhibits.

Musée des Arts et Métiers (p161) Europe's oldest science and technology museum.

Best Residence Museums

Musée National Eugène Delacroix (p232) The romantic artist's home and studio con-tains many of his more intimate works.

Musée Bourdelle (p249) Monu-mental bronzes in the house and workshop of sculptor Antoine Bourdelle.

Maison de Victor Hugo (p160) Victor Hugo's former quarters.

Maison de Balzac (p86) Novelist Honoré de Balzac's spa house.

Musée Yves Saint Laurent Paris (p85) In the fashion designer's studios.

Bœuf bourguignon

Dining Out

The inhabitants of some cities rally around local sports teams, but in Paris they rally around la table – and everything on it. Pistachio macarons, shots of tomato consommé, decadent bœuf bourguignon, a gooey wedge of Camembert running onto the cheese plate...food isn't fuel here; it's the reason you get up in the morning.

Pistachio macarons

Paris: A Culinary Renaissance

Home to one of the world's great culinary traditions, France has shaped Western cooking techniques and conceptions of what good food is for centuries – whether it's a multicourse gourmet meal or a crusty baguette. Blessed with a rich and varied landscape, farmers with a strong sense of regional identity and a culture that celebrates life's daily pleasures, it's no surprise that French chefs have long been synonymous with gastronomic genius.

In recent decades, though, restaurant culture started to slip. Frozen and industrially prepared ingredients, stultifying business regulations and an over-reliance on formulaic dishes led to a general decline in both quality and innovation. Alarmed by these forbidding trends, a new generation of chefs emerged, re-emphasising market-driven, *fait maison* (homemade) cuisine and displaying a willingness to push the boundaries of traditional tastes, while at the same time downplaying the importance of Michelin stars and the formal, chandelier-studded dining rooms of yesteryear.

More and more of these chefs – and, just as importantly, more and more diners – are open to culinary traditions originating outside France. Some have trained abroad, while others hail from Japan, the US or elsewhere. The latter group has come to Paris specifically because they love French cooking, but none are so beholden to its traditions that they are afraid to introduce new concepts or techniques from back home. French cuisine has finally come to the realisation

NEED TO KNOW

Opening Hours

➡ Restaurants generally open from noon to 2pm for lunch and from 7.30pm to 10.30pm for dinner. Peak Parisian dining times are 1pm and 9pm.

➡ Most restaurants shut for at least one full day (usually Sunday). August is the peak holiday month and many places are consequently closed during this time.

Price Ranges

The following price ranges refer to the cost of a two-course meal.

€	less than €20
€€	€20–€40
€€€	more than €40

Reservations

➡ Midrange restaurants will usually have a free table for lunch (arrive by 12.30pm); book a day or two in advance for dinner.

➡ Reservations up to one or two months in advance are crucial for lunch and dinner at popular/high-end restaurants. You may need to reconfirm on the day.

Tipping

A *pourboire* (tip) on top of the bill is not necessary as service is always included. But it is not uncommon to round up the bill if you were pleased with your waiter.

Paying the Bill

Trying to get *l'addition* (the bill) can be maddeningly slow. Do not take this personally. The French consider it rude to bring the bill immediately – you have to be persistent when it comes to getting your server's attention.

Prix-Fixe Menus

➡ Daily *formules* or *menus* (*prix-fixe* menus) typically include two- to four-course meals. In some cases, particularly at market-driven neobistros, there is no *carte* (menu).

➡ Lunch *menus* are often a fantastic deal and allow you to enjoy *haute cuisine* at very affordable prices.

that a global future doesn't necessarily mean a loss of identity – decadent work-of-art pastries and the divine selection of pungent cheeses aren't going anywhere. Instead, there is an opportunity to once again create something new.

How to Eat & Drink Like a Parisian

Eating well is of prime importance to most French people, who spend an inordinate amount of time thinking about, discussing and enjoying food and wine. Yet dining out doesn't have to be a ceremonious occasion or one riddled with pitfalls for the uninitiated. Approach food with even half the enthusiasm *les français* do, and you will be welcomed, encouraged and exceedingly well fed.

WHEN TO EAT

Petit déjeuner (breakfast) The French kick-start the day with a slice of baguette smeared with unsalted butter and jam and *un café* (espresso) or – for kids – hot chocolate. Parisians might grab a coffee and croissant on the way to work, but otherwise croissants (eaten straight, never with butter or jam) are more of a weekend treat or *goûter* (afternoon snack) along with *pains au chocolat* (chocolate-filled croissants) and other *viennoiseries* (sweet pastries).

Déjeuner (lunch) The traditional main meal of the day, lunch incorporates a starter and main course with wine, followed by a short, sharp *café*. During the work week this is less likely to be the case – many busy Parisians now grab a sandwich to go and pop off to run errands – but the standard hour-long lunch break, special *prix-fixe* menus and *tickets restaurant* (company-funded meal vouchers) ensure that many restaurants fill up at lunch.

Apéritif Otherwise known as an *apéro*, the premeal drink is sacred. Cafes and bars get packed out from around 5pm onwards as Parisians wrap up work for the day and relax over a glass of wine or beer.

Diner (dinner) Traditionally lighter than lunch, but a meal that is being treated more and more as the main meal of the day. In restaurants the head chef will almost certainly be in the kitchen, which is not always the case during lunch.

WHERE TO EAT

Bistro (or *bistrot*) A small neighbourhood restaurant that serves French standards (duck confit, *steak-frites*). The setting is usually casual; if you're looking for a traditional French meal, a bistro is the place to start. Don't expect *haute cuisine* service; most simply do not have the staff to cater to a diner's every whim.

Crêperie, Latin Quarter (p211)

Brasserie Much like a cafe except it serves full meals, drinks and coffee from morning until 11pm or later. Typical fare includes *choucroute* (sauerkraut) and sausages.

Cafe Many visitors will naturally gravitate towards cafes (which become bars around 5pm) because of the alluring ambience and buzzy sun-kissed terraces. Meals are inexpensive but often consist of industrially prepared food that's simply reheated, so stick to the drinks.

Crêperie A quintessentially Parisian snack is the street crêpe made to order, slathered with Nutella and folded up in a triangular wedge. Crêpes can be so much more than this, however, as a trip to any authentic crêperie will reveal. Savoury crêpes, known as *galettes*, are made with buckwheat flour; dessert crêpes are made with white flour – usually you order one of each accompanied by a bowl of cider.

Gastronomic Pierre Gagnaire, Guy Savoy, Pascal Barbot...Paris has one of the highest concentrations of culinary magicians in the world. Designed to amaze your every sense, many of these restaurants are once-in-a-lifetime destinations – even for Parisians – so do your homework and reserve well in advance.

Market Fantastic places to wander: here you'll find all the French culinary specialities in the same place, in addition to meals and snacks cooked on-site. Scores of food markets set up in the city. Most are open twice weekly from 8.30am to 1pm, though covered markets keep longer hours, reopening around 4pm. For a complete list, visit www.paris.fr/equipements/marches-alimentaires.

Neobistro Generally small and relatively informal, these are run by young, talented chefs who aren't afraid to experiment. The focus is on market-driven cuisine, hence choices are often limited to one or two dishes per course. Some specialise in small plates designed for sharing.

Wine bar The focus is on sampling wine; the style of cuisine, while often excellent, can be wildly different. Some *caves à manger* serve nothing more than plates of cheese and charcuterie (*saucisson*, pâté); other *bars à vins* are full-on gastronomic destinations with a talented chef running the kitchen.

MENU ADVICE

Carte Menu, as in the written list of what's cooking, listed in the order you'd eat it: starter, main course, cheese, then dessert. Note that an entrée is a starter, not the main course (as in the US).

Menu Not at all what it means in English, *le menu* in French is a *prix-fixe* menu: a multicourse meal at a fixed price. It's by far the best-value dining there is and most restaurants chalk one on the board. In some cases, particularly at neobistros, there is no *carte* – only a stripped-down *menu* with one or two choices.

À la carte Order whatever you fancy from the menu (as opposed to opting for a *prix-fixe* menu).

Text in right margin: PLAN YOUR TRIP DINING OUT

THE FIVE BASIC CHEESE TYPES

Charles de Gaulle once famously asked how it was possible to govern a country with 246 types of cheese (now countless more). A more relevant question for visitors: how do you come to grips with a shop that sells such a head-spinning variety? The choices on offer at a *fromagerie* (cheese shop) can be overwhelming, but vendors will always allow you to sample before you buy, and they are usually very generous with their guidance and pairing advice.

In shops, cheeses are typically divided into five main groups:

Fromage à pâte demi-dure 'Semi-hard cheese' means uncooked, pressed cheese. Among the finest are Tomme de Savoie, made from either raw or pasteurised cow's milk; Cantal, a cow's-milk cheese from Auvergne that tastes something like cheddar; St-Nectaire, a pressed cheese that has a strong, complex taste; and Ossau-Iraty, a ewe's-milk cheese made in the Basque Country.

Fromage à pâte dure 'Hard cheese' is always cooked and then pressed. Among the most popular are Beaufort, a grainy cow's-milk cheese with a slightly fruity taste from Rhône-Alpes; Comté, a cheese made with raw cow's milk in Franche-Comté; Emmental, a cow's-milk cheese made all over France; and Mimolette, an Edam-like dark-orange cheese from Lille that can be aged for up to 36 months.

Fromage à pâte molle 'Soft cheese' is moulded or rind-washed. Camembert, a classic moulded cheese from Normandy that for many is synonymous with 'French cheese', and Brie de Meaux are both made from raw cow's milk. Munster from Alsace, mild Chaource and strong-smelling Langres from Champagne, and the odorous Époisses de Bourgogne are rind-washed, fine-textured cheeses.

Fromage à pâte persillée 'Marbled' or 'blue cheese' is so called because the veins often resemble *persille* (parsley). Roquefort is a ewe's-milk veined cheese that is to many the king of French cheeses. Fourme d'Ambert is a mild cow's-milk cheese from Rhône-Alpes. Bleu du Haut Jura (also called Bleu de Gex) is a mild, blue-veined mountain cheese.

Fromage de chèvre 'Goat's-milk cheese' is usually creamy and both sweet and slightly salty when fresh, but it hardens and gets much saltier as it matures. Among the best varieties are Ste-Maure de Touraine, a creamy, mild cheese from the Loire region; Crottin de Chavignol, a classic though saltier variety from Burgundy; Cabécou de Rocamadour from Midi-Pyrénées, often served warm with salad or marinated in oil and rosemary; and Chabichou, a soft, slightly aged cheese from Poitou.

Formule Similar to a *menu, une formule* is a cheaper lunchtime option comprising a main plus starter or dessert. Wine or coffee is sometimes included.

Plat du jour Dish of the day, invariably good value.

Menu enfant Two- or three-course meal for kids (generally up to the age of 12) at a fixed price; usually includes a drink.

Menu dégustation Fixed-price tasting menu served in many top-end restaurants, consisting of at least five modestly sized courses.

DINING TIPS

Bread Order a meal and within seconds a basket of fresh bread will be brought to the table. Butter is rarely an accompaniment. Except in the most upmarket of places, don't expect a side plate – simply put it on the table.

Water Asking for *une carafe d'eau* (jug of tap water) is perfectly acceptable, although some waiters will presume you don't know this and only offer mineral water, which you have to pay for. Should you prefer bubbles, ask for *de l'eau gazeuze* (fizzy mineral water). Ice (*glaçons*) can be hard to come by.

Service To state the obvious, France is not a service-oriented country. No one is working for tips here, so to get around this, think like a Parisian – acknowledge the expertise of your *serveur* by asking for advice (even if you don't really want it) and don't be afraid to flirt. In France, flirtation is not the same as picking someone up; it is both a game that makes the mundane more enjoyable and a vital life skill to help you get what you want (such as the bill). Being witty and speaking French with an accent will often help your cause.

Dress Smart casual is best. How you look is very important, and Parisians favour personal style above all else. But if you're going somewhere dressy, don't assume this means suit and tie – that's more business-meal attire. At the other end of the spectrum, running shoes may be too casual, unless, of course, they are more hip than functional, in which case you may fit right in.

Vegetarians & Vegans

Vegetarians and vegans make up a small minority in a country where *viande* (meat) once also meant 'food', but in recent years they have been increasingly well catered for with a slew of new vegetarian and vegan

---

DAILY BREAD (& PASTRIES TOO)

Few things in France are as tantalising as the smell of just-baked buttery croissants wafting out of an open bakery door. With roughly 1200 *boulangeries* (bakeries) in Paris – or 11.5 per sq km – you'll likely find yourself inside one at some point during your stay. And, as you'll notice in the extravagant display windows, bakeries bake much more than baguettes: they also sell croissants, chocolate éclairs, quiches, pizzas and an astounding array of pastries and cakes. If you're eating lunch on the cheap, a trip to the closest bakery will do you right.

Specialist patisseries (pastry shops), often headed by big-name pastry chefs, create astonishing works of art. Their delicacies fall into several categories: *bavarois* (gelatin-set, cream-based desserts), *gateaux* (literally 'cakes', but spanning everything from a sponge-based chocolate-and-coffee *opéra* to layered-pastry *millefeuille*), cookie-style treats like shell-shaped madeleine cakes and macarons, *choux* (puff pastry, such as éclairs and profiteroles), *entremets* (eg flans) and *viennoiseries* (yeast-based baked goods including croissants and *pains au chocolat*).

When buying bread from a *boulangerie,* try to familiarise yourself with the varieties on sale while you're standing in the queue – not all baguettes are created equal. Most Parisians today will ask for a *baguette tradition* (traditional-style baguette), distinguished by its pointy tips and coarse, handcrafted surface. Other breads you'll see include *boules* (round loaves), *pavés* (flattened rectangular loaves) and *ficelles* (skinny loaves that are half the weight of a baguette).

The shape of a baguette (literally 'stick' or 'wand') evolved when Napoléon Bonaparte ordered army bakers to create loaves for soldiers to stuff down their trouser legs on the march.

Every spring *boulangers* (bakers) battle it out in the official Grand Prix de la Meilleure Baguette de Paris (Best Baguette in Paris). The winner is not only awarded a cash prize but also provides the French president with baguettes for a year.

addresses, from casual vegan burger, pizza and hot-dog joints to gourmet vegetarian and vegan restaurants. More and more modern places are also offering vegetarian choices on their set *menus*. Another good bet is non-French cuisine; Middle Eastern cuisine, in particular, is currently a red-hot trend. See www.happycow.net for a guide to vegan options in Paris.

Gluten-Free

Gluten-free dining options are steadily becoming more prevalent: try NoGlu (p185) for starters, and bakery Chambelland (p168) for breads and cakes.

Gluten-free addresses are mapped at www.glutenfreeinparis.com.

Cooking Classes

What better place to discover the secrets of *la cuisine française* than in Paris, the capital of gastronomy? Courses are available at different levels and for various durations. The following are taught in English:

Cook'n With Class (☏01 42 57 22 84; www. cooknwithclass.com; 6 rue Baudelique, 18e; ⊙2hr classes from €109; ⓜSimplon, Jules Joffrin) A bevy of international chefs, small classes and an enchanting Montmartre location are ingredients for success at this informal cooking school, which organises family classes for parents and kids, cheese and wine courses, market visits, gourmet food tours and six-course dinners with the chef and sommelier as well as regular cookery classes.

Le Cordon Bleu (Map p414; ☏01 85 65 15 00; www.cordonbleu.edu/paris; 13-15 quai André Citroën, 15e; 3hr classes from €55, 2-day courses from €470; ⓜJavel–André Citroën, RER Javel) One of the world's foremost culinary arts schools, founded in 1895. Themed three-hour classes span food and wine pairing, vegetarian cuisine, éclairs, choux pastry and more.

Top: Fromagerie (cheese shop), Île St-Louis (p204)
Middle: Vegan sweets on display
Bottom: Cooking course at Le Cordon Bleu

La Cuisine Paris (Map p386; ☏01 40 51 78 18; www.lacuisineparis.com; 80 quai de l'Hôtel de Ville, 4e; 2hr cooking class/walking tour from €99; ⓜPont Marie, Hôtel de Ville) Classes range from how to make bread and croissants to macarons as well as market classes and gourmet 'foodie walks'.

Le Foodist (Map p400; ☏06 71 70 95 22; www. lefoodist.com; 59 rue du Cardinal Lemoine, 5e; ⓜCardinal Lemoine) Classes at this culinary school include classic French cookery and patisserie courses, allowing you to create your own éclairs and choux pastry, macarons or croissants. Market tours, and wine and cheese tastings and pairings, are also available. Three-hour classes start at €99.

Eating by Neighbourhood

Montmartre & Northern Paris
Neobistros, wine bars and world cuisine
(p139)

Champs-Élysées & Grands Boulevards
Big-name chefs and backstreet bistros
(p100)

Louvre & Les Halles
Trendy restaurants on the rise (p121)

Le Marais, Ménilmontant & Belleville
Premier foodie destination
(p164)

Eiffel Tower & Western Paris
Gastronomic addresses and museum restaurants
(p89)

St-Germain & Les Invalides
Chic cafes plus *haute cuisine* (p235)

The Islands
Romantic setting but limited options
(p202)

Latin Quarter
Cheap eats and Left Bank treasures
(p211)

Bastille & Eastern Paris
Balances tradition and innovation
(p183)

Montparnasse & Southern Paris
Historic brasseries and neighbourhood favourites (p253)

PARIS' WHOLESALE MARKETS

Covering an area bigger than Monaco (234 hectares), **Marché International de Rungis** (☎08 25 05 44 05; www.visite rungis.com; av des Maraîchers, Rungis; tour €85; ⊗by reservation) is sectioned into vast halls for meat, cheese, fish, fruit and vegetables, organic fruit and vegetables, plants and cut flowers. Fascinating behind-the-scenes tours of its operations are in English and French. Prices include a three-hour market tour, a 45-minute breakfast and bus transport to and from central Paris. Pick-up is at 4am from place Denfert-Rochereau, 14e, returning around 10am. Wear warm clothes (and comfortable shoes!). No children under 13.

The markets are otherwise off-limits to the public.

Useful Websites

David Lebovitz (www.davidlebovitz.com) Expat US pastry chef and cookbook author. Good insights and recommendations.

Le Fooding (www.lefooding.com) The French movement that's giving Michelin a run for its money. Le Fooding's mission is to shake up the ossified establishment, so expect a good balance of quirky, under-the-radar reviews and truly fine dining.

La Fourchette (www.thefork.com) Website offering user reviews and great deals of up to 50% off in Paris restaurants.

Paris by Mouth (www.parisbymouth.com) Capital dining and drinking with articles and recommendations searchable by *arrondissement*.

Lonely Planet's Top Choices

Restaurant Guy Savoy (p238) Resplendent triple-Michelin-starred flagship in the neoclassical mint.

Bouillon Racine (p236) Classical French cooking in an art nouveau showpiece.

Berthillon (p202) Arguably the world's most sublime ice cream.

Restaurant AT (p215) Abstract-art-like masterpieces made from rare ingredients.

Substance (p90) Boundary-pushing flavour combinations by rising-star chef Matthias Marc.

Best By Budget

€

Ladurée (p100) The original creator of the lighter-than-air macaron.

Le Petit Pan (p253) Superb small sharing plates and wines by the glass.

Populus (p255) Local hotspot serving French classics.

L'Avant-Poste (p140) Eco-conscious seasonal cooking.

€€

Maison Maison (p123) Seine-side restaurant hidden by the Pont Neuf.

Au Passage (p166) A springboard for talented chefs.

Le Cassenoix (p254) *Terroir* specialist footsteps from the Eiffel Tower.

La Cantine du Troquet (p236) Tip-top bistro fare from chef Christian Etchebest.

Kitchen Ter(re) (p213) Innovative creations using ancient-grain pastas.

€€€

Le Jules Verne (p83) Michelin-starred cuisine inside the Eiffel Tower.

Septime (p188) A beacon of modern cuisine.

Frenchie (p125) The bijou bistro that redefined Parisian dining.

Lasserre (p100) Fine dining and flawless service beneath a retractable roof.

Maison (p170) Adventurous palates flock to the 'home' of chef Sota Atsumi.

Best for Traditional French

Chez La Vieille (p123) Homage to the former wholesale markets Les Halles.

Le Bon Georges (p102) For those who thrive on nostalgia.

Le Temps au Temps (p188) Traditional and excellent-value bistro fare on foodie street rue Paul Bert.

Le Verre Volé (p140) Unpretentious wine-bar dining.

Chez Dumonet (Joséphine) (p238) The Parisian bistro of your dreams.

Best for Seafood

L'Écailler du Bistrot (p186) Extraordinary seafood in a traditional setting.

L'Avant Comptoir de la Mer (p235) Chic St-Germain seafood-tapas bar.

Le Dôme (p255) Magnificent shellfish platters in a timeless art deco brasserie.

Clamato (p189) Seafood-tapas sibling of Michelin-starred Septime.

Best for Crêpes

Breizh Café (p164) Authentic Breton crêpes, with several branches around town.

Crêperie Pen-Ty (p142) Northern Paris' best crêperie.

Little Breizh (p236) Innovative twists such as Breton sardines.

Crêperie Josselin (p254) In the 'Little Brittany' neighbourhood near Gare Montparnasse.

Best for Vegetarian & Vegan

Abattoir Végétal (p142) Plant-filled vegan cafe in Montmartre.

Le Potager de Charlotte (p147) Gourmet vegan restaurant.

Soul Kitchen (p142) Market-driven vegetarian dishes.

Yumi (p142) New-generation coffee shop and veg canteen.

VGT Bowl (p235) Végétal Gourmand Tonique' lives up to its name.

Best for Pastries

Cédric Grolet Opéra (p121) Queues stretch down the street for Cédric Grolet's elaborate creations.

Stohrer (p122) Rue Montorgueil landmark in business since 1730.

Jacques Genin (p164) Assembled-to-order *millefeuilles*.

Fou de Pâtisserie (p122) One-stop-shop for treats by some of France's top pastry chefs.

Starting the day at an alfresco cafe

Bar Open

For the French, drinking and eating go together like wine and cheese, and the line between a cafe, salon de thé (tearoom), bistro, brasserie, bar and even a wine bar is blurred. The boundary between drinking and clubbing is often nonexistent – a cafe that's quiet mid-afternoon might have DJ sets in the evening and dancing later on.

Wine pairing

Drinking

For most Parisians living in tiny apartments, cafes and bars have traditionally served as the *salon* they don't have – a place where they can meet with friends over *un verre* (glass of wine), read for hours over a *café au lait,* debate politics while downing an espresso, swill cocktails during *apéro* (apéritif; predinner drink) or get the party started aboard a floating club on the Seine.

COFFEE & TEA

Coffee has always been Parisians' drink of choice to kick-start the day. So it's surprising, particularly given France's fixation on quality, that Parisian coffee long lagged behind world standards, with burnt, poor-quality beans and unrefined preparation methods. However, Paris' coffee revolution has seen local roasteries like Belleville Brûlerie and Coutume priming cafes citywide for outstanding brews made by professional baristas, often using cutting-edge extraction techniques. Caffeine fiends are now spoilt for choice and while there's still plenty of substandard coffee in Paris, you don't have to go far to avoid it.

Surprisingly, too, tea – more strongly associated with France's northwestern neighbours the UK and Ireland – is extremely popular in Paris. Tearooms offer copious varieties; learn about its history at the tea museum within the original Marais branch of **Mariage Frères** (Map p386; www.mariagefreres.com; 30, 32 & 35 rue du Bourg Tibourg, 4e; ⊙10.30am-7.30pm; ⓂHôtel de Ville).

NEED TO KNOW

Opening Hours

Closing time for cafes and bars tends to be 2am, though some have licences until dawn. Club hours vary depending on the venue, day and event.

Tiered Pricing

Drinking in Paris essentially means paying the rent for the space you take up. So it costs more to sit at a table than to stand at the counter, more for coveted terrace seats, more on a fancy square than a back-street, more in the 8e than the 18e.

Average Costs

An espresso starts at around €2, a glass of wine from €3.50, a cocktail €9 to €16 and a *demi* (half-pint) of beer €3.50 to €7. In clubs and chic bars, prices can be double. Admission to clubs is free to around €20 and is often cheaper before 1am.

Happy 'Hour'

Most mainstream bars and international-styled pubs have a 'happy hour' – called just that (no French translation) – which ushers in reduced-price drinks for a good two or three hours, usually between around 5pm and 8pm.

Top Tips

➡ Some wine bars offer free corkage; otherwise, it typically costs around €4.50 to €7.

➡ Although most places serve at least small plates (often full menus), it's normally fine to order a coffee or alcohol if you're not dining.

➡ The French rarely go drunk-wild and tend to frown upon it.

Coffee Decoded

Un café Single shot of espresso.

Un café allongé Espresso lengthened with hot water (sometimes served separately).

Un café au lait Coffee with milk.

Un café crème Shot of espresso lengthened with steamed milk.

Un double Double shot of espresso.

Une noisette Shot of espresso with a spot of milk.

Above: Shopping for tea at a branch of Mariage Frères (p55)

Left: Les Deux Magots (p240)

WINE

Wine is easily the most popular beverage in Paris and house wine can cost less than bottled water. Of France's dozens of wine-producing regions, the principal ones are Burgundy, Bordeaux, the Rhône and the Loire valleys, Champagne, Languedoc, Provence and Alsace. Wines are generally named after the location of the vineyard rather than the grape varietal. The best wines are Appellation d'Origine Contrôlée (AOC; also labelled Appellation d'Origine Protégée, AOP), meaning they meet stringent regulations governing where, how and under what conditions they're grown, fermented and bottled.

Les vins naturels (natural wines) have a fuzzy definition – no one really agrees on the details, but the general idea is that they are produced from organically grown grapes using few or no pesticides or additives. This means natural wines do not contain sulphites, which are added as a preservative in most wines. The good news is that this gives natural wines a much more distinct personality (or *terroir,* as the French say); the bad news is that these wines can also be more unpredictable. For more specifics, see the website www.morethanorganic.com.

BEER

Beer hasn't traditionally had a high profile in France and mass-produced varieties such as Kronenbourg 1664 (5.5%), brewed in Strasbourg, dominate. Paris' growing *bière artisanale* (craft beer) scene, however, is going from strength to strength, with an increasing number of city breweries, such as Brasserie BapBap (p175) and Brasserie la Goutte d'Or (p150), microbreweries and cafes offering limited-production brews on tap and by the bottle. The city's artisan-beer fest, the Paris Beer Festival (p27), takes place in brasseries, bars and specialist beer shops throughout the city. An excellent resource for hopheads is www.hoppyparis.com.

COCKTAILS

Paris' resurgent cocktail scene spans glitzy hotel bars and neobistros, super-cool backstreet speakeasies and former hostess bars in the hip SoPi ('south Pigalle') neighbourhood. Sample forgotten French liqueurs, fresh fruit, and homemade infusions and syrups at the best of the bunch. Aficionados won't want to miss Paris Cocktail Week (p26), held the last week of January.

Nightlife

Paris' residential make-up means nightclubs aren't ubiquitous. Lacking a mainstream scene, clubbing here tends to be underground and extremely mobile. The best DJs and their followings have short stints in a certain venue before moving on, and the scene's hippest *soirées clubbing* (clubbing events) float between venues – including the many dance-driven bars.

The growing suburban scene is much more alternative and spontaneous in nature but also harder to reach.

Wherever you wind up, the beat is strong. Electronic music is of a particularly high quality in Paris' clubs, with some excellent local house and techno. Funk and groove are also popular, and the Latin scene is huge; salsa-dancing and Latino-music nights pack out plenty of clubs. World music also has a following in Paris, where everything goes at clubs. R&B and hip-hop pickings are decent, if not extensive.

ROOFTOP BARS

Innovative drinking and dining spaces are carving out their place on the city's rooftops, with panoramic views over the skyline strung with Parisian landmarks.

One of the best rooftop bars is Le Perchoir (p174), atop a former industrial building in Ménilmontant. The same team also runs the rooftop bar Le Perchoir Marais (p172) at department store BHV, and the 2020-opened bar and restaurant at Pavilion 6 of the trade-fair and exhibition centre Paris Expo Porte de Versailles, 15e, utilising produce grown on-site at the 14,000-sq-metre biodiverse urban rooftop farm (the world's largest).

Seasonal rooftop bar-restaurants set up at department stores Galeries Lafayette (p104) and Le Printemps (p104). Other warm-weather hotspots are the rooftop terrace of cultural centre Point Éphémère (p150) on the banks of Canal St-Martin, and Perchoir de l'Est, above railway station Gare de l'Est.

An increasing number of Paris' hotels also have spectacular rooftop bars, such as Hôtel des Grands Boulevards (p282), Mama Shelter (p288) and Terrass'' Hôtel (p285), among others.

Drinking by Neighbourhood

Montmartre & Northern Paris
Local gems include canal-side cafes
(p148)

Champs-Élysées & Grands Boulevards
Swanky hotel bars and glam nightclubs
(p102)

Louvre & Les Halles
Eclectic mix of bars and clubs
(p127)

Le Marais Ménilmontant & Belleville
Hip drinking and nightlife venues
(p171)

Eiffel Tower & Western Paris
Classy bars and cocktail lounges
(p90)

St-Germain & Les Invalides
Historic literary cafes and stylish bars
(p240)

● Louvre

The Islands
Quaint tearooms and wine bars
(p203)

Latin Quarter
Spirited student pubs and bars
(p216)

Bastille & Eastern Paris
Lively clubs and bars galore
(p189)

Montparnasse & Southern Paris
Boulevard-facing brasseries and backstreet cafes
(p258)

BEFORE, L'AFTER & AFTER D'AFTERS

Seasoned Parisian clubbers, who tend to have a finely tuned sense of the absurd, split their night into three parts. First, *la before* – drinks in a bar that has a DJ playing. Second, they head to a club for *la soirée,* which rarely kicks off before 1am or 2am. When the party continues (or begins) at around 5am and goes until midday, it's *l'after.* Invariably, though, given the lack of any clear-cut distinction between Parisian bars and clubs, the before and after can easily blend into one without any real 'during'. *After d'afters,* meanwhile, kicks off in bars and clubs on Sunday afternoons and evenings, with a mix of strung-out hardcore clubbers pressing on amid those looking for a party that doesn't take place in the middle of the night.

CLUBBING WEBSITES

Track tomorrow's hot 'n' happening soirée with these Parisian-nightlife links:

Paris DJs (www.parisdjs.com) Free downloads to get you in the groove.

Paris Bouge (www.parisbouge.com) Comprehensive listings site.

Sortir à Paris (www.sortiraparis.com) Click on 'Soirées & Bars', then 'Nuits Parisiennes'.

Tribu de Nuit (www.tribudenuit.com) Parties, club events and concerts galore.

INDIE CLUBBING SCENE

The following informal venues and collectives organise parties in the northern *banlieues* (suburbs):

Otto 10 (www.facebook.com/otto10events)

75021 (www.facebook.com/75021Paris)

Le 6B (www.le6b.fr)

Lonely Planet's Top Choices

Bar Hemingway (p127) Legendary cocktails inside the Ritz.

Le Pavillon Puebla (p148) Pavilion opening to two terraces in the leafy Parc des Buttes Chaumont.

Le Baron Rouge (p189) Wonderfully convivial barrel-filled wine bar.

Le Perchoir (p174) Rooftop bar best visited at sunset.

Les Deux Magots (p240) Watch St-Germain go by from this famous cafe's terrace.

Candelaria (p171) Clandestine cocktail bar hidden behind a taqueria (taco restaurant).

Best Wine Bars

Au Sauvignon (p240) Original zinc bar and hand-painted ceiling.

Le Garde Robe (p128) Affordable natural wines and unpretentious vibe.

Augustin Marchand D'Vins (p242) Atmospheric decor and excellent wines.

Septime La Cave (p189) Wine and gourmet nibbles just off rue de Charonne.

La Cave des Climats (p242) Classy imbibing and dining.

Ô Chateau (p129) Lively wine bar with guided tastings and tours.

Best Cocktails

Le Syndicat (p148) Cocktails incorporate rare French spirits.

Baby Doll (p127) Concoctions and decor inspired by French musician Serge Gainsbourg.

Le Mary Céleste (p171) Innovative cocktails in the hip Haut Marais.

Experimental Cocktail Club (p127) Speakeasy that spawned an international empire.

Tiger (p241) Gin specialist with 130 varieties.

Cod House (p241) Sake-based cocktails pair with gourmet small plates.

Best Beer

Paname Brewing Company (p149) Craft-brewery taproom in a 19th-century waterside granary with a floating pontoon.

Brasserie la Goutte d'Or (p150) Northern Paris brewery and taproom.

Les Cuves de Fauve (p189) Great house brews in the burgeoning Fairdherbe neighbourhood.

Micro Brasserie Balthazar (p175) Crowdfunded microbrewery with guest Parisian beers.

Best Pavement Terraces

Scilicet (p127) Right on the Seine with a spectacular Parisian panorama.

Chez Prune (p146) The boho cafe that put Canal St-Martin on the map.

L'Ébouillanté (p173) Among Paris' prettiest cafe terraces, with homemade ginger lemonade.

Café des Anges (p190) The terrace of this Bastille cafe buzzes night and day.

Shakespeare & Company Cafe (p216) Live the Parisian Left Bank literary dream.

Best Nightclubs

Le Rex Club (p129) Renowned house and techno club with a phenomenal sound system.

Bridge (p102) Huge 2000-capacity club beneath the Pont Alexandre III bridge.

La Machine du Moulin Rouge (p150) In the Moulin Rogue's former boiler room.

Bateau El Alamein (p259) Floating club on the Seine.

Best Coffee

Belleville Brûlerie (p153) Groundbreaking roastery with Saturday-morning tastings.

Beans on Fire (p175) Collaborative roastery and cafe.

La Caféothèque (p172) Coffee house and roastery with an in-house coffee school.

Coutume Café (p242) Artisan roastery with a flagship Left Bank cafe.

Honor (p102) Outdoor coffee bar in an elegant rue du Faubourg St-Honoré courtyard.

Café Lomi (p149) Coffee roastery and cafe in the multi-ethnic La Goutte d'Or neighbourhood.

Best Tearooms

Mariage Frères (p55) Paris' oldest and finest tearoom, founded in 1854.

Nina's (p128) Utlises produce from the Château de Versailles' gardens.

La Mosquée (p215) Sip sweet mint tea and nibble delicious pastries at Paris' mosque.

Jacques Genin (p164) Famed chocolatier with an on-site tearoom.

Palais Garnier (p103)

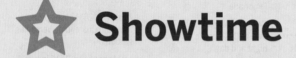

⭐ Showtime

Catching a performance in Paris is a treat. French and international opera, ballet and theatre companies and cabaret dancers take to the stage in fabled venues, while elsewhere a flurry of young, passionate, highly creative musicians, thespians and other artists make the city's fascinating fringe art scene what it is.

Moulin Rouge (p151)

Cabarets

Whirling lines of feather-boa-clad, high-kicking dancers at grand-scale cabarets like cancan creator Moulin Rouge are a quintessential fixture on Paris' entertainment scene – for everyone but Parisians. Still, the dazzling sets, costumes and dancing guarantee an entertaining evening (or matinee).

Tickets to these spectacles start at around €90 (from around €165/190 with lunch/dinner), with the option of Champagne. Reserve ahead.

Live Music

Festivals for just about every musical genre ensure that everyone gets to listen in. Street music is a constant in this busker-filled city, with summer adding stirring open-air concerts along the Seine and in city parks to the year-round serenade of accordions.

JAZZ & BLUES

Jazz emerged in Paris during WWI, with the city becoming Europe's most important jazz centre after WWII. Its clubs still lure international stars.

Admission generally ranges from free to around €30 depending on artist, time and venue. Concerts are listed at www.parisjazzclub.net.

Download podcasts, tunes, concert information and all that jazz from Paris' jazz radio station, TSF (www.tsfjazz.com).

FRENCH CHANSONS

While *chanson* literally means 'song' in French, it also specifically refers to a style of heartfelt, lyric-driven music typified by Édith Piaf, Maurice Chevalier, Charles Az-

NEED TO KNOW

Opening Hours

Entertainment opening hours vary widely, depending on the genre, venue and individual event; confirm times when planning and making bookings.

Listings

Paris' top listings guide, *L'Officiel des Spectacles* (www.offi.fr; €1), is published in French but is easy to navigate. It's available from news stands on Wednesday, and is crammed with everything that's on in the capital, including concert, theatre and cinema listings.

Useful Websites

LYLO (www.lylo.fr) Short for Les Yeux, Les Oreilles (meaning 'eyes and ears'), offering the low-down on concerts, festivals and more.

Le Figaro (www.lefigaro.fr/culture) Music, cinema and theatre listings.

Paris Nightlife (www.parisnightlife.fr) All-encompassing listings site.

Tickets

The most convenient place to purchase concert, theatre and other cultural and sporting-event tickets is from electronics and entertainment megashop **Fnac** (www.fnactickets.com), whether in person at the *billeteries* (ticket offices) or online. There are branches throughout Paris, including in the Forum des Halles. Tickets generally can't be refunded.

Discount Tickets

On the day of performance, theatre, opera and ballet tickets are sold for half price (plus €3.50 commission) at the Kiosque Théâtre Madeleine (p103); there are branches at the main tourist office (p338) and at Montparnasse.

navour et al. You'll come across some rousing live covers of their most famous songs at traditional venues. Contemporary twists on the genre include the fusion of dance beats with traditional *chanson* melodies. The term also covers intimate cabarets such as Montmartre's Au Lapin Agile (p151).

Admission ranges from free to around €30 depending on artist, time and venue.

ROCK, POP & INDIE

AccorHotels Arena (p191), **Stade de France** (☎01 55 93 00 00; www.stadefrance. com; St-Denis La Plaine; 1½hr stadium tours adult/child €15/10; Ⓜ St-Denis-Porte de Paris) and Le Zénith (p136) in Parc de la Villette are among the largest venues but also the most impersonal; newer additions include La Seine Musicale (p259) and **Paris La Défense Arena** (www.parisladefense-arena.com; 99 Jardins de l'Arche, Nanterre; Ⓜ La Défense–Grande Arche). Smaller concert halls with real history and charm include La Cigale (p151) and L'Olympia (p103) among numerous others.

CLASSICAL MUSIC

The city hosts dozens of orchestral, organ and chamber-music concerts each week. In addition to theatres and concert halls, Paris' beautiful, centuries-old stone churches have magnificent acoustics; posters outside advertise upcoming events with ticket information, or visit www.ampconcerts.com, where you can make online reservations. Tickets cost around €23 to €30.

Larger venues include the Jean Nouvel–designed 2400-seat Philharmonie de Paris (p150) concert hall and La Seine Musicale.

WORLD & LATINO

Musiques du monde (world music) has a huge following in Paris, where everything – from Algerian raï and other North African music to Senegalese *mbalax* and West Indian *zouk* – goes at clubs. Many venues have salsa classes.

Cinema

The film lover's ultimate city, Paris has some wonderful movie houses to catch new flicks, avant-garde cinema and priceless classics.

First-run cinema tickets cost around €11.50 for adults (€13.50 for 3D). Students and over 60s get discounted tickets (usually around €8.50) from 7pm Sunday to 7pm Friday. Discounted tickets for children and teens have no restrictions. Most cinemas have across-the-board discounts before noon.

Foreign films (including English-language films) screened in their original language with French subtitles are labelled 'VO' *(version originale)*. Films labelled 'VF' *(version française)* are dubbed in French.

Music festival Rock en Seine (p28)

Lost in Frenchlation (www.lostinfrenchlation.com) regularly hosts English-subtitled screenings of French films accompanied by drinks – check upcoming events online.

Opera & Ballet

France's Opéra National de Paris and Ballet de l'Opéra National de Paris perform at Paris' two opera houses: the Palais Garnier (p103) and Opéra Bastille (p191). The season runs between September and July.

Theatre

Theatre productions, including those originally written in other languages, are invariably performed in French. Only occasionally do English-speaking troupes play at smaller venues in and around town.

Non-French speakers should check out **Theatre in Paris** (TIP; ☎01 85 08 66 89; www.theatreinparis.com; tickets €20-100; ☉phone enquiries 10am-7pm Mon-Fri), whose bilingual hosts provide an English-language program and direct you to your seats. Typically there are upwards of 10 shows on offer, from French classics to contemporary comedies and Broadway-style productions with English surtitles. Book via its English online ticketing platform.

Buskers in Paris

Paris' gaggle of clowns, mime artists, living statues, acrobats, in-line skaters, buskers and other street entertainers can be loads of fun and cost substantially less than a theatre ticket (a few coins in the hat is appreciated). Some excellent musicians perform in the long, echo-filled corridors of the metro (artists audition for the privilege). Outside, you can be sure of a good show at the following:

Place Georges Pompidou, 4e The huge square in front of the Centre Pompidou.

Pont St-Louis, 4e The bridge linking Paris' two islands.

Place Joachim du Bellay, 1er Musicians and fire-eaters near the Fontaine des Innocents.

Parc de la Villette, 19e African drummers at the weekend.

Place du Tertre, 18e Montmartre's original main square is Paris' busiest busker stage.

Entertainment by Neighbourhood

Champs-Élysées & Grands Boulevards (p103) Famous revues and Paris' palatial 1875-built opera house take top billing here.

Louvre & Les Halles (p129) Swinging jazz clubs, centuries-old theatres and cinemas mix it up with pumping nightclubs.

Montmartre & Northern Paris (p150) Show-stopping cabarets, mythologised concert halls and cutting-edge cultural centres.

Le Marais, Ménilmontant & Belleville (p175) Rockin' live-music venues, old-style *chansons* and arts centres.

Bastille & Eastern Paris (p191) Opera, old-time tea dancing and France's national cinema institute are big drawcards.

Latin Quarter (p218) Swing bands, cinema retrospectives and jam sessions are among the Latin Quarter's offerings.

St-Germain & Les Invalides (p242) Atmospheric cinemas, cultural centres and theatres inhabit this chic, sophisticated neighbourhood.

Montparnasse & Southern Paris (p259) Some of this area's most happening venues are aboard boats moored on the Seine.

PLAN YOUR TRIP SHOWTIME

Philharmonie de Paris (p150)

Lonely Planet's Top Choices

Palais Garnier (p103) Paris' premier opera house is an artistic inspiration.

Point Éphémère (p150) Ubercool cultural centre on the banks of Canal St-Martin.

Moulin Rouge (p151) The can-can creator razzle-dazzles with spectacular sets, costumes and choreography.

Café Universel (p218) Brilliant jazz club showcasing a diverse range of styles.

Best Cinemas

La Cinémathèque Française (p191) The national cinema institute has a host of cinematic offerings.

Le Louxor (p151) Neo-Egyptian art deco treasure; look for films accompanied by a live pianist.

Le Champo (p218) Beloved art deco icon screening independent films.

Forum des Images (p130) The Paris film archive of movies set in the French capital, with a five-screen cinema.

Le Grand Rex (p130) Art deco landmark with behind-the-scenes tours.

Best for French Chansons

Au Lapin Agile (p151) Legendary Montmartre cabaret.

Chez Louisette (p152) Classic *chansons* at northern Paris' vast flea market, the Marché aux Puces de St-Ouen.

Le Vieux Belleville (p176) Old-fashioned bistro and *musette* atop Parc de Belleville.

Best Jazz Clubs

Café Universel (p218) Intimate club with unpretentious vibe and no cover.

New Morning (p151) Solid and varied line-up of everything from postbop and Latin to reggae.

Le Baiser Salé (p129) Reputable venue that focuses on Caribbean and Latin sounds.

Sunset & Sunside (p129) Blues, fusion and world sounds, as well as straight-up jazz.

Cave du 38 Riv' (p176) Rue de Rivoli jazz club with concerts and jam sessions.

Duc des Lombards (p129) Intimate, sophisticated club.

Best for Rock, Pop & Indie

Le Motel (p191) Beloved indie venue near Bastille.

Le Divan du Monde (p150) Great indie shows at this hybrid cabaret-club in Pigalle.

Cabaret Sauvage (p136) Giant yurt that hosts hip-hop, funk and world concerts.

Bus Palladium (p151) Eclectic rock venue.

La Maroquinerie (p176) Tiny but trendy venue in Ménilmontant with cutting-edge gigs.

Nouveau Casino (p176) Underground and up-to-the-minute acts.

Best for Classical Music

Philharmonie de Paris (p150) Home to the Orchestre de Paris.

La Seine Musicale (p259) Landmark venue with many classical offerings.

Sainte-Chapelle (p200) Unforgettable classical concerts amid jewel-like stained glass.

Maison de la Radio (p91) Top performers recorded live for national radio.

Église St-Eustache (p119) Sunday-afternoon organ concerts.

Église de la Madeleine (p98) Memorable organ recitals.

Best Theatre, Dance & Opera

Palais Garnier (p96) Fabled home of the phantom of the opera, offering an unforgettable experience.

Opéra Bastille (p191) Paris' main, modern opera house, seating an audience of 3400.

Comédie Française (p130) Historic state-run theatre dating from the 17th century.

Théâtre National de Chaillot (p87) Modern dance.

La Seine Musical (p259) Ballets, musicals and more.

Best for World & Latino

Favela Chic (p176) Latin, funk and Brazilian pop.

Cabaret Sauvage (p136) From reggae and raï to dance-till-dawn DJ nights.

La Java (p176) Live salsa nights followed by Latin and electro DJs.

La Chapelle des Lombards (p191) Afro jazz, reggae and Latin grooves.

Passage des Panoramas (p67)

Treasure Hunt

Paris has it all: broad boulevards lined with international chains, luxury avenues studded with designer fashion houses, famous grands magasins (department stores) and fabulous markets. But the real charm lies in strolling the city's backstreets, where tiny speciality shops and quirky boutiques selling everything from strawberry-scented wellington boots to heavenly fragranced candles are wedged between cafes, galleries and churches.

NEED TO KNOW

Opening Hours

Generally, shops open 10am to 7pm Monday to Saturday. Smaller shops may shut on Monday and/or close from around noon to 2pm for lunch. Shops in ZTIs (international tourist zones, eg Le Marais) open late and on Sundays.

Sales

Paris' twice-yearly *soldes* (sales), which last for four weeks, start in mid-January (the second Wednesday, or first Wednesday if the second occurs after 12 January) and again in late June (the last Wednesday, or second-last if the last occurs after 28 June).

Tax Refunds

Non-EU residents may be eligible for a TVA (*taxe sur la valeur ajoutée;* value-added tax) refund.

Top Shopping Tips

➡ Head to a *cabine d'essayage* (fitting room), or check sizes at www.online conversion.com/clothing.

➡ Most shops offer free (and very beautiful) gift wrapping – ask for *un paquet cadeau.*

➡ A *ticket de caisse* (receipt) is essential for returning/exchanging an item (within one month of purchase).

Shopping Etiquette

➡ If you're happy browsing, tell sales staff, '*Je regarde*' – 'I'm just looking'.

➡ Bargaining is only acceptable at flea markets.

➡ In smaller, exclusive shops, shopkeepers may not appreciate your touching the merchandise until invited to do so.

Parisian Souvenirs

For authentic distinctive and/or nostalgic souvenirs, visit the City of Paris' Paris Rendez-Vous boutique at the Hôtel de Ville (p161). Its online boutique ships worldwide.

At major museums, the Boutiques de Musées (www.boutiquesdemusees.fr) have high-quality replicas and a digital painting-and-frame service: browse masterpieces, choose a frame style and have it mailed to your home.

Vintage dress

Fashion

Fashion shopping is Paris' forte. Yet although its well-groomed residents make the city at times look and feel like a giant catwalk, fashion here is about style and quality first and foremost, rather than status or brand names. A good place to get an overview of Paris fashion is at the city's famous *grands magasins.*

Paris is aiming to become the world's most sustainable fashion capital by 2024. Its initiative Paris Good Fashion sets out to improve sourcing and traceability, make processes more eco-friendly and create a circular economy. The city's fashion entrepreneurs continue to rise to the challenge.

Although tickets for Paris' high-profile *haute couture* and prêt-à-porter fashion shows are like hens' teeth, you can still see some runway action: reserve ahead to attend fashion shows (p104) at Galeries Lafayette.

Parisian fashion doesn't have to break the bank: there are fantastic bargains at secondhand and vintage boutiques (generally, the more upmarket the area, the better quality the cast-offs). Outlet shops sell previous seasons' collections, surpluses and seconds by name-brand designers. **Arlettie** (Map p366; ☏01 84 16 12 12; www. arlettie.fr; 17 av Raymond Poincaré; ☉hours vary; Ⓜ Trocadéro) holds big-name designer overstock sales.

Covered Passages

Dating from the 19th century, Paris' glass-roofed *passages couverts* (covered passages) were the precursors to shopping malls and are treasure chests of small, exquisite boutiques. Beautifully preserved arcades include Paris' oldest, **Passage des Panoramas** (Map p372; btwn 10 rue St-Marc, 2e & 11 bd Montmartre, 9e; ⓂGrands Boulevards, Richelieu Drouot), dating from 1800.

Markets

Nowhere encapsulates Paris' village atmosphere more than its markets. Not simply places to shop, the city's street markets are social gatherings for the entire neighbourhood, and visiting one will give you a true appreciation of Parisian life.

Nearly every little quarter has its own street market at least once a week (never Monday) where tarpaulin-topped trestle tables bow beneath fresh, cooked and preserved delicacies. *Marchés biologiques* (organic markets) are increasingly sprouting up across the city. Many street markets also sell clothes, accessories, homewares and more. Markets in Paris' more multicultural neighbourhoods are filled with the flavours and aromas of continents beyond Europe.

Bric-a-brac, antiques, retro clothing, jewellery, cheap brand-name clothing, footwear, African carvings, DVDs, electronic items and much more are laid out at the city's flea markets. Watch out for pickpockets!

The website www.paris.fr/pages/les-marches-parisiens-2428 lists every Parisian market, including speciality markets such as flower markets, as well as schedules of ephemeral *brocantes* (secondhand markets) and *vide-greniers* ('empty the attic' sales).

Gourmet Goods

Food, wine and tea shops make for mouth-watering shopping. Pastries might not keep, but items you can take home (customs regulations permitting) include light-as-air macarons, chocolates, jams, preserves and, of course, fabulous French cheeses. Many of the best *fromageries* (cheese shops) can provide vacuum packing.

PLAN YOUR TRIP TREASURE HUNT

Bouquiniste (p220)

Shopping by Neighbourhood

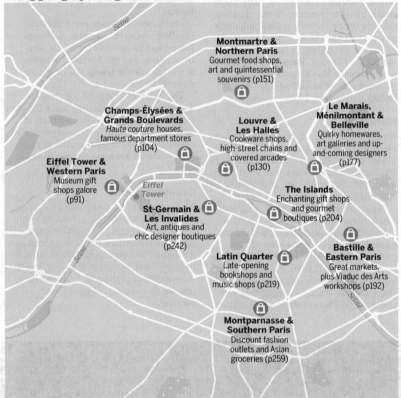

Montmartre & Northern Paris
Gourmet food shops, art and quintessential souvenirs (p151)

Champs-Élysées & Grands Boulevards
Haute couture houses, famous department stores (p104)

Louvre & Les Halles
Cookware shops, high-street chains and covered arcades (p130)

Le Marais, Ménilmontant & Belleville
Quirky homewares, art galleries and up-and-coming designers (p177)

Eiffel Tower & Western Paris
Museum gift shops galore (p91)

Eiffel Tower

St-Germain & Les Invalides
Art, antiques and chic designer boutiques (p242)

The Islands
Enchanting gift shops and gourmet boutiques (p204)

Latin Quarter
Late-opening bookshops and music shops (p219)

Bastille & Eastern Paris
Great markets, plus Viaduc des Arts workshops (p192)

Montparnasse & Southern Paris
Discount fashion outlets and Asian groceries (p259)

Art & Antiques

From venerable antique dealers to edgy art galleries, there's a wealth of places in this artistic city to browse and buy one-off conversation pieces and collectibles. A good starting point is the Carré Rive Gauche ('Left Bank Square'), bounded by quai Voltaire and rues de l'Université, des St-Pères and du Bac, in St-Germain, where you'll find scores of specialist merchants.

Homewares & Design

Paris has a trove of design shops selling inspired homewares to brighten your living and/or working environment. Parisian creativity comes to the fore during Paris Design Week (www.maison-objet.com/en/paris-design-week), held in fact over 10 days in early September and featuring launches, workshops and other events. Other design showcases accessible to the public include the 12-day Foire de Paris (www.foiredeparis.fr) contemporary living fair from late April to early May at the Parc des Expositions at Porte de Versailles, 15e.

Lonely Planet's Top Choices

Bouquinistes (p220) Vintage advertising posters and other treasures along the banks of the Seine.

Le Bonbon au Palais (p219) Artisan sweets from regions throughout France in a geography-classroom-themed boutique.

La Grande Épicerie de Paris (p245) Glorious food emporium.

Magasin Sennelier (p245) Historic art-supply shop with paints, canvases and paraphernalia galore.

Shakespeare & Company (p219) A 'wonderland of books', as Henry Miller described it.

Galeries Lafayette (p104) Monumental department store topped by a stained-glass dome.

Best Concept & Design Stores

Merci (p177) Fabulously fashionable and unique: all profits go to a children's charity in Madagascar.

Empreintes (p177) Emporium showcasing some 6000 French artists and designers.

L'Exception (p130) Fashion, homewares, books and more from over 400 French designers.

O/HP/E (p152) Designer homewares, stationery, cosmetics and gourmet goods in the buzzing Château d'Eau neighbourhood.

Thanks (p152) Homewares, gifts and jewellery all made in France.

Le Bazar Français (p243) Homewares, fashion, accessories and jewellery at this shop are all designed and made in France.

Best Sustainable Paris-Designed Fashion

Sézane (p131) Eco-conscious, affordable fashion by Parisian entrepreneur-designer Morgane Sézalory.

Les Récupérables (p152) Sustainable fashion made from unused fabrics.

Samy Chalon (p177) Haut Marais atelier fusing ethical upcycling with luxury couture.

Faguo (p178) Recycled and vegan lines, and a tree-planting project.

Best Secondhand & Vintage Boutiques

Didier Ludot (p131) Couture creations of yesteryear.

Kiliwatch (p131) New and used streetwear; vintage hats and boots.

Chercheminippes (p244) Several specialist boutiques on one street.

Catherine B (p244) Stocking only Chanel and Hermès vintage pieces.

Le Dépôt-Vente de Buci (p244) Clothing from the 1960s on.

Best For Kids

Bonton (p179) Vintage-inspired fashion, furnishings and knick-knacks for babies, toddlers and children.

Album (p220) Superb collection of *bandes desinées* (comic strips) and related collectibles.

Finger in the Nose (p244) Streetwise Parisian label for kids.

Smallable Concept Store (p244) A one-stop shop for babies, children and teens.

Best Gourmet Shops

La Grande Épicerie de Paris (p245) Now with an outpost on the Right Bank, too.

Place de la Madeleine (p101) Single-item specialist shops and famous emporiums.

La Manufacture de Chocolat (p192) Alain Ducasse's bean-to-bar chocolate factory.

Fromagerie Goncourt (p179) Contemporary *fromagerie* styled like a boutique.

La Dernière Goutte (p243) Wines from small, independent French producers.

Best Art & Antiques

Hôtel Drouot (p104) Famous auction house.

Galerie Teo Leo (p242) Treasures from the 1940s onwards.

Marché de la Création (p261) Market selling handmade arts and crafts.

Best Flea Markets

Marché aux Puces de St-Ouen (p152) One of Europe's largest flea markets, with more than 2500 stalls.

Marché aux Puces d'Aligre (p193) Retro and antique homewares are among the finds at this small, central 12e flea market.

Marché aux Puces de la Porte de Vanves (p260) Friendly southern Paris flea market.

Marché aux Puces de Montreuil (p193) Eastern Paris flea market.

LGBTIQ+ Travellers

The city known as 'gay Paree' lives up to its name. Paris is so open that there's less of a defined 'scene' here than in other cities where it's more underground. While Le Marais is the mainstay of gay and lesbian nightlife, you'll find LGBTIQ+ venues throughout the city attracting a mixed crowd.

Background

Paris was the first European capital to vote in an openly gay mayor when Bertrand Delanoë was elected in 2001. The city itself is very open – same-sex couples commonly display affection in public and checking into a hotel room is unlikely to raise eyebrows. In fact, the only challenge you may have is working out where straight Paris ends and gay Paris starts, as the city is so stylish and sexy.

In 2013 France became the 13th country in the world to legalise same-sex marriage (and adoption by same-sex couples), and polls show that the majority of French citizens support marriage equality. Typically, at least one partner needs to be a resident to get married here. And, of course, there's no end of romantic places to propose.

Drinking & Nightlife

Le Marais, especially the areas around the intersection of rue Ste-Croix de la Bretonnerie and rue des Archives, and eastwards to rue Vieille du Temple, has long been Paris' main centre of LGBTIQ+ nightlife and is still its epicentre. There's also a handful of bars and clubs close by to its west, particularly around Châtelet. The lesbian scene is less prominent than its gay counterpart, and centres on a few cafes and bars; rue des Écouffes is a good starting point. Bars and clubs are generally all gay- and lesbian-friendly.

Events

By far the biggest event on the gay and lesbian calendar is Gay Pride Day, in late June, when the annual Marche des Fiertés (p27) through Paris via Le Marais provides a colourful spectacle, and plenty of parties take place.

Year-round, check LGBTIQ+ websites or ask at gay and lesbian bars and other venues to find out about events.

Organisations & Resources

Centre **LGBT Paris-Île de France** (☎01 43 57 21 47; www.centrelgbtparis.org; 63 rue Beaubourg, 3e; ☻3.30-8pm Mon-Fri, 1-7pm Sat; Ⓜ Rambuteau) is the single best source of information for gay and lesbian travellers in Paris, with a large **library** (☻6-8pm Mon-Wed, 5-7pm Fri & Sat) of books and periodicals and a sociable bar. It also has details of hotlines, helplines, gay and gay-friendly medical services and politically oriented activist associations.

Guided Tours

For an insider's perspective on gay life in Paris, and recommendations on where to eat, drink, sightsee and party, take a tour with the **Gay Locals** (www.thegaylocals.com; 2/3hr tour €240/300). English-speaking residents lead two tours of 'the Gaybourhood' Le Marais or Montmartre, as well as longer tours, and itinerary planning (from €40 per day) based on your interests. Its website is a good source of nightlife info.

Lonely Planet's Top Choices

Open Café (p172) The wide terrace is prime for talent-watching.

Gibus Club (p172) One of Paris' biggest gay parties.

La Champmeslé (p128) Cabaret nights, fortune-telling and art exhibitions attract an older lesbian crowd.

Best Weekend in Le Marais

Loustic (p174) Among the best coffee (and espresso-bar interior design) in town.

Place des Vosges (p160) Soak up the romance of this charming city square.

Faguo (p178) Shop for fashion, footwear and more at this eco-responsible boutique.

Cimetière du Père Lachaise (p157) Oscar Wilde's winged-angel-topped tomb is a highlight.

Le Perchoir Marais (p172) Take in the city and Seine views over a cocktail at this rooftop bar.

Derrière (p168) Play ping-pong between courses at this stellar restaurant.

Best Gay Hang-Outs

Café Cox (p172) The meeting place for an interesting (and interested) cruisy crowd throughout the evening, from dusk onward.

Raidd Bar (p172) Upstairs is a pulsating den of DJs, dancing, themed parties, raunchy shower shows...

LABO (p128) Nightly events include karaoke and drag shows.

El Hombre (p128) The dance floor gets packed at this bear bar.

Best Lesbian Hang-Outs

3w Kafé (p172) Flagship cocktail bar–pub.

La Champmeslé (p128) A fixture on Paris' lesbian scene since the '70s.

Le Tango (p172) Mingle with a mixed and cosmopolitan gay and lesbian crowd.

Ici (p128) Stylish Châtelet newcomer with vaulted lounge and dance areas.

La Mutinerie (p128) Shoot pool at this sociable bar.

Best Apéros

Open Café (p172) With a four-hour happy hour kicking off daily at 6pm, how can you possibly go wrong?

Raidd Bar (p172) Has a laid-back lounge-style ground-floor bar.

LABO (p128) The terrace at this gay hang-out is lively from the afternoon on.

Best Clubs

Open Café (p172) The only place to be, late on a Saturday night.

Le Tango (p172) Set in a historic 1930s dance hall.

Gibus Club (p172) Get ready to party.

Best Party Spots Elsewhere in Paris

Ménilmontant Edgy urban cool.

Pigalle Montmartre's sexy southern neighbour.

Champs-Élysées Glam bars and clubs.

Bastille Lively local vibe.

Canal St-Martin Arty, indie venues.

St-Germain Quintessential Parisian style.

Parks & Activities

In the run-up to Paris' 2024 Summer Olympics and Summer Paralympics, you'll find ample opportunities to watch spectator sports or take part yourself. To unwind with the Parisians, check out the city's green spaces, where you can thwack a tennis ball, stroll in style, admire art, or break out some wine and cheese.

Parks

For apartment-dwelling Parisians, the city's parks act as communal backyards. Popular inner-city spaces include the enchanting Jardin du Luxembourg (p228), stately Jardin des Tuileries (p118) and elegant Parc Monceau (p137), as well as the sprawling botanical gardens, greenhouses and museums that make up the Jardin des Plantes (p209). The city's two forests, the western Bois de Boulogne (p88) and eastern Bois de Vincennes (p184), offer easy escapes from the concrete into nature.

Spectator Sports

Paris hosts a great variety of sporting events throughout the year, from the French Open and Paris Masters to local football matches. There's a handful of stadiums in and around the city; for upcoming events, click on Sports & Games (under the Going Out menu) at www.parisinfo.com. If you can read French, sports daily *L'Équipe* (www.lequipe.fr) will provide more depth.

Local teams include football's Paris Saint-Germain (www.psg.fr) and rugby's sky-blue-and-white-dressed Racing 92 (www.racing92.fr) and pink-clad Stade Français Paris (www.stade.fr). Catch France's national football team, Les Bleus (www.fff.fr), at the Stade de France.

The city's three horse-racing tracks can make for a thrilling afternoon. The Hippodrome d'Auteuil and the Hippodrome de Longchamp are in the Bois de Boulogne; the Hippodrome de Paris-Vincennes is in the Bois de Vincennes. Every October the Prix de l'Arc de Triomphe (www.prixarcdetriomphe.com), Europe's most prestigious horse race, is held at the Hippodrome de Longchamp.

Cycling

Everyone knows that the Tour de France races up the Champs-Élysées at the end of July every year, but you don't need Chris Froome's leg muscles to enjoy Paris on two wheels. Between the Paris bike-share scheme Vélib' (p341), and the hundreds of kilometres of urban bike paths, cycling around the city has never been easier. Sign up for one of the great city bike tours (p336) or hire a bike yourself (p333). Some streets are closed to vehicle traffic on Sundays – see www.paris.fr/pages/paris-respire-2122 – great news for cyclists! Bring your own helmet.

Skating

The next-most popular activity after cycling has to be skating, whether on the street or on ice. Rent a pair of in-line skates at Nomadeshop (p179) and join the Friday-evening skate, **Pari Roller** (Map p412; www.pari-roller.com; place Raoul Dautry, 14e; ☺9.30pm-midnight Fri; Ⓜ Montparnasse Bienvenüe) FREE, that zooms through the Paris streets, or join the more laid-back Sunday-afternoon skate, Rollers & Coquillages (www.rollers-coquillages.org).

During the winter holidays, several temporary outdoor rinks are installed around Paris. Venues change from year to year; check www.paris.fr for locations.

Hammams & Spas

Whether you want to hobnob with the stars at a *spa de luxe* or get a *savon noir* (black soap) exfoliation at the neighbourhood *hammam* (Turkish steambath), Paris has spaces to suit every whim.

A *hammam* generally charges an entrance fee, which grants you admission to a steam bath and sauna. Extras – exfoliation scrubs, orange-blossom massages, and mint tea and North African pastries – are tacked onto the initial price (but they're worth it!). Most *hammams* are primarily for women; if men are admitted it's usually only once or twice a week, and only rarely at the same time as women.

Swimming

If you plan to go swimming at either your hotel or in a public pool, you'll need to don a *bonnet de bain* (bathing cap) – even if you don't have any hair. You shouldn't need to buy one ahead of time as they are generally sold at most pools. Men are required to wear skin-tight trunks (Speedos); loose-fitting Bermuda shorts are not allowed.

Boules

You'll often see groups of earnest Parisians playing boules (aka *pétanque*, France's most popular traditional game, similar to lawn bowls) in the Jardin du Luxembourg and other parks and squares with suitably flat, shady patches of gravel. The Arènes de Lutèce (p210) *boulodrome* in a 2nd-century Roman amphitheatre in the Latin Quarter is a fabulous spot to absorb the scene. There are usually places to play at **Paris Plages** (www.parisinfo.com; ⊙mid-Jul–early Sep).

If you want to try out the sport indoors, head to Chez Bouboule (p126), which has a packed-sand *boulodrome* and a bar.

NEED TO KNOW

Resources

The city of Paris website (www.paris.fr/sport) has info on everything from skating and badminton to stadiums and equipment rental. Also useful is http://quefaire.paris.fr/sports, which lists venues for football and climbing, and has info on swimming pools open at night and other activities.

Tickets

Tickets for big events can generally be purchased through the venue's website. Reserve well in advance, before you leave for Paris. If you want to try your luck once here, head to the box office at a Fnac store (www.fnac.com; follow the Magasins link to locate a branch near you).

Parks & Activities by Neighbourhood

Eiffel Tower & Western Paris (p88) Escape to the Bois de Boulogne.

Louvre & Les Halles (p118) Superb vistas unfold from the elegant Jardin des Tuileries.

Montmartre & Northern Paris (p136) Large parks include beautiful Parc Monceau, hilly Parc des Buttes Chaumont and futuristic Parc de la Villette.

Le Marais, Ménilmontant & Belleville (p179) Departure point for in-line skating.

Bastille & Eastern Paris (p182) The elevated walkway Promenade Plantée, expansive Bois de Vincennes, Parc Floral and a host of other great parks.

Latin Quarter (p209) Stroll the Jardin des Plantes.

St-Germain & Les Invalides (p228) Home to the city's most iconic swath of green, the Jardin du Luxembourg.

Montparnasse & Southern Paris (p256) The rails-to-trails Petite Ceinture, Parc Montsouris and unique swimming pools.

Paris' oldest bridge, Pont Neuf (p201)

The Seine

The lifeline of Paris, the Seine sluices through the city, spanned by 37 bridges. Its Unesco World Heritage–listed riverbanks offer picturesque promenades, parks, activities and events, including summertime beaches. After dark, watch the river dance with the watery reflections of city lights and tourist-boat flood lamps.

Riverbank Rejuvenation

Long harbouring busy traffic-choked freeways, the Seine's *berges* (banks) were reborn with the 2013 creation of the completely car-free 2.5km stretch of the Left Bank from the Pont de l'Alma to the Musée d'Orsay (linked to the water's edge by a grand staircase that doubles as amphitheatre seating). This innovative promenade is dotted with restaurants and bars (some aboard boats), and there are ball-game courts, a skate ramp, a kids' climbing wall, a 100m running track and floating gardens on 1800 sq metres of artificial islands. Temporary events as diverse as film screenings and knitting workshops take place throughout the year.

The city of Paris followed up this success in 2017 by banishing cars on the Right Bank, now with a car-free total of 4.5km between the quai des Tuileries and Port de l'Arsenal (from where cruises depart to the Bassin de la Villette via Canal St-Martin). There are cycle and walking paths, *pétanque* (a game similar to bowls) and other sporting facilities, along with kids' play areas, restaurants and bars, and some nifty audiovisual 'timescope' binoculars covering the city's history.

Promenading & Pausing

The Seine's riverbanks are where Parisians come to cycle, jog, in-line skate and stroll; staircases along the banks lead down to the water's edge.

Particularly picturesque spots for a riverside promenade include the areas around Paris' two elegant inner-city islands, the **Île de la Cité** and **Île Saint-Louis**. Up at street level, the city's Right and Left Banks are lined with the distinctive green-metal *bouquiniste* (p220) stalls selling antiquarian books, sheet music and old advertising posters.

A lesser-known island stroll is the artificial Île aux Cygnes (p250) via its tree-shaded walkway, the Allée des Cygnes. Walking from west to east gives you a stunning view of the Eiffel Tower.

The river also acts as a giant backyard for apartment-dwelling Parisians. All along its banks you'll find locals reading, picnicking, canoodling or just basking in the sunshine. Among the best-loved spots is the tiny triangular park square du Vert-Galant (p201), beneath the Pont Neuf.

Summertime Beaches

Each summer, the Paris Plages (Paris Beaches; p27) see *pétanque,* pop-up bars and cafes, sun lounges, parasols, water fountains and sprays line the river from around mid-July to early September (exact dates vary from year to year).

The Paris Plages were established in 2002 for Parisians who couldn't escape to the coast to cool off in the summer months. They now typically set up at the Parc Rives de Seine (between the Pont de Solferino and Pont Alexandre III on the Left Bank, and between the Pont de Sully to the Pont Neuf on the Right Bank), as well as along the quays by the Bassin de la Villette in the 19e, where there are three clean-water-zoned swimming pools of varying depths, accommodating children and swimmers with disabilities. The pools are patrolled by life guards and are typically open 11am to 9pm during the Paris Plages season. Check the annual program at www.parisinfo.com.

Although swimming is otherwise banned in the waterways due to maritime traffic and water quality, efforts are being made

PLAN YOUR TRIP THE SEINE

to ensure the Seine is clean enough to host open-water swimming events during the 2024 Summer Olympics.

Seine-Side Entertainment

In addition to riverside park activities, entertainment options include nightclubs aboard boats moored in the 13e, such as Bateau El Alamein (p259), with live-music gigs, a floating swimming pool, Piscine Joséphine Baker (p261), and more bars and restaurants along the Parc Rives de Seine on both river banks.

Riverside venues also include Les Docks (p252), incorporating vast outdoor terraces and a rooftop bar.

River Cruises & Tours

The best way to become acquainted with the Seine is to take a cruise along its waters. A plethora of companies run day- and night-time boat tours (p336), usually lasting around an hour, with commentary in multiple languages. Many cruise companies also offer brunch, lunch and dinner cruises.

An alternative to traditional boat tours is the Batobus (p334), a handy hop-on, hop-off service that stops at quintessentially Parisian attractions: the Eiffel Tower, Invalides, Musée d'Orsay, St-Germain des Prés, Notre Dame, Jardin des Plantes, Hôtel de Ville, Musée du Louvre and place de la Concorde. Single- and multiday tickets allow you to spend as long as you like sightseeing between stops.

CHERYL RAMALHO/GETTY IMAGES ©

Explore Paris

PARIS'
TOP EXPERIENCES

Haussmannian façade (p299)

Neighbourhoods at a Glance

❶ Eiffel Tower & Western Paris p80

Home to very well-heeled Parisians, this *grande dame* of a neighbourhood is where you can get up close and personal with the city's symbolic tower as well as more contemporary architecture in the high-rise business district of La Défense just outside the *périphérique* (ring road) encircling central Paris.

❷ Champs-Élysées & Grands Boulevards p92

Baron Haussmann famously reshaped the Parisian cityscape around the Arc de Triomphe, from which 12 avenues radiate like the spokes of a wheel, including the glamorous Champs-Élysées. To its east are gourmet shops garlanding the Église de la Madeleine and the Grands Boulevards' art nouveau department stores.

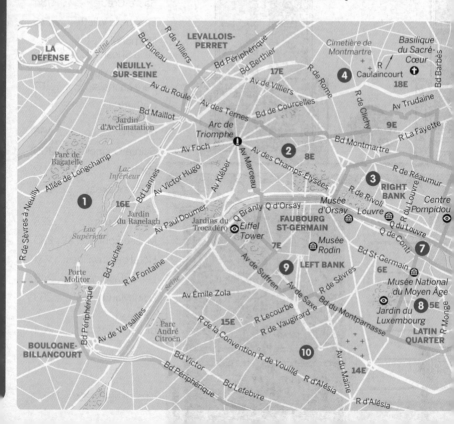

❸ Louvre & Les Halles p106

Paris' splendid line of monuments, the *axe historique* (historic axis; also called the grand axis), passes through the Tuileries gardens before reaching IM Pei's glass pyramid at the entrance to Paris' most monumental museum, the Louvre. Near the Forum des Halles shopping mall and park is the magnificent church Église St-Eustache.

❹ Montmartre & Northern Paris p132

Montmartre's lofty views, wine-producing vines and hidden village squares have lured painters since the 19th century. Crowned by the Sacré-Cœur basilica, Montmartre is the city's steepest quarter, and its slinking streets lined with crooked ivy-clad buildings retain a fairy-tale charm. The grittier neighbourhoods of Pigalle and Canal St-Martin are hotbeds of creativity with a trove of hip drinking, dining and shopping addresses.

❺ Le Marais, Ménilmontant & Belleville p154

Fashionable bars and restaurants, emerging designers' boutiques, and thriving gay and Jewish communities all squeeze into Le Marais' narrow medieval lanes. Neighbouring Ménilmontant has some of the city's most happening nightlife, while hilly Belleville is vibrant and multicultural.

❻ Bastille & Eastern Paris p180

Fabulous markets, intimate bistros and cutting-edge drinking and dancing venues make this neighbourhood one of the best places to discover the Parisians' Paris.

❼ The Islands p194

Paris' geographic and spiritual heart is here in the Seine. The larger of the two inner-city islands, Île de la Cité, is home to Notre Dame and the exquisite stained glass of Sainte-Chapelle. Serene little Île St-Louis is graced with charming boutiques.

❽ Latin Quarter p205

So named because international students communicated in Latin here until the French Revolution, it remains Paris' hub of academic life. This lively area is also home to museums and churches, plus a beautiful art deco mosque and botanic gardens.

❾ St-Germain & Les Invalides p222

Literary buffs, antique collectors and fashionistas flock to this legendary part of Paris, where the presence of writers such as Sartre, de Beauvoir and Hemingway still lingers in historic cafes.

❿ Montparnasse & Southern Paris p246

Fabled Montparnasse has brasseries from its mid-20th-century heyday and re-energised backstreets that buzz with local life. The 13e is the premium *arrondissement* for edgy street art.

Eiffel Tower & Western Paris

EIFFEL TOWER | LA DÉFENSE | BOIS DE BOULOGNE | 16E

Neighbourhood Top Five

1 **Eiffel Tower** (p82) Ascending the icon at dusk to watch its sparkling lights blink across Paris.

2 **Musée du Quai Branly – Jacques Chirac** (p84) Finding inspiration in traditional art and artisanship from around the world.

3 **Cité de l'Architecture et du Patrimoine** (p85) Wandering past cathedral portals, gargoyles and intricate scale models in this standout museum dedicated to French architecture.

4 **Bois de Boulogne** (p88) Exploring western Paris' oasis of greenery: from bike

rides, rowing boats and horse races to an amusement park kids will adore!

5 **Musée Marmottan Monet** (p86) Taking a trip to see the world's largest collection of Monet canvases, alongside other impressionist and postimpressionist painters.

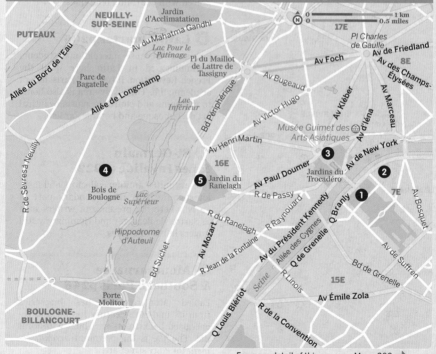

For more detail of this area see Map p366.

Explore Eiffel Tower & Western Paris

With its hourly sparkles that illuminate the evening skyline, the Eiffel Tower (p82) needs no introduction. Ascending to its viewing platforms will offer you a panorama over the whole of Paris, with the prestigious neighbourhood of Passy (the 16e *arrondissement*) stretching along the far banks of the Seine to the west. In the 18th and 19th centuries, Passy was home to luminaries such as Benjamin Franklin and Balzac. Defined by its sober, elegant buildings from the Haussmann era, it was only annexed to the city in 1860.

Fabulous museums here include the Musée Marmottan Monet (p86), with the world's largest collection of Monet paintings; the hip Palais de Tokyo (p85), with modern art installations; the Musée Guimet des Arts Asiatiques (p87), France's standout Asian art museum; the underrated Cité de l'Architecture et du Patrimoine (p85), with captivating sculptures and murals; and a host of smaller collections. On the Left Bank is the prominent Musée du Quai Branly – Jacques Chirac (p84), introducing indigenous art and culture from outside Europe, while at the city's western edge is the leafy refuge of the Bois de Boulogne (p88). Beyond this lies the business district of La Défense.

Local Life

Museum hopping Parisians flock to this part of town for its fine museums (p85).

Green space Leafy Bois de Boulogne (p88) is where city-dwellers escape the concrete on bikes, skates or by *footing* (jogging).

Business district Skyscrapers rub shoulders with modern art at business hub La Défense (p91).

Getting There & Away

Metro Line 6 runs south from Charles de Gaulle–Étoile past the Eiffel Tower (views are superb from the elevated section); line 9 runs southwest from the Champs-Élysées. Line 1 terminates at La Défense.

RER RER A runs west past La Défense; RER C runs east–west along the Left Bank, with a stop at the Eiffel Tower.

Bus Scenic bus 69 runs from the Champ de Mars (Eiffel Tower) along the Left Bank, crosses the Seine at the Louvre, and continues east to Père Lachaise.

Bicycle Handy Vélib' stations include 2 av Octave Creard (for the Eiffel Tower) and 3 av Bosquet (for Musée du Quai Branly).

Boat The hop-on, hop-off **Batobus** (Map p366; Port de la Bourdonnais, 7e; Mléna, RER Pont de l'Alma) has an Eiffel Tower stop.

Lonely Planet's Top Tip

There are excellent top-end restaurants in the 16e, but it is substantially more affordable – and fun in nice weather – to follow the local flock and picnic. Build your own feast with sweet and savoury goodies from *boulangeries* (bakeries), *fromageries* (cheese shops), markets, speciality food shops or takeaway delis.

✖ Best Places to Eat

➜ Le Jules Verne (p83)

➜ Substance (p90)

➜ Bustronome (p90)

➜ Brasserie Cézanne (p89)

For reviews, see p89.

🍷 Best Places to Drink

➜ St James Paris (p90)

➜ Bô Zinc Café (p90)

➜ Frog XVI (p90)

For reviews, see p90.

👁 Best Museums

➜ Musée du Quai Branly – Jacques Chirac (p84)

➜ Cité de l'Architecture et du Patrimoine (p85)

➜ Musée Marmottan Monet (p86)

➜ Musée Guimet des Arts Asiatiques (p87)

➜ Palais de Tokyo (p85)

➜ Musée Yves Saint Laurent Paris (p85)

For reviews, see p84.

TOP EXPERIENCE
MAKE IT TO THE TOP OF THE EIFFEL TOWER

There are different ways to experience the Eiffel Tower, from a daytime trip to an evening ascent amid twinkling lights to a meal in one of its restaurants. And even though some seven million people come annually, few would dispute that each visit is unique – and something that simply has to be done when in Paris.

Metal Asparagus

Named after its designer, Gustave Eiffel, the Tour Eiffel was built for the 1889 Exposition Universelle (World's Fair). It took 300 workers, 2.5 million rivets and two years of nonstop labour to assemble. Upon completion, the tower became the tallest human-made structure in the world (324m) – a record held until the 1930 completion of New York's Chrysler Building. A symbol of the modern age, it faced opposition from Paris' artistic and literary elite, and the 'metal asparagus', as some snidely called it, was originally slated to be torn down in 1909. It was spared only because it proved an ideal platform for the transmitting antennas needed for the newfangled science of radiotelegraphy.

1st Floor

Of the tower's three floors, the 1st (57m) has the most space but least impressive views. The glass-enclosed **Pavillon Ferrié** houses an immersion film along with a small cafe and souvenir shop, while the outer walkway features a discovery circuit to help visitors learn more about the tower's ingenious design. Check out the sections of glass flooring that provide a dizzying view of the ant-like people walking

DON'T MISS

➜ 1st-floor Pavillon Ferrié
➜ 2nd-floor panorama
➜ Top-floor Champagne bar

PRACTICALITIES

➜ Map p366, F5
➜ ☎08 92 70 12 39
➜ www.toureiffel.paris
➜ Champ de Mars, 5 av Anatole France, 7e
➜ adult/child lift to top €25.90/13, lift to 2nd fl €16.60/8.30, stairs to 2nd fl €10.40/5.20
➜ ⏱lifts & stairs 9am-12.45am mid-Jun–Aug, lifts 9.30am-11.45pm, stairs 9.30am-6.30pm Sep–mid-Jun
➜ Ⓜ Bir Hakeim, RER Champ de Mars–Tour Eiffel

on the ground far below. This level also hosts the restaurant **58 Tour Eiffel** (Map p366; www.restaurants-toureiffel.com; ✏ 🍴). The 1st floor's commercial areas are powered by two sleek wind turbines within the tower.

2nd Floor
Views from the 2nd floor (115m) are the best – impressively high but still close enough to see the city below. Telescopes and panoramic maps pinpoint locations in Paris and beyond. Story windows give an overview of the lifts' mechanics, and the vision well allows you to gaze through glass panels to the ground. Also up here are toilets, a souvenir shop, a macaron bar and Michelin-starred restaurant **Le Jules Verne** (Map p366; ✏ 01 83 77 34 34; www.restaurants-toureiffel.com; 3-course weekday lunch menu €135, 5-/7-course menus €190/230; ⏱ noon-1.30pm & 6-9.30pm).

Top Floor
Views from the wind-buffeted top floor (276m) stretch up to 60km on a clear day, though at this height the panoramas are more sweeping than detailed. Celebrate your ascent with a glass of bubbly (€13 to €22) from the Champagne bar (open 10.15am to 10.15pm). Afterwards peep into Gustave Eiffel's restored top-level office where lifelike wax models of Eiffel and his daughter Claire greet Thomas Edison.

Tickets & Queues
Visitors must pass through security at the bullet-proof glass barriers surrounding the tower's base. The two entrances to the glass enclosure are on av Gustave Eiffel; the two exits are on quai Branly.

Ascend as far as the 2nd floor (either on foot or by lift), from where there's a separate lift to the top floor (closed during heavy winds). Pushchairs must be folded in lifts and bags or backpacks larger than aeroplane-cabin size aren't allowed. Note that the top floor and stairs aren't accessible to people with limited mobility.

Pre-purchasing tickets online gives you an allocated time slot and means you only have to queue for security. Print your ticket or show it on your phone. If you can't reserve your tickets ahead of time, expect lengthy waits for tickets in high season.

Stair tickets can't be reserved online. Buy them at the south pillar, where the staircase can also be accessed: the climb consists of 360 steps to the 1st floor and another 360 steps to the 2nd floor.

If you have reservations for either restaurant, you're granted direct post-security access to the lifts.

MAN ON WIRE
In 2017, French adventurer Nathan Paulin covered 670m between the tower and Trocadéro on a slackline at a maximum height of 70m, establishing the record for the world's longest urban slackline crossing while raising money for charity.

Every hour on the hour, the entire tower sparkles for five minutes with 20,000 6-watt lights. They were first installed for Paris' millennium celebration in 2000 – it took 25 mountain climbers five months to install the current bulbs and 40km of electrical cords. For the best view of the light show, head across the Seine to the Jardins du Trocadéro.

PAINT
Sporting six different colours throughout its lifetime, the tower has been painted red and bronze since 1968. Work is underway to strip the previous 19 coats and apply the yellow-brown shade originally conceived by Gustave Eiffel, giving it a new golden hue in time for the 2024 Olympics.

TOP EXPERIENCE
LOOK AND LEARN AT MUSÉE DU QUAI BRANLY

No other museum in Paris provides such inspiration for travellers, armchair anthropologists and those who simply appreciate the beauty of traditional craftwork. A tribute to the incredible diversity of human culture, the Musée du Quai Branly – Jacques Chirac presents an overview of indigenous and folk art from around the world.

Divided into four main sections (Oceania, Asia, Africa and the Americas), the museum showcases an impressive array of masks, carvings, weapons, jewellery and more, all displayed in a refreshingly unique interior without rooms or high walls. Although its sheer vastness can be intimidating, there are numerous aids on hand to help you navigate the collection and delve deeper into particular sections. Strategically placed multimedia touch screens provide more context for certain pieces, while tailored walks (available online and upon request at the entrance) focus on specific themes, from masks and funerary objects to jewellery and musical instruments.

Highlights to look out for include remarkable carvings from Papua New Guinea (Oceania); clothing, jewellery and textiles from ethnic groups from India to Vietnam (Asia); an impressively diverse collection of masks (Africa); and artefacts from the great American civilisations – the Mayas, Aztecs and Incas.

Must-sees include temporary exhibits and performances, which are generally excellent.

DON'T MISS
⇒ The Papua New Guinea collection, Oceania

⇒ The Evenk shaman cloak, Asia (Siberia)

⇒ West African masks, Africa

⇒ The grizzly totem pole, Americas

PRACTICALITIES
⇒ Map p366, G4

⇒ 📞 01 56 61 70 00

⇒ www.quaibranly.fr

⇒ 37 quai Branly, 7e

⇒ adult/child €12/free, 1st Sun of month free

⇒ ⏰10.30am-7pm Tue, Wed & Fri-Sun, to 10pm Thu, plus 10.30am-7pm Mon during school holidays

⇒ M Alma Marceau, RER Pont de l'Alma

◉ SIGHTS

The Eiffel Tower may get top billing here, but it's the incredible assortment of museums that ensures repeat visitors. Most destinations are found on the Right Bank of the Seine. Further west is the Musée Marmottan Monet and the leafy expanse of the Bois de Boulogne. Northwest again, Paris' business district La Défense, begun in the 1950s, is a forest of skyscrapers.

EIFFEL TOWER TOWER
See p82.

MUSÉE DU QUAI BRANLY – JACQUES CHIRAC MUSEUM
See p84.

**MUSÉE
YVES SAINT LAURENT PARIS** MUSEUM
Map p366 (☎01 44 31 64 00; www.museeysl paris.com; 5 av Marceau, 16e; adult/child €10/7; ⊙11am-6pm Tue-Thu, Sat & Sun, to 9pm Fri; MAlma-Marceau) Housed in the legendary designer's studios (1974–2002), this museum holds retrospectives of YSL's avant-garde designs, from early sketches to finished pieces. Temporary exhibitions give an insight into the creative process of designing a *haute couture* collection and the history of fashion throughout the 20th century. The building can only accommodate a small number of visitors at a time, so buy tickets online or expect to queue outside.

**MUSÉE D'ART MODERNE
DE LA VILLE DE PARIS** GALLERY
Map p366 (☎01 53 67 40 00; www.mam.paris.fr; 11 av du Président Wilson, 16e; ⊙10am-6pm Tue, Wed & Fri-Sun, to 10pm Thu; Ména) FREE The permanent collection at Paris' modern-art museum displays works representative of just about every major artistic movement of the 20th and 21st centuries, with works by Modigliani, Matisse, Braque and Soutine. The real jewel, though, is the room hung with canvases by Dufy and Bonnard. Look out for cutting-edge temporary exhibitions (not free). Download the free multilingual app online.

PALAIS DE TOKYO GALLERY
Map p366 (☎01 81 97 35 88; www.palaisdetokyo. com; 13 av du Président Wilson, 16e; adult/child €12/free; ⊙noon-9pm Wed-Mon; Ména) The Tokyo Palace, created for the 1937 Exposition Internationale des Arts et Techniques dans

---

◉ TOP EXPERIENCE
UNDERSTAND FRENCH ARCHITECTURE

In the eastern wing of the Palais de Chaillot, directly across from the Eiffel Tower, **Cité de l'Architecture et du Patrimoine** is devoted to French architecture and heritage. The burgundy walls and skylit rooms showcase 350 plaster casts taken from the country's greatest monuments, a collection whose seeds were sown following the desecration of many buildings during the French Revolution.

Some of the original details from which the casts were made, such as sculptures from the Reims Cathedral, were later destroyed in the wars that followed. Although they're not in situ, wandering through such a magnificent collection of church portals, gargoyles, and saints and sinners from around France is an incomparable experience for anyone interested in the elemental stories that craftspeople chose to preserve in stone.

On display on the upper floors are reproduced murals and stained-glass windows from some of France's most important monuments, which are arranged in an intriguing labyrinthine layout. One of the most beautiful reproductions in this section is the Cathédrale of St-Etienne cupola.

DON'T MISS
➡ Casts Gallery
➡ Murals and Stained-Glass Galleries
➡ Cathédrale of St-Étienne cupola

PRACTICALITIES
➡ Map p366, E4
➡ ☎01 58 51 52 00
➡ www.citedel architecture.fr
➡ 1 place du Trocadéro et du 11 Novembre, 16e
➡ adult/child €8/free, 1st Sun of month free
➡ ⊙11am-7pm Wed & Fri-Mon, to 9pm Thu
➡ MTrocadéro

la Vie Moderne (International Exposition of Art and Technology in Modern Life), has no permanent collection. Instead, its shell-like interior of concrete and steel is a stark backdrop to interactive contemporary-art exhibitions and installations.

The art- and design-focused bookshop is fabulous, and its eating, drinking and entertainment options – including sustainably themed Mediterranean restaurant **Les Grands Verres** (Map p366; www.quixotic-projects.com; 2-/3-course lunch menu €23/29, mains €19-28; ⊙noon-2.30pm & 7-11pm, bar to 1am), with a compacted-earth bar, and basement nightclub **Yoyo** (Map p366; www.facebook.com/yoyoconcertparis; ⊙hours vary) – are magic.

PARC DU CHAMP DE MARS PARK

Map p366 (Champ de Mars, 7e; ⊙24hr; MÉcole Militaire, RER Champ de Mars–Tour Eiffel) Running southeast from the Eiffel Tower, the grassy Champ de Mars – an ideal summer picnic spot – was originally used as a parade ground for the cadets of the 18th-century **École Militaire**, the vast French-classical building at the southeastern end of the park, which counts Napoléon Bonaparte among its graduates.

Until 2024, the park is hosting a **temporary Grand Palais** while the original undergoes renovations.

Check for scheduled children's **puppet shows** (Map p366; ☑ 06 25 10 70 52; www.guignol duchampdemars.fr; allée du Général Margueritte, 7e; show €5; MÉcole Militaire, RER Champ de Mars–Tour Eiffel).

PALAIS GALLIERA MUSEUM

Map p366 (☑ 01 56 52 86 00; www.palaisgalliera. paris.fr; 10 av Pierre 1er de Serbie, 16e; adult/child €14/free; ⊙10am-6pm Tue, Wed, Sat & Sun, to 8pm Thu & Fri; Ména) Paris' Fashion Museum warehouses some 200,000 outfits (spanning court costumes through to contemporary *haute couture* by designers such as Jean Paul Gaultier and accessories (including canes, umbrellas fans and gloves) from the late 17th century to the present day. The sumptuous Italianate palace and gardens date from the mid-19th century.

MAISON DE BALZAC MUSEUM

Map p366 (☑ 01 55 74 41 80; www.maisonde balzac.paris.fr; 47 rue Raynouard, 16e; adult/child €6/free; ⊙10am-6pm Tue-Sun; MPassy, RER Avenue Président Kennedy) This pretty, three-storey spa house is where realist novelist Honoré de Balzac (1799–1850) lived and worked from 1840 to 1847, editing the entire *Comédie Humaine*. There's a lot of memorabilia, letters, prints and portraits – perfect for die-hard Balzac fans.

◉ TOP EXPERIENCE
MARVEL AT MONET'S MASTERPIECES

Housed in the duc de Valmy's former hunting lodge (well, let's call it a mansion), the intimate **Musée Marmottan Monet** houses the world's largest collection of Monet paintings and sketches. It provides an interesting if patchy cross-section of his work, beginning with paintings such as the seminal *Impression, Soleil Levant* (1873) and *Promenade près d'Argenteuil* (1875), passing through numerous water-lily studies, before moving on to the rest of the collection, which is considerably more abstract and dates to the early 1900s. Some of the masterpieces to look out for include *La Barque* (1887), *Cathédrale de Rouen* (1892), *Londres, le Parlement* (1901) and the various *Nymphéas* – many of these were smaller studies for the works now on display in the Musée de l'Orangerie (p118).

Temporary exhibitions, included in the admission price and always superb, are generally shown either in the basement or on the 1st floor. Also on display are a handful of canvases by Renoir, Pissarro, Gauguin and Morisot, and a collection of 13th- to 16th-century illuminations, which are quite lovely if somewhat out of place.

DON'T MISS
→ *Impression, Soleil Levant*
→ *Promenade près d'Argenteuil*
→ *Londres, le Parlement*

PRACTICALITIES
→ Map p366, C5
→ ☑ 01 44 96 50 33
→ www.marmottan.fr
→ 2 rue Louis Boilly, 16e
→ adult/child €12/8.50; audioguides €3
→ ⊙10am-6pm Tue, Wed & Fri-Sun, to 9pm Thu
→ MLa Muette

TOP EXPERIENCE
ADMIRE ASIAN ARTS AT MUSÉE GUIMET

France's foremost Asian arts museum, **Musée Guimet des Arts Asiatiques**, has a superb collection of sculptures, paintings and religious articles that originated in the vast stretch of land between Afghanistan and Japan. In fact, it's possible to observe the gradual transmission of both Buddhism and artistic styles along the Silk Road in some of the museum's pieces, from the 1st-century Gandhara Buddhas from Afghanistan and Pakistan to the later Central Asian, Chinese and Japanese Buddhist sculptures and art.

Other strong points of the museum include the Southeast Asian statuary on the ground floor (which has the world's largest collection of Khmer artefacts outside Cambodia), the Nepalese and Tibetan bronzes and mandalas, and the vast China collection, which encompasses everything from ink paintings and calligraphy to funerary statuary and early bronzes. Audioguides are free.

Part of the collection, comprised of Chinese furniture, teaware and temporary exhibits, is housed in the nearby **Hôtel d'Heidelbach** (Map p366; www.guimet.fr; 19 av d'Iéna, 16e; incl in Musée Guimet admission; ⊘10am-6pm Wed-Mon, garden to 5pm; Ⓜléna). Don't miss the wonderful Japanese garden here.

DON'T MISS

➡ Afghan collection
➡ Southeast Asian statuary
➡ China collection
➡ Himalayan mandalas and thangkas

PRACTICALITIES

➡ Map p366, F4
➡ 🖉01 56 52 54 33
➡ www.guimet.fr
➡ 6 place d'Iéna, 16e
➡ adult/child €8.50/ free, 1st Sun of month free
➡ ⊘10am-6pm Wed-Mon
➡ Ⓜléna

PALAIS DE CHAILLOT   HISTORIC BUILDING

Map p366 (place du Trocadéro et du 11 Novembre, 16e; ⓂTrocadéro) The two curved, colonnaded wings of this building (built for the 1937 International Expo) and central terrace afford an exceptional panorama of the **Jardins du Trocadéro**, Seine and Eiffel Tower. The eastern wing houses the standout Cité de l'Architecture et du Patrimoine (p85), devoted to French architecture and heritage, as well as the **Théâtre National de Chaillot** (Map p366; 🖉01 53 65 31 00; www.theatre-chaillot. fr) staging dance and theatre. The western wing houses the Musée de l'Homme (and the **Musée de la Marine** (Maritime Museum; Map p366; www.musee-marine.fr), which is due to reopen in 2022.

MUSÉE DE L'HOMME   MUSEUM

Map p366 (Museum of Humankind; 🖉01 44 05 72 72; www.museedelhomme.fr; 17 place Trocadéro et du 11 Novembre, 16e; adult/child €10/7; ⊘11am-7pm Wed-Mon; ⓂPassy, léna) Opened in 1882, this museum traces the evolution of humankind through artefacts gathered from around the world. Fascinating pieces on display include a Cro-Magnon shell necklace, delicately carved mammoth tusks and reindeer jawbones, a variety of Paleolithic stone tools and a Peruvian mummy. Eiffel Tower views extend from the ground-floor restaurant and 2nd-floor cafe.

MUSÉE DU VIN   MUSEUM

Map p366 (🖉01 45 25 63 26; www.museeduvin paris.com; 5 sq Charles Dickens, 16e; adult/child €10/free, incl glass of wine adult €13.90; ⊘10am-6pm Tue-Sun; ⓂPassy) The Wine Museum, headquarters of the prestigious International Federation of Wine Brotherhoods, introduces visitors to the fine art of viticulture with mock-ups and tool displays in 15th-century vaulted cellars. Two-hour tasting courses (English available) take place by appointment on Saturdays (€63). If you lunch in the attached restaurant (noon to 3pm Tuesday to Saturday, three-course menu including wine from €37), museum admission is free.

FLAME OF LIBERTY MEMORIAL   MONUMENT

Map p366 (place de l'Alma, 8e; ⓂAlma Marceau) This bronze sculpture, a replica of the one topping the Statue of Liberty, was placed here in 1987 as a symbol of friendship between France and the USA. More famous is its location, above the place d'Alma tunnel

WORTH A DETOUR

BOIS DE BOULOGNE

The 845-hectare **Bois de Boulogne** (Map p366; www.paris.fr/equipements/bois-de-boulogne-2779; bd Maillot, 16e; MPorte Maillot) owes its informal layout to Baron Haussmann, who, inspired by London's Hyde Park, planted 400,000 trees here in the 19th century. Along with various gardens and other sights, the park has 15km of cycle paths and 28km of bridle paths through 125 hectares of forested land.

Be warned that the area can be a distinctly adult playground day and night, especially along the allée de Longchamp running northeast from the Étang des Réservoirs (Reservoirs Pond), where sex workers cruise for clients.

The Bois de Boulogne is served by metro lines 1 (Porte Maillot, Les Sablons), 2 (Porte Dauphine), 9 (Michel-Ange-Auteuil) and 10 (Michel-Ange-Auteuil, Porte d'Auteuil), and the RER C (Avenue Foch, Avenue Henri Martin). Vélib' stations are found near most of the park entrances, but not within the park itself.

Jardin d'Acclimatation (Map p366; ✆01 40 67 90 85; bd des Sablons, 16e; admission €5.20, per attraction €3; ⊙10am-6pm Mon-Fri, to 7pm Sat, Sun & school holidays; MLes Sablons) Families adore this green, flowery amusement park on the Bois de Boulogne's northern fringe, which was renovated in 2018. There are swings, roundabouts, playgrounds, a paddling pool, a petting zoo and puppet shows several times per week.

Lac Inférieur (Map p366; ✆06 95 14 00 01; Carrefour du Bout des Lacs; 1hr €12, plus deposit €50; ⊙noon-6pm mid-Mar–Oct; MAvenue Henri Martin) Rent an old-fashioned rowing boat to explore Lac Inférieur, the largest of Bois de Boulogne's lakes – romance guaranteed.

Parc de Bagatelle (Map p366; rte de Sèvres à Neuilly, 16e; adult/child Apr-Sep €6/3, Oct-Mar €2.50/1.50; ⊙9.30am-8pm Apr-Sep, shorter hours rest of year; MPorte Maillot) Irises bloom in May, roses between June and October, and water lilies in August and September at this park created as the result of a wager in 1775 between Marie Antoinette and the Count of Artois.

Pré Catelan (Catelan Meadow; Map p366; rte de Suresnes, 16e; ⊙9.30am-8pm Apr-Oct, Jardin Shakespeare 2-4pm, shorter hours Nov-Mar; MRanelagh) FREE This area within Parc de Bagatelle has a wonderful Jardin Shakespeare where plants, flowers and trees mentioned in Shakespeare's plays are cultivated. Watch for summer performances in the attached open-air theatre.

Jardin des Serres d'Auteuil (Map p366; ✆01 40 72 16 16; av de la Porte d'Auteuil, 16é; ⊙8am-8.30pm summer, shorter hours rest of year; MPorte d'Auteuil) FREE Located at the southeastern end of the Bois de Boulogne is the Jardin des Serres d'Auteuil, a garden with impressive conservatories that opened in 1898 and are home to a large collection of tropical plants. Six contemporary greenhouses are set around the Stade Roland Garros, home of the French Open.

Fondation Louis Vuitton (Map p366; ✆01 40 69 96 00; www.fondationlouisvuitton.fr; 8 av du Mahatma Gandhi, 16e; adult/child €14/5; ⊙usually 11am-8pm Mon, Wed & Thu, 11am-9pm Fri, 10am-8pm Sat & Sun; MLes Sablons) Emerging behind the Jardin d'Acclimatation, this 'cloud-like' glass-panelled building hosts temporary shows such as the MOMA in Paris, the Sergei Shchukin collection and Art/Africa. Check online for the latest exhibit. A shuttle runs between the Arc de Triomphe and the museum during opening hours.

where, on 31 August 1997, Diana, Princess of Wales, was killed in a car accident.

AQUARIUM DE PARIS CINÉAQUA AQUARIUM
Map p366 (✆01 40 69 23 23; www.cineaqua.com; av des Nations Unies, 16e; adult/child €20.50/16; ⊙10am-7pm; ♠; MTrocadéro) Paris' aquarium, on the eastern side of the Jardins du Trocadéro, has a shark tank and 500-odd fish species to entertain families on rainy days. Three cinemas screen ocean-related and other films (dubbed in French, with subtitles). On Saturday nights, nocturnal visits (7pm and 10pm; adult/child €27.90/22.90) include a glass of bubbly or a soft drink.

EATING

In addition to the pickings of the 16e *arrondissement*, the many restaurants of Les Invalides and the buzzing market street of rue Cler (7e) are a short walk from the Eiffel Tower. For a truly memorable experience, dine in the icon itself.

MALITOURNE
PASTRIES €

Map p366 (www.patisserie-malitourne.com; 30 rue de Chaillot, 16e; pastries €3.50-5.50; ⊘7.30am-7pm Mon-Fri; MAlma-Marceau) Indulge in something sweet at this great little patisserie, chocolate-maker and *traiteur* (caterer), going strong since 1976. Along with sweet pastries, it has quiches and filled baguettes.

LES DEUX ABEILLES
CAFE €

Map p366 (☎01 45 55 64 04; 189 rue de l'Université, 7e; 3-course lunch menu €24, dishes €16-21; ⊘9am-7pm Mon-Sat; MAlma Marceau, RER Pont d'Alma) A refuge from the Eiffel Tower crowds, delightfully old-fashioned tearoom the Two Bees has floral-patterned wallpaper, terracotta-tiled floors and white-clothed tables. It serves a variety of soups, salads, quiches, omelettes and gratins, along with homemade cakes and *citronnade* (ginger lemonade) throughout the day. In warm weather, take a seat on the pavement terrace, shaded by a dark-green awning.

BRASSERIE CÉZANNE
BRASSERIE €€

Map p366 (☎01 43 59 58 43; www.brasserie cezanne.fr; 45 av Kléber, 16e; mains €18-27; ⊘noon-midnight; MBoissière) Pastel shutters, ochre walls, olive-green velvet seating and terracotta pots of lavender recreate a little slice of sun-baked southern France – as do the Provençal dishes (simply grilled sardines with bread and butter, tender pink lamb with rosemary, entrecôte with roast tomato and artichoke salad), and delightful reds, whites and rosés from Provence, Languedoc-Roussillon and the Rhône Valley.

LA GARE
INTERNATIONAL €€

Map p366 (☎01 42 15 15 31; www.lagare-paris. com; 19 Chaussée de la Muette, 16e; small plates €4-14, mains €18-34; ⊘restaurant noon-2.30pm & 7-10.30pm, cafe 3.30-11pm; 🛜; MLa Muette) A former Petite Ceinture steam-train station, the 19th-century, red-brick Gare Passy–La Muette, with soaring vaulted ceilings and a park-facing terrace, provides the inspiration for the restaurant-cafe it now houses. 'Travel-themed' dishes from around the world include Périgord roast chicken, Argentine fillet and American barbecued ribs cooked on the 11m-long charcoal outdoor rotisserie.

ARNAUD NICOLAS
FRENCH €€

Map p366 (☎01 45 55 59 59; www.arnaudnicolas. paris; 46 ave de la Bourdonnais, 7e; 2-/3-course weekday lunch menu €32/35, mains €22-35; ⊘restaurant 7-9.45pm Mon, noon-1.45pm & 7-9.45pm Tue-Sat, shop 5-9pm Mon, 10am-3pm & 5-9pm Tue-Sat; 🚼; MÉcole Militaire) Charcuterie maestro Arnaud Nicolas has an upmarket boutique and restaurant with a menu that changes every two weeks. A meal might start with scallop quenelles with red-squash foam, move on to foie gras and pigeon pie with green cabbage, and finish with apple sautéed in butter with fresh apple and chestnut crème. Reservations are a must.

LE PETIT RÉTRO
BISTRO €€

Map p366 (☎01 44 05 06 05; www.petitretro.fr; 5 rue Mesnil, 16e; 2-/3-course menus lunch €26/31, mains €19-31; ⊘noon-2.30pm & 7-10.30pm Mon-Sat; 🚼; MVictor Hugo) From the gorgeous 'Petit Rétro' emblazoned on the zinc bar to the ceramic, floral art nouveau tiles on the wall, this 1904-opened old-style bistro is fittingly a historic monument. Seasonal ingredients are used to prepare dishes both classic (lamb brochette with buttery pommes Anna) and contemporary (langoustine ravioli with seaweed butter and green asparagus tips).

DAROCO
ITALIAN €€

Map p366 (☎01 44 14 91 91; www.daroco.fr; 3 place Clément Ader, 16e; pizza €11-18, mains €14-28; ⊘noon-11pm; 🥢; MMirabeau, RER Gare D'Avenue du Président Kennedy) Framed by a cobalt-blue façade, with floor-to-ceiling windows and hanging plants, stylish Daroco is an inexpensive 16e stop for authentic Italian cuisine. Along with piping-hot pizzas, there are handmade pastas (eg hazelnut and raisin ravioli), risottos (confit lemon and pecorino) and mains such as spring lamb with grilled polenta, or sea bream with mandarin and caper foam.

FIRMIN LE BARBIER
FRENCH €€

Map p366 (☎01 45 51 21 55; www.firminlebarbier. fr; 20 rue de Monttessuy, 7e; 3-/6-course menu €35/64, mains €25-28; ⊘noon-2pm & 7-10.30pm Wed-Fri & Sun, 7-10.30pm Sat; 🚼; MÉcole Militaire or RER Pont de l'Alma) A five-minute walk from the Eiffel Tower, this brick-walled bistro was opened by a retired surgeon turned gourmet whose passion is apparent in everything from the personable service to the wine list. Market-driven dishes prepared in the open kitchen are traditional French (pike soufflé, beef cheek with bone marrow). There are just eight tables, so reserve ahead.

★ SUBSTANCE
FRENCH €€€

Map p366 (📞01 47 20 08 90; www.substance. paris; 18 rue de Chaillot, 16e; mains €24-40, 5-/7-course menu €79/95, with paired wines €124/150; ⏱noon-2pm & 7.30-10.30pm Mon-Fri; Mléna, Alma-Marceau) A striking contemporary dining room in shades of muted blue is the backdrop for truly original cooking by young-gun chef Matthias Marc: Normandy scallop carpaccio with smoked sea urchin roe and hay vinaigrette; foie gras and Ardennes pheasant pie with purple cauliflower, kale and quince relish; and hazelnut-crème-stuffed cabbage, with Corsican clementine and citrusy calamansi sorbet. Book ahead.

LES OMBRES
FRENCH €€€

Map p366 (📞01 47 53 68 00; www.lesombres-restaurant.com; 27 quai Branly, 7e; 3-course menu lunch/dinner €46/74, mains €32-46; ⏱noon-2.15pm & 7-10.30pm; Mléna, RER Pont de l'Alma) This glass-enclosed rooftop restaurant on the 5th floor of the Musée du Quai Branly is named the 'Shadows' after the patterns cast by the Eiffel Tower's webbed ironwork. Dramatic tower views are complemented by creations such as scorpion fish in bouillabaisse broth, and slow-cooked pork shoulder with apricot and foie gras stuffing. Be sure to book.

🍷 DRINKING & NIGHTLIFE

Aside from the illuminated Eiffel Tower, the wealthy, predominantly residential 16e doesn't have much going on after dark. The pace picks up around the Palais de Tokyo, and the lively bars and cafes of St-Germain are a short metro ride away.

★ ST JAMES PARIS
BAR

Map p366 (www.saint-james-paris.com; 43 av Bugeaud, 16e; ⏱7pm-1am; 🛜; MPorte Dauphine) Hidden behind a stone wall, this historic mansion-turned-hotel opens its bar nightly to nonguests – and the setting redefines extraordinary. Winter drinks are in the wood-panelled library; summer drinks are on the impossibly romantic 300-sq-metre garden terrace with giant balloon-shaped gazebos (the first publicly displayed hot-air balloons took flight here). It has 35 house cocktails and a premium wine list.

BÔ ZINC CAFÉ
BAR

Map p366 (📞01 42 24 69 05; www.facebook.com/ bozinc.cafe; 59 av Mozart, 16e; ⏱7am-1am Mon-Fri, from 8am Sat & Sun; MRanelagh) With its soft sage-green façade, long, curved bar and buzzing pavement terrace, Bô Zinc is one of those great hybrid addresses – perfect for hanging with locals over coffee, tea or after-work cocktails. Seating is a mix of wooden bistro chairs and 'flop-in' armchairs. Top-notch food is served from noon to 11pm.

FROG XVI
PUB

Map p366 (www.frogpubs.com; 110bis av Kléber, 16e; ⏱9am-1am Mon-Wed, 9am-2am Thu & Fri, 10am-2am Sat, 10am-1am Sun; 🛜; MTrocadéro) This popular Parisian microbrewery has

---

MOVEABLE FEASTS

Bustronome (Map p366; 📞09 54 44 45 55; www.bustronome.com; 2 av Kléber, 16e; 4-course lunch menu €65, 6-course dinner menu €100; ⏱by reservation 3hr tour 12.15pm, 12.45pm, 7.45pm & 8.45pm daily; 📷♿; MKléber, Charles de Gaulle–Étoile) A true moveable feast, Bustronome is a voyage into French gastronomy aboard a glass-roofed bus, with Paris' famous monuments – the Arc de Triomphe, Palais Garnier and Eiffel Tower among them – gliding by as you dine on seasonal creations prepared in the purpose-built vehicle's lower-deck galley. Children's menus for lunch/dinner cost €40/50; vegetarian, vegan and gluten-free menus are available.

Ducasse sur Seine (Map p366; 📞01 58 00 22 08; www.ducasse-seine.com; Port Debilly, 16e; 3-course lunch menu €100, with paired wines €150, 5-course dinner menu €190, with paired wines €290; ⏱12.45-2.30pm & 8.30-10.30pm; MTrocadéro) Launched by multi-Michelin-starred chef Alain Ducasse, 'floating restaurant' Ducasse sur Seine sails through the city past icons such as the Louvre at lunch and dinner, served at white-clothed tables.

LA DÉFENSE

The high-rise business district of La Défense is undergoing a multiyear overhaul that will see its public art–filled promenade and public spaces become greener and more accessible. Get updates at **Info Défense** (☏01 47 74 84 24; www.parisladefense.com; place de la Défense; ⏱9am-6pm Mon-Fri, 11am-5pm Sat & Sun; Ⓜ La Défense Grande Arche).

La Défense's landmark edifice is the marble **Grande Arche** (☏01 40 90 52 20; www.lagrandearche.fr; 1 Parvis de la Défense; adult/child €15/7; ⏱10am-7pm; Ⓜ La Défense Grande Arche), a cube-like arch built in the 1980s to house government offices. The arch marks the western end of the *axe historique* (historic axis), though Danish architect Johan-Otto von Sprekelsen deliberately placed the Grande Arche fractionally out of alignment. A lift whisks you up for spectacular views from the rooftop. Temporary photojournalism exhibits are held in the museum (included in the rooftop visit).

several locations, but for beer drinkers this one is a saving grace in the posh 16e. Its own-brewed beers include Dark de Triomphe (stout); the big screen shows live sports. Happy hour runs from 5pm to 8pm on weekdays.

CAFÉ JACQUES   CAFE

Map p366 (☏01 47 53 68 01; www.quaibranly.fr; 27 quai Branly, 7e; ⏱10am-6.30pm Tue, Wed & Fri-Sun, to 9.30pm Thu; Ⓜ Iéna or RER Pont de l'Alma) Peacefully set in the modernist garden at the rear of the Musée du Quai Branly, this casual spot has ringside views of the Eiffel Tower. Alongside wine, beer and the usual hot drinks, it serves good cafe-style food throughout the day, and Grom ice lollies for the kids.

⭐ ENTERTAINMENT

MAISON DE LA RADIO   LIVE MUSIC

Map p366 (☏01 56 40 15 16; www.maisondelaradio.fr; 116 av du Président Kennedy, 16e; concerts from €10; Ⓜ Passy or RER Avenue du Président Kennedy) Catch a classical concert at Radio France's concert space. With some 200 annual performances, expect a wide variety of music, from organ and chamber music to appearances by the national orchestra.

🛍 SHOPPING

The best and most varied options for shopping in western Paris will be in the many museum gift shops. Apart from this, the area is largely residential.

MARCHÉ PRÉSIDENT WILSON   MARKET

Map p366 (av du Président Wilson, 16e; ⏱7am-2.30pm Wed, to 3pm Sat; Ⓜ Iéna, Alma-Marceau) This open-air market across from Palais de

Tokyo is the most convenient in the neighbourhood. Organic wines, heirloom vegetables and artisanal charcuterie are some of the many temptations.

LA GRANDE ÉPICERIE RIVE DROITE   FOOD & DRINKS

Map p366 (☏01 44 14 38 00; www.lagrandeepicerie.com; 80 rue de Passy, 16e; ⏱8.30am-9pm Mon-Sat, 9am-12.45pm Sun; Ⓜ La Muette or RER Boulainvilliers) Topped by a dome made up of 2336 glass prisms and filled with tiled panels, frescoes and mosaics, the Right Bank branch of the beloved gourmet emporium (p245) on the Left Bank has four floors of premium products and a handful of eat-in options, including a restaurant.

LA TABLE DE MAÎTRE CORBEAU   CHEESE

Map p366 (52 rue St-Didier, 16e; ⏱9.30am-8pm Mon-Fri, from 8.30am Sat; Ⓜ Victor Hugo) Modern white-tiled *fromagerie* La Table de Maître Corbeau specialises in rare French cheeses, such as crumbly Gaec de la Grande Casse bleu de Termignon, truffled Baron Edmond de Rothschild brie de Meaux, and log-shaped Ste-Maure de Touraine – ash-covered goat's cheese perforated by hay.

LORETTE & JASMIN   VINTAGE

Map p366 (☏06 14 08 06 22; www.loretteetjasmin.com; 6 rue François Millet, 16e; ⏱10.30am-12.45pm & 2.15-7pm Tue-Fri, 10.30am-7pm Sat; Ⓜ Jasmin, Mirabeau) One of the most well-known consignment stores in Paris, Lorette & Jasmin carries a diverse range of gently used luxury brands (Louis Vuitton, Dior, Chanel) yet remains small and personable enough to make browsing pleasant. Lorette's bag bar will let you rent that designer handbag you've always coveted for up to several days.

Champs-Élysées & Grands Boulevards

CHAMPS-ÉLYSÉES | GRANDS BOULEVARDS | TRIANGLE D'OR

Neighbourhood Top Five

❶ Arc de Triomphe (p94) Climbing to the top of Napoléon's triumphal arch to survey the *axe historique,* extending from the Louvre to La Défense, and paying tribute to the Tomb of the Unknown Soldier.

❷ Palais Garnier (p96) Taking in a performance or touring the mythic 19th-century opera house, where Chagall's ceiling fresco is on display.

❸ Galeries Lafayette (p104) Catching a free fashion show showcasing seasonal trends at the magnificent art nouveau department store and admiring the rooftop panorama.

❹ Hôtel de la Marine (p96) Touring this magnificent palace on place de la Concorde.

❺ Champs-Élysées (p96) Strolling the over-the-top avenue – you can't leave Paris without doing it once.

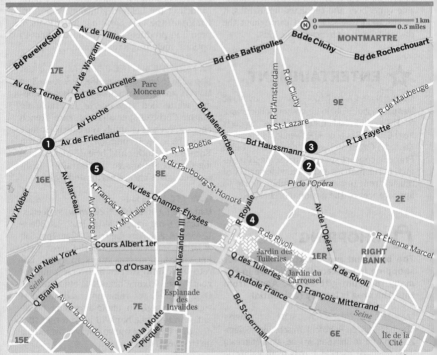

For more detail of this area see Map p368 and p370 ➡

Explore Champs-Élysées & Grands Boulevards

The Champs-Élysées and Grands Boulevards area is grandiose in layout – it's possible to play an epically proportioned game of connect the dots here. The main landmarks – the Arc de Triomphe, place de la Concorde, place de la Madeleine and the Palais Garnier – are joined by majestic boulevards, each lined with harmonious rows of Haussmann-era buildings.

Monumental vistas will keep your eyes occupied, but high-end shops and elegant department stores are this district's *raison d'être* and you will soon find your gaze slipping to the luxury display windows. Dior, Chanel, Louis Vuitton...fans of *haute couture* will find themselves pulled into the famed Triangle d'Or (Golden Triangle), south from the Champs-Élysées. Further east along the Grands Boulevards are the historic *grands magasins* (department stores) like Le Printemps and Galeries Lafayette, which will appeal to shoppers interested in a broader overview of French fashion.

Entertainment, too, has a strong tradition in this area, the most notable venue being the famed 19th-century opera house, the Palais Garnier. While non-French speakers will skip the theatres along the Grands Boulevards, there are plenty of music venues – from classical to rock – that require no language skills to appreciate.

Local Life

Epicurean life Shop for luxury gourmet goods at the exclusive shops and emporiums surrounding Place de la Madeleine (p101).

Art life Parisians' thirst for art is unquenchable – join locals viewing exhibitions in museums like the Petit Palais (p97), home to the Musée des Beaux-Arts de la Ville de Paris, the city's fine-arts museum.

Park life Unwind in the tiny, secreted Jardin de la Nouvelle France (p97).

Getting There & Away

Metro & RER Metro line 1 follows the Champs-Élysées below ground, while lines 8 and 9 serve the Grands Boulevards. RER A stops at Auber (Opéra) and Charles de Gaulle–Étoile.

Bicycle You'll find Vélib' stations on side streets off the Champs-Élysées.

Boat The hop-on, hop-off Batobus Champs-Élysées stop is just east of Pont Alexandre III.

Lonely Planet's Top Tip

Haute cuisine – and *haute* prices – are the rule in the 8e, but if you eat at one of the finer restaurants for lunch on a weekday, you'll save a bundle and still get to treat your tastebuds to an extraordinary meal. Make sure to reserve.

✖ Best Places to Eat

➡ Richer (p101)

➡ Ladurée (p100)

➡ Le Hide (p100)

➡ Mamou (p101)

➡ Lasserre (p100)

For reviews, see p100.➡

🍷 Best Places to Drink

➡ Honor (p102)

➡ Bridge (p102)

➡ Le Rouge à Lèvres (p102)

For reviews, see p102.➡

🔒 Best Shopping

➡ Galeries Lafayette (p104)

➡ Le Printemps (p104)

➡ Triangle d'Or (p105)

➡ Place de la Madeleine (p101)

➡ À la Mère de Famille (p104)

For reviews, see p104.➡

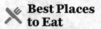

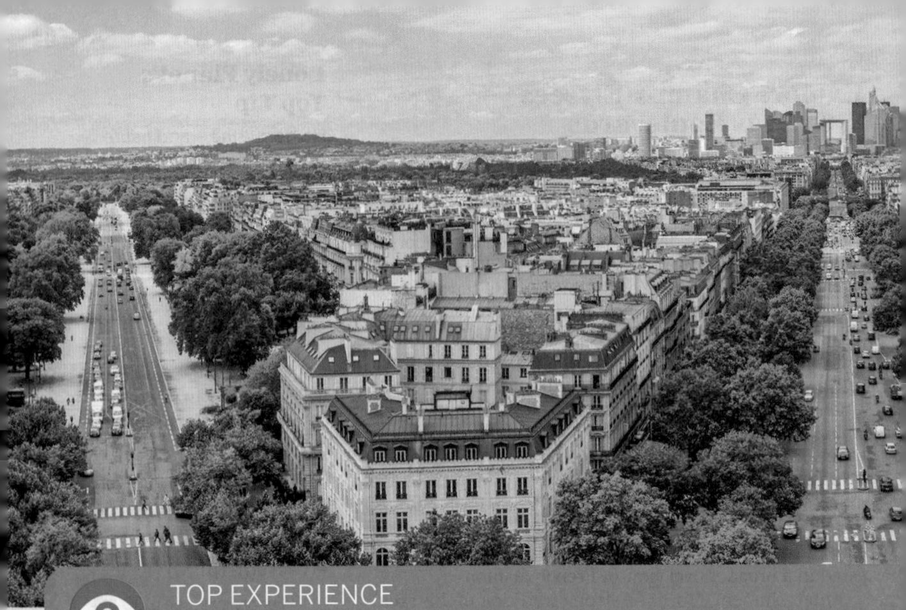

DISCOVER THE PANORAMAS ATOP THE ARC DE TRIOMPHE

Napoléon's armies never did march through the Arc de Triomphe showered in honour, but the monument has nonetheless come to stand as the very symbol of French patriotism. It's not for nationalistic sentiments, however, that so many visitors huff up the narrow, spiralling staircase. Rather it's the sublime panoramas from the top that make the arch such a notable attraction.

History

The arch was first commissioned in 1806 in the style of a Roman triumphal arch, following Napoléon's victory at Austerlitz the year before. At the time, the victory seemed like a watershed moment that confirmed the tactical supremacy of the French army, but a mere decade later, Napoléon had already fallen from power and his empire had crumbled.

The Arc de Triomphe was never fully abandoned – simply laying the foundations, after all, had taken an entire two years – and in 1836, after a series of starts and stops under the restored monarchy, the project was finally completed. In 1840 Napoléon's remains were returned to France and passed under the arch before being interred at Invalides.

Beneath the Arch

Beneath the arch at ground level lies the **Tomb of the Unknown Soldier**. Honouring the 1.3 million French soldiers who lost their lives in WWI, the Unknown Soldier was laid to rest in 1921, beneath an eternal flame that is rekindled daily at 6.30pm.

Also here are a number of bronze plaques laid into the ground. Take the time to try and decipher some: these mark significant moments in modern French history, such as the

DON'T MISS

➜ Tomb of the Unknown Soldier
➜ The sculptures
➜ Viewing platform

PRACTICALITIES

➜ Map p368, A2
➜ www.paris-arc-de-triomphe.fr
➜ place Charles de Gaulle, 8e
➜ viewing platform adult/child €13/free, 1st Sun of month Nov-Mar free
➜ ⊙10am-11pm Apr-Sep, to 10.45pm Oct-Mar
➜ Ⓜ Charles de Gaulle–Étoile

proclamation of the Third French Republic (4 September 1870) and the return of Alsace and Lorraine to French rule (11 November 1918).

The most notable plaque is the text from Charles de Gaulle's famous London broadcast on 18 June 1940, which sparked the French Resistance to life: 'Believe me, I who am speaking to you with full knowledge of the facts, and who tell you that nothing is lost for France. The same means that overcame us can bring us victory one day. For France is not alone! She is not alone!'

The Sculptures

The arch is adorned with four main sculptures, six panels in relief, and a frieze running beneath the top. Each was designed by a different artist; the most famous sculpture is the one to the right as you approach from the Champs-Élysées: *La Marseillaise* (Departure of the Volunteers of 1792). Sculpted by François Rude, it depicts soldiers of all ages gathering beneath the wings of victory, en route to drive back the invading armies of Prussia and Austria.

The higher panels depict a series of important victories for the Revolutionary and imperial French armies, from Egypt to Austerlitz, while the detailed frieze is divided into two sections: the *Departure of the Armies* and the *Return of the Armies*.

Don't miss the **multimedia section** beneath the viewing platform, which provides more detail and historical background for each of the sculptures.

Viewing Platform

Climb the 284 steps to the viewing platform at the top of the 50m-high arch and you'll be suitably rewarded with magnificent panoramas over western Paris. From here, a dozen broad avenues – many of them named after Napoléonic victories and illustrious generals – radiate towards every compass point.

The Arc de Triomphe is the highest point in the line of monuments known as the *axe historique* (historic axis, also called the grand axis); it offers views that swoop east down the Champs-Élysées to the gold-tipped obelisk at place de la Concorde (and beyond to the Louvre's glass pyramid), and west to the skyscraper district of La Défense, where the colossal Grande Arche marks the axis' western terminus.

Lift access to the top is only for visitors with limited mobility and parents with young children.

ARCH ACROBATICS

On 7 August 1919, three weeks after the WWI victory parade, Charles Godefroy flew a biplane through the arch (14.5m wide) to honour the French pilots who had fought in the war. It was no easy feat: Jean Navarre, the pilot originally chosen to perform the flight, crashed his plane while practising and died.

Don't cross the traffic-choked roundabout above ground if you value your life! Stairs lead from the northern side of the Champs-Élysées to pedestrian tunnels (not linked to metro tunnels) that bring you out safely beneath the arch. Tickets to the viewing platform are sold in the tunnel (you can also pre-purchase them online).

BASTILLE DAY CELEBRATION

The military parade commemorating Bastille Day (14 July) kicks off from the arch, which is adorned by a billowing tricolour.

◎ SIGHTS

Strolling down the Champs-Élysées from the Arc de Triomphe will leave you in the museum-rich neighbourhood surrounding the unparalleled vistas of place de la Concorde. Just west of the square are three architectural beauties from fin-de-siècle Paris: the Grand Palais, Petit Palais and Palais de la Découverte. North of Concorde is place de la Madeleine, with its neoclassical Église de la Madeleine. Further east towards the Grands Boulevards is the legendary Palais Garnier, the city's 19th-century opera house.

◎ Champs-Élysées

ARC DE TRIOMPHE   LANDMARK
See p94.

AVENUE DES CHAMPS-ÉLYSÉES   STREET
Map p368 (8e; Ⓜ Charles de Gaulle–Étoile, George V, Franklin D Roosevelt, Champs-Élysées–Clemenceau) No trip to Paris is complete without strolling this broad, tree-shaded avenue lined with luxury shops. Named for the Elysian Fields ('heaven' in Greek mythology), the Champs-Élysées was laid out in the 17th century and is part of the *axe historique,* linking place de la Concorde with the Arc de Triomphe. It's where presidents and soldiers parade on Bastille Day, where the Tour de France holds its final sprint, and where Paris turns out for organised and impromptu celebrations.

Cars are banished on the first Sunday of the month and plans approved by Paris' mayor in 2021 will transform the avenue into an 'extraordinary garden' by 2030.

HÔTEL DE LA MARINE   PALACE
Map p368 (🕿01 44 61 20 00; www.hotel-de-la-marine.paris; 2 place de la Concorde, 8e; 90-minute grand tour adult/child €17/free; ⏰10.30am-7pm Sat-Thu, to 10pm Fri, courtyard 9am-midnight daily; Ⓜ Concorde) Built to house the Garde-Meuble de la Couronne (royal furnishings), the Hôtel de la Marine is one of two grand-scale palaces (along with the Hôtel de Crillon, now a luxury hotel) commissioned by Louis XV in the late 18th century to grace place de la Concorde. After the building was looted

---

◉ TOP EXPERIENCE
SEE A SHOW AT PALAIS GARNIER

Few other Paris monuments have provided artistic inspiration in the way that the Palais Garnier has. From Degas' ballerinas to Gaston Leroux' Phantom and Chagall's ceiling, the layers of myth painted on gradually over the decades have bestowed a particular air of mystery and drama to its ornate interior. Designed in 1860 by Charles Garnier (then an unknown 35-year-old architect), the opera house was part of Baron Haussmann's massive urban renovation project.

The opera house is open to visitors during the day, and the building is a fascinating place to explore even if you're not taking in a show. Highlights include the opulent **Grand Staircase**, the **library-museum** (1st floor) and the horseshoe-shaped **auditorium** (2nd floor), with its extravagant gilded interior and red velvet seats. Above the massive chandelier is Chagall's gorgeous **ceiling mural** (1964), which depicts scenes from 14 operas.

Visits are either unguided (audioguides available; €5), or you can reserve a spot online for a two-hour English-language guided tour. Check the website for updated schedules.

DON'T MISS
➡ Grand Staircase
➡ Library-Museum
➡ Chagall's ceiling fresco

PRACTICALITIES
➡ Map p370, C4
➡ 🕿08 92 89 90 90
➡ www.operadeparis.fr
➡ cnr rues Scribe & Auber, 9e
➡ adult/child self-guided tours €14/10, guided tours €17/9.50
➡ ⏰10am-6pm mid-Jul–early Sep, to 4pm early Sep–mid-Jul, English tours 11am & 2.30pm
➡ Ⓜ Opéra

OLYMPIC RELOCATIONS

Paris' magnificent **Grand Palais** (Map p368; www.grandpalais.fr; 3 av du Général Eisenhower, 8e; MChamps-Élysées–Clemenceau), first built for the 1900 Exposition Universelle (World's Fair), will be a landmark venue of the 2024 Olympic and Paralympic games (p315), and will be closed for renovations until 2024.

During this time, a **temporary Grand Palais** will set up on the Parc du Champ de Mars (p86), adjacent to the Eiffel Tower. This 20m-high, 10,000-sq-metre building will also have an additional temporary structure added to the main structure each year in order to to expand it to some 18,000 sq metres. The space will host headlining exhibitions and events, as well as the Olympic judo and wrestling competitions.

Also on the move is the children's science museum **Palais de la Découverte** (www.palais-decouverte.fr), which is setting up a 770-sq-metre temporary home in the Parc André Citroën (p250) until 2024. It will open to the public by registration on weekends and during school holidays.

during the French Revolution, the French navy was headquartered here until 2015. Audioguide tours provide an insight into its history – prebook online.

Key events to have taken place in the building include the signing of *le décret d'abolition de l'esclavage* (decree of the abolition of slavery) in 1848. German troops were installed here from 1940 to 1944 during the Nazi Occupation of Paris.

In all, 6200 sq metres are visitable, including its ceremonial rooms and 18th-century apartments, and an exhibition space. A ground-floor passage with a tearoom, restaurants and a bookshop will connect rue Royale and rue St-Florentin.

PLACE DE LA CONCORDE   SQUARE

Map p368 (8e; MConcorde) Paris spreads around you, with views of the Eiffel Tower, the Seine and along the Champs-Élysées, when you stand in the city's largest square. Its 3300-year-old pink granite obelisk was a gift from Egypt in 1831. The square was first laid out in 1755 and originally named after King Louis XV, but its royal associations meant that it took centre stage during the Revolution – Louis XVI was the first to be guillotined here in 1793.

During the following two years, 1343 more people, including Marie Antoinette, Danton and Robespierre, also lost their heads here. The square was given its present name after the Reign of Terror in the hope that it would become a place of peace and harmony. The corners of the square are marked by eight statues representing what were once the largest cities in France.

PETIT PALAIS   GALLERY

Map p368 (☎01 53 43 40 00; www.petitpalais.paris.fr; av Winston Churchill, 8e; ⊙10am-6pm Tue-Sun, temporary exhibitions to 9pm Fri; MChamps-Élysées–Clemenceau) **FREE** This architectural stunner was built for the 1900 Exposition Universelle, and is home to the **Musée des Beaux-Arts de la Ville de Paris** (City of Paris Museum of Fine Arts). It specialises in medieval and Renaissance *objets d'art,* such as porcelain and clocks, tapestries, drawings, and 19th-century French paintings and sculpture; there are also paintings by such artists as Rembrandt, Colbert, Cézanne, Monet, Gauguin and Delacroix. An audioguide costs €5.

The cafe here has lovely garden seating.

PONT ALEXANDRE III   BRIDGE

Map p368 (btwn cours la Reine, 8e & quai d'Orsay, 7e; MChamps-Élysées–Clemenceau, Invalides) Built for the 1900 Exposition Universelle (World's Fair) to link the Grand Palais and Petit Palais with Les Invalides on the Left Bank, this Beaux Arts–style single-span steel bridge – a listed historical monument – is emblazoned with cherubs and nymphs, with four 17m-high pylons topped with statues of gilded winged horses. From the bridge there are sensational views of the Eiffel Tower. Art nouveau lamps illuminate it at night.

JARDIN DE LA NOUVELLE FRANCE   PARK

Map p368 (cnr av Franklin D Roosevelt & cours la Reine, 8e; ⊙24hr; MFranklin D Roosevelt) Descending rustic, uneven staircases (by the white-marble Alfred de Musset sculpture on av Franklin D Roosevelt, or the upper garden off cours la Reine) brings you to the tiny 0.7-hectare Jardin de la Nouvelle

France, an unexpected wonderland of lilacs, and lemon, orange, maple and weeping beech trees. There's a wildlife-filled pond, waterfall, wooden footbridge and benches to soak up the serenity.

BOUQUET OF TULIPS
SCULPTURE

Map p368 (1 av Dutuit, 8e; Ⓜ Champs-Élysées–Clemenceau) Reaching 11m high and weighing 61 tonnes, this bronze, aluminium and stainless steel sculpture of an outsized hand holding aloft a bouquet of colourful, high-gloss tulips was gifted to the city of Paris by its creator, American artist Jeff Koons, following the 2015 terrorist attacks. It was installed opposite the Petit Palais in 2019, with 80% of the commercial copyright proceeds going to the victims' families.

STATUE OF GÉNÉRAL CHARLES DE GAULLE
STATUE

Map p368 (place Clemenceau, 8e; Ⓜ Champs-Élysées–Clemenceau) Created by Jean Cardot, this 3.7m-high bronze statue (2000), set atop a 3.85m-high pedestal, depicts a striding Général Charles de Gaulle, who led the French Resistance against Nazi Germany in World War II. Nearby stands a statue of Winston Churchill (1988) by the same sculptor.

⊙ Grands Boulevards

MUSÉE NATIONAL GUSTAVE MOREAU
GALLERY

Map p370 (☏01 48 74 38 50; www.musee-moreau.fr; 14 rue de la Rochefoucauld, 9e; adult/child €7/free; ⊙10am-6pm Wed-Mon; Ⓜ Trinité) Symbolist painter Gustave Moreau's former studio is crammed with 4800 of his paintings, drawings and sketches – although symbolism received more attention as a literary movement in France (Baudelaire, Verlaine, Rimbaud). A particular highlight is *La Licorne* (The Unicorn), inspired by *La Dame à la Licorne* (The Lady with the Unicorn) cycle of tapestries in the Musée National du Moyen Âge. Note that it's not accessible to wheelchair users as there's no lift.

ÉGLISE DE LA MADELEINE
CHURCH

Map p370 (Church of St Mary Magdalene; www.eglise-lamadeleine.com; place de la Madeleine, 8e; ⊙9.30am-7pm; Ⓜ Madeleine) Place de la Madeleine is named after the 19th-century neoclassical church at its centre, the Église de la Madeleine. Constructed in the style of a massive Greek temple, 'La Madeleine' was consecrated in 1842 after almost a century of design changes and construction delays.

The church is a popular venue for classical-music concerts (some free); check the posters outside or the website for dates.

On the south side, the monumental staircase affords one of the city's most quintessential Parisian panoramas. From here, you can see down rue Royale to place de la Concorde and its obelisk and across the Seine to the Assemblée Nationale. The Invalides' gold dome appears in the background.

NOUVEAU MUSÉE DU PARFUM
MUSEUM

Map p370 (☏01 40 06 10 09; https://musee-parfum-paris.fragonard.com; 3-5 square de l'Opéra Louis Jouvet, 9e; ⊙9am-6pm Mon-Sat; Ⓜ Opéra or RER Auber) 𝗙𝗥𝗘𝗘 If the art of fragrance entices, stop by Fragonard's perfume museum. One of a trio of Paris locations, it has 30-minute guided tours (English available) that walk visitors through the history of perfume making, the layers of perfume composition and the processes of distilling a flower's fragrance. Tours finish in the shop, where you can test your nose on different scents. At 1pm on Saturdays, it also runs 90-minute English-language workshops where you can create and bottle your own perfume.

Two other wings can be found at **rue Scribe** (Map p370; ☏01 47 42 04 56; www.fragonard.com; 9 rue Scribe, 9e; ⊙9am-6pm Mon-Sat, to 5pm Sun; Ⓜ Opéra or RER Auber) 𝗙𝗥𝗘𝗘, an old townhouse with a collection of copper distillery vats and antique flacons, and the **Théâtre-Musée des Capucines** (Map p370; ☏01 42 60 37 14; www.fragonard.com; 39 blvd des Capucines, 2e; ⊙9am-6pm Mon-Sat; Ⓜ Opéra or RER Auber) 𝗙𝗥𝗘𝗘, which concentrates on the bottling and packaging side of perfume production.

CHAPELLE EXPIATOIRE
CHAPEL

Map p370 (☏01 42 65 35 80; www.chapelle-expiatoire-paris.fr; 29 rue Pasquier, 8e; adult/child €6/free; ⊙10am-12.30pm & 1.30-6.30pm Tue-Sat Apr-Sep, to 5pm Oct-Mar; Ⓜ St-Augustin) The austere, neoclassical Atonement Chapel, opposite 36 rue Pasquier, sits atop the section of a cemetery where Louis XVI, Marie Antoinette and many other victims of the Reign of Terror were buried after their executions in 1793. It was erected by Louis' brother, the restored Bourbon king Louis XVIII, in 1815. Two years later the royal bones were removed to the Basilique de St-Denis.

🚶 Neighbourhood Walk
Arc de Triomphe to Palais Garnier

START ARC DE TRIOMPHE
END PALAIS GARNIER
LENGTH 4.2KM; TWO HOURS

Paris is at its most glamorous along this walk, which takes you from the Arc de Triomphe along the famed av des Champs-Élysées to the opulent Palais Garnier opera house.

The city's grandeur peaks beneath the mighty ❶**Arc de Triomphe** (p94). Access is via the pedestrian tunnels beneath the roundabout.

A dozen avenues radiate from the Étoile, including tree-lined ❷**avenue des Champs-Élysées** (p96). Take your time strolling this broad avenue past luxury shops.

Parkland unfolds at the Champs-Élysées Marcel Dassault roundabout; turn right on av Franklin D Roosevelt then left on av du Général Eisenhower: on your right is the 1900-built, glass-roofed ❸**Grand Palais** (p97), currently being renovated as a Paris 2024 Olympic venue.

Heading south across av Winston Churchill, you'll arrive at the smaller but equally striking art nouveau ❹**Petit Palais** (p97), likewise built for the 1900 World's Fair.

Beyond the Petit Palais, turn left on av Dutuit and rejoin the Champs-Élysées, continuing east to ❺**place de la Concorde** (p97), the vast square between the Champs-Élysées and the Jardin des Tuileries, with views taking in the Eiffel Tower and the Seine. The pink granite obelisk marks the site of a French Revolution guillotine.

Turn left on rue Royale to place de la Madeleine. The Greek-temple-style ❻**Église de la Madeleine** (p98) dominates the centre, while the place itself is home to exquisite gourmet shops, and a colourful flower market.

Continue north along rue Tronchet and right onto bd Haussmann. On your left you'll see the *grands magasins* (department stores) Le Printemps then ❼**Galeries Lafayette** (p104) – be sure to head inside and up to Galeries Lafayette's rooftop for a fabulous, free panorama.

Turn right on rue Halévy to reach the resplendent ❽**Palais Garnier** (p96).

✖ EATING

The Champs-Élysées area is known for its big-name chefs and culinary icons, but there are a few under-the-radar restaurants too, where Parisians who live and work in the area dine on a regular basis. Rue de Ponthieu, running parallel to the Champs-Élysées, is a good spot to hunt for casual eateries, bakeries and cafes.

Head to the Grands Boulevards for a more diverse dining selection – everything from hole-in-the-wall wine bars to organic cafes.

✖ Champs-Élysées

★ LADURÉE   PASTRIES €

Map p368 (📱01 40 75 08 75; www.laduree.fr; 75 av des Champs-Élysées, 8e; pastries €7-10.50, mains €19-33; ⊘tearoom noon-9pm, shop 8am-7.30pm; 📶; MGeorge V) One of Paris' oldest patisseries, Ladurée has been around since 1862 and first created the lighter-than-air, ganache-filled macaron in the 1930s. Its tearoom is the classiest spot to indulge on the Champs in pastries or more formal meals. Alternatively, pick up some pastries to go – its trademark macarons (€2.60), in particular, are heavenly.

CRÊPE AVENUE   CRÊPES €

Map p368 (📱01 42 65 20 27; www.facebook.com/crepeavenue; 4 rue de Surène, 8e; galettes €6-11.50, crêpes €4.50-9, 2-course lunch menu €14; ⊘noon-3.30pm & 7-11.30pm Mon-Sat; 📶🍽🎧; MMadeleine) With a whitewashed, contemporary dining space, this is an excellent find for savoury galettes named for Parisian quartiers such as Concorde (goat's cheese and tomato), Champs-Élysées (spinach and crème fraîche) and Madeline (mushrooms and egg), along with sweet crêpes.

LE HIDE   FRENCH €€

Map p368 (📱01 45 74 15 81; www.lehide.fr; 10 rue du Général Lanrezac, 17e; 2-/3-course menu €34/38, mains €26; ⊘6.30-11pm Mon, Tue & Sat, noon-2pm & 6.30-11pm Wed-Fri; MCharles de Gaulle–Étoile) A perpetual favourite, Le Hide is a tiny neighbourhood bistro serving scrumptious traditional French fare: lobster bisque with shaved black truffles, veal kidneys sautéed in mustard and baked shoulder of lamb. Unsurprisingly, this place fills up faster than you can scamper down the steps of the nearby Arc de Triomphe – reserve well in advance.

CONTRASTE   FRENCH €€

Map p368 (📱01 42 65 08 36; www.contraste.paris; 18 rue d'Anjou, 8e; mains €24-39, 5-course menu €79, with paired wines €124; ⊘noon-2pm & 7.30-10.30pm Mon-Fri; MMadeleine) The dining room juxtaposes old (embossed timber panelling, gilt-framed mirrors) with new (designer lighting and lounge music) but the real contrast here is the cuisine, which reflects the origins of its two chefs, who are from Brittany and the Pyrenees. The result? Dishes like mountain trout with shards of citrus-infused buckwheat galettes, or Bigorre pork with sea herbs and oysters.

LASSERRE   GASTRONOMY €€€

Map p368 (📱01 43 59 53 43; www.restaurant-lasserre.com; 17 av Franklin D Roosevelt, 8e; mains €78-112, 4-/6-course menu €145/195, with paired wines €260/350; ⊘7-10pm Tue-Sat; MFranklin D Roosevelt) Since 1942, this exceedingly elegant Triangle d'Or restaurant has hosted style icons (including Audrey Hepburn) and is still a superlative choice for a Michelin-starred meal to remember. A bellhop-attended lift, white-and-gold chandeliered decor, extraordinary retractable roof and flawless service set the stage for creations such as braised sea bass with caviar or crêpes Suzette flambéed tableside. Observe the dress code.

ORIGINES   FRENCH €€€

Map p368 (📱09 86 41 63 04; www.origines-restaurant.com; 6 rue de Ponthieu, 8e; 3-course lunch menu €44, 6-course dinner menu €85, mains €39-46; ⊘12.15-2pm & 7.30-10pm Mon-Fri; MFranklin D Roosevelt) Chef Julien Boscus, who earned a Michelin star at Left Bank restaurant Les Climats, opened his own debonair blue- and grey-hued Right Bank premises in 2019. Black-truffle brioche with chardonnay-poached oysters, veal sweetbreads with hazelnut and lemon butter, and roast venison with burnt-pear puree are among the menu highlights. The three-course lunch is a superb deal.

✖ Grands Boulevards

CHEZ PLUME   ROTISSERIE €

Map p370 (📱01 48 78 65 43; www.chezplume.fr; 6 rue des Martyrs, 9e; dishes €7.50-12.50, sides €3.50-9; ⊘10.15am-2.30pm & 5-9pm Mon-Fri, 9.30am-9pm Sat, 9.30am-3pm Sun; MNotre

LOCAL KNOWLEDGE

GOURMET FOOD SHOPS: PLACE DE LA MADELEINE

Ultragourmet food shops garland **Place de la Madeleine** (Map p370; MMadeleine) in the 8e; many have in-house dining options. Notable names include truffle dealers La Maison de la Truffe (Map p370; ☎01 42 65 53 22; www.maison-de-la-truffe.com; 19 place de la Madeleine, 8e; ⊙10am-10.30pm Mon-Sat, closed mid-late Aug); mustard specialist Boutique Maille (Map p370; www.maille.com; 6 place de la Madeleine, 8e; ⊙10am-7pm Mon-Sat, 11am-6pm Sun); and extravagant chocolate sculptures at Patrick Roger (Map p370; ☎09 67 08 24 47; www.patrickroger.com; 3 place de la Madeleine, 8e; ⊙11am-7pm). Famous caterer Fauchon has a grand cafe (Map p370; ☎01 87 86 28 23; www.grandcafefauchon.fr; 11 place de la Madeleine, 8e; 2-/3-course lunch menu €45/55, 4-/5-course dinner menu €48/78; ⊙7am-midnight; 🖉🖉) here.

Nearby is La Maison du Miel (Map p370; www.maisondumiel.fr; 24 rue Vignon, 9e; ⊙9.30am-7pm Mon-Sat), in the honey business since 1898.

Dame de Lorette) This long-standing rotisserie specialises in free-range chicken from southwest France, prepared in a variety of fashions: simply roasted, as a crumble, or even in a quiche or sandwich. It's wonderfully casual: add a side or two (potatoes, polenta, seasonal veggies) and pull up a counter seat.

CHÉRI CHARLOT
SANDWICHES €

Map p370 (☎09 80 41 78 27; www.facebook.com/chericharlot; 33 rue Richer, 9e; dishes €6-11; ⊙10am-4pm Mon & Tue, to 9pm Wed-Fri; MCadet) If every French cheese had a charcuterie soulmate, who would be paired up with whom? This tiny deli seeks to answer this question with its excellent choice of sandwiches: Le Serra (St-Nectaire, Serrano ham), Le Rami (Comté, pastrami) and Le Chon (Reblochon, smoked bacon) are just some of its winning combinations. A sandwich (or quiche) with a drink costs €9.

LE VALENTIN
CAFE €

Map p370 (☎01 47 70 88 50; www.facebook.com/salondethelevalentin; 30-32 passage Jouffroy, 9e; pastries €3-4.60, dishes €8-14.50; ⊙8.30am-7.30pm Mon-Sat, 9.30am-7pm Sun; MGrands Boulevards) Inside beautiful covered arcade passage Jouffroy, this enchanting, two-storeyed *salon de thé* (tea house) slash patisserie slash *chocolaterie* is an equally lovely spot for breakfast, light lunches like quiches, salads, *feuilletés* (savoury-filled puff pastries) and brochettes (skewers), and dozens of varieties of tea, accompanied by exquisite *tartelettes* and delectable cakes.

★RICHER
BISTRO €€

Map p370 (www.lericher.com; 2 rue Richer, 9e; mains €17-25; ⊙noon-2.30pm & 7.30-10.30pm; MPoissonnière, Bonne Nouvelle) Richer's pared-back, exposed-brick decor is a smart setting for genius creations including wild plaice cerviche with fennel puree and confit tomato jelly or lacquered pork with chorizo curry. It doesn't take reservations, but it serves snacks and Chinese tea, and has a full bar (open until midnight). It's run by the same team as across-the-street neighbour **L'Office** (Map p370; ☎01 47 70 67 31; www.office-resto.com; 3 rue Richer, 9e; mains €19-29.50; ⊙noon-2.30pm & 6.30-10.30pm Mon-Fri; MPoissonière, Bonne Nouvelle).

ABRI SOBA
JAPANESE €€

Map p370 (10 rue Saulnier, 9e; dishes €9-18; ⊙noon-2pm & 7-9.30pm Tue-Sat, 7-9.30pm Sun; MCadet) A team of Japanese chefs in blue aprons calls out orders from Katsuaki Okiyama's open kitchen, while in the natural-wood interior, diners feast on soba noodles in one of 16 ways – such as cold with sesame sauce – alongside lightly battered, crisp tempura vegetables or an assortment of sashimi. No reservations; arrive early to beat the inevitable queues.

MAMOU
BISTRO €€

Map p370 (☎01 44 63 09 25; www.mamou-restaurant.com; 42 rue Taitbout, 9e; 2-/3-course lunch menu €21/23, mains €23-28; ⊙noon-2.30pm Mon & Tue, noon-2.30pm & 7.30-10.30pm Wed-Fri; MChaussée d'Antin) Fans of *haute cuisine* sans *haute* attitude should seek out this casual bistro by the Palais Garnier.

Accomplished chef Romain Lalu runs the kitchen, and diners can expect well-executed flavour combinations, such as trout with white asparagus and radishes or veal terrine with wild mushroom sauce. There's an excellent natural wine selection. Reserve ahead.

LE BON GEORGES
BISTRO €€

Map p370 (☑01 48 78 40 30; www.lebongeorges. com; 45 rue St-Georges, 9e; 2-course lunch menu €23, mains €24-36; ⊗noon-3pm & 7-11pm; MSt-Georges) Le Bon Georges thrives on nostalgia, focusing on personable service (the proprietor works the room himself) and a hearty bistro menu featuring classic French dishes like duck hearts with calf's liver, pigeon with cherry sauce, and red-wine-poached pears. Beef from the Polmard butchers (who raise their own cattle) and seasonal produce are guaranteed.

COCO
BRASSERIE €€

Map p370 (☑01 42 68 86 80; www.coco-paris. com; 1 place Jacques Rouché, 9e; mains €22-36; ⊗7.30am-2am; ⊛; MOpéra, Chaussée d'Antin) Transformed in the style of Napoléon III, the Palais Garnier's on-site restaurant has velvet lounges; tasselled lamps; interior palms, monstera and ferns; carpets inspired by the opera house wallpapers and a magnificent box-hedge-framed terrace. Food is served throughout the day (including classic layered Opéra cake from lunchtime on). It's a sublime setting even if you're not attending a performance.

🍷 DRINKING & NIGHTLIFE

The Champs-Élysées is home to a mix of exclusive nightspots, tourist haunts and a handful of large dance clubs. As a rule, you'll want to look as chic as possible to get in the door. Bars in the Grands Boulevards area tend to be more relaxed.

🍷 Champs-Élysées

HONOR
COFFEE

Map p368 (www.honor-cafe.com; 54 rue du Faubourg St-Honoré, 8e; ⊗10am-5pm Mon-Thu & Sat, 9am-3pm Fri; MMadeleine) Hidden off ritzy rue du Faubourg St-Honoré, in a court-

yard adjoining fashion house Comme des Garçons, is this opaque-plastic-sheltered black-and-white timber kiosk brewing coffee from small-scale producers around the globe. It also serves sourdough crumpets topped with combinations like avocado and serrano ham and luscious cakes (dishes €4 to €7.50), along with fresh juices, wine and beer.

BRIDGE
CLUB

Map p368 (☑06 40 46 44 62; www.facebook. com/pg/bridgeparisclub; Pont Alexandre III, 8e; ⊗11pm-6am Fri & Sat; MChamps-Élysées–Clemenceau, Invalides) Buried beneath Paris' most elaborate bridge, Pont Alexandre III, this cavernous 1500-sq-metre space, with a capacity of 2000 clubbers, is one of the city's top nightlife destinations. Check its agenda online for DJs, video installations, parties and other events. It also opens on Sunday nights before public-holiday Mondays.

BUGSY'S
PUB

Map p368 (www.bugsys.fr; 15 rue Montalivet, 8e; ⊗noon-1am Mon-Sat; MMiromesnil) There aren't many bars in western Paris that come attitude-free, so if you're in search of a friendly welcome to pair with a beer and burger, Bugsy's is for you. It gets crowded, though.

🍷 Grands Boulevards

AU GÉNÉRAL LA FAYETTE
BAR

Map p370 (☑01 47 70 59 08; www.augenerallafayette.fr; 52 rue la Fayette, 9e; ⊗7am-2am; ⊛; MLe Peletier) With its archetypal belle époque decor (brass fittings, polished wood, large murals) and excellent wines by the glass, this old-style brasserie is an atmospheric spot for a coffee stop or evening drink.

LE ROUGE À LÈVRES
WINE BAR

Map p370 (www.lerougealevres.com; 6 rue Rougemont, 9e; ⊗6pm-1am Tue-Sat; ⊛; MGrands Boulevards) Stylised wine bar Le Rouge à Lèvres has an eye-popping decor of foliage-print wallpaper, bamboo-and-straw light fittings and a fairy-lit indoor tree. Pair 60-plus natural wines by the glass or bottle with small sharing plates like stuffed peppers or swordfish tataki.

IBRIK
CAFE

Map p370 (☎01 73 71 84 60; www.ibrik.fr; 43 rue Laffitte, 9e; ⊗8.30am-4.30pm Mon-Fri, noon-5.30pm Sat; 🗟; MNotre-Dame-de-Lorette) Nothing will warm your heart more on a rainy day than popping into this two-floor coffee shop for a shot of cortado or rich hot chocolate (it also does smoothies and fresh juices). Bare concrete floors and a single coat of primer on the walls add to the quirky appeal.

ARCHIBON
WINE BAR

Map p370 (www.archibon.fr; 13 rue Rougemont, 9e; ⊗6pm-midnight Mon-Fri, to 10pm Sat; MGrands Boulevards) Head to this lively little backstreet wine bar for sustainably sourced, natural wines from around France to accompany simple but delicious cheese, charcuterie and cold seafood platters. Wines are available by the glass or bottle, and to take away.

☆ ENTERTAINMENT

Entertainment in the Champs-Élysées and Grands Boulevards neighbourhoods revolves around the landmark Palais Garnier, which stages opera and ballet performances. A handful of smaller music venues are located further east, where you can catch lesser-known acts passing through Paris.

PALAIS GARNIER
OPERA, BALLET

Map p370 (www.operadeparis.fr; place de l'Opéra, 9e; MOpéra) The city's original opera house (p96) is smaller than its Bastille counterpart, but has perfect acoustics. Due to its odd shape, some seats have limited or no visibility – book carefully. Ticket prices and conditions (including last-minute discounts) are available from the **box office** (Map p370; ☎international calls 01 71 25 24 23, within France 08 92 89 90 90; www.operadeparis.fr; cnr rues Scribe & Auber; ⊗10am-6.30pm Mon-Sat; MOpéra). Online flash sales (*les rendez-vous du mercredi*) are held from noon on Wednesdays.

L'OLYMPIA
LIVE MUSIC

Map p370 (☎08 92 68 33 68; www.olympiahall.com; 28 bd des Capucines, 9e; MMadeleine, Opéra) Opened by the founder of the Moulin Rouge in 1888, the Olympia has hosted all the big names over the years, from Édith Piaf to Jimi Hendrix, Jeff Buckley and the Arctic Monkeys, though it's small enough to put on a fairly intimate show.

SALLE GAVEAU
CONCERT VENUE

Map p368 (☎01 49 53 05 07; www.sallegaveau.com; 45 rue La Boétie, 8e; MMiromesnil) Exceptional acoustics make this 1907-built concert hall a superb place to catch chamber music, piano recitals, orchestras and theatre performances. It has a capacity of 900 over three levels. Check performances and buy tickets online.

THÉÂTRE MARIGNY
THEATRE

Map p368 (☎01 76 49 47 12; www.theatremarigny.fr; av de Marigny, 8e; MChamps-Élysées-Clemenceau) This 12-sided pavilion-style theatre was built in 1883 by Charles Garnier (who designed Paris' Palais Garnier opera house). The main theatre, with a capacity of 1023, hosts musicals and opera, while the smaller studio, seating 311 people, presents concerts and plays.

SALLE PLEYEL
LIVE MUSIC

Map p368 (☎08 92 97 60 63; www.sallepleyel.com; 252 rue du Faubourg St-Honoré, 8e; 🗟; MTernes) This concert hall has hosted performers such as Patricia Kaas, the Pretenders, Status Quo and Jamiroquai, as well as acts like the Ballet Nacional de Cuba.

FOLIES-BERGÈRE
LIVE MUSIC

Map p370 (☎08 92 68 16 50; www.foliesbergere.com; 32 rue Richer, 9e; MCadet) This is the legendary club where Charlie Chaplin, WC Fields and Stan Laurel appeared on stage together one night in 1911, and where Josephine Baker – accompanied by her diamond-collared pet cheetah and wearing only stilettos and a skirt made from bananas – bewitched audience members, including Ernest Hemingway. Today shows span everything from solo acts such as Ben Harper to musicals.

KIOSQUE THÉÂTRE MADELEINE
BOOKING SERVICE

Map p370 (www.kiosqueculture.com; opposite 15 place de la Madeleine, 8e; ⊗12.30-2.30pm & 3-7.30pm Tue-Sat, 12.30-3.45pm Sun; MMadeleine) Pick up half-price tickets for same-day performances of ballet, opera and music at this free-standing kiosk.

🔒 SHOPPING

Both French and global chains line the Champs-Élysées, but it's the luxury fashion houses in the Triangle d'Or and on rue du Faubourg St-Honoré that have made Paris famous. The area around Opéra and the Grands Boulevards is where you'll find flagship *grands magasins* (department stores).

⭐ GALERIES LAFAYETTE   DEPARTMENT STORE

Map p370 (📞01 42 82 34 56; http://hauss mann.galerieslafayette.com; 40 bd Haussmann, 9e; ⊙9.30am-8.30pm Mon-Sat, 11am-8pm Sun; 🛜; MChaussée d'Antin, RER Auber) Grande-dame department store Galeries Lafayette is spread across the main store (its magnificent neo-byzantine stained-glass dome dates from 1912), its **men's store**, and **homewares store** with **gourmet emporium**.

Catch modern art in the 1st-floor **Galerie des Galeries** (Map p370; 📞01 42 82 87 98; www.galeriedesgaleries.com; ⊙11am-7pm Wed-Mon) **FREE**, take in a **fashion show** (Map p370; 40 bd Haussmann; adult/child €14/9; ⊙3pm Fri mid-Feb–mid-Dec by online reservation), ascend to a free, windswept rooftop panorama or take a break at one of its many restaurants and cafes.

For the best views of the dome, walk along the free, 9m-long glass walkway extending below it on the 3rd floor.

Check online for details of 70-minute behind-the-scenes store tours (adult/child €13.50/9), available in English.

A branch of Galeries Lafayette is located on the **avenue des Champs-Élysées** (Map p368; 📞01 83 65 61 00; www.galerieslafayette champselysees.com; 60 av Champs-Élysées, 8e; ⊙10.30am-11pm Tue-Sat, to 10pm Sun & Mon; MFranklin D Roosevelt).

LE PRINTEMPS   DEPARTMENT STORE

Map p370 (📞01 42 82 50 00; www.printemps france.com; 64 bd Haussmann, 9e; ⊙9.35am-8pm Mon-Wed, Fri & Sat, 9.35am-8.45pm Thu, 11am-8pm Sun; 🛜; MHavre Caumartin) Famous department store Le Printemps encompasses Le Printemps de la Mode, for women's fashion; Le Printemps de la Beauté et Maison, for beauty and homewares, with a staggering display of perfume, cosmetics and accessories; Le Printemps de l'Homme, for men's fashion; and the gourmet emporium Le Printemps du Goût, with two floors dedicated to artisan French produce.

Guided 90-minute tours (adult/child €13.50/9) of the historic building, getting you up-close to highlights like its glass dome, are available in English.

There's a free panoramic rooftop terrace and numerous luxury eateries.

LAULHÈRE   HATS

Map p368 (www.laulhere-france.com; 14-16 rue du Faubourg St-Honoré, 8e; ⊙11am-7pm Mon-Sat; MMadeleine) Founded in 1840, beret maker Laulhère still supplies the French army with the iconic headwear. Handcrafted from soft, durable and water-resistant merino wool, varieties range from plain to jewel-encrusted versions. The boutique is hidden within a courtyard off rue du Faubourg St-Honoré.

À LA MÈRE DE FAMILLE   FOOD & DRINKS

Map p370 (📞01 47 70 83 69; www.lamerede famille.com; 35 rue du Faubourg Montmartre, 9e; ⊙9.30am-8pm Mon-Sat, 10am-7.30pm Sun; MLe Peletier) Founded in 1761, this is the original location of Paris' oldest chocolatier. Its beautiful belle époque shop (a listed historic monument) is as enchanting as the rainbow of sweets, caramels and chocolates inside.

GUERLAIN   PERFUME

Map p368 (📞spa 01 45 62 52 57; www.guerlain. com; 68 av des Champs-Élysées, 8e; ⊙10am-8pm Mon-Sat; MFranklin D Roosevelt) Guerlain is Paris' most famous parfumerie, and its shop (dating from 1912) is one of the most beautiful in the city. With its shimmering mirror-and-marble art deco interior, it's a reminder of the former glory of the Champs-Élysées. For total indulgence, make an appointment at its sublime spa.

HÔTEL DROUOT   ANTIQUES

Map p370 (📞01 48 00 20 20; www.drouot.com; 7-9 rue Drouot, 9e; ⊙11am-6pm Mon-Wed & Fri, to 8pm Thu; MRichelieu Drouot) Selling everything from antiques and jewellery to rare books and art, Paris' most established auction house has been in business for more than a century. Viewings are from 11am to 6pm the day before and 11am to noon the morning of the auction. Pick up the catalogue in-house or online.

HISTORIC HAUTE COUTURE

A stroll around the legendary Triangle d'Or (bordered by avs George V, Champs-Élysées and Montaigne, 8e) or on rue du Faubourg St-Honoré, 8e, and its eastern extension rue St-Honoré, 1er, constitutes the walk of fame of exclusive French fashion.

Balmain (Map p368; www.balmain.com; 44 rue François 1er, 8e; ⊙10.30am-7pm Mon-Sat; MFranklin D Roosevelt) Founded by French designer Pierre Balmain in 1945, this is the groundbreaking ultra-feminine label's flagship store.

Chanel (Map p372; www.chanel.com; 19 rue Cambon, 1er; ⊙10am-7pm Mon-Sat, 11am-7pm Sun; MMadeleine) This gleaming 1500-sq-metre flagship, with entrances on rues St-Honoré, Duphot and Cambon, is footsteps from Coco Chanel's original boutique at 31 rue Cambon (which remains the fashion house's design HQ today).

Chloé (Map p368; ☑01 47 23 00 08; www.chloe.com; 50 av Montaigne, 8e; ⊙10.30am-7pm Mon-Sat, 1-7pm Sun; MFranklin D Roosevelt) Established in the 1950s, this Parisian label has contemporary street cred.

Dior (Map p368; ☑01 45 63 12 51; www.dior.com; 44 av Montaigne, 8e; ⊙10am-7pm Mon-Sat, 11am-7pm Sun; MFranklin D Roosevelt) Post-WWII, Christian Dior's creations re-established Paris as the world fashion capital. Its flagship address, 30 av Montaigne, 8e, was under renovation at the time of writing, with plans to move its headquarters to Champs-Élysées.

Givenchy (Map p368; ☑01 44 43 99 90; www.givenchy.com; 36 av Montaigne, 8e; ⊙10am-7pm Mon-Sat, 1-7pm Sun; MFranklin D Roosevelt) The first to present a luxurious collection of women's prêt-à-porter.

Hermès (Map p368; ☑01 40 17 46 00; www.hermes.com; 24 rue du Faubourg St-Honoré, 8e; ⊙10.30am-6.30pm Mon-Sat; MConcorde) Founded in 1837 by a saddle-maker, Hermès' famous scarves are *the* fashion accessory.

Lanvin (Map p368; ☑01 44 71 31 73; www.lanvin.com; 22 rue du Faubourg St-Honoré, 8e; ⊙10.30am-7pm Mon-Sat; MConcorde) Established by milliner-turned-designer for women's and children's clothing Jeanne Lanvin at the turn of the 20th century.

Louis Vuitton (Map p368; ☑09 77 40 40 77; www.louisvuitton.com; 101 av des Champs-Élysées, 8e; ⊙10am-8pm Mon-Sat, 11am-8pm Sun; MGeorge V) Take home a Real McCoy canvas bag with the 'LV' monogram.

Saint Laurent (Map p368; ☑01 42 65 74 59; www.ysl.com; 38 rue du Faubourg St-Honoré, 8e; ⊙10.30am-7.30pm Mon-Sat; MConcorde) One of the top Parisian designers from the 1960s on, YSL was the first to incorporate non-European styles into his work.

LANCEL FASHION & ACCESSORIES
Map p368 (☑01 42 25 18 35; www.lancel.com; 4 Rond Point des Champs-Élysées, 8e; ⊙10am-7pm; MFranklin D Roosevelt) Open racks of luscious totes fill this handbag designer's gleaming premises.

MARCHÉ AUX FLEURS MADELEINE MARKET
Map p370 (place de la Madeleine, 8e; ⊙8am-7.30pm Mon-Sat; MMadeleine) This colourful flower market has been trading since the early 19th century.

PUBLICIS DRUGSTORE DEPARTMENT STORE
Map p368 (☑01 44 43 75 07; www.publicis drugstore.com; 133 av des Champs-Élysées, 8e; ⊙8am-2am Mon-Fri, 10am-2am Sat & Sun; MCharles de Gaulle-Étoile) An institution since 1958, Publicis incorporates cinemas and late-opening shops, including an *épicerie* (specialist grocer), pharmacy, beauty counter, international newsagent, a wine *cave* (cellar) and cigar bar.

Louvre & Les Halles

LOUVRE | LES HALLES | RIGHT BANK

Neighbourhood Top Five

1 Musée du Louvre
(p108) Exploring the Louvre's little-visited quiet corners, with timeless masterpieces every which way you turn.

2 Centre Pompidou
(p116) Contemplating Europe's largest collection of modern art and admiring the view from the top of one

of the city's most whimsical buildings.

3 Jardin des Tuileries
(p118) Finally meeting Monet's water lilies, picnicking in the park and revelling in Paris at its symmetrical best.

4 Église St-Eustache
(p119) Feasting on exquisite sacred art and soulful music

in this landmark Gothic church.

5 Jardin du Palais Royal
(p120) Browsing designer boutiques beneath the arcaded galleries and letting the kids run free amid Daniel Buren's zebra-striped columns.

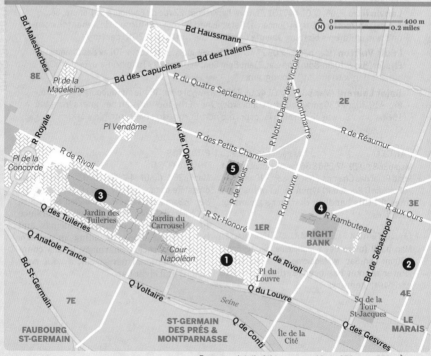

For more detail of this area see Map p372 and p376.

Explore Louvre & Les Halles

The banks of the Seine make an enchanting starting point. A wonderful exploratory loop snakes westwards along quai des Tuileries, past the sculptures and green lawns, pools and fountains of Jardin des Tuileries (p118). Continue north to ritzy place Vendôme, then east along shop-chic rue St-Honoré.

Set aside at least half a day for the Musée du Louvre (p108), followed by a visit to the exquisite, arcade-flanked Jardin du Palais Royal (p120). Art lovers will likewise want to set aside another half-day minimum for the Centre Pompidou (p116), which contains Europe's largest collection of modern and contemporary art. Yet more contemporary art awaits at the Collection Pinault – Paris (p120).

Beyond it, the timeless sophistication of the Louvre area disappears in a flash, replaced by bright lights, jostling crowds and swinging jazz clubs. Day and night the mainly pedestrian zone between the Centre Pompidou and Forum des Halles is packed with people, just as it was for the 850-odd years when Paris' main *halles* (marketplace) for foodstuffs was here.

Local Life

After-work drinks Rue Montorgueil has a good selection of cafe-bars, but it's rue St-Saveur's cocktail clubs (p127) and the hip bars on rue Montmartre that steal the late-night show.

Museums Forget Tuesday when the Louvre (p108) and Centre Pompidou (p116) are closed; go local and visit during less-crowded late-night openings or one-off cultural events.

Little Tokyo Rue Ste-Anne, just west of Jardin du Palais Royal, is loaded with Japanese eateries, with more in the side streets, such as Ryo (p125).

Getting There & Away

Metro & RER The Louvre has two metro stations: Palais Royal–Musée du Louvre (lines 1 and 7) and Louvre Rivoli (line 1). Numerous metro and RER lines converge at Paris' main hub, Châtelet–Les Halles.

Bus Major bus lines include the 27 from rue de Rivoli (for bd St-Michel and place d'Italie) and the 69 near the Louvre Rivoli metro (for Invalides and Eiffel Tower).

Bicycle Stations at 1 place Ste-Marguerite de Navarre and 2 rue de Turbigo are best placed for the Châtelet–Les Halles metro/RER hub; for the Louvre pedal to/from 165 rue St-Honoré.

Boat The hop-on, hop-off **Batobus** (Map p372; quai du Louvre, 1er; MTuileries, Pont Neuf) stops outside the Louvre.

Lonely Planet's Top Tip

The busy transport hub beneath the Forum des Halles, incorporating metro stations Châtelet and Les Halles, along with RER station Châtelet–Les Halles, is a maze of tunnels, staircases and platforms; neighbouring metro stations are inevitably quicker and easier to access, even if the walk above ground is slightly further from your destination.

✗ Best Places to Eat

➡ Frenchie (p125)
➡ Cédric Grolet Opéra (p121)
➡ Maison Maison (p123)
➡ Verjus (p126)
➡ Balagan (p123)

For reviews, see p121.➡

☕ Best Places to Drink

➡ Bar Hemingway (p127)
➡ Scilicet (p127)
➡ Experimental Cocktail Club (p127)
➡ Baby Doll (p127)
➡ Harry's New York Bar (p127)
➡ L'Ivress (p128)

For reviews, see p127.➡

☆ Best Entertainment

➡ Le Grand Rex (p130)
➡ La Place (p129)
➡ Comédie Française (p130)
➡ Le Baiser Salé (p129)

For reviews, see p129.➡

TOP EXPERIENCE
GET LOST IN ART AT THE MUSÉE DU LOUVRE

Paris' *pièce de résistance* is one of the world's largest and most diverse museums, showcasing 35,000 works of art in palatial surrounds, including some of the best-known works ever created. It would take nine months to glance at every piece, rendering advance planning essential.

Palais du Louvre

The Louvre today rambles over four floors and through three wings: the **Sully Wing** creates the four sides of the Cour Carrée (literally, 'Square Courtyard') at the eastern end of the complex; the **Denon Wing** stretches 800m along the Seine to the south; and the northern **Richelieu Wing** skirts rue de Rivoli. The building started life as a fortress built by Philippe-Auguste in the 12th century – medieval remnants are still visible on the lower ground floor (Sully). In the 16th century it became a royal residence and after the Revolution, in 1793, it was turned it into a national museum. Its booty was no more than 2500 paintings and *objets d'art*.

Over the centuries French governments amassed the paintings, sculptures and artefacts displayed today. The 'Grand Louvre' project inaugurated by the late President Mitterrand in 1989 doubled the museum's exhibition space, and both new and renovated galleries have since opened, including the state-of-the-art **Islamic art galleries** (lower ground floor, Denon) in the stunningly restored Cour Visconti.

Mona Lisa

Easily the Louvre's most admired work is Leonardo da Vinci's *La Joconde* (in French; *La Gioconda* in Italian), the lady with that enigmatic smile known as *Mona Lisa* (Room 711, 1st floor, Denon).

DON'T MISS

➡ Mesopotamian and Egyptian collections

➡ 1st floor, Denon Wing

➡ Napoléon III Apartments

PRACTICALITIES

➡ Map p372, F7

➡ ☎01 40 20 53 17

➡ www.louvre.fr

➡ rue de Rivoli & quai des Tuileries, 1er

➡ adult/child €15/free, 6-9.45pm 1st Sat of month free

➡ ⊙9am-6pm Mon, Thu, Sat & Sun, to 9.45pm Wed, Fri & 1st Sat of month

➡ Ⓜ Palais Royal–Musée du Louvre

Mona (*monna* in Italian) is a contraction of *madonna,* and Gioconda is the feminine form of the surname Giocondo. Scientists used infrared technology to peer through paint layers and confirm *Mona Lisa's* identity as Lisa Gherardini (1479–1542?), wife of Florentine merchant Francesco de Giocondo. It was also confirmed her dress was covered in a transparent gauze veil typically worn in early-16th-century Italy by pregnant women or new mothers, suggesting the work was painted to commemorate the birth of her second son around 1503, when she was aged about 24.

Its immense popularity has led to controversial suggestions it should be moved to an external location, given the pressure on the Louvre's visitor numbers. You'll need to queue to see the painting; once in front of it, you'll have around two minutes before being moved on.

Priceless Antiquities

Whatever your plans are, don't rush by the Louvre's astonishing cache of treasures from antiquity: both **Mesopotamia** (ground floor, Richelieu) and **Egypt** (ground and 1st floors, Sully) are well represented, as seen in the *Code of Hammurabi* (Room 227, ground floor, Richelieu) and *The Seated Scribe* (Room 635, 1st floor, Sully). Room 307 (ground floor, Sully) holds impressive friezes and an enormous **two-headed-bull column** from the Darius Palace in ancient Iran, while a huge seated **statue of Pharaoh Ramesses II** highlights the temple room (Room 324, ground floor, Sully).

Also worth a look are the mosaics and figurines from the Byzantine empire (lower ground floor, Denon), and the Greek statuary collection, culminating with the world's most famous armless duo, the **Venus de Milo** (Room 346, ground floor, Sully) and the **Winged Victory of Samothrace** (Room 703, 1st floor, Denon).

French & Italian Masterpieces

The **1st floor of the Denon Wing**, where the *Mona Lisa* is found, is easily the most popular part of the Louvre – and with good reason. Rooms 700 through 702 are hung with monumental French paintings, many iconic: look for the *Consecration of the Emperor Napoléon I* (David), *The Raft of the Medusa* (Géricault) and *Grande Odalisque* (Ingres).

Rooms 710, 711, 712 and 716 are also must-visits. Filled with classic works by **Renaissance** masters (Raphael, Titian, Uccello, Botticini), this area culminates in the crowds around the *Mona Lisa*. But you'll find plenty else to contemplate, such as the superbly detailed *Wedding Feast at Cana* (Room 711). Botticelli's frescoes grace Room 706.

THE PYRAMID INSIDE & OUT

Almost as stunning as the masterpieces inside is the 21m-high glass pyramid designed by Chinese-American architect IM Pei (1917–2019) that crowns the main entrance to the Louvre. Beneath Pei's Grande Pyramide is the **Hall Napoléon**, the museum's main entrance area. To revel in another Pei pyramid of equally dramatic dimensions, head towards the **Carrousel du Louvre** (Map p372; www.carrouseldulouvre.com; 99 rue de Rivoli, 1er; ◷10am-8pm Wed-Mon, 11am-7pm Tue; ⌨; ⓜPalais Royal–Musée du Louvre), a busy shopping mall that loops underground from the Grande Pyramide to the **Arc de Triomphe du Carrousel** (Map p372; place du Carrousel, 1er; ⓜPalais Royal–Musée du Louvre) – its centrepiece is Pei's **Pyramide Inversée** (inverted glass pyramid).

From October to June each year, the Louvre's innovative cultural education space, the Petite Galerie, mounts a major exhibition with interactive displays plus related Louvre-wide tours, alongside storytelling, readings, films and other events for all ages. Keep an eye on the website for details.

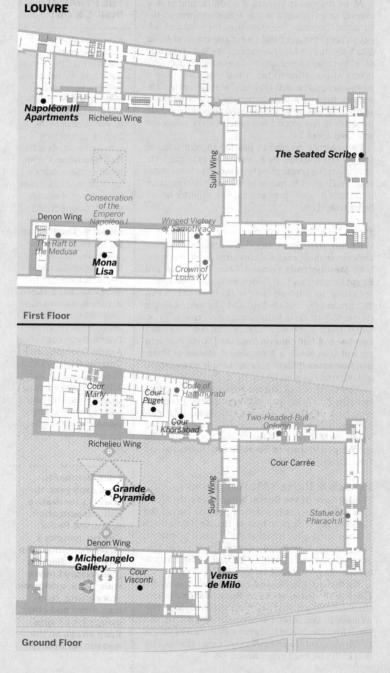

LOUVRE & LES HALLES MUSÉE DU LOUVRE

LOUVRE

Napoléon III Apartments Richelieu Wing

The Seated Scribe •

Sully Wing

Consecration of the Emperor Napoléon I

Denon Wing

Winged Victory of Samothrace

The Raft of the Medusa

Mona Lisa

Crown of Louis XV

First Floor

Cour Marly

Cour Puget

Code of Hammurabi

Cour Khorsabad

Two-Headed-Bull Column

Richelieu Wing

Cour Carrée

Grande Pyramide •

Denon Wing

Statue of Pharaoh II

Sully Wing

• **Michelangelo Gallery**

Cour Visconti

Venus de Milo •

Ground Floor

Porte des Lions entrance

Northern European Painting

The 2nd floor of the Richelieu Wing, directly above the gilt and crystal of the **Napoléon III Apartments** (1st floor), allows for a quieter meander through the Louvre's inspirational collection of Flemish and Dutch paintings spearheaded by the works of Peter Paul Rubens and Pieter Bruegel the Elder. Vermeer's *The Lacemaker* can be found in Room 837, while Room 845 is devoted chiefly to works by Rembrandt.

Trails & Tours

Self-guided thematic trails range from Louvre masterpieces and the art of eating to family-friendly topics. Download trail brochures in advance from the website. Another good option is to rent a Nintendo 3DS multimedia guide (€5; ID required). More formal, English-language **guided tours** (Map p372; tour excl museum entry adult/child €12/7; ⊘11am & 2pm daily except 1st Tue & Sun of month, plus 7pm Wed; ⓂPalais Royal–Musée du Louvre) depart from the Hall Napoléon. Reserve a spot online up to 14 days in advance or sign up on arrival at the museum.

Louvre Auditorium

Off the main entrance hall, the **Louvre Auditorium** (Map p372; ☑01 40 20 55 00; www.louvre.fr/musiques; Hall Napoléon, Musée du Louvre, rue de Rivoli & quai des Tuileries, 1er; ⓂPalais Royal–Musée du Louvre) is an excellent place to catch classical concerts from September to April or May, such as its Thursday lunchtime concerts costing a mere €15/6 per adult/child, which feature up-and-coming composers and musicians.

ACCESSING THE LOUVRE

The Louvre embarked on a 30-year renovation plan in 2014, with the aim of modernising the museum to make it more accessible, including increasing the number of museum entrances. Security queues at the underground Carrousel du Louvre entrance (p109) and the **Porte des Lions entrance** (quai François Mitterrand; ⊘9am-5.30pm Wed-Mon) are typically shorter than the main Grande Pyramide entrance. To guarantee entry, you'll need to pre-purchase a ticket with an allocated time slot on the museum's website (€2 surcharge) or make a time slot reservation using a Paris Museum Pass. Tickets are only valid for the duration of your visit (you can no longer come and go as you please throughout the day).

French kings wore their crowns only once – at their coronation. Lined with embroidered satin and topped with openwork arches and a fleur-de-lis, and crafted in 1722, Louis XV's crown (Room 705, 1st floor, Denon) was originally adorned with pearls, sapphires, rubies, topazes, emeralds and diamonds.

KIEVVICTOR / SHUTTERSTOCK ©

1. Glass-ceilinged hall
The Palais du Louvre itself is a building of historic and architectural importance.

2. Winged Victory of Samothrace
Despite having long-since lost its head and arms, this statue of the goddess Nike remains impressive.

3. A portrait by Francisco Goya
This Spanish artist was an important figure in the romantic period.

4. *Death of Sardanapalus* by Eugène Delacroix
The legend of decadent Assyrian king Sardanapalus and his outrageous demise also inspired a play by Byron.

The Louvre

A HALF-DAY TOUR

Successfully visiting the Louvre is a fine art. Its complex labyrinth of galleries and staircases spiralling across three wings and four floors renders discovery a snakes-and-ladders experience. Initiate yourself with this three-hour itinerary – a playful mix of *Mona Lisa*–obvious and up-to-the-minute unexpected.

Arriving in the ❶ **Cour Napoléon** beneath IM Pei's glass pyramid, pick up colour-coded floor plans at an information stand, then ride the escalator up to the Sully Wing and swap passport or credit card for a multimedia guide (there are limited descriptions in the galleries) at the wing entrance.

The Louvre is as much about spectacular architecture as masterful art. To appreciate this, zip up and down Sully's Escalier Henri II to admire ❷ **Venus de Milo**, then up parallel Escalier Henri IV to the palatial displays in ❸ **Cour Khorsabad**. Follow signs for the escalator up to the 1st floor and the opulent ❹ **Napoléon III apartments**. Next traverse 25 consecutive galleries (thank you, floor plan!) to flip conventional contemplation on its head with Cy Twombly's ❺ **The Ceiling**, and the hypnotic ❻ **Winged Victory of Samothrace**, which brazenly insists on being admired from all angles. End with the impossibly famous ❼ **Raft of the Medusa**, ❽ **Mona Lisa** and ❾ **Virgin & Child**.

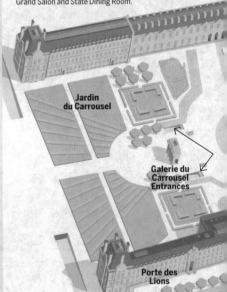

Napoléon III Apartments
Rooms 544 & 547, 1st Floor, Richelieu
Napoléon III's gorgeous gilt apartments were built from 1854 to 1861, featuring an over-the-top decor of gold leaf, stucco and crystal chandeliers that reaches a dizzying climax in the Grand Salon and State Dining Room.

Jardin du Carrousel

Galerie du Carrousel Entrances

Porte des Lions

TOP TIPS

➡ Floor plans for navigating the Louvre's maze of galleries are free from the information desks in the Hall Napoléon.

➡ The Denon Wing is always packed; visit on late nights (Wednesday or Friday) or trade Denon in for the notably quieter Richelieu Wing.

LOUVRE AUDITORIUM

Classical-music concerts are staged several times a week at the Louvre Auditorium (off the main entrance hall). Don't miss the Thursday lunchtime concerts featuring emerging composers and musicians. The season runs from September to April or May, depending on the concert series.

Mona Lisa
Room 711, 1st Floor, Denon
No smile is as enigmatic or bewitching as hers. Da Vinci's diminutive *La Joconde* hangs opposite the largest painting in the Louvre – sumptuous, fellow Italian Renaissance artwork *The Wedding at Cana*.

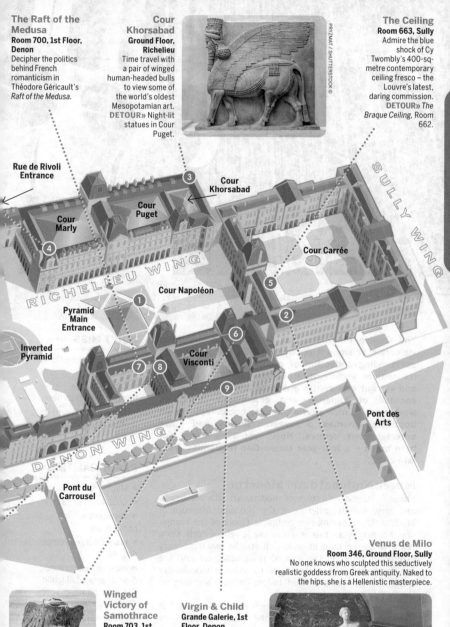

The Raft of the Medusa
Room 700, 1st Floor, Denon
Decipher the politics behind French romanticism in Théodore Géricault's *Raft of the Medusa*.

Cour Khorsabad
Ground Floor, Richelieu
Time travel with a pair of winged human-headed bulls to view some of the world's oldest Mesopotamian art. DETOUR» Night-lit statues in Cour Puget.

The Ceiling
Room 663, Sully
Admire the blue shock of Cy Twombly's 400-sq-metre contemporary ceiling fresco – the Louvre's latest, daring commission. DETOUR» *The Braque Ceiling*, Room 662.

Rue de Rivoli Entrance

SULLY WING

Cour Khorsabad

③

Cour Puget

Cour Marly

④

Cour Carrée

RICHELIEU WING

⑤

Cour Napoléon

①

Pyramid Main Entrance

②

Inverted Pyramid

⑥

Cour Visconti

⑦ ⑧

⑨

Pont des Arts

DENON WING

Pont du Carrousel

Venus de Milo
Room 346, Ground Floor, Sully
No one knows who sculpted this seductively realistic goddess from Greek antiquity. Naked to the hips, she is a Hellenistic masterpiece.

Winged Victory of Samothrace
Room 703, 1st Floor, Denon
Draw breath at the aggressive dynamism of this headless, handless Hellenistic goddess. DETOUR» The razzle-dazzle of the Apollo Gallery's crown jewels.

Virgin & Child
Grande Galerie, 1st Floor, Denon
In the spirit of artistic devotion save the Louvre's most famous gallery for last: a feast of Virgin-and-child paintings by Da Vinci, Raphael, Domenico Ghirlandaio, Giovanni Bellini and Francesco Botticini.

TOP EXPERIENCE
BE DELIGHTED AT THE CENTRE POMPIDOU

The Centre Pompidou has amazed and delighted visitors ever since it opened in 1977, not just for its outstanding collection of modern art but also for its radical architectural statement. The dynamic and vibrant arts centre enthralls with its irresistible cocktail of galleries and exhibitions, hands-on workshops, dance performances, bookshop, design boutique, cinemas, a research library and other entertainment venues. Note, you'll need to get here quick – a four-year renovation is planned from late 2023.

Musée National d'Art Moderne
Europe's largest collection of modern art fills the bright and airy, well-lit galleries of the National Museum of Modern Art, covering two complete floors of the Pompidou. For art lovers, this is one of the jewels of Paris. On a par with the permanent collection are the two temporary exhibition halls (on the ground floor/basement and the top floor), which showcase some memorable blockbuster exhibits. Also of note is the fabulous children's gallery on the 1st floor.

The permanent collection changes every two years, but the basic layout generally stays the same. The 5th floor showcases artists active between 1905 and 1970 (give or take a decade); the 4th floor focuses on more contemporary creations, roughly from the 1990s onward.

The dynamic presentation of the 5th floor mixes up works by Picasso, Matisse, Chagall and Kandinsky with lesser-known contemporaries from as far afield as Argentina and Japan, as well as more famous cross-Atlantic names such as Arbus, Warhol, Pollock and Rothko.

DON'T MISS

➡ Musée National d'Art Moderne
➡ Cutting-edge temporary exhibitions
➡ The 6th floor and its sweeping panorama of Paris

PRACTICALITIES

➡ Map p376, F7
➡ 📞 01 44 78 12 33
➡ www.centre pompidou.fr
➡ place Georges Pompidou, 4e
➡ museum, exhibitions & panorama adult/child €14/free, panorama only €5/free
➡ ⏰11am-9pm Wed-Mon, temporary exhibits to 11pm Thu
➡ Ⓜ Rambuteau

One floor down on the 4th, you'll find monumental paintings, installation pieces, sculpture and video taking centre stage. The focus here is on contemporary art, architecture and design.

Architecture & Views

Former French President Georges Pompidou wanted an ultracontemporary artistic hub and he got it: competition-winning architects Renzo Piano and Richard Rogers designed the building inside out, with utilitarian features like plumbing, pipes, air vents and electrical cables forming part of the external façade. The building was renovated in 2020.

Viewed from a distance (such as from Sacré-Cœur), the Centre Pompidou's primary-coloured, box-like form amid a sea of muted grey Parisian rooftops makes it look like a child's Meccano set abandoned on someone's elegant living-room rug. Although the Centre Pompidou is just six storeys high, the city's low-rise cityscape means stupendous views extend from its roof (reached by external escalators enclosed in tubes). Rooftop admission is included in museum and exhibition admission – or buy a panorama ticket (€5) just for the roof.

Atelier Brancusi

West of the Centre Pompidou main building, this reconstruction of the **studio** (Map p376; www.centre pompidou.fr; 55 rue de Rambuteau, 4e; ⊙2-6pm Wed-Mon; Ⓜ Rambuteau) ᴳᴿᴱᴱ of Romanian-born sculptor Constantin Brancusi (1876–1957) – known for works such as *The Kiss* and *Bird in Space* – contains over 130 sculptures in stone and wood. You'll also find drawings, pedestals and photographic plates from his original Paris studio.

Children's Activities

On the 1st floor, the Galerie des Enfants, open from 11am to 7pm Wednesday to Monday, is an exhibition area aimed at children aged two to 10, which encourages interactive experimentation; various workshops take place on Wednesday, Saturday and Sunday.

For teenagers aged 13 to 16, Studio 13/16, open 2pm to 6pm Wednesday, Saturday and Sunday on the lower ground floor, has visual, multimedia and performing art kits and opportunities to meet artists.

Tours

Guided tours in English take place at 2pm on Saturday and sometimes Sunday (€4.50; reserve online). Audioguided tours are downloadable on the website (you'll need your own smartphone and earphones).

ENTERTAINMENT

A keystone of the Centre Pompidou's popularity with Parisians as well as visitors is its entertainment options. Along with two **cinemas** screening single films, retrospectives, documentaries and more, it hosts a packed calendar of concerts, theatre and dance.

The full-monty Pompidou experience is as much about hanging out in the busy streets and squares around it, packed with souvenir shops and people, as absorbing the centre's contents. West of the Centre Pompidou, fun-packed place Georges Pompidou and its nearby pedestrian streets attract bags of buskers, musicians, jugglers and mime artists. Don't miss place Igor Stravinsky with its fanciful mechanical fountains of skeletons, hearts, treble clefs, and a big pair of ruby-red lips by Jean Tinguely and Niki de Saint Phalle.

LOUVRE & LES HALLES THE CENTRE POMPIDOU

TOP EXPERIENCE
WANDER THE JARDIN DES TUILERIES

Filled with fountains, classical sculptures and magnificent panoramas every way you turn, this quintessentially Parisian park was laid out in 1664 by André Le Nôtre, who also created the gardens at Vaux-le-Vicomte and Versailles.

The 16th-century Palais des Tuileries (home to Napoléon, among others) stood at the garden's western end until 1871, when it was razed during the upheaval of the Paris Commune. All that remains of the palace today are two buildings, both museums. The ensemble now forms part of the Banks of the Seine Unesco World Heritage site.

The **Musée de l'Orangerie** (Map p368; ☎01 44 77 80 07; www.musee-orangerie.fr; place de la Concorde, 1er; adult/child €9/free; ☺9am-6pm Wed-Mon; Ⓜ Concorde), set in a 19th-century edifice built to shelter the garden's orange trees in winter, is a treat. The two oval rooms of the purpose-built top floor are the show-stealer; here you'll find eight of Monet's enormous, ethereal *Water Lilies* canvases bathed in natural light.

Downstairs is the private collection of art dealer Paul Guillaume (1891–1934), with works by all the big names of early modern art: Cézanne, Matisse, Picasso, Renoir, Modigliani, Soutine and Utrillo.

There's always a queue, so arrive early. A combination ticket covering admission to the Musée d'Orsay costs €18.

The other museum is the wonderfully airy **Jeu de Paume** (Map p368; ☎01 47 03 12 50; www.jeudepaume.org; 1 place de la Concorde, 1er; Ⓜ Concorde), set in the palace's erstwhile royal tennis court. It stages innovative photography exhibitions.

DON'T MISS

➜ Monet's *Water Lilies*
➜ Paul Guillaume collection
➜ Jeu de Paume
➜ Picnic or stroll in the park

PRACTICALITIES

➜ Map p372, C5
➜ rue de Rivoli, 1er
➜ ☺7am-11pm Jun-Aug, 7am-9pm Apr, May & Sep, 7.30am-7.30pm Oct-Mar
➜ Ⓜ Tuileries, Concorde

TOP EXPERIENCE
ATTEND AN ORGAN RECITAL AT ST-EUSTACHE

Just north of the open green spaces of the Jardin Nelson Mandela next to the city's old marketplace, now the Forum des Halles, is one of the most beautiful churches in Paris. Majestic, architecturally magnificent and musically outstanding, Église St-Eustache has made spirits soar for centuries.

Tales of spiritual pomp and circumstance are plentiful. It was here that Richelieu and Molière were baptised, Louis XIV celebrated his first Holy Communion and Colbert was buried. Mozart chose St-Eustache for the funeral Mass of his mother and in 1855 Berlioz' *Te Deum* premiered here – the church's acoustics are extraordinary.

Built between 1532 and 1637, the church is primarily Gothic, though a neoclassical façade was added on the western side in the mid-18th century. Artistic highlights include a work by Rubens, Raymond Mason's colourful bas-relief of market vendors (1969) and Keith Haring's bronze triptych (1990) in the side chapels. Outside is a gigantic sculpture of a head and hand entitled *L'Écoute* (Listen; 1986) by Henri de Miller. Audioguides (€3) are available from reception.

One of France's largest organs is above the church's western entrance; it has 101 stops and 8000 pipes dating from 1854. Free organ recitals at 5pm on Sunday are a must for music lovers, as is June's Festival des 36 Heures de St-Eustache – 36 hours of nonstop music embracing a symphony of genres.

DON'T MISS

➡ *L'Écoute*

➡ Free Sunday-afternoon organ recitals

➡ Artwork in the side chapels

PRACTICALITIES

➡ Map p376, C5

➡ ☑ 01 42 36 31 05

➡ www.saint-eustache.org

➡ 146 rue Rambuteau, 1er

➡ ⊙ 9.30am-7pm Mon-Fri, 10am-7.15pm Sat, 9am-7.15pm Sun

➡ Ⓜ Les Halles, RER Châtelet–Les Halles

⊙ SIGHTS

MUSÉE DU LOUVRE MUSEUM
See p108.

CENTRE POMPIDOU MUSEUM
See p116.

JARDIN DES TUILERIES PARK
See p118.

ÉGLISE ST-EUSTACHE CHURCH
See p119.

MUSÉE DES ARTS DÉCORATIFS GALLERY
Map p372 (MAD; ☎01 44 55 57 50; www.mad-paris.fr; 107 rue de Rivoli, 1er; adult/child €14/free; ⊙11am-6pm Tue, Wed & Fri-Sun, to 9pm Thu; MPalais Royal–Musée du Louvre) Privately administered collections of applied arts and design, advertising and graphic design, and fashion and textiles are displayed in the Rohan Wing of the vast Palais du Louvre at the Musée des Arts Décoratifs (aka MAD). Art nouveau and art deco pieces are among its highlights.

For an extra €6, you can scoop up a combo ticket that also includes the Musée Nissim de Camondo (p138) in the 8e.

JARDIN DU PALAIS ROYAL GARDENS
Map p372 (www.domaine-palais-royal.fr; 2 place Colette, 1er; ⊙8am-10.30pm Apr-Sep, to 8.30pm Oct-Mar; MPalais Royal–Musée du Louvre) The Jardin du Palais Royal is a perfect spot to sit, contemplate and picnic between boxed hedges, or to shop in the trio of beautiful arcades that frame the garden: the **Galerie de Valois** (east), **Galerie de Montpensier** (west) and **Galerie Beaujolais** (north). However, it's the southern end of the complex, polka-dotted with sculptor Daniel Buren's 260 black-and-white striped columns, that has become the garden's signature feature.

This elegant urban space is fronted by the neoclassical **Palais Royal** (closed to the public), constructed in 1633 by Cardinal Richelieu but mostly dating to the late 18th century. Louis XIV lived here in the 1640s; today it is home to the **Conseil d'État** (Council of State; Map p372; 1 place du Palais Royal, 1er; MPalais Royal–Musée du Louvre).

The Galerie de Valois is the most upmarket arcade, with designer boutiques like Stella McCartney and Pierre Hardy. Across the garden, in the Galerie de Montpensier, the Revolution broke out on a warm mid-July day, just three years after the galleries opened, in the Café du Foy. The third ar-

cade, tiny Galerie Beaujolais, is crossed by **Passage du Perron**, a passageway above which the writer Colette (1873–1954) lived out the last dozen years of her life.

BOURSE DE COMMERCE
PINAULT COLLECTION MUSEUM
Map p376 (www.boursedecommerce.fr; 2 rue de Viarmes, 1er; adult/child €14/free; ⊙11am-7pm Mon-Sun, to 9pm Fri; MLes Halles, RER Châtelet-Les Halles) This much-anticipated art museum opened in 2021. It occupies the Bourse de Commerce, an 18th-century rotunda that once held the city's grain market and stock exchange. Japanese architect Tadao Ando designed the ambitious interior, where three floors of galleries will display contemporary works collected by François Pinault, who previously teamed up with Ando to open Venice's Palazzo Grassi and Punta della Dogana. Exhibitions span varying scales and media, from painting, sculpture, photography and video to installations.

ÉGLISE ST-GERMAIN
L'AUXERROIS CHURCH
Map p376 (www.saintgermainauxerrois.cef.fr; 2 place du Louvre, 1er; ⊙9am-7pm; MLouvre Rivoli, Pont Neuf) Built between the 13th and 16th centuries in a mixture of Gothic and Renaissance styles and with similar dimensions and ground plans to those of Notre Dame, this once royal parish church stands on a site at the eastern end of the Louvre that has been used for Christian worship since about 500 CE. The church has been hosting Notre Dame's worship services since the cathedral's devastating fire of 2019.

MUSÉE EN HERBE GALLERY
Map p376 (☎01 40 67 97 66; www.museeenherbe.com; 23 rue de l'Arbre Sec, 1er; €7; ⊙10am-7pm; ⊞; MLouvre Rivoli, Pont Neuf) One of the city's great backstreet secrets, this children's museum is a surprise gem for art lovers of every age. Its permanent exhibition changes throughout the year and focuses on the work of one artist or theme through a series of interactive displays.

PLACE VENDÔME SQUARE
Map p372 (1er; MTuileries, Opéra) Octagonal place Vendôme and the arcaded and colonnaded buildings around it were constructed between 1687 and 1721. In March 1796 Napoléon married Josephine, Viscountess Beauharnais, in the building at No 3. Today the buildings surrounding the square

house the posh Hôtel Ritz Paris and some of the city's most fashionable boutiques.

The 43.5m-tall **Colonne Vendôme** (Vendôme Column; Map p372) in the centre of the square consists of a stone core wrapped in a 160m-long bronze spiral made from hundreds of Austrian and Russian cannons captured by Napoléon at the Battle of Austerlitz in 1805.

TOUR JEAN SANS PEUR
TOWER

Map p376 (Tower of John the Fearless; ☑01 40 26 20 28; www.tourjeansanspeur.com; 20 rue Étienne Marcel, 2e; adult/child €6/4; ⊙1.30-6pm Wed-Sun; ⓂÉtienne Marcel) This 29m-high Gothic tower was built during the Hundred Years' War by the Duke of Bourgogne so that he could take refuge from his enemies – such as the supporters of the Duke of Orléans, whom he had assassinated. Part of a splendid mansion in the early 15th century, it is one of the few examples of feudal military architecture extant in Paris. Climb 140 steps up the spiral staircase to the top turret (no views).

TOUR ST-JACQUES
TOWER

Map p376 (☑01 83 96 15 05; 39 rue de Rivoli, 4e; adult/child €12/10; ⊙by reservation 10am-5pm Sat & Sun Jun-early Nov; ⓂChâtelet) Just north of place du Châtelet, the Flamboyant Gothic, 54m-high St James Tower is all that remains of the Église St-Jacques la Boucherie, built by the powerful butchers guild in 1523 as a starting point for pilgrims setting out for the shrine of St James at Santiago de Compostela in Spain. Guided 40-minute tours (in French; book online at www.desmotsetdesarts.com) take visitors up 300 stairs to an expansive panorama. Children must be 10 years or older.

FORUM DES HALLES
NOTABLE BUILDING

Map p376 (www.forumdeshalles.com; 1 rue Pierre Lescot, 1er; ⊙shops 10am-8.30pm Mon-Sat, 11am-7pm Sun; ⓂLes Halles, RER Châtelet–Les Halles) Paris' main wholesale food market stood here for nearly 800 years before being replaced by this underground shopping mall in 1971. Long considered an eyesore by many Parisians, the mall's exterior was finally demolished in 2011 to make way for its golden-hued translucent canopy, unveiled in 2016. Below, four floors of stores (125 in total), 23 restaurants, cafes and fast-food outlets, and entertainment venues including cinemas and a swimming pool, extend down to the city's busiest metro/RER hub. Spilling out from the canopied centre is

LIVING WALL

On the corner of rue des Petits Carreaux (the northern extension of foodie street rue Montorgueil), this extraordinary *mur végétal* ('vertical garden') was installed on a 25m-high blank building façade by the modern innovator of the genre, French botanist Patrick Blanc, in 2013. **L'Oasis d'Aboukir** (Map p376; 83 rue d'Aboukir, 2e; ⓂSentier) has since flourished to cover a total surface area of 250 sq metres in greenery. Subtitled *Hymne à la Biodiversité* (Ode to Biodiversity), the 'living wall' incorporates some 7600 plants from 237 different species.

the **Jardin Nelson Mandela** (Map p376; 1er; ⊙24hr; ⓂLes Halles, RER Châtelet–Les Halles).

59 RIVOLI
GALLERY

Map p376 (www.59rivoli.org; 59 rue de Rivoli, 1er; ⊙1-8pm Tue-Sun; ⓂChâtelet, Pont Neuf) **FREE** In such a classical part of Paris, 59 Rivoli is a bohemian breath of fresh air. Watch artists at work in the 30 ateliers (studios) spread over six floors of this long-abandoned bank building, now a legalised squat where some of Paris' most creative talent works (but doesn't live). The ground-floor gallery hosts a new exhibition every fortnight and free gigs, concerts and shows pack the place out at weekends.

EATING

The dining scene in central Paris is excellent, and there is no shortage of choices, from eat-on-the-go bakeries to casual foodie favourites to Michelin-starred cuisine. By all means reserve a table at a big-name restaurant, but also try wandering food streets like rue Montorgueil or rue Ste-Anne, aka 'Little Tokyo'.

★CÉDRIC GROLET OPÉRA
PASTRIES €

Map p372 (www.cedric-grolet.com; 35 av de l'Opéra, 2e; pastries €4-17; ⊙10am-5pm Tue-Sat; ⓂOpéra, Pyramides) Palace hotel Le Meurice's executive pastry chef, wunderkind Cédric Grolet, opened his *boulangerie-pâtisserie* in 2019, showcasing his *viennoiseries*

RUE MONTORGUEIL

A splinter of the historic Les Halles, rue Montorgueil was once the oyster market and the final stop for seafood merchants hailing from the coast. Immortalised by Balzac in *La Comédie humaine,* this vibrant strip still draws Parisians to eat and shop – it's lined with *fromageries* and other shops with stalls on the street, cafes, and some revered patisseries and restaurants.

Stohrer (Map p376; www.stohrer.fr; 51 rue Montorgueil, 2e; pastries €2.50-6; ⊘7.30am-8.30pm; Ⓜ Étienne Marcel, Sentier) Opened in 1730 by Nicolas Stohrer, the Polish pastry chef of queen consort Marie Leszczyńska (wife of Louis XV), this place offers house-made specialities, including its own inventions *baba au rhum* (rum-soaked sponge cake) and *puits d'amour* (caramel-topped, vanilla-cream-filled puff pasty). The beautiful pastel murals were added in 1864 by Paul-Jacques-Aimé Baudry, who also decorated the Palais Garnier's Grand Foyer.

Fou de Pâtisserie (Map p376; www.foudepatisserieboutique.fr; 45 rue Montorgueil, 2e; pastries €4.50-11.50; ⊘10am-8pm; Ⓜ Les Halles, Sentier, RER Châtelet–Les Halles) Single-name patisseries scatter across the city, but for a greatest-hits range from its finest pastry chefs – Cyril Lignac, Christophe Adam (L'Éclair de Génie), Jacques Genin, Pierre Hermé and Philippe Conticini included – head to this one-stop concept shop.

L'Escargot (Map p376; ☑01 42 36 83 51; www.escargotmontorgueil.com; 38 rue Montorgueil, 1er; snails per half-dozen €12-18, mains €23-37; ⊘noon-11pm; Ⓜ Étienne Marcel) A rue Montorgueil landmark, the giant golden snail atop this restaurant's jet-black façade leaves you in no doubt of its signature cuisine. Dating from 1832, it replenished market workers at the former *halles,* and keeps the tradition alive with snails prepared in a variety of ways, from classic garlic and parsley butter to truffles, foie gras or pungent blue cheese.

Au Rocher de Cancale (Map p376; ☑01 42 33 50 29; 78 rue Montorgueil, 2e; dozen oysters €18-40, seafood platter €32-80; ⊘8am-2am; Ⓜ Sentier, Les Halles, RER Châtelet–Les Halles) This 19th-century timber-lined restaurant (first opened in 1804 at No 59) is the last remaining legacy of the old oyster market. You can feast on oysters and seafood from Cancale (in Brittany) as well as other *plats du jour.*

including *pains au chocolat,* magnificent filled still-warm baguettes, and signature pastries, such as caramel-and-Tahitian-vanilla St-Honoré. Upstairs is a herringbone-floored tearoom.

SALATIM
ISRAELI €

Map p376 (☑01 42 36 30 03; www.facebook.com/SalatimParis; 15 rue des Jeûneurs, 2e; mains €9-16; ⊘11am-3.30pm Mon-Fri; Ⓜ Sentier) Chipped plates and organised chaos reign at Yariv Berreby's overflowing sardine-tin-sized eatery. It takes its name from the Hebrew word for salad, and you'd be remiss not to try the eponymous mixed plate (eggplant caviar, pickled red cabbage, hummus etc), or its chocolate *babka* (braided Jewish bread). If you can't get a seat, the takeaway window beckons.

PETIT BAO
CHINESE €

Map p376 (www.petitbao.com; 116 rue St-Denis, 2e; dishes €6-13; ⊘noon-3pm & 7-11pm Mon-Fri, noon-11pm Sat & Sun; Ⓜ Étienne Marcel) Steaming Shanghai-style bao buns, by the pair or half-dozen, are the star of this little white-tiled restaurant's show (watch staff hand-kneading them in the open kitchen). Flavours span pork, prawn and ginger to pumpkin, shiitake and green onion. Other choices include Chinese aubergine sautéed in soy and garlic, and stir-fried noodles with choy sum, broccoli and oyster sauce. No reservations.

CRÊPE DENTELLE
CRÊPES €

Map p376 (☑01 40 41 04 23; 10 rue Léopold Bellan, 2e; crêpes €8.20-15, 2-course lunch menu €12; ⊘noon-3pm & 7.30-11pm Mon-Fri; Ⓜ Sentier) Named after a style of crêpe that's as delicate as fine lace *(dentelle),* this is probably not the place to go if you're starving. However, it is an excellent choice for a light and inexpensive lunch. Arrive by 12.15pm or you may not get a seat.

MAAFIM
ISRAELI €

Map p376 (☑01 42 36 40 83; www.facebook.com/maafimparis; 5 rue des Forges, 2e; 2-/3-course lunch menu €18/21, mains €13; ☺8.30am-4pm Mon, 8.30am-10pm Tue-Thu, 8.30am-3pm Fri, 9am-4pm Sun; Ⓜ Sentier) Parisians' love affair with Israeli cuisine shows no signs of abating, and Maafim is a perfect place to see why. Delicious dishes span *shakshouka* (tomato- and chilli-poached eggs served in the pan) to *denesse* (yoghurt- and mint-baked sea bream) and a fantastic chocolate *babka*.

CLOUD CAKES
VEGAN €

Map p376 (www.cloudcakes.fr; 8 rue Mandar, 2e; dishes €5.50-13, Sunday brunch €26; ☺9am-7pm Mon-Sat; 🛜 🍴; Ⓜ Sentier) Behind its sky-blue façade, this little tiled cafe serves plant-based cuisine at breakfast (avocado and coriander toast, pancakes with fresh fruit and flaked almonds) and lunch (soups, salad bowls and grilled vegan cheese sandwiches), along with cupcakes, slices and cookies.

DAME TARTINE
CAFE €

Map p376 (☑01 77 18 88 59; www.dame-tartine.com; 2 rue Brisemiche, 4e; tartines €9.90-14; ☺9am-11.30pm; 🛜; Ⓜ Hôtel de Ville) One of the few reasonable dining options near the Centre Pompidou, Dame Tartine makes the most of its lively location across from the whimsical Stravinsky Fountain. Its speciality – the tartine (open-face sandwich) – hits the spot after visiting the museum.

BONESHAKER DOUGHNUTS
PASTRIES €

Map p376 (www.boneshakerparis.com; 77 rue d'Aboukir, 2e; doughnuts €3-4.50; ☺8.30am-6pm Tue-Fri, from 10am Sat; Ⓜ Sentier) Boneshaker creates dazzling small-batch, homemade doughnuts in fun flavour combinations such as cardamom and vanilla cream; chocolate and stout with torched marshmallows; summer berry crumble; and peach and basil. Come early before the day's bake sells out.

PANTAGRUEL
FRENCH €€

Map p376 (☑01 73 74 77 28; www.restaurant-pantagruel.com; 24 rue du Sentier, 2e; 2-/3-course lunch menu €29/34, mains €32-39; ☺12.15-2.30pm & 7.30-10.30pm Tue-Sat; Ⓜ Grands Boulevards) While the dining room is austere, dazzling ceramics showcase Pantagruel's gastronomic creations. Mains arrive at the table in three parts, for example lobster ceviche with lime caviar, followed by lobster medallions with cress oil and brown-

butter foam, and roast lobster with crispy zander and seaweed tempura shards, as do desserts (sated caramel pudding, sake ice cream and rum baba).

★MAISON MAISON
MEDITERRANEAN €€

Map p376 (☑09 67 82 07 32; www.maisonmaison.fr; 63 Parc Rives de Seine, 1er; small plates €9-19; ☺kitchen noon-11.30pm Tue-Sat, to 6pm Sun, bar to 2am; Ⓜ Pont Neuf) Halfway down the stairs by Pont Neuf is this wonderfully secret space beneath the *bouquinistes* (used-book sellers), where you can watch the *bateaux-mouches* (river-cruise boats) float by as you dine on creations such as butternut squash and blue cheese *millefeuille* or smoked black mullet with radish dressing. In nice weather, don't miss a cocktail on the glorious riverside terrace.

★BALAGAN
ISRAELI €€

Map p372 (☑01 40 20 72 14; www.balagan-paris.com; 9 rue d'Alger, 1er; mains €24-33; ☺noon-2pm & 7-10pm; Ⓜ Tuileries) Navy blues and creamy diamond tiling characterise this Israeli hotspot. Delectable starters – deconstructed kebabs, crispy halloumi cheese with dates, onion confit Ashkenazi chicken liver, spicy tuna tartare with pistachios – are followed by mains such as lamb with smoked-almond yoghurt or octopus with bone-marrow crumble. Pair them with knockout cocktails like a Bloody Balagan (mezcal, sherry vinegar, beetroot syrup and lime).

CHEZ LA VIEILLE
FRENCH €€

Map p376 (☑01 42 60 15 78; www.chezlavieille.fr; 1 rue Bailleul, 1er; mains €26-39; ☺noon-2pm & 6-10.30pm Tue-Sat, closed Aug; Ⓜ Louvre Rivoli) In salvaging this history-steeped spot within a 16th-century building, star chef Daniel Rose pays homage to the former wholesale markets, erstwhile legendary owner Adrienne Biasin (many of her timeless dishes have been updated, from terrines and rillettes to veal blanquette), and the soul of Parisian bistro cooking itself. Dine at the street-level bar or upstairs in the peacock-blue dining room.

AU PIED DE COCHON
BRASSERIE €€

Map p376 (☑01 40 13 77 00; www.pieddecochon.com; 6 rue Coquillière, 1er; mains €19-36.50, seafood platters per person €30-80; ☺24hr; 🛜; Ⓜ Les Halles, RER Châtelet–Les Halles) Enduring brasserie Au Pied de Cochon, with huge mirrors, crimson banquettes and

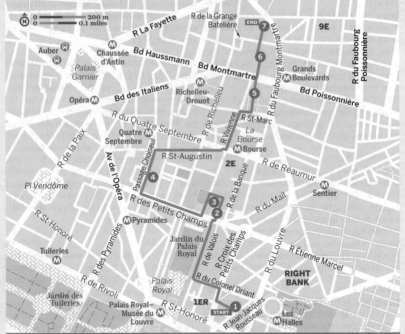

Neighbourhood Walk
Right Bank Covered Passages

START GALERIE VÉRO DODAT
END PASSAGE VERDEAU
LENGTH 2.2KM; TWO HOURS

The Right Bank's sumptuously decorated *passages couverts* (covered arcades) offer a stroll through early-19th-century Paris. Avoid Sundays, when some arcades are shut.

At 19 rue Jean-Jacques Rousseau, the 1826-built **1 Galerie Véro Dodat** retains its 19th-century skylights, ceiling murals, Corinthian columns, tiled floor, gas globe fittings (now electric) and bijou shopfronts. Continue to the Jardin du Palais Royal, and follow the arcades to Passage des Deux Pavillons and up the stairs to rue des Petits Champs. Turn right and duck into **2 Galerie Vivienne** (1826), decorated with floor mosaics and bas-reliefs on the walls. Don't miss wine shop Legrand Filles & Fils, Wolff et Descourtis, selling silk scarves, and florist Emilio Robba.

Exit on rue Vivienne and peek in at **3 Galerie Colbert** (1823), featuring a huge glass dome and rotunda. West along rue des Petits Champs is **4 Passage Choiseul** (1824), a 45m-long covered arcade, now filled with cheap eateries. Paul Verlaine (1844–96) drank absinthe here and Céline (1894–1961) grew up in his mother's lace shop at No 62.

Continue to **5 Passage des Panoramas**, Paris' oldest covered arcade (1800) and the first to be lit by gas (1817). It was expanded in 1834 with four interconnecting passages – Feydeau, Montmartre, St-Marc and Variétés – and is full of excellent restaurants and unusual shops.

Enter at 10-12 bd Montmartre into **6 Passage Jouffroy**, Paris' last major passage (1847). There's a wax museum, the Musée Grévin, and wonderful boutiques, including bookshops, silversmiths and MG Segas, where Toulouse-Lautrec bought his walking sticks.

Cross the road to the 1847-opened **7 Passage Verdeau**. There's lots to explore: vintage comic books, antiques, old postcards and more. The northern exit is at 31bis rue du Faubourg Montmartre.

frosted-glass lamps, opens around the clock, just as it did when workers at the former Les Halles wholesale markets started and ended their day here. Specialities include sensational crouton-filled onion soup topped with melted Emmental cheese, pigs' trotters, tails, ears and snouts, and spectacular shellfish platters.

LA MAISON PLISSON ST-HONORÉ
CAFE, DELI €€

Map p372 (www.lamaisonplisson.com; 35 place du Marché St-Honoré, 1er; 2-course lunch €24, mains €13-27; ⏱cafe & deli 9.30am-9pm Mon, 8.30am-11.30pm Tue-Sat, 9am-8pm Sun; 🔊📶; Ⓜ Pyramides) On elegant place du Marché St-Honoré, this gourmet emporium's bushels of fresh fruit and vegetables, house-baked breads and pastries, meats, cheeses and exquisite condiments are utilised by its on-site cafe in dishes like spiced honey–marinated duckling with roasted quince.

BAMBOU
SOUTHEAST ASIAN €€

Map p376 (📞01 40 28 98 30; www.bambouparis.fr; 23 rue des Jeûneurs, 2e; mains €12-24; ⏱kitchen noon-2.30pm & 7-11.30pm Mon-Sat, bar to 2am Mon-Sat; 🔊📶; Ⓜ Sentier) This spectacular restaurant occupies a 500-sq-metre former fabric warehouse, with vintage birdcages and a giant metal dragon adorning the main dining room, a downstairs billiards room–bar, a vast terrace and a Zen-like garden. Specialities include squid with black pepper and basil, and aromatic pad thai, along with cocktails like Chang Mai Mule (lemongrass-infused vodka, ginger beer and lime leaves).

TRADI
BISTRO €€

Map p376 (📞01 44 82 07 83; www.tradi.paris; 4 rue du Mail, 2e; mains €20-31; ⏱noon-3pm & 7-11pm Tue-Sat; Ⓜ Sentier) 🍴 This reborn traditional bistro only uses sustainable French produce, which can be traced from farm to plate. Everything is made on-site, including the pâtés, smoked salmon and freshly baked bread. The blackboard menu changes daily but might feature line-caught dorade with tarragon leaves and white beans or honey-roasted quail.

LE COCHON À L'OREILLE
FRENCH €€

Map p376 (📞01 40 15 98 24; 15 rue Montmartre, 1er; mains €16-22; ⏱noon-2pm Mon, noon-2pm & 7-10.30pm Tue-Sat; Ⓜ Les Halles, RER Châtelet–Les Halles) A Parisian jewel and listed monument, the hole-in-the-wall Le Cochon à l'Oreille retains 1890-laid tiles depicting vibrant market scenes of the old *halles*, while an iron staircase leads to a second dining room upstairs. Bistro-style dishes are traditional French (the steak tartare is excellent), and are accompanied by well-chosen wines. Cash only.

RYO
JAPANESE €€

Map p372 (📞01 40 20 91 86; www.ryoparis.wordpress.com; 7 rue des Moulins, 1er; mains €22-32, sushi €5.50-11; ⏱noon-2.30pm & 7-10.30pm Tue-Sat; Ⓜ Pyramides) Footsteps from rue Ste-Anne in Paris' 'Little Tokyo' neighbourhood, this unassuming two-level restaurant decked out in white (symbolising Japan) and wood (nature) is run by former Nobu chef Toyofumi Ozuru. As well as hand-rolled sushi, authentic Japanese flavours include miso-glazed aubergine, yuzu-marinated black cod and seared beef with ginger, daikon (white radish) and amazu (vinegar-based sweet-and-sour sauce).

LA TOUR DE MONTLHÉRY – CHEZ DENISE
FRENCH €€

Map p376 (📞01 42 36 21 82; 5 rue des Prouvaires, 1er; mains €23-28; ⏱noon-2.30pm & 7.30pm-5am Mon-Fri mid-Aug–mid-Jun; Ⓜ Les Halles, RER Châtelet–Les Halles) The most traditional eatery near the former Les Halles marketplace, this boisterous old half-timbered bistro with red-chequered tablecloths stays open until dawn and has been run by the same family since 1966. If you're ready to feast on all the French classics – snails in garlic sauce, veal liver, steak tartare, braised beef cheeks and house-made pâté – reservations are in order.

L'ÉCUME
SEAFOOD €€

Map p372 (📞01 42 61 93 87; www.ecume-saint-honore.fr; 6 rue de Marché St-Honoré, 1er; oysters per half-dozen €17-37, shellfish platters €25; ⏱restaurant 11am-7pm Tue-Thu, to 10pm Fri & Sat, shop 9.30am-8pm Tue-Thu, to 10pm Fri & Sat, closed Aug; Ⓜ Tuileries) From the outside this green-awning-shaded place looks simply like a fishmongers, with wicker baskets of oysters out front, and glass counters with shellfish on beds of shaved ice inside. At the back, however, is a hidden dining space with colourful coastal-scene murals and a seagull soundtrack, where you can order oysters by the half-dozen, piled-high platters and crisp white wine.

⭐FRENCHIE
BISTRO €€€

Map p376 (📞01 40 39 96 19; www.frenchie-ruedunil.com; 5 rue du Nil, 2e; 3-/5-course menu €57/95; ⏱6-10pm Mon-Wed, noon-2pm & 6-10pm

LOCAL KNOWLEDGE

RUE D'ARGOUT & RUE MONTMARTRE

A slip of a street from the 13th century, rue d'Argout is one of those short, stumble-upon strips where there's always something happening.

Favourite hang-outs here include pocket-handkerchief-size **Blend** (Map p376; ☑01 40 26 84 57; www.blendhamburger.com; 44 rue d'Argout, 2e; burgers €10-14, fries €4-5; ☉noon-11pm; ☎; ⓜSentier), one of the original progenitors of Paris' enduring gourmet burger trend. Nearby is **Chez Bouboule** (Map p376; www.chezbouboule.fr; 46 rue d'Argout, 2e; ☉noon-2am Mon, 5.30pm-2am Tue-Sat; ⓜSentier), where you can play an all-weather indoor game of *pétanque* on its sandy indoor *boulodrome* while sipping cocktails like the Bouboule Special (Lillet Rosé, grapefruit, fresh mint and lime). A few steps away is buzzing coffee specialist **Matamata** (Map p376; ☑01 71 39 44 58; www.matamatacoffee. com; 58 rue d'Argout, 2e; ☉8am-5pm Mon-Fri, from 9am Sat & Sun; ☎; ⓜSentier).

Just beyond is rue Montmartre, clad with numerous places to sip coffee and cocktails. Two of the longest running are the Crazy Heart, aka **Le Cœur Fou** (Map p376; ☑01 42 33 04 98; www.facebook.com/lecoeurfou; 55 rue Montmartre, 2e; ☉5pm-2am; ⓜÉtienne Marcel), a tiny gallery-bar, and **Le Tambour** (Map p376; ☑01 42 33 06 90; 41 rue Montmartre, 2e; ☉8.30am-5.30am; ⓜÉtienne Marcel, Sentier), a vintage mecca for Parisian night owls with its long hours (food until 3am).

Thu & Fri; ⓜSentier) Tucked down an inconspicuous alley, this tiny bistro with wooden tables and old stone walls is always packed and for good reason: Gregory Marchand's modern, market-driven, unpretentious dishes, which have earned him a Michelin star. Only five-course menus are available at dinner. Reserve well in advance. Alternatively, head to neighbouring **Frenchie Bar à Vins** (Map p376; www.frenchie-bav.com; 6 rue du Nil, 2e; small plates €11-34; ☉6.30-11pm; ⓜSentier).

There are no reservations at Frenchie Bar à Vins – for the best chance of nabbing a seat, arrive by 6pm, when a queue starts forming, or after 10pm.

During the day, swing by its adjacent deli-style takeaway outlet **Frenchie to Go** (Map p376; ☑01 42 21 96 92; www.frenchie-ftg. com; 9 rue du Nil, 2e; dishes €8.50-22; ☉10am-6pm; ☎; ⓜSentier).

Its northern Paris outpost **Frenchie Pigalle** (small plates €7-19, mains €21-27; ☉noon-2.30pm & 6-9pm; ☎) in the Grand Hôtel Pigalle (p285), also takes walk-in diners only.

★**VERJUS**   INTERNATIONAL €€€

Map p372 (☑01 42 97 54 40; www.verjusparis. com; 52 rue de Richelieu, 1er; menu €78, with wine €133; ☉7-11pm Mon-Fri; ⓜBourse, Pyramides) Opened by American duo Braden Perkins and Laura Adrian, Verjus was born out of their former clandestine supper club, the Hidden Kitchen. The restaurant builds on that tradition, offering a chance to sample some excellent, creative cuisine in a casual space. The tasting menu is a series of small plates, using ingredients sourced straight from producers. Reserve well in advance.

If you're just after an apéritif or a prelude to dinner, the downstairs **Verjus Bar à Vins** (Map p372; 47 rue de Montpensier, 1er; ☉6-11pm Mon-Fri; ⓜBourse, Pyramides) serves a handful of charcuterie and cheese plates. For lunch or a more casual dinner, don't miss nearby **Ellsworth** (Map p372; ☑01 42 60 59 66; www.ellsworthparis.com; 34 rue de Richelieu, 1er; 2-/3-course lunch menu €24/30, mains €24-28; ☉12.15-2.15pm & 7-10.30pm Tue-Sat, 11.30am-3pm Sun; ⓜPyramides), Verjus' sister restaurant.

LE GRAND VÉFOUR   GASTRONOMY €€€

Map p372 (☑01 42 96 56 27; www.grand-vefour. com; 17 rue de Beaujolais, 1er; lunch/dinner menu €115/315, mains €102-126; ☉noon-2.30pm & 7.30-10.30pm Mon-Fri; ⓜPyramides) Holding two Michelin stars, this 18th-century jewel on the northern edge of the Jardin du Palais Royal has been a dining favourite since 1784; the names ascribed to each table span Napoléon and Victor Hugo to Colette (who lived next door). Expect a voyage of discovery from chef Guy Martin in one of the most beautiful restaurants in the world.

KEI   GASTRONOMY €€€

Map p376 (☑01 42 33 14 74; www.restaurant-kei. fr; 5 rue Coq Héron, 1er; 5-/8-course lunch menu €58/125, 6-/8-course dinner menu €150/230; ☉12.30-2pm & 7.30-9pm Tue, Wed, Fri & Sat, 7.30-9pm Thu; ⓜLes Halles, RER Châtelet–Les Halles) Lit by a Venetian chandelier, this white-

and grey-toned restaurant became France's first restaurant helmed by a Japanese chef, Kei Kobayashi, to gain three Michelin stars in 2020. Exquisite dishes might include poached oysters with seawater jelly and sea lettuce, and miso-lacquered pigeon, matched with rare French vintages.

YAM'TCHA
FUSION €€€

Map p376 (✆01 40 26 08 07; www.yamtcha.com; 121 rue St-Honoré, 1er; lunch/7-course dinner €70/150; ⊙noon-1.30pm Wed-Fri, 8-9.30pm Wed-Sat; ⓂLouvre Rivoli) Adeline Grattard's ingeniously fused French and Cantonese flavours (scallops with coconut milk and lemongrass smoke) have gained her critical praise along with a Michelin star. Reserve one month ahead (minimum) and pair dishes with wine or tea. Alternatively, indulge in *bāozi* (steamed buns) and oolong at **Boutique Yam'Tcha** (Map p376; ✆01 40 26 06 06; 4 rue Sauval, 1er; steamed buns €4-6, dishes €12-14; ⊙noon-6pm Wed-Fri, to 8pm Sat; ⓂLouvre Rivoli), or head to casual cafe-bistro **Café Lai'Tcha** (Map p376; ✆01 40 26 05 05; www.facebook.com/cafelaitcha; 7 rue du Jour, 1er; wonton bar dishes €6-14, tasting menus €50-60, Sunday brunch €42; ⊙wonton bar noon-7pm Tue-Sat, cafe 7-10pm Tue, noon-2.30pm & 7-10pm Wed-Sat, 11am-4pm Sun; ⓂLes Halles, RER Châtelet–Les Halles) with an all-day wonton bar.

🍷 DRINKING & NIGHTLIFE

The area north of Les Halles is a prime destination for night owls. Cocktails predominate, but you'll also find wine and Champagne bars, studenty hang-outs, open-till-dawn local dives and a smattering of nightclubs. Rue St-Sauveur, rue Tiquetonne and rue Montmartre make good starting points.

★BAR HEMINGWAY
COCKTAIL BAR

Map p372 (www.ritzparis.com; Hôtel Ritz Paris, 15 place Vendôme, 1er; ⊙6pm-2am; ⓢ; ⓂOpéra) Black-and-white photos and memorabilia (hunting trophies, old typewriters and framed handwritten letters by the great writer) fill this snug bar inside the Ritz. Head bartender Colin Peter Field mixes monumental cocktails, including three different Bloody Marys made with juice from freshly squeezed seasonal tomatoes. Legend has it that Hemingway himself,

wielding a machine gun, helped liberate the bar during WWII.

★SCILICET
BAR

Map p376 (www.scilicet.fr; 134 voie Georges Pompidou, 1er; ⊙noon-2am daily Jun-Aug, 6pm-2am Wed-Fri, 4pm-2am Sat Sep-May; ⓢ; ⓂChâtelet, RER Châtelet–Les Halles) An elongated stone archway houses this hidden riverside bar, with digital light displays projected on the ceiling, and DJs spinning from 8pm nightly in summer and regularly through the rest of the year. Its greatest asset, though, is its sprawling Seine-side terrace, with front-row views of quintessential Parisian landmarks like the turreted Conciergerie and Eiffel Tower, spectacularly illuminated at night.

★BABY DOLL
COCKTAIL BAR

Map p372 (www.babydollparis.com; 16 rue de Daunou, 2e; ⊙6pm-2am Tue-Thu & Sun, to 5am Fri & Sat; ⓢ; ⓂOpéra) Paying homage to immortal Parisian musician Serge Gainsbourg (1928–91), this seductive bar has foliage-print carpets replicated from his 7e mansion, ruby and emerald velvet banquettes, pleated leather armchairs and a smooth soundtrack. Gainsbourg-inspired cocktails include Couleur Café (chocolate-infused tequila, mezcal and coriander) and Bloody & G (a reinvented Bloody Mary with caper- and horseradish-infused gin).

EXPERIMENTAL COCKTAIL CLUB
COCKTAIL BAR

Map p376 (ECC; www.experimentalgroup.com; 37 rue St-Sauveur, 2e; ⊙7pm-2am Mon-Thu, 7pm-4am Fri & Sat, 8pm-2am Sun; ⓂRéaumur Sébastopol) Behind black curtains, this retro-chic speakeasy is a sophisticated flashback to those *années folles* (crazy years) of Prohibition New York. Cocktails are individual and fabulous, and DJs keep the party going until dawn at weekends. It's not a large space, however, and fills to capacity quickly.

HARRY'S NEW YORK BAR
COCKTAIL BAR

Map p372 (✆01 42 61 71 14; www.facebook.com/HarrysNewYorkBarParis; 5 rue Daunou, 2e; ⊙noon-2am Mon-Sat, 4pm-1am Sun; ⓂOpéra) One of the most popular American-style bars in the pre-war years, Harry's once welcomed writers including F Scott Fitzgerald and Ernest Hemingway, who no doubt sampled the bar's unique cocktail and creation: the Bloody Mary. The Cuban mahogany interior dates from the mid-19th century and was brought over from a Manhattan bar in 1911.

GAY & LESBIAN CHÂTELET

To the west of Paris' traditional LGBTIQ+ epicentre Le Marais are a cluster of venues around Châtelet.

For men, hotspots include pink-lit **LABO** (Map p376; www.thelabo.fr; 37 rue des Lombards, 1er; ⊙3pm-3am Tue & Wed, to 4am Thu, to 6am Fri-Sun; 🛱; Ⓜ Châtelet, RER Châtelet–Les Halles), with nightly events including karaoke and drag parties, and bear bar **El Hombre** (Map p376; www.elhombreparis.com; 15 rue de la Reynie, 4e; ⊙4pm-3am Sun-Thu, to 5am Fri & Sat; 🛱; Ⓜ Châtelet, RER Châtelet–Les Halles), with disco balls, teddy bears and a dance floor.

Women may want to check out classy **Ici** (Map p376; www.facebook.com/delonmarie. fr; 6 rue de la Tacherie, 4e; ⊙5pm-midnight Tue-Thu, to 2am Fri & Sat; Ⓜ Hôtel de Ville, Châtelet, RER Châtelet–Les Halles), with several vaulted lounge and dance areas, and sociable lesbian dive bar **La Mutinerie** (Map p376; www.lamutinerie.eu; 176 rue St-Martin, 3e; ⊙5pm-2am; 🛱; Ⓜ Rambuteau), with a pool table. Further west is **La Champmeslé** (Map p372; 🖉01 42 96 85 20; www.lachampmesle.fr; 4 rue Chabanais, 2e; ⊙4pm-4am Mon-Sat; Ⓜ Pyramides), Paris' first lesbian bar, dating from 1979.

L'IVRESS
WINE BAR

Map p376 (🖉06 61 40 27 97; www.livress.fr; 5 rue Poissonnière, 2e; ⊙6pm-1am Mon-Sat; Ⓜ Sentier) Make sure to reserve an armchair or oak barrel (for those who prefer to stand) at this cosy bar and wine shop, otherwise your chances of getting a table may be slim. A choice selection of wines from independent vineyards and quality nibbles keep the after-work crowd lingering long past happy hour. Book by text message.

NINA'S
TEAHOUSE

Map p372 (🖉01 55 04 80 55; www.ninasparis.com; 29 rue Danielle Casanova, 1er; ⊙11am-7pm Mon-Fri; Ⓜ Opéra) With a history dating back to 1672, this tea specialist off place Vendôme still owns the rights to harvest essential oils, flowers and fruit from Le Potager du Roi (the King's Kitchen Garden) at the Château de Versailles. Its exquisite pink-and-white upstairs tearoom serves Marie Antoinette's favourite apple-and-rose tea blend and apple cake with rose icing.

LE SHERWOOD
BAR

Map p372 (www.lesherwood.fr; 3 rue Daunou, 2e; ⊙7pm-5am Tue-Sun; Ⓜ Opéra) Crimson lamps glow in 1930s-styled Le Sherwood's piano bar, where live jazz plays nightly, and in its atmospheric vaulted cellar. House cocktails like Luxury Parisian (rosé Champagne, St-Germain liqueur and strawberry and raspberry puree) complement the extensive wine list. Classic French food is served until 3am.

HOPPY CORNER
CRAFT BEER

Map p376 (🖉09 83 06 90 39; www.facebook. com/hoppycorner; 34 rue des Petits Carreaux, 2e; ⊙5pm-midnight Mon & Tue, to 2am Wed-Fri, 2pm-2am Sat; Ⓜ Sentier) Mainly French beers rotate on the 15 taps of this convivial craft-beer specialist, such as Indigo IPA from Deck & Donohue, made in Montreuil just east of central Paris. A handful of European (and occasionally American) brews also make the blackboard listing the day's offerings; super-knowledgable staff can help you decide. Dried hops are served as bar snacks.

LE GARDE ROBE
WINE BAR

Map p376 (🖉01 49 26 90 60; www.legarderobe. fr; 41 rue de l'Arbre Sec, 1er; ⊙noon-3pm & 5pm-midnight Mon-Fri, 4pm-midnight Sat; Ⓜ Louvre Rivoli) At Le Garde Robe you can expect excellent, affordable natural wines, a casual atmosphere and a good selection of food, ranging from cheese and charcuterie plates to adventurous options (Chinese five spice and soy-marinated cockles).

CAFÉ LA FUSÉE
BAR

Map p376 (🖉01 42 76 93 99; 168 rue St-Martin, 3e; ⊙9am-2am Mon-Sat, from 10am Sun; Ⓜ Rambuteau, Étienne Marcel) A short walk from the Centre Pompidou, the Rocket is a lively, laid-back indie hang-out with an awning-shaded terrace strung with fairy lights outside. You can grab simple, inexpensive meals here, and it's got a decent wine selection by the glass.

MABEL
COCKTAIL BAR

Map p376 (🖉01 42 33 24 33; www.mabelparis. com; 58 rue d'Aboukir, 2e; ⊙7pm-midnight Mon-Wed, to 1am Thu, to 2am Fri & Sat; Ⓜ Sentier) Find your inner corsair in one of the countless varieties of rum here (the selection spans 35 countries) or perhaps the gooey goodness of an accompanying grilled cheese sandwich – a favourite of plunderers everywhere.

MA CAVE FLEURY
WINE BAR

Map p376 (☑01 40 28 03 39; www.macavefleury. wordpress.com; 177 rue St-Denis, 2e; ☺5-10pm Mon, 11am-1pm & 5-10pm Tue-Thu, 11am-10pm Fri & Sat; Ⓜ Réamur Sébastopol) Morgane Fleury opened this welcoming little place in 2009 to promote organic and biodynamic wines. The emphasis is on Champagne – her family has been producing biodynamic bubbly for decades – but you can also sample a decent selection of organic wines from around France. Watch for pop-ups, concerts and other events, including some on Sundays.

Ô CHATEAU
WINE BAR

Map p376 (☑01 44 73 97 80; www.o-chateau. com; 68 rue Jean-Jacques Rousseau, 1er; ☺4pm-midnight Mon-Sat; ☎; Ⓜ Les Halles, RER Châtelet–Les Halles) Wine aficionados can thank this young, fun, cosmopolitan wine bar for bringing affordable tasting to Paris. Choose from over 50 *grands vins* served by the glass (or 1000-plus by the bottle!). Or sign up in advance for a 'tour de France' of French wines (€59) or a guided cellar tasting in English over lunch (€75) or dinner (€99).

Other options include Champagne cruises along the Seine (€65) and a day trip to Champagne (€245).

ANGELINA
TEAHOUSE

Map p372 (☑01 42 60 82 00; www.angelina-paris. fr; 226 rue de Rivoli, 1er; ☺10.30am-6.30pm Tue-Fri, to 7.30pm Sat & Sun; Ⓜ Tuileries) Clink china with lunching ladies, their posturing poodles and half the students from Tokyo University at Angelina, a grande-dame tearoom with bevelled mirrors and beautiful frescoes dating from 1903. Decadent pastries are available, but it's the super-thick 'African' hot chocolate, served with a pot of whipped cream and a carafe of water, that prompts the constant queue for a table.

LE REX CLUB
CLUB

Map p376 (☑01 42 36 10 96; www.rexclub.com; 5 bd Poissonnière, 2e; ☺midnight-7am Thu-Sat; Ⓜ Bonne Nouvelle) Attached to the art deco Grand Rex cinema, with a capacity of 850 clubbers, this is Paris' premier house and techno venue where some of the world's hottest DJs strut their stuff on a 70-speaker, multidiffusion sound system.

⭐ ENTERTAINMENT

Les Halles has a handful of good entertainment options, starting with the two underground cinemas in the shopping centre, one of which is the city's film archive. Further north, near the Grands Boulevards, is the mythic Grand Rex, a must visit for cinephiles. Live jazz, classical, opera and dance performances are on almost nightly at the various venues scattered throughout the neighbourhood.

LA PLACE
ARTS CENTRE

Map p376 (☑01 70 22 45 48; www.laplace.paris; Forum des Halles, 10 passage de la Canopée, 1er; ☺bar 1-7pm Tue-Sat, concert hours vary; Ⓜ Les Halles, RER Châtelet–Les Halles) Under the Forum des Halles' custard-yellow glass canopy, Paris' inaugural hip-hop cultural centre has a 400-capacity concert hall, a 100-capacity broadcast studio, several recording studios and street-art graffiti workrooms, along with a relaxed bar. Some concerts are free, while ticket prices vary for others – check the program online.

RUE DES LOMBARDS JAZZ CLUBS

Rue des Lombards is the street to swing by for live jazz. **Le Baiser Salé** (Map p376; ☑01 42 33 37 71; www.lebaisersale.com; 58 rue des Lombards, 1er; ☺hours vary; Ⓜ Châtelet, RER Châtelet–Les Halles), meaning the Salty Kiss, is known for its Afro and Latin jazz, and jazz fusion concerts. You'll find two venues in one at well-respected **Sunset & Sunside** (Map p376; ☑01 40 26 46 60; www.sunset-sunside.com; 60 rue des Lombards, 1er; concerts €7-25; ☺hours vary; Ⓜ Châtelet, RER Châtelet–Les Halles): electric jazz, fusion and occasional salsa downstairs at Sunset; acoustics and concerts on the ground floor at Sunside. Founded in 1984, intimate, sophisticated jazz club **Duc des Lombards** (Map p376; ☑01 42 33 22 88; www.ducdeslombards.com; 42 rue des Lombards, 1er; ☺7-11.30pm Mon-Thu, to 3.30am Fri & Sat; Ⓜ Châtelet, RER Châtelet–Les Halles) typically hosts two concerts per night and regular free jam sessions (you'll need to buy a drink).

COMÉDIE FRANÇAISE
THEATRE

Map p372 (www.comedie-francaise.fr; 1 place Colette, 1er; MPalais Royal–Musée du Louvre) Founded in 1680 under Louis XIV, this state-run theatre bases its repertoire on the works of classic French playwrights. The theatre has its roots in an earlier company directed by Molière at the Palais Royal.

The French playwright and actor was seized by a convulsion on stage during the fourth performance of the *Imaginary Invalid* in 1673 and died later at his home on nearby rue de Richelieu.

FORUM DES IMAGES
CINEMA

Map p376 (☑01 44 76 63 00; www.forumdes-images.fr; Forum des Halles, 2 rue du Cinéma, Porte St-Eustache, 1er; cinema tickets adult/child €6.50/4.50; ⏰5-9pm Tue & Thu, from 1pm Wed, from 4pm Fri, from 10.30am Sat & Sun; MLes Halles, RER Châtelet–Les Halles) A five-screen cinema showing films set in Paris is the centrepiece of the city's film archive. Created in 1988 to establish an audiovisual archive of the city, the complex has a library and research centre with newsreels, documentaries and advertising. Its online program lists thematic series, festivals and events.

THÉÂTRE DU CHÂTELET
PERFORMING ARTS

Map p376 (☑01 40 28 28 28; www.chatelet.com; 2 rue Edouard Colonne, 1er; MChâtelet, RER Châtelet–Les Halles) Stunningly renovated, this 2046-capacity venue stages concerts, operas, musicals, theatre and dance.

BACKSTAGE AT THE FLICKS

Visiting 1932 art deco cinematic icon **Le Grand Rex** (Map p376; ☑01 45 08 93 58; www.legrandrex.com; 1 bd Poissonnière, 2e; adult/child tours €11/9, cinema tickets €15/12; ⏰tours 10am-6pm Wed, Sat & Sun, extended hours during school holidays; MBonne Nouvelle) is like no other trip to the flicks. Screenings aside, the cinema runs 50-minute behind-the-scenes tours (English soundtracks available) during which visitors – tracked by a sensor slung around their neck – are whisked right up (via a lift) behind the giant screen, tour a soundstage and get to have fun in a recording studio. Whizz-bang special effects along the way will stun adults and kids alike.

THÉÂTRE DE LA VILLE
DANCE

Map p376 (☑01 48 87 59 50; www.theatredelaville-paris.com; 2 place du Châtelet, 4e; MChâtelet, RER Châtelet–Les Halles) It hosts theatre and music too, but this venue is best known for its contemporary dance productions.

🔒 SHOPPING

The 1er and 2e *arrondissements* are mostly about fashion. Indeed Sentier is the city's traditional garment-making district. Rue Étienne Marcel, place des Victoires and rue du Jour flaunt prominent labels and shoe shops. Nearby rue Montmartre and rue Tiquetonne have streetwear and avant-garde designs; the easternmost part of the 1er around Palais Royal has luxury vintage and conservative label fashion.

LA SAMARITAINE
DEPARTMENT STORE

Map p376 (www.lasamaritaine.com; 19 rue de la Monnaie, 1er; MPont Neuf) One of Paris' four big department stores, the 10-storey La Samaritaine has finally emerged from its much-contested and drawn-out multi-million euro overhaul. Pritzker Prize-winning Japanese firm Sanaa has preserved much of the building's gorgeous art nouveau and art deco features, including the glass ceiling topping the central Hall Jourdain.

Luxury hotel Cheval Blanc opened its doors here in 2021.

L'EXCEPTION
DESIGN

Map p376 (☑01 40 39 92 34; www.lexception.com; 24 rue Berger, 1er; ⏰11am-7pm Mon-Sat, 1-7pm Sun; MLes Halles, RER Châtelet–Les Halles) Over 400 different French designers come together under one roof at this light-filled concept store, which showcases rotating collections of men's and women's fashion along with accessories including lingerie and swimwear, shoes, eyewear, gloves, hats, scarves, belts, bags, watches and jewellery. It also sells design books, cosmetics, candles, vases and other gorgeous homewares, and has a small in-house coffee bar.

LEGRAND FILLES & FILS
FOOD & DRINKS

Map p376 (☑01 42 60 07 12; www.caves-legrand.com; 1 rue de la Banque, 2e; ⏰11am-7pm Mon, 10am-7.30pm Tue-Sat; MBourse) Tucked inside Galerie Vivienne since 1880, Legrand sells fine wine and all the accoutrements: corkscrews, tasting glasses, decanters etc. It also has a fancy wine bar, *école du vin* (wine school; courses from €65 for two hours) and *éspace dégustation* with several tastings a month, some accompanied by live concerts (from €25 for 90 minutes); check its website for details.

DIDIER LUDOT
VINTAGE

Map p372 (☎01 42 96 06 56; www.didierludot.fr; 20 & 24 Galerie de Montpensier, 1er; ☺10.30am-7pm Mon-Sat; Ⓜ Palais Royal–Musée du Louvre) In the rag trade since 1975, collector Didier Ludot sells the city's finest couture creations of yesteryear, hosts exhibitions and has published a book portraying the evolution of the little black dress.

E DEHILLERIN
HOMEWARES

Map p376 (☎01 42 36 53 13; www.edehillerin.fr; 18-20 rue Coquillière, 1er; ☺9am-12.30pm & 2-6pm Mon, 9am-7pm Tue-Fri, 9am-6pm Sat; Ⓜ Les Halles, RER Châtelet–Les Halles) Founded in 1820, this extraordinary two-level store – more like an old-fashioned warehouse than a shiny, chic boutique – carries an incredible selection of professional-quality *matériel de cuisine* (kitchenware). Poultry scissors, turbot poacher, professional copper cookware or an Eiffel Tower–shaped cake tin – it's all here.

SÉZANE
FASHION & ACCESSORIES

Map p376 (www.sezane.com; 1 rue St-Fiacre, 2e; ☺8am-8.30pm Tue-Sat; Ⓜ Grands Boulevards) ✒ Affordable French fashion label Sézane, founded by Parisian entrepreneur-designer Morgane Sézalory, has cult status in Paris. Its chic women's tops, trousers, skirts, dresses, knitwear, outerwear, handbags, shoes and homewares such as bed linen are all sustainably sourced, with many proceeds donated to Demain, its own children's charity (there's also an adjoining charity shop selling past collections).

SEPT CINQ
FASHION & ACCESSORIES

Map p376 (☎09 83 00 44 01; www.sept-cinq.com; 26 rue Berger, 1er; ☺11am-7.30pm Mon-Sat, 1-7pm Sun; ☏; Ⓜ Les Halles, RER Châtelet–Les Halles) Scarves, designer T-shirts, Paris-themed

stationery and locally made jewellery make this boutique worth a peek. The in-house tearoom also serves light lunches and sweet nibbles.

KILIWATCH
FASHION & ACCESSORIES

Map p376 (☎01 42 21 17 37; www.kiliwatch.paris; 64 rue Tiquetonne, 2e; ☺10.30am-7pm Mon, to 7.30pm Tue-Sat; Ⓜ Étienne Marcel) A Parisian institution, Kiliwatch gets jam-packed with hip guys and gals rummaging through racks of new and used streetwear, along with vintage hats and boots plus art and photography books, eyewear and the latest sneakers.

YASMINE ESLAMI
FASHION & ACCESSORIES

Map p372 (www.yasmine-eslami.com; 35 rue de Richelieu, 1er; ☺noon-7pm Mon-Sat; Ⓜ Pyramides) Parisian designer Yasmine Eslami founded her lingerie label in 2011 and branched into swimwear in 2015. At her own boutique you'll find her contemporary, figure-flattering designs using European textiles, including French lace from Calais. Her ranges are also stocked in department stores such as Galeries Lafayette.

ALTERMUNDI
GIFTS & SOUVENIRS

Map p376 (www.altermundi.com; 140 voie Georges Pompidou, 1er; ☺11am-2pm & 3-7.30pm Wed-Sun; Ⓜ Châtelet, RER Châtelet–Les Halles) ✒ Wedged beneath quai de la Mégisserie in a stone archway, this little boutique is perfect for picking up Parisian gifts, such as children's colouring maps of Paris and France, framed and unframed prints and posters of the city, and Paris-emblazoned T-shirts and bags, along with jewellery, ceramics and more. Its all-French and European designs are Fair Trade and ethically sourced.

ANTOINE
FASHION & ACCESSORIES

Map p372 (☎01 42 96 01 80; www.antoine1745.com; 10 av de l'Opéra, 1er; ☺10.30am-1pm & 2-6.30pm Mon-Sat; Ⓜ Pyramides, Palais Royal–Musée du Louvre) Antoine has been the Parisian master of bespoke canes, umbrellas, fans and gloves since 1745.

Montmartre & Northern Paris

MONTMARTRE | CLICHY BATIGNOLLES | CANAL ST-MARTIN | 10E | 17E | 18E | 19E

Neighbourhood Top Five

1 Basilique du Sacré-Cœur (p134) Hiking up the steps for panoramic city view, with some of the city's finest street entertainers outside and a glittering mosaic within.

2 Parc de la Villette (p136) Enjoying a performance or exhibit at the city's largest cultural playground or taking the kids to its world-class science museum.

3 Musée Jacquemart-André (p137) Stepping into opulent surrounds at this elegant art museum, a rare snapshot of 19th-century Parisian high society.

4 Basilique de St-Denis (p139) Discovering the tombs of French royalty at this popular pilgrimage site in St-Denis.

5 Le Mur des je t'aime Learning how to say 'I love you' in every language under the sun in a pretty city park in Montmartre.

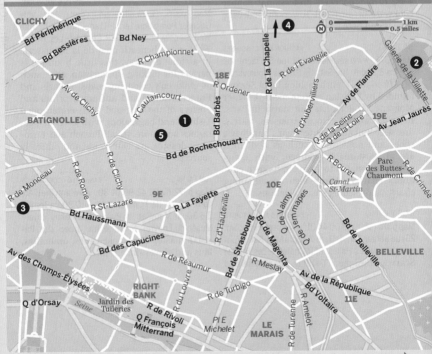

For more detail of this area see Map p380.

Explore Montmartre & Northern Paris

One of the wellsprings of Parisian myth, Montmartre has always stood apart. Bohemians, revolutionaries, artists, cancan dancers and headless martyrs have all played a role in its story, and vestiges of the original village – ivy-clad buildings, steep narrow streets – remain. A romantic base, Montmartre is rich in sights, cuisine, shopping and entertainment. Most visitors spend half a day exploring the side streets that tumble from the summit, with stunning city vistas. When the crowds get too much, explore rarely visited streets on the backside of the Butte (as the hill is known) and excellent lesser-known museums to the southwest. Immediately north of place de Clichy is the *'nouveau quartier'* (new district) of Clichy-Batignolles, with Paris' strikingly modern law courts by architect Renzo Piano at its epicentre.

After dark, night owls will enjoy drinking cocktails and dining in style in south Pigalle (aka 'SoPi'). Or head east into the 10e *arrondissement*, another traditional working-class area, though gentrified in pockets with trendsetting bistros, bars and pop-up design stores – the area immediately around rue des Petites Écuries and its continuation, rue du Château d'Eau, has never been as hot as right now. For *bobo* (bourgeois bohemian) lifestyle, meander east again to Canal St-Martin.

Local Life

Canal lounging Cycle, stroll, picnic and chill along the picturesque quays of Canal St-Martin (p146).

Sustainable dining Join Gen Z foodies in the burgeoning 10e, where eco-responsible bistros L'Avant-Poste (p140) and Les Résistants (p145) have been packed from day one.

Tapas Ditch traditional sit-down dining for shared plates at fashionable *bar à manger* (dining bar) Déviant (p148) or Django (p145).

Le Goutte d'Or Explore this predominantly North African *quartier,* with its craft brewery, coffee roaster and iconic fashion label Maison Château Rouge (p153).

Getting There & Away

Metro Lines 2, 4 and 12 serve Montmartre; 5 and 7 serve northeastern Paris; 4 and 5 serve Gare du Nord. Clichy museums are accessed via lines 2 and 13.

RER B and D link Gare du Nord with central Paris.

Bicycle Vélib' stations dot Canal St-Martin, place République and place Jacques Bonsergent.

Lonely Planet's Top Tip

Although not quite as pretty as Seine-side Paris, the neighbourhoods in north and northeast Paris remain fairly safe as far as big cities go; just use your common sense. Stay on your guard at the foot of the hill leading up to Sacré-Cœur and on Montmartre's place du Tertre – pickpockets and con artists do work the crowds here.

✕ Best Places to Eat

➡ L'Avant-Poste (p140)
➡ Holybelly (p140)
➡ Trattoria Libertino (p140)
➡ Coretta (p144)
➡ Django (p145)
➡ Le Verre Volé (p140)

For reviews, see p139.➡

⬤ Best Places to Drink

➡ Déviant (p148)
➡ Le Très Particulier (p148)
➡ Le Pavillon Puebla (p148)
➡ Le Syndicat (p148)
➡ Gravity Bar (p149)

For reviews, see p148.➡

☆ Best Entertainment

➡ Philharmonie de Paris (p150)
➡ Point Éphémère (p150)
➡ La Cigale (p151)
➡ Le Divan du Monde & Chez Madame Arthur (p150)
➡ Moulin Rouge (p151)

For reviews, see p150.➡

MONTMARTRE & NORTHERN PARIS

TOP EXPERIENCE
CLIMB THE STAIRCASE AT SACRÉ-CŒUR

More than just a place of worship, the distinctive dove-white domed Basilique du Sacré-Cœur (Sacred Heart Basilica) is a veritable experience. Reached by 270 steps, the *parvis* (forecourt) in front of the basilica provides a postcard-perfect city panorama. Buskers and street artists perform on the steps, while picnickers spread out on the hillside park.

DON'T MISS

➡ Paris views from the *parvis*

➡ The apse mosaic *Christ in Majesty*

➡ The dome

History

It may appear to be a place of peacefulness and quiet contemplation today, but Sacré-Cœur's foundations were laid amid bloodshed and controversy. Its construction began in 1875, in the wake of France's humiliating defeat by Prussia and the subsequent chaos of the Paris Commune. Following Napoléon III's surrender to von Bismarck in September 1870, angry Parisians, with the help of the National Guard, continued to hold out against Prussian forces – a harrowing siege that lasted four long winter months. By the time a ceasefire was negotiated in early 1871, the split between the radical working-class Parisians (supported by the National Guard) and the conservative national government (supported by the French army) had become insurmountable.

Over the next several months, the rebels, known as Communards, managed to overthrow the reactionary government and take over the city. It was a particularly chaotic and bloody moment in Parisian history, with mass executions on both sides and a wave of rampant destruction that spread throughout Paris. Montmartre was a key Communard stronghold. It was on the future site of Sacré-Cœur that the rebels won their first victory and it was consequently the first neighbourhood to be targeted when the French army returned in full force in May 1871. Ultimately, many Communards were buried alive in the gypsum mines beneath the Butte.

PRACTICALITIES

➡ Map p378, F3

➡ ☎01 53 41 89 00

➡ www.sacre-coeur-montmartre.com

➡ Parvis du Sacré-Cœur, 18e

➡ basilica free, dome adult/child €6/4

➡ ⊙basilica 6am-10.30pm, dome 10.30am-8.30pm

➡ ⓜAnvers, Abbesses

Following the 2019 fire at Notre Dame cathedral, Sacré-Cœur became Paris' most visited building. In 2020, it was announced that the process was underway for the basilica to be protected as a historic monument.

The Basilica

Within the historical context, the construction of an enormous basilica to expiate the city's sins seemed like a gesture of peace and forgiveness – indeed, the seven million French francs needed to construct the church's foundations came solely from the contributions of local Catholics. However, the Montmartre location was certainly no coincidence: the conservative old guard desperately wanted to assert its power in what was then a hotbed of revolution. The battle between the two camps – Catholic versus secular, royalist versus republican – raged on and in 1882 the construction of the basilica was even voted down by the city council on the grounds that it would continue to fan the flames of civil war. It was overturned in the end by a technicality.

The Romano-Byzantine–style basilica's travertine stone exudes calcite, ensuring it remains white despite weathering and pollution. Six successive architects oversaw construction of the basilica, and it wasn't until 1919 that Sacré-Cœur was finally consecrated, contrasting the surrounding area's bohemian lifestyle.

While criticism of its design and white travertine stone has continued throughout the decades (one poet called it a giant baby's bottle for angels), the interior is enlivened by the glittering apse mosaic *Christ in Majesty,* designed by Luc-Olivier Merson in 1922 and one of the largest in the world.

Above the high altar is displayed the Blessed Sacrament. The prayer 'cycle' that began in 1885 before the basilica's completion still continues around the clock, with perpetual adoration of this sacrament by the faithful – including at night.

On Sundays, you can hear the organ being played during Mass and Vespers.

The Dome & Crypt

Outside, to the west of the main entrance, 300 spiralling steps climb up to to the basilica's **dome**, which affords one of Paris' most spectacular panoramas; it's said you can see for 30km on a clear day. Weighing in at 19 tonnes, the bell in the tower above, called La Savoyarde, is the largest in France.

To the left of the basilica's main entrance, steps lead down to the huge chapel-lined **crypt** (typically closed to visitors).

DEVOUT BELIEVERS

The basilica was constructed on the highest point in the city, early believers thinking the 130m-high hill was nearer to God. Find the names of thousands of devout Parisians who financed the church engraved on the walls inside the church.

DIVINE INTERVENTION?

In 1944, 13 Allied bombs were dropped on Montmartre, falling just next to Sacré-Cœur. Although the stained-glass windows all shattered from the force of the explosions, miraculously no one died and the basilica sustained no other damage.

NIGHT ADORATION

To spend a night at the basilica and take your turn praying in front of the Blessed Sacrament, check into the basilica guesthouse (dorm €4 to €6, single €16, breakfast €4) between 8.45pm and 9.45pm. Mass is celebrated at 10pm and next day at 7am. Pilgrims are issued with a time-slot pass to enter the basilica during the night. Register online at least 48 hours in advance.

TOP EXPERIENCE

CATCH A CONCERT IN PARC DE LA VILLETTE

The vast green Parc de la Villette is a cultural centre, kids playground and landscaped urban space rolled into one. The French love of geometric forms defines the layout – the colossal mirror-like sphere of the Géode cinema, an undulating strip of corrugated steel stretching for hundreds of metres, the bright-red cubical pavilions known as *folies* – but the intersection of two canals, the Ourcq and the St-Denis, brings the most natural and popular element: water.

Although it's a fair hike from central Paris, consider the trip here to attend one of the many events (world, rock and classical music concerts; art exhibits; outdoor cinema; circuses; modern dance). Throughout the year, events are staged in the wonderful old Grande Halle, **Le Zénith** (Map p384; www.le-zenith.com; 211 av Jean Jaurès, 19e; Ⓜ Porte de Pantin), the **Cabaret Sauvage** (Map p384; ☏ 01 42 09 03 09; www.cabaretsauvage.com; 211 av Jean Jaurès, 19e; Ⓜ Porte de la Villette) and Paris' stunning, cutting-edge Cité de la Musique – Philharmonie de Paris complex. Inside the latter, the **Musée de la Musique** (Map p384; ☏ 01 44 84 44 84; www.philharmoniedeparis.fr; 221 av Jean Jaurès, 19e; adult/child €8/free; ⊘ noon-6pm Tue-Fri, from 10am Sat & Sun; Ⓜ Porte de Pantin) displays some 1000 of its 7000-odd collection of rare musical instruments, many of which you can hear being played on the music museum's audioguide (included in admission).

The park is also a winner with families. In fine weather, children (and adults) will enjoy exploring the numerous themed gardens, the best of which double as playgrounds. For kids, however, the star attraction is **Cité des Sciences** (Map p384; ☏ 01 85 53 99 74; www.cite-sciences.fr; 30 av Corentin Cariou, 19e; per attraction adult/child €12/9; ⊘ 10am-6pm Tue-Sat, to 7pm Sun, La Géode 10.30am-8.30pm Tue-Sun; ♿; Ⓜ Porte de la Villette) and its attached cinemas. The brilliant Cité des Enfants is the most popular section, with a construction site, a TV studio, robots and water-based physics experiments, all designed for children.

DON'T MISS

➡ Evening performances
➡ The themed gardens
➡ Cité des Sciences

PRACTICALITIES

➡ Map p384, B1
➡ www.lavillette.com
➡ 211 av Jean Jaurès, 19e
➡ ⊘ 6am-1am
➡ Ⓜ Porte de la Villette, Porte de Pantin

◉ SIGHTS

The hilltop neighbourhood of Montmartre safeguards some of Paris' most iconic sights, including the white-domed Sacré-Cœur basilica and a Parisian vineyard. The *quartier's* museums evoke its fabled artistic heritage and it's easy to stroll between them. West, past place de Clichy and beyond to Parc Monceau, there are a couple of excellent lesser-known art museums at home in historic mansions. Canal St-Martin, a sight in itself with its vintage bridges and canal boats, flows to the east.

BASILIQUE DU SACRÉ-CŒUR BASILICA
See p134.

PARC DE LA VILLETTE PARK
See p136.

★MUSÉE DE MONTMARTRE MUSEUM
Map p378 (☏01 49 25 89 39; www.museede montmartre.fr; 12 rue Cortot, 18e; adult/child €13/7, garden only €5; ◷11am-6pm Wed-Fri, to 7pm Sat & Sun Apr-Sep, to 6pm Wed-Sun Oct-Mar; Ⓜ Lamarck–Caulaincourt) This delightful 'village' museum showcases paintings, lithographs and documents illustrating Montmartre's bohemian, artistic and hedonistic past – one room is dedicated entirely to the French cancan. It's housed in a 17th-century manor where several artists, including Renoir and Raoul Dufy, had their studios in the 19th century. You can also visit the studio of painter Suzanne Valadon, who lived and worked here with her son Maurice Utrillo and partner André Utter between 1912 and 1926.

Allow ample time to stroll the museum gardens, named after Renoir, who painted his masterpieces *Bal du Moulin de la Galette* and *Jardin de la rue Cortot* while working in his studio here from 1875 to 1877. Find the tree strung with a swing to evoke the impressionist painter's famous work *La Balançoire,* also painted here. Follow the path to the end of the garden for a stunning 'secret' view of the Clos Montmartre vineyards and end your visit with a drink or light bite in the garden's enchanting Café Renoir. Museum admission includes an audioguide.

★MUSÉE JACQUEMART-ANDRÉ MUSEUM
Map p385 (☏01 45 62 11 59; www.musee-jacque mart-andre.com; 158 bd Haussmann, 8e; adult/child incl audioguide €12/7.50; ◷10am-6pm, to 8.30pm Mon during temporary exhibitions; Ⓜ Miromesnil) The home of art collectors Nélie Jacquemart and Édouard André, this opulent late-19th-century residence combines elements from different eras – seen here in the presence of Greek and Roman antiquities, Egyptian artefacts, period furnishings and portraits by Dutch masters. Its 16 rooms offer an absorbing glimpse of the lifestyle of Parisian high society: from the library, hung with canvases by Rembrandt and Van Dyck, to the marvellous Jardin d'Hiver – a glass-paned garden room backed by a magnificent double-helix staircase.

PARC MONCEAU PARK
Map p385 (www.paris.fr/equipements/parc-mon ceau-1804; 35 bd de Courcelles, 8e; ◷7am-10pm May-Aug, to 9pm Sep, to 8pm Oct-Apr; Ⓜ Monceau) Marked by a neoclassical rotunda at its main bd Courcelles entrance, beautiful Parc Monceau sprawls over 8.2 lush

---

ⓘ CANAL CRUISES

Seine boat rides are well known, but for something different, take a canal cruise. Two companies run seasonal 2½-hour trips along the Canal St-Martin between central Paris and Parc de la Villette. Boats pass through four double locks, two swing bridges and an underground section with an art installation.

Canauxrama (Map p382; ☏01 42 39 15 00; www.canauxrama.com; 13 quai de la Loire, 19e; adult/child €18/9; ◷hours vary; Ⓜ Jaurès) Cruises depart from Bassin de la Villette near Parc de la Villette and from Port de l'Arsenal; summertime evening weekend cruises are particularly enchanting. Gourmand and thematic cruises too.

Paris Canal Croisières (Map p384; ☏01 42 40 29 00; www.pariscanal.com; Parc de la Villette, 19e; adult/child €22/14; ◷mid-Mar–mid-Dec; Ⓜ Porte de Pantin) Cruises depart from Parc de la Villette and from quai Anatole France near the Musée d'Orsay.

hectares. It was laid out by Louis Carrogis Carmontelle in 1778–79 in English style with winding paths, ponds and flower beds. An Egyptian-style pyramid is the only original folly remaining today, but other distinctive features include a bridge modelled after Venice's Rialto, a Renaissance arch and a Corinthian colonnade. There are play areas, a carousel and scheduled puppet shows for kids.

MUSÉE NISSIM DE CAMONDO   GALLERY

Map p385 (☑01 44 55 57 50; www.madparis.fr; 63 rue de Monceau, 8e; adult/child incl audioguide €12/free; ⊙10am-5.30pm Wed-Sun; ⓂMonceau, Villiers) Housed in a sumptuous mansion modelled on the Petit Trianon at Versailles, this museum displays 18th-century furniture, wood panelling, tapestries, porcelain and other *objets d'art* collected by Count Moïse de Camondo, a Sephardic Jewish banker who moved from Constantinople to Paris in the late 19th century.

MUSÉE DE LA VIE ROMANTIQUE   MUSEUM

Map p378 (☑01 55 31 95 67; www.vie-romantique. paris.fr; 16 rue Chaptal, 9e; ⊙10am-6pm Tue-Sun; ⓂBlanche, St-Georges) FREE Framed by green shutters, this mansion where painter Ary Scheffer once lived sits in a cobbled courtyard at the end of a tree-shaded alley. The objects exhibited create a wonderful flashback to romantic-era Paris, when George Sand (Amantine Lucile Aurore Dupin), Chopin (Sand's lover), Delacroix et al attended salons here. Temporary exhibitions command an admission fee (adult/reduced €9/7). End with tea and cake in the museum café's enchanting summer garden.

November to June, classical music concerts are held in the 19th-century mansion.

PARC DES BUTTES CHAUMONT   PARK

Map p384 (www.paris.fr/equipements/parc-des-buttes-chaumont-1757; rue Manin & rue Botzaris, 19e; ⊙7am-10pm May-Aug, to 9pm Sep & Apr, to 8pm Oct-Mar; ⓂButtes Chaumont, Botzaris) Buttes Chaumont is one of the city's largest green spaces, with landscaped slopes hiding grottoes, waterfalls, a lake and even an island topped with a temple to Sibylle. Once a gypsum quarry and rubbish dump, it was given its present form by Baron Haussmann in time for the opening of the 1867 Exposition Universelle. The tracks of the abandoned 19th-century Petite Ceinture railway line, which once circled Paris, run through the park.

It's a favourite with Parisians, who come here to practise tai chi, take the kids to a puppet show, grab a sundowner and pizza at trendy Le Pavillon Puebla (p148) or simply to relax with a bottle of wine and a sundown picnic.

LE 104   GALLERY

Map p382 (☑01 53 35 50 00; www.104.fr; 5 rue Curial, 19e; ⊙noon-7pm Tue-Fri, 11am-7pm Sat & Sun; ⓂRiquet) A funeral parlour turned city-funded alternative art space, Le 104 is a hive of activity. It essentially supports and encourages young artists, and a meander through its public areas uncovers breakdancers, wacky art installations and rehearsing actors. Check the schedule for theatre, circus, concerts and other events. Culinary needs are well taken care of with a pizza truck, retro 1950s-styled cafe and loft-like restaurant-bar.

CIMETIÈRE DE MONTMARTRE   CEMETERY

Map p378 (www.paris.fr/equipements/cimetiere-de-montmartre-5061; 20 av Rachel, 18e; ⊙8am-6pm Mon-Fri, to 6.30pm Sat, 9am-6pm Sun

---

STREET ART

The banks of Canal St-Martin and Pigalle seethe with impromptu street art: where else boasts a basketball court such as Pigalle's **Playground Duperré** (Map p378; 22 rue Duperré, 9e; ⊙10am-8pm May-Sep, shorter hours Oct-Apr; ⓂPigalle), recast as a street-art installation in eye-popping shades of yellow, blue, indigo and fuchsia-pink?

North of place de Clichy, Batignolles' **rue Biot** is a fantastic spot to admire Jérôme Mesnager's distinctive white skeletal figures, Mosko's exotic animal stencils, Invader mosaics and wall murals by Franco-Congolese artist Kouka Ntadi all in one place.

Nearby, street art and post-graffiti get their own dedicated space at **Art 42** (www. art42.fr; 96 bd Bessières, 17e; ⊙tours every 2nd Tue in English 7pm, in French 6-9pm; ⓂPorte de Clichy) FREE, with works by Banksy, Bom.K, Miss Van, Swoon and other boundary-pushing urban artists. Reserve a free guided tour (1½ to two hours) of the 4000 sq metres of subterranean rooms in advance online.

BASILIQUE DE ST-DENIS

Once one of France's most sacred sites, the **Basilique de St-Denis** (☎01 48 09 83 54; www.saint-denis-basilique.fr; 1 rue de la Légion d'Honneur; basilica free, tombs adult/child €9.50/free, 1st Sun of month Nov-Mar free; ☺10am-6.15pm Mon-Sat, noon-6.15pm Sun Apr-Sep, 10am-5.15pm Mon-Sat, noon-5.15pm Sun Oct-Mar; MBasilique de St-Denis) was built atop the tomb of St Denis, the 3rd-century martyr and alleged first bishop of Paris who was beheaded by Roman priests. By the 6th century it had become the royal necropolis. Almost all of France's kings and queens from Dagobert I (r 629–39) to Louis XVIII (r 1814–24) are buried here (42 kings and 32 queens in total).

The single-towered basilica, begun around 1136, was the first major structure in France to be built in the Gothic style. The tombs in the crypt are Europe's largest collection of funerary art and the real reason to make the trip out here. Adorned with *gisants* (recumbent figures), those made after 1285 were carved from death masks and are thus fairly lifelike; earlier sculptures are depictions of how rulers might have looked.

Note that the metro line splits in two at La Fourche, so be sure to board a metro bound for St-Denis-Université.

---

mid-Mar–Oct, 8am-5.30pm Mon-Sat, 9am-5.30pm Sun Nov–mid-Mar; MPlace de Clichy) **FREE** This 11-hectare cemetery opened in 1825. It contains the graves of writers Émile Zola (whose ashes are now in the Panthéon), Alexandre Dumas *fils* and Stendhal; composers Jacques Offenbach and Hector Berlioz; artists Edgar Degas and Gustave Moreau; film director François Truffaut and dancer Vaslav Nijinsky, among others.

Steps from the rue Caulaincourt road bridge, built in 1888, lead down to the entrance on av Rachel, just off bd de Clichy.

MUSÉE CERNUSCHI
MUSEUM

Map p385 (☎01 53 96 21 50; www.cernuschi.paris.fr; 7 av Vélasquez, 8e; suggested donation €2; ☺10am-6pm Tue-Sun; MVilliers) **FREE** The recently renovated Cernuschi Museum comprises an excellent and rare collection of ancient Chinese art (funerary statues, bronzes, ceramics), much of which predates the Tang dynasty (618–907), in addition to diverse pieces from Japan. Milan banker and philanthropist Henri Cernuschi (1821–96), who settled in Paris before the unification of Italy, assembled the collection during an 1871–73 world tour.

Temporary exhibitions command an admission fee (adult/reduced €9/7).

DALÍ PARIS
GALLERY

Map p378 (☎01 42 64 40 10; www.daliparis.com; 11 rue Poulbot, 18e; adult/child €13/9; ☺10am-6pm; MAbbesses) More than 300 works by Salvador Dalí (1904–89), the flamboyant Catalan surrealist printmaker, painter, sculptor and self-promoter, are on display at this basement museum located just west of place du Tertre. The private collection includes Dalí's strange sculptures, lithographs, and many of his illustrations and furniture, including the famous *Mae West Lips Sofa*. An audioguide costs €3.

HALLE ST-PIERRE
GALLERY

Map p378 (☎01 42 58 72 89; www.hallesaintpierre.org; 2 rue Ronsard, 18e; adult/child €9/6; ☺11am-6pm Mon-Fri, to 7pm Sat, noon-6pm Sun; MAnvers) Founded in 1986, this museum and gallery is in a lovely former covered market. It focuses on the primitive and Art Brut schools; there is no permanent collection, but the museum stages several temporary exhibitions a year. It also has an auditorium, a cafe that's a lovely place to chill over a laptop and an excellent art bookshop.

✗ EATING

Western Paris' culinary scene evolves slowly, but once you cross over that invisible border somewhere in the middle of the 9th *arrondissement*, it's a different world, with a constant flurry of new openings in south Pigalle, along Canal St-Martin and in the cosmopolitan 10e west of place de la République: young chefs here head up some of the most exciting dining venues in Paris today. *Rues commerçantes* (shopping streets), where food stalls set up on the pavement outside shops include rue des Martyrs and, in the 17e, rue Poncelet.

LOCAL KNOWLEDGE

URBAN FARMING

Mingle with green-thumbed, eco-conscious locals at **La REcyclerie** (📞01 42 57 58 49; www.larecyclerie.com; 83 bd Ornano, 18e; ⏱8am-midnight Mon-Thu, to 2am Fri & Sat, to 10pm Sun; 🚇Porte de Clignancourt) 🍴, a groundbreaking urban farm and alternative cultural centre at home in an abandoned Petite Ceinture train station. The repurposed eco-hub has community-tended vegetable and herb gardens and chickens along the old railway line, and provides ingredients for its on-site, predominantly vegetarian cafe-canteen. Tables stretch trackside in summer and the station houses a cavernous dining space. In turn, food scraps replenish the chickens and gardens, and beehives on the roof produce honey. Watch for regular upcycling and repair workshops, flea markets and various other events – or sign up (in advance, online) for a free guided tour in French, departing at 4pm on Tuesday and Saturday.

★L'AVANT-POSTE　　　FRENCH €

Map p382 (📞0981410107; www.lavantposteparis.fr; 7 rue de la Fidélité, 10e; 2-/3-course lunch menu €16.50/18.50, mains €9-14; ⏱noon-2pm & 7-10pm Tue-Sat; 🚇Bonne Nouvelle) 🍴 'Eco-responsible' is the tasty buzzword at the second outpost of Les Résistants (p145), in a former wig shop in the earthy 10e. Fresh, seasonal produce is sourced from artisan producers and the menu changes daily – waste is just not a word here. Tuck into seaweed-spiked beetroot borsch (soup) or Corsican *panzetta* (pork) with an old-fashioned mix of spelt, mushrooms, courgette and chard. Reservations vital.

★TRATTORIA LIBERTINO　　　ITALIAN €

Map p382 (📞01 42 63 92 87; www.bigmammagroup.com/en/trattorias/libertino; 44 rue de Paradis, 10e; pizza €13-20, mains €11-17; ⏱noon-2.30pm & 6.45-10.45pm Mon-Wed, to 11pm Thu & Fri, noon-3.15pm & 6.45-11pm Sat, noon-3.15pm & 6.45-10.45pm Sun; 🚇Poissonnière) In Italian 'Libertino' means a pleasure-seeking, fun-loving gigolo and this is precisely the infectious vibe of this latest address by the brilliantly successful Big Mamma group. A riot of faux foliage, paintings and ceramics fills the flamboyant interior to bursting and the menu features all the Italian trattoria classics and Roman-style pizzas.

The artichoke salad, bruschetta topped with truffle shavings and *cacio e pepe* (spaghetti with cheese and pepper) for two served in a parmesan crust bowl are all exceptional. Chefs in the open kitchen and waiting staff are Italian, and the desserts – lemon tiramisu, *île flottante* with caramelised popcorn – are gigantesque, utterly decadent and not to be refused.

★HOLYBELLY　　　INTERNATIONAL €

Map p382 (www.holybellycafe.com; 5 & 19 rue Lucien Sampaix, 10e; dishes €6-16.50; ⏱9am-5pm; 🍴📶; 🚇Jacques Bonsergent) Friendly vibes, sassy breakfast 'n' lunch dishes and specialist coffee define this duo. Holybelly at No 5 cooks all-day pancakes and eggs, while the Holybelly original at No 19 serves more creative, seasonal dishes to share. Last orders 4pm. No reservations.

Be it Holybelly's signature bacon cured in organic maple syrup, kasha porridge with poached pear or winter asparagus with hazelnut dukkah, dining here is never dull. Craft beers, natural wines and some funky cocktails, using celery-infused gin or mixing iced filter coffee with absinthe, make the drinks menu equally irresistible.

★PAPILLES　　　INTERNATIONAL €

Map p378 (📞09 50 78 16 32; www.papilles-restaurant.com; 77 rue de Rochechouart, 9e; dishes €7.50-15, sides €2-4; ⏱9am-5pm; 🍴📶; 🚇Anvers) No spot in northern Paris satisfies brunch cravings like this hipster coffee house with exposed red brick, velour seating and a menu signed off by Franco-Vietnamese chef Céline Pham. The sassy brunch menu is served all day and fabulously mixes French, Vietnamese and world flavours. The *oeufs bené bené* (poached eggs on toast with lemon sabayon) and *bánhnìnì* (marinated chicken, coriander and pickle toasted sandwich) are highlights. Weekends (no reservations) get packed out.

★LE VERRE VOLÉ　　　BISTRO €

Map p382 (📞01 48 03 17 34; www.leverrevole.fr; 67 rue de Lancry, 10e; mains €14-21, sandwiches €6-12; ⏱kitchen 12.30-2.30pm & 7.30-11.30pm, bar 9.30am-2am; 📶; 🚇Jacques Bonsergent) The tiny 'Stolen Glass' – a wine shop with a few tables – is one of Paris' most popular wine bar/restaurants, with outstanding natural and unfiltered wines and expert

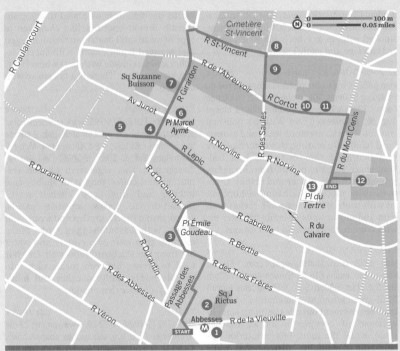

🏃 Neighbourhood Walk
Mythic Montmartre

START ABBESSES METRO STATION
END PLACE DU TERTRE
LENGTH 1KM; ONE HOUR

Begin on ➊ **place des Abbesses**, where Hector Guimard's iconic art nouveau metro entrance still stands. Learn how to say 'I love you' in several languages at ➋ **Le Mur des je t'aime**. Head up passage des Abbesses to place Émile Goudeau; at No 13 is ➌ **Le Bateau Lavoir** (https://museede montmartre.fr/en/bateau-lavoir), where Max Jacob, Amedeo Modigliani and Pablo Picasso – who painted his seminal *Les Dem-oiselles d'Avignon* (1907) here – once had art studios.

Climb up rue Lepic to Montmartre's two surviving windmills: ➍ **Moulin Radet** (83 rue Lepic), now a restaurant, and, 50m west, ➎ **Moulin Blute Fin**. In the 19th century, the latter had an open-air dance hall, immortalised by Renoir in his 1876 *Bal du Moulin de la Galette* (in the Musée d'Orsay).

Just north, on place Marcel Aymé, a man pops out of a stone wall: the sculpture ➏ **Le**

Passe-Muraille ('The Walker Through Walls') portrays the hero of Aymé's short story of the same name. Local lore says it brings luck to rub the figure's left (hence highly polished) hand. Continue along rue Girardon to Sq Suzanne Buisson, home to a ➐ **statue of St-Denis**, the 3rd-century martyr beheaded by Roman priests.

After passing Cimetière St-Vincent you'll see celebrated cabaret ➑ **Au Lapin Agile** (p151), with a mural of a rabbit jumping out of a cooking pot by caricaturist André Gill. Opposite is ➒ **Clos Montmartre**, a 1933 vineyard that produces an average of 800 bottles of wine each October.

Uphill is Montmartre's oldest building, a 17th-century manor house. One-time home to painters Renoir, Utrillo and Raoul Dufy, it's now the ➓ **Musée de Montmartre** (p137). Continue past composer ⑪ **Eric Satie's former residence** (No 6) and turn right onto rue du Mont Cenis; you'll soon come to historic ⑫ **Église St-Pierre de Mont-martre**. End on busy ⑬ **place du Tertre**, the former main square of the village.

advice. Unpretentious *plats du jour* are excellent and seasonal specials include house-smoked salmon gravlax with lime-pickled red cabbage and cauliflower.

52 FAUBOURG ST-DENIS
BISTRO €

Map p382 (www.faubourgstdenis.com; 52 rue du Faubourg St-Denis, 10e; mains €18-22; ⊗kitchen noon-2.30pm & 7-11pm, bar 8am-midnight, closed Aug; ⊛; MChâteau d'Eau) With its polished concrete floors, raw stone walls and ginger-hued banquette seating, this contemporary neighbourhood cafe-restaurant is a brilliant space to hang out in, from breakfast through to lunch, dinner and drinks. Creative cuisine might include tuna sashimi salad with beetroot jelly, egg-yolk ravioli with ham and mushrooms or lamb-shoulder pie with cinnamon-fig jus. No reservations.

ABATTOIR VÉGÉTAL
VEGAN €

Map p378 (www.abattoirvegetal.com; 61 rue Ramey, 18e; mains €15-17; ⊗noon-4pm & 7-10pm Tue-Sat, 11am-3.30pm Sun; ⊛⊅; MJules Joffrin) Mint-green wrought-iron chairs and tables line the pavement outside the 'plant slaughterhouse' (it occupies a former butcher shop), while the light, bright interior has bare-bulb downlights, distempered walls and greenery-filled hanging baskets. Cold-pressed juices, 'wellness lattes', a delicious ginger pear cider and other artisan drinks accompany creative, 100% raw vegan dishes, served alongside natural wines.

ALIX ET MIKA
FRENCH €

Map p378 (⊅01 73 71 19 90; www.alixetmika.com; 37 rue Lamarck, 18e; tartares €6-10, sides €4-5; ⊗7-10.30pm Wed-Fri, noon-3pm & 7-10.30pm Sat & Sun; MLamarck-Caulaincourt) 'French cut lovers' is the strapline of this corner bistro specialising in hand-cut tartares, served with fantastic duck-fat-cooked fries and boutique French cheeses to follow. The tartare menu is pick-and-mix style, offering a tantalising choice of organic meats (beef, veal) and fish (salmon, tuna, white fish) prepared a dozen different ways: French, Italian, Mexican etc.

CRÊPERIE PEN-TY
CRÊPES €

Map p378 (⊅01 48 74 18 49; www.creperiepenty.com; 65 rue de Douai, 9e; crêpes €5-9, galettes €4-13; ⊗noon-2.30pm & 7-11.15pm Mon-Fri, 12.30-4pm & 6.30-11.30pm Sat, to 10.30pm Sun; MPlace de Clichy) Consistently hailed as the best crêperie in northern Paris (it's been around since 1976), old-world Pen-Ty is well

worth the detour. Book ahead to enjoy authentic Breton apéritifs like *chouchen* (a type of mead) and *pastis marin* (an aniseed and seaweed liquor), along with superb savoury *galettes* (made with buckwheat flour) and sweet crêpes. There is a takeaway window too.

SOUL KITCHEN
VEGETARIAN €

Map p378 (⊅01 71 37 99 95; www.facebook.com/soulkitchenparis; 33 rue Lamarck, 18e; 2-course lunch menu €14.50; ⊗8.45am-6pm Mon-Fri, 10am-6pm Sat & Sun; ⊛⊅⊞; MLamarck-Caulaincourt) This vegetarian kitchen restaurant and coffee shop with shabby-chic interior and tiny open kitchen serves market-driven dishes: creative salads, soups, savoury tarts, gratins and wraps – all packed with seasonal veggies. Order at the counter, grab your own cutlery and water jug from the sideboard, and wait for your food to arrive. Between meals tuck into granola bowls, muffins, cakes and mint-laced *citronnade* (lemonade).

YUMI
VEGETARIAN €

Map p382 (⊅01 86 76 72 29; www.yumi.fr; 27 rue du Château d'Eau, 10e; sandwiches, soups & bowls €3.50-11; ⊗8.30am-6pm Mon-Fri, 10am-7pm Sat, 10am-6pm Sun; ⊛⊅; MJacques Bonsergent, Château d'Eau) Be it a dirty chai latte, peppery ginger shot, breakfast bowl of chia pudding with fresh fruit or brunch brimming with organic veg, this new-generation coffee shop and canteen packs a punch. Huge floor-to-ceiling windows flood the trendy shabby-chic interior and the vase with freshly cut flowers is a welcome touch.

SCARAMOUCHE
ICE CREAM €

Map p378 (www.glaces-scaramouche.com; 22 rue la Vieuville, 18e; ice cream 1/2/3/4 scoops €3/5/6.50/8; ⊗noon-midnight Apr-Dec; MAbbesses) Raw Jersey milk, organic eggs and fresh fruit, and wild herbs from southern France go into this Provençal ice-cream maker's sublime *glaces* (ice creams). Some 40 flavours are available each day, such as black sesame, geranium and pistachio, lemon and ginger, saffron, chilli pepper and hazelnut, black truffle, fennel seed, even hibiscus mojito. Expect lengthy queues (well worth the wait).

SAWADEE KHAP
THAI €

Map p378 (⊅09 87 33 81 03; https://sawadeekhap.eatbu.com; 65 rue de Douai, 9e; soups & salads €8, mains €10; ⊗noon-3pm & 6-10pm

CLICHY-BATIGNOLLES

Batignolles didn't become part of Paris proper until 1860, during Haussmann's re-modelling of the capital, and change is once again afoot in the district immediately north of place de Clichy, in the 17e *arrondissement*. In 2018 the City of Paris relocated its law courts – historically on Île de la Cité (p200) – to a dazzling, purpose-built, L-shaped glass skyscraper here, designed by Italian architect Renzo Piano. Metro line 14 has also been extended north, with new metro station Pont Cadinet (next to **Parc Martin Luther-King** on rue Cadinet) ensuring a fast link between the rapidly changing suburb and central Paris since late 2020.

For an authentic taste of this increasingly appealing 'hood, take a stroll along main streets rue Biot and rue des Dames (watch for the much-anticipated mid-2020 opening of iconic Bistro des Dames and Hôtel Eldorado at No 18, after a year of renovation). Linger with locals over drinks at wine bar **Les Caves Populaires** (Map p385; 01 53 04 08 32; www.facebook.com/lescaves.populaires; 22 rue des Dames, 17e; 8.30am-2am Mon-Fri, 10am-2am Sat, 11am-2am Sun; Place de Clichy), **Chez Poupette** (Map p385; 01 44 71 94 37; www.chez-poupette.fr; 20 rue Biot, 17e; 2-/3-course menu €15.90/19.90; 10am-2am Mon-Sat; Place de Clichy), or raucous sports pub **Lush** (Map p385; 01 43 87 49 46; www.lushbarparis.com; 16 rue des Dames, 17e; 5.30pm-1.30am; Place de Clichy). For meals, the seasonal bistro fare of chef Clement Eymery at **Strobi** (Map p385; 01 72 38 59 86; www.le-strobi.fr; 12 rue Biot, 17e; mains €12-19; noon-2.30pm & 7-11pm; Place de Clichy), Breton crêpes at **Breizh Café** (Map p385; 01 40 07 11 69; www.breizhcafe.com; 31 rue des Batignolles, 17e; lunch menu €19, crêpes & galettes €6-18.50; 11.30am-11pm Mon-Fri, 10am-11pm Sat & Sun; Rome, Place de Clichy), or modern French cuisine at Batignolles' latest head-turner Coretta (p144), are all fabulous choices.

Coffee shop **Dose** (Map p385; www.dose.paris; 82 place du Dr Félix Lobligeois, 17e; 8am-6pm Tue-Fri, 9am-7pm Sat & Sun; Rome) is a popular spot for *un café* or brunch, after you've had a frolic in the grassy **square des Batignolles** city park across the street.

Mon-Sat; Place de Clichy) Pretty much packed to the rafters ever since it opened, this pocket-sized newbie on Paris' thriving street-food scene wins big with flavoursome Thai soups, salads, curries and satay sticks for takeaway. The *tom kha khai* (chicken, coconut milk and lemon grass soup), *som tam* (green papaya, tomato and peanut salad), mirin-marinated ribs and caramelised pork are all authentic and delicious.

FRIC-FRAC
SANDWICHES €

Map p382 (01 42 85 87 34; www.fricfrac.fr; 79 quai de Valmy, 10e; sandwiches €9-14; noon-3pm & 7.30-10.30pm Mon-Thu, noon-10.30pm Fri-Sun; Jacques Bonsergent) French snack croque monsieur (toasted cheese-and-ham sandwich) gets a contemporary makeover at this canal-side space. Gourmet Winnie (Crottin de Chavignol cheese, dried fruit, chestnut honey, chives and rosemary) and exotic Shaolin (king prawns, lemongrass paste, shiitake mushrooms and Thai basil) are among the creative combos served with salad and fries. Eat in or head to the canal.

L'ÉTÉ EN PENTE DOUCE
CAFE €

Map p378 (01 42 64 02 67; http://lete-en-pente-douce.business.site; 8 rue Paul Albert, 18e; mains €10.70-18.50; noon-midnight; Château Rouge) Parisian terraces don't get finer than 'Summer on a Gentle Slope' (named after the 1987 French film): look for the colourful rainbow of metal tables and chairs hidden on a car-free square wedged between two flights of steep Montmartre staircases. Come dusk, fairy lights twinkle between trees. Quiches, salads, roast chicken and several vegetarian dishes define the kitchen.

BOUILLON PIGALLE
BRASSERIE €

Map p378 (01 42 59 69 31; www.bouillonpigalle.com; 22 bd de Clichy, 18e; mains €8.70-13.50; noon-midnight; Pigalle) Brilliant prices, all-day service and quality ingredients used in unapologetically traditional dishes – snails with garlic and parsley butter, veal liver and mash, *pot-au-feu* (hotpot) and *tête de veau* (boiled calf's head) – are the keys to the success of this new-generation *bouillon*

LOCAL KNOWLEDGE

NEW-GEN BAKERIES

Rekindling ancient recipes and innovating with bold new pastries and leavening methods is what Paris' new generation of gourmet bakers are about. Be it for picnic supplies, a light takeaway lunch or sweet bite to enjoy with coffee, these are our favourite *boulangeries*.

Du Pain et des Idées (Map p382; ☎01 42 40 44 52; www.dupainetdesidees.com; 34 rue Yves Toudic, 10e; breads €1.20-7, pastries €2.50-6.50; ⊙6.45am-8pm Mon-Fri, closed Aug; MJacques Bonsergent) This traditional bakery with an exquisite 19th-century interior is famed for its naturally leavened bread, orange-blossom brioche and flavoured *escargots* (scroll-like 'snails'). Its mini savoury *pavés* (breads) flavoured with Reblochon cheese and fig, or goat's cheese, sesame and honey, are perfect for lunch on the run.

Sain Boulangerie (Map p382; ☎07 61 23 49 44; www.sain-boulangerie.com; 15 rue Marie et Louise, 10e; pastries from €1.50; ⊙7.30am-2.30pm & 4.15-8pm Tue-Sat, 8am-1pm Sun; MGoncourt, Jacques Bonsergent) Forever innovative, chef Anthony Courteille has morphed the pocket-sized space where he headed up *table d'hôte* restaurant Matière à into his very own bijou bakery instead. Artisanal breads and pastries, using natural yeast and inspired by ancient recipes, are the passionate bread-maker's speciality and his crisp, caramelised *chaussons aux pommes* (apple turnovers) and tonka-bean shortbread alone are worth the two-minute detour from Canal St-Martin.

Mamiche (Map p378; ☎01 53 21 03 68; www.mamiche.fr; 45 rue Condorcet, 9e; pastries €2-5; ⊙8am-8pm Tue-Fri, to 7pm Sat; MAnvers) Take one bite into a cinnamon roll, apricot crostata or signature *babka* (orange-blossom and chocolate brioche) at this new-generation *boulangerie* and you'll be hooked. Young entrepreneurs Cécile Khayat and Victoria Effantin quit their day jobs to open this neighbourhood bakery and their artisan *pains* and pastries are now the hottest thing here since sliced bread.

Pain Pain (Map p378; ☎01 42 23 62 81; www.pain-pain.fr; 88 rue des Martyrs, 18e; breads & pastries €1.20-8; ⊙7am-8pm Tue-Sat, 7.30am-7.30pm Sun; MAbbesses) Sébastien Mauvieux, famed for his baguettes, also bakes outstanding corn bread, rye and seasonal chestnut loaves and other varieties of *pain* at his notably chic, boutique-styled bakery. Grab a sandwich or decadent slice of layered Opéra cake with yuzu and raspberries to take away, perhaps, or savour a stylish moment on cushioned seating amid pink-flamingo and turquoise-bird wallpaper.

(workers' canteen-style 'soup kitchen'). It doesn't take reservations, so arrive outside peak times or expect to queue.

PINK FLAMINGO
PIZZA €

Map p382 (☎01 42 02 31 70; www.pinkflamingopizza.com; 67 rue Bichat, 10e; pizzas €11.50-17.50; ⊙7-11.30pm Mon-Thu, noon-2.30pm & 7-11.30pm Fri & Sat, noon-11.30pm Sun; MJacques Bonsergent) Once the weather warms up, the Flamingo unveils its secret weapon – pink helium balloons that delivery staff use to locate you and your perfect canal-side picnic spot (GPS not needed). Order a Poulidor (duck, apple and chèvre) or a Basquiat (Gorgonzola, figs and cured ham), and pop into Le Verre Volé (p140) across the canal for the perfect bottle of vino.

MARCHÉ ST-MARTIN
MARKET €

Map p382 (31-33 rue du Château d'Eau, 10e; half-dozen oysters & glass of wine €10; ⊙9am-8pm Mon-Sat, to 2pm Sun; MChâteau d'Eau, Jacques Bonsergent) This lovely covered market, built in 1859 and revamped in 1880, is a delightful spot to mooch around stalls selling high-quality food produce. Join locals for breakfast, brunch, lunch or – in winter – a plate of seasonal, freshly shucked oysters and glass of white wine at the market's *bar à huîtres* (oyster bar).

★CORETTA
BISTRO €€

Map p385 (☎01 42 26 55 55; www.restaurantcoretta.com; 151bis rue Cardinet, 17e; lunch menu €30, 2-/3-course dinner menu €37/43; ⊙noon-2pm & 7.30-10pm Mon-Fri, to 10.30pm Sat & Sun; 🛜; MPont Cadinet) 🌿 This dazzling contemporary bistro with two floors, huge windows and a sharp Scandinavian-design interior has been an icon for Batignolles' renaissance from urban underdog to hipster 'hood ever since it opened. Modern French bistro fare, exquisitely presented on bright white plates, is packed with seasonal products. Chefs work hard to be ecologically responsible (zero waste, local produce etc).

'Coretta', if you're wondering, pays homage to Coretta Scott King, the author, activist and civil rights leader who was also married to Martin Luther King Jr (after whom the adjoining city park is named).

★DJANGO   FRENCH €€

Map p378 (☑01 74 64 64 84; www.django-pigalle. fr; 24 rue Victor Massé, 9e; shared plates €9-16; ☻kitchen 6-11pm, bar to 2am daily; MPigalle) A former Pigalle guitar shop has morphed into a stylish *bar à manger* (dining bar) where fashionistas hobnob until the wee hours over craft cocktails, natural wines and inventive shared plates by chef Khélil Morin. Offerings might include leeks in fig vinaigrette with tangy 12-month-aged Comté, shrimp ravioli or roast cauliflower with piquillo pepper and caraway 'ketchup'.

CHEVAL D'OR   FUSION €€

Map p384 (☑09 54 12 21 77; www.chevaldor paris.com; 21 rue de la Villette, 19e; dishes €7-28; ☻7.30-11pm Wed-Fri, 12.30-2pm & 7.30-11pm Sat & Sun) With its old signage, it might look like just another *'restaurant Chinois'* (Chinese restaurant) on the fringe of multicultural Belleville, but look again. Inside the designer interior, foodies lounge on stools around the open kitchen feasting on stunning French-Asian cuisine from Japanese chef Taku Sekine. His creative spins on traditional pork noodles, bao buns and crème caramel are already legendary.

LES RÉSISTANTS   FRENCH €€

Map p382 (☑01 77 32 77 61; www.lesresistants. fr; 16-18 rue du Château d'Eau, 10e; 2-/3-course lunch menu €16.50/18.50, mains €19-25; ☻noon-2pm & 7-10.30pm Tue-Sat; MChâteau d'Eau) Natural oak, marble and stone blend seamlessly with a profusion of over-sized wicker lampshades and green foliage at this wildly popular, contemporary restaurant in the increasingly foodie 10e. Fresh seasonal produce used by chef Clément Desbans is responsibly sourced from artisan producers all over France or elsewhere, to magical effect.

LE FAHAM   FUSION €€

Map p385 (☑01 53 81 48 18; www.lefaham.com; 108 rue Cardinet, 17e; 2-/3-course weekday lunch menu €26/32, 6-course tasting menu €69, mains €29-32; ☻noon-2pm & 7.30-9.30pm Tue-Sat; MVilliers, Pont Cardinet) Named after an orchid used to flavour rum on the Île de la Réunion, this modern bistro is the love child of *Top Chef* candidate Kelly Rangama and *pâtissier* Jérôme Devreese, who take your tastebuds to the Indian Ocean and beyond with dishes like scallops with spicy black pudding and bourbon-beer sauce. For dessert: cinnamon-laced sweet-potato *tatin* and sorbet. Reservations essential.

ABRI   BISTRO €€

Map p382 (☑01 83 97 00 00; www.abrirestau rant.fr; 92 rue du Faubourg Poissonnière, 9e; tasting menu lunch/dinner €55/65, dinner mains €17-22; ☻12.15-2pm & 7.15-10pm Tue-Sat; MPoissonnière) It's no bigger than a shoebox and the decor is borderline nonexistent, but that's all part of the charm. Katsuaki Okiyama is a seriously talented chef with an artistic flair, and his surprise tasting menus are exceptional. On Saturdays, a giant gourmet sandwich (€14) is all that's served for lunch.

MARROW   BISTRO €€

Map p382 (☑09 81 34 57 00; 128 rue du Faubourg St-Martin, 10e; mains €15-19; ☻kitchen 6-10pm Tue-Sat, bar to 2am, closed Aug; MGare de l'Est) Hay-smoked quail with peat vinaigrette, grilled octopus with fennel confit, and roast bone marrow are among the adventurous flavour combinations from Hugo Blanchet, who partnered with mixologist Arthur Combe to open this gourmet neobistro. Cheese aficionados won't be able to resist the caramelised *chèvre frais* (fresh goat's cheese) as the *fromage* course.

BELLE MAISON   SEAFOOD €€

Map p378 (☑01 42 81 11 00; 4 rue de Navarin, 9e; mains €22-23; ☻12.30-2pm & 7.30-10pm Tue-Sat; MSt-Georges) With hip blue-and-white-tiled decor in happening SoPi (south Pigalle), Belle Maison is always busy. It's named after a small beach on Île d'Yeu, off France's Atlantic coast, where the owners holiday. Here, the kitchen cooks up scallops, oysters, cockles and other shellfish aplenty. Sophisticated mains include Earl Grey–marinated mullet and grilled mackerel with crispy wasabi root and miso caramel.

MONTMARTRE & NORTHERN PARIS EATING

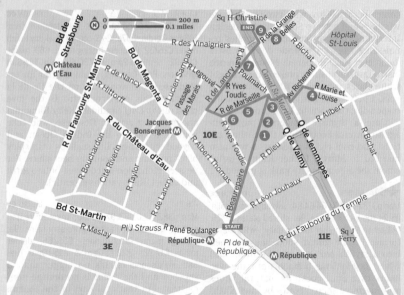

Local Life
Exploring Canal St-Martin

Bordered by shaded towpaths and criss-crossed with iron footbridges, Canal St-Martin wends through the city's northern neighbourhoods. Stroll among this rejuvenated *quartier*'s fashionable cafes, bars and boutiques to appreciate why it's so beloved by Parisian creatives.

❶ Vintage Fashion
Flip through colour-coded racks of brand-name cast-offs at vintage boutique **Frivoli** (Map p382; www.facebook.com/frivolidepot; 26 rue Beaurepaire, 10e; ⊙1-7pm Mon, 11am-7pm Tue-Fri, 2-7pm Sat & Sun; Ⓜ République, Jacques Bonsergent) on boutique-lined rue Beaurepaire, a lively street for fashion and homewares shopping.

❷ Culture Vulture
Local artwork is displayed at **Espace Beaurepaire** (Map p382; ☎01 42 45 59 64; www.espacebeaurepaire.com; 28 rue Beaurepaire, 10e; Ⓜ Jacques Bonsergent) FREE, a gallery and cultural centre that also hosts events such as book signings, pop-up concept stores and dance performances.

❸ Canal-side Cafes
Watch the passing boats from **Chez Prune** (Map p382; 36 rue Beaurepaire, 10e; ⊙8am-2am Mon-Sat, 10am-2am Sun; Ⓜ Jacques Bon-

sergent, République), the vibrant vintage cafe that put Canal St-Martin on the map.

❹ Baker at Work
Cross the canal to watch artisan bakers at work and grab an out-of-this-world *chausson aux pommes* (apple turnover) to go at Sain (p144), the gourmet kitchen-bakery of chef Anthony Courteille.

❺ Alternative Médecine
Among the famous Parisian brands on boutique-laden rue de Marseille, don't miss the gorgeous handmade jewellery at studio-showroom **Medecine Douce** (Map p382; www.bijouxmedecinedouce.com; 10 rue de Marseille, 10e; ⊙11am-7pm Mon-Sat; Ⓜ Jacques Bonsergent).

❻ L'Heure du Gôuter
Join locals snacking on sweet *escargots* ('snails'), croissants and other pastries at Belle Époque bakery Du Pain et des Ideés (p144).

Canal St-Martin

7 Designer Books & Looks

Artazart (Map p382; www.artazart.com; 83 quai de Valmy, 10e; ☉10.30am-7.30pm Mon-Fri, from 11am Sat, from 1pm Sun; Ⓜ Jacques Bonsergent) is Paris' leading design bookshop and also stocks quirky collector's items, such as pinhole cameras and upcycled messenger bags.

8 Specialist Coffee

Lively coffee shop **Ten Belles** (Map p382; ☎09 83 08 86 69; www.tenbelles.com; 10 rue de la Grange aux Belles, 10e; dishes €3-7; ☉8.30am-5pm Mon-Fri, 9am-6pm Sat & Sun; ☎; Ⓜ Jacques Bonsergent), with pavement tables a stone's skim from the canal, serves Belleville Brûlerie coffee and house-baked scones, cakes and savoury light bites.

9 Historic Hotel & Cafe

Watch the canal's vintage road bridge swing open to let boats pass from the terrace of historic hotel-turned-bistro **Hôtel du Nord** (Map p382; ☎01 40 40 78 78; www.hoteldunord.org; 102 quai de Jemmapes, 10e; ☉10am-1.30am; ☎; Ⓜ Jacques Bonsergent), the setting for Marcel Carné's 1938 film of the same name.

CUISINE   BISTRO €€

Map p378 (☎01 44 63 75 64; www.restaurant cuisine.fr; 50 rue Condorcet, 9e; 2-/3-course lunch menu €18/22, mains €21-23; ☉7.30-10pm Mon, noon-2pm & 7.30-10pm Tue-Fri; Ⓜ Pigalle, Anvers) The menu might be short – just a handful of starters, desserts and two mains – but chef Takao Inazawa carefully selects every last organic product to produce startling Japanese-French fusion dishes like horse-mackerel tartare spiced with mint-shiso and Japanese ginger or veal-brain tempura. Snag a table on the pavement terrace to admire the bistro's gorgeous soft-green, 1960s marble façade while dining.

LE BON, LA BUTTE   BISTRO €€

Map p378 (☎09 70 93 55 52; www.lebonlabutte. fr; 102ter rue Lepic, 18e; lunch/dinner menu €20/30, mains €20-40; ☉7pm-1am Wed & Thu, noon-2.30pm & 7pm-1am Fri & Sat, noon-4pm & 7pm-1am Sun; Ⓜ Abbesses) It's hard to resist the traditional mushroom-painted façade and line-up of emerald-green wine bottles in the window of this neighbourhood bistro. Plunge into its vintage interior, complete with wooden bar, tables and chairs, and enjoy delicious cooking by chef David, paired with interesting biodynamic wines by small French producers courtesy of sommelier Thibaut.

BOUILLON 47   BISTRO €€

Map p378 (☎09 51 18 66 59; www.restaurant bouillon.fr; 47 rue de Rochechouart, 9e; 2-/3-course midweek lunch menu €21/28, dinner menu €42, mains €26; ☉noon-2.30pm & 7-11pm Tue-Sat; Ⓜ Cadet, Anvers) It seats little more than 20 people inside and out, making reservations essential at this popular bistro known for its seasonal French cuisine. Begin with seared scallops in a watercress sauce, followed by pigeon with stuffed cabbage and candied garlic. French boutique cheeses served with sweet fig confit or pear *tatin* and verbena ice cream make for an admirable finale.

LE POTAGER DE CHARLOTTE   VEGAN €€

Map p378 (☎01 44 65 09 63; www.lepotagerde charlotte.fr; 12 rue de la Tour d'Auvergne, 9e; mains €18-21, Sunday brunch €30; ☉7-10pm Tue-Thu, noon-2.30pm & 7-10pm Fri & Sat, 11am-3pm Sun; ☎; Ⓜ Cadet) Vegan brothers David and Adrien are dedicated to gourmet plant-based cuisine. Farmers market–sourced ingredients come together in dishes like chickpea and rice pancakes with cashew cream, and quinoa with pomegranate, marinated tofu and roasted hazelnuts. Sunday brunch is an all-in feast of granola, pancakes, avocado, hummus and more (also available à la carte).

RESTAURANT KEN KAWASAKI FUSION €€€

Map p378 (📞09 70 95 98 32; www.restaurant kenkawasaki.fr; 15 rue Caulaincourt, 18e; 5-/8-course tasting menu €45/90; ⏱12.30-1.30pm & 7.30-9.30pm Tue-Sat; MAbbesses, Blanche) Japanese minimalism at its finest: this tiny restaurant with one large shared table and crisp white walls adorned with Monet-style oils showcases the Michelin-starred cuisine of chef Ken Kawasaki. The surprise menu changes monthly and excites tastebuds with a melody of French and Japanese flavours. For the ultimate treat, marry your meal with a trio of wine or sake pairings (€30).

ASPIC BISTRO €€€

Map p378 (📞09 82 49 30 98; www.aspic-restau rant.fr; 24 rue de la Tour d'Auvergne, 9e; 7-course tasting menu €75, with wine €118; ⏱7.30-10pm Tue-Sat; 📶; MAnvers) Chef Quentin Giroud ditched the high-flying world of finance for the stoves, and this small, vintage-style space with semi-open kitchen is testament to his conviction – as is his Michelin star. No-choice, weekly changing tasting menus feature inspired creations like salt-roasted beetroot with lobster bisque mousse, skin-on plaice with popcorn capers, and celeriac with mustard shoots and grated raw cauliflower.

🍷 DRINKING & NIGHTLIFE

Crowded around place Pigalle at the foot of Montmartre you'll find an eclectic selection of nightlife options, from local cafes and hipster dives to dance clubs and hostess bars. In contrast, the trend around the Canal St-Martin is more barista-run cafes, though wonderful summer nights (and days) see everyone decamp to the canal-side quays with blankets, baguettes and bottles of wine. In the 10e, parallel rue du Faubourg St-Martin and rue du Faubourg St-Denis and surrounding streets are speckled with cocktail bars, hybrid bistro-bars and hip cafes.

★DÉVIANT WINE BAR

Map p382 (📞01 48 24 66 79; www.vivantparis. com/deviant; 39 rue des Petites Écuries, 10e; ⏱7pm-late Tue-Sat; MPoissonnière, Bonne Nouvelle) The latest creation of talented chef Pierre Touitou of nearby Vivant, this jam-packed wine bar lures foodies and fashionistas with its huge selection of natural wines by the glass and exquisite small plates to share. Don't expect tables – the drinking, dining 'n' hobnobbing action goes on around a spectacular, long black-and-white marble bar.

★LE TRÈS PARTICULIER COCKTAIL BAR

Map p378 (📞01 53 41 81 40; www.hotelparticu lier.com; 23 av Junot, 18e; ⏱6pm-2am Tue-Sat; MLamarck–Caulaincourt) The clandestine cocktail bar of boutique Hôtel Particulier Montmartre is an entrancing spot for a summertime alfresco cocktail. Each cocktail is inspired by a film and comes with tasting notes. Ring the buzzer at the unmarked black gated entrance and make a beeline for the 1871 mansion's flowery walled garden (or, if it's raining, the lavish conservatory-style interior).

★LE PAVILLON PUEBLA BEER GARDEN

Map p384 (📞01 42 39 34 20; www.leperchoir.fr; 39 av Simon Bolivar, 19e; ⏱6pm-midnight Tue-Sat, 1-9pm Sun; 📶; MButtes Chaumont, Pyrénées) The folks running the hugely successful rooftop bar Le Perchoir (p174) are also behind this enchanting, self-proclaimed 'temple du bonheur' (temple of happiness), evocative of an old-fashioned guinguette (outdoor tavern/dance venue) in Parc des Buttes Chaumont. Fairy lights illuminate, while Moroccan decor with contemporary furniture gives the interior of the 19th-century pavilion a cool 21st-century edge. DJs play Fridays and Saturdays.

Cocktails, craft beers and pizza keep the bar staff busy all night, and kids are catered for with activities (workshops, games, colouring and shared pizzas) on Sundays.

★LE SYNDICAT COCKTAIL BAR

Map p382 (www.syndicatcocktailclub.com; 51 rue du Faubourg St-Denis, 10e; ⏱6pm-2am; MChâteau d'Eau) Plastered top to bottom in peeling posters, an otherwise unmarked façade conceals one of Paris' hottest cocktail bars, but it's no fly-by-night. Le Syndicat's subtitle, Organisation de Défense des Spiritueux Français, reflects its impassioned commitment to French spirits. Ingeniously crafted (and named) cocktails include Saix en Provence (Armagnac, chilli-spiced watermelon syrup, lemon and lavender). Table reservations highly recommended.

GRAVITY BAR
COCKTAIL BAR

Map p382 (☑06 98 54 92 49; www.facebook.com/gravitybar; 44 rue des Vinaigriers, 10e; ⊙6pm-2am Wed-Sat, 5pm-midnight Sun & Mon; MJacques Bonsergent) Gravity's wave-like interior, crafted from slats of plywood descending to the curved concrete bar, threatens to distract from the business at hand – serious cocktails, such as Back to My Roots (Provence herb–infused vodka, vermouth, raspberry puree and lemon juice), best partaken in the company of excellent and inventive tapas-style small plates such as octopus croquettes.

PANAME BREWING COMPANY
BREWERY

Map p384 (☑01 40 36 43 55; www.panamebrewingcompany.com; 41bis quai de la Loire, 19e; ⊙11am-2am; ☎; MCrimée, Laumiere) Spectacularly situated in an industrial 1850s former granary on Bassin de la Villette, Paname's taproom has floor-to-ceiling windows and opens on to a terrace shaded by an ancient cherry tree and a floating table-strewn pontoon. Its five seasonal beers typically include a pilsner, session, märzen, Berliner Weisse, pale ale or IPA (look out for them around Paris too).

LA FONTAINE DE BELLEVILLE
COFFEE

Map p382 (☑09 81 75 54 54; www.cafesbelleville.com; 31-33 rue Juliette Dodu, 10e; ⊙8am-10pm Wed-Sun; ☎; MColonel Fabien) This seemingly traditional neighbourhood cafe with gold lettering, woven sky-blue-and-cream bistro chairs and vintage fittings is so much more than that. Showcasing expertly roasted beans by Parisian coffee roastery Belleville Brûlerie, it's a hotspot for excellent coffee, all-day food and fantastic live jazz every Saturday from 4.30pm to 7.30pm.

LULU WHITE
COCKTAIL BAR

Map p378 (www.luluwhite.bar; 12 rue Frochot, 9e; ⊙7pm-2am Mon, Wed, Thu & Sun, to 4am Fri & Sat; MPigalle) Sip absinthe-based cocktails in Prohibition-era New Orleans surrounds at this elegant, serious and supremely busy cocktail bar named for an infamous early-20th-century brothel owner. It hosts regular live jazz and folk music – bring your dancing shoes.

LOCAL KNOWLEDGE

ROOFTOP BARS

As if this edgy part of Paris doesn't already offer a kaleidoscope of drinking possibilities on ground level, its rooftops hide away a bevy of sunset-hot rooftop bars. Those atop Le Grand Quartier (p284), Terrass" Hôtel (p285) and Generator Hostel (p283) are perfect places to end the day with a mellow, early-evening apéritif. After dark, the party pace quickens at rooftops bars La Machine du Moulin Rouge (p150) and Point Éphémère (p150).

LIPSTICK
COCKTAIL BAR

Map p378 (www.facebook.com/Lipstickbar; 5 rue Frochot, 9e; ⊙6pm-5am Tue-Sat; MPigalle) If the name isn't a clue, the decor certainly is: its bordello-like leopard-print lounges, red-velour drapes and a pole in the centre of the bar reflect its former incarnation as a brothel in this gentrifying red-light district. Stupendous cocktails (€8 to €10) include Lip Smash (rum, Angostura bitters, ginger, lime and red-fruit coulis).

Happy hour cocktails from 6pm to 10pm kick off the party; DJs play on Fridays and Saturdays from 11pm.

CAFÉ LOMI
COFFEE

Map p382 (☑09 51 27 46 31; www.lomi.coffee; 3ter rue Marcadet, 18e; ⊙8am-6pm Tue-Sat; ☎; MMarcadet–Poissonnière) Lomi's internationally sourced beans are roasted here on-site in multiethnic La Goutte d'Or, adjacent to its cafe. Brews include filter coffee (mug, Aeropress or Chemex) and wacky creations like Bleu d'Auvergne cheese dipped in espresso or tonic water with espresso. Laptops are welcome and it serves breakfast, lunch and weekend brunch, making it a popular chill-work address in the 18e.

DIRTY DICK
COCKTAIL BAR

Map p378 (☑01 48 78 74 58; www.facebook.com/dirtydickparis; 10 rue Frochot, 9e; ⊙6pm-2am; MPigalle) A steely black façade, dim interior lighting and tropical decor inject an exotic vibe into the city's favourite tiki bar. Punch bowls serve up to four people; tropical cocktails include the Monkey Seed (pineapple-infused whisky with banana and salted caramel).

MONTMARTRE & NORTHERN PARIS DRINKING & NIGHTLIFE

BERLINER PIGALLE
BAR

Map p378 (www.berliner.paris; 14 rue Frochot, 9e; ☺6pm-2am Mon-Sat; MPigalle) For a change from the craft-cocktail norm on bar-lined rue Frochot, duck into this Berliner bar for a beer and *currywurst* (sausage with curry sauce), Berliner dog or salt-spiked *bretzel* (large pretzel). Like its big sister Berliner Wunderbar in Bastille, it sports dozens of different German beers, on tap and bottled, plus cocktails and Hamburg's original Fritz-Kola in various flavours.

HARDWARE SOCIÉTÉ
COFFEE

Map p378 (☎01 42 51 69 03; 10 rue Lamarck, 18e; ☺9.30am-3.30pm Thu, Fri & Mon, to 4pm Sat & Sun; ☎; MChâteau Rouge) A handy refreshment stop pre- or post-visit to Sacré-Cœur, this Parisian outpost of Melbourne's Hardware Société cooks up barista-crafted coffee (using beans from Melbourne's Padre roastery) and bountiful breakfasts and lunches in a cramped interior with jazzy, Christian Lacroix butterfly wallpaper. Brunch aficionados swear by both the sweet pan-fried brioche and the pork belly with fried eggs sunny-side-up.

LA MACHINE DU MOULIN ROUGE
CLUB

Map p378 (☎01 53 41 88 89; www.lamachinedu moulinrouge.com; 90 bd de Clichy, 18e; ☺club midnight-6am Fri & Sat, bar 6pm-midnight Wed & Thu, 6pm-2am Fri, noon-2am Sat, noon-4pm Sun; MBlanche) Part of the original Moulin Rouge (well, the boiler room, anyway), this club packs 'em in on weekends with a dance floor, concert hall, the Bar à Bulles (aka Champagne bar), an outdoor terrace and rooftop. Live sounds include rock, metal, hip-hop and jazz. Check the club agenda and buy tickets online.

> **BEER TALK**
> ....
> An earthy reflection of northern Paris' gutsy, multi-ethnic *quartier* of La Goutte d'Or, craft brewery **Brasserie la Goutte d'Or** (Map p382; ☎09 80 64 23 51; www.brasserielagouttedor.com; 28 rue de la Goutte d'Or, 18e; ☺4-7pm Tue-Sat; MChâteau Rouge, Barbès-Rochechouart) FREE is the brainchild of brewmaster Thierry Roche, who turns to the local 'hood for inspiration: spicy red beer 'Château Rouge' is named after the local metro station; fruity India pale ale 'Ernestine' evokes the street in La Goutte d'Or where beer was brewed in the early 1900s; 'Petite Pigalle' evokes the cabarets of Pigalle. Taste and buy in its taproom, and check its Facebook page for upcoming events, including themed pairings, live music, informal guided tours and so on.

⭐ ENTERTAINMENT

Diverse venues in this vast neighbourhood range from iconic cabarets and hallowed concert halls to intimate jazz clubs, edgy arts centres and a host of stages at Parc de la Villette.

⭐PHILHARMONIE DE PARIS
CONCERT VENUE

Map p384 (☎01 44 84 44 84; www.philharmonie deparis.fr; 221 av Jean Jaurès, 19e; ☺box office noon-6pm Tue-Fri, 10am-6pm Sat & Sun, plus concerts; MPorte de Pantin) Major complex Cité de la Musique – Philharmonie de Paris hosts an eclectic range of concerts, from classical to North African and Japanese, in the Philharmonie building's Grande Salle Pierre Boulez, with an audience capacity of 2400 to 3600. The adjacent Cité de la Musique's Salle des Concerts has a capacity of 900 to 1600.

POINT ÉPHÉMÈRE
LIVE MUSIC

Map p382 (☎01 40 34 02 48; www.pointephemere. org; 200 quai de Valmy, 10e; ☺noon-2am Mon-Sat, to 11pm Sun; ☎; MJaurès, Louis Blanc) On the banks of Canal St-Martin in a former fire station and later squat, this arts and music venue attracts an underground crowd for concerts, dance nights and art exhibitions. There's a restaurant and hip rooftop bar, Le Top, which buzzes with activity in fine weather.

LE DIVAN DU MONDE & MADAME ARTHUR
LIVE MUSIC

Map p378 (☎01 40 05 08 10; www.madamearthur. fr; 75 rue des Martyrs, 18e; cabaret before 10pm €20, club from midnight Fri & Sat/Wed & Thu €15/free; ☺8pm-6am Wed-Sat; MPigalle) Very much an iconic, cross-cultural address at the foot of Montmartre, this hybrid cabaret-club has played host to cabaret troupe Madame Arthur since 1946. The first show is at 8pm, and the dance floor thrives with clubbers from midnight. Soirées are themed around a music genre, band or artist: 100% *musique française,* Britney Spears, 1980s

French pop group Les Rita Mitsouko, Françoise Hardy etc.

Dress code: no shorts, flip-flops or sports trainers/sneakers.

MOULIN ROUGE   CABARET

Map p378 (☑01 53 09 82 82; www.moulinrouge.fr; 82 bd de Clichy, 18e; show only from €88, dinner & show from €190; ☺show only 9pm & 11pm, dinner & show 7pm; ⓂBlanche) Immortalised in Toulouse-Lautrec's posters and later in Baz Luhrmann's film, Paris' legendary cabaret twinkles beneath a 1925 replica of its original red windmill. Yes, it's packed with bus-tour crowds, but from the opening bars of music to the last high cancan kick, it's a whirl of fantastical costumes, sets, choreography and Champagne. Book in advance and dress smartly (no trainers/sneakers).

No entry for children under six years.

LA CIGALE   LIVE MUSIC

Map p378 (☑01 49 25 89 99; www.lacigale.fr; 120 bd de Rochechouart, 18e; ⓂPigalle) Now classed as a historical monument, this music hall dates from 1887 but was redecorated a century later by Philippe Starck. Artists who have performed here include Ryan Adams, Ibrahim Maalouf and the Dandy Warhols.

LE LOUXOR   CINEMA

Map p382 (☑01 44 63 96 98; www.cinemalouxor.fr; 170 bd de Magenta, 10e; tickets adult/child €9.90/5; ⓂBarbès-Rochechouart) Built in neo-Egyptian art deco style in 1921 and saved from demolition by a neighbourhood association seven decades later, this historical monument is a palatial place to catch new releases, classics, piano-accompanied 'ciné-concerts', short-film festivals, special workshops (such as singalongs) or live-music performances. Don't miss a drink at its bar, which opens onto an elevated terrace overlooking Sacré-Cœur.

BUS PALLADIUM   LIVE MUSIC

Map p378 (☑01 45 26 80 35; www.buspalladium.com; 6 rue Pierre Fontaine, 9e; ☺Tue-Sat; ⓂPigalle, Blanche) The place to be in the 1960s (Dalí, Hallyday and Jagger all hung out here), the Bus is back in business half-a-century later, with a mixed bag of performances by DJs and indie and pop groups.

NEW MORNING   JAZZ, BLUES

Map p382 (☑01 45 23 51 41; www.newmorning.com; 7 & 9 rue des Petites Écuries, 10e; ☺hours vary; ⓂChâteau d'Eau) This highly regarded auditorium with excellent acoustics hosts big-name jazz concerts (Ravi Coltrane, Lake Street Dive) as well as a variety of blues, rock, funk, salsa, Afro-Cuban and Brazilian music.

AU LAPIN AGILE   CABARET

Map p378 (☑01 46 06 85 87; www.au-lapin-agile.com; 22 rue des Saules, 18e; adult €28, student except Sat €20; ☺9pm-1am Tue-Sun; ⓂLamarck–Caulaincourt) Named after *Le Lapin à Gill*, a mural of a rabbit jumping out of a cooking pot by caricaturist André Gill, which can still be seen on the western exterior wall, this rustic cabaret venue was favoured by artists and intellectuals in the early 20th century and traditional *chansons* are still performed here. The evening-long show includes singing and poetry.

LA SCALA PARIS   PERFORMING ARTS

Map p382 (☑01 40 03 44 30; www.lascala-paris.com; 13 bd de Strasbourg, 10e; ⓂStrasbourg–St-Denis) Dance, circus arts, concerts and multimedia productions all feature at this 550-capacity theatre.

🛍 SHOPPING

Montmartre screams crass keyring-filled souvenir shops, but there are quality specialist boutiques selling everything from handcrafted jewellery to antique perfume bottles, plus classic vinyl and vintage fashion to be found. Gourmets will enjoy the food shops on rue des Martyrs in Pigalle, while rue Beaurepaire and rue de Marseille by Canal St-Martin are for discerning fashion lovers. For alternative and/or sustainable fashion, design and pop-up concept stores, the edgiest strips to watch are rue du Château d'Eau, 10e, and rue des Dames in upcoming Batignolles. North of all this sprawls Paris' gargantuan Marché aux Puces de St-Ouen flea market.

★SÉZANE   FASHION & ACCESSORIES

Map p385 (Le Libre Service; www.sezane.com; 63 bd Batignolles, 17e; ☺11am-8pm Mon-Sat; ⓂVilliers) As if fashionistas needed any confirmation that northern Paris' *'nouveau quartier'* Clichy-Batignolles is the place to be: iconic fashion brand Sézane has opened its first self-service concept store in a cavernous space overlooking place Prosper-Goubaux. Alongside the season's collection

FLEA MARKET

Spanning nine hectares, vast **Marché aux Puces de St-Ouen** (www.pucesdeparis-saintouen.com; rue des Rosiers, St-Ouen; ☉Sat-Mon; ⓂPorte de Clignancourt) was founded in 1870 and is said to be Europe's largest flea market. More than 2000 stalls are grouped into 15 *marchés* (markets) selling everything from 17th-century furniture to 21st-century clothing. Each market has different opening hours – check the website for details. There are miles upon miles of 'freelance' stalls; come prepared to spend some time. Dining options include the legendary **Chez Louisette** (☏01 40 10 12 14; Marché Vernaison, allée 10, 136 av Michelet, St-Ouen; mains €14.50-20; ☉11am-7pm Sat-Mon; ⓂPorte de Clignancourt), a popular 1930s *guinguette* (cafe-bar with outdoor dancing) where singers perform rousing French *chansons* with the merry accompaniment of an accordion.

for women, there's the brand's signature knitwear wall, a jewellery bar and racks of upcycled vintage wear.

★ **LES RÉCUPÉRABLES** FASHION & ACCESSORIES
Map p382 (www.lesrecuperables.com; 11 rue des Gardes, 18e; ☉10am-6pm Mon-Wed, to 7.30pm Thu & Fri, noon-7.30pm Sat; ⓂChâteau Rouge, Barbès–Rochechouart) 🌿 Eco-conscious Parisian designer Anaïs Dautais Warmel takes unwanted fabric scraps from upholstery workshops and *haute couture* fashion houses in Paris and transforms them into wildly trendy, petrol-blue bomber jackets, cute Dior-inspired dresses, tartan-print trench coats and the like.

★ **THANKS** CONCEPT STORE
Map p378 (www.thanks.paris; 42 rue Condorcet, 9e; ☉10.30am-7.30pm Tue-Sat; ⓂPigalle, Anvers) Former financial-trader-turned-jeweller Arnaud Soulignac is the creative mastermind behind this tiny boutique specialising in stylish and unique homewares, gifts and jewellery – all made in France. The origami-inspired unicorn, swan and triceratops pendants are by the owner himself, and the choice of handmade greeting cards and inspirational posters is particularly tempting.

O/HP/E CONCEPT STORE
Map p382 (www.facebook.com/ohpeparis10; 27 rue du Château d'Eau, 10e; ☉2-7pm Tue, 8.30am-7pm Wed-Fri, 9.30am-7.30pm Sat, 9.30am-6.30pm Sun; ⓂJacques Bonsergent) White-on-white concept store O/HP/E ('Objets Homemade Pâtisserie Épicerie') stocks chic homewares – ceramics, textiles, light fittings, candles and kitchenware – alongside beautiful cosmetics, stationery, gifts

and gourmet delicacies (preserves, nougats, sugar-coated olives and chocolates). Ponder your purchases over coffee and a hazelnut praline tart or other tempting cake in its stylish cafe.

BALADES SONORES MUSIC
Map p378 (☏01 83 87 94 87; www.baladessonores.com; 1-3 av Trudaine, 9e; ☉noon-8pm Mon-Sat, plus 2-7pm 1st Sun of month; ⓂAnvers) One of Paris' best vinyl shops, Balades Sonores sprawls over two adjacent buildings. The ground floor of 1 av Trudaine stocks contemporary pop, rock, metal, garage and French music (all genres). Its basement holds secondhand blues, country, new wave and punk from the '60s to '90s. Next door, No 3 has soul, jazz, funk, hip-hop, electronica and world music.

PIGALLE FASHION & ACCESSORIES
Map p378 (www.pigalle-paris.com; 7 rue Henry Monnier, 9e; ☉noon-8pm Mon-Sat, from 2pm Sun; ⓂSt-Georges) Pick up a hoodie emblazoned with the black-and-white Pigalle logo from this leading Parisian menswear brand, created by designer and basketball player Stéphane Ashpool, who grew up in the 'hood.

LA SEINOGRAPHE ET ATELIER MOUTI CONCEPT STORE
Map p378 (www.shop.la-seinographe.fr; 41 Rue Notre Dame de Lorette, 9e; ☉11am-7.30pm Tue-Sat; ⓂSt-Georges) Bringing together the carefully curated 'Made in France' homewares of lifestyle-blog-turned-boutique La Seinographe and the exquisite paper creations of Atelier Mouti, this stylish boutique is a wonderful spot for gift shopping, with fanciful paper products and textiles, jewellery and other homewares, all crafted in Paris or France.

BELLEVILLE BRÛLERIE   COFFEE

Map p382 (Le Quartier Général; ☎01 42 85 79 37; www.cafesbelleville.com; 14 rue Lally Tollendal, 19e; ⏰10.30am-1pm & 2-6.30pm Wed-Sun; ⓂJaurès) Belleville Brûlerie brought good coffee to Paris and its beans go into some of the best espressos in town. Here at its headquarters, Le Quartier Général, where roasting takes place, you can taste its blends and buy beans to take home.

SPREE   FASHION & ACCESSORIES

Map p378 (www.spree.fr; 16 rue de la Vieuville, 18e; ⏰11am-7.30pm Tue-Sat, 3-7pm Sun; ⓂAbbesses) Allow plenty of time to browse this boutique-gallery, with a carefully selected collection of designer fashion put together by stylist Roberta Oprandi and artist Bruni Hadjadj. What makes shopping here fun is that all the furniture – vintage 1950s to 1980s pieces by Eames and other mid-century designers – is also for sale, as is the contemporary artwork on the walls.

MAISON CHÂTEAU ROUGE   DESIGN

Map p382 (www.maison-chateaurouge.com; 40bis rue Myrha, 18e; ⏰11am-7pm Mon-Sat; ⓂChâteau Rouge) A celebration of grassroots Afro-Parisian culture, contemporary urban fashion label Maison Château Rouge was launched in Paris in 2015 by Youssouf Fofana and his brother, Mamadou. Along with vividly patterned men's and women's clothing (T-shirts, trousers, skirts, dresses and raincoats), its colourful concept store also sells Senegalese music, Bana-Bana bissap juice, African crafts and more.

CENTRE COMMERCIAL   FASHION & ACCESSORIES

Map p382 (www.centrecommercial.cc; 2 rue de Marseille, 10e; ⏰1-7.30pm Mon, 11am-8pm Tue-Sat, 2-7pm Sun; ⓂJacques Bonsergent) 🖊 Just off Canal St-Martin, this concept store is first choice for sustainable French-made fashion for men and women, and lifestyle objects for the home. It was founded by the same eco-conscious duo behind the sustainable footwear brand Veja (p177). Peppermint- and pine-perfumed mug candles, handmade in Paris, make beautiful gifts to take home.

SERGEANT PAPER   STATIONERY

Map p382 (☎01 83 89 99 55; www.sergeantpaper.com; 26 rue du Château d'Eau, 10e; ⏰noon-8pm Tue-Sat, 11am-6pm Sun; ⓂChâteau d'Eau) Framed posters and prints – many featuring the French capital or some aspect of that enviable Parisian lifestyle by top French graphic artists – are for sale at this crisp white space in the alternative 10e.

Le Marais, Ménilmontant & Belleville

Neighbourhood Top Five

❶ Cimetière du Père Lachaise (p157) Admiring tomb art while paying your respects to the rich, famous and infamous in the world's most visited cemetery.

❷ Musée National Picasso (p160) Immersing yourself in the life and art of one of the world's most eccentric modern artists, Pablo Picasso, and admiring the museum's grand 17th-century mansion.

❸ Place des Vosges (p160) Lapping up the grace and architectural beauty of Paris' most elegant square, not missing afternoon tea beneath the arches and a peek around Victor Hugo's former home.

❹ Hôtel de Ville (p161) Taking in a world-class art exhibition for free at Paris' neo-Renaissance city hall.

❺ Mémorial de la Shoah (p156) Gaining a poignant insight into German-occupied Paris and Holocaust horrors.

For more detail of this area see Map p386 and p390. ⇒

Explore Le Marais, Ménilmontant & Belleville

Sublime place des Vosges is a perfect starting point – this elegant city square is a triumph of architectural symmetry. Meander west along busy rue de Rivoli or backstreet rue du Roi de Sicile, with shops, cafes and bars. Essential for history buffs are Mémorial de la Shoah (p156) and Musée Carnavalet (p161).

Bearing north towards the fashionable Haut Marais, strips laden with hip drinking and dining options include rue Vieille du Temple near the Musée National Picasso and rue des Rosiers in the historic Jewish quarter Pletzl. From Haut Marais, bar-busy rue Oberkampf and rue Jean-Pierre Timbaud duck east into grittier Ménilmontant; the crowds disappear in vibrant, multicultural Belleville. Pencil in a half-day for the Cimetière du Père Lachaise (p157) and, in fine weather, stroll alone the river banks, summer host to the Paris Plages (p27) beaches.

Local Life

River life Stroll along the riverside Parc Rives de Seine (p160), play *pétanque* (boules) and sip drinks at water's edge.

Alfresco picnics In hilltop Parc de Belleville (p170) or bandstand-clad square Maurice Gardette (p163).

Zero-waste dining Enjoy wildly different, sustainable dishes by upcoming chefs at pioneering kitchen lab For the Love of Food (p164).

Rooftop cocktails Join Parisians on a fashionable rooftop like Le Perchoir (p174), Le Perchoir Marais (p172) or Au Top (p166).

Franco-Asian cuisine Explore contemporary neobistro culture with Japanese chefs at Maison (p170) and Double Dragon (p168).

Getting There & Away

Metro Lower Marais stops include Hôtel de Ville (lines 1, 11), St-Paul (line 1) and Rambuteau (line 11); for Haut Marais, Filles du Calvaire and St-Sébastien-Froissart (line 8) and Temple (line 3). For Ménilmontant, use Ménilmontant (line 2), Parmentier (line 3) and Oberkampf (lines 5 and 9).

Bus Bus 76 from rue de Rivoli to the 20e and Porte de Bagnolet.

Bicycle Vélib' stations include place de l'Hôtel de Ville, Filles du Calvaire metro station and bd de Belleville.

Boat Hop-on, hop-off **Batobus** (Map p396; quai de l'Hôtel de Ville, 4e; MHôtel de Ville) stops at the Hôtel de Ville.

Lonely Planet's Top Tip

Le Marais is flat, but Ménilmontant becomes hilly and Belleville is (for Paris) super-steep. Save your calf muscles by catching the metro to your easternmost destination to walk or cycle west downhill.

LE MARAIS, MÉNILMONTANT & BELLEVILLE

✕ Best Places to Eat

➡ Jacques Genin (p164)
➡ Breizh Café (p164)
➡ Au Passage (p166)
➡ Au Top (p166)
➡ Maison (p170)

For reviews, see p164.➡

🍷 Best Places to Drink

➡ Le Perchoir (p174)
➡ Grand Café Tortoni (p171)
➡ Le Mary Céleste (p171)
➡ Candelaria (p171)
➡ La Commune (p174)
➡ Bambino (p171)

For reviews, see p171.➡

🔒 Best Shopping

➡ Merci (p177)
➡ Empreintes (p177)
➡ Veja (p177)
➡ Fromagerie Goncourt (p179)
➡ Kerzon (p177)
➡ Samy Chalon (p177)

For reviews, see p177.➡

TOP EXPERIENCE

REFLECT ON THE HOLOCAUST AT MÉMORIAL DE LA SHOAH

Founded in 1956 as a memorial to the unknown Jewish martyr, the Mémorial de la Shoah is now one of Europe's most important Holocaust museums and documentation centres. A vast permanent collection and well-thought-out temporary exhibits all pertain to the Holocaust and the German occupation of parts of France and Paris during WWII.

Victims of the Shoah – a Hebrew word meaning 'catastrophe' that's synonymous in France with the Holocaust – are remembered on the **Mur des Noms** (Wall of Names), a wall of stone from Jerusalem inscribed with the names of 76,000 Jews, including 11,000 children, deported from France to Nazi extermination camps during WWII. Renovation work in late 2019 and early 2020 saw the stone replaced with new Jerusalem stone, allowing 175 since-discovered missing names to be inscribed (in addition to adding 1498 missing birth dates and correcting the spelling of hundreds of existent names). Most victims died in Auschwitz and other camps between 1942 and 1944; only 2500 survived deportation.

Deep in the appropriately sombre, bunker-like building lies the **crypt** and **tomb to the unknown Jewish martyr** – all six million Jews with no grave of their own. Ashes from some Jews who died in death camps and also the Warsaw ghetto are entombed in the Star of David, sculpted from black marble and pierced in its centre with an eternal flame.

DON'T MISS

→ Mur des Noms
→ Crypt
→ Ninety-minute guided tour in English, 3pm second Sunday of month

PRACTICALITIES

→ Map p386, B7
→ 01 42 77 44 72
→ www.memorialdela shoah.org
→ 17 rue Geoffroy l'Asnier, 4e
→ admission free
→ 10am-6.30pm Sun-Wed & Fri, to 10pm Thu
→ M Pont Marie, St-Paul

STOCKBYM/GETTY IMAGES ©

TOP EXPERIENCE
VISIT THE ATMOSPHERIC CIMETIÈRE DU PÈRE LACHAISE

The world's most visited cemetery opened in 1804. Its 44 hectares hold more than 70,000 ornate tombs and a stroll here is akin to exploring a verdant sculpture garden. Père Lachaise was intended as a response to local neighbourhood graveyards being full – at the time, it was groundbreaking for Parisians to be buried outside the *quartier* in which they'd lived.

Among the 800,000-odd buried here are composer Chopin; playwright Molière; poet Apollinaire; writers Balzac, Proust, Gertrude Stein and Colette; and *chanteuse* Édith Piaf alongside her two-year-old daughter. The grave of Irish playwright and humorist **Oscar Wilde** (1854–1900), division 89, is surrounded by a glass barrier to prevent fans impregnating the stone with red lipstick imprints. The other big hitter is 1960s rock star **Jim Morrison** (1943–71), who died in **Le Marais** (Map p386; 17 rue Beautreillis, 4e; Ⓜ St-Paul), division 6. Up in division 92 lies the grave of **Monsieur Noir**, aka journalist Yvan Salman (1848–70), shot aged 22 by Pierre Bonaparte, great-nephew of Napoléon. Legend says women who stroke the amply filled crotch of Monsieur Noir's prostrate bronze effigy will enjoy increased fertility. The **Mur des Fédérés** is a plain brick wall against which Communard insurgents were lined up, shot and buried in a mass grave in 1871.

Approaching the cemetery along bd de Ménilmontant, the **Monument aux Morts Parisiens de la Première Guerre Mondiale** was unveiled on the cemetery's outside western wall on the 2018 centenary of the armistice marking the end of WWI. The 280m-long, black metal panel, engraved with the names of the 94,415 known Parisians killed in combat and another 8000 missing, runs the entire length of the street.

DON'T MISS

→ Jim Morrison
→ Édith Piaf
→ Oscar Wilde
→ Monsieur Noir
→ Mur des Fédérés & war memorials

PRACTICALITIES

→ Map p390, G8
→ ☎ 01 55 25 82 10
→ www.pere-lachaise.com
→ 8 bd de Ménilmontant & 16 rue du Repos, 20e
→ admission free
→ ⏱ 8am-6pm Mon-Fri, from 8.30am Sat, from 9am Sun mid-Mar–Oct, shorter hours Nov–mid-Mar
→ Ⓜ Père Lachaise, Gambetta

Cimetière du Père Lachaise

A HALF-DAY TOUR

There is a certain romance to getting lost in this jungle of graves spun from centuries of tales. But to search for one grave amid the million in this 44-hectare land of the dead requires guidance.

Approaching the main entrance on bd de Ménilmontant, pay your respects at the ❶ **Monument aux Morts Parisiens de la Première Guerre Mondiale**. Inside the cemetery, head up av Principle and turn right onto av du Puits to grab a map at the ❷ **Bureaux de la Conservation**.

Backtrack along av du Puits, turn right onto av Latérale du Sud, scale the stairs and bear right along chemin Denon to New Realist artist ❸ **Arman**, film director ❹ **Claude Chabrol** and ❺ **Chopin**.

Follow chemin Méhul downhill, cross av Casimir Périer and bear right onto chemin Serré. Take the second left (chemin Lebrun – unsigned), head uphill and near the top leave the footpath to weave through graves on your right to rock star ❻ **Jim Morrison**. Back on chemin Lauriston, continue uphill to roundabout ❼ **Rond-Point Casimir Périer**.

Admire the funerary art of contemporary photographer ❽ **André Chabot**, av de la Chapelle. Continue uphill for energising city views from the ❾ **chapel** steps, then zigzag to ❿ **Molière & La Fontaine**, on chemin Molière.

Cut between graves onto av Tranversale No 1 – spot potatoes atop ⓫ **Parmentier's** headstone. Continue straight onto av Greffülhe and left onto av Tranversale No 2 to rub ⓬ **Monsieur Noir's** shiny crotch.

Navigation to ⓭ **Édith Piaf** and the ⓮ **Mur des Fédérés** is straightforward. End with angel-topped ⓮ **Oscar Wilde** near the Porte Gambetta entrance.

TOP TIPS

➡ Père Lachaise is a photographer's paradise any time of the day or year, but best are sunny autumn mornings after the rain.

➡ Cemetery lovers will appreciate themed guided tours (two hours) led by entertaining cemetery historian Thierry Le Roi (www.necro-romantiques.com).

BRUNO DE HOGUES / GETTY IMAGES ©

Chopin, Division 11
Add a devotional note to the handwritten letters and flowers brightening the marble tomb of Polish composer/pianist Frédéric Chopin (1810–49), who spent his short adult life in Paris. His heart is buried in Warsaw.

Jim Morrison, Division 6
The original bust adorning the disgracefully dishevelled grave of Jim Morrison (1943–71), lead singer of The Doors, was stolen. Pay your respects to rock's greatest legend – no chewing gum or padlocks please.

HUANG ZHENG / SHUTTERSTOCK ©

André Chabot, Division 20
Contemporary photographer André Chabot (b 1941) shoots funerary art, hence the bijou 19th-century chapel he's equipped with monumental granite camera – and a QR code in preparation for the day he departs.

Molière & La Fontaine, Division 25
Parisians refused to leave their local *quartier* for Père Lachaise so in 1817 the authorities moved in popular playwright Molière (1622–73) and poet Jean de la Fontaine (1621–95). The marketing strategy worked.

Oscar Wilde, Division 89
Irish writer Oscar Wilde (1854–1900) was forever scandalous: check the enormous packet of the sphinx on his tomb, sculpted by British-American sculptor Jacob Epstein 11 years after Wilde died.

av des Combattants Étrangers morts pour la France

Porte Gambetta Entrance

av Circulaire

Crematorium

88

Chapel

av Feuillant

av Tranversale No 3

89

15

90

av Carette

93

av Tranversale No 1

av Tranversale No 2

50

51

9

av de Saint Morys

92

12

Monsieur Noir, Division 92
Cemetery sex stud Mr Black, alias 21-year-old journalist Victor Noir (1848–70), was shot by Napoléon III's nephew in a botched duel. Urban myth means women rub his crotch to boost fertility.

24

chemin Molière

25

av de la Chapelle

21

8

20

10

42

av Greffülhe

26

11

95

Rond-Point Casimir Périer

7

41

av Pacthod

97

39

13

14

chemin Auriston

14

chemin Lesseps

chemin Maison

6

6

96

av Circulaire

5

35

76

chemin Lebrun

Édith Piaf, Division 97
The archbishop of Paris might have refused Parisian diva Édith Piaf (1915–63) the Catholic rite of burial, but that didn't stop more than 100,000 mourners attending her interment at Père Lachaise.

chemin Serré

Mur des Fédérés, Division 76
This plain brick wall was where 147 Communard insurgents were lined up and shot in 1871. Equally emotive is the sculpted walkway of commemorative war memorials surrounding the mass grave.

Porte de la Réunion

Famille CASSION-PIAF

⊙ SIGHTS

The majority of sights in this neighbourhood concentrate in the narrow, medieval streets and sheltered squares of Le Marais, which are easily accessed on foot. Museums here include an increasing number of cutting-edge art galleries. The Cimetière du Père Lachaise sprawls northeast in the 20e.

⊙ Le Marais

MÉMORIAL DE LA SHOAH   MUSEUM
See p156.

★MUSÉE NATIONAL PICASSO-PARIS   MUSEUM

Map p386 (✆01 85 56 00 36; www.museepicasso paris.fr; 5 rue de Thorigny, 3e; adult/child €14/free; ⊙10.30am-6pm Tue-Fri, from 9.30am Sat & Sun; Ⓜ Chemin Vert, St-Paul) One of Paris' most treasured art collections is showcased inside the mid-17th-century Hôtel Salé, an exquisite private mansion owned by the city since 1964. The Musée National Picasso is a staggering art museum devoted to Spanish artist Pablo Picasso (1881–1973), who spent much of his life living and working in Paris. The collection includes more than 5000 drawings, engravings, paintings, ceramic works and sculptures by the *grand maître* (great master), although they're not all displayed at the same time.

The extraordinary cache of works was donated to the French government by the artist's heirs in lieu of paying inheritance taxes. In addition to the permanent collec-tion, the museum mounts two major tem-porary exhibitions a year (included in the admission price). An audioguide costs €5.

PARC RIVES DE SEINE   PARK

Map p386 (Ⓜ Quai de la Rapée, Pont Marie, Pont Neuf) Following the success of the former expressway turned park on the Left Bank (p233), this 4.5km stretch of Unesco-listed Right Bank is also now a car-free Parisian playground. The park has cycling and walk-ing paths, *pétanque* and other sporting fa-cilities, along with kids play areas, climbing walls, huge chalkboards to write or draw on to your heart's content, plus year-round bars, and hammocks, sunloungers and umbrella-shaded tables in summer.

PLACE DES VOSGES   SQUARE

Map p386 (4e; Ⓜ Bastille, Chemin Vert) Inaug-urated in 1612 as place Royale and thus Paris' oldest square, place des Vosges is a strikingly elegant ensemble of 36 sym-metrical houses with ground-floor arcades, steep slate roofs and large dormer windows arranged around a leafy square with four symmetrical fountains and an 1829 copy of a mounted statue of Louis XIII. The square received its present name in 1800 to honour the Vosges *département* (administrative di-vision) for being the first in France to pay its taxes.

MAISON DE VICTOR HUGO   MUSEUM

Map p386 (✆01 42 72 10 16; www.maisonsvictor hugo.paris.fr; 6 place des Vosges, 4e; ⊙10am-6pm Tue-Sun; Ⓜ Bastille) Between 1832 and 1848, the celebrated novelist and poet Vic-tor Hugo lived in an apartment in Hôtel

---

STREET ART

Unsurprisingly, this creative wedge of Paris has a couple of iconic walls representative of the capital's dynamic street-art scene. To date hundreds of murals have been paint-ed on **Le MUR** (Map p390; www.lemur.fr; rue Oberkampf, 11e; Ⓜ Parmentier), on the south-ern side of the building housing Café Charbon (p175) in Le Marais. 'MUR' ('wall') also stands for Modulable Urbain Réactif (Modular Urban Reactive). Nearby, **Le Mur du Marais** (Map p386; 2 rue des Quatre Fils, 3e; Ⓜ Rambuteau) FREE is another wall-turned-bold street-art canvas, two minutes' walk from the Musée National Picasso (p160).

Heading into Belleville, **rue Dénoyez** (Map p390; 20e; Ⓜ Belleville) was known for years as Paris' most dazzling street art, with everything on the tiny cobbled street – from litter bins and flower pots to lamp posts and window shutters – smothered in colourful graffiti. Commercial development means just one side of the street retains its psychedelic street art. Not far away, on place Fréhel overlooking rue de Belleville, the sharp-tongued **art installation** (Map p390) FREE reading *Il faut se méfier des mots* (Be wary of words), by Niçois artist Ben, is a place of pilgrimage for every self-respecting street-art devotee.

de Rohan-Guéménée, a townhouse overlooking one of Paris' most elegant squares. Hugo moved here a year after the publication of *Notre Dame de Paris* (The Hunchback of Notre Dame), completing *Ruy Blas* during his stay. The museum here, with Hugo's personal drawings and portraits, reopened after extensive renovations, including a new cafe, in 2021.

MUSÉE CARNAVALET
MUSEUM

Map p386 (☑01 44 59 58 58; www.carnavalet. paris.fr; 23 rue de Sévigné, 3e; ☻10am-6pm Tue-Sun, last ticket sales 5.15pm; ⓂSt-Paul, Chemin Vert) Paris' history museum, spanning Gallo-Roman times onwards, rambles over a pair of remarkable *hôtels particuliers* (private mansions), the 1560-built **Hôtel Carnavalet** and 1688-built **Hôtel Le Peletier de St-Fargeau**. The museum reopened in 2021 after a multi-year renovation.

MUSÉE DES ARTS ET MÉTIERS
MUSEUM

Map p386 (☑01 53 01 82 75; www.arts-et-metiers. net; 60 rue de Réaumur, 3e; adult/child €8/free, 6-9pm Fri & 1st Sun of month free; ☻10am-6pm Tue-Thu, Sat & Sun, to 9pm Fri; ⓂArts et Métiers) The Arts and Crafts Museum, dating to 1794 and Europe's oldest science and technology museum, is a must for families – or anyone with an interest in how things tick or work. Housed inside the sublime 18th-century priory of St-Martin des Champs, some 2400 instruments, machines and working models from the 18th to 20th centuries are displayed across three floors. In the priory's attached church is Foucault's original pendulum, introduced to the world at the Universal Exhibition in Paris in 1855.

LAFAYETTE ANTICIPATIONS
ARTS CENTRE

Map p386 (Fondation d'entreprise Galeries Lafayette; ☑01 57 40 64 17; www.lafayetteanticipati ons.com; 9 rue du Plâtre, 4e; ☻11am-7pm Mon, Wed, Sat & Sun, to 8pm Thu & Fri; ⓂRambuteau) FREE The corporate foundation of French retailer Galeries Lafayette opened this unique multidisciplinary space for producing, experimenting with and exhibiting new works of contemporary art, design and fashion. Transformed in 2018 by architect Rem Koolhaas, the 1891 building now has 2500 sq metres of exhibition space and a striking 18m-high glass tower. Three to four free exhibitions take place annually, alongside ticketed performances and workshops.

FROM MARSH TO À LA MODE

The Marais (meaning 'marsh' or 'swamp' in French) was exactly what its name implies until the 13th century, when it was converted to farmland. In the early 17th century, Henri IV built place Royale (today's place des Vosges), turning the area into Paris' most fashionable residential address. When the aristocracy moved out of Paris to Versailles and Faubourg St-Germain in the 18th century, Le Marais' townhouses passed into the hands of ordinary Parisians. The 110-hectare area was given a major facelift in the late 1960s and early '70s, and today it is one of the city's most coveted, fashionable and à la mode addresses.

HÔTEL DE VILLE
ARCHITECTURE

Map p386 (www.paris.fr; place de l'Hôtel de Ville, 4e; ⓂHôtel de Ville) FREE Paris' beautiful town hall was gutted during the Paris Commune of 1871 and rebuilt in luxurious neo-Renaissance style between 1874 and 1882. The ornate façade is decorated with 108 statues of illustrious Parisians, and its temporary exhibitions (admission free; enter at 29 rue de Rivoli) have a Parisian theme.

MUSÉE COGNACQ-JAY
MUSEUM

Map p386 (☑01 40 27 07 21; www.museecognac qjay.paris.fr; 8 rue Elzévir, 3e; ☻10am-6pm Tue-Sun; ⓂSt-Paul, Chemin Vert) FREE This museum inside the Hôtel de Donon displays oil paintings, pastels, sculpture, *objets d'art*, jewellery, porcelain and furniture from the 18th century, assembled by Ernest Cognacq (1839–1928), founder of La Samaritaine department store, and his wife Louise Jay. Although Cognacq appreciated little of his collection, boasting that he had never visited the Louvre and was only acquiring collections for the status, the artwork and *objets d'art* give a good idea of upper-class tastes during the Age of Enlightenment.

PAVILLON DE L'ARSENAL
MUSEUM

(www.pavillon-arsenal.com; 21 bd Morland, 4e; ☻11am-7pm Tue-Sun; ⓂSully–Morland) FREE Built in 1879 as a museum, this magnificent glass-roofed building with arched wrought-iron girders wasn't actually used as one until over a century later, when it opened as a centre for Parisian urbanism and architecture. Exhibitions (30 per year) showcase the city's

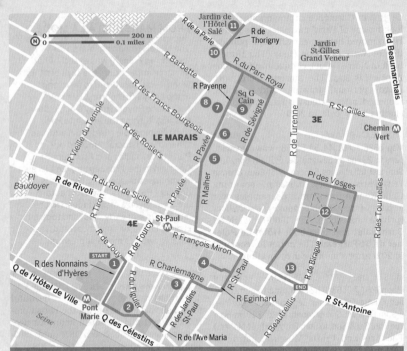

Neighbourhood Walk
Medieval Marais Meanderings

START HÔTEL D'AUMONT
END HÔTEL DE SULLY
LENGTH 2.6KM; TWO HOURS

While Henri IV was busy building place Royale (today's place des Vosges), aristocrats were commissioning *hôtels particuliers* (private mansions) – beautiful Renaissance structures that lend Le Marais a notable architectural harmony. At 7 rue de Jouy stands majestic ❶ **Hôtel d'Aumont**, built in 1648 for a king's councillor. Continue south along rue des Nonnains d'Hyères and turn left onto rue de l'Hôtel de Ville; at 1 rue du Figuier is ❷ **Hôtel de Sens**, the oldest Marais mansion with geometric gardens and neogothic turret. It was begun around 1475 for the archbishops of Sens and restored in 1930.

Head northeast along rue des Jardins de St-Paul. To the left, two truncated towers are all that remain of Philippe-Auguste's ❸ **enceinte**, a fortified wall built between 1190 and 1209 and once guarded by 77 towers. Cross rue Charlemagne, duck into

rue Eginhard and follow it to rue St-Paul and ❹ **Église St-Paul St-Louis** (1641). At the end of rue St-Paul, turn left, then walk north up rue Malher and rue Pavée, the first cobbled road in Paris. At No 24 is late-Renaissance ❺ **Hôtel Lamoignon**, built for Diane de France (1538–1619), the legitimised daughter of Henri II.

North along rue Payenne is the rear of the ❻ **Musée Carnavalet** (p161); the Revolutionary-era 'Temple of Reason' ❼ **Chapelle de l'Humanité** at No 5; and the back of the ❽ **Musée Cognacq-Jay** (p161). From grassy ❾ **square George Cain** opposite 11 rue Payenne, walk northwest to more spectacular 17th-century *hôtels particuliers*: ❿ **Hôtel de Libéral Bruant** (1 rue de la Perle) and Hôtel Salé, aka the ⓫ **Musée National Picasso** (p160).

Retrace your steps to rue du Parc Royal, walk south down rue de Sévigné and follow rue des Francs Bourgeois eastwards to end with sublime ⓬ **place des Vosges** (p160) and ⓭ **Hôtel de Sully**.

past, present and future. Interpretative information is in French but it's fascinating for anyone with an interest in the evolution of Paris. There's a small but excellent architectural bookshop on the ground floor.

MAISON EUROPÉENNE DE LA PHOTOGRAPHIE
MUSEUM

Map p386 (MEP; www.mep-fr.org; 5-7 rue de Fourcy, 4e; adult/child €10/6; ⊙11am-8pm Wed & Fri-Sun, to 10pm Thu; MSt-Paul) The European House of Photography, housed in the overly renovated Hôtel Hénault de Cantobre (dating – believe it or not – from the early 18th century), has cutting-edge temporary exhibits (usually retrospectives on single photographers), as well as an enormous permanent collection on the history of photography and its connections with France.

FONDATION HENRI CARTIER-BRESSON
MUSEUM

Map p386 (☑01 40 61 50 50; www.henricartier-bresson.org; 79 rue des Archives, 3e; adult/child €9/free; ⊙11am-7pm Tue-Sun; MArts et Métiers) Founded by renowned French humanist photographer Henri Cartier-Bresson (1908–2004) and his portrait-photographer wife Martine Franck (1938–2012), this gallery displays their works and also mounts rotating exhibitions by French and international photographers. Cartier-Bresson pioneered artistic photojournalism, set up a photography department for the Resistance and co-founded the collective agency Magnum.

MUSÉE DES ARCHIVES NATIONALES
MUSEUM

Map p386 (☑01 40 27 60 96; www.archives-nation-ales.culture.gouv.fr; 60 rue des Francs Bourgeois, 3e; adult/child €5/free; ⊙10am-5.30pm Mon & Wed-Fri, from 2pm Sat & Sun; MRambuteau) France's National Archives and small museum are set in a stunning pair of *hôtels particuliers* amid beautiful gardens. Dating from the early 18th century, Hôtel de Soubise and Hôtel de Rohan (closed for renovation until 2023) are extravagantly painted and gilded in the rococo style inside, with antique furniture and 18th-century paintings alongside a fascinating collection of documents on display, such as the Edict of Nantes and Marie Antoinette's final letter.

The audiovisual room screens films and has multimedia exhibits. Admission is more expensive during temporary exhibitions. Note that the museum inside Hôtel de Soubise remains open while its sister mansion undergoes extensive renovation work.

⊙ Ménilmontant & Belleville

CIMETIÈRE DU PÈRE LACHAISE
CEMETERY

See p157.

★ATELIER DES LUMIÈRES
MUSEUM

Map p390 (☑01 80 98 46 00; www.atelier-lumi eres.com; 38-40 rue St-Maur, 11e; adult/child €15/10; ⊙10am-6pm Mon-Thu, to 10pm Fri & Sat, to 7pm Sun; MVoltaire) A former foundry dating from 1835 that supplied iron for the French navy and railroads now houses Paris' first digital-art museum. The 1500-sq-metre La Halle mounts dazzling light projections that take over the bare walls. Long programs lasting around 30 minutes are based on historic artists' works; there's also a shorter contemporary program. Screenings are continuous. In the separate Le Studio space, you can discover emerging and established digital artists.

SQUARE MAURICE GARDETTE
PARK

Map p390 (rue du Général Blaise, 11e; ⊙8am-9.30pm Mon-Fri, 9am-9.30pm Sat & Sun May-Aug, to 8.30pm Apr & Sep, shorter hours Oct-Mar; MSt-Ambroise, Rue St-Maur) In the heart of the vibrant 11e, this square was first laid out in 1872 on the former site of the Ménilmontant slaughterhouses, and in 1979 was transformed into the charming little park you see today. Filled with elms, chestnuts, silver birches and magnolias, with hollyhocks, irises and asters blooming in spring and summer, it's a favourite with locals and makes an idyllic spot for a picnic. Dating from 1899, the wrought-iron bandstand at its centre hosts occasional concerts.

MUSÉE ÉDITH PIAF
MUSEUM

Map p390 (☑01 43 55 52 72; 5 rue Crespin du Gast, 11e; ⊙by reservation 1-6pm Mon-Wed, closed Jun & Sep; MMénilmontant) FREE This private museum in Ménilmontant, some 1.5km from the birthplace of the iconic singer Édith Piaf and closer to her final resting place in Père Lachaise, follows the life and career of the 'urchin sparrow' through memorabilia, recordings, personal objects, letters and other documentation. Admission is by reservation only at least several days in advance; you'll receive the door codes upon booking. Donations are welcome. Be aware that there are several flights of stairs, and that only French is spoken.

✖ EATING

Packed with eateries of every imaginable type, Le Marais is one of Paris' premier dining neighbourhoods, with many restaurants and bistros requiring a reservation. Despite the huge concentration of eating addresses, it's a popular area for new openings. Multi-ethnic Belleville is tops for Asian fare. Some of the Bastille and Eastern Paris neighbourhood's best neobistros are within easy walking distance of Cimetière du Père Lachaise.

✖ Le Marais

★ JACQUES GENIN   PASTRIES €

Map p386 (📞01 45 77 29 01; www.jacquesgenin. fr; 133 rue de Turenne, 3e; pastries €9; ⊙11am-7pm Tue-Fri & Sun, to 7.30pm Sat; MOberkampf, Filles du Calvaire) Wildly creative *chocolatier* Jacques Genin is famed for his flavoured caramels, *pâtes de fruits* (fruit jellies) and exquisitely embossed *bonbons de chocolat* (chocolate sweets). But what completely steals the show at his elegant chocolate showroom is the *salon de dégustation* (aka tearoom), where you can order a pot of outrageously thick hot chocolate and legendary Genin *millefeuille,* assembled to order.

★ BREIZH CAFÉ   CRÊPES €

Map p386 (📞01 42 72 13 77; www.breizhcafe.com; 109 rue Vieille du Temple, 3e; crêpes & galettes €6.80-19; ⊙11.30am-11pm Mon-Sat, to 10pm Sun; MSt-Sébastien–Froissart) Everything at the Breizh ('Breton' in Breton) is 100% authentic, including its organic-flour crêpes and *galettes* (savoury buckwheat crêpes) that top many Parisians' lists for the best in the city. Other specialities include Cancale oysters and 20 types of cider. Tables are limited and there's often a wait; book ahead or try its deli, **L'Épicerie** (Map p386; 📞01 42 71 39 44; 111 rue Vieille du Temple, 3e; crêpes & galettes €6.80-19; ⊙11.30am-10pm; MSt-Sébastien–Froissart), next door.

FOR THE LOVE OF FOOD   INTERNATIONAL €

Map p386 (www.fortheloveoffood.paris; 80 rue des Tournelles, 3e; 2-/3-course lunch €20/24, 4-course dinner menu €38; ⊙12.15-2.30pm & 7-11pm Fri-Sun; MChemin Vert) ✐ This groundbreaking place, opened in late 2019, is all about sustainability and innovation. Dubbed Paris' first chef-incubator restaurant for 'curious gastronomes', it invites a different trio of chefs each month to create its menu. Produce must be seasonal and responsibly sourced, and meals are ordered in advance online to ensure zero waste. Dining is in an attractive, minimalist space around shared wooden tables.

Check its website for the month's chefs, their cuisine (French, Filipino, Mexican, vegetarian, anything goes) and menus.

MIZNON   ISRAELI €

Map p386 (📞01 42 74 83 58; www.facebook. com/miznonparis; 22 rue des Écouffes, 4e; pita sandwiches €6-12.50; ⊙noon-11pm Sun-Thu, to 3.30pm Fri; ✐; MSt-Paul, Hôtel de Ville) Parisians can't get enough of this hip outpost of celebrity chef Eyal Shani's famed Tel Aviv restaurant. Head past the grocery crates to the bar to order a warm, fluffy pita (with lamb, fish, vegetarian ratatouille or roasted cauliflower) and phenomenal house-made hummus. Don't miss the sweet *banane au chocolat* pita to finish. Takeaway's available if you can't get a seat.

L'AS DU FALLAFEL   FELAFEL €

Map p386 (📞08 99 34 43 64; www.l-as-du-fallafel. zenchef.com; 34 rue des Rosiers, 4e; takeaway €5.50-8.50, mains €12-18; ⊙noon-midnight Sun-Thu, to 4pm Fri; ✐; MSt-Paul) The lunchtime queue stretching halfway down the street from this place says it all. This Parisian favourite, 100% worth the inevitable wait, is the address for kosher, perfectly deep-fried felafel (chickpea balls) and chicken or lamb shawarma sandwiches. Do as every Parisian does and get them to take away.

OKOMUSU   JAPANESE €

Map p386 (📞09 67 40 97 27, 01 57 40 97 27; 11 rue Charlot, 3e; mains €13.80-17.80; ⊙7.30-10pm Tue-Thu, noon-2pm & 7.30-10pm Fri-Sun; MSt-Sébastien–Froissart) Once full – which happens within seconds of chef Hiroko Tabuchi opening her *table d'hôte* – all eyes are on the chef as she deftly whips up steaming plates of sautéed noodles and her speciality, *okonomiyaki* (a wheat-flour pancake with cabbage, chives, ginger, dried fish shavings and pork, prawn or squid), while hungry diners sit at the bar. Vegetarians can order a meat-free version.

BIGLOVE CAFFÉ   ITALIAN €

Map p386 (Amore; 📞01 44 78 08 97; www.big mammagroup.com; 30 rue Debelleyme, 3e; pizza & pasta €12-18; ⊙noon-2.30pm & 7-10.45pm

LOCAL KNOWLEDGE

MARCHÉ DES ENFANTS ROUGES

Built in 1615, Paris' oldest covered market, **Marché des Enfants Rouges** (Map p386; 39 rue de Bretagne & 33bis rue Charlot, 3e; ⊗8.30am-1pm & 4-7.30pm Tue-Sat, 8.30am-2pm Sun, individual stall hours vary; Ⓜ Filles du Calvaire), is secreted behind an inconspicuous green-metal gate. A glorious maze of 20-odd food stalls selling ready-to-eat dishes from around the globe (Moroccan couscous, Japanese bento boxes and more), as well as produce, cheese and flower stalls, it's a great place to meander and to dine with locals around communal tables. The monster sandwiches and *galettes* (savoury crêpes) whipped up on a sizzling griddle by retired baker Alain while you wait at **Chez Alain Miam Miam** (Map p386; ☑01 83 97 04 15; www.facebook.com/ChezAlainMiamMiam; dishes €3.50-9.50; ⊗9am-3.30pm Wed-Fri, to 5.30pm Sat, to 3pm Sun, closed Aug; ☑), inside the market or around the corner at Alain's sit-down **cafe** (Map p386; 26 rue Charlot, 3e; sandwiches & galettes €3.50-11.50; ⊗8.30am-5pm Tue-Sun), are legends in their own right.

Otherwise, tucked down the rear right-hand side of the covered market, **Les Enfants du Marché** (Map p386; www.lesenfantsdumarche.fr; mains €15-32; ⊗9am-5pm Tue, Wed & Sun, to 9pm Thu-Sat) is a sizzling-hot *comptoir* (counter) with bamboo stools. Pair natural wines, artisan French spirits, craft beers and cocktails with charcuterie, cheese and seafood platters or mains like herb-roasted Gascon pig or Loire Valley hare with foie gras and truffles.

Mon-Wed, to 11pm Thu & Fri, 10am-3.30pm & 6.45-11pm Sat, 10am-3.30pm & 7-10.45pm Sun; Ⓜ Filles du Calvaire) There is no sign of the popularity of this insanely busy, Italian-run trattoria by the Big Mamma group flagging. From day one, Parisians have queued up outside (no reservations) waiting to snag a table in the festive, grocery-styled space to feast on wood-fired, gluten-free pizzas and terrific brunch dishes such as blackberry pancakes with ricotta and maple syrup or eggs Benedict with feta.

PASTELLI MARY
GELATERIA   GELATO €
Map p386 (☑09 83 89 05 05; www.facebook.com/pastellimarygelateria; 60 rue du Temple, 3e; gelato 1/2/3/4 scoops €3.50/5/6.50/8; ⊗11am-10pm; Ⓜ Rambuteau) The youngest winner of Milan's prestigious Cone d'Oro (Golden Cone), artisan gelato maker Mary Quarta has more than 100 different flavours in her all-natural repertoire, and serves around a dozen different freshly made small batches each day at her light, white-painted Haut-Marais shop. Standouts include avocado, black sesame, peach Champagne bellini, plum and kiwi.

BAGNARD   MEDITERRANEAN €
Map p386 (☑01 55 43 90 47; www.yonisaada.com/bagnard; 58 rue de Saintonge, 3e; pans bagnats €16, mains €16-21; ⊗11.30am-2.30pm & 7-11pm Mon-Fri, 11.30am-11.30pm Sat, 11.30am-

11pm Sun; Ⓜ Filles du Calvaire) Slate blue-and-white walls, herringbone parquet and an on-trend mix of worn wood and leather create a cosy vibe at this trendy *'cantine Méditerranean'* in Haut Marais. A handsomely stuffed LuLu Le Bagnard – an olive oil-drenched tuna, egg and anchovy *pan bagnat* (sandwich typical to Nice) – is chef Yoni Saada's signature dish, but his tapas, salads and meats are equally hard to resist.

COSI   SANDWICHES €
Map p386 (5 rue des Filles du Calvaire, 3e; sandwiches €6.50-9, lunch menus €10.50-13; ⊗noon-10pm; Ⓜ Filles du Calvaire) The *rive gauche's* indisputable Italian sandwich king has expanded across the river with this bright and spacious Right Bank sandwich den. Choose your sandwich vibe – easy, *tranquille* or posh – and the creative mix you fancy inside the homemade focaccia bread. Wackily named sandwiches include Naked Willi, Tom Dooley and Cheesy English.

HANKBURGER   VEGAN €
Map p386 (☑09 72 44 03 99; www.hankrestaurant.com; 55 rue des Archives, 3e; burgers €8.50; ⊗noon-10pm Sun-Fri, to 11pm Sat; ☏☑; Ⓜ Rambuteau) 🍃 No animal products are involved in the vegan burgers at Hank, an acronym for 'Have A Nice Karma'. Soy-based burgers include La Catcheuse (alfalfa and sweet mustard sauce) and Tata Monique (minced black olives and basil sauce). The stylish

LOCAL KNOWLEDGE

TASTY BREAKFAST DATES

Gramme (Map p386; ☑09 50 92 20 23; www.facebook.com/pg/grammeparis/; 86 rue des Archives, 3e; ⊗9am-4pm Mon & Wed-Fri, 10am-5pm Sat & Sun; 🛜; MArts et Métiers, Temple) Lomi coffee and homemade rose lemonade kickstart the day at this on-trend coffee shop, bursting at the seams at weekends with Haut-Marais hipsters who pile into the tiny retro space to breakfast, brunch or lunch on world-inspired signature dishes such as Le Banh Mi Dog (hot dog stuffed with pulled pork, pickled veg and green coriander mayo) and *brioche perdue* (pan-fried eggy bread).

Kitchen (Map p386; ☑09 52 55 11 66; www.kitchenparis.com; 74 rue des Gravilliers, 3e; dishes €4-14; ⊗8am-3pm Mon-Fri, to 4pm Sat & Sun; 🖉; MArts et Métiers) Sweet and savoury US-style pancakes – all milk- and gluten-free – are served in this tiny breakfast kitchen alongside granola with coconut yoghurt, several avocado toast variations and stuffed bagels. Lunch kicks in from 11.30am with creative vegetarian and vegan dishes. Vegan protein shakes, cold-pressed juices, smoothies and Lomi coffee flesh out an excellent drinks *carte*.

The Hood (Map p390; www.thehoodparis.com; 80 rue Jean-Pierre Timbaud, 11e; mains €9.50-15, brunch €23; ⊗8am-6pm Mon, Wed & Sun, to 10pm Thu-Sat; 🛜; MParmentier) Fusion French-Asian grub gives an alternative twist to this easy-going neighbourhood coffee shop with vintage moulded ceiling, pea-green wall and mismatched flea-market furnishings. Coffee beans are roasted by London's Climpsons & Sons, and breakfast faves include kaya toast, rice pudding, and granola with syrupy *gula melaka* (palm sugar). Vietnamese pork and chicken *banh mi* (sandwiches) and Singapore-inspired chicken bulk out the all-day menu.

Marlette (Map p386; ☑01 43 31 06 64; www.marlette.fr; 6 rue du Forez, 3e; ⊗8.30am-6.30pm Mon-Fri, from 9.30am Sat & Sun; 🛜; MFilles du Calvaire) This snug, two-room ode to good coffee (by Parisian roasters Coutume) in Haut Marais is the latest opening by coffee-shop empire Marlette from Brittany's Île de Ré. Seating mixes regular tables with comfy cushioned 'sofas' to kick back on over a breakfast cappuccino, cream-filled carrot cake or veg-powered lunchtime bowl. Laptops are welcome, and 'weekend' brunch (€22.90 to €26.90) is a daily fixture (until 3pm, weekends 4pm).

space is a pleasure to linger in and the kitchen works strictly with fresh, organic and often local produce.

★AU TOP   MEDITERRANEAN €€
Map p386 (☑01 43 56 50 50; www.au-top.paris; 93 rue Vieille du Temple, 3e; small plates €9-18, mains €22-31; ⊗kitchen 6-11pm Mon-Fri, 9am-11pm Sat & Sun, bar to 2am daily; 🛜; MRambuteau) This clandestine rooftop restaurant/lounge bar – roofless and star-topped on summer nights – enjoys a 360-degree skyline view. Sit around the open kitchen or at marble-topped tables to feast on Mediterranean cuisine such as spicy sea bass tartare in yuzu cream, oven-roasted Breton artichoke, and steaks grilled over a charcoal fire. An eclectic playlist by Nova provides a party-loving ambience. Reservations essential.

To find Au Top, step through the red door at No 93, search out the lift at the far right back of the courtyard and ride it to the 5th floor.

★AU PASSAGE   BISTRO €€
Map p386 (☑01 43 55 07 52; www.restaurant-au passage.fr; 1bis passage St-Sébastien, 11e; small plates €8-24, meats to share €25-70; ⊗12.30-2pm & 7-10pm Wed-Sat; MSt-Sébastien–Froissart) Rising-star chefs continue to make their name at this *petit bar de quartier* (little neighbourhood bar). Choose from a good-value, uncomplicated selection *of petites assiettes* (small tapas-style plates) of cold meats, raw or cooked fish, vegetables and more, and larger meat dishes such as slow-roasted lamb shoulder or *côte de bœuf* (rib-eye steak) to share. Reservations are essential.

CLOWN BAR   FRENCH €€
Map p386 (☑01 43 55 87 35; www.clown-bar-paris.com; 114 rue Amelot, 11e; mains €28-36; ⊗kitchen noon-2.30pm & 7-10.30pm Wed-Sun, bar 8am-2am; MFilles du Calvaire) The former staff dining room of the city's winter circus, the 1852-built Cirque d'Hiver, is a historic

monument with colourful clown-themed ceramics and mosaics, painted glass ceilings and its original zinc bar. Modern French cuisine spans scallops with finger lime and watercress dressing to Mesquer pigeon stuffed with figs. The pavement terrace gets packed out on sunny days.

CAM
ASIAN **€€**

Map p386 (☑06 26 41 10 66; 55 rue au Maire, 3e; mains €10-24; ☺7pm-midnight Wed-Sun, closed Aug; MArts et Métiers) Don't be fooled by the tatty façade reading 'CAM Import Export' – this former miniature Eiffel Tower wholesaler has been stripped back to create a hip space for small pan-Asian plates that fire up the spice (bonito head with spring onion relish; smoked cuttlefish with ginger dressing; fermented soy-marinated steak with lettuce, mint and cilantro) accompanied by well-priced natural wines. No reservations.

BRASSERIE BOFINGER
BRASSERIE **€€**

Map p386 (☑01 42 72 87 82; www.bofinger paris.com; 5-7 rue de la Bastille, 4e; 2-/3-course menus €19.90/33, mains €18.50-37; ☺noon-3pm & 6.30pm-midnight Mon-Fri, noon-3.30pm & 6.30pm-midnight Sat, noon-11pm Sun; 🖥🚻; MBastille) Founded in 1864, Bofinger is reputedly Paris' oldest brasserie, though its polished art nouveau brass, glass and mirrors indicate redecoration a few decades later. Alsatian-inspired specialities include six kinds of *choucroute* (sauerkraut), along with oysters (€16.80 to €28.20 per half-dozen) and magnificent seafood platters (€30 to €90). Ask for a seat downstairs beneath the *coupole* (stained-glass dome).

ROBERT ET LOUISE
FRENCH **€€**

Map p386 (☑01 42 78 55 89; www.robertetlouise. com; 64 rue Vieille du Temple, 3e; mains €18-26; ☺7.30-10pm Tue-Fri, 12.30-3pm & 7.30-10pm Sat & Sun; MRambuteau) Going strong since 1958, this wonderfully convivial 'country inn' with red gingham curtains and rustic timber beams offers simple and inexpensive French food, including *côte de bœuf* (side of beef for two or three people) cooked on an open fire. Arrive early to snag the farmhouse table next to the fireplace – the makings of a real jolly Rabelaisian evening.

BONTEMPS
PASTRIES **€€**

Map p386 (☑01 42 74 10 68; www.facebook.com/ bontempspatisserie; 57 rue de Bretagne, 3e; tea or coffee & cake €20; ☺11am-7.30pm Wed-Fri, from 10am Sat, 10am-6pm Sun; MTemple) As pretty as a picture, with freshly cut flowers adorning marble tables and glass lampshades overhead, this salon serves buttery *sablés* (shortbread biscuits), a punchy *tarte au citron* (lemon tart) and other exquisite treats from its adjoining jewel-box-like patisserie. Everything is served on floral bone china with gold trim and summertime spoils at peppermint-green tables in a romantic courtyard.

ISTR
SEAFOOD **€€**

Map p386 (☑01 43 56 81 25; www.istr.paris; 41 rue Notre Dame de Nazareth, 3e; half-dozen oysters €12-44, mains €19-35, 2-/3-course lunch menus €19/24; ☺kitchen noon-2.30pm & 6-10pm Mon-Fri, 6-11pm Sat & Sun, bar to 2am daily; MTemple) Fabulously patterned wallpaper and a gleaming zinc bar set the stage for innovative Breton-inspired cuisine. The region's

LE MARAIS, MÉNILMONTANT & BELLEVILLE EATING

JEWISH PLETZL

Cacher (kosher) grocery shops, butchers, restaurants, delis and takeaway felafel joints cram the narrow streets of Pletzl (from the Yiddish for 'little square'), home to Le Marais' long-established Jewish community. It starts in rue des Rosiers and continues along rue Ste-Croix de la Bretonnerie to rue du Temple. Don't miss the **art nouveau synagogue** (Agoudas Hakehilos Synagogue; Map p386; 10 rue Pavée, 4e; MSt-Paul) designed in 1913 by Hector Guimard, who was also responsible for the city's famous metro entrances.

For an in-depth look at Jewish history, visit the **Musée d'Art et d'Histoire du Judaïsme** (Map p386; ☑01 53 01 86 60; www.mahj.org; 71 rue du Temple, 3e; adult/child €10/free; ☺11am-6pm Tue-Fri, from 10am Sat & Sun; MRambuteau), housed in Pletzl's sumptuous Hôtel de St-Aignan, dating from 1650. Highlights include documents relating to the Dreyfus Affair, and artworks by Chagall, Modigliani and Soutine. The museum also runs guided walking tours of the 'hood (including museum entrance €23/17; English available).

famed *istr* ('oyster' in Breton) is the star of the show here, served natural, as a Bloody Mary–style shot, or with sauces such as soy and ginger. Other creations include buckwheat chips with smoked haddock fishcakes. It doubles as a rocking bar.

DERRIÈRE
FRENCH €€

Map p386 (☑01 44 61 91 95; www.derriere-resto. com; 69 rue des Gravilliers, 3e; mains €18-36, weekend brunch €34; ☉7.30-11.30pm Tue-Fri, noon-4pm & 7.30-11.30pm Sat, noon-4pm Sun; MArts et Métiers) Play table football, sit on the side of the bed, glass of Champers in hand, or lounge between bookcases at this apartment-style restaurant in a beautiful courtyard. Chilled vibe aside, Derrière ('behind') is deadly serious in the kitchen. Classic French bistro dishes and more inventive creations are excellent, as is weekend brunch.

VANTRE
BISTRO €€

Map p390 (☑01 48 06 16 96; www.vantre.fr; 19 rue de la Fontaine au Roi, 11e; 2-/3-course lunch menu €17/21, mains €26-32; ☉noon-2pm & 8-10pm Mon-Fri; MGoncourt) Behind its crimson façade, backstreet neobistro Vantre has a stripped-back dining room of bare boards and cream walls, leaving the focus squarely on the food. Daily changing menus might start with bacon-stuffed cuttlefish with avocado and kumquat dressing, followed by saddle of lamb with chicory, quince and salsify, and a flourless Valrhona chocolate and barley cake.

VINS DES PYRÉNÉES
BISTRO €€

Map p386 (☑01 42 72 64 94; www.vinsdespyr enees.com; 25 rue Beautreillis, 4e; mains €17-35; ☉kitchen noon-2.30pm & 7.30-10pm, bar 7am-2am; MBastille) Originally opened in 1905, this beautifully restored bistro has a reinvigorated menu (beef tartare with anchovies and smoked egg yolk, duck breast with pumpkin and hazelnuts). A spiralling metal staircase leads upstairs to its cocktail bar and a heated terrace with a retractable roof. Its tequila-fuelled Les Gens Sont Étranges (People Are Strange) is named for former regular Jim Morrison, who lived nearby.

CARBÓN
BISTRO €€

Map p386 (☑01 42 72 49 12; www.carbonparis. com; 14 rue Charlot, 3e; 2-/3-course lunch menu €26/33, mains €22, dinner sharing plates small €11-26, large €52-120; ☉noon-2pm & 7pm-2am Tue-Sat, noon-2.30pm Sun; MFilles du Calvaire) Exposed stone walls, leather seating, marble-topped tables and indoor plants (plus cocktail bar La Mina in the vaulted cellar) give Carbón a rustic appeal. Many dishes, such as mezcal-marinated tuna, guinea fowl with quince and hay-infused duck with pontoise cabbage, are smoked over beech wood. Dinner, with enticing sharing plates to choose from, is a fun and sociable affair.

✕ Ménilmontant & Belleville

DOUBLE DRAGON
ASIAN €€

Map p390 (www.doubledragonparis.com; 52 rue St-Maur, 11e; 3-course lunch menu €18, mains €15.50-28; ☉noon-2.30pm Wed, noon-2.30pm & 7.30-10.30pm Thu-Sun; MRue St-Maur) Sisters Tatiana and Katia Levha, who run nearby bistro Le Servan (p186), fire up the spice on organic produce at this on-trend place. Barbecued duck hearts, pan-fried mussels, crispy pig's-ear dumplings or simple veggie red curries are typical dishes on the frequently changing menu. No reservations (expect to wait).

FRENCH BASTARDS
BAKERY €

Map p390 (61 rue Oberkampf, 11e; pastries €1.50-5.50, sandwiches €7.50-9; ☉7.30am-8.30pm Mon-Wed & Fri, from 8.30am Sat, 8.30am-7.30pm Sun; MParmentier) Traditional treats such as *pains au chocolat* (chocolate-filled pastries) sit alongside innovations like 'cruffins' (a cross between croissants and muffins) and *pains au cinnamon* (snail-shaped cinnamon scrolls) at this young and fun, thoroughly modern lifestyle bakery with sofa, books to browse, coffee machine and a single shared table. Fantastic sandwiches include Italian charcuterie with Corsican cheese.

CHAMBELLAND
BAKERY €

Map p390 (☑01 43 55 07 30; www.chambelland. com; 14 rue Ternaux, 11e; lunch menu €10-12, pastries €2.50-9; ☉8.30am-7.30pm Mon-Sat, 9am-6pm Sun; MParmentier) Using rice and buckwheat flour from its own mill in southern France, this pioneering 100% gluten-free bakery creates exquisite cakes and pastries as well as sourdough loaves and brioches peppered with nuts, seeds, chocolate and fruit. Stop for lunch at one of the handful of plastic tables in this relaxed space, strewn with sacks of flour and books.

MARCHÉ DE BELLEVILLE
MARKET €

Map p390 (bd de Belleville, 11e & 20e; ⊙7am-2.30pm Tue & Fri; Ⓜ Belleville) Belleville Market has filled busy thoroughfare bd de Belleville with open-air fruit, veg and other fresh-produce stalls since 1860. Food shopping aside, it provides a fascinating insight into the large, vibrant community of this eastern neighbourhood, home to artists, students and immigrants from Africa, Asia and the Middle East.

L'ATELIER LIBANAIS
LEBANESE €

Map p390 (📞01 44 65 95 25; www.atelier-libanais.com; 91 rue de Belleville, 19e; ⊙noon-11pm Sun-Thu, to midnight Fri & Sat) Colourful woven straw bags, lamps straight from the souk in Beirut and a tiny corner shop selling rose syrup, Aleppo soap and the like infuse a colourful dose of Lebanese *art de vivre* into this canteen-styled eatery in Belleville. Tuck into tasty bowls of hummus, labneh and other aromatic mezes, or go for a generously filled pita bread.

You'll find a second branch at 47 rue Oberkampf, 11e.

LA CANTINE DE BELLEVILLE
FRENCH €

Map p390 (📞01 43 15 99 29; www.lacantinebelleville.fr; 108 bd de Belleville, 20e; 2-/3-course menus lunch €12/14, dinner €15/18, mains lunch/dinner €10/12; ⊙kitchen 10am-10pm, bar to 2am; 🛜; Ⓜ Belleville) Belleville's local 'canteen' is a vibrant one-stop shop for dining, drinking and dancing after dark. Old-school chairs, vintage lighting, exposed brickwork and posters covering the walls give the place a garage vibe. Cuisine is classic French; excellent steaks include a *côte de boeuf* for two. Happy hour runs from 5pm to 8.30pm. Regular concerts take place in the vaulted cellar.

TAI YIEN
CANTONESE €

Map p390 (📞01 42 41 44 16; 5 rue de Belleville, 20e; mains €8.50-13.80; ⊙10am-11.30pm Sun-Thu, to 1.30am Fri & Sat; Ⓜ Belleville) Crispy-skinned ducks and roast pork hang in the windows of this wholly authentic Hong Kong–style 'steam restaurant' in Belleville's Chinatown. *Har gow* (prawn dumplings) and *sui mai* (minced pork dumplings) are served alongside specialities such as hen's feet and turnip cakes. Arrive early or late to beat the lunchtime crush.

MASSALE
BISTRO €€

Map p390 (📞01 73 79 87 90; 5 rue Guillaume Bertrand, 11e; 2-/3-course lunch menu €18/23, mains €24-30; ⊙noon-2.30pm & 7.30-10pm Mon-Fri; Ⓜ St-Maur) Enchantingly vintage in design, with bar and overhead ceiling fan, this is a tasty little neobistro delightfully off the tourist-trodden track. *'Massale'* is the ancient process of sorting the best seeds to re-plant next season, and selecting exceptional produce is precisely what owners Thomas and Arthur, together with Finnish chef Marlo Snellman in the kitchen, uphold.

The day's menu might include a poached egg in pecorino cream, followed by guinea fowl from Les Landes in southwest France married with spinach and roasted walnuts. End with a 120-day-aged Morbier, or a Sicilian-orange rice pudding with caramelised pistachios. Massale is a top insider choice for lunch before or after nearby Atelier des Lumières (p163).

FIEF
FRENCH €€

Map p390 (📞01 47 00 03 22; www.fiefrestaurant.fr; shared plates €7-20, 6-course tasting menu €68; ⊙6.30-11pm Tue-Sat; 🖐; Ⓜ St-Ambroise) 🍃 The industrial-style red-brick-and-stone interior is as striking as the modern French cuisine of head-turning young chef Victor Mercier. Debut venture of the 2018 *Top Chef* finalist, eco-conscious Fief (an acronym for *'fait ici en France'* or 'made here in France') is a radical showcase for French produce – strictly no imports here, coffee and chocolate fiends.

Choose from plates to share in the dining room, a bar stool at the open kitchen or a six-course tasting menu around a shared table (reserve in advance). Equally enticing veg, vegan and meaty bites include

ASIAN EAT STREETS

Paris' largest Chinatown is on the Left Bank in the 13e but on the Right Bank, Belleville is home to a small but thriving Chinatown around the Belleville metro station, at the nexus of the 10e, 11e, 19e and 20e *arrondissements*, with hole-in-the-wall eateries through to large restaurants and Asian supermarkets. In the 3e, rue au Maire, 3e (metro Arts et Métiers), is a small restaurant- and shop-lined street with authentic Chinese food.

LOCAL KNOWLEDGE

A HILLTOP PICNIC

A few blocks east of bd de Belleville, the lovely but little-known **Parc de Belleville** (Map p390; 47 rue des Couronnes & rue Piat, 20e; ⊙8am-9.30pm May-Aug, shorter hours Sep-Apr; MCouronnes, Pyrénées) unfolds across a hill 128m above sea level amid 4.5 hectares of greenery. Climb to the top for some of the best views of the city armed with a bread-and-cheese picnic bought in Belleville from two of the finest in their field: boulangerie (bakery) **Au 140** (Map p390; www.au140.com; 140 rue de Belleville, 20e; sandwiches €3-5.50; ⊙7am-8pm Tue-Fri, from 7.30am Sat, 7am-7pm Sun; MJourdain) and **Fromagerie Beaufils** (Map p390; ☎01 46 36 61 71; www.fromagerie-beaufils.com; 118 rue de Belleville, 20e; ⊙8.30am-1pm & 3.30-7.45pm Tue-Sat, to 1pm Sun; MJourdain).

pumpkin in sweet hazelnut and praline vinaigrette, stuffed cabbage, and chicken in a barbecue apple sauce. Cocktail pairings by mixologist Stephen Martin are sublime.

PIERRE SANG
FRENCH €€

Map p390 (☎09 67 31 96 80; www.pierresang. com; 55 rue Oberkampf, 11e; 2-/3-/5-course lunch menus €20/25/35, 6-course dinner menus €39; ⊙noon, 7pm & 9.30pm; ☞; MParmentier, Oberkampf) At *Top Chef* finalist Pierre Sang's flagship, modern French cuisine has a strong fusion lilt thanks to his French and Korean background, and the vibe is casual and fun. He also has a neighbouring French-Korean atelier (workshop) annex at 6 rue Gambey, and experimental 'signature' restaurant at 8 rue Gambey. Kids under eight years eat free here and at the atelier.

BIDOCHE
FRENCH €€

Map p386 (☎09 81 12 59 81; www.bidoche. fr; 7 rue Jean-Pierre Timbaud, 11e; 2-/3-course menu €14.90/17.90, mains €12.90-26; ⊙noon-2pm Mon-Thu, noon-2pm & 7.30-10pm Fri & Sat; MOberkampf) Banker-turned-butcher Alexandre can invariably be found, knife in hand, at this artisanal butcher's restaurant where meat, sourced from small French producers by Alexandre personally, is king. Admire the day's available cuts in the gleaming *boucherie* (butcher's shop) out front, chat to the butcher perhaps, then

duck behind the counter to dine in the clandestine bistro.

A mixed charcuterie platter makes a fantastic start to any meal, followed by a trio of house-seasoned, hand-cut tartares (beef, veal and lamb, beef) or your own bespoke cut of grilled meat (personally selected and priced by weight). Advance reservations recommended.

LA CAVE DE L'INSOLITE
BISTRO €€

Map p390 (☎01 53 36 08 33; www.facebook. com/lacavedelinsolite; 30 rue de la Folie Méricourt, 11e; 2-/3-course midweek lunch menu €18/20, mains €18-26; ⊙12.15-2.30pm & 7.30-10.30pm Tue-Sat, 12.15-2.30pm & 7.30-10pm Sun; ☞; MSt-Ambroise, Parmentier) Brothers Axel and Arnaud, who have worked at some of Paris' top addresses, run this rustic-chic wine bar with barrels, timber tables and a wood-burning stove. Duck pâté with cider jelly, haddock rillettes with lime and endive confit, and beef with mushroom and sweetbread sauce are among the seasonal dishes; its 100-plus hand-harvested wines come from small-scale French vineyards.

BØTI
BISTRO €€

Map p390 (☎06 65 49 12 29; www.facebook. com/BOTI.paris; 74 bd de Ménilmontant, 20e; 2-/3-course menu lunch €12/16, dinner €23/27; ⊙noon-3pm & 8pm-midnight Wed-Sat; MPère Lachaise) There's always at least one vegetarian option (such as black sesame polenta) on the small but superb weekly menu at this welcoming little stone-walled bistro footsteps from Père Lachaise, alongside meat and poultry dishes like confit spiced lamb shoulder or duck terrine with pickled lotus root. Wines are excellent; artisanal beers include a quinoa-based gluten-free brew. Cash only.

★MAISON
FUSION €€€

Map p390 (☎01 43 38 61 95; www.maison-sota. com; 3 rue St-Hubert, 11e; lunch/dinner menu €55/125; ⊙12.30-2pm & 7.30-9.30pm Wed-Sun; MRue St-Maur) Ring to enter this epicurean loft (as one would any '*maison*' or 'home'), take the monumental staircase to a mezzanine crowned with a glass skylight, and savour the open-kitchen show of Japanese chef Sota Atsumi. The *tomettes* (terracotta tiles) covering floor *and* walls are as sensational as the kaleidoscope of exquisitely presented, fusion small plates. Single fixed *menus* change daily.

LE CHATEAUBRIAND
BISTRO €€€

Map p390 (☎01 43 57 45 95; www.lechateau briand.net; 129 av Parmentier, 11e; tasting menu €75; ⊗7-11pm Tue-Sat; ⓂGoncourt) Michelin-starred Le Chateaubriand is an elegantly tiled, art deco dining room with strikingly imaginative cuisine. Basque chef Iñaki Aizpitarte is well travelled and his dishes display global exposure again and again in their unexpected combinations (watermelon and mackerel, milk-fed veal with langoustines and truffles). Reservations open 21 days in advance and are obligatory.

Should more casual (and more affordable) tapas dishes or a lighter meal beckon, head to Le Chateaubriand's stylish *comptoir,* **Le Dauphin** (Map p390; ☎01 55 28 78 88; 131 av Parmentier, 11e; small plates €3.50-20; ⊗6pm-2am Tue, 12.30-3pm & 6pm-2am Wed-Sat; ⓂGoncourt), on the same street.

🍷 DRINKING & NIGHTLIFE

Le Marais is a spot *par excellence* when it comes to a good night out – the lively scene embraces everything from gay-friendly and gay-only venues to arty cafes, eclectic bars and raucous pubs. Rue Oberkampf and parallel rue Jean-Pierre Timbaud are hubs of the Ménilmontant bar crawl, a scene that is edging out steadily through cosmopolitan Belleville.

🍷 Le Marais

★GRAND CAFÉ TORTONI
CAFE

Map p386 (☎01 42 72 28 92; www.facebook.com/ grandcafetortoni; 45 rue de Saintonge, 3e; ⊗9am-7pm Tue-Sat, 11am-6pm Sun; ⓂFilles du Calvaire) A favourite address with hobnobbing socialites in the 19th century, this historic Italian cafe is suddenly the trendiest spot in Haut Marais to linger over coffee or an egg-and-pastry breakfast at the red marble-topped bar, or to shop for exquisite Officine Universelle Buly fragrances and candles in the polished, old-world setting.

Wood panelling and shelves lined with glass jars of unusual dried ingredients that go into the natural body butters, perfumes and so on evoke a centuries-old apothecary, and a calligrapher scribes a beautiful dedication on the packaging of each item purchased. Oh, and florist Miyoko works her magic in the hidden courtyard out back.

★LE MARY CÉLESTE
COCKTAIL BAR

Map p386 (www.quixotic-projects.com/venue/ le-mary-celeste; 1 rue Commines, 3e; ⊗bar 6pm-2am Mon-Fri, noon-2am Sat & Sun, kitchen 7-11.30pm Mon-Fri, noon-11.30pm Sat & Sun; ⓂFilles du Calvaire) Snag a stool at the central circular bar at this eternally fashionable, brick-and-timber-floored cocktail bar or reserve one of a handful of tables online. Innovative cocktails mix weird and wonderful ingredients (curry leaves, green cardamom, dried Iranian lemon, turmeric syrup), often seasonal, and there are lovely natural wines too – all perfect partners to tapas-style dishes (grilled duck hearts, devilled eggs).

★CANDELARIA
COCKTAIL BAR

Map p386 (www.quixotic-projects.com/candel aria; 52 rue de Saintonge, 3e; ⊗bar 6pm-2am, taqueria noon-10.30pm Sun-Wed, to 11.30pm Thu-Sat; ⓂFilles du Calvaire) A lime-green taqueria serving homemade tacos, quesadillas and tostadas conceals one of Paris' coolest cocktail bars through an unmarked internal door. Phenomenal cocktails made from agave spirits, including mezcal, are inspired by Central and South America, such as a Guatemalan El Sombrerón (tequila, vermouth, bitters, hibiscus syrup, pink-pepper-infused tonic and lime). Weekend evenings kick off with DJ sets.

BAMBINO
WINE BAR

Map p386 (☎01 43 55 68 20; www.facebook.com/ bambinorestaurantparis; 25 rue St-Sébastien, 11e; ⊗6pm-2am Thu-Tue; ⓂSt-Sébastien–Froissart) A cool new headquarters for devotees of both *vin* (wine) and vinyls, Bambino mixes music with an outstanding wine list packed with natural wines. Linger by the polished concrete bar and watch the DJ at work, spinning old-fashioned vinyl on the turntable. Delicious tapas to share – parsley-laced duck hearts, artichokes, creamy polenta and so on – provides the icing on the cake.

LITTLE RED DOOR
COCKTAIL BAR

Map p386 (☎01 42 71 19 32; www.lrdparis.com; 60 rue Charlot, 3e; ⊗6pm-1am Thu-Sun; ⓂFilles du Calvaire) Behind an inconspicuous timber façade, a tiny crimson doorway is the illusionary portal to this low-lit, bare-brick drinking den filled with flickering candles. Ranked among the World's 50 Best Bars, it's a must for serious mixology fans. Its annual collection of 11 cocktails, in themes from 'art' to 'architecture', are intricately crafted from ingredients such as glacier ice and paper syrup.

LE PERCHOIR MARAIS   ROOFTOP BAR

Map p386 (☏01 48 06 18 48; www.leperchoir.fr; 37 rue de la Verrerie, 4e; ☺8.15pm-1.30am Mon-Sat, 7.15pm-1.30am Sun; MHôtel de Ville) Run by the talented mixologists behind Le Perchoir (p174), this sky deck sits atop department store BHV (p179). Seine and city views, with cocktail in hand, are second to none, and in winter a tarpaulin cocoons the outdoor seating, whose decor changes seasonally.

BOOT CAFÉ   COFFEE

Map p386 (www.facebook.com/bootcafe; 19 rue du Pont aux Choux, 3e; ☺10am-6pm; ☏; MSt-Sébastien–Froissart) Born in a former cobblers' shop, bijou Boot is a fashionable spot to grab a quality coffee and an accompanying sweet morsel. Colombian beans are roasted by the Fuglen Roastery in Oslo and monster cookies – the salted caramel is sinful – are by Paris' imitable Emperor Norton. Just two tables and a handful of plastic stools squeeze into the box interior.

LA CAFÉOTHÈQUE   COFFEE

Map p386 (☏01 53 01 83 84; www.lacafeotheque. com; 52 rue de l'Hôtel de Ville, 4e; ☺9am-6pm; ☏; MPont Marie, St-Paul) From the industrial grinder to elaborate tasting notes, this coffee house and roastery is serious. Grab a

GAY & LESBIAN MARAIS

Open Café (Map p386; www.opencafe.fr; 17 rue des Archives, 4e; ☺11am-2am Sun-Thu, to 3am Fri & Sat; MHôtel de Ville) A gay venue for all types at all hours, this spacious bar-cafe, with twinkling disco balls strung from the starry ceiling, has bags of appeal – including a big, awning-shaded pavement terrace that's always busy, an all-day kitchen and a four-hour happy 'hour' kicking in daily at 6pm.

Le Tango (Map p386; ☏01 48 87 25 71; www.boite-a-frissons.fr; 13 rue au Maire, 3e; admission Fri & Sat €10, Sun €6; ☺10pm-5am Fri & Sat, 6-11pm Sun; MArts et Métiers) Billing itself as a *boîte à frissons* (club of thrills), Le Tango hosts a mixed and cosmopolitan, gay and lesbian crowd in a historic 1930s dancehall. Its atmosphere and style is retro and festive, with waltzing, salsa and tango from the moment it opens. From about 12.30am onwards DJs play. Sunday's gay tea dance is legendary.

3w Kafé (Map p386; www.facebook.com/3wkafe; 8 rue des Écouffes, 4e; ☺7pm-3am Wed & Sun, to 4am Thu, to 6.30am Fri & Sat; MSt-Paul) The name of this flagship cocktail-bar-pub means 'women with women'. It's relaxed and there's no ban on men (but they must be accompanied by a woman). On weekends there's dancing downstairs with a DJ. Themed evenings take place regularly; check its Facebook page for events.

Gibus Club (Map p386; ☏01 77 15 73 09; www.gibusclub.fr; 18 rue du Faubourg du Temple, 11e; ☺11pm-7am Thu-Sat; MRépublique) What started out as a summer party thrown by Scream Club has since morphed into a permanent fixture on the city's gay scene, rebranded as Gibus Club and still working hard to stay top dog as one of Paris' biggest gay parties.

Raidd Bar (Map p386; 23 rue du Temple, 4e; ☺6pm-4am, to 5am Fri & Sat; MHôtel de Ville) Don't be deceived by the laid-back lounge atmosphere of the ground-floor bar, one of the busiest gay hang-outs in Le Marais. Upstairs, it is a pulsating den of DJs and electro dance music, themed parties, disco nights, Brazilian soirées, raunchy shower shows and all sorts. Happy 'hour' runs from 6pm to 10pm.

Quetzal (Map p386; 10 rue de la Verrerie, 4e; ☺5pm-4am; MHôtel de Ville) This perennial favourite gay bar is opposite rue des Mauvais Garçons (Bad Boys' Street), named after the brigands who congregated here in 1540. It's always busy, with house and dance music playing at night ('80s and '90s tunes on Thursdays), and cruisy at all hours. Plate-glass windows allow you to check out the talent before it arrives.

Happy hours run from 5pm to 6pm and from 11pm to midnight.

Café Cox (Map p386; www.coxbar.fr; 15 rue des Archives, 4e; ☺5pm-2am; MHôtel de Ville) This small gay bar with decor that changes every quarter is the meeting place for an interesting (and interested) crowd throughout the evening from dusk onwards. Happy 'hour' runs from 6pm to 10pm (until 2am Sunday).

seat, and pick your bean, filtration method (Aeropress, V60 filter, piston or drip) and preparation style. The in-house coffee school has tastings and various courses including two-hour weekend tasting initiations (five *terroirs*, five extraction methods) for €60 (English available).

SHERRY BUTT
COCKTAIL BAR

Map p386 (☑09 63 38 47 80; www.sherrybutt paris.com; 20 rue Beautreillis, 4e; ⊙6pm-2am Tue-Sat, from 8pm Sun & Mon; ⓂBastille) Named for the sherry-seasoned oak casks used to age whisky, this dimly lit, stone-walled bar is one for serious cocktail connoisseurs. Seasonal menus might include Sherring is Caring (sweet and dry sherries, tonka bean syrup, lemon and soda) or Nux Aeterna (cognac, sweet sherry, red-wine-based Byrrh, dry vermouth and chocolate liqueur). It's standing room only on weekends when DJs play.

AUX DEUX AMIS
CAFE

Map p390 (☑01 58 30 38 13; 45 rue Oberkampf, 11e; ⊙9.30am-2am Tue-Fri, from noon Sat; ⓂOberkampf, Parmentier) From the well-worn, tiled floor to the day's menu scrawled in marker on the vintage mirror, quintessential neighbourhood cafe Aux Deux Amis is perfect for a coffee, a glass of natural wine or tapas-style dishes including the house speciality – *tartare de cheval* (hand-chopped, herb-seasoned horse meat).

L'ÉBOUILLANTÉ
CAFE

Map p386 (www.facebook.com/Ebouillante; 6 rue des Barres, 4e; ⊙noon-10pm Tue-Sun Jun-Aug, to 7pm Tue-Sun Sep-May; ☎; ⓂPont Marie, Hôtel de Ville) Set on a pedestrian, stone-flagged street just footsteps from the Seine, with one of the city's prettiest terraces, cornflower-blue-painted L' Ébouillanté buzzes with Parisians sipping refreshing glasses of homemade *citronnade* (ginger lemonade), hibiscus-flower cordial and over two dozen varieties of tea. Delicious cakes, jumbo salads and savoury crêpes complement the long drinks menu.

FRENCH RIVIERA
COCKTAIL BAR

Map p386 (☑06 19 28 28 05; www.facebook.com/ frenchriviera.marais; 14 rue Froissart, 3e; ⊙6pm-2am Tue-Sat; ⓂFilles du Calvaire) Female mixologist Adèle Fardeau is the creative energy behind this stylish newcomer. Vintage posters for Nice, Menton and other beach resorts on the French Riviera decorate the walls, and cocktails – Cannes, Pampelonne

APÉRO HOUR

Clad with benches and shaded by trees, pretty pedestrian square **place du Marché Ste-Catherine** (Map p386; 4e; ⓂSt-Paul) is framed on three sides by atmospheric cafe pavement terraces that are perfect for that all-essential early-evening *apéro* (predinner drink) beneath the fairy lights at dusk.

and so on (€13) – are equally evocative of France's hot south. Antibes packs a punch with rum, cointreau, mango syrup, lemon, passion fruit and a sprinkling of *herbes de Provence*.

LE BALLON ROUGE
WINE BAR

Map p386 (☑09 86 29 13 01; www.leballonrouge. fr; 51 rue Notre Dame de Nazareth, 3e; ⊙kitchen 7-11.30pm Mon-Fri, noon-4pm & 7pm-midnight Sat, bar 3pm-midnight Mon-Fri, noon-midnight Sat; ⓂStrasbourg–St-Denis) Sleek new-generation wine bar Le Ballon Rouge has dozens of natural-wine references covering every major French region, and hosts regular tastings with winemakers. Wines by the glass and bottle pair with gourmet sharing plates (€8 to €12) such as leeks in a caper sauce or oven-roasted St-Marcellin cheese with rosemary honey. Mixed cheese, charcuterie and seafood platters (€15 to €19.50) are equally tempting.

LE LOIR DANS LA THÉIÈRE
CAFE

Map p386 (www.leloirdanslatheiere.com; 3 rue des Rosiers, 4e; ⊙9am-7.30pm; ☎; ⓂSt-Paul) The *Alice in Wonderland*–inspired Dormouse in the Teapot is a wonderful old space filled with retro toys, wooden tables, mismatched chairs and comfy couches. Its dozen different teas, poured in the company of excellent savoury tarts and desserts, including its signature lemon meringue pie, ensure a constant queue on the street outside, especially for weekend brunch.

FLUCTUAT NEC MERGITUR
CAFE

Map p386 (☑01 42 06 42 81; www.fluctuat-cafe. paris; 18 place de la République, 10e; ⊙9am-11pm Mon-Fri; ☎; ⓂRépublique) On pedestrianised place de la République, this glass-box cafe-bar and sprawling terrace overlook the square's 9.4m-high bronze statue of Marianne, symbol of the French Republic. Parisian beers include Demory and Gallia;

LOCAL KNOWLEDGE

RIVERSIDE DRINKS

Come the warm days of spring, enchanting cafe and bar terraces mushroom down by the water's edge. Opening hours naturally fluctuate, depending on the weather, but **Les Nautes** (Map p386; ☎01 42 74 59 53; www.lesnautes-paris.com; 1 quai des Célestins, 4e; ⏰5pm-2am Wed-Sun; 📶; MSully–Morland) is a top Seine-side spot to chill with over a cocktail, glass of house punch or organic wine, cheese or charcuterie platter and awesome river views. DJs, bands and the occasional orchestra at weekends.

If afloat rocks your boat more, join the jet set aboard **Peniche Marcounet** (Map p386; ☎06 60 47 38 52; www.peniche-marcounet.fr; Port des Célestins, 4e; ⏰bar 10am-4am year-round, riverside terrace 10am-midnight May-Sep; 📶; MPont Marie), a beautiful 1925-built timber barge moored by the Pont Marie with cosy cabin bar and fabulous umbrella-shaded summer terrace on the banks with tables made from wooden pallets. Year-round, live gigs range from jazz, blues and tango to French *chanson* swing. Craft beers, cocktails and natural wines complement a barbecue-skewed menu and fantastic weekend brunch.

locally inspired cocktails range from the namesake République (chartreuse, gin, cucumber syrup and Perrier) to the vodka-laced Rive Droite (Right Bank; with lemon) and Rive Gauche (Left Bank; with lime).

LOUSTIC   COFFEE
Map p386 (☎09 80 31 07 06; www.cafeloustic.com; 40 rue Chapon, 3e; ⏰8.30am-6pm Mon-Fri, from 9.30am Sat, from 10am Sun; 📶; MArts et Métiers) Brit-born, Paris-adopted Channa Galhenage is the barista energy behind this north Marais espresso bar. Hermès wallpaper, geometric prints and 'golden oldie' French films screened on one wall make Loustic (old Breton for 'smart Alec') a beautiful space for lounging or laptop-ing over excellent Caffènation coffee (roasted in Antwerp).

WILD & THE MOON   JUICE BAR
Map p386 (☎01 43 20 50 01; www.wildandthe moon.fr; 138 rue Amelot, 11e; ⏰9am-8.30pm; 📶; MFilles du Calvaire) 🍃 Wild & The Moon's largest space yet occupies a former wine bar, complete with original vintage signage and a generously sized pavement terrace. Nut milks, 'superhero' vitality shots, fruit and vegetal smoothies and cold-pressed juices are the specialities, and raw food – power bowls, granola, gluten-free avocado toast is served all day.

Find other Le Marais branches at 25 rue des Gravilliers and 55 rue Charlot, both in the 3e *arrondissement*.

LE 10H10   CAFE
Map p386 (☎01 44 49 92 59; www.le10h10.com; 210 rue St-Martin, 3e; ⏰9am-8pm Mon-Fri, from 10am Sat, 1-8pm Sun; 📶; MRambuteau, Réaumur–Sébastopol) Lightning-fast wi-fi, the use of a scanner, colour printer, lockers and an on-site kitchen, and coffee, soft drinks and snacks are included in the rate at this popular co-working cafe, which charges €5/25 per hour/day. Wallpapered in groovy '70s-style prints and strewn with retro sofas and lava lamps, it sports an informal lounge vibe.

🍷 Ménilmontant & Belleville

⭐LE PERCHOIR   ROOFTOP BAR
Map p390 (☎01 48 06 18 48; www.leperchoir.fr; 14 rue Crespin du Gast, 11e; ⏰6pm-2am Mon-Thu, 4pm-2am Fri & Sat, 4pm-midnight Sun; 📶; MMénilmontant) Sunset is the best time to hit this 7th-floor bar for drinks overlooking Paris' rooftops and Saturday-night DJ sets. In winter, it's covered by a sail-like canopy and warmed by burning fires in metal drums. Below, the wildly popular 6th-floor restaurant morphs into a club by night. The entrance is hidden in an inner courtyard (take the lift or stairs).

Great cocktails include Beale Street (JD, San Pellegrino Limonata and cherry juice) and Suzebucker (gin, absinthe, lemon juice and ginger ale).

LA COMMUNE   COCKTAIL BAR
Map p390 (www.syndicatcocktailclub.com/la-commune; 80 bd de Belleville, 20e; ⏰6pm-2am Tue-Sat; 📶; MCouronnes) An atrium-style covered timber deck strewn with plants and comfy sofas marks the entrance to La Commune. Like its 10e sibling Le Syndicat (p148), cocktails made from French spirits

are its *raison d'être*. Here, the speciality is punch bowls containing five to eight glasses, such as Bisso Na Bissap (Corsican cedar brandy, apricot liqueur, French whisky, bissap juice and fresh citrus).

CAFÉ CHARBON
BAR

Map p390 (☑01 43 57 55 13; www.lecafecharbon. fr; 109 rue Oberkampf, 11e; ⊗8am-2am Mon-Wed, to 5am Thu, to 6am Fri & Sat; ☜; ⓜParmentier) Night owls, this is *your* address. Canopied by a gold-stencilled navy-blue awning, veteran Charbon remains one of the best bars in Ménilmontant and is always crowded thanks to a fantastic Belle Époque decor (high ceilings, chandeliers and leather booths) and buzzing ambience. Happy 'hour' is 5pm to 8pm; DJs and musicians play Friday and Saturday.

BEANS ON FIRE
COFFEE

Map p390 (www.thebeansonfire.com; 7 rue du Général Blaise, 11e; ⊗9am-3pm Tue-Sat; ☜; ⓜSt-Ambroise) Outstanding coffee is guaranteed at this innovative space. Not only a welcoming local cafe, it's also a collaborative roastery, where movers and shakers on Paris' reignited coffee scene come to roast their beans (ask about two-hour roasting workshops, available in English, if you're keen to roast your own). Its park-facing terrace is a neighbourhood hotspot on sunny days. Cash only.

Breakfast – granola, coffee-laced rice pudding, eggs, scones etc – is served until 3pm; lunch from noon.

LE 50
COFFEE

Map p390 (☑01 42 85 79 37; www.cafesbelleville. com; 50 rue de Belleville, 20e; ⊗8am-5pm Wed-Sun; ☜; ⓜBelleville) HQ for discerning coffee lovers in Belleville since 2019, this vintage corner cafe with wood panelling and signature blue bistro tables is a simple yet highly convivial affair. Regulars hover around the zinc bar, sipping espresso, noisette or filter coffee made with 'French Toast', 'Body Builder' or the latest creative roast from the 'hood's very own roaster, Belleville Brûlerie (p153).

Warm toasted and buttered *pain d'épices* (ginger bread), granola bowls and exceptional *sables* (shortbread) hit the light breakfast spot.

☆ ENTERTAINMENT

Repurposed art nouveau markets, 19th-century concert halls, jazz cellars and the city's winter circus (p34) are all on the bill in this buzzing neighbourhood.

LE BATACLAN
LIVE MUSIC

Map p386 (☑01 43 14 00 30; www.bataclan.fr; 50 bd Voltaire, 11e; ⓜOberkampf, Filles du Calvaire) Built in 1864, intimate concert, theatre and dance hall Le Bataclan was Maurice Chevalier's debut venue in 1910. The 1497-capacity venue reopened with a concert by Sting on

LOCAL BREWS

Brasserie BapBap (Map p390; ☑01 77 17 52 97; www.bapbap.paris; 79 rue St-Maur, 11e; guided tours €15; ⊗90min guided tours in English 4.30pm Sat, shop & tasting room 6-10pm Mon-Sat; ⓜRue St-Maur) BapBap, whose name means 'Brassée à Paris, Bue à Paris' (Brewed in Paris, Beloved in Paris; the latter a twist on 'drunk in Paris', as in 'consumed in Paris'), occupies an iron-girdered 20th-century warehouse turned garage. Tours show you the filtering, boiling, whirlpool and fermentation tanks, plus four tastings. Its street-front shop sells its brews and also offers *dégustation* (tasting).

Micro Brasserie Balthazar (Map p390; ☑01 71 24 90 82; www.facebook.com/MBBalthazar; 90 bd Ménilmontant, 20e; ⊗5pm-1am Mon-Sat; ⓜPère Lachaise) Balthazar's house brews, such as La Vibe (fruity pale ale), La Badas (black IPA), La Pickpocket (a double IPA), L'Ibu Profane (session IPA) and La Tiramistout (milk stout with aromas of coffee and chocolate) rotate on the taps at this crowdfunded microbrewery, along with guest beers from other French breweries, including Brasserie la Goutte d'Or.

La Beer Fabrique (Map p390; ☑01 71 27 71 02; www.labeerfabrique.com; 6 rue Guillaume Bertrand, 11e; 2hr/4hr brewing course €60/160; ⊗by reservation; ⓜRue St-Maur) During a two-hour course at this brewing school, you'll brew your own beer (and take it away with you, along with three of La Beer Fabrique's own beers), and enjoy six tastings accompanied by charcuterie. Four-hour courses will see you brew 15L of beer that you also get to take with you. Instruction is in English and French.

> **LOCAL KNOWLEDGE**
>
> ### GET CULTURAL
>
> Look out for exhibitions, concerts, workshops, fashion pop-ups, yoga classes, all sorts, at cultural centre **Le Carreau du Temple** (Map p386; ☑01 83 81 93 30; www.carreaudutemple.eu; 2 rue Perrée, 3e; ☺10am-10pm Mon-Fri, from 9am Sat, box office 10am-6pm Mon-Sat; Ⓜ Temple), in a former art nouveau covered market in Haut Marais, and in Ménilmontant at **La Bellevilloise** (☑01 46 36 07 07; www.labellevilloise.com; 19-21 rue Boyer, 20e; ☺7pm-1am Wed & Thu, to 2am Fri, 11am-2am Sat, 11.30am-midnight Sun; Ⓜ Gambetta), complete with summer garden and Sunday brunch accompanied by toe-tapping live jazz.

12 November 2016, almost a year to the day following the tragic 13 November 2015 terrorist attacks that took place here, and it once again hosts French and international rock and pop legends.

L'ALIMENTATION GÉNÉRALE
LIVE MUSIC

Map p390 (☑09 81 86 42 50; www.alimentation-generale.net; 64 rue Jean-Pierre Timbaud, 11e; admission Wed, Thu & Sun free, Fri & Sat €10; ☺7pm-2am Wed, Thu & Sun, to 5am Fri & Sat; Ⓜ Parmentier) This true hybrid, known as the Grocery Store to Anglophones, is a massive space, fronted at street level by its in-house Italianate canteen-bar with big glass windows and retro 1960s Belgian furniture. But music is the big deal here, with an impressive line-up of live gigs and DJs spinning pop, rock, electro, soul and funk to a packed dance floor.

LA MAROQUINERIE
LIVE MUSIC

(☑01 40 33 35 05; www.lamaroquinerie.fr; 23 rue Boyer, 20e; ☺6pm-2am; Ⓜ Gambetta) This tiny but trendy venue in Ménilmontant entices a local crowd with cutting-edge gigs – many bands kick off their European tours here. Past acts have included PJ Harvey, Bruno Mars, Pete Doherty and Coldplay. Also here are an alfresco courtyard and a restaurant with a short but excellent menu.

FAVELA CHIC
WORLD MUSIC

Map p386 (☑01 40 21 38 14; www.favelachic.com; 18 rue du Faubourg du Temple, 11e; ☺7.30pm-2am Tue-Thu, to 5am Fri & Sat; Ⓜ République) Favela Chic opens as a convivial restaurant and quickly morphs into caipirinha- and mojito-fuelled flirting and dancing (mostly on the long tables). The music is typically bossa nova, samba, *baile* (dance), funk and Brazilian pop, and it can get hot and crowded. The pace ramps up another gear on Saturday's club night (admission €15) when DJs spin tunes from 11pm until dawn.

LA JAVA
WORLD MUSIC

Map p390 (☑01 42 02 20 52; www.la-java.fr; 105 rue du Faubourg du Temple, 11e; concerts free-€10; ☺8pm-dawn Mon-Sat; Ⓜ Goncourt) Built in 1922, this is the dance hall where Édith Piaf got her first break, and it now reverberates to the sound of live salsa, rock and world music. Live concerts usually take place at 8pm or 9pm during the week. Afterwards a festive crowd gets dancing to electro, house, disco and Latino DJs.

NOUVEAU CASINO
LIVE MUSIC

Map p390 (☑01 43 57 57 40; www.nouveaucasino.net; 109 rue Oberkampf, 11e; Ⓜ Parmentier) This club-concert annexe of Café Charbon (p175) is revered for its live-music concerts (usually Tuesday, Thursday and Friday) and lively club nights on weekends. Electro, pop, deep house, rock – the program is eclectic, underground and always up to the minute.

LE VIEUX BELLEVILLE
LIVE MUSIC

Map p390 (☑01 44 62 92 66; www.le-vieux-belleville.com; 12 rue des Envierges, 20e; ☺concerts 8.30pm-2am Tue, Fri & Sat; Ⓜ Pyrénées) This old-fashioned bistro and *musette* at the top of Parc de Belleville is an atmospheric venue for performances of *chansons* featuring accordions and an organ grinder three times a week. It's a lively favourite with locals; reserve in advance.

CAVE DU 38 RIV'
JAZZ

Map p386 (☑01 48 87 56 30; www.38riv.com; 38 rue de Rivoli, 4e; concerts €15-30; ☺concerts from 8.30pm Mon-Sat, from 5pm Sun; Ⓜ Hôtel de Ville) On busy rue de Rivoli, a tiny street frontage gives way to a fantastically atmospheric vaulted stone cellar with jazz concerts most nights; check the agenda online. Jam sessions with free admission typically take place on Mondays, Thursdays and Fridays.

🛍️ SHOPPING

Le Marais and Haut Marais enjoy a strong fashion presence, with tiny ateliers and boutiques with rising and just-established designers at work; find many on and around rue Charlot and rue de Turenne, 3e. To the south, in the 4e, is department store BHV (p179). Both areas enjoy late-night and Sunday trading.

North of place de la République, fashion designers pepper rue de Marseille and rue Beaurepaire near Canal St-Martin; rue du Château d'Eau, 10e, is the street to find edgy concept stores, pop-ups and alternative design boutiques.

🏠 Le Marais

⭐MERCI   CONCEPT STORE

Map p386 (☑01 42 77 00 33; www.merci-merci. com; 111 bd Beaumarchais, 3e; ☺10am-7.30pm Mon-Sat; Ⓜ St-Sébastien–Froissart) 🌿 A Fiat Cinquecento marks the entrance to this unique concept store, which donates all its profits to a children's charity in Madagascar. Shop for fashion, accessories, linens, lamps and nifty designs for the home. Complete the experience with a coffee in its hybrid used-bookshop-cafe, a juice at its **Cinéma Café** (Map p386; ☺10am-7pm Mon-Sat) or lunch in its stylish **La Cantine de Merci** (Map p386; 111 bd Beaumarchais, 3e; mains €14-20; ☺10am-6pm Mon-Sat).

⭐EMPREINTES   DESIGN

Map p386 (www.empreintes-paris.com; 5 rue de Picardie, 3e; ☺11am-1pm & 2-7pm Tue-Sat; Ⓜ Temple) Spanning four floors, this design emporium is a concept store for unique, hand-crafted pieces by emerging and established French artists and designers. Exquisite jewellery, fashion and art are displayed alongside striking homewares (ceramics, cushions, furniture, lighting, books and more).

⭐VEJA   FASHION & ACCESSORIES

Map p386 (www.veja-store.com/fr_fr/; 15 rue de Poitou, 3e; ☺11am-8pm Mon-Sat, 2-7pm Sun; Ⓜ Filles du Calvaire) 🌿 Living proof that Parisian fashionistas are increasingly green: every Saturday and Sunday huge queues snake outside this 2019-opened store, much-loved for its ecofriendly, unisex trainers (sneakers) and plastic-free running

shoes – all made in Brazil and crafted from organic raw materials (cotton, rubber, recycled polyester fabrics etc), hence their sustainable '100% vegan' unique selling point.

Global brand Veja, whose name means 'look' in Brazilian, was founded by French entrepreneurs Sébastien Kopp and François Ghislain Morilion in 2004.

⭐KERZON   HOMEWARES

Map p386 (www.kerzon.paris; 68 rue de Turenne, 3e; ☺11.30am-7.30pm Tue-Sat; Ⓜ St-Sébastien–Froissart) Candles made from natural, biodegradable wax in Parisian scents such as Jardin du Luxembourg (with lilac and honey), Place des Vosges (rose and jasmine) and Parc des Buttes-Chaumont (cedar and sandalwood) make aromatic souvenirs of the city. The pretty white and sage-green boutique also stocks room fragrances, scented laundry liquids, and perfumes, soaps, bath oils and other toiletries.

LA GARÇONNIÈRE   CONCEPT STORE

Map p386 (www.la-garconniere.fr; 47bis rue des Archives, 3e; ☺11am-8pm Mon-Sat; Ⓜ Rambuteau) One of those achingly way-too-cool-for-school addresses, this concept store sizzles with gift ideas for your *homme*: clever board games, French wine-tasting kits, Image Republic posters, Parisian Carmen gins infused with pepper or grapefruit, alongside a carefully curated selection of clothing, accessories and footwear. Find a cafe here too, plus table football and a barber.

SAMY CHALON   FASHION & ACCESSORIES

Map p386 (☑01 44 59 39 16; 24 rue Charlot, 3e; ☺11.30am-7.30pm Tue-Sat; Ⓜ St-Sébastien–Froissart) 🌿 With a brilliant mix of ethical upcycling and luxury couture, French designer Samy Chalon transforms second-hand Hermès scarves, Chanel dresses and other iconic fashion pieces into whimsical tops, flowing skirts, unusual knits and downright cool frocks oozing femininity and sass. His workshop is right above the boutique.

HEUREUX LES CURIEUX   CONCEPT STORE

Map p386 (www.heureuxlescurieux.com; 23 rue du Pont aux Choux, 3e; ☺11am-7pm Tue-Sat, noon-6pm Sun; Ⓜ St-Sébastien Froissart) Shopping at this innovative concept store wedged between designer boutiques in Haut Marais is a different experience each time: every few weeks its bright white interior showcases a different brand or designer, be it with a

CATHERINE LE NEVEZ/LONELY PLANET ©

Dining at Maison Plisson

focus on fashion, homewares, lifestyle, gastronomy, tech and so on. 'Made in France' seems to be a common theme, but anything goes.

MAISON PLISSON
FOOD & DRINKS

Map p386 (☑01 71 18 19 09; www.facebook. com/LaMaisonPlisson; 93 bd Beaumarchais, 3e; mains €7-15, weekend brunch €29; ⊙9.30am-9pm Mon, 8.30am-9pm Tue-Sat, 9.30am-8pm Sun; MSt-Sébastien–Froissart) Framed by glass-canopied wrought-iron girders, this gourmet emporium incorporates a covered-market-style, terrazzo-floored food hall filled with exquisite, mostly French produce: meat, vegetables, cheese, wine, chocolate, jams, freshly baked breads and much more. If your appetite's whetted, its cafe, opening to twin terraces, serves charcuterie, foie gras and cheese platters, bountiful salads and delicacies such as Noilly Prat–flambéed sardines.

EATALY
FOOD & DRINKS

Map p386 (☑01 83 65 81 00; www.eataly.net/fr_ fr/magasins/paris-marais; 37 rue Ste-Croix de la Bretonnerie, 4e; ⊙10am-10pm, restaurant hours vary; MHôtel de Ville) Lovers of Italian food will have a field day in this culinary paradise combining several eateries with market counters selling meat, breads, cheese, fresh pasta, pizza slices, buxom fruit and veg, deli goods and so on. There's an extensive Italian wine cellar, plus a cooking school offering various themed two-hour classes (from €35) for adults and children.

FAGUO
FASHION & ACCESSORIES

Map p386 (☑01 42 71 10 42; www.faguo-store. com; 81 rue Vieille du Temple, 3e; ⊙10.30am-7.30pm; MSt-Paul) ✿ Few brands are as conscious of their carbon footprint as this Paris-based fashion company that plants a tree in France for each product it sells, and has vegan and recycled lines in its seasonal collection of clothing, footwear, accessories and luggage for men and women. A recycling terminal in its Marais boutique ensures a second life for old, unwanted clothes.

ANDREA CREWS
FASHION & ACCESSORIES

Map p386 (☑01 45 26 36 68; www.andreacrews. com; 83 rue de Turenne, 3e; ⊙1-7.30pm Wed-Fri, to 7pm Sat; MSt-Sébastien–Froissart) Using everything from discarded clothing to electrical fittings and household bric-a-brac, this bold art and fashion collective sews, recycles and reinvents to create the most extraordinary pieces. Watch out for 'happenings' in its Marais boutique.

L'ÉCLAIREUR
FASHION & ACCESSORIES

Map p386 (☑01 48 87 10 22; www.leclaireur. com; 40 rue de Sévigné, 3e; ⏱11am-7pm Mon-Sat, from 2pm Sun; MSt-Paul) Part art space, part lounge and part deconstructionist fashion statement, this shop is known for having the next big thing first. Two tonnes of wooden planks, 147 TV screens and walls that move to reveal the men's and women's collection all form part of the stunning interior design by Belgian artist Arne Quinze.

EDWART
CHOCOLATE

Map p386 (☑01 42 78 48 92; www.edwart.fr; 17 rue Vielle du Temple, 4e; ⏱11am-noon & 1-8pm Mon-Wed, 11am-8pm Thu-Sun; MHôtel de Ville) Wunderkind chocolatiers Edwin Yansané and Arthur Heinze (collectively 'Edwart') take their inspiration from Paris (and – as a global melting pot – by extension, the world). Feisty chocolates using unique ingredients such as Indian curry, Iranian saffron and Japanese whisky are sparingly displayed in their sleek Marais boutique.

BONTON
CHILDREN'S CLOTHING

Map p386 (www.bonton.fr; 5 bd des Filles du Calvaire, 3e; ⏱10am-7pm Mon-Sat; MSt-Sébastien–Froissart) Chic concept store Bonton stocks vintage-inspired fashion, furnishings and knick-knacks for babies, toddlers and children. Don't leave without donning an old-fashioned, floppy sunhat or pair of oversized sunglasses and getting your photo snapped in its retro photo booth. Parents will find a bathroom with a changing mat in the basement.

🏠 Ménilmontant & Belleville

★FROMAGERIE GONCOURT
CHEESE

Map p390 (☑01 43 57 91 28; www.facebook.com/lafromageriegoncourt; 1 rue Abel Rabaud, 11e; ⏱9am-1.30pm & 3.30-8pm Tue-Fri, 9am-8pm Sat; MGoncourt) Styled like a boutique, this contemporary *fromagerie* is a must-discover. Clément Brossault ditched a career in banking to become a *fromager* and his seasonal cheese selection – 70-plus types – is superb. Cheeses flagged with a bicycle symbol are varieties he discovered in situ during a two-

month French cheese tour he embarked on as part of his training.

BHV
DEPARTMENT STORE

(Map p386; www.bhv.fr; 52 rue de Rivoli, 4e; ⏱9.30am-8pm Mon-Sat, 11am-7.30pm Sun; MHôtel de Ville) BHV (pronounced bay-ash-vay) is a vast, straightforward department store in Le Marais where you can buy everything from guidebooks on Paris to men's, women's and kids' clothing and accessories, stationery, luggage and every imaginable type of hammer, power tool, nail, plug and hinge.

Drink and dine at the rooftop cocktail bar Le Perchoir Marais (p172) or the covered courtyard with street-food stalls.

🏃 SPORTS & ACTIVITIES

SEIZE
ARTS & CRAFTS

Map p386 (☑01 48 06 86 19; www.seizeparis. com; 16 rue de Crussol, 11e; ⏱2-7pm Tue-Fri, from 11am Sat; MOberkampf) Natural light floods into this attractive arts space, strung with an eye-catching collection of fashionably eclectic wicker lampshades above one long shared table. This is where Parisians gather to mingle with other like-minded souls over creative ateliers (workshops) in knitting, macramé, embroidery, scrapbooking, flower arranging, paper crafting, jewellery making etc. Ateliers (€50 to €90) last two to three hours.

NOMADESHOP
SKATING

Map p386 (☑01 44 54 07 44; www.nomadeshop. com; 37 bd Bourdon, 4e; half-/full-day skate hire from €8/15; ⏱11am-1.30pm & 2.30-7.30pm Tue-Fri, 10am-7pm Sat; MBastille) Nomadeshop rents and sells in-line equipment and accessories, including wheels, helmets, elbow and knee guards; a rental deposit of €150 is required. Multiday rentals are available. It can also help set up skating lessons and has details of the three-hour roller *randonnées* organised by in-line skating club Rollers & Coquillages (www. rollers-coquillages.org), departing from in front of the shop each Sunday at 2.30pm.

Bastille & Eastern Paris

BASTILLE | BOIS DE VINCENNES | 12E

Neighbourhood Top Five

① **Opéra Bastille** (p191) Taking in a backstage tour or performance at this modern monolith, on the landmark square where revolutionaries stormed the Bastille in 1789.

② **Promenade Plantée** (p182) Joining Parisians for a stroll along the foliage-laced path of this elevated city park, uniquely positioned atop a 19th-century railway viaduct.

③ **Château de Vincennes** (p184) Exploring Paris' only medieval castle, complete with a prerequisite keep and a sublime 16th-century royal chapel.

④ **Parc Zoologique de Paris** (p184) Spotting lions, white rhinos, giraffes and wolverines at the city's state-of-the-art zoo in the Bois de Vincennes.

⑤ **Cinémathèque Française** (p182) Catching timeless cinematic classics at this little-known cinema museum and screening complex.

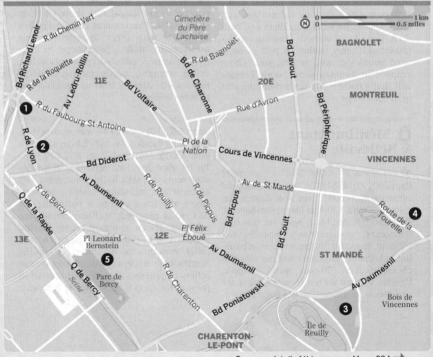

For more detail of this area see Map p394.➡

Explore Bastille & Eastern Paris

Bastille isn't known for its sights, but it's nonetheless a fascinating area to explore on foot. As it's still authentically residential in most parts, a wander will give you a taste of everyday life in one of Paris' most dynamic neighbourhoods. For a bird's-eye perspective, ascend to elevated park Promenade Plantée (p182), which looks down on the surrounding streets.

Yet Bastille's main attraction is not aimless *flâneurie* (urban strolling): the area's real appeal is dipping your toes into a vibrant restaurant scene dominated by young, creative chefs; its scores of popular, inexpensive bars and cafes; and the profusion of evening entertainment, from avant-garde opera to indie rock.

You may be reluctant to leave the city behind with so much to explore, but an easy trip to the Bois de Vincennes (p184), the city's largest park, never disappoints. From a castle and a zoo to outdoor concerts, bike excursions, pick-up football matches and picnics, it's one of the most-loved spots in the capital to unwind alfresco.

Local Life

Bistros The 11e and 12e have an unusually high number of old-school bistros that have preserved much of their original decor, such as Chez Paul (p186) and Le Bistrot du Peintre (p185).

Markets Fabulous markets in this neighbourhood include the twice-weekly Marché Bastille (p192), and daily (bar Sunday) Marché d'Aligre (p193), as well as bi-weekly organic market Marché Biologique Place du Père Chaillet (p193).

Green spaces Eastern Paris is blessed with some superb parks. The Promenade Plantée (p182) and Parc de Bercy (p182) are easy escapes; on weekends many Parisians decamp to the much larger Bois de Vincennes (p184), with the family favourite Parc Floral de Paris (p184) at its heart.

Getting There & Away

Metro Lines 1, 5 and 8 serve Bastille; lines 1 and 8 are major east–west arteries, while line 5 heads south across the Seine and north to the Gare du Nord. Line 14 links Bercy with St-Lazare in the northwest and the 13e in southeastern Paris.

RER The east–west RER A stops at Nation and Gare de Lyon en route to central and western Paris, while RER D links Gare de Lyon with Gare du Nord.

Bicycle You'll find Vélib' stations around place de la Bastille on bd Richard Lenoir, bd Bourdon and rue de Lyon.

Lonely Planet's Top Tip

While the area immediately surrounding place de la Bastille has spawned a clutch of faceless bars and restaurant chains, walking east along rue de Charonne or rue du Faubourg St-Antoine brings you to to the 11e's Faidherbe *quartier* (quarter), a much more interesting neighbourhood filled with all the exciting dining addresses, atmospheric cafes and quirky, unusual shops that make a city great.

BASTILLE & EASTERN PARIS

✖ Best Places to Eat

➡ Septime (p188)
➡ Mokonuts (p186)
➡ Le Servan (p186)
➡ Madito (p183)
➡ Chez Paul (p186)
➡ Le Bistrot Paul Bert (p186)

For reviews, see p183.➡

🍷 Best Places to Drink

➡ Le Baron Rouge (p189)
➡ La Manufacture de Café (p189)
➡ Bluebird (p190)
➡ Les Cuves de Fauve (p189)

For reviews, see p189.➡

🔒 Best Shopping

➡ Marché Bastille (p192)
➡ Marché d'Aligre (p193)
➡ La Manufacture de Chocolat (p192)
➡ Viaduc des Arts (p192)

For reviews, see p192.➡

◉ SIGHTS

Historic place de la Bastille – at the intersection of the 4e, 11e and 12e *arrondissements* – is the obvious place to start exploring. Take a waterside stroll south along the city's only pleasure port, Port de l'Arsenal. Southeast of here is the busy Gare de Lyon station area, with the unusual Promenade Plantée, which can be followed on foot for 4.5km to Bois de Vincennes on the far eastern fringe of this neighbourhood. Several key sights are clustered in and around the green urban woodland.

PROMENADE PLANTÉE   PARK

Map p394 (Coulée Verte René-Dumont; cnr rue de Lyon & av Daumesnil, 12e; ⊙8am-9.30pm Mon-Fri, from 9am Sat & Sun Mar-Oct, 8am-5.30pm Mon-Fri, from 9am Sat & Sun Nov-Feb; Ⓜ Bastille, Gare de Lyon, Daumesnil) The disused 19th-century Vincennes railway viaduct was reborn in 1993 as the world's first elevated park, planted with a fragrant profusion of cherry trees, maples, rose trellises, bamboo corridors and lavender. Three storeys above ground, it provides a unique aerial vantage point on the city. Along the first, northwestern section, above av Daumesnil, art-gallery workshops beneath the arches form the Viaduc des Arts (p192). Staircases provide access (lifts here invariably don't work).

Officially the Coulée Verte René-Dumont, it's better known as the Promenade Plantée. Waking southeast, look out for the spectacular art deco–style police station at the start of rue de Rambouillet, which was built in 1991 and is topped with a dozen huge, identical telamones (male figures used as pillars) based on Michelangelo's *Dying Slave*.

The viaduct later drops back to street level at Jardin de Reuilly (1.5km); it's possible to follow it all the way (4.5km) to the Bois de Vincennes (p184). This latter section can also be done on a bike or in-line skates. A 1.7km section of the former **Petite Ceinture** (PC 12; btwn rue des Meuniers & Villa du Bel-Air, 12e; ⊙8am-sunset Mar-Oct, from 9am Nov-Feb; Ⓜ Michel Bizot), the steam railway line that encircled central Paris from the late 19th century until the line closed to passenger trains in 1934 and freight trains in the early 1990s, intersects the promenade 200m north of square Charles Péguy.

CINÉMATHÈQUE FRANÇAISE   MUSEUM

(✆01 71 19 33 33; www.cinematheque.fr; 51 rue de Bercy, 12e; adult/child €5/2.50, 1st Sun of month free, with film €8; ⊙noon-7pm Wed-Mon; Ⓜ Bercy) A little-known gem near Parc de Bercy, the Cinémathèque Française was originally created in 1936 by film archivist Henri Langlois. Devoted to the history of cinema, its museum, relaunching in 2021, takes inspiration from director Georges Méliès (whose classic *A Trip to the Moon* featured in 2011's *Hugo*). Displays include costumes, props, early equipment, old advertising posters and short clips. Temporary exhibitions usually take a behind-the-scenes look at a particular film. Enter via place Léonard-Bernstein by the park.

Its cinema (p191) screens up to 10 films daily.

OPÉRA BASTILLE   NOTABLE BUILDING

Map p394 (✆01 71 25 24 23; www.operadeparis.fr; 2-6 place de la Bastille, 12e; tours adult/child €17/12; ⊙tours Sep–mid-Jul; Ⓜ Bastille) Designed by architect Carlos Ott, this concrete, glass and steel opera house (p191) is Paris' largest, with a 2745-seat main auditorium. During his presidency, François Mitterrand instigated its creation as one of his *grands projets* (great projects), and inaugurated it on 13 July 1989, the eve of the 200th anniversary of the storming of the Bastille prison. The date was symbolic as the new opera house was intended to strip opera of its elitist airs.

Guided tours (in French) lasting 1½ hours take you behind the scenes. Tour schedules are online; the box office sells tickets 10 minutes beforehand.

PARC DE BERCY   PARK

(rues Paul Belmondo, de l'Ambriosie & François Truffaut, 12e; ⊙24hr; Ⓜ Cour St-Émilion, Bercy) Built on the site of a former wine depot, this large, landscaped park is a great place to break for a picnic and let the kids run free. Vestiges of its former incarnation are spread across the park and the Cour St-Émilion, where the warehouses were located. In some spots you'll see the old railroad tracks; in others you'll find grape vines.

Bercy reached its height as the 'world's wine cellar' in the 19th century: it was right on the Seine, close to Paris yet outside the city walls, meaning that shipping was convenient and commerce tax-free.

LES PASSAGES DE LA BASTILLE

The area east of the Bastille was originally outside city limits and under the control of the nearby Abbey de Saint-Antoine (now the St-Antoine Hospital). In 1471, King Louis XI granted the abbey an unusual privilege: craftsmen living on the abbey's land were granted exemption from city taxes and, more importantly, from the stringent guild regulations that stifled innovation. Cabinetmakers, gilders, varnishers and others flocked here, and the result was a flurry of creativity that resulted in the introduction of prized new furniture styles over the centuries, such as Louis XIV, Louis XV and Louis XVI.

The passages and courtyards once inhabited by artisans still exist – you'll find plenty if you look closely while walking along rue du Faubourg St-Antoine – but the sounds of hammer and saw have largely been replaced by the secluded live-work spaces of architects and graphic designers.

PLACE DE LA BASTILLE   SQUARE

Map p394 (12e; MBastille) A 14th-century fortress built to protect the city gates, the Bastille became a prison under Cardinal Richelieu, which was mobbed on 14 July 1789, igniting the French Revolution. At the centre of the square is the 52m-high **Colonne de Juillet**, a green-bronze column topped by a gilded, winged Liberty. Revolutionaries from the uprising of 1830 are buried beneath. Major redevelopments now link the square to the Bassin de l'Arsenal.

The location of the old fortress prison of the Bastille is marked on the ground, and the foundations are also marked below ground in the Bastille metro station, on the platform of line 5.

EATING

Bastille dining tends to swing between a highly lauded group of up-and-coming chefs, who run the hip neobistros that have reinspired Parisian cooking, and the die-hard traditionalists, who rarely venture beyond the much-loved standards of French cuisine. The neighbourhood caters to all budgets, tastes and time constraints – along with the area's sensational markets, speciality food shops and **boulangeries** (bakeries), you'll find gourmet burger, sandwich and pizza addresses in the mix too.

★MADITO   LEBANESE €

Map p394 (☑01 45 35 89 72; www.madito.fr; 38 rue de Citeaux, 12e; mains €11-15, tasting menu €28; ⊙noon-3pm & 7-11pm Tue-Sat; ☑; MFaidherbe-Chaligny) Teensy Madito prepares startlingly good Lebanese cuisine daily from scratch (there's no microwave or freezer on the premises). With just 20 seats, you'll need to book ahead to feast on starters such as *makdous* (aubergine stuffed with red peppers and walnuts) or *warak enab* (vine-leaf-wrapped rice and spiced beef), followed by mains like *tawouk* (lemon- and yoghurt-marinated chicken).

Vegetarian choices are plentiful. Finish with desserts like *aish as-saraya* (rosewater-syrup-soaked bread pudding) or *sfouf* (almond semolina cake).

FARINE & O   BAKERY €

Map p394 (www.facebook.com/FarineetO; 153 rue du Faubourg St-Antoine, 11e; pastries €2-5.50, sandwiches & salads €5.50-7.50; ⊙7.30am-8.30pm Wed-Mon; MLedru-Rollin) *Pâtissier* Olivier Magne, a winner of the prestigious Meilleur Ouvrier de France master craftsman competition, hails from the Cantal region of France and has brought his talents to the capital. Magne's stunning creations include a mini choux pastry Paris-Brest with chestnut cream, blackcurrant and lemon brioche, and strawberry and pistachio tarts, along with his signature sourdough loaves.

BREIZH CAFÉ PAUL BERT   CRÊPES €

Map p394 (☑01 42 78 27 49; www.breizhcafe.com; 23 rue Paul Bert, 11e; crêpes & galettes €6-18.50; ⊙11.30am-11pm; ☑; MCharonne) Fronted by its distinctive French navy–blue façade, authentic Breton crêperie Breizh's outpost in the hip Faidherbe neighbourhood serves stunning savoury *galettes* and sweet crêpes made with artisan ingredients: truffled ham, Normandy scallops, Basque chorizo, St-Malo seaweed, smoked herring, organic Breton honey, Valrhona chocolate and Madagascan vanilla, as well as homemade salted caramel.

WORTH A DETOUR

BOIS DE VINCENNES

Originally royal hunting grounds, Paris' eastern woodlands, **Bois de Vincennes** (av Daumesnil, 12e; M Porte de Charenton, Porte Dorée), were annexed by the army following the Revolution and then donated to the city in 1860 by Napoléon III. A fabulous place to escape the endless stretches of Parisian concrete, the woods also contain a handful of notable sights, including a bona fide royal château.

Metro lines 1 (St-Mandé, Château de Vincennes) and 8 (Porte Dorée, Porte de Charenton) will get you to the edges of the park. Pick up picnic supplies on rue de Midi, Vincennes' main shopping street.

Château de Vincennes (01 48 08 31 20; www.chateau-de-vincennes.fr; 1 av de Paris; adult/child €9.50/free; 10am-6pm mid-May–mid-Sep, to 5pm mid-Sep–mid-May; M Château de Vincennes) This fortified royal residence on Paris' fringe, originally a 12th-century hunting lodge, was expanded several times throughout the centuries until it reached its present size under Louis XIV. Notable features of the striking medieval château include the beautiful 52m-high keep (1370) and royal chapel (1552). Note that the chapel is only open between 10.30am and 1pm, and 2pm and 5.30pm mid-May to mid-September (until 4.30pm mid-September to mid-May).

Parc Zoologique de Paris (Zoo de Vincennes; 08 11 22 41 22; www.parczoologiquede paris.fr; cnr av Daumesnil & rte de Ceinture du Lac Daumesnil, 12e; adult/child €20/17; 9.30am-8.30pm May-Aug, shorter hours Sep-Apr; M Porte Dorée) Paris' largest, state-of-the-art zoo focuses on the conservation of species and habitats, with camouflaged vantage points (no peering through fences). Its biozones include Patagonia (sea lions, pumas); the Sahel-Sudan savannah (lions, white rhinos, giraffes); forested Europe (wolves, lynxes, wolverines); rainforested Amazon-Guyana (jaguars, monkeys, anacondas); and Madagascar (lemurs). Tickets are slightly cheaper online.

Parc Floral de Paris (01 49 57 25 50; www.parcfloraldeparis.com; Esplanade du Chateau de Vincennes/rte de la Pyramide; adult/child May-Oct €2.50/1.50, Nov-Apr free; 9.30am-8pm Apr-Sep, to 6.30pm Oct, to 5pm Nov-Feb, to 6.30pm Mar; ; M Château de Vincennes) This magnificent botanical park is a highlight of the Bois de Vincennes. Natural landscaping, a Japanese bonsai pavilion, an azalea garden and several ponds with water lilies and lotuses impress garden lovers, while Paris' largest play area (slides, jungle gyms, sandboxes) thrills families with young children. For bigger kids, there are plenty of paid-for activities too, including minigolf (featuring Parisian landmarks), a ropes course and table tennis (equipment rental available). Free open-air concerts staged throughout summer make it a first-rate picnic destination. Not all facilities open outside the warmer months.

Lac Daumesnil (www.barques.org; rte de Ceinture du Lac Daumesnil, 20e; hourly boat hire for 2-/4-person boat €13.20/14.20; boat hire 10am-1hr before dark mid-Feb–mid-Nov; M Porte Dorée) Like something out of a Renoir painting, the largest lake in Bois de Vincennes is a popular destination for walks and rowboat excursions in warmer months (cash only; €20 deposit required). A Buddhist temple is nearby.

Hippodrome de Vincennes (01 49 77 17 17; www.vincennes-hippodrome.com; 2 rte de la Ferme, 12e; adult/child €3/free; ; M Château de Vincennes or RER Joinville-le-Pont) First opened in 1863 and rebuilt in 1879 following the Franco-Prussian War, this hippodrome hosts horse races and trotting races. Binoculars are available for hire. Free shuttle buses run from the metro and RER stations.

Musée de l'Histoire de l'Immigration (01 53 59 58 60; www.histoire-immigration.fr; 293 av Daumesnil, 12e; adult/child €6/free, 1st Sun of month free; 10am-5.30pm Tue-Fri, to 7pm Sat & Sun) Not actually part of the park but near Porte Dorée station, this heavyweight museum documents the hot-potato topic of immigration. The informative gallery of personal items donated by members of the public particularly stands out. It's housed in the lavish 1931 Palais de la Porte Dorée along with the **Aquarium Tropical** (01 53 59 64 30; www.aquarium-tropical.fr; adult/child €7/5.50; 10am-5.30pm Tue-Fri, to 7pm Sat & Sun). Admission prices rise during temporary exhibitions.

NANINA
CHEESE €

Map p394 (☑07 78 46 46 36; www.facebook. com/nanina75011; 24bis rue Basfroi, 11e; lunch menus €7.50-13.50, panini €6-9; ⊗10am-3pm & 5-8.30pm Mon-Thu, 10am-3pm & 5-10pm Fri, 10am-10pm Sat, closed Aug; MVoltaire) Nanina's creamy mozzarella and ricotta, made from Auvergne-sourced buffalo milk and hand-made here on the premises, supply some of Paris' most prestigious restaurants. You can taste the cheeses here on their own, in panini or as part of a lunch *menu* that might include lasagne or pasta. Staff are happy to show you around and explain the cheese-making process.

NOGLU
CAFE €

Map p394 (☑01 42 36 52 50; www.noglu.fr; 15 rue Basfroi, 11e; pastrites €2.50-8, dishes €8.50-17, weekend brunch €28; ⊗9am-4.30pm Mon-Fri, 10am-6pm Sat; 🛜🍴; MCharonne) The clue is in the name: everything NoGlu serves for breakfast (granola, porridge, *tartines*), lunch (Buddha bowls, soups, quiches, burgers and pastas) and weekend brunch is gluten-free, with dairy-free and vegan options. The rose-pink dining room is styled like a Parisian living room.

CAFÉ MIRABELLE
CAFE €

Map p394 (www.cafemirabelleparis.wixsite.com; 16 rue la Vacquerie, 11e; pastries €2.50-7.50, 2-course lunch menu €15.80, weekend brunch €29; ⊗8am-6pm Wed-Fri, from 9am Sat & Sun; 🛜; MPhilippe Auguste, Voltaire) A black-and-white stencilled outline of Paris' skyline stretches across one wall of this charming cafe, whose home-baked treats include custard- and banana-filled croissants, Grand Marnier gateau and yuzu meringue pie. Its *gianduja* (choc-hazelnut) hot chocolate is a winter warmer; in summer, cool down with a freshly squeezed juice.

LE BAR À SOUPES
SOUP €

Map p394 (www.lebarasoupes.com; 33 rue de Charonne, 11e; soups €4.90-7.80, 2-course lunch menu €14; ⊗noon-3pm & 6.30-10.30pm Mon-Sat; 🍴; MLedru-Rollin) With six different soups served daily, chances are you'll find something here to warm you up. Choices might include leek, potato and chorizo, pumpkin-chestnut borscht, cauliflower and Bleu d'Auvergne cheese, and the vodka-laced Bloody Mary. There's a handful of tables; otherwise pick up a steaming cup to take away.

LES DOMAINES QUI MONTENT
FRENCH €

Map p394 (☑01 43 56 89 15; www.lesdomaines quimontent.com; 136 bd Voltaire, 11e; 2-course lunch menu €16.90; ⊗kitchen noon-3pm Mon-Sat, shop 10.30am-7.30pm Mon, 10am-8pm Tue-Thu, 10am-8.30pm Fri & Sat; MVoltaire) Les Domaines Qui Montent was around before the *cave à manger* trend began, and while it's not as trendy as most newcomers, it is very much the real thing. Above all a wine shop, it offers simple two-course lunch *menus* made from premium ingredients like smoked black Bigorre pork sausage that you can pair with any of its available bottles.

CRÊPERIE BRETONNE FLEURIE DE L'EPOUSE DU MARIN
CRÊPES €

Map p394 (☑01 43 55 62 29; 67 rue de Charonne, 11e; crêpes €4.50-13.50; ⊗noon-2pm & 7-11pm Mon-Sat, noon-2pm & 7-10pm Sun; MCharonne) Authentic down to its savoury buckwheat *galettes* and sweet crêpes smothered with fillings such as chestnut puree and cara-melised hazelnut, this delightful Breton crê-perie with a sky-blue façade, half-timbered walls and lace curtains is filled with emo-tive black-and-white photos of Brittany.

LES GALOPINS
BISTRO €

Map p394 (☑01 47 00 45 35; 24 rue des Taillandiers, 11e; 2-/3-course lunch menus €13.50/17, mains €14.50-23.50; ⊗noon-3pm & 7.30-11pm Mon-Fri, 7.30-11pm Sat & Sun; MBastille) Vin-tage posters on the walls give a retro am-bience to this warm and buzzing bistro filled with locals feasting on huge platefuls of traditional French country fare. Hearty appetites should order the *côté de bœuf* (rib steak) served with Béarnaise sauce or *épaule d'agneau* (lamb shoulder) for two. Staff go out of their way to please.

VG PÂTISSERIE
PASTRIES €

Map p394 (www.vgpatisserie.fr; 123 bd Voltaire, 11e; pastries €3.50-6; ⊗1-7pm Tue, 9am-7pm Wed-Sat, 9am-5pm Sun; 🍴; MVoltaire) 🌿 Organic treats at this *pâtisserie végétale*, including *pains au chocolat* and croissants, cinnamon and nutmeg *millefeuille* (layered pastry), blood-orange meringue tarts and macrons, are eggless, butterless and often vegan and/or gluten-free. Zero-waste discounts apply if you bring your own containers and bags.

LE BISTROT DU PEINTRE
BISTRO €

Map p394 (☑01 47 00 34 39; www.bistrotdupein tre.com; 116 av Ledru-Rollin, 11e; mains €11.50-18; ⊗kitchen noon-2.30pm & 7-10.30pm, bar 7am-2am Mon-Sat, from 8am Sun; 🛜; MLedru-Rollin)

The 1902 art nouveau bar, elegant terrace, classic value-for-money bistro dishes, including its signature *pot au feu,* confit duck leg with sautéed potatoes and time-honoured desserts (*tarte à l'orange, crème caramel* and chocolate-drizzled profiteroles...), and a finely honed wine list make this Belle Époque treasure an atmospheric stop day or night.

★MOKONUTS   CAFE €€
Map p394 (☎09 80 81 82 85; www.mokonuts. com; 5 rue St-Bernard, 11e; pastries €2.50-7, mains €20-25; ⊗9am-4pm Mon-Fri, closed Aug; ☏; ⓂFaidherbe-Chaligny) ✦ Much-loved hole-in-the-wall Mokonuts, with a beautiful mosaic-tiled floor, makes a cosy refuge for snacks like flourless chocolate layer cake, clementine almond cake and white-chocolate and roasted-almond cookies. Sea bream with chickpeas and capers, and lamb shoulder with hummus are among the all-organic lunchtime mains (book well ahead). Natural wines and craft beers feature on the drinks list. Bookings are recommended.

Alternatively, head around the corner to its offspring **Mokoloco** (Map p394; 74 rue de Charonne, 11e; sandwiches €7.50-10.50; ⊗11.30am-5pm Tue-Sat; ⓂCharonne) for gourmet sandwiches, salads and famous cookies – look for the same mint-green façade.

★LE SERVAN   BISTRO €€
Map p394 (☎01 55 28 51 82; www.leservan.fr; 32 rue St-Maur, 11e; 3-course lunch menu €29, mains €24-35; ⊗noon-10.30pm; ⓂVoltaire, Rue St-Maur, Père Lachaise) Ornate cream-coloured ceilings with moulded cornices and pastel murals, huge windows and wooden floors give this neighbourhood neobistro near Père Lachaise a light, airy feel on even the greyest Parisian day. Seared mackerel with yuzu and miso dressing, and duck and coriander dumplings are among the inventive creations on the daily changing menu. Reserve to avoid missing out.

LE BISTROT PAUL BERT   BISTRO €€
Map p394 (☎01 43 72 24 01; 18 rue Paul Bert, 11e; 2-/3-course menu €19/42; ⊗noon-2pm & 7.30-11pm Tue-Thu, 7.30-11pm Fri, noon-2.30pm Sat, closed Aug; ⓂFaidherbe-Chaligny) When food writers list Paris' best bistros, Paul Bert's name consistently pops up. The timeless decor and classic dishes, such as *steak-frites* (steak and chips) and hazelnut-cream Paris-Brest pastry, reward booking ahead. Siblings in the same street: **L'Écailler du Bistrot** (Map p394; ☎01 43 72 76 77; 22 rue Paul Bert, 11e; oysters per half-dozen €9-22, mains €28-41, seafood platters per person from €42; ⊗noon-2.30pm & 7.30-11pm Tue-Sat) for seafood; **La Cave Paul Bert** (Map p394; ☎01 58 53 50 92; 16 rue Paul Bert, 11e; ⊗noon-midnight, kitchen noon-2pm & 7.30-11.30pm), a wine bar with small plates; and **Le 6 Paul Bert** (Map p394; ☎01 43 79 14 32; www.le6paulbert.com; 6 rue Paul Bert, 11e; 3-course weekday lunch menu €22, small plates €8-28; ⊗noon-2pm & 7.30-11pm Tue-Fri, 7.30-11pm Sat) for modern cuisine.

Produce for all three restaurants is grown on its farm in Normandy.

PASSERINI   ITALIAN €€
Map p394 (☎01 43 42 27 56; www.passerini.paris; 65 rue Traversière, 12e; lunch menus €26-48, dinner mains €18-32; ⊗7.30-10.15pm Tue, noon-2.15pm & 7.30-10.15pm Wed-Sat, closed early May & Aug; ⓂLedru-Rollin) Rome native Giovanni Passerini is one of the finest Italian chefs cooking in Europe today. Delectable specialities include roast pigeon with smoked ricotta, and red Sicilian shrimp ravioli with pumpkin and bergamot sauce, and are complemented by natural wines sourced from small vineyards. Pastas are made fresh and are also sold at its adjoining deli, Pastificio Passerini.

BUFFET   BISTRO €€
Map p394 (☎01 83 89 63 82; www.restaurant buffet.fr; 8 rue de la Main d'Or, 11e; mains €15-22; ⊗7-11pm Tue-Sat; ⓂLedru-Rollin) Tucked away on a charming Bastille backstreet behind a mulberry-coloured façade, Buffet has burgundy leather seating, wooden tables, mirrors and terrazzo floors. Despite its name, there's no smorgasbord but a short daily changing blackboard menu of bistro dishes like lemon sole with hand-cut chips, roast duck with prunes, and chestnut-chocolate mousse that belies the complexity of the cooking.

CHEZ PAUL   BISTRO €€
Map p394 (☎01 47 00 34 57; www.chezpaul.com; 13 rue de Charonne, 11e; 2-/3-course weekday lunch menu €18/21, mains €17.50-26; ⊗noon-1am; ⓂLedru-Rollin) This is Paris as your grandmother knew it: chequered red-and-white napkins, faded photographs on the walls, old red banquettes and traditional French dishes such as pig trotters, *andouillette* (a feisty tripe sausage) and *tête de veau et cervelle* (calf head and brains). If offal isn't for you, alternatives include a steaming bowl of *pot au feu* (beef stew).

VLASTAS/SHUTTERSTOCK ©

Château de Vincennes (p184)

COUP D'ŒIL
FRENCH €€

Map p394 (☎01 43 57 59 68; www.coupdoeil.paris; 80 rue Sedaine, 11e; 3-course weekday lunch menu €18, small plates dinner €7-14; ⏰noon-3pm & 6-10pm, bar to 2am; ☎; MVoltaire) Traditional decor (exposed brick, patterned tiles) meets contemporary design (wave-form timber ceiling panels) at this striking wine bar. Cider-steamed cockles, fennel-marinated grilled octopus, and potato and cheese soufflé with crab sauce are among the dishes that accompany all-natural wines. Live jazz, blues and soul often plays on Saturday nights.

L'ÉBAUCHOIR
BISTRO €€

Map p394 (☎01 43 42 49 31; www.lebauchoir. com; 43-45 rue de Citeaux, 12e; lunch menus €15-29, mains €22-25; ⏰8-11pm Mon, noon-2.30pm & 8-11pm Tue-Thu, noon-2.30pm & 7.30-11pm Fri & Sat; MFaidherbe-Chaligny) Drop in to this convivial gourmet bistro for inventive creations from chef Thomas Dufour. French classics form the base of his dishes, such as seared scallops with toasted wild almonds or whole roasted veal kidneys with citrus compote and *dolce forte* (chocolate, vinegar and raisin) sauce. In the evening, there's usually at least one vegetarian main on the à la carte menu.

Across the street, the same team offers walk-in wine-bar dining at **Le Siffleur de Ballons** (Map p394; www.lesiffleurdeballons.

fr; 34 rue de Citeaux, 12e; 2-course lunch menu €14, dishes €6-14; ⏰5.30-11.30pm Tue, 10.30am-3pm & 5.30-11.30pm Wed-Fri, 10.30am-11pm Sat; MFaidherbe-Chaligny).

LE SQUARE TROUSSEAU
FRENCH €€

Map p394 (☎01 43 43 06 00; www.squaretrousseau.com; 1 rue Antoine Vollon, 12e; mains €25-38; ⏰kitchen noon-2.30pm & 7-10pm, bar 8.30am-2am; ☎⑂; MLedru-Rollin) With etched glass, a zinc bar and polished wood panelling, this Belle Époque cafe-restaurant dating from 1907 is a local landmark. A real all-rounder, this is a place where Parisians flock for a coffee-and-croissant breakfast, a classic French meal like frogs' legs or veal with mushrooms, or an after-work drink on the delightful terrace overlooking a lovely leafy square.

À LA BANANE IVOIRIENNE
AFRICAN €€

Map p394 (☎01 43 70 49 90; www.facebook.com/ALaBananeIvoirienne; 10 rue de la Forge Royale, 11e; menu €29.50, mains €12.50-15; ⏰kitchen 7-11pm Tue-Sat, bar to 1am Fri & Sat; MFaidherbe-Chaligny) An institution in Paris since 1989, À la Banane Ivoirienne dishes up the best Ivorian food in Paris along with fabulous live music and dancing on Friday nights. West African specialities – including stuffed crab, braised *attiéké* (fermented cassava

Le Baron Rouge

pulp), *alloco* (fried plaintain) and plenty of fiery meats and fish – are dished up in a colourful interior bristling with gewgaws.

LE TEMPS AU TEMPS
BISTRO €€

Map p394 (☎01 43 79 63 40; 13 rue Paul Bert, 11e; 2-/3-course menu lunch €20/22, dinner €28/32, mains €24-29; ◷7.30-11.30pm Tue, 11.45am-1.30pm & 7.30-11.30pm Wed-Sat; ⓂFaidherbe-Chaligny) Foodie street rue Paul Bert is the perfect spot for this delightfully traditional and excellent-value bistro with a quaint timber façade and a menu chalked on a blackboard outside. Lunch *menus* include a glass of wine – just the job for washing down a deliciously garlicky snail fricassee or sea bream with braised endives and spicy chorizo.

À LA RENAISSANCE
CAFE €€

Map p394 (☎01 43 79 83 09; 87 rue de la Roquette, 11e; mains €20-32, platters €8-16; ◷kitchen 8am-10pm, bar to 2am; ⓂVoltaire) This vintage neighbourhood place with a curvaceous zinc bar, a ceramic tile floor and an enclosed terrace is a great place to dine on quintessential Paris cafe fare. Along with cheese and charcuterie platters, it serves wild boar terrine, steak tartare and duck-heart *cassoulet* (slow-cooked casserole).

RHINO ROUGE
BARBECUE €€

Map p394 (☎01 43 44 28 55; www.facebook.com/rhinorougeparis; 2 rue Théophile Roussel, 12e; mains €10-29; ◷noon-2.30pm & 7-11pm Tue-Sat; ⓂLedru-Rollin) Meats supplied by star butcher Olivier Metzger are smoked for up to 12 hours in Rhino Rouge's fire-engine-red in-house smoker. Menu standouts include beef brisket, pork ribs, pulled-pork burgers and Black Angus steaks, as well as Cajun chicken. Be sure to order a side of 'Rebel Potatoes' (a cross between fries and wedges), which are also cooked in the smoker.

LE CHARDENOUX
BISTRO €€

Map p394 (☎01 43 71 49 52; www.restaurantlechardenoux.com; 1 rue Jules Vallès, 11e; mains €20-28; ◷noon-2.30pm & 7-11pm; ⓂCharonne) Dating from 1908, this picture-perfect Parisian bistro with a polished-timber façade, patterned tiled floors, ceiling frescoes, mirrored walls, bevelled frosted-glass screens and a centrepiece zinc bar is a listed historic monument. Star chef Cyril Lignac creates inventive surf (mussels au gratin, Guérande salt–crusted sea bass) and some turf (seared rib-eye with kombu seaweed, fresh wasabi and green-apple relish).

It's across the road from Lignac's combined chocolate boutique and tearoom **La Chocolaterie Cyril Lignac** (Map p394; www.lachocolateriecyrillignac.com; 25 rue Chanzy, 11e; pastries €3-5.50; ◷8am-6pm Tue-Fri, to 7pm Sat & Sun; ⓂCharonne), to the east, and from his bakery–pastry shop **La Pâtisserie** (Map p394; www.cyrillignac.com; 24 rue Paul Bert, 11e; pastries €3-6.50; ◷7am-8pm Tue-Sun; ⓂCharonne, Faidherbe-Chaligny), to the south.

BRASSERIE ROSIE
BRASSERIE €€

Map p394 (☎07 49 19 19 62; www.brasserierosie.com; 53 rue du Faubourg St-Antoine, 11e; mains €13-22; ◷noon-midnight; 🛜👶; ⓂLedru-Rollin, Bastille) Neo-retro chequerboard-tiled floors, a timber bar, green-marble tables and shell-pink booths at this 2020-opened brasserie complement its homage to classic dishes: *œufs mayonnaise*, onion soup, truffled ham croquettes, *magret de canard* (seared duck breast), *pithivier chanmô* (pigeon and pork pie) and *tarte citron meringuée* (lemon meringue pie). Produce is sourced directly from 130 farms around Paris. High chairs are on hand for families.

★SEPTIME
GASTRONOMY €€€

Map p394 (☎01 43 67 38 29; www.septime-charonne.fr; 80 rue de Charonne, 11e; mains €24-28,

5-course lunch menu with/without wine €105/60, 7-course dinner menu €155/95; ⊙7.30-10pm Mon, 12.15-2pm & 7.30-10pm Tue-Fri; Ⓜ Charonne) The alchemists in Bertrand Grébaut's Michelin-starred kitchen produce truly beautiful creations, served by blue-aproned waitstaff. The menu reads like an obscure shopping list: each dish is a mere listing of three ingredients, while the mystery *carte blanche* dinner *menu* puts you in the hands of the innovative chef. Reservations require planning and perseverance – book at least three weeks in advance.

Its nearby wine bar **Septime La Cave** (Map p394; 📱01 43 67 14 87; www.septime-la cave.fr; 3 rue Basfroi, 11e; ⊙4-11pm; Ⓜ Charonne) is ideal for a pre- or post-meal drink. For stunning small seafood plates, its walk-in sister restaurant **Clamato** (Map p394; www.clamato-charonne.fr; 80 rue de Charonne, 11e; small plates €14-23, dozen oysters €24-58; ⊙noon-2.30pm & 7-11pm Mon-Fri, noon-11pm Sat & Sun; Ⓜ Charonne) is right next door.

DERSOU
BISTRO €€€

Map p394 (📱09 81 01 12 73; www.dersouparis. com; 21 rue St-Nicolas, 12e; 5-/6-/7-course tasting menu with paired cocktails €95/115/135, mains €16-30, Sunday brunch €20; ⊙7.30-11pm Tue-Fri, noon-3pm & 7.30-11pm Sat, noon-3pm Sun, closed Aug; Ⓜ Ledru-Rollin) Much of the seating at this hotspot, which turns out creative fusion cuisine, is at the counter, where you get first-class views of chef Taku Sekine at work. Intricately constructed tasting menus are a highlight, with each course exquisitely paired with a bespoke cocktail. Reservations are essential.

TABLE
FRENCH €€€

Map p394 (📱01 43 43 12 26; www.table.paris; 3 rue de Prague, 12e; mains €79-89; ⊙noon-3pm & 7.45-10.30pm Tue-Fri, 7.30-10pm Sat; Ⓜ Ledru-Rollin) Unusual and rare artisan products sourced from all over France decide the day's menu at Michelin-starred Table, styled like a contemporary *table d'hôte,* with diners seated at the curvaceous zinc bar while talented food writer and chef Bruno Verjus performs in his open kitchen. Verjus grows herbs and flowers in his own garden, and delights in talking food with diners.

LE TRAIN BLEU
FRENCH €€€

Map p394 (📱01 43 43 09 06; www.le-train-bleu. com; 1st fl, Gare de Lyon, 26 place Louis Armand, 12e; 2-/3-/6-course menu €49/65/110, mains €29-46; ⊙restaurant 11.30am-2.45pm & 7-10.45pm, bar 7.30am-10pm; 🛜🚻; Ⓜ Gare de Lyon) This spectacular Belle Époque train-station restaurant has been an elegant port of call since 1901. Cuisine is traditional French – Salers beef tartare is prepared at your table – and even if you can't dine here, indulging in a silver pot of tea or a cocktail in its comfortable lounge-bar is well worth the top-end prices.

🍷 DRINKING & NIGHTLIFE

Bastille invariably draws a crowd, particularly along rue de Lappe, 11e, which is awash with raucous bars. Continue further east and the options become much more stylish and appealing, with wine bars, intimate clubs and backstreet cocktail dens.

⭐ LE BARON ROUGE
WINE BAR

Map p394 (www.lebaronrouge.net; 1 rue Théophile Roussel, 12e; ⊙5-10pm Mon, 10am-2pm & 5-10pm Tue-Fri, 10am-10pm Sat, 10am-4pm Sun; Ⓜ Ledru-Rollin) Just about the ultimate Parisian wine-bar experience, this wonderfully unpretentious local meeting place, where everyone is welcome, has barrels stacked against the bottle-lined walls and serves cheese, charcuterie, and oysters on weekends in season. It's especially busy on Sunday after the Marché d'Aligre wraps up. For a small deposit, you can fill up 1L bottles straight from the barrel.

LA MANUFACTURE DE CAFÉ
COFFEE

Map p394 (www.lecafe-alainducasse.com; 12 rue St-Sabin, 11e; ⊙10.15am-6.45pm Tue-Sun; Ⓜ Bréguet–Sabin) Legendary French chef Alain Ducasse's ongoing expansion of his empire includes this 2019-launched coffee roastery, using beans sourced from his travels to sustainable small-scale plantations. Glass windows at the back of the cafe let you see the roasting in action, while expert staff guide you through the menu of coffees, accompanied by chocolates made at Ducasse's nearby La Manufacture de Chocolat (p192).

LES CUVES DE FAUVE
MICROBREWERY

Map p394 (www.fauvebiere.com; 64 rue de Charonne, 11e; ⊙5.30pm-2am Mon-Fri, 11.30am-2am Sat & Sun; 🛜) Watch the brewing in action while you try Fauve's permanent range, such as Bon Esprit (pilsner), Force Majeure (raspberry stout) and Coup d'Éclat (IPA), and seasonal beers like La Petite Charonne (Parisian

RUE DE LAPPE

Although at night it's one of the rowdiest bar-hopping streets in Paris, rue de Lappe is actually quite peaceful during the day. Like most streets in the area, it dates back to the 17th century and was originally home to cabinetmakers, who first moved there to escape the taxes and restrictions imposed by guilds operating within the city limits.

In the centuries that followed, the street was gradually taken over by metalworkers, who equipped the city with its zinc bars, copper piping and the like: one of the busiest bars on the street, **Bar des Ferrailleurs** (Map p394; ☎01 48 07 89 12; www.bardes ferrailleurs.fr; 18 rue de Lappe, 11e; ⏰6pm-2am; MBastille), is a hip homage to these workers. At the same time, immigrants from the central French region of Auvergne also moved in, opening up *cafés-charbons*, places where you could go for a drink and buy coal at the same time. In this way, the street eventually became a popular drinking strip, and its accordion-driven dance halls were to become famous throughout Paris. The dance hall Le Balajo (p192) dates back to 1936 and continues to host weekly *thés dansants* (tea dances).

You can still find an Auvergne speciality shop here, **Chez Teil** (Map p394; 6 rue de Lappe, 11e; ⏰10am-1pm & 4-8pm Tue-Sat; MBastille), at No 6, as well as a beautiful old cafe-bar and bistro, **Les Sans-Culottes** (Map p394; ☎01 48 05 42 92; www.bistrotles sansculottes.fr; 27 rue de Lappe, 11e; ⏰8am-2am Mon-Sat; MBastille), at No 27.

Pale Ale). Each beer comes in its own style of glass featuring work by a different artist. Soak them up with snacks like homemade sausages with red-onion ketchup.

BLUEBIRD
COCKTAIL BAR

Map p394 (12 rue St-Bernard, 11e; ⏰6pm-2am Sun-Thu, to 3am Fri & Sat; MFaidherbe-Chaligny) The ultimate neighbourhood hang-out, Bluebird is styled like a 1950s apartment with retro decor, a fish tank along one wall, and a soundtrack of smooth lounge music. Cocktail recipes date from the 1800s and early 1900s and change seasonally. Guest bartenders often drop by for a stint; ask about cocktail masterclasses.

LA FÉE VERTE
BAR

Map p394 (☎01 43 72 31 24; www.facebook.com/ feeverteparis; 108 rue de la Roquette, 11e; ⏰7am-2am Mon-Wed, from 8am Thu-Sun; ☎; MVoltaire) Absinthe is the speciality of the Green Fairy, a thronging neighbourhood bar with dark-wood furniture, huge mirrors and a zinc bar. It serves over 20 different types of the devilish drink (served traditionally, with slotted spoons and sugar cubes) as well as good food, including house-speciality burgers. Happy hour runs from 5pm to 8pm.

LOUVE
WINE BAR

Map p394 (☎01 43 38 90 80; www.louve.vin; 17 rue Bréguet, 11e; ⏰4.30-10.30pm Mon, 10.30am-1pm & 4.30pm-midnight Tue & Wed, 10.30am-1pm & 4.30pm-1am Thu, 10.30am-1pm & 4.30pm-3.30pm Fri; ☎; MBréguet–Sabin) Hundreds of wines

from winemakers across France, including up to a dozen by the glass, can be paired with charcuterie and/or cheese platters at this spiffing glass-and-steel wine bar with floor-to-ceiling windows and timber-topped tables. It's also a great place to buy bottles to take away, along with gourmet treats from its on-site deli. Hours can fluctuate.

LE PURE CAFÉ
CAFE

Map p394 (www.lepurecafe.fr; 14 rue Jean Macé, 11e; ⏰7am-2am; MCharonne) A classic Parisian corner cafe, Le Pure is a charming spot to drop into for a morning coffee, apéritif, contemporary bistro meal or weekend brunch. Its selection of wines by the glass (including natural and organic varieties) is particularly good. Film buffs might recognise its cherry-red façade and vintage-wood and zinc bar from the Richard Linklater film *Before Sunset*.

TWENTY ONE SOUND BAR
CLUB

Map p394 (☎01 43 70 78 01; www.facebook.com/ twentyonesoundbar; 20 rue de la Forge Royale, 11e; ⏰9pm-2am Tue-Sat; MFaidherbe-Chaligny) Stark steel and concrete amp up the acoustics at this hip-hop haven, with regular drinks specials and big-name DJs mixing on the decks.

CAFÉ DES ANGES
CAFE

Map p394 (www.cafedesangesparis.com; 66 rue de la Roquette, 11e; ⏰7.30am-2am; ☎; MBastille) With its pastel green–shaded paintwork and locals sipping coffee beneath the red awning on its busy pavement terrace, Angels Cafe lives up to the 'quintessential Paris cafe' dream. In winter wrap up beneath a blanket outside, or squeeze through the crowds at the zinc bar to snag a coveted table inside. Happy hour runs from 5pm to 9pm.

KABANE
CAFE
Map p394 (www.facebook.com/Kabane.cafe; 23 rue Faidherbe, 11e; ⏰10am-6pm Mon-Fri, to 7pm Sat & Sun; 🖥; Ⓜ Faidherbe-Chaligny) With exposed stone and 19th-century brickwork, and a glassed-in rear courtyard, Kabane is a stylish spot for Fair Trade, single-origin coffee. It also has loose-leaf, Oolong and Pu-erh teas, and deliciously rich, thick organic hot chocolate. Drinks are served in beautiful artisan pottery by French ceramicist Michel Cohen.

LES CAVES DE PRAGUE
WINE BAR
Map p394 (📞01 72 68 07 36; 8 rue de Prague, 12e; ⏰10am-1pm & 4-11pm Tue & Wed, 4-11pm Thu-Sat) Take a seat surrounded by floor-to-ceiling shelves stocked with thousands of bottles of wine, or out on the terrace on rue de Prague in fine weather, to sample vintages from all over France, accompanied by artisan charcuterie, cheeses and pâtés served on slate. Look for the bright violet façade.

# ☆ ENTERTAINMENT

Paris' east is home to major venues such as the AccorHotels Arena and Opéra Bastille, as well as a host of smaller spaces staging intimate gigs. Other highlights include screenings at the national film institute La Cinémathèque Française.

OPÉRA BASTILLE
OPERA
Map p394 (📞01 71 25 24 23; www.operadeparis. fr; 2-6 place de la Bastille, 12e; ⏰box office noon-6.30pm Mon-Sat, 1hr prior to performances Sun; Ⓜ Bastille) Paris' premier opera hall, Opéra Bastille's 2745-seat main auditorium also stages ballet and classical concerts. Online tickets go on sale up to three weeks before telephone or box-office sales (from noon on Wednesdays); online flash sales offer significant discounts. Limited standing-only tickets (*places débouts*; €5) are available 90 minutes before performances. French-language 90-minute guided tours (p182) take you backstage.

Significant discounts are available for those aged under 28 and over 65.

BADABOUM
LIVE MUSIC
Map p394 (📞01 48 06 50 70; www.badaboum. paris; 2bis rue des Taillandiers, 11e; ⏰club 11pm-6am Thu-Sun, concerts vary; Ⓜ Ledru-Rollin) The onomatopoeically named Badaboum hosts a mixed bag of concerts on its up-close-and-personal stage, but focuses on electro, funk and hip-hop. Great atmosphere, super cocktails and a super-chic white-tiled restaurant, too.

SUPERSONIC
LIVE MUSIC
Map p394 (📞01 49 23 41 90; www.supersonic-club.fr; 9 rue Biscornet, 12e; ⏰7pm-midnight Sun-Wed, to 4am Thu, to 6am Fri & Sat; 🖥; Ⓜ Bastille) With a capacity of 250, post-industrial venue Supersonic hosts mostly indie, rock, garage, electro-pop and tribute bands; the first three concerts of the evening are free (though you're expected to buy a drink), with paid-for concerts typically following. DJs draw clubbers from midnight on Fridays and Saturdays.

LA CINÉMATHÈQUE FRANÇAISE
CINEMA
(📞01 71 19 33 33; www.cinematheque.fr; 51 rue de Bercy, 12e; tickets adult/child €7/4; ⏰noon-10pm; Ⓜ Bercy) This national institution (p182) is a temple to the 'seventh art' and always screens its foreign offerings in their original versions. Up to 10 films a day are shown, usually retrospectives (eg Spielberg, Altman, Eastwood) mixed in with related but more obscure films.

LE MOTEL
LIVE MUSIC
Map p394 (www.lemotel.fr; 8 passage Josset, 11e; ⏰6pm-2am Tue-Sun; Ⓜ Ledru-Rollin) This hole-in-the-wall venue in the hot-to-boiling-point 11e has become the go-to indie bar around Bastille. It's especially well loved for its comfy sofas, inexpensive but quality drinks (craft beers on tap and craft cocktails; happy hour is from 6pm to 9pm) and excellent music, with live bands and DJs Tuesday to Saturday (plus quiz nights and other events on Sunday).

LA CHAPELLE DES LOMBARDS
LIVE MUSIC
Map p394 (📞01 43 57 24 24; www.la-chapelle-des-lombards.com; 19 rue de Lappe, 11e; ⏰11pm-2am Tue & Wed, to 5.30am Thu-Sat, 6.30pm-1.30am Sun; Ⓜ Bastille) World music dominates at this perennially popular Bastille dance club, with happening Latino DJs and live reggae, funk and Afro jazz concerts. Prices vary from night to night; when admission is free, you're expected to buy a drink.

LE BALAJO
LIVE MUSIC

Map p394 (☑01 47 00 07 87; www.balajo.fr; 9 rue de Lappe, 11e; ☺hours vary; Ⓜ Bastille) A mainstay of Parisian nightlife since 1936, this ancient ballroom is devoted to Latin American music and dance classes (Bachata; Cuban salsa) during the week, with clubbing on weekends when the dance floor rocks until *aube* (dawn). But the best time to visit is for its old-fashioned *thés dansants* (tea dances), held from 2pm to 7pm on Mondays.

ACCORHOTELS ARENA
STADIUM

(☑01 49 97 51 91; www.accorhotelsarena.com; 8 bd de Bercy, 12e; ☎; Ⓜ Bercy) This 20,300-seat indoor sports arena, whose sloping exterior is covered with lawns, hosts the largest concerts and events to come through Paris (Cirque du Soleil, Lenny Kravitz, Elton John, Lady Gaga, Adele, Drake), as well as various sporting competitions and matches. Also here is an ice rink.

🛍 SHOPPING

Superb markets aside, Bastille and eastern Paris are not really known for shopping, but there's a select choice of unique boutiques and specialist shops. Key fashion brands have stores on the western end of trendy rue de Charonne, between av Ledru-Rollin and rue du Faubourg St-Antoine, and arts and crafts studio-showrooms are tucked under the viaduct arches beneath the Promenade Plantée.

★ MARCHÉ BASTILLE
MARKET

Map p394 (bd Richard Lenoir, 11e; ☺7am-2.30pm Thu, to 3pm Sun; Ⓜ Bastille, Bréguet–Sabin) If you only get to one open-air street market in Paris, this one – stretching between the Bastille and Richard Lenoir metro stations – is among the very best. Its 150-plus stalls are piled high with fruit and vegetables, meats, fish, shellfish, cheeses and seasonal specialities such as truffles. You'll also find clothing, leather handbags and wallets, and a smattering of antiques.

LA MANUFACTURE DE CHOCOLAT
CHOCOLATE

Map p394 (www.lechocolat-alainducasse.com; 40 rue de la Roquette, 11e; ☺10.30am-7pm Mon-Sat; Ⓜ Bastille) If you dine at superstar chef Alain Ducasse's restaurants, the chocolate will have been made here at Ducasse's own chocolate factory (the first in Paris to produce 'bean-to-bar' chocolate), which he set up with his former executive pastry chef Nicolas Berger. Deliberate over ganaches, pralines and truffles and no fewer than 47 flavours of chocolate bar.

VIADUC DES ARTS
ARTS & CRAFTS

Map p394 (www.leviaducdesarts.com; 1-129 av Daumesnil, 12e; ☺hours vary; Ⓜ Bastille, Gare de Lyon) Located beneath the red-brick arches of the Promenade Plantée (p182) elevated park, the Viaduc des Arts' 1.5km-long line-up of traditional artisans and contemporary designers – including furniture and tapestry restorers, interior designers, cabinetmakers, violin- and flute-makers, embroiderers and jewellers – carries out

---

RECORD COLLECTIONS

Bastille has a great collection of vinyl shops. **Souffle Continu** (Map p394; www.souffle continu.com; 20-22 rue Gerbier, 11e; ☺noon-8pm Mon-Sat; Ⓜ Philippe Auguste, Voltaire) owners Bernard Ducayron and Théo Jarrier have their own record label, and stock genres as diverse as avant-garde garage, industrial poetry and medieval metal. Unearth jazz, blues, soul, funk, indie rock and garage at **Le Silence de la Rue** (Map p394; 39 rue Faidherbe, 11e; ☺11am-7.30pm Mon-Sat; Ⓜ Faidherbe-Chaligny). **Music Fear Satan** (Map p394; www.musicfearsatan.com; 4bis rue Richard Lenoir, 11e; ☺11.30am-7.30pm Mon-Sat; Ⓜ Charonne) specialises in metal (all genres), indie rock and hardcore punk. New releases, rereleases and secondhand '60s, '70s and '80s vinyl are stocked at haphazardly catalogued **Hands & Arms** (Map p394; www.handsandarms.com; 72 rue Crozatier, 12e; ☺11am-7pm Tue-Sat, to 2pm Sun; Ⓜ Faidherbe-Chaligny). **Citeaux Sphere** (Map p394; ☑06 11 76 65 89; 45 rue de Citeaux, 12e; mains €12-18; ☺11am-5pm Mon & Sun, to 11pm Tue-Sat; ☎; Ⓜ Faidherbe-Chaligny) combines a vinyl shop with a wine bar and laid-back cafe.

antique renovations and creates new items using time-honoured methods.

LA BOTTE GARDIANE   SHOES

Map p394 (www.labottegardiane.com; 25 rue de Charonne, 11e; ⏱11am-2pm & 3-8pm Mon-Fri, 11am-8pm Sat; Ⓜ Ledru-Rollin) A designated Entreprise du Patrimoine Vivant (Living Heritage Enterprise), La Botte Gardiane handcrafts shoes, sandals and boots for men, women and children using traditional techniques and all-French products such as Degermann leather and natural vegetable dyes.

MARCHÉ BIOLOGIQUE
PLACE DU PÈRE CHAILLET   MARKET

Map p394 (place du Père Chaillet, 11e; ⏱10am-8pm Wed, 7am-2.30pm Sat; Ⓜ Voltaire) 🍃 Since its launch in late 2018, this *marché biologique* (organic market) has become a neighbourhood favourite for fresh, seasonal fruit, veggies and other all-natural products sold by around 20 traders.

SO WE ARE   FASHION & ACCESSORIES

Map p394 (www.soweare-shop.fr; 13 rue Keller, 11e; ⏱11.30am-7.30pm Mon-Sat; Ⓜ Ledru-Rollin) Founded by friends Hélène and Magali, So We Are specialises in hard-to-find French and European women's fashion labels. Look out for embroidered T-shirts by Keur Paris, art deco–inspired geometric jewellery from Paris-based Aurélie Joliff, dresses and jackets by La Petite Française, knitwear from Belgian-based Roos Vandekerckhove, and trousers, shirts and shoes from Danish designers Samsøe & Samsøe.

HAMS   FOOD & DRINKS

Map p394 (Maison de Jambon; ☎09 61 68 70 35; 21 rue Paul Bert, 11e; ⏱10am-8pm Tue & Wed, to 9.30pm Thu-Sat, to 5pm Sun; Ⓜ Charonne) Jean-François Le Goeff's aromatic deli specialises in premium hams, such as Noir de Bigoerre (from the French Pyrenees), Culatello di Zibello (Italy) and Pata Negra Bellota (Spain), alongside other artisan meats, cheeses, wines and preserves. Better still, you can dine in-house on charcuterie platters and gourmet sandwiches, or pick them up to take away.

MARCHÉ AUX
PUCES DE MONTREUIL   MARKET

(av du Professeur André Lemierre, 20e; ⏱7am-5pm Sat-Mon; Ⓜ Porte de Montreuil) Trading since 1860, this flea market has scores of stalls selling everything from furniture to

MARCHÉ D'ALIGRE

A favourite with chefs and locals, the stalls at this chaotic street **market** (Map p390; rue d'Aligre, 12e; ⏱7.30am-1.30pm Tue-Fri, to 2.30pm Sat & Sun; Ⓜ Ledru-Rollin) are piled with fruit, vegetables and seasonal delicacies such as truffles. Behind them, specialist shops stock cheeses, coffee, chocolates, meat, seafood and wine. More are located in the adjoining covered market hall, Marché Beauvau (Map p394; place d'Aligre, 12e; ⏱9am-1pm & 4-7.30pm Tue-Fri, 9am-1pm & 3.30-7.30pm Sat, 9am-1.30pm Sun). The small but bargain-filled flea market Marché aux Puces d'Aligre (Map p394; place d'Aligre, 12e; ⏱7.30am-1.30pm Tue-Fri, to 2.30pm Sat & Sun) takes place on the square.

books, comics, stamps, coins, art and vinyl, as well as cheap vintage and new clothing.

It's just outside the bd Périphérique but still within the 20e.

BERCY VILLAGE   SHOPPING CENTRE

(www.bercyvillage.com; Cour St-Émilion, 12e; ⏱shops & cinema 10am-8pm, restaurants & bars 11am-2am; Ⓜ Cour St-Émilion) Set in the former Bercy wine warehouses, this popular outdoor mall has a multiplex cinema, restaurants, bars and a string of stores catering to the needs of Parisian families: home design, clever kitchen supplies, quality toy stores and more.

🏃 SPORTS & ACTIVITIES

ARKOSE   CLIMBING

(☎01 71 93 14 34; www.nation.arkose.com; 35 rue des Grands Champs, 20e; 90min session adult/child €15/8, shoe hire €3, lessons per hr €15; ⏱8am-midnight; Ⓜ Buzenval) A great way to stay active on a rainy day, this indoor bouldering centre (no ropes) occupies a 1000-sq-metre space with a maximum height of 4.5m. Of its 200 challenging routes spanning six levels of difficulty, 25 are rerouted each week; the popular children's area is shaped like a castle. It also hosts yoga classes and has an organic cafe.

The Islands

ÎLE DE LA CITÉ | ÎLE ST-LOUIS

Neighbourhood Top Five

❶ Cathédrale Notre Dame de Paris (p196) Revelling in the crowning glory of medieval Gothic architecture, and thanking the heavens that the structure survived the devastating fire in 2019.

❷ Sainte-Chapelle (p200) Reading richly coloured biblical tales, exquisitely told through stained-glass imagery with a grace and beauty impossible to find elsewhere.

❸ Conciergerie (p201) Learning how Marie Antoinette and thousands of others spent their final days at this 14th-century palace turned prison before being beheaded.

❹ Berthillon (p202) Savouring the sweetness of this famous Parisian ice cream during a riverbank stroll.

❺ Marché aux Fleurs Reine Elizabeth II (p204) Shop for romantic blooms to say *'je t'aime'* the old-fashioned way at Paris' oldest flower market.

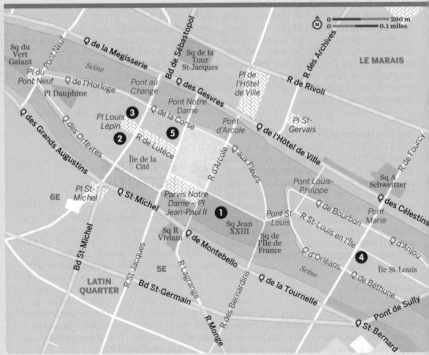

For more detail of this area see Map p396

Explore the Islands

Where better to start your explorations than Notre Dame (p196)? The interior will be off limits for years to come, but the massive towers and dramatic flying buttresses can still be marvelled at from behind the fence. For beautiful 13th-century stained glass, don't miss exquisite Sainte-Chapelle (p200), a few footsteps from French Revolution prison, the Conciergerie (p201).

Cross Pont St-Louis (p202) to enchanting little Île St-Louis. After brunch or lunch at deliciously Parisian hang-out Café Saint Régis (p202), browse the island's boutiques and buy an iconic Berthillon (p202) ice cream to enjoy by the river's edge.

Come late afternoon, stroll back over Pont St-Louis – where you're likely to catch buskers – for a pre-dinner apéritif at Le Bar du Caveau (p204); allow ample time to lap up the quaint, old-world vibe of pretty, car-free place Dauphine. Afterwards, head to gastronomic Sequana (p203) for dinner, followed by late-night cocktails and live music at trendy Quai de Bourbon (p203).

Local Life

Art life Europe's largest surviving medieval hall, the Conciergerie (p201), hosts contemporary art exhibitions.

Weekend brunch Enjoy a deliciously slow start to the weekend over brunch at Café Saint Régis (p202).

Street entertainment Pont au Double (linking Notre Dame with the Left Bank) and Pont St-Louis (linking both islands) buzz with street performers in summer.

Picnic life Buy sandwiches and tarts from Boulangerie Huré (p203) to eat in a park with river view: try square du Vert-Galant (Île de la Cité).

Getting There & Away

Metro Metro Cité (line 4) on Île de la Cité is the Islands' only metro station. Pont Marie (line 7) on the Right Bank is Île St-Louis' closest station.

Bus Bus 47 links Île de la Cité with Le Marais and Gare de l'Est; bus 21 with Opéra and Gare St-Lazare. On Île St-Louis it's bus 67 to Jardin des Plantes and place d'Italie; bus 87 via the Latin Quarter to Champ de Mars.

Bicycle Handy Vélib' stations can be found at the Cité metro and 41 quai de l'Horloge.

Boat The hop-on, hop-off Batobus stops opposite Notre Dame on the Left Bank.

Lonely Planet's Top Tip

Queues to swoon over spectacular stained glass in Sainte-Chapelle can be staggeringly long. To speed things up, visit the Conciergerie first and buy a ticket covering admission to both the old prison and the chapel. With this *billet jumelé* you can skip Sainte-Chapelle's ticket queue and enter via the 'priority access' line open to Paris Museum Pass holders, those under 26 years or with prepaid or combination tickets.

✖ Best Places to Eat

➤ Berthillon (p202)
➤ Café Saint Régis (p202)
➤ Boulangerie Huré (p203)
➤ Les Fous de l'Île (p203)
➤ Le Caveau du Palais (p203)
➤ Sequana (p203)

For reviews, see p202.➡

🔒 Best Shopping

➤ Marché aux Fleurs Reine Elizabeth II (p204)
➤ 38 Saint Louis (p204)
➤ L'Îles aux Images (p204)
➤ L'embrasser (p204)

For reviews, see p204.➡

◉ Best For Romance

➤ Pont Neuf (p201)
➤ Square du Vert-Galant (p201)
➤ Vedettes du Pont Neuf (p202)

For reviews, see p201.➡

TOP EXPERIENCE
WITNESS THE HISTORIC RECONSTRUCTION OF CATHÉDRALE NOTRE DAME DE PARIS

Majestic and monumental, Paris' iconic French Gothic Cathédrale Notre Dame de Paris was the capital's most visited unticketed site until 2019 when fire swept through it, leaving the cathedral interior inaccessible for years to come. The 14 million annual visitors who once crossed its threshold can now only admire its darkened, scaffolding-draped exterior from afar.

Architecture
Built on a site occupied by earlier churches and, a millennium prior, a Gallo-Roman temple, Notre Dame was begun in 1163 and largely completed by the early 14th century. The cathedral was badly damaged during the Revolution, prompting architect Eugène Emmanuel Viollet-le-Duc to oversee extensive renovations between 1845 and 1864. There are good views of the magnificent forest of ornate **flying buttresses** encircling the cathedral chancel and supporting its walls from the riverside (eastern) end of rue du Cloître Notre Dame and quai de l'Archevêché.

Notre Dame is known for its sublime balance, though in accordance with standard Gothic practice, minor asymmetrical elements were introduced to avoid monotony. These include the slightly different shapes of the three main **portals**, whose statues were once brightly coloured to make them more effective as a *Biblia pauperum* – a 'Bible of the poor' to help the illiterate faithful understand Old Testament stories, the Passion of the Christ and the lives of the saints.

Fire of April 2019
On the evening of 15 April 2019, a blaze broke out under the cathedral's roof. Firefighters were able to control the fire and ultimately save the church, including its two bell towers, spectacular rose windows and western façade. But the damage remained devastating:

DON'T MISS
➡ Flying buttresses
➡ Cathedral views from rue de la Cité, rue du Cloître Notre Dame, Pont St-Louis & Pont de l'Archevêché

PRACTICALITIES
➡ Map p396, D4
➡ www.notredamedeparis.fr
➡ 6 Parvis Notre Dame – place Jean-Paul II, 4e
➡ ⊙closed indefinitely
➡ Ⓜ Cité

both the roof and iconic spire – actually a 19th-century addition – were completely destroyed and the interior was severely damaged. Several statues and artefacts had already been removed from the cathedral as part of a restoration program underway prior to the fire. While flames engulfed the cathedral, Paris firefighters and the fire brigade's chaplain formed a human chain to save many of the remaining cathedral treasures.

Rebuilding Notre Dame

After the fire, French President Emmanuel Macron said he'd like the cathedral to be rebuilt by 2024, in time for the Olympic Games. Within days of the fire, private donors had pledged some €600 million to assist with this and by early 2020 the fund had hit €922 million. It took more than two years to clean and stabilise the structure, and construction was expected to commence in early 2022.

Salvaged Treasures

Notre Dame's sacred relics – displayed in the cathedral **treasury** until 2019 – and priceless artworks survived the fire remarkably intact and were transferred to vaults in the Louvre for safekeeping and/or restoration work. Among them were several **Mays** – huge 3m-tall paintings commemorating one of the Acts of the Apostles, accompanied by a poem or literary explanation – offered to Notre Dame by city goldsmiths. By the early 18th century, when the brotherhood of goldsmiths was dissolved, the cathedral had received 76 such monumental paintings; 13 were on display at the time of the fire.

Pilgrims flocked to Église St-Germain l'Auxerrois (p120), the former parish church of the Louvre, in September 2019 for an exceptional veneration of Notre Dame's **Ste-Couronne** (Holy Crown), purportedly the crown of thorns placed on Jesus' head before he was crucified. Originally preserved in the cathedral treasury and exhibited at the cathedral on the first Friday of each month, every Friday during Lent and on Good Friday, the relic now remains in a safe at the Louvre and will only be shown during Lent at the St-Germain l'Auxerrois church.

Notre Dame Music

Music has been a sacred part of Notre Dame's soul since birth. The best day to appreciate its musical heritage is on Sunday at a Gregorian or polyphonic Mass (10am and 6.30pm, respectively), transferred until further notice to Église St-Germain l'Auxerrois. Check the cathedral's website for its monthly agenda. If you can't make it in person, tune into Sunday's 6.30pm Mass on Radio Notre Dame 1 (100.7 FM), or streamed on the cathedral's website.

POINT ZERO

Notre Dame has always been deemed the very heart of Paris – so much so that distances from Paris to every part of metropolitan France are measured from Parvis Notre Dame-place Jean-Paul II, the vast square in front of the cathedral. A bronze star embedded in the ground marks the exact location of **Point Zéro des Routes de France** (Map p396; Parvis Notre Dame – place Jean-Paul II, 4e; Ⓜ Cité). The same square is graced by a statue of Charlemagne (742–814 CE), emperor of the Franks, on horseback.

Stand on rue de la Cité to admire Notre Dame's fun collection of grimacing and grinning gargoyles, sculpted in stone around the cathedral's bell towers on the rooftop Galerie des Chimères (Gargoyles Gallery) in the 19th century. These grotesque statues divert rainwater from the roof, with the water exiting through their elongated open mouths. They also, purportedly, ward off evil spirits.

Notre Dame

TIMELINE

1160 Maurice de Sully becomes bishop of Paris. Mission: to grace growing Paris with a lofty new cathedral.

1182–90 The choir with double ambulatory is finished and work starts on the nave and side chapels.

1200–50 The ❶ **west façade**, with rose window, three portals and two soaring towers, goes up. Everyone is stunned.

1345 Some 180 years after the foundation stone was laid, the Cathédrale de Notre Dame is complete. It is dedicated to *notre dame* (our lady), the Virgin Mary.

1789 Revolutionaries smash the original Gallery of Kings, pillage the cathedral and melt all its bells except the great bell ❷ **Emmanuel**. The cathedral becomes a Temple of Reason and then a warehouse.

1831 Victor Hugo's novel *The Hunchback of Notre Dame* inspires new interest in the half-ruined Gothic cathedral.

1845–64 Architect Viollet-le-Duc undertakes its restoration. Twenty-eight new kings are sculpted for the west façade. The heavily decorated ❸ **portals** and spire are reconstructed. The neogothic treasury is built.

1860 The area in front of Notre Dame is cleared to create the ❹ **parvis**, an alfresco classroom where Parisians can learn a catechism illustrated on sculpted portals.

1935 A rooster bearing part of the relics of the Crown of Thorns, St Denis and Ste Geneviève is put on top of the cathedral spire to protect those who pray inside.

1991 The architectural masterpiece of Notre Dame and its Seine-side riverbanks become a Unesco World Heritage Site.

2013 Notre Dame celebrates 850 years since construction began with a bevy of new bells and restoration works.

2019 A fire causes devastating damage to the cathedral interior, destroys most of the roof and topples the spire.

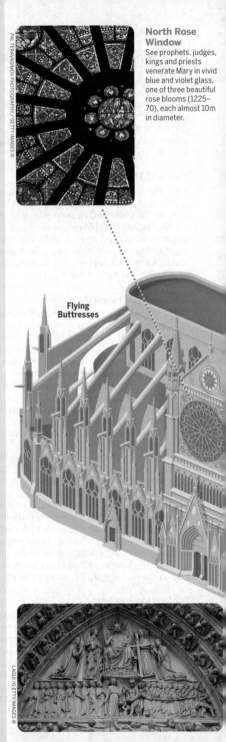

North Rose Window
See prophets, judges, kings and priests venerate Mary in vivid blue and violet glass, one of three beautiful rose blooms (1225–70), each almost 10m in diameter.

Flying Buttresses

Treasury

The cash reserve of French kings – who ordered chalices, crucifixes, baptism fonts and other sacred gems to be melted down in the Mint during times of financial strife (war, famine and so on) – was stored in the Notre Dame treasury.

In the April 2019 fire, priceless relics, such as the prized Ste-Couronne (Holy Crown), purportedly the wreath of thorns placed on Jesus' head before he was crucified, were saved by a human chain of rescue workers.

Spire & Roof

Two-thirds of the roof, and the 19th-century spire, were destroyed in the 2019 fire.

BRIAN A JACKSON / SHUTTERSTOCK ©

SYAOCHKA / SHUTTERSTOCK ©

Great Bell

The peal of Emmanuel, the cathedral's great bell, is so pure thanks to precious gems and jewels Parisian women threw into the pot when it was recast from copper and bronze in 1631. Admire its original siblings in square Jean XXII.

Chimera Gallery

The north tower is graced with grimacing gargoyles and grotesque chimera, including celebrity chimera Stryga, who has wings, horns, a human body and sticking-out tongue. This bestial lot wards off demons.

South Tower

North Tower

Great Gallery

West Rose Window

North Tower Staircase

Portal of St-Anne (Entrance)

Portal of the Last Judgement

Portal of the Virgin (Exit)

 Parvis Notre Dame

Three Portals

Play 'I spy' (Greed, Cowardice et al) beneath these sculpted doorways, which illustrate the seasons, life and the 12 vices and virtues alongside the Bible.

BATHE IN COLOURED LIGHT AT SAINTE-CHAPELLE

No single sight is as dazzling as this bijou Holy Chapel, hidden away like a precious gem – which it is – within the city's original, 13th-century Palais de Justice (Law Courts). Paris' oldest, finest stained glass laces its exquisite Gothic interior – best viewed on sunny days when the light floods in to create a mesmerising rainbow of bold colour throughout. Sainte-Chapelle was built in just six years (compared with nearly 200 years for Notre Dame) and consecrated in 1248.

History

The chapel was conceived by Louis IX to house his personal collection of holy relics, including the famous Ste-Couronne (Holy Crown), acquired by the French king in 1239 from the emperors of Constantinople for a sum of money easily exceeding the amount it cost to build the chapel. Formerly safeguarded in the treasury at Cathédrale Notre Dame de Paris, the wreath of thorns was transferred to a safe inside the Louvre for safekeeping following the devastating cathedral fire of April 2019.

Stained Glass

Statues, foliage-decorated capitals, angels and so on decorate this sumptuous, bijou chapel. But it is the 1113 biblical scenes, from Genesis through to the resurrection of Christ, depicted in its 15 floor-to-ceiling stained-glass windows – 15.5m high in the nave, 13.5m in the apse – and monumental, 9m-wide rose window that stun visitors. From the bookshop in the former ground-floor chapel reserved for palace staff, head up the narrow spiral staircase signposted 'Chapelle Haute' to the upper chapel, where only the king and his close friends were allowed.

DON'T MISS

➡ 13th-century stained glass
➡ 15th-century rose window
➡ Concerts of classical and sacred music

PRACTICALITIES

➡ Map p396, C2
➡ ☎01 53 40 60 80, concerts 01 42 77 65 65
➡ www.sainte-chapelle.fr
➡ 8 bd du Palais, 1er
➡ adult/child €11.50/ free, combined ticket with Conciergerie €17/ free
➡ ⏰11am-7pm
➡ Ⓜ Cité

SIGHTS

Île de la Cité was the site of the first settlement in Paris (c 3rd century BCE) and later the centre of Roman Lutetia. The island remained the hub of royal and ecclesiastical power, even after the city spread to both banks of the Seine in the Middle Ages. Smaller Île St-Louis was actually two uninhabited islets called Île Notre Dame (Our Lady Isle) and Île aux Vaches (Cows Island) in the early 17th century – until a building contractor and two financiers worked out a deal with Louis XIII to create one island and build two stone bridges to the mainland.

The eventual rebuild of the city's fire-ravaged cathedral is not the only momentous change that the Parisian islands, unchanged for centuries, are experiencing. The recent departure of the law courts and police HQ from Île de la Cité to the suburb of Batignolles, coupled with the agreed future redevelopment of part of historic hospital Hôtel Dieu into commercial offices, shops and restaurants, heralds a new era for the island.

CATHÉDRALE
NOTRE DAME DE PARIS   CATHEDRAL
See p196.

SAINTE-CHAPELLE   CHAPEL
See p200.

CONCIERGERIE   MONUMENT
Map p396 (📞01 53 40 60 80; www.paris-concier-gerie.fr; 2 bd du Palais, 1er; adult/child €9.50/free, combined ticket with Sainte-Chapelle €17/free; ☺10.30am-6.30pm; MCité) A royal palace in the 14th century, the Conciergerie later became a prison. During the Reign of Terror (1793–94) alleged enemies of the Revolution were incarcerated here before being brought before the Revolutionary Tribunal next door in the 13th-century **Palais de Justice**. Top-billing exhibitions take place in the beautiful, Rayonnant Gothic **Salle des Gens d'Armes**, Europe's largest surviving medieval hall.

Of the almost 2800 prisoners held in the dungeons during the Reign of Terror (in various 'classes' of cells, no less) before being sent in tumbrels to the guillotine, the star prisoner was Queen Marie Antoinette – you can see a reproduction of her cell. As the Revolution began to turn on its own, radicals Danton and Robespierre made an appearance at the Conciergerie and, finally, the judges of the tribunal themselves.

To get the most out of your visit, rent a HistoPad (a tablet-device guide; €5) to explore the Conciergerie in augmented reality and take part in an interactive, 3D treasure hunt.

CRYPTE ARCHÉOLOGIQUE   MUSEUM
Map p396 (Archaeological Crypt; 📞01 55 42 50 10; www.crypte.paris.fr; 7 Parvis Notre Dame – place Jean-Paul II, 4e; adult/child incl exhibition €9/free; ☺10am-6pm Tue-Sun; MCité) Beneath the large square in front of Notre Dame lies an archaeological crypt. The 117m-long and 28m-wide area displays the remains of structures built on this site during the Gallo-Roman period, a 4th-century enclosure wall, the foundations of the medieval foundlings hospice and original sewers sunk by Haussmann. In 2020, the crypt reopened after Notre Dame's catastrophic 2019 fire with an exhibition on the cathedral's 19th-century revival following the publication of Victor Hugo's novel *The Hunchback of Notre Dame*.

SQUARE DU VERT-GALANT   PARK
Map p396 (place du Pont Neuf, 1er; MPont Neuf) Chestnut, yew, black walnut and weeping willow trees grace this picturesque park at the westernmost tip of the Île de la Cité, along with migratory birds including mute swans, pochard and tufted ducks, black-headed gulls and wagtails. Sitting at the islands' original level, 7m below their current height, the waterside park is reached by stairs leading down from the Pont Neuf. It's romantic at any time of day, but especially so in the evening as the sun sets over the river.

PONT NEUF   BRIDGE
Map p396 (MPont Neuf) Paris' oldest bridge, misguidingly named 'New Bridge', has linked the western end of Île de la Cité with both riverbanks since 1607, when the king, Henri IV, inaugurated it by crossing the bridge on a white stallion. View the bridge's arches (seven on the northern stretch and five on the southern span), decorated with 381 *mascarons* (grotesque figures) depicting barbers, dentists, pickpockets, loiterers etc, from a spot along the river or afloat.

The inaugural crossing is commemorated by an equestrian **statue of Henri IV**, known to his subjects as the Vert Galant ('jolly rogue' or 'dirty old man', perspective depending).

Pont Neuf and nearby place Dauphine were used for public exhibitions in the 18th century. In the last century the bridge became an *objet d'art* in 1963, when School of Paris artist Nonda built, exhibited and lived in a huge Trojan horse of steel and wood on the bridge; in 1985 when Bulgarian-born 'environmental sculptor' Christo famously wrapped the bridge in beige fabric; and in 1994 when Japanese designer Kenzo covered it with flowers.

MÉMORIAL DES MARTYRS
DE LA DÉPORTATION   MONUMENT
Map p396 (☑01 46 33 87 56; square de l'Île de France, 1er; ⊙10am-7pm Apr-Sep, to 5pm Tue-Sun Oct-Mar; MCité, RRER St-Michel–Notre Dame) FREE The Memorial to the Victims of the Deportation, erected in 1962, remembers the 200,000 French residents (including 76,000 Jews, of whom 11,000 were children) who were deported to and murdered in Nazi concentration camps during WWII. A single barred 'window' separates the bleak, rough-concrete courtyard from the waters of the Seine. Inside lies the **Tomb of the Unknown Deportee**.

PONT ST-LOUIS   BRIDGE
Map p396 (MPont Marie) This postcard-perfect bridge connects Île de la Cité and Île St-Louis. Dating from 1969, it is the seventh bridge built on this spot to link the two islands. The first – made from wood – went up in the 1630s.

ÉGLISE ST-LOUIS EN L'ÎLE   CHURCH
Map p396 (☑01 46 34 11 60; www.saintlouis enlile.catholique.fr; 19 rue St-Louis en l'Île, 4e; ⊙9.30am-1pm & 2-7.30pm Mon-Sat, 9am-1pm &

2-7pm Sun; MPont Marie) French baroque Église St-Louis en l'Île, under renovation until 2022 (hence the veil of scaffolding outside), was built between 1664 and 1726. It hosts classical music and organ concerts, and offers a free guided tour of its interior (in French) one Sunday a month at 3pm; check the agenda online.

✗ EATING

Île St-Louis is a pleasant, if pricey and unexceptional, and often touristy place to dine. Otherwise lacking in decent eating places, Île de la Cité has a handful of lovely addresses on its western tip.

Self-caterers will find a couple of *fromageries* (cheese shops), chocolate shops and a small grocery store on rue St-Louis en l'Île, 4e.

★BERTHILLON   ICE CREAM €
Map p396 (☑01 43 54 31 61; www.berthillon.fr; 29-31 rue St-Louis en l'Île, 4e; 1/2/3/4 scoops takeaway €3/4.50/6/7.50; ⊙10am-8pm Wed-Sun, closed mid-Feb–early Mar & Aug; MPont Marie) Founded here in 1954, this esteemed *glacier* (ice-cream maker) is still run by the same family today. Its 70-plus all-natural, chemical-free flavours include fruit sorbets (pink grapefruit, raspberry and rose) and richer ice creams made from fresh milk and eggs (salted caramel, candied Ardèche chestnuts, Armagnac and prunes, gingerbread, liquorice, praline and pine kernels). Watch for tempting new seasonal flavours.

Breakfast, afternoon tea and cake, not to mention the most sumptuous ice-cream sundaes topped with lashings of *chantilly* (sweetened whipped cream) and homemade fruit coulis, are served in its adjoining, timber-fronted tearoom.

★CAFÉ SAINT RÉGIS   CAFE €
Map p396 (☑01 43 54 59 41; www.lesaintregis-paris.com; 6 rue Jean du Bellay, 4e; dishes €10-15, mains €19-29; ⊙kitchen 7am-midnight, bar to 2am; 🛜; MPont Marie) Waiters in long white aprons, a ceramic-tiled interior and retro vintage decor make hip Le Saint Regis a deliciously Parisian hang-out any time of the day, from breakfast pastries, organic omelettes and mid-morning croques monsieurs (ham-and-cheese toasties) to Parisian classics – garlicky snails, onion soup, fried-egg-topped *steak à cheval* – and late-night cocktails.

ℹ ROMANCE ON THE SEINE

There is nothing more romantic or quintessentially Parisian than a cruise along the River Seine. One-hour cruises run by **Vedettes du Pont Neuf** (Map p396; ☑01 46 33 98 38; www.vedettesdu pontneuf.com; square du Vert Galant, 1er; adult/child €14/7; ⊙10.30am-10.30pm; MPont Neuf) depart year-round from Vedettes' centrally located dock at the western tip of Île de la Cité; commentary is in French and English. Tickets are cheaper if you buy in advance online (adult/child €14/7). Check the website for details of its lunch cruises (€42/29), evening Champagne cruises (€24.50) and dinner cruises (€72/35).

BOULANGERIE HURÉ   BAKERY €

Map p396 (www.facebook.com/HureCreateur
DePlaisir; 1 rue d'Arcole, 4e; sandwiches €3.90-
5.20, lunch menus €8.50-10.80; ⏱6.30am-8pm
Mon-Sat; MSt-Michel Notre Dame, Châtelet)
'Createur de plaisir' (creator of pleasure) is
the enticing strapline of this contemporary
boulangerie (bakery) where glass cabinets
burst with feisty savoury quiches and pizza slices, jumbo salads, 26 types of *sables*
(cookies), lavish fruit tarts (pear or banana
and chocolate perhaps, or apple crumble?)
and a rainbow of cakes.

For a light, takeaway lunch to eat in a
park, you'll be hard-pushed to find a better-
value spot. There are two other branches in
Paris, one handily by the Centre Pompidou
and another on place d'Italie in the 13e.

LES FOUS DE L'ÎLE   FRENCH €€

Map p396 (✆01 43 25 76 67; www.lesfousdelile.
com; 33 rue des Deux Ponts, 4e; 2-/3-course menus lunch €21/26, dinner €29/36, mains €17-22;
⏱noon-11pm; 🛜; MPont Marie) Families flock
to this island bistro, which features a rustic
cockerel theme celebrating the French national symbol and chef Steven Rouquier in
the kitchen. Inventive French fare includes
steak tartare with smoked duck, roast avocado and fried seaweed, followed perhaps
by marinated sardines in chickpea cream
and, for dessert, tangy Abondance cheese
from the Alps and apple-cider ice cream.

Handily, service is continuous from noon
to 11pm.

LE CAVEAU DU PALAIS   FRENCH €€

Map p396 (✆01 43 26 04 28; www.caveaudu
palais.fr; 19 place Dauphine, 1er; mains €21-27;
⏱noon-2.30pm & 7-10pm; MPont Neuf) Le
Caveau's half-timbered dining areas and
(weather permitting) alfresco terrace are
invariably packed with diners tucking
into bountiful fresh fare: pan-seared scallops with artichokes, mushroom ravioli in
creamy chestnut sauce, or duck with roast
figs. The divinely flaky *millefeuille maison*
or crème brûlée are typically sweet Parisian
ways to end any meal here.

More informal dishes are served at its
adjacent wine bar, Le Bar du Caveau (p204).

MA SALLE À MANGER   BISTRO €€

Map p396 (✆01 43 29 52 34; 26 place Dauphine,
1er; 2-/3-course menu €29.50/37.50, mains €21-
23; ⏱9am-10.30pm; MPont Neuf) Framed by
a pretty blue-and-white striped awning, My
Dining Room chalks its daily bistro menu
on a blackboard. No-fuss dishes include
French onion soup, bœuf bourguignon and
a feather-light crème brûlée. It also cooks
up sandwiches and crêpes to take away.

Its terrace overlooking place Dauphine,
with red metal furniture and cheery win-
tertime rugs to cuddle up in on friskier
days, is enchanting.

L'ÎLOT VACHE   FRENCH €€

Map p396 (✆01 46 33 55 16; www.lilotvache.fr; 35
rue St-Louis en l'Île, 4e; menu €39, mains €24.50-
35; ⏱7-11pm; 🕿; MPont Marie) Named for one
of the Île St-Louis' previous two islands and
decorated with cow statuettes, this former
butcher shop flickers with candles that
give its exposed stone walls and dark wood
beams a romantic glow. Traditional French
classics range from Burgundy snails in parsley butter to bœuf bourguignon 'grandma-
style', duck confit and a glorious homemade
tarte tatin (upside-down apple tart).

SEQUANA   MODERN FRENCH €€€

Map p396 (✆01 43 29 78 81; www.sequana.paris;
72 quai des Orfèvres, 1er; 2-/3-course lunch menu
€24/32, 4-/6-course dinner menu €55/75; ⏱noon-
2.30pm & 7-10pm Tue-Fri, 7-10pm Sat; MPont Neuf)
At home in a chic steel-grey dining room
with retro red-velour armchairs and 1950s-
style turquoise banquet-seating on Île de la
Cité's southwestern tip, fine-dining Sequana
evokes the Gallo-Roman goddess of the
River Seine. In the kitchen are well-travelled
Philippe and Eugénie, whose childhood in
Senegal finds its way into colourful combos
such as mallard and butternut pumpkin or
parsnip and black tea.

🍷 DRINKING & NIGHTLIFE

**Drinking venues on the islands are in
short supply. They do exist, but use
them as a starting point – few places
here stay open late (with one exception).**

★**QUAI DE BOURBON**   WINE BAR

Map p396 (✆01 40 51 05 05; www.quaidebour
bon.fr; 1 quai de Bourbon; ⏱5pm-2am Tue-Sat;
MPont Marie) With its worn petrol-blue façade and decorative vintage ironwork (look
for the bunch of grapes), Quai de Bourbon
appears to be just another quintessential
Parisian neighbourhood bar. But enter the
fashionably minimalist interior lit by two

giant naked lightbulbs, and descend to the basement to uncover the island's coolest music and cocktail bar.

There are live gigs most nights and the roster ticks off most music genres. The cocktail menu includes a detailed history of each cocktail (€10) and smoked beef, black-truffle-spiked ham and mixed cheese platters are among the tasty morsels served alongside.

LE BAR DU CAVEAU
WINE BAR

Map p396 (www.caveaudupalais.fr; 17 place Dauphine, 1er; ⊗bar 8am-6.30pm Mon-Fri, kitchen noon-4pm Mon-Fri; MPont Neuf) The wine bar of neighbouring restaurant Le Caveau du Palais (p203) is an enchanting spot for a glass of wine from France's flagship regions accompanied by light dishes (€9 to €14) like salads, a Poilâne-bread *tartine* (open-faced sandwich) or warming croque monsieur.

In warm weather, chill on its pavement terrace overlooking the island's prettiest square.

🛍 SHOPPING

Île St-Louis is a shopper's delight for craft-filled boutiques and tiny, charming specialist stores. Head to Île de la Cité for souvenirs and tourist kitsch.

★ MARCHÉ AUX FLEURS REINE ELIZABETH II
MARKET

Map p396 (www.facebook.com/Marche.Aux. Fleurs.Reine.Elizabeth.2; place Louis Lépine et quai de la Corse, 4e; ⊗9.30am-7pm Mon-Sat, 8am-7pm Sun; MCité) Blooms have been sold at this quaint flower market since 1808, making it the oldest market of any kind in Paris.

★ 38 SAINT LOUIS
FOOD & DRINKS

Map p396 (✆01 46 33 30 00; 38 rue St-Louis en l'Île, 4e; ⊗8.30am-10pm Tue-Sat, 9.30am-4pm Sun; MPont Marie) Not only does this contemporary, creamy white-fronted *fromagerie* run by young, dynamic, food-driven duo Didier Grosjean and Thibault Lhirondelle have an absolutely superb selection of first-class French cheese, it also offers Saturday wine tastings, artisan fruit juices and prepared dishes to go, such as sheep's-cheese salad with truffle oil, and wooden boxes filled with vacuum-packed cheese to take home.

L'ÎLES AUX IMAGES
ART

Map p396 (✆01 56 24 15 22; www.vintage-photos-lithos-paris.com; 51 rue St-Louis en l'Île, 4e; ⊗2-7pm Mon-Sat & by appointment; MPont Marie) Original and rare vintage posters, photographs and lithographs dating from 1850 onwards from artists including Man Ray, Salvador Dalí, Paul Gauguin and Picasso are stocked at this gallery-boutique. Many depict Parisian scenes and make evocative home decorations. Framing can be arranged.

L'EMBRASSER
ART

Map p396 (✆01 42 38 87 95; www.facebook.com/lembrasser; 24 rue St-Louis en l'Île, 4e; ⊗11am-7pm Wed-Sun) A glass-and-steel façade opens onto a minimalist interior at this stylish gallery dedicated to Japanese art: think prints, paintings, pottery and ceramics. Check its Facebook page for the month's exhibition.

LIBRAIRIE ULYSSE
BOOKS

Map p396 (✆06 27 31 35 95, 01 43 25 17 35; www.ulysse.fr; 26 rue St-Louis en l'Île, 4e; ⊗2-8pm Tue-Fri, mornings & Sat by appointment; MPont Marie) Stuffed to the rafters with antiquarian and new travel guides, *National Geographic* back editions and maps, this bijou boutique was the world's first travel bookshop when it was opened in 1971 by the intrepid Catherine Domaine. Hours vary, but ring the bell and Catherine will open up if she's around.

CLAIR DE RÊVE
TOYS

Map p396 (✆01 43 29 81 06; www.clairdereve.com; 35 rue St-Louis en l'Île, 4e; ⊗11am-1pm & 2-7pm Mon-Sat; MPont Marie) Stringed marionettes made of papier mâché, leather and porcelain bob from the ceiling of this endearing little shop. It also sells wind-up toys and music boxes.

UPPER
CONCEPT STORE

Map p396 (✆01 42 49 29 96; www.upperconcept.com; 19 rue des Deux Ponts, 4e; ⊗11am-7pm Tue-Sat; MPont Marie) Part boutique, art gallery, cafe (serving coffee, tea, beer, wine and cocktails) and co-working space (where you pay by the hour or day), Upper spreads over three floors. Men's and women's fashion, hats, handbags, jewellery, sunglasses, stationery and homewares, such as lamps and pot plant holders, are displayed alongside works by Parisian, French and international artists.

Latin Quarter

LATIN QUARTER | 5E

Neighbourhood Top Five

❶ Panthéon (p207) Paying homage to France's greatest thinkers buried beneath this domed neo-classical mausoleum.

❷ Shakespeare & Company (p219) Browsing the shelves of Paris' most magical bookshop and refuelling at its inspirational, literary-themed cafe.

❸ Institut du Monde Arabe (p208) Visiting the fascinating exhibits inside the stunning Jean Nouvel–designed building before heading to the roof to admire the incredible panorama.

❹ Jardin des Plantes (p209) Strolling around Paris' sprawling botanical gardens and visiting its historic greenhouses, zoo and the many branches of the Natural History Museum located here.

❺ Caveau de la Huchette (p218) Lapping up the Latin Quarter vibe and dancing after dark at a jazz gig in a mythical medieval cellar.

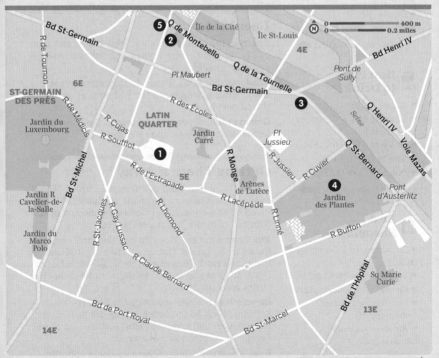

For more detail of this area see Map p398 and p400 ➡

Lonely Planet's Top Tip

While hungry first-time visitors are often drawn into the maze of tiny streets between the Seine, rue St-Jacques and bd St-Germain, you'd be wise to simply avoid this heavily touristed, overpriced area altogether. Instead, grab some bread, cheese, charcuterie and wine from local speciality shops and enjoy some multimillion-dollar views with your meal. Best bets? The quays along the Seine, place du Panthéon (a student fave) and the leafy Jardin des Plantes.

✖ Best Places to Eat

➜ Restaurant AT (p215)
➜ La Bête Noire (p211)
➜ Café de la Nouvelle Mairie (p211)
➜ Baieta (p215)
➜ Kitchen Ter(re) (p213)

For reviews, see p211.➜

🍷 Best Places to Drink

➜ Nuage (p216)
➜ Shakespeare & Company Café (p216)
➜ Le Verre à Pied (p216)
➜ Strada Café (p216)
➜ Pub St-Hilaire (p217)

For reviews, see p216➜

🔒 Best Shopping

➜ Shakespeare & Company (p219)
➜ Le Bonbon au Palais (p219)
➜ Bières Cultes Jussieu (p219)
➜ Fromagerie Laurent Dubois (p219)
➜ Au Vieux Camper Librairie (p220)

For reviews, see p219.➜

Explore Latin Quarter

The Latin Quarter has been student central for Parisian higher education since the Middle Ages. Rub shoulders with some of France's greatest literati at the neoclassical Panthéon (p207), followed by *un café* at Café de la Nouvelle Mairie (p211); if hunger strikes, this is a top spot for lunch too. Meander south to thriving market street rue Mouffetard (p221), the finest strip for Latin Quarter aromas, tastes and local-life vibes. Flit from open-air market food stall to tantalising food shop, stopping for lunch at a restaurant here. (Skip on Mondays, when the market stalls are shut.) End with an espresso at *nouvelle génération* coffee shop Dose (p217).

Parisian men gather to play boules (similar to lawn bowls), as they have done so for centuries, at Roman amphitheatre Arènes de Lutèce (p210). Catch a game, then while away a serene afternoon exploring Jardin des Plantes (p209). Don't miss the magnificent 18th-century greenhouses, the Natural History Museum's Grande Galerie de l'Évolution (p209) and a sweet mint tea in the Mosquée de Paris (p214).

Kick off the evening with a guided tasting of six French wines and Champagne at Wine Tasting in Paris (p221). Dine in a local bistro, then descend into a medieval cellar for a jazz and jam session or into one of the quarter's lively pubs to hobnob with local students.

Local Life

Sporting life Join the locals playing boules and football in the 2nd-century Roman amphitheatre Arènes de Lutèce (p210).

Academic life Clink drinks during extended Latin Quarter happy hours with the Sorbonne academic sitting next to you.

Cinema life Independent cinemas in the Latin Quarter screen cult, classic and rare films.

Getting There & Away

Metro The most central metro stations are St-Michel by the Seine, Cluny–La Sorbonne or Maubert-Mutualité on bd St-Germain; and Censier Daubenton or Gare d'Austerlitz by the Jardin des Plantes.

Bus Convenient bus stops include the Panthéon for the 89 to Jardin des Plantes and 13e; bd St-Michel for the 38 to Centre Pompidou, Gare de l'Est and Gare du Nord; and rue Gay Lussac for the 27 to Île de la Cité, Opéra and Gare St-Lazare.

Bicycle Handy Vélib' stations include 42 rue St-Severin, 5e, off bd St-Michel; 40 rue des Boulangers, 5e, near Cardinal Lemoine metro station; and 27 rue Lacépède, 5e, near place Monge.

Boat The hop-on, hop-off Batobus docks opposite Notre Dame on quai de Montebello.

TOP EXPERIENCE
PAY RESPECTS TO HISTORY'S GREAT THINKERS AT THE PANTHÉON

Elegant and regal in equal measure, the massive neoclassical dome of the Left Bank's iconic Panthéon is an icon of the Parisian skyline. Louis XV originally commissioned the vast architectural masterpiece around 1750 as an abbey dedicated to Ste Geneviève in thanksgiving for his recovery from an illness. Due to financial and structural problems, it wasn't completed until 1789.

The Panthéon reverted to religious duties twice after the Revolution but has played a secular role ever since 1885. Its **crypt** serves as the resting place of some of France's greatest thinkers, including Voltaire, Rousseau, Braille and Hugo.

The first woman to be interred in the Panthéon based on achievement was two-time Nobel Prize–winner Marie Curie (1867–1934), reburied here, along with her husband, Pierre, in 1995. Also interred here are Resistance fighters Pierre Brossolette and Jean Zay, as well as the symbolic interments of Resistance fighters Germaine Tillion and Geneviève de Gaulle-Anthonioz, with soil from their graves.

In 2018, Auschwitz survivor, feminist icon and human rights activist Simone Veil became the fifth woman to be interred in the Panthéon.

A copy of **Foucault's pendulum**, first hung from the dome in 1851 to demonstrate the rotation of the earth, takes pride of place.

Until the Eiffel Tower was built, the Panthéon was the highest building in Paris. Its colonnaded dome, accessible via 206 steps, is open to visitors (€3) between April and October – predictably, the city panorama is swooningly good. Take a 1½-hour DIY guided tour of the mausoleum with the excellent audioguide (€3), available at the entrance.

DON'T MISS

➡ The architecture
➡ Foucault's Pendulum
➡ Crypt

PRACTICALITIES

➡ Map p400, C1
➡ ☎01 44 32 18 00
➡ www.paris-pantheon.fr
➡ place du Panthéon, 5e
➡ adult/child €11.50/free
➡ ⏰10am-6.30pm Apr-Sep, to 6pm Oct-Mar
➡ Ⓜ Maubert-Mutualité or RER Luxembourg

SIGHTS

The Latin Quarter's Roman and medieval roots can be seen throughout the neighbourhood. Natural history buffs won't want to miss the museums making up the Muséum National d'Histoire Naturelle in the beautifully green Jardin des Plantes. Watch for the 2022 reopening after extensive renovation of the neighbourhood's premier museum and France's finest medieval-history museum, the Musée National du Moyen Âge.

MUSÉE NATIONAL DU MOYEN ÂGE MUSEUM
Map p398 (☑01 53 73 78 00; www.musee-moyen age.fr; 28 rue du Sommerard, 5e; adult/child €5/ free, 1st Sun of month free; ⊙9.15am-5.45pm Wed-Mon; ⋒Cluny–La Sorbonne) The National Museum of the Middle Ages is undergoing renovations through at least early 2022 and may be partially open when you visit. Check the website for updates.

It showcases a series of sublime treasures, from medieval statuary, stained glass and *objets d'art* to its celebrated series of tapestries, *The Lady with the Unicorn* (1500). Other highlights include ornate 15th-century mansion Hôtel de Cluny and the *frigidarium* (cold room) of an enormous Roman-era bathhouse.

Designed by architect Bernard Desmoulin, the contemporary entrance building houses the ticket office, bookshop, souvenir boutique and visitors' cloakroom. When renovation works are complete, the museum will have a state-of-the-art layout with enhanced explanatory panels and interactive displays, and will again provide access to the Hôtel de Cluny's 1st floor, late-Gothic chapel, La Chapelle de l'Hôtel de Cluny, with rich carvings of Christ on the cross, 13 angels, and floral and foliage ornaments.

Outside are the museum's beautiful medieval gardens.

MOSQUÉE DE PARIS MOSQUE
Map p400 (☑01 45 35 78 17; www.mosqueede paris.net; 2bis place du Puits de l'Ermite, 5e; adult/ child €3/2; ⊙9am-6pm Sat-Thu; ⋒Place Monge) Paris' central mosque, with a striking 33m-high minaret, was completed in 1926 in an ornate art deco Moorish style. You can visit the interior to admire the intricate tile work and calligraphy. A separate entrance leads to the wonderful North African–style *hammam* (Turkish bathhouse), restaurant and tea-

---

TOP EXPERIENCE
LEARN ABOUT THE ARAB WORLD AT THE INSTITUT DU MONTE ARABE

The groundbreaking **Institut du Monte Arabe** is a one-stop shop for learning about the Arab world, both today and a millennia ago. It was created in 1980, in partnership with 18 Middle Eastern and North African nations, to foster cross-cultural dialogue. Its museum (on the 4th to 7th floors) focusses on art, artisanship and science, with everything from pre-Islamic ceramics to ancient astronomical instruments, from regional music displays to Arabic calligraphy. Temporary exhibitions complement the permanent collections.

You certainly can't miss the building: this is one of the city's many architectural landmarks, with French architect Jean Nouvel using traditional Arabic latticed-wood windows (*mashrabiya*) as his inspiration for the eye-catching glass façade. Dazzling when the sun shines, the imposing façade incorporates thousands of photo-electrically sensitive apertures that allow those inside the building to peer out without being seen. Electric motors open and close the apertures to regulate the amount of light and heat that reach the institute's interior.

DON'T MISS

➡ Museum
➡ Top-floor observation terrace
➡ Temporary exhibitions

PRACTICALITIES

➡ Arab World Institute
➡ Map p398, F3
➡ ☑01 40 51 38 52
➡ www.imarabe.org
➡ 1 place Mohammed V, 5e
➡ adult/child €8/free
➡ ⊙1-6pm Tue-Sun
➡ ⋒Jussieu

room, and a small souk (actually more of a gift shop). Visitors must be modestly dressed.

JARDIN DES PLANTES   PARK

Map p400 ([📞]01 40 79 56 01; www.jardindesplantes deparis.fr; place Valhubert & 36 rue Geoffroy-St-Hilaire, 5e; ⊙8am-7.30pm Apr-Sep, shorter hours winter; [M]Gare d'Austerlitz, Censier Daubenton, Jussieu) Founded in 1626 as a medicinal herb garden for Louis XIII, Paris' 24-hectare botanic gardens – visually defined by the double alley of plane trees that runs the length of the park – are an idyllic spot to stroll around, break for a picnic (watch out for the automatic sprinklers!) and escape the city concrete for a spell. Three museums from the Muséum National d'Histoire Naturelle and a small zoo, La Ménagerie, add to its appeal.

Other attractions include peony and rose gardens, an alpine garden, and the gardens of the École de Botanique, used by students of the school and green-fingered Parisians. The beautiful glass-and-metal Grandes Serres, a series of four greenhouses, have been in use since 1714; several of Henri Rousseau's jungle paintings, sometimes on display in the Musée d'Orsay, were inspired by his frequent visits here.

LA MÉNAGERIE   ZOO

Map p400 (Le Zoo du Jardin des Plantes; [📞]01 40 79 56 01; www.mnhn.fr; 57 rue Cuvier, 5e; adult/child €13/10; ⊙9am-6pm Mon-Sat, to 6.30pm Sun Mar-Oct, to 5pm Nov-Feb; [M]Gare d'Austerlitz) Like the Jardin des Plantes in which it's located, this 170-species zoo is more than a tourist attraction; it also doubles as a research centre for the reproduction of rare and endangered species. During the Prussian siege of 1870, the animals of the day were themselves endangered, when almost all were eaten by starving Parisians.

MUSÉUM NATIONAL
D'HISTOIRE NATURELLE   MUSEUM

Map p400 (www.mnhn.fr; place Valhubert & 36 rue Geoffroy-St-Hilaire, 5e; [M]Gare d'Austerlitz, Censier Daubenton, Jussieu) Despite the name, the National Museum of Natural History is not a single building, but a collection of sites throughout France. Its historic home is in the Jardin des Plantes, and it's here that you'll find the greatest number of branches: taxidermied animals in the excellent Grande Galerie de l'Évolution (Map p400; [📞]01 40 79 54 79; www.grandegalerie delevolution.fr; 36 rue Geoffroy-St-Hilaire, 5e; adult/child €10/7, incl Galeries des Enfants €12/9;

⊙10am-6pm Wed-Mon; [♿]; [M]Censier Daubenton); fossils and dinosaur skeletons in the Galerie de Paléontologie et d'Anatomie Comparée (Map p400; [📞]01 40 79 56 01; www. mnhn.fr; 2 rue Buffon, 5e; adult/child €9/free; ⊙10am-6pm Wed-Mon; [M]Gare d'Austerlitz); and meteorites and crystals in the Galerie de Minéralogie et de Géologie (Map p400; [📞]01 40 79 56 01; www.galeriedemineralogieet geologie.fr; 36 rue Geoffroy-St-Hilaire, 5e; adult/child €7/free; ⊙10am-6pm Wed-Mon Mar-Oct, to 5pm Nov-Feb; [M]Censier Daubenton).

Created in 1793, the National Museum of Natural History became a site of significant scientific research in the 19th century. Of the three museums here, the four-floor Grande Galerie de l'Évolution is a particular winner if you're travelling with kids: life-sized elephants, tigers and rhinos play safari, and imaginative exhibits (including a virtual reality room, reserve; €5) fill 6000 sq metres. The temporary exhibits are generally excellent. Within this building is a separate attraction, the Galerie des Enfants (Map p400; [📞]01 40 79 56 01; www.mnhn.fr; adult/child €12/9, combination ticket with Grande Galerie de l'Évolution €12/9; ⊙10am-6pm Wed, Sat & Sun, plus school holidays; [M]Censier Daubenton) – a hands-on science museum tailored to children aged from six to 12 years.

MUSÉE DE LA
SCULPTURE EN PLEIN AIR   SCULPTURE

Map p398 (quai St-Bernard, 5e; [M]Gare d'Austerlitz) [FREE] Along quai St-Bernard, this open-air sculpture museum (also known as the Jardin Tino Rossi) has more than 50 late-20th-century unfenced sculptures. It could be a great picnic spot, but unfortunately is not always well maintained.

ABBAYE ROYALE DU
VAL-DE-GRÂCE   CHURCH

Map p400 ([📞]01 40 51 51 92; www.ecole-valde-grace.sante.defense.gouv.fr; 1 place Alphonse Laveran; adult/child €5/2.50; ⊙noon-6pm Tue-Thu, Sat & Sun Sep-Jul; [M]RER Port Royal) One of the city's grandest remnants of pre-Revolution Paris, Chapelle de la Val-de-Grâce was built in 1645 to celebrate the birth of Anne of Austria and King Louis XIII's first son after 23 years of childless marriage. After the revolution, in 1795, the royal abbey became a military hospital. A small museum in the original abbey cloister, the Musée du Service de Santé des Armées, explores its work; this is the only section open to the public.

Once a month music concerts are held in the chapel (October to June); check the website for schedules.

ÉGLISE ST-ÉTIENNE DU MONT CHURCH

Map p400 (☑01 43 54 11 79; www.saintetiennedu mont.fr; 1 place Ste-Geneviève, 5e; ⊗2.30-7.30pm Mon, 8.30am-7.30pm Tue-Fri, 8.30am-1pm & 2-8pm Sat & Sun; ⓂCardinal Lemoine) FREE The Church of Mount St Stephen, built between 1492 and 1655, contains Paris' only surviving rood screen (1521–45), separating the chancel from the nave; the others were removed during the late Renaissance because they prevented the faithful in the nave from seeing the priest celebrate Mass.

In the nave's southeastern corner, the tomb of Ste Geneviève lies in a chapel.

The patron saint of Paris, Ste Geneviève was born at Nanterre in 422 CE and turned away Attila the Hun from Paris in 451 CE.

A highly decorated reliquary near her tomb contains all that is left of her earthly remains – a finger bone.

Fans of the Woody Allen film *Midnight in Paris* will recognise the stone steps on the northwestern corner as the place where Owen Wilson's character is collected by vintage car and transported back to the 1920s.

ARÈNES DE LUTÈCE RUINS

Map p400 (49 rue Monge, 5e; ⊗8am-8.30pm May-Aug, shorter hours rest of year; ⓂPlace Monge) FREE The 2nd-century Roman amphitheatre Lutetia Arena once seated 10,000 people for gladiatorial combats and other events. Found by accident in 1869 when rue Monge was under construction, it's now used by locals playing football and, especially, boules. Hours can vary.

LATIN QUARTER LITERARY ADDRESSES

Like its Left Bank neighbours, the Latin Quarter is steeped in literary history.

James Joyce's flat (Map p400; 71 rue du Cardinal Lemoine, 5e; ⓂCardinal Lemoine) Somewhat fittingly, squint through the wrought-iron gates of 71 rue du Cardinal Lemoine to see the courtyard flat where a near-blind James Joyce finished editing *Ulysses*. The Irish writer and his wife, Nora, were put up rent-free by French novelist Valery Larbaud, who owned the apartment marked with an 'E'. It's not open to the public, but Joyce is said to have scribbled away at the manuscript with his head laid almost sideways as it was the only way he was able to see what he had written.

Ernest Hemingway's apartment (Map p400; 74 rue du Cardinal Lemoine, 5e; ⓂCardinal Lemoine) A few doors down from chez Joyce, at 74 rue du Cardinal Lemoine, is the townhouse where Ernest Hemingway (1899–1961) and his first wife, Hadley, lived it up between January 1922 and August 1923. Conveniently for the party-loving novelist, his 3rd-floor apartment was right above one of the hottest dance halls in town, the Bal au Printemps: Hemingway was one of the most loyal regulars at the parties and literary soirées thrown many Friday nights here by English writer and editor Ford Madox.

Paul Verlaine's garret (Map p400; 39 rue Descartes, 5e; ⓂCardinal Lemoine) Hemingway might have lived on rue du Cardinal Lemoine in the 1920s but his writing desk was around the corner, in a top-floor garret of a hotel at 39 rue Descartes – today a traditional French restaurant with vintage decor and plenty of time-faded old photographs on the wall. A popular stopover for impoverished writers, French poet Paul Verlaine (1844–96) lived for a while – and then died – in the same hotel.

Place de la Contrescarpe Rue Descartes runs south into place de la Contrescarpe (place Monge), now a well-scrubbed square with four Judas trees and a fountain, but once a 'cesspool' (said Hemingway), especially Café des Amateurs at 2–4 place de la Contrescarpe.

George Orwell's boarding house (Map p400; 6 rue du Pot de Fer, 5e; ⓂPlace Monge) George Orwell (1903–50) arrived in Paris in spring 1928 and checked into a cheap boarding house above 6 rue du Pot de Fer, where he stayed until he moved to London in December 1929. Despite its slumminess, the boarding house – or 'Hotel X' as he called it in *Down and Out in Paris and London* (1933) – seemed 'like a holiday' after a day slaving away washing dishes at a restaurant on nearby rue du Commerce.

SQUARE RENÉ VIVIANI
PARK

Map p398 (quai de Montebello, 5e; ⊘24hr; MSt-Michel) Opened in 1928 on the site of the former graveyard of adjoining church Église St-Julien le Pauvre (p218), this picturesque little park is home to the oldest tree in Paris, a black locust *(Robinia pseudoacacia)*. Royal gardener Jean Robin planted it here in 1602 following a trip to the American colonies. It has been severely pruned back but, despite initial appearances, it is still alive. A fountain by Georges Jeanclos installed in 1995 depicts the legend of St Julien.

ÉGLISE ST-SÉVERIN
CHURCH

Map p398 (⊘01 42 34 93 50; 1 rue des Prêtres St-Séverin, 5e; ⊘9.30am-7.30pm Mon-Sat, 9am-8pm Sun; MCluny–La Sorbonne) FREE Extensively renovated in the 15th century, this Gothic church contains one of the oldest bells in Paris, cast in 1412. Also of note are the seven modern stained-glass windows depicting the seven sacraments, designed by Jean René Bazaine in 1970.

SORBONNE
UNIVERSITY

Map p398 (www.sorbonne.fr; 12 rue de la Sorbonne, 5e; MCluny–La Sorbonne or RER Luxembourg) The *crème de la crème* of academia flock to this distinguished university, one of the world's most famous. Today 'La Sorbonne' embraces most of the 13 autonomous universities – some 45,000 students in all – created when the University of Paris was reorganised after the student protests of 1968. Visitors are not permitted to enter.

CHAPELLE DE LA SORBONNE
CHURCH

Map p398 (www.sorbonne.fr; place de la Sorbonne, 5e; MCluny–La Sorbonne) The Sorbonne university's distinctive domed church was built between 1635 and 1642. The remains of Cardinal Richelieu (1585–1642) lie in a tomb with an effigy of a cardinal's hat suspended above. You may visit only on a 1½-hour guided tour (in French; €15); see the website for information on booking.

COLLÈGE DES BERNARDINS
HISTORIC BUILDING

Map p398 (⊘01 53 10 74 44; www.collegedesbernardins.fr; 18-24 rue de Poissy, 5e; ⊘10am-6pm Mon-Sat; MCardinal Lemoine) FREE Dating back to 1248, this former Cistercian college originally served as living quarters and place of study for novice monks. It's now an art gallery and Christian culture centre with events ranging from lectures to film screenings and music performances; check schedules online.

✕ EATING

From chandelier-lit palaces loaded with history to cheap-eat student haunts, the 5e *arrondissement* caters to every budget and culinary taste. Rue Mouffetard is famed for its food market and food shops, though you'll have to trek down side streets for the neighbourhood's best meals.

★CAFÉ DE LA NOUVELLE MAIRIE
CAFE €

Map p400 (⊘01 44 07 04 41; 19 rue des Fossés St-Jacques, 5e; small plates €8-11, mains €14-22; ⊘kitchen noon-3pm & 8-10.30pm Mon-Fri, bar 8am-midnight Mon-Fri; MCardinal Lemoine) Shhhh...just around the corner from the Panthéon but hidden away on a small, fountained square, this hybrid cafe-restaurant and wine bar is a tip-top neighbourhood secret, serving natural wines and delicious seasonal bistro fare, from oysters and ribs (*à la française*) to grilled lamb sausage over lentils. It takes reservations for dinner but not lunch – arrive early.

LA BÊTE NOIRE
MEDITERRANEAN €

Map p412 (⊘06 15 22 73 61; www.facebook.com/labetenoireparis; 58 rue Henri Barbusse, 5e; lunch mains €12-15, dinner menu €25-45, brunch €25; ⊘8am-5pm Tue, 8am-11pm Wed-Fri, 9.30am-5.30pm Sat & Sun; 🔊; MRER Port Royal) A small, fashionably minimalist interior with open kitchen and funky music ensure bags of soul at this off-the-radar *cantine gastronomique,* a showcase for the sensational home cooking of passionate chef-owner Maria. Inspired by her Russian-Maltese heritage, she cooks just one meat and one vegetarian dish daily using seasonal ingredients from local farmers and small producers, washed down with Italian wines.

End with one of Maria's extraordinary homemade cakes – a soft, rich Sicilian-inspired almond cookie or sweet whirl of a chocolate-and-pistachio pastry perhaps – and a serious craft coffee poured by Italian barista Bartolomeo. Reservations recommended, especially for weekend brunch.

ONOPOKÉ
HAWAIIAN €

Map p400 (⊘09 82 29 81 87; www.onopoke.fr; 167 rue St-Jacques, 5e; mains €10-15.50; ⊘noon-5pm Mon-Fri, to 8pm Sat; MCardinal Lemoine) Head here for creative beans, grains, pulses and veg topped with raw or smoked fish (tuna, salmon, white fish) and your chosen sprinkling of fried onions, chilli, sunflower seeds or wasabi-laced sesame seeds. Always rammed with cent-smart students from the neighbouring Sorbonne, OnoPoké prepares turbo-sized salad bowls inspired by traditional Hawaiian *poke* (raw diced fish with sushi rice) in a hip, laid-back space.

Order at the counter, grab a seat at a shared table and await your made-to-measure bowl. Meat lovers will appreciate the French duck or *viande séchée* (air-dried meat) bowl, and there is tofu-peppered *poke* for vegetarians. Takeaway too.

CIRCUS BAKERY BAKERY €

Map p398 (63 rue Galande, 5e; pastries €4-8.50, sandwiches €14; ⏱7am-8pm; Ⓜ Maubert-Mutualité) Spectacular sourdough cinnamon rolls are the showstoppers at this bakery with a rustic dark-timber exterior and exposed stone and brick interior. Other treats include apple tarts and breads, such as chocolate-marbled varieties, and Parisianroasted Hexagone coffee to take away. The wood-fired pita sandwiches are definitely pricey, but stuffed to bursting with scrumptious marinated veggies.

NUMÉRO 220 CAFE €

Map p400 (☎06 66 93 58 71; www.facebook. com/numero220; 220 rue St-Jacques, 5e; mains €7-14; ⏱8.30am-6pm Tue-Fri, 10.30am-5pm Sat; 🖉; Ⓜ RER Luxembourg) For a casual breakfast or vegetarian lunch, this cafe hits the spot. Temptations run from sweet-potato curry, salads and slices of quiche to sweet and savoury pancakes and French toast for breakfast. Coffee to go, too!

CROQ' FAC SANDWICHES €

Map p398 (160 rue St-Jacques, 5e; sandwich menu €5.50; ⏱8am-7pm Mon-Sat; Ⓜ Cardinal Lemoine) Latin Quarter students pack out this *sandwicherie* (sandwich bar) at lunchtime, and for good reason. Delicious, made-to-measure sandwiches embrace dozens of bread types (wraps, ciabatta, panini, bagels, *pan bagnat* etc) and fillings (the world's your oyster). Arrive before noon to ensure a table – inside or on the people-watching pavement terrace – otherwise you can take away.

LES BAUX DE PARIS FRENCH €

Map p400 (☎01 47 07 91 58; 71 rue Mouffetard, 5e; mains €8.50-13; ⏱11.30am-2am; Ⓜ Censier Daubenton) Centuries-old wooden beams and exposed stone add instant charm to this busy restaurant-bar on rue Mouffetard, a market street. Be it a deep-fried squid, tuna tataki or traditional *magret de canard*

(duck breast) with figs and pecan nuts, there is a dish or small plate to suit every taste.

LE POT O'LAIT CRÊPES €

Map p400 (☎09 83 26 76 80; 41 rue Censier, 5e; lunch menus €11.50-14, galettes €8.50-11.50; ⏱11.30am-2.30pm & 7-10.30pm; Ⓜ Censier Daubenton) A bright, contemporary spot, the Milk Can is the business when it comes to *galettes* (savoury buckwheat crêpes) – try smoked salmon or goat's cheese and bacon – and sweet crêpes (pistachio ice cream, zesty orange, hot chocolate and whipped cream). Salads are spectacular; kids will love the ice-cream sundaes.

BOULANGERIE ERIC KAYSER BAKERY €

Map p398 (www.maison-kayser.com; 8 rue Monge, 5e; ⏱6.45am-8.15pm Mon & Wed-Fri, from 6.30am Sat & Sun; Ⓜ Maubert–Mutualité) This original branch of Eric Kayser – now a household name in Paris with 16 addresses across the city and several more worldwide – is one of the best bakeries that's reasonably close to the Seine and the islands. A few doors down is a second **shop** (Map p398; 14 rue Monge, 5e; ⏱7am-8.15pm Tue, from 7.30am Wed-Sun; Ⓜ Maubert–Mutualité), with seating, coffee and light, flaky pastries.

BOULANGERIE BRUNO SOLQUES BAKERY €

Map p400 (☎01 43 54 62 33; 243 rue St-Jacques, 5e; ⏱8am-7pm Mon-Fri; Ⓜ Place Monge or RER Luxembourg) Inventive *pâtissier* Bruno Solques crafts wonderfully rustic breads (sold by weight measured on old-fashioned scales) using only organic flours. The small, bare-boards shop is also filled with Solques' creatively shaped flat tarts with mashed fruit, fruit-filled brioches and subtly spiced gingerbread. It's on the pricey side but worth it – kids from the school across the way can't get enough.

PETITS PLATS DE MARC CAFE €

Map p400 (☎01 43 36 60 79; www.facebook.com/ LesPetitsPlatsDeMarc; 6 rue de l'Arbalète, 5e; mains €11-15, weekend brunch €18-23; ⏱10am-3pm Mon & Tue, 8am-4pm Wed, to 6pm Thu-Sat, to 5pm Sun; 🛜; Ⓜ Censier Daubenton) This tiny pit stop off rue Mouffetard is wonderfully cosy and a change from the usual humdrum tourist spots; the homemade soups, quiches, pastries and salads are delicious and easy on the wallet. Tea and coffee are served throughout the day; weekend brunch is among Paris' finest. To brunch on the cheap (€15.50 to €19), dine and leave before noon.

BISTRO LE MAUZAC
BISTRO €

Map p400 (☎01 46 33 75 22; www.bistro-mauzac. com; 7 rue de l'Abbé de l'Epée, 5e; 2-course lunch menu €16, mains €11-27; ⏱7am-11pm Mon-Sat; ☎; ⓂPlace Monge or RER Luxembourg) With a moon-shaped zinc bar and traditional furnishings, Le Mauzac is a quintessential old-school Parisian bistro. Drinks and food are served nonstop, kicking off with egg-fuelled breakfasts (€2 to €14), followed by lunchtime steaks, hearty bowls of *soupe à l'oignon* (onion soup) and croques-monsieurs (grilled ham and cheese) made with Poilâne bread. Sweet crêpes, pastries and ice cream, too.

ODETTE
PATISSERIE €

Map p398 (☎01 43 26 13 06; www.odette-paris. com; 77 rue Galande, 5e; 1/6/12 pastry puffs €1.90/10.90/19.80; ⏱9am-8pm Mon, Fri & Sat, 11am-8pm Tue-Thu; ⓂSt-Michel) Odette's ground-floor space sells *choux* (pastry puffs) with seasonal flavoured cream fillings, such as coffee, lemon, green tea, salted caramel, pistachio and forest berries (nine on offer at a time). Upstairs, its art deco tearoom plays 1920s music and serves *choux* along with tea, coffee and Champagne. The black-painted timber façade and a geranium-filled 1st-floor window box are charming.

BONJOUR VIETNAM
VIETNAMESE €

Map p400 (☎01 43 54 78 04; 6 rue Thouin, 5e; mains €8-14; ⏱noon-2.30pm & 7-11pm Wed-Mon; ⓂCardinal Lemoine) Stop by this lauded Vietnamese spot for a bowl of *pho* (noodle soup with thin slices of rare beef, mint, anise and lime) or *bobun* (cold rice-noodle salad with marinated beef). There's only a handful of tables; reserve.

CHEZ NICOS
CRÊPES €

Map p400 (☎01 45 87 28 13; 44 rue Mouffetard, 5e; crêpes €1.50-6; ⏱10am-2am; ⓂPlace Monge) The signboard outside crêpe artist Nicos' unassuming little shop lists dozens of fillings but ask for his masterpiece by name: 'La Crêpe du Chef', stuffed with aubergines, feta, mozzarella, lettuce, tomatoes and onions. There's a handful of tables inside; otherwise get it wrapped up in foil and head to a nearby park.

LE PUITS DE LÉGUMES
VEGETARIAN, ORGANIC €

Map p398 (☎01 43 25 50 95; https://le-puits-de-lgumes.zenchef.com; 18 rue du Cardinal Lemoine, 5e; lunch menus €13.50-20, mains €13-21; ⏱noon-4pm & 7-10pm Mon-Sat; ☎; ⓂCardinal Lemoine) 🌿 Homemade tarts, quiches, omelettes, fish and rice dishes loaded with fresh seasonal vegetables are the draw of the 'Vegetable Well', an all-organic vegetarian (plus fish) option with a cheery apple-green façade. From the tiny kitchen a comforting waft of homemade cooking pervades the simple dining room, filled with a handful of condiment-laden tables. Specials are chalked on the board outside.

★ KITCHEN TER(RE)
GASTRONOMY €€

Map p398 (☎01 42 39 47 48; www.zekitchen galerie.fr; 26 bd St-Germain, 5e; 2-/3-course lunch menu €26/30, mains €21; ⏱12.15-2pm & 7.15-10pm Tue-Sat; ⓂMaubert-Mutualité) William Ledeuil's third project, Kitchen Ter(re) showcases pasta dishes made from six varieties of ancient grains. But don't write it off as another tired riff on Italian cuisine: instead expect a marvellous procession of out-of-the-box flavour and colour combinations, ranging from citrusy girolette with pumpkin, peanut paste and a fourme d'Ambert cream, or conchiglioni with cockles, green curry and nori-roasted cabbage.

LES PAPILLES
BISTRO €€

Map p400 (☎01 43 25 20 79; www.lespapilles paris.fr; 30 rue Gay Lussac, 5e; 2-/4-course menu €28/35; ⏱noon-2pm & 7-10.30pm Tue-Sat; ⓂRaspail or RER Luxembourg) This hybrid bistro, wine cellar and *épicerie* (specialist grocer) with a sunflower-yellow façade is one of those fabulous Parisian dining experiences. Meals are served at simply dressed tables wedged beneath bottle-lined walls, and fare is market driven: each weekday sees a different *retour du marché* (back-from-the-market menu). But what really sets it apart is its exceptional, mostly natural wine list.

It only seats around 15 people; reserve a few days in advance to guarantee a table. After your meal, stock your own *cave* (wine cellar) at Les Papilles' *cave à vins*.

LE BEL ORDINAIRE
FRENCH €€

Map p400 (☎09 81 11 72 78; www.lebelordinaire. com; 5 rue de Bazeilles, 5e; 2-/3-course lunch menu €21/26, dinner mains €22-26; ⏱noon-2pm & 7.30-10pm Tue-Sat; ⓂCensier Daubenton) The owners here clearly have a different definition of the word 'ordinary' than the rest of us: pop in for market-driven delights like sardines in an almond-milk sauce, deconstructed lasagne or fried broccoli with kimchi, paired with a glass of organic wine.

Great location at the foot of rue Mouffetard. Reserve at dinner.

LE COUPE-CHOU
FRENCH €€

Map p398 (☑01 46 33 68 69; www.lecoupechou. com; 9 & 11 rue de Lanneau, 5e; mains €22-36.50; ☺7-10.30pm; Ⓜ Maubert-Mutualité) This maze of candlelit rooms inside a vine-clad 17th-century townhouse is overwhelmingly romantic. Ceilings are beamed, furnishings are antique, open fireplaces crackle and background classical music mingles with the intimate chatter of diners. As in the days when Marlene Dietrich dined here, reservations are essential. Timeless French dishes include Burgundy snails, steak tartare and bœuf bourguignon.

Finish off with fabulous cheeses sourced from *fromagerie* (cheese shop) Quatre-homme and a silken crème brûlée.

Le Coupe-Chou, incidentally, has nothing to do with cabbage *(chou);* it's named after the barber's razor once wielded in one of its seven rooms.

L'AGRUME
BISTRO €€

Map p400 (☑01 43 31 86 48; www.restaurant-lagrume.fr; 15 rue des Fossés St-Marcel, 5e; 2-/3-course lunch menu €23/26, dinner menu €48; ☺noon-2.30pm & 7.30-10.30pm Tue-Sat; Ⓜ Censier Daubenton) Reserve a table in advance (online or by telephone) at this chic bistro where you can watch chefs work with seasonal products in the open kitchen while you dine at a table or the *comptoir* (counter). Lunch is magnificent value and a real gourmet experience. Evening dining is an exquisite, no-choice *dégustation* (tasting) medley of five courses that changes daily.

BONVIVANT
BISTRO €€

Map p398 (☑01 43 26 51 34; www.bonvivant. paris; 7 rue des Écoles, 5e; mains €16-22; ☺9am-2am; Ⓜ Cardinal Lemoine) Braised duck in black-currrant sauce, mushroom polenta, cheese and charcuterie plates – this casual bar makes for an inviting place to converse while enjoying hearty bistro fare over a glass of wine or beer. Across rue des Écoles is Bonvivant Pizza, where you can grab some focaccia to go (€8.50) or a whole pie.

DESVOUGES
FRENCH €€

Map p400 (☑01 47 07 91 25; www.facebook.com/ restaurantdesvouges; 6 rue des Fosses St-Marcel, 5e; mains €20-25; ☺11.30am-2pm Mon, 11.30am-2pm & 7.30-9.30pm Tue-Fri; Ⓜ St-Marcel, Les Gobelins) Expect a healthy dose of humour

as well as top-notch bistro cuisine and *'fromages qui puent un peu'* ('stinky cheeses') at this neighbourhood bistro, the passion of Jérôme Desvouges, who ditched a 17-year career in IT journalism to open his own restaurant. Sea bass roasted in honey and *confit de canard* cannelloni are among the treats on the creative menu.

LE BUISSON ARDENT
FRENCH €€

Map p400 (☑01 43 54 93 02; www.lebuisson ardent.paris; 25 rue Jussieu, 5e; 2-/3-course lunch menus €19/24, mains €22-38; ☺noon-2.30pm & 7.30-10.30pm; Ⓜ Jussieu) Housed in a former coach house, this time-worn bistro (front-room murals date to the 1920s) serves classy, exciting French fare. The menu changes every week and includes varied dishes such as grilled tuna with capers and black olives, veal cutlets with candied ginger sauce and beef in porto. Stop by after 5pm for a happy-hour apéritif.

LES PIPOS
FRENCH €€

Map p398 (☑01 43 54 11 40; www.facebook. com/lespiposbaravins; 2 rue de l'École Polytechnique, 5e; 2-course weekday menu €14.50, mains €10.90-19.90; ☺9.30am-midnight Mon-Fri, from noon Sat; Ⓜ Maubert-Mutualité) Natural wines are the speciality of this *bar à vins*, which it keeps in its vaulted stone cellar. First-rate food – served from noon onward – includes a fish of the day and oysters from Brittany, along with standards such as confit of duck and a mouth-watering cheese board, which includes all the French classics (Comté, Bleu d'Auvergne, Brie de Meaux, Rocamadour and St-Marcellin).

LE PETIT PONTOISE
BISTRO €€

Map p398 (☑01 43 29 25 20; www.lepetitpon toise.fr; 9 rue de Pontoise, 5e; 2-/3-course weekday lunch menu €26/34, mains €23-36; ☺noon-2.30pm & 6.30-10.30pm; Ⓜ Maubert-Mutualité) Entering this tiny bistro with traditional lace curtains and simple wooden tables is like stepping into old-world Paris. And the kitchen lives up to expectation with fantastic old-fashioned classics including calf kidneys, veal liver cooked in raspberry vinegar, roast quail, *cassoulette d'escargots* (snail stew) and honey- and almond-baked camembert (out of this world). Everything is deliciously *fait maison* (homemade).

MOSQUÉE DE PARIS
NORTH AFRICAN €€

Map p400 (☑01 45 35 75 17; 39 rue Geoffroy-St-Hilaire, 5e; mains €11-28; ☺kitchen noon-midnight; Ⓜ Censier Daubenton, Place Monge) Dig into one of 10 types of couscous or choose a meaty grill at this richly decorated North African restaurant tucked within the walls of the city's art deco–Moorish mosque (p208). The atmosphere is wonderful, though better North African cuisine can be had elsewhere in Paris. Lighter appetites can enjoy mint tea and a *pâtisserie orientale* beneath the trees in the **tearoom** (Map p400) courtyard.

Feeling decadent? Book a *formule orientale* (€68), which includes a body scrub, 10-minute massage and a lounge in the women-only *hammam* (p221), as well as lunch, mint tea and a sweet pastry.

ANAHUACALLI
MEXICAN €€

Map p398 (📞 01 43 26 10 20; 30 rue des Bernardins, 5e; mains €17-22; ⏱ 7-10.30pm Mon-Sat, 11.30am-2.30pm Sun; 🍴; Ⓜ Maubert-Mutualité) This restaurant behind a discreet rosemary-coloured façade cooks up some of the only upmarket Mexican cuisine in Paris. Enjoy elegantly presented enchiladas, tamales and mole poblano in a sparingly decorated interior lined with mirrors and statuettes. Fish lovers, you'll adore the *pescado à la veracruzana* (fish of the day flambéed with tequila).

LA RÔTISSERIE D'ARGENT
ROTISSERIE €€

Map p398 (📞 01 43 54 17 47; www.rotisserie dargent.com; 19 quai de la Tournelle, 5e; mains €19-35; ⏱ noon-2.15pm & 7-10pm; Ⓜ Cardinal Lemoine) Spit-roasted suckling pigs, chickens, ducks, shoulder of lamb, pigeons and more turn on rotating skewers over an open flame within view of your table at this relaxed quayside bistro run by its Michelin-starred neighbour La Tour d'Argent. Order off the daily chalkboard and save room for classic desserts like crème brûlée or lavish seasonal fruit tarts.

The wine list is extensive and excellent.

★ RESTAURANT AT
GASTRONOMY €€€

Map p398 (📞 01 56 81 94 08; www.atsushitanaka. com; 4 rue du Cardinal Lemoine, 5e; 6-course lunch menu €65, 12-course dinner tasting menu €115, with paired wines €185; ⏱ 12.30-1.30pm & 8-9.30pm Tue-Sat; Ⓜ Cardinal Lemoine) Trained by some of the biggest names in gastronomy (Pierre Gagnaire included), chef Atsushi Tanaka showcases abstract artlike masterpieces incorporating rare ingredients (charred bamboo, kohlrabi turnip cabbage, juniper berry powder, wild purple fennel,

Nepalese Timut pepper) on stunning outsized plates in a blank-canvas-style dining space. Reservations are essential.

★ BAIETA
FRENCH €€€

Map p398 (📞 01 42 02 59 19; www.restaurant-baieta-paris.fr; 5 rue de Pontoise, 5e; 2-/4-course weekday lunch menu €29/45, 7-course dinner menu €85, mains €29-42; ⏱ noon-2.30pm & 7-10.30pm Tue-Sat; Ⓜ Maubert-Mutualité) Baieta means 'little kiss' in the patois of Nice, the home town of culinary sensation Julia Sedefdjian, who at 21 was France's youngest Michelin-starred chef when she helmed Paris' Les Fables de La Fontaine. Opened in 2018, her timber- and charcoal-toned Latin Quarter premises showcase her Niçoise roots in creations like confit octopus with crab gnocchi, and smoked-quail *barbajuan* (ricotta-filled pastry).

PROSPER ET FORTUNÉE
MODERN FRENCH €€€

Map p400 (📞 01 43 37 70 39; 50 rue Broca, 5e; menus €60; ⏱ 8.30-10.30pm Tue-Sat; Ⓜ Les Gobelins) 🌿 Eric Lévy's 20-seat premises is effectively a clandestine supper club where you can watch the chef prepare daily changing dishes (raw mackerel with yuzu and lemon confit; prime fillet with black radish) using mostly organic premium produce in his open kitchen. Dinner kicks off at a fixed time (8.30pm); reservations essential.

LE VENT D'ARMOR
SEAFOOD €€€

Map p398 (📞 01 46 34 50 99; www.le-vent-darmor. com; 25 quai de la Tournelle, 5e; 2-/3-course weekday lunch menu €30/36, 4-course dinner menu €70, mains €34-52; ⏱ 7.30-10pm Mon, noon-2pm & 7.30-10pm Tue-Sat; Ⓜ Maubert-Mutualité) Porthole- and lantern-style light fittings are among the contemporary nautical design elements at this sleek Seine-side restaurant. Premium seafood dishes include Marennes Oléron oysters with Pernod foam, grilled Brittany sole with truffle-butter sauce, Normandy St-Pierre (John Dory) with roasted black garlic *crème,* and scallop tartare with smoked haddock hearts.

LA TOUR D'ARGENT
GASTRONOMY €€€

Map p398 (📞 01 43 54 23 31; www.latour dargent.com; 15 quai de la Tournelle, 5e; lunch menu €105, dinner menus €290-360, mains €88-125; ⏱ 12.30-2pm & 7-10pm Tue-Sat, closed Aug; Ⓜ Cardinal Lemoine) The venerable Michelin-starred 'Silver Tower' is famous for its *caneton* (duckling), rooftop garden with glimmering island views and fabulous history harking back to 1582 – from Henry III's inauguration of the first fork in France to inspiration for the winsome animated film *Ratatouille*. Its wine cellar is one of Paris' best; dining is dressy and exceedingly fine.

Reserve eight to 10 days ahead for lunch, three weeks ahead for dinner.

Buy fine food, accessories and Champagne from its own vineyard in **Le Comptoir** (Map p398; ☑01 46 33 45 58; 17 Quai de la Tournelle, 5e; ⊙noon-8pm Tue-Sat; ⓂCardinal Lemoine), La Tour d'Argent's boutique on the same street, and dine for a snip of the price at its casual bistro La Rôtisserie d'Argent (p215).

LA TRUFFIÈRE   GASTRONOMY €€€

Map p400 (☑01 46 33 29 82; www.la-truffiere.fr; 4 rue Blainville, 5e; lunch menu €45, dinner menus €72-105; ⊙noon-1.30pm & 7-9.30pm Tue-Sat; ⓂPlace Monge) As its name implies, truffles are the centrepiece of this Michelin-starred restaurant's menu, featuring in most (albeit not all) of its weekly changing dishes, from classic Italian gnocchi to miso and sake-marinated tuna with samphire, roast venison with juniper berries and smoked Jerusalem artichokes, and oxtail stew with mash. To go all-out, order the seven-course black truffle tasting menu (€225).

🍷 DRINKING &
⚘ NIGHTLIFE

Rive Gauche romantics, well-heeled cafe-society types and students by the gallon drink in the 5e *arrondissement*, where nostalgic haunts, swish bars and new-generation coffee shops ensure a deluge of early-evening happy hours and a quintessential Parisian soirée.

★ SHAKESPEARE
& COMPANY CAFE   CAFE

Map p398 (www.shakespeareandcompany.com; 37 rue de la Bucherie, 5e; ⊙10am-7pm; 🛜; ⓂSt-Michel) 🌱 Instant history was made when this literary-inspired cafe opened in 2015 adjacent to magical bookshop Shakespeare & Company (p219), designed from long-lost sketches to fulfil late bookshop founder George Whitman's 1960s dream. Organic chai tea, turbo-power juices and specialist coffee by Parisian roaster Café Lomi marry with soups, salads, bagels and pastries by Bob's Bake Shop.

Not to be missed: a Golden Latte (€6), aka milky coffee spiced with turmeric, cinnamon, ginger, nutmeg, black pepper and coconut oil. Before leaving, you might want to buy a 250g bag of 'Assemblage Shakespeare' coffee beans (€13) to take home as a Parisian souvenir.

★ NUAGE   CAFE

Map p398 (☑09 82 39 80 69; www.nuagecafe.fr; 14 rue des Carmes, 5e; ⊙9am-7pm Mon-Fri, 11am-8pm Sat & Sun; 🛜; ⓂMaubert-Mutualité) One of a crop of co-working cafes to mushroom in Paris, Nuage (Cloud) lures a loyal following of nomadic digital creatives with its cosy, home-like spaces in an old church (and subsequent school where Cyrano de Bergerac apparently studied). Payment is by the hour (€5) or day (€25), craft coffee is by Parisian roaster Coutume (p242) and gourmet snacks stave off hunger pangs.

Super-fast wi-fi, books to browse, games to play, music and a silent zone only add to the appeal.

LE VERRE À PIED   CAFE

Map p400 (☑01 43 31 15 72; www.facebook.com/leverreapied.fr; 118bis rue Mouffetard, 5e; ⊙10am-10pm Tue, 10am-10.30pm Wed, 9.30am-10.30pm Thu-Sat, 9.30am-4pm Sun; ⓂCensier Daubenton) This *café-tabac* (cafe and tobacconist) is a pearl of a place where little has changed since 1870. Its nicotine-hued mirrored wall, moulded cornices and original bar make it part of a dying breed, but it epitomises the charm, glamour and romance of an old Paris everyone loves, including stallholders from the rue Mouffetard market who yo-yo in and out.

Contemporary photography and art adorns one wall. Lunch (*plat du jour* €16) is a busy, lively affair thanks to the kitchen's wholesome homemade cuisine. Live music quickens the pulse a couple of evenings a week.

STRADA CAFÉ   COFFEE

Map p398 (www.facebook.com/stradacafe94; 24 rue Monge, 5e; ⊙8am-6.30pm Mon-Fri, 9.30am-6.30pm Sat & Sun; 🛜; ⓂCardinal Lemoine) Beans from Parisian roastery L'Arbre à Café and Lyon's Mokxa roastery underpin the success of this sunlit corner cafe, strewn with an eclectic mix of armchairs and wooden-chair seating. Electrical sockets are plentiful (no laptops at weekends, however) and international baristas are passionate about their brews. There's breakfast, salad-and-soup lunches, weekend brunch and gluten-free cakes.

BREWBERRY
BAR

Map p400 (☑06 62 46 75 13; www.facebook.com/brewberrylebar; 11 rue du Pot de Fer, 5e; ⊙5pm-midnight Tue-Sat; ⓂPlace Monge) If you're feeling homesick for your favourite IPA, there's a chance they might have it here, with 24 craft beers on tap from as far off as Colorado and Hawaii.

LE VIOLON DINGUE
PUB

Map p398 (☑01 43 25 79 93; www.facebook.com/TheViolonDingue; 46 rue de la Montagne Ste-Geneviève, 5e; ⊙5pm-5am Tue-Sat; ⓂMaubert-Mutualité) Students pack out the loud, lively 'Crazy Violin', with big-screen sports upstairs and the flirty 'Dingue Lounge' downstairs. Its name is a pun on the expression *le violon d'Ingres,* meaning 'hobby' in French because the celebrated painter Jean-Auguste-Dominique Ingres played fiddle in his spare time. Happy hour is 5pm to 10pm Tuesday to Saturday. Expect beer pong and other anglophone pub antics.

CAVE LA BOURGOGNE
BAR

Map p400 (☑01 47 07 82 80; 144 rue Mouffetard, 5e; ⊙7am-2am Mon-Sat, to 11pm Sun; ⓂCensier Daubenton) A prime spot for soaking up rue Mouffetard's contagious 'saunter-all-day' spirit, this neighbourhood hang-out sits on square St-Médard, one of the Latin Quarter's loveliest, with flower-bedecked fountain, centuries-old church and market stalls spilling across one side. Inside, locals and their pet dogs meet for coffee around dark wood tables alongside a local wine-sipping set. In summer everything spills outside.

PUB ST-HILAIRE
PUB

Map p398 (☑01 46 33 52 42; www.facebook.com/pubsthilaire; 2 rue Valette, 5e; ⊙3pm-2am Mon-Thu, 4pm-4am Fri & Sat; ⓂMaubert-Mutualité) 'Buzzing' fails to do justice to the pulsating vibe inside this student-loved pub. Generous happy hours last from 5pm to 9pm and the place is kept packed with a trio of pool tables, board games, music on two floors, hearty bar food and various gimmicks to rev up the party crowd (a metre of cocktails, 'be your own barman' etc).

L'ACADÉMIE DE LA BIÈRE
PUB

Map p400 (☑01 43 54 66 65; www.academie-biere.com; 88bis bd de Port Royal, 5e; ⊙10am-

RUE MOUFFETARD

Originally a Roman road, the sloping, cobbled rue Mouffetard acquired its name in the 18th century, when the now underground River Bièvre became the communal waste disposal for local tanners and wood pulpers. The odours gave rise to the name Mouffette ('skunk'), which evolved into Mouffetard. The street's now filled with market stalls (except Mondays), cheap eateries and lively bars.

2am; ⓂVavin or RER Port Royal) Serious students of Belgian beer should head to this 'beer academy' to try its 15 on tap or choose from more than 150 bottled varieties, including Trappist (monk-made) beers like prized Westmalle, abbey beers including Grimbergen and Leffe, fruit beers, and Cantillon gueuze (double-fermented Lambic beer made in Brussels). Happy hour is an early starter, from 3.30pm to 7.30pm.

In true Belgian tradition, it also serves *moules* (mussels), delivered and cleaned each morning, cooked in creative ways including with mustard, curry or Roquefort, and served continuously.

DOSE
COFFEE

Map p400 (www.dosedealerdecafe.fr; 73 rue Mouffetard, 5e; ⊙8am-6pm Tue-Fri, 9am-7pm Sat & Sun; ☎; ⓂPlace Monge) Artisan Breton roastery Caffè Cataldi supplies the beans for a potent dose of caffeine at this hip coffee shop and organic juice bar. Plump for a lovely cushioned bench seat in the heated alley outside or join the line-up of digital creatives hooked up to various devices or browsing bookshelves in the inside galley space.

Great choice of milks (including almond), tea, beer and light bites (waffles, cakes, open sandwiches, avocado toast).

LA BRÛLERIE DES GOBELINS
COFFEE

Map p400 (☑01 43 31 90 13; www.comptoirsrichard.fr/magasin-brulerie-des-gobelins; 2 av des Gobelins, 5e; ⊙9.30am-7.30pm Tue-Sat; ⓂGobelins) It might be part of Comptoirs Richard today, but this historic Parisian roastery has been the place in the 5e *arrondissement* to savour serious coffee made from beans roasted in situ for the last five decades or so. Post-espresso with aromatic notes of cinnamon, honey, cocoa and vanilla, purchase a bag of coffee to take home – beans are ground to order.

TEA CADDY
TEAHOUSE

Map p398 (✏01 43 54 15 56; 14 rue St-Julien le Pauvre, 5e; ⊙11am-7pm; 🐾; 🅜St-Michel) Arguably the most English of the 'English' tearooms in Paris, this institution, founded by a certain Miss Klinklin in 1928, is a fine spot to break for light meals like omelettes or a genteel cream tea with a Devon scone after viewing nearby Sainte-Chapelle or the Conciergerie. Weekend brunch (€28.80) is served until 4pm.

LE PIANO VACHE
BAR

Map p398 (✏01 46 33 75 03; www.facebook.com/pianovacheparis5; 8 rue Laplace, 5e; ⊙5pm-2am Mon-Sat; 🅜Maubert-Mutualité) Down the hill from the Panthéon, this shabby backstreet bar is covered in old posters and drenched in 1970s and '80s rock ambience. A real student fave, it has bands and DJs playing mainly rock, plus some goth, reggae and pop. Happy hour runs from 5pm to 9pm.

☆ ENTERTAINMENT

Jazz and independent cinema are the twin strengths of the Latin Quarter's entertainment scene, with a host of venues for both.

★CAFÉ UNIVERSEL
JAZZ

Map p400 (✏01 71 32 64 38; www.cafeuniversel.org; 267 rue St-Jacques, 5e; ⊙7pm-midnight Tue-Sat, to 2pm Sun; 🐾; 🅜Censier Daubenton, RER Port Royal) Café Universel hosts a brilliant array of live concerts with everything from bebop and Latin sounds to vocal jazz sessions (check the schedule online). Plenty of freedom is given to young producers and artists, and its convivial, relaxed atmosphere attracts a mix of students and jazz lovers. Concerts are free, but you should tip the artists when they pass the hat around.

CAVEAU DE LA HUCHETTE
JAZZ

Map p398 (✏01 43 26 65 05; www.caveaudelahuchette.fr; 5 rue de la Huchette, 5e; admission €13-15; ⊙9pm-2am Sun-Thu, to 4am Fri & Sat; 🅜St-Michel) Housed in a medieval *caveau* (cellar) that was used as a courtroom and torture chamber during the Revolution, this club is where many of the jazz greats

(Count Basie, Art Blakey) have played since the end of WWII. It attracts its fair share of tourists, but the atmosphere can be more electric than at the more serious jazz clubs. Sessions start at around 9.30pm.

ÉGLISE ST-JULIEN LE PAUVRE
CLASSICAL MUSIC

Map p398 (✏01 42 26 00 00; www.concertinparis.com; 1 rue St-Julien le Pauvre, 5e; hours vary; 🅜St-Michel) Piano recitals (Chopin, Liszt) are staged at least two evenings a week in one of the oldest churches in Paris. Higher-priced tickets directly face the stage. Payment is by cash only at the door.

L'ÉPÉE DE BOIS
CINEMA

Map p400 (✏08 92 68 75 35; www.cine-epeedebois.fr; 100 rue Mouffetard, 5e; adult/child €8.90/5; 🅜Censier Daubenton) Even locals find it easy to miss the small doorway leading to rue Mouffetard's little two-screen cinema, which shows art-house flicks such as Julie Delpy–directed films, as well as major new releases. Show times are posted online.

LE PETIT JOURNAL ST-MICHEL
JAZZ, BLUES

Map p400 (✏01 43 26 28 59; www.petitjournalsaintmichel.fr; 71 bd St-Michel, 5e; admission incl 1 drink €20-25, with dinner €59-69; ⊙7.30pm-1am Mon-Sat; 🅜Cluny–La Sorbonne or RER Luxembourg) Classic jazz concerts kick off at 9pm in the atmospheric downstairs cellar of this sophisticated jazz venue across from the Jardin du Luxembourg (p228). Everything, ranging from Dixieland and vocals to big band and swing, sets patrons' toes tapping. Dinner is served at 7.30pm, but it's the music that's the real draw.

LE CHAMPO
CINEMA

Map p398 (www.cinema-lechampo.com; 51 rue des Écoles, 5e; tickets adult/child €9/4; 🅜Cluny–La Sorbonne) This is one of the most popular of the many Latin Quarter cinemas, featuring classics and retrospectives looking at the films of such actors and directors as Alfred Hitchcock, Jacques Tati, Alain Resnais, Frank Capra and Tim Burton. One of the two *salles* (cinemas) has wheelchair access.

LE GRAND ACTION
CINEMA

Map p398 (www.legrandaction.com; 5 rue des Écoles, 5e; tickets adult/child €9.50/6; 🅜Cardinal Lemoine) Cult films screen in their original languages at this cinephiles' favourite.

🛍 SHOPPING

Bookworms will love this part of the Left Bank, home to some wonderful bookshops. Other student-frequented shops include camping stores, comic shops, old-school vinyl shops where collectors browse for hours and cheap, colourful homewares stores, interspersed with the occasional *droguerie-quincaillerie* (hardware store) – easily spotted by the jumble of laundry baskets, buckets etc piled on the pavement out the front.

⭐SHAKESPEARE & COMPANY   BOOKS

Map p398 (📞01 43 25 40 93; www.shakespeare andcompany.com; 37 rue de la Bûcherie, 5e; ⏰10am-10pm Mon-Sat, 12.30-8pm Sun; Ⓜ St-Michel) Enchanting nooks and crannies overflow with new and secondhand English-language books. The original shop (12 rue l'Odéon, 6e; closed by the Nazis in 1941) was run by Sylvia Beach and became the meeting point for Hemingway's 'Lost Generation'. Readings by emerging and illustrious authors regularly take place, and there's a wonderful cafe (p216) next door.

The bookshop is fabled for nurturing writers, and at night its couches turn into beds where 'Tumbleweeds' (aspiring writers and book-mad students) overnight in exchange for stacking shelves.

American-born George Whitman opened the present incarnation in 1951, attracting a beat-poet clientele, and scores of authors have since passed through its doors. In 2006 Whitman was awarded the Officier des Arts et Lettres by the French Minister of Culture, recognising his significant contribution to the enrichment of the French cultural inheritance. Whitman died in 2011, aged 98; he is buried in division 73 of Cimetière du Père Lachaise (p157). Today his daughter, Sylvia Beach Whitman, maintains Shakespeare & Company's serendipitous magic.

⭐LE BONBON AU PALAIS   FOOD

Map p398 (📞01 78 56 15 72; www.lebonbonau palais.com; 19 rue Monge, 5e; ⏰10.30am-7.30pm Tue-Sat; Ⓜ Cardinal Lemoine) Kids and kids-at-heart will adore this sugar-fuelled *tour de France*. The school-geography-themed boutique stocks rainbows of artisanal sweets from around the country. Old-fashioned glass jars brim with treats like *calissons* (diamond-shaped, icing-sugar-topped ground fruit and almonds from Aix-en-Provence), *rigolettes* (fruit-filled pillows from Nantes), *berlingots* (striped, triangular boiled sweets from Carpentras and elsewhere) and *papalines* (herbal liqueur-filled pink-chocolate balls from Avignon).

FROMAGERIE
LAURENT DUBOIS   CHEESE

Map p398 (📞01 43 54 50 93; www.fromages laurentdubois.fr; 47ter bd St-Germain, 5e; ⏰8am-7.30pm Tue-Sat, 8.30am-1pm Sun; Ⓜ Maubert-Mutualité) One of the best *fromageries* in Paris, this cheese-lover's nirvana is filled with to-die-for delicacies, such as St-Félicien with Périgord truffles. Rare, limited-production cheeses include blue Termignon and Tarentaise goat's cheese. All are appropriately cellared in warm, humid or cold environments. Branches include one in the 15e.

BIÈRES CULTES JUSSIEU   DRINKS

Map p400 (📞09 51 27 04 84; www.bierescultes. fr; 44 rue des Boulangers, 5e; ⏰4-8pm Mon, 4-9.30pm Tue-Thu, 11am-2pm & 4-11pm Fri, 11am-2pm & 4-9.30pm Sat; Ⓜ Cardinal Lemoine) At any one time this beer-lovers' fantasyland stocks around 500 different craft and/or international brews, along with four on tap to taste on the spot. Just some of its wares when you visit might include US-brewed Alaskan Smoked Porter, German smoked Aecht Schlenkerla Rauchbier from Bamberg and New Zealand Monteith's. Check its website and Facebook page for events and seasonal releases.

MOCOCHA   CHOCOLATE

Map p400 (📞01 47 07 13 66; www.chocolats mococha.com; 89 rue Mouffetard, 5e; ⏰11am-8pm Tue-Sat, to 6pm Sun; Ⓜ Censier Daubenton) A mouth-watering range of chocolates by several *maîtres chocolatiers* (master chocolate-makers) are laid out like jewels at this chocolate shop.

ANDROUET   CHEESE

Map p400 (📞01 45 87 85 05; www.androuet. com; 134 rue Mouffetard, 5e; ⏰9.30am-1.30pm & 3.30-7.30pm Tue-Thu, 9.30am-7.30pm Fri & Sat, 9.30am-1.30pm Sun; Ⓜ Censier Daubenton) All of the cheeses at this great *fromagerie* can be vacuum-packed for free to take home – look up to admire the murals on the building's cherry-red façade. Androuet is one of three tantalising cheese shops on rue Mouffetard.

DELIZIUS
FOOD & DRINKS

Map p400 (☎01 42 17 00 23; 134 rue Mouffetard, 5e; ⊙9.30am-8pm Tue-Sat, 9am-2pm Sun; MCensier Daubenton) Stuffed olives and capsicums and marinated aubergine are among the picnic goodies at this gourmet Italian deli, which also sells ready-to-eat hot meals and fresh and dried pasta.

AU VIEUX CAMPEUR
SPORTS & OUTDOORS

Map p398 (☎01 53 10 48 48; www.auvieux campeur.fr; 48 rue des Écoles, 5e; ⊙11am-8pm Mon-Wed & Fri, 11am-9pm Thu, 10am-8pm Sat; MMaubert-Mutualité) This outdoor store has colonised the Latin Quarter, with some two dozen different boutiques scattered around its original shop that opened on rue St-Jacques in 1941 (actually a few doors down at No 38). Each space is devoted to a different sport: climbing, skiing, diving, camping, biking, water sports and so on.

Ask cashiers for a list (in French) and map of the various stores.The **branch** (Map p398; ☎01 53 10 48 21; 50 rue des Écoles, 5e) next door sells everything imaginable for running and cycling.

AU VIEUX CAMPER LIBRAIRIE
BOOKS

Map p398 (☎01 53 10 48 27; 2 rue de Latran, 5e; ⊙11am-7.30pm Mon-Wed & Fri, to 9pm Thu, 10am-7.30pm Sat; MMaubert-Mutualité) For anyone planning an adventure in France, this bookshop is an invaluable resource. Detailed IGN topo maps and guides for climbing, via ferrata, hiking, ski touring, snowshoeing and more fill the maze-like premises. Guidebooks are in multiple languages, including English.

MAYETTE LA BOUTIQUE DE LA MAGIE
GAMES

Map p398 (☎01 43 54 13 63; www.mayette. com; 8 rue des Carmes, 5e; ⊙2-7.30pm Tue-Sat; MMaubert-Mutualité) One of a kind, this 1808-established magic shop is said to be the world's oldest. Since 1991 it's been in the hands of world-famous magic pro Dominique Duvivier. Professional and hobbyist magicians flock here to discuss king sandwiches, reverse assemblies, false cuts and other card tricks with Duvivier and his daughter, Alexandra.

Should you want to learn the tricks of the trade, Duvivier has magic courses up his sleeve.

ALBUM
COMICS

Map p398 (☎01 53 10 00 60; www.albumcomics. com; 67 bd St-Germain, 5e; ⊙10am-8pm Mon-Sat, noon-7pm Sun; MCluny–La Sorbonne) Album specialises in *bandes dessinées* (comic strips), which have an enormous following in France, with everything from Tintin and Babar to erotic comics and the latest Japanese manga. Serious comic collectors – and anyone excited by Harry Potter wands, *Star Wars, Superman* and other superhero figurines and T-shirts (you know who you are!) – shouldn't miss it.

LIBRAIRIE EYROLLES
BOOKS

Map p398 (☎01 44 41 11 74; www.eyrolles.com; 55-61 bd St-Germain, 5e; ⊙10am-8pm Mon-Sat; MMaubert-Mutualité) One of Paris' largest bookshops sells titles in English, has stacks of browsing space, and stocks an exceptional range of maps, guides and travel lit.

BOUQUINISTES

Bouquinistes (Map p376; quai Voltaire, 7e, to quai de la Tournelle, 5e, & Pont Marie, 4e, to quai du Louvre, 1er; ⊙11.30am-dusk) With some 3km of forest-green boxes lining the Seine – containing over 300,000 secondhand (and often out-of-print) books, rare magazines, postcards and old advertising posters – Paris' *bouquinistes* (used-book sellers) are as integral to the cityscape as the Panthéon. Many open only from spring to autumn (and many shut in August), but year-round you'll still find some to browse.

The *bouquinistes* have been in business since the 16th century, when they were itinerant peddlers selling their wares on Parisian bridges; back then their sometimes subversive (eg Protestant) materials could get them into trouble with the authorities. By 1859 the city had finally wised up: official licences were issued, space (10m of railing) was rented and eventually the permanent green boxes were installed.

Today, *bouquinistes* (the official count ranges from 200 to 240) are allowed to have four boxes, only one of which can be used to sell souvenirs. Look hard enough and you just might find some real treasures: old comic books, forgotten first editions, maps, stamps, erotica and prewar newspapers – as in centuries past, it's all there, waiting to be rediscovered.

MARCHÉ MAUBERT
MARKET

Map p398 (place Maubert, 5e; ⊙7am-2.30pm Tue & Thu, 7am-3pm Sat; Ⓜ Maubert-Mutualité) Shop for fruit and veg (some organic), cheese, bread and so on at this welcoming, village-like food market that spills across place Maubert thrice weekly.

MARCHÉ MONGE
MARKET

Map p400 (place Monge, 5e; ⊙7am-2pm Wed, Fri & Sun; Ⓜ Place Monge) Open-air Marché Monge is laden with wonderful cheeses, baked goods and a host of other temptations.

ABBEY BOOKSHOP
BOOKS

Map p398 (☑01 46 33 16 24; https://abbeybookshop.wordpress.com; 29 rue de la Parcheminerie, 5e; ⊙10am-7pm Mon-Sat; Ⓜ Cluny–La Sorbonne) Inside 18th-century Hôtel Dubuisson, this chaotic but welcoming Canadian-run bookshop serves free coffee (sweetened with maple syrup) to sip while you browse thousands upon thousands of new and used books. Watch for occasional literary events.

AUX MERVEILLEUX DE FRED
FOOD

Map p398 (☑01 43 54 63 72; www.auxmerveilleux.com; 2 rue Monge, 5e; ⊙7.30am-8pm Tue-Sat, to 7pm Sun; Ⓜ Maubert-Mutualité) This chandeliered boutique – one of several in Paris – concentrates on one dessert, the marvellous *merveilleux*: meringue layered with whipped cream and rolled in one of six seasonal flavours, such as chocolate flakes, *speculoos* (spiced biscuit) powder, almond slivers, caramel dust or rose sugar crystals. Watch staff hand-making the delicacy while you queue.

NICOLAÏ
PERFUME

Map p400 (☑01 44 55 02 00; www.pnicolai.com; 240 rue St-Jacques, 5e; ⊙10.30am-2pm & 3-6.30pm Mon-Sat; Ⓜ Place Monge) Established in Paris in 1986 by esteemed *parfumeuse* Patricia de Nicolaï, whose great-grandfather Pierre-François Pascal Guerlain founded Guerlain 150 years earlier, Nicolaï remains a family-run business today. Recent fragrances include Cococabana (with notes of ylang-ylang, palm, vanilla and tonka flower), Kiss Me Tender (orange blossom, almond, jasmine and cloves) and Musc Monoï (lemon, magnolia, coconut and sandalwood).

CROCODISC
MUSIC

Map p398 (www.crocodisc.com; 40 & 42 rue des Écoles, 5e; ⊙11am-7pm Tue-Sat, closed late Jul–mid-Aug; Ⓜ Maubert-Mutualité) Music might be more accessible than ever before in the digital age, but for many, digital recordings will never replace rummaging through racks for treasures. New and secondhand CDs and vinyl discs at 40 rue des Écoles span world music, rap, reggae, salsa, soul and disco, while No 42 has pop, rock, punk, new wave, electro and soundtracks.

Its nearby sister shop **Crocojazz** (Map p398; ☑01 43 54 47 95; www.crocodisc.com; 64 rue de la Montagne Ste-Geneviève, 5e; ⊙11am-1pm & 2-7pm Tue-Sat, closed late Jul–mid-Aug; Ⓜ Maubert-Mutualité) specialises in jazz, blues, gospel and timeless crooners, with books and DVDs as well as recordings.

MARCHÉ MOUFFETARD
MARKET

Map p400 (rue Mouffetard, 5e; ⊙8am-7.30pm Tue-Sat, to noon Sun; Ⓜ Censier Daubenton) Grocers, butchers, fishmongers and other food purveyors set their goods out on street stalls during this almost-daily market. Many stalls close from lunchtime onwards.

🏃 SPORTS & ACTIVITIES

HAMMAM DE LA MOSQUÉE DE PARIS
SPA

Map p400 (☑01 43 31 38 20; www.la-mosquee.com; 39 rue Geoffroy-St-Hilaire, 5e; entry €20, spa packages €48-68; ⊙10am-9pm Wed-Mon; Ⓜ Place Monge) Massages, including an exfoliating body scrub, are the key draw at this atmospheric *hammam*. Bring a swimsuit but hire a towel/dressing gown. Women only.

WINE TASTING IN PARIS
WINE

Map p400 (☑06 76 93 32 88; www.wine-tasting-in-paris.com; 14 rue des Boulangers, 5e; tastings from €47; ⊙hours vary; Ⓜ Jussieu) Find this wine-tasting school on a winding cobblestone backstreet. With the knowledgeable Thierry from wine-rich Burgundy at the helm, themed tastings and tours do not disappoint. The comprehensive French Wine Tour (€62, 2½ hours, six wines, 5pm) covers tasting methodology, wine vocabulary and French winegrowing regions. Foodies will adore the tasty, lunchtime cheese–wine pairing (€47, 1½ hours, four wines, noon).

All classes are in English; book online.

St-Germain & Les Invalides

ST-GERMAIN | LES INVALIDES | FAUBOURG ST-GERMAIN | LEFT BANK

Neighbourhood Top Five

1 **Musée d'Orsay** (p224) Revelling in a wealth of world-famous impressionist masterpieces and art nouveau architecture at this glorious national museum.

2 **Jardin du Luxembourg** (p228) Strolling through the chestnut groves and orchards, past ponds and statues, at the city's most popular park.

3 **Musée Rodin** (p230) Indulging in an exquisitely Parisian moment in the sculpture-filled gardens of the magnificently renovated Hôtel Biron.

4 **La Grande Épicerie de Paris** (p245) Feasting your eyes on the fantastical displays at this food emporium attached to Paris' first department store, Le Bon Marché, designed by Gustave Eiffel.

5 **Hôtel des Invalides** (p231) Visiting Napoléon's elaborate tomb within the monumental complex housing France's largest military museum.

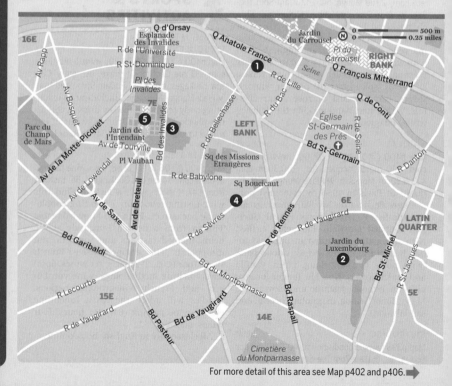

For more detail of this area see Map p402 and p406.

Explore St-Germain & Les Invalides

Despite gentrification since its early-20th-century bohemian days, there remains a startling cinematic quality to this soulful part of the Left Bank where artists, writers, actors and musicians cross paths.

This is one of those neighbourhoods whose very atmosphere is an attraction in itself, so allow plenty of time to stroll its side streets and stop at its fabled literary cafes, prêt-à-porter stores, gourmet shops, covered market and grand department store Le Bon Marché (p244), with its vast white spaces showcasing interior design. Nearby, admire the exquisite art nouveau façade of Hôtel Lutetia (1910), a glittering stunning pearly cream after recent renovation: built to accommodate wealthy customers from Le Bon Marché, the luxurious palace hotel was one of the capital's first 'modern' luxury hotels. View Delacroix' works at the Église St-Sulpice (p232) and his former studio, the Musée National Eugène Delacroix (p232); linger in the masterpiece-filled sculpture garden of the Musée Rodin (p230).

Check out the breathtaking collections of the exceptional Musée d'Orsay (p224), before dining at the area's stylish restaurants and swizzling cocktails at its bars.

Local Life

River life Join locals jogging, skating, cycling, bar-hopping or just Zenning out along the riverside promenade Les Berges de Seine (p233).

Market life Street markets where St-Germain denizens stock up on bountiful fresh produce include Marché Raspail (p244) and rue Cler.

Fashion life Scour the racks for designer cast-offs at St-Germain's secondhand boutiques.

Getting There & Away

Metro This area is especially well served by metro and RER. Get off at metro stations St-Germain des Prés, Mabillon or Odéon for its busy bd St-Germain heart. RER line C shadows the Seine along the Left Bank and is a fast way to get from St-Michel–Notre Dame to the Musée d'Orsay.

Bicycle Convenient Vélib' stations include 141 bd St-Germain, 6e; opposite 2 bd Raspail, 6e; and 62 rue de Lille, 7e.

Boat Batobus boats dock by quai Malaquais for St-Germain des Prés and quai Anatole France for the Musée d'Orsay.

Lonely Planet's Top Tip

The St-Germain and Les Invalides neighbourhood's two biggest-hitting museums – the impressionist-filled Musée d'Orsay and magnificently renovated Musée Rodin – offer a discounted combination ticket costing €18. But you don't need to cram both into one day; the joint ticket is valid for a single visit to each museum within three months.

✖ Best Places to Eat

➡ Bouillon Racine (p236)
➡ Tomy & Co (p239)
➡ Clover Green (p238)
➡ Beaupassage (p236)
➡ Café Constant (p239)
➡ La Cantine du Troquet (p236)

For reviews, see p235.➡

🍷 Best Places to Drink

➡ Coutume Café (p242)
➡ Le Bar des Prés (p241)
➡ Les Deux Magots (p240)
➡ Au Sauvignon (p240)
➡ La Cave des Climats (p242)
➡ Augustin Marchand D'Vins (p242)

For reviews, see p240.➡

🔒 Best Shopping

➡ Le Bon Marché (p244)
➡ La Grande Épicerie de Paris (p245)
➡ Bonne Gueule (p243)
➡ Cantin (p245)
➡ Cire Trudon (p243)

For reviews, see p242.➡

TOP EXPERIENCE
ENJOY ART IN THE MUSÉE D'ORSAY

Resplendently set in a former railway station overlooking the Seine, the Musée d'Orsay is a one-stop shop for some of the world's most celebrated paintings by impressionist, postimpressionist and art nouveau artists. The museum's cavernous interiors, vintage monumental clocks and contemporary styled galleries are as dazzling as the art itself.

History

The Gare d'Orsay railway station was designed by competition-winning architect Victor Laloux. Even on its completion, just in time for the 1900 Exposition Universelle, painter Edouard Detaille declared that the new station looked like a Palais des Beaux Arts. But although it had its own hotel and all the mod cons of the day – including luggage lifts and passenger elevators – by 1939 the increasing electrification of the rail network meant the platforms were too short for mainline trains, and within a few years all rail services ceased.

The station was used as a mailing centre during WWII, and in 1962 Orson Welles filmed Franz Kafka's *The Trial* in the then-abandoned building. Fortunately, it was saved from being demolished and replaced with a hotel complex by a Historical Monument listing in 1973, before the government set about establishing the palatial museum.

Transforming the languishing building into the country's premier showcase for art from 1848 to 1914 was the grand project of President Valéry Giscard d'Estaing, who signed off on it in 1977. The museum opened its doors in 1986.

Far from resting on its laurels, major renovations at the Musée d'Orsay between 2008 and 2011 incorporated a re-energised layout and increased exhibition space. Nine rooms on the 5th floor were completely renovated in 2019. World-renowned paintings now gleam from

DON'T MISS

➜ The building
➜ Painting collections
➜ Decorative-arts collections
➜ Sculptures
➜ Graphic-arts collections

PRACTICALITIES

➜ Map p406, G2
➜ ☎01 40 49 48 14
➜ www.musee-orsay.fr
➜ 1 rue de la Légion d'Honneur, 7e
➜ adult/child €16/free
➜ ⊘9.30am-6pm Tue, Wed & Fri-Sun, to 9.45pm Thu
➜ Ⓜ Assemblée Nationale or RER Musée d'Orsay

richly coloured walls that create an intimate, stately home–like atmosphere, with high-tech illumination literally casting the masterpieces in a new light.

Paintings

Most visitors make a beeline for the world's largest collection of impressionist and postimpressionist art, the highlights of which include Manet's *On the Beach* and *Woman with Fans;* Monet's gardens at Giverny and *Rue Montorgueil, Paris, Celebration of June 30, 1878;* Cézanne's card players, *Apples and Oranges* and *Blue Vase;* Renoir's *Ball at the Moulin de la Galette* and *Young Girls at the Piano;* Degas' ballerinas; Toulouse-Lautrec's cabaret dancers; Pissarro's *The Seine and the Louvre;* Sisley's *View of the Canal St-Martin;* and Van Gogh's self-portraits, *Bedroom in Arles* and *Starry Night over the Rhône.*

Decorative & Graphic Arts

Household items such as hat and coat stands, candlesticks, desks, chairs, bookcases, vases, pot-plant holders, free-standing screens, wall mirrors, water pitchers, plates, goblets and bowls become works of art in the hands of their creators, who incorporated exquisite design elements from the era.

Drawings, pastels and sketches from major artists are another of the d'Orsay's lesser-known highlights. Look for Georges Seurat's *The Black Bow* (c 1882), which uses crayon on paper to define forms by contrasting between black and white, and Paul Gaugin's poignant self-portrait (c 1902–03), drawn near the end of his life.

Sculptures

The cavernous former station is a magnificent setting for sculptures, including works by Degas, Gaugin, Camille Claudel, Renoir and Rodin.

Dining

Grab a snack or light bite at the ground-floor Café de l'Ours, overlooking François Pompon's sculpted *Polar Bear* (1923–33).

On the 5th floor, one of the Orsay's two monumental clocks keeps watch in the shimmering **Café Campana** (Map p406; mains €14-19; ⊙10.30am-5pm Tue, Wed & Fri-Sun, to 9pm Thu; ⓜAssemblée Nationale, RER Musée d'Orsay), serving salads and international fare.

Furniture and menu aside, time has scarcely changed at the Orsay's original **Le Restaurant** (Map p406; ☑01 45 49 47 03; www.facebook.com/Restaurants. Musee.Orsay; mains €17-29, lunch menus €24.50-31, dinner menu €49; ⊙11.45am-5.30pm Tue, Wed & Fri-Sun, 11.45am-2.45pm & 7-9.30pm Thu; ☑ⓜ; ⓜAssemblée Nationale, RER Musée d'Orsay).

GUIDED TOURS

For a thorough introduction to the museum, 90-minute 'Masterpieces of the Musée d'Orsay' guided tours (€6) in English run at 11.30am and 2.30pm on Tuesday. Kids under 13 years aren't permitted on adult tours; look out for family tours (six to 12 years; €4.50) and themed children's workshops (six to eight years; €7) instead. An audioguide costs €5.

Photography is allowed, but no flash and no selfie sticks please – both are forbidden.

VIEWS

Look down on Paris (spot Montmartre's Sacré-Cœur) through the former railway station's two giant glass clock faces – one in Café Campana, with adjacent roof terrace (closed in winter), and another immediately after the impressionist galleries.

1. *Woman with Fans* **by Édouard Manet**
Manet often depicted middle-class Parisians.

2. *Ball at the Moulin de la Galette* **by Pierre-Auguste Renoir**
Take a stroll through Montmartre to see the Moulin Blute Fin (p141), the inspiration for this painting.

3. *The Garden at Giverny* **by Claude Monet**
A leading figure in the impressionist movement, Monet was inspired by his garden.

4. *On the Beach* **by Édouard Manet**
Manet's works are among the Musée d'Orsay's extensive collection of impressionist paintings.

PHOTODED MICHAL BEDNAREK/SHUTTERSTOCK©

 TOP EXPERIENCE
STROLL THE JARDIN DU LUXEMBOURG

Playing the quintessential French *flâneur* (indulgent stroller or meanderer) in this romantic city park is a classic 'I'm in Paris!' moment. Elegant and timeless in equal measure, the 23-hectare large garden squirrels away a lush medley of pea-green lawns and crunchy gravel paths, formal terraces and chestnut groves, ornamental ponds and orchards – with their own charm in every season.

History

The Jardin du Luxembourg's history stretches further back than Napoléon's dedication. The gardens are a backdrop to the Palais du Luxembourg, built in the 1620s for Marie de Médicis, Henri IV's consort, to assuage her longing for the Pitti Palace in Florence. The Palais is now home to the French Senate.

Numerous overhauls across the centuries have given the Jardin du Luxembourg a blend of traditional French- and English-style gardens that is unique in Paris.

All of the gardens' nostalgic childhood activities are still here today, as well as modern play equipment, tennis and other sporting and games venues.

Grand Bassin

It is for good reason that the Luxembourg Gardens hold a place in the heart of every Parisian: for centuries, this is where children (and grown-up 'children') have come to while away a weekend afternoon chasing **toy sailboats** (Map p402; www.lesvoiliersduluxembourg.fr; sailboat rental per 30min €4; ⏲11am-6pm Apr-Oct; ⓂNotre Dame des Champs, RER Luxembourg) on the octagonal **Grand Bassin** (Map p402; ⓂMabillon, RER Luxembourg), a serene ornamental pond. Nearby, younger children and tots can take **pony rides** (Map p402; ☑06 07 32 53 95; www.animaponey.com; 600m/900m pony ride €6/8.50; ⏲3-6pm Wed, Sat, Sun & school holidays; ⓂNotre Dames des Champs, RER Luxembourg) or romp around the **playgrounds** (Map p402; adult/child

DON'T MISS

➜ Grand Bassin
➜ Puppet shows
➜ Orchards
➜ Palais du Luxembourg
➜ Musée de Luxembourg

PRACTICALITIES

➜ Map p402, E6
➜ www.senat.fr/visite/jardin
➜ 6e
➜ ⏲hours vary
➜ ⓂMabillon, St-Sulpice, Rennes, Notre Dame des Champs, RER Luxembourg

€1.50/2.50; ⏱hours vary; Ⓜ Notre Dame des Champs, RER Luxembourg) – the green half is for kids aged seven to 12 years, the blue half for under-sevens.

Puppet Shows

Puppetry is an ancient tradition in France and shows at the Jardin du Luxembourg's bijou **Théâtre du Luxembourg** (Map p402; 📞01 43 29 50 97; www.marion nettesduluxembourg.fr; tickets €6.80; ⏱Wed, Sat & Sun, daily during school holidays; Ⓜ Notre Dame des Champs) are entertaining regardless of whether you speak French or are a child. Check the program online.

Orchards

Dozens of apple varieties grow in the **orchards** (Map p402; Ⓜ Notre Dame des Champs, RER Luxembourg) in the gardens' south. Bees have produced honey in the nearby apiary, the **Rucher du Luxembourg** (Map p402; Ⓜ Notre Dame des Champs, RER Luxembourg), since the 19th century. The annual Fête du Miel (Honey Festival) offers two days of tasting and buying its sweet harvest around late September in the ornate **Pavillon Davioud** (Map p402; 55bis rue d'Assas, 6e; Ⓜ Notre Dame des Champs, RER Luxembourg).

Palais du Luxembourg

The **Palais du Luxembourg** (Map p402; www.senat. fr; rue de Vaugirard, 6e; Ⓜ Mabillon, RER Luxembourg) was built in the 1620s and has been home to the Sénat (French Senate) since 1958. It's occasionally visitable by guided tour.

East of the palace is the ornate, Italianate **Fontaine des Médicis** (Map p402; Ⓜ Mabillon, RER Luxembourg), built in 1630. During Baron Haussmann's 19th-century reshaping of the roads, the fountain was moved 30m and the pond and dramatic statues of the giant bronze Polyphemus discovering the white-marble lovers Acis and Galatea were added.

Musée du Luxembourg

Top-billing temporary art exhibitions, such as 'Cézanne et Paris', are held in the beautiful **Musée du Luxembourg** (Map p402; 📞01 40 13 62 00; www. museeduluxembourg.fr; 19 rue de Vaugirard, 6e; most exhibitions adult/child €13/free; ⏱10.30am-7pm Tue-Sun, to 10pm Mon; Ⓜ St-Sulpice, RER Luxembourg).

Around the back of the museum, lemon and orange trees, palms, grenadiers and oleanders shelter from the cold in the palace's **orangery** (Map p402; Ⓜ St-Sulpice, RER Luxembourg). Nearby, the heavily guarded **Hôtel du Petit Luxembourg** was where Marie de Médicis lived while the Palais du Luxembourg was being built. The president of the Senate has called it home since 1825.

PHOTOGRAPHY EXHIBITIONS

Photography exhibitions showcasing the works of world-renowned artists are held twice a year in the Jardin du Luxembourg. Life-sized pictures are installed along the railings near the Senate building.

If you fancy taking home a classic Jardin du Luxembourg chair, pick one up from Fermob (p243).

JARDIN & LES MIS

The Jardin du Luxembourg plays a pivotal role in Victor Hugo's Les Misérables: the novel's lovers Marius and Cosette meet here for the first time.

The gardens are studded with more than 100 sculptures. Look out for statues of Stendhal, Chopin, Baudelaire and Delacroix.

TOP EXPERIENCE
VISIT RODIN'S 'THE THINKER'

Even if you're not an art lover, it is worth visiting this high-profile Musée Rodin art gallery to lose yourself in its romantic gardens. One of the most peaceful green oases in Paris, the formal flowerbeds and boxed-hedge arrangements framing 18th-century mansion Hôtel Biron house original sculptures by sculptor, painter, sketcher, engraver and collector Auguste Rodin. This is where he lived and worked while in Paris.

Sculptures

The first large-scale cast of Rodin's famous sculpture **The Thinker** (*Le Penseur*), made in 1902, resides in the garden – the perfect place to contemplate this heroic naked figure conceived by Rodin to represent intellect and poetry.

The Gates of Hell (*La Porte de l'Enfer*) was commissioned in 1880 as the entrance for a never-built museum, and Rodin worked on his sculptural masterpiece up until his death in 1917. Standing 6m high and 4m wide, its 180 figures comprise an intricate scene from Dante's *Inferno*.

Marble monument to love **The Kiss** (*Le Baiser*) was originally part of *The Gates of Hell*. The sculpture's entwined lovers caused controversy on completion due to Rodin's then-radical depiction of women as equal partners in ardour. The museum also features many sculptures by Camille Claudel, Rodin's protégé and muse.

Collections

In 1908 Rodin donated his entire art collection to the French state on the proviso that they dedicate his former workshop and showroom, the 18th-century mansion Hôtel Biron (1730), to displaying his works. In addition to Rodin's own paintings and sketches, don't miss his prized collection of works by artists including Van Gogh and Monet.

DON'T MISS

➡ *The Thinker*
➡ *The Gates of Hell*
➡ *The Kiss*
➡ Camille Claudel sculptures
➡ Collections

PRACTICALITIES

➡ Map p406, D4
➡ ☎01 44 18 61 10
➡ www.musee-rodin.fr
➡ 79 rue de Varenne, 7e
➡ adult/child €13/free, garden only €5/free
➡ ⏲10am-6.30pm Tue-Sun
➡ Ⓜ Varenne, Invalides

TOP EXPERIENCE
SEE NAPOLÉON'S TOMB

Named after the 4000 *invalides* (disabled war veterans) for whom it was built to accommodate in the 1670s, Hôtel des Invalides stands sentry over the grandiose, pea-green of Esplanade des Invalides. On 14 July 1789, it was from this monumental edifice that revolutionaries famously pilfered 32,000 rifles before charging to place de la Bastille to storm the city prison.

Église du Dôme

South of the main courtyard is the **Église du Dôme** (Map p406; incl in Hôtel des Invalides entry; ◷10am-6pm Wed-Mon, to 9pm Tue Apr-Oct, 10am-5pm Nov-Mar; Ⓜ Varenne), which, with its golden dome (1677–1735), is one of the finest religious edifices erected under Louis XIV.

Also south of the main courtyard is the **Église St-Louis des Invalides**, once used by soldiers.

Tombeau de Napoléon 1er

The extremely extravagant tomb of Napoléon (pictured) comprises six coffins fitting into one another like a Russian nesting doll. Find it in the centre of the Église du Dôme.

Musée de l'Armée

Sobering wartime footage screens at this **army museum** (Map p406; incl in Hôtel des Invalides entry; ◷10am-6pm Apr-Oct, to 5pm Nov-Mar), north of the main courtyard, which also has weaponry, flag and medal displays as well as a multimedia area dedicated to Charles de Gaulle. This is the nation's largest collection on French military history.

Musée des Plans-Reliefs

Within the Hôtel des Invalides itself, the esoteric **Musée des Plans-Reliefs** is full of scale models of towns, fortresses and châteaux across France.

DON'T MISS

➔ Musée de l'Armée
➔ Église du Dôme
➔ Tombeau de Napoléon 1er
➔ Musée des Plans-Reliefs

PRACTICALITIES

➔ Map p406, D4
➔ ☎ 01 44 42 38 77
➔ www.musee-armee.fr
➔ 129 rue de Grenelle, 7e
➔ adult/child €14/free
➔ ◷10am-6pm Apr-Oct, to 5pm Nov-Mar
➔ Ⓜ Varenne, La Tour Maubourg

◉ SIGHTS

Chart-topping sights in this stately neighbourhood include the impressionist-art-filled Musée d'Orsay, massive military complex Hôtel des Invalides (home to Napoléon's tomb) and romantic, sculpture-strewn Musée Rodin. Look out for smaller, lesser-known gems too, such as the Musée National Eugène Delacroix, and some exquisite churches. Allow ample time for ambling in the city's most beautiful park, timeless Jardin du Luxembourg.

◉ St-Germain

JARDIN DU LUXEMBOURG   PARK
See p228.

MONNAIE DE PARIS   MUSEUM
Map p402 (☑01 40 46 56 66; www.monnaiede
paris.fr; 11 quai de Conti, 6e; adult/child €12/free;
⊙11am-7pm Tue & Thu-Sun, to 9pm Wed; Ⓜ Pont
Neuf) The 18th-century royal mint, Monnaie de Paris, houses the **Musée du 11 Conti**, an interactive museum exploring the history of French coinage from antiquity onwards, plus edgy contemporary-art exhibitions. The impeccably restored, neoclassical building, with one of the longest façades on the Seine, stretching 116m long, squirrels away five sumptuous courtyards, the Hôtel de Conti designed by Jules Hardouin-Mansart in 1690, engraving workshops, the original foundry (now the museum boutique), Guy Savoy's flagship restaurant (p238) and fashionable cafe Frappé par Bloom (p241).

Coins were minted at the Monnaie de Paris until 1973 when manufacturing was moved to the town of Pessac on the Atlantic coast. The Ministry of Finance still uses the Paris mint, however, to produce commemorative medals and coins, many of which are sold in the museum's stylish boutique alongside glass jars of honey from hives on the building's rooftop, medallions featuring the Louvre or Eiffel Tower, and other classy souvenirs.

Skip ticket queues by buying tickets online or from one of the automatic ticket machines, tucked away at the foot of the grandiose, red-carpeted staircase swirling up to Guy Savoy's Michelin-star restaurant.

MUSÉE NATIONAL EUGÈNE DELACROIX   MUSEUM
Map p402 (☑01 44 41 86 50; www.musee-dela
croix.fr; 6 rue de Furstenberg, 6e; adult/child €7/free; ⊙9.30am-5.30pm Wed-Mon; Ⓜ Mabillon) In a courtyard off a tree-shaded square, this museum is housed in the romantic artist's home and studio at the time of his death in 1863. It contains a collection of his oil paintings, watercolours, pastels and drawings, including *L'Education de la Vierge* (1842) and his paintings of Morocco.

As well as the Musée du Louvre, you can see Delacroix's works at the Musée d'Orsay and frescoes at Église St-Sulpice.

ÉGLISE ST-SULPICE   CHURCH
Map p402 (☑01 42 34 59 98; www.pss75.fr/saint-sulpice-paris; place St-Sulpice, 6e; ⊙7am-7.30pm; Ⓜ St-Sulpice) FREE In 1646 work started on the twin-towered Church of St Sulpicius, lined inside with 21 side chapels, and it took six architects 150 years to finish. It's famed for its striking Italianate façade with two rows of superimposed columns, its Counter Reformation–influenced neoclassical decor, its frescoes by Eugène Delacroix – and its setting for a murderous scene in Dan Brown's *The Da Vinci Code*. You can hear the monumental, 1781-built organ during 10.30am Mass on Sunday or the occasional Sunday-afternoon concert.

The frescoes in the Chapelle des Sts-Anges (Chapel of the Holy Angels), first to the right as you enter the chapel, depict Jacob wrestling with the angel (to the left) and Michael the Archangel doing battle with Satan (to the right), and were painted by Delacroix between 1855 and 1861. Free guided tours of the church (in English) depart on the first Sunday of each month at 12.45pm. To delve into the crypt, sign up in advance for a tour (in French) on the second and fourth Sundays of the month at 3pm.

MUSÉE ATELIER ZADKINE   MUSEUM
Map p402 (☑01 55 42 77 20; www.zadkine.paris.fr; 100bis rue d'Assas, 6e; ⊙10am-6pm Tue-Sun; Ⓜ Vavin) FREE Russian cubist sculptor Ossip Zadkine (1890–1967) arrived in Paris in 1908 and lived and worked in this cottage for almost 40 years. Zadkine produced an enormous catalogue of sculptures made from clay, stone, bronze and wood. The museum covers his life and work; one room displays figures he sculpted in contrast-

ing walnut, pear, ebony, acacia, elm and oak. Admission is only free when there is no temporary exhibition; otherwise adult/child admission is €8/free.

LE BATEAU IVRE
MONUMENT

Map p402 (btwn 2 & 4 rue Férou, 6e; M St-Sulpice) Arthur Rimbaud's 1871 poem *Le Bateau Ivre* (The Drunken Boat), depicting a fantastical and frightening sea voyage of a sinking boat from the first-person narration of the boat itself using rich imagery and symbolism, occupies a 300m-long wall spanning an entire block in the heart of St-Germain. Rimbaud wrote the poem at age 16 after being inspired by Jules Verne's recently published novel *Twenty Thousand Leagues Under the Sea*. The 100-line poem was hand painted on the wall in 2012.

BIBLIOTHÈQUE MAZARINE
LIBRARY

Map p402 (☎01 44 41 44 06; www.bibliotheque-mazarine.fr; 23 quai de Conti, 6e; ◷10am-6pm Mon-Fri; M Mabillon) FREE Within the **Institut de France** (Map p402; www.institut-de-france.fr), the Mazarine Library is France's oldest public library, founded in 1643. You can visit the bust-lined, late-17th-century reading room during opening times.

◉ Les Invalides

MUSÉE RODIN
MUSEUM

See p230.

MUSÉE D'ORSAY
MUSEUM

See p224.

HÔTEL DES INVALIDES
MONUMENT, MUSEUM

See p231.

PARC RIVES DE SEINE
PARK

Map p406 (◉information point noon-7pm Tue-Sun May-Sep, shorter hours Oct-Apr; M Solférino, Assemblée Nationale, Invalides) A breath of fresh air, this 2.5km-long expressway-turned-riverside-promenade on the Left Bank is a favourite spot in which to run, cycle, skate, climb (there's a climbing wall at pont des Invalides), play board games or take part in a packed program of events. It's also simply a great place to hang out – on the archipelago of floating gardens or at the burgeoning restaurants and bars (some floating aboard boats and barges).

FLUCTUART
CULTURAL CENTRE

Map p406 (☎07 67 02 44 37; www.fluctuart.fr; pont des Invalides, 7e; ◷noon-midnight Wed-Sun

---

◉ TOP EXPERIENCE
DISCOVER NOTRE DAME'S PRECURSOR

The sheer magnificence and magnitude of Paris' cathedral on Île de la Cité makes it hard to believe that this humble 'village' church, built in the 11th century on the site of a 6th-century abbey, was the primary place of worship for Parisians up until the 14th century (when Notre Dame was completed). The Romanesque church, officially called **Église St-Germain des Prés** (St Germanus of the Fields), has undergone numerous facelifts over the centuries.

Chapelle de St-Symphorien, part of the original abbey, is believed to be the resting place of St Germanus (496–576), the first bishop of Paris. The Merovingian kings were buried here during the 6th and 7th centuries, but their tombs disappeared during the Revolution.

Over the western entrance, the bell tower has changed little since 990, although the spire dates only from the 19th century.

Until the late 17th century the abbey owned most of the land in the Left Bank west of what's now bd St-Michel, and donated some of its lands along the Seine – the Pré aux Clercs (Fields of the Scholars) – to house the University of Paris (hence the names of the nearby streets, rues du Pré aux Clercs and de l'Université).

DON'T MISS

➡ Chapelle de St-Symphorien
➡ Bell tower

PRACTICALITIES

➡ Map p402, D3
➡ ☎01 55 42 81 18
➡ www.eglise-saint germaindespres.fr
➡ 3 place St-Germain des Prés, 6e
➡ ◷9am-8pm
➡ M St-Germain des Prés

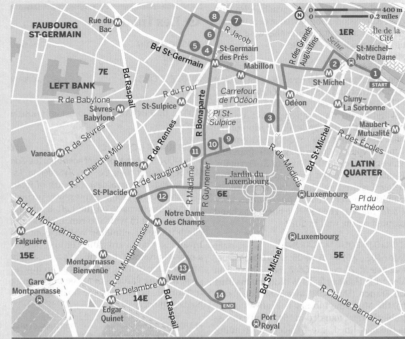

Neighbourhood Walk
Left Bank Literary Loop

START QUAI ST-MICHEL
END 113 RUE NOTRE DAMES DES CHAMPS
LENGTH 5KM; ONE TO TWO HOURS

To retrace the footsteps of Left Bank literary luminaries, begin by following the Seine-
side trail of *bouquinistes* (secondhand
booksellers, loved by Ernest Hemingway)
along quai St-Michel from **1** **Notre Dame**
(p196) to place St-Michel.

Continue west then cross the street and
duck south along rue Gît-le-Cœur to the
'Beat Hotel', today **2** **Relais Hôtel du
Vieux Paris**, where Allen Ginsberg, Jack
Kerouac, William S Burroughs and others
holed up in the 1950s.

At **3** **12 rue de l'Odéon** stood the
original Shakespeare & Company bookshop where owner Sylvia Beach lent books
to Hemingway, and edited, retyped and
published *Ulysses* for James Joyce in
1922. It was closed during the occupation
when Beach refused to sell her last copy of
Joyce's *Finnegan's Wake* to a Nazi officer.

Bd St-Germain's **4** **Les Deux Magots**
(p240) and **5** **Café de Flore** (p241) were

favourite cafes of postwar intellectuals
Jean-Paul Sartre and Simone de Beauvoir.

At **6** **36 rue Bonaparte** Henry Miller
stayed in a 5th-floor mansard room in 1930,
which he later wrote about in *Letters to Emil*
(1989). **7** **L'Hôtel** (p291), the former Hôtel
d'Alsace, is where Oscar Wilde died in 1900.
Hemingway spent his first night in Paris
in room 14 of the **8** **Hôtel d'Angleterre**
(p291) in 1921.

In 1925 William Faulkner stayed several
months at what's now the posh **9** **Hôtel
Luxembourg Parc**, and Hemingway's
last years in Paris were at **10** **6 rue Férou**.
F Scott and Zelda Fitzgerald lived at **11** **58
rue de Vaugirard** in 1928, near **12** **27 rue
de Fleurus**, where Gertrude Stein lived and
entertained artists and writers including
Matisse, Picasso, Braque, Gauguin, Fitzgerald, Hemingway and Ezra Pound.

Pound lived at **13** **70bis rue Notre
Dame des Champs** in a flat filled with Japanese paintings, while Hemingway's first
apartment in this area was above a sawmill
at **14** **113 rue Notre Dame des Champs**.

winter, daily summer; Ⓜ Invalides) **FREE** Opened in 2019, this hip cultural centre occupying a *péniche* (barge) off pont des Invalides brought an unexpected dash of coolness to an otherwise institutional neighbourhood. It claims to be the first floating urban art centre in the world and hosts the works and creations of all kinds of emerging artists. There are exhibition spaces as well as a vibrant bar and a restaurant.

MUSÉE MAILLOL
MUSEUM

Map p406 (Fondation Dina Vierny; www.musee maillol.com; 61 rue de Grenelle, 7e; adult/child €13.50/11.50; ☉10.30am-6.30pm Sat-Thu, to 8.30pm Fri; Ⓜ Rue du Bac) Located in the stunning 18th-century Hôtel Bouchardon, this splendid little museum focuses on the work of sculptor Aristide Maillol (1861–1944), whose creations primarily occupy several rooms on the 2nd floor, and also includes works by Matisse, Gauguin, Kandinsky, Cézanne and Picasso. All are from the private collection of Odessa-born Dina Vierny (1919–2009), Maillol's principal model for 10 years from the age of 15. Major temporary exhibitions (included in the admission price) regularly take place here.

IMMEUBLE LAVIROTTE
NOTABLE BUILDING

Map p406 (29 av Rapp, 7e; Ⓜ École Militaire) Let your eyes settle on the aesthetic minutiae of the fantastic art nouveau façade of this building, which is one of the most photogenic private edifices in the *arrondissement*. It was built in 1901.

 EATING

This neighbourhood's streets are lined with everything from quintessential Parisian bistros to chic designer restaurants and flagship establishments with Michelin-starred chefs. Some charming places hide inside Cour du Commerce St-André, a glass-covered passageway built in 1735 to link two *jeu de paume* (old-style tennis) courts, and the much more recent Beaupassage, with upmarket cafes, restaurants and shops. For snacks and fast food to munch on the move, head to rue St-André des Arts, a lively street peppered with taco, Lebanese, crêpe and felafel takeaways.

✕ St-Germain

★ L'AVANT COMPTOIR DE LA TERRE
TAPAS €

Map p402 (www.camdeborde.com; 3 Carrefour de l'Odéon, 6e; tapas €5-15; ☉noon-11pm; Ⓜ Odéon) Squeeze in around the zinc bar and feast on amazing tapas (fried squid, egg and mushrooms, and veal breast with green cabbage) and wines by the glass in a chaotically sociable atmosphere. There are only a few seats around the bar and it's tiny.

For seafood tapas, head to adjacent **L'Avant Comptoir de la Mer** (Map p402; tapas €5-15, oysters per half-dozen €18-26; ☉noon-11pm); for porcine tapas, nearby **L'Avant Comptoir du Marché** (Map p402; 15 rue Lobineau, 6e; tapas €5-15; ☉noon-11pm; Ⓜ Mabillon). Or for gourmet bistro dining, try for a lunchtime table or evening reservation at **Le Comptoir** (Map p402; ☎01 44 27 07 97; 5 Carrefour de l'Odéon, 6e; mains €20-36; ☉noon-11pm; Ⓜ Odéon).

LA LAITERIE SAINTE CLOTILDE
FRENCH €

Map p406 (☎01 45 51 74 61; www.lalaiteriesainte clotilde.fr; 64 rue de Bellechasse, 7e; mains €19-22, menus €24-28; ☉noon-2pm & 8-10pm Mon-Fri, 8-10pm Sat; Ⓜ Solférino) Your neighbours might be diplomats or civil servants working in a ministry nearby – not a bad sign. In a very institutional area, La Laiterie is a beacon of character and cosiness, with an atmospheric decor harking back to the 1970s and French classics cooked to perfection.

VGT BOWL
VEGETARIAN €

Map p402 (☎01 47 03 92 07; https://vgt-bowl. business.site; 22 rue de Beaune, 7e; mains €12-18; ☉11.30am-4pm Mon-Sat; ✔; Ⓜ Rue du Bac) V stands for 'Végétal', G for 'Gourmand' and T for 'Tonique' – this gives you an idea of what's on offer at this quirky, buzzy and colourful vegetarian den. Enjoy a bowl replete with healthy ingredients while sampling a delicious fruit cocktail. And there's nothing better than finishing on a sweet note with, say, an apple crumble.

BISTROT ERNEST
BISTRO €

Map p402 (☎01 56 24 47 47; www.facebook.com/ bistroternest; 21 rue de Seine, 6e; mains €13-19; ☉noon-3pm & 6-10pm Tue-Sun; Ⓜ Odéon) An unpretentious yet characterful bistro with affordable mains in the heart of the 6e is an increasingly rare treat. A hot fave among art dealers and gallerists, Bistrot Ernest fulfils many a Francophile dream. Old-fashioned bookshelves and bistro tables, a curvy zinc bar and an affable patron all give the place an essential Parisian buzz.

The cuisine is wholly simple but people come here to absorb the atmosphere.

MAISON MULOT
PASTRIES €

Map p402 (☑01 43 26 91 03; www.gerard-mulot. com; 76 rue de Seine, 6e; items from €1.80; ☺7am-8pm; MOdéon) Fruit tarts (peach, lemon, apple), croissants, cakes and *amaryllis* (the house signature dessert) are among this celebrated pastry chef's specialities sold at his delightfully quaint patisserie with candyfloss pink-and-white striped canopy. Also sells quiches and gourmet sandwiches.

LITTLE BREIZH
CRÊPES €

Map p402 (☑01 43 54 60 74; www.facebook. com/littlebreizhcreperie; 11 rue Grégoire de Tours, 6e; crêpes & galettes €6-17; ☺noon-2.15pm & 7-10.30pm Tue-Sat, closed Aug; ☑; MOdéon) As authentic as you'd find in Brittany, but with some innovative twists (such as Breton sardines, olive oil and sundried tomatoes, or smoked salmon, dill cream, pink peppercorns and lemon), the crêpes at this sweet spot are infinitely more enticing than those sold on nearby street corners. The decor is no less appealing, with beams, subdued lighting and blonde stone walls.

SIMPLE
VEGETARIAN €

Map p406 (☑01 45 44 79 88; www.facebook. com/cantinesimple; 86 rue du Cherche Midi, 6e; mains €15-20; ☺noon-11pm; ☎☑; MSt-Placide) Amid the many eateries on fashionable rue du Cherche Midi, Simple stands out for its super-healthy, fully organic salads, soup of the day and detox veggie bowls. Dozens of fresh flowers in vases decorate wooden tables inside and the pavement terrace is a perfect spot to people-watch over a Veggie Detox *assiette* (plate).

LA CRÈMERIE
FRENCH €

Map p402 (☑01 43 54 99 30; www.facebook. com/lacremerieparis; 9 rue des Quatre Vents, 6e; small plates €10-21; ☺6-10pm Mon, 11.30am-2pm & 6-10pm Tue-Sat; MOdéon) Beneath an original glass-covered ceiling, this marble-walled *caviste* (wine cellar) is a delicious flashback to 1880s Paris. With a stock of 400-odd wines and an exquisite array of France's finest gourmet goods, it is a de-lightful spot for an early-evening *apéro* (predinner drink) accompanied by tapas-style dishes or a fully fledged meal.

LES ANTIQUAIRES
BISTRO €

Map p402 (☑01 42 61 08 36; www.lesantiquaires. net; 13 rue du Bac, 7e; mains €18-21; ☺7am-11.30pm; MRue du Bac) Before you do anything else, sidle up to the bar or bag a seat on the terrace for a potent mojito or a glass of wine. This place is lively and hip, and will put you in the mood for some perfectly cooked bistro fare, including beef fillet and oysters, with a creative twist. Bonus: it's open *'en continu'* (nonstop).

★BEAUPASSAGE
FOOD HALL €€

Map p406 (www.beaupassage.fr; 53-57 rue de Grenelle, 7e; ☺passage 7am-11pm, individual hours vary; MSèvres–Babylone) Some of France's finest chefs, artisans and purveyors occupy this open-air 'mini district'. Look out for Yannick Alléno (with a restaurant, wine cellar and art gallery), Anne-Sophie Pic (gastronomy), Olivier Bellin (seafood), Thierry Marx (bakery-patisserie), Pierre Hermé (pastries, including his signature macarons, with a sit-down cafe), Nicole Barthélémy (cheeses) and renowned butcher Alexandre Polmard (with an attached restaurant).

Also accessible via Beaupassage is Coya, a Peruvian bar-restaurant in a former church.

★LA CANTINE DU TROQUET
BISTRO €€

Map p406 (☑01 43 27 70 06; www.lacantinedu-troquet.com; 79 rue du Cherche Midi, 6e; mains €19-25; ☺noon-2pm & 7-10pm Mon-Fri; MSt-Placide) One of six eateries run by chef Christian Etchebest in Paris, La Cantine du Troquet is a favoured spot for fans of bistro fare made with top-notch ingredients and sourced from the best producers around the country. Classics include pig loin and grilled razor clams. There are sturdy desserts such as *riz au lait* (milk rice) and a great wine list.

★BOUILLON RACINE
BRASSERIE €€

Map p402 (☑01 44 32 15 60; www.bouillonracine. fr; 3 rue Racine, 6e; 3-course €35, mains €17-33; ☺noon-11pm; ☑; MCluny–La Sorbonne) Inconspicuously situated in a quiet street, this heritage-listed art nouveau 'soup kitchen', with mirrored walls, floral motifs and ceramic tiling, was built in 1906 to feed market workers. Despite the magnificent

PARIS' OLDEST RESTAURANT & CAFE

St-Germain claims both the city's oldest restaurant and its oldest cafe.

À la Petite Chaise (Map p402; ☑01 42 22 13 35; www.alapetitechaise.fr; 36 rue de Grenelle, 7e; 2-/3-course lunch menu €25.50/33.50, 3-course dinner menu €36.50, mains €21-28; ⊙noon-2pm & 7-11pm; MSèvres-Babylone) In 1860 wine merchant Georges Rameau took the innovative move of serving food (to accompany his wares) to customers coming to his shop – and so the oldest restaurant still standing in the capital was born. The kitchen remains firmly grounded in timeless French classics like onion soup and fillet of veal.

Le Procope (Map p402; ☑01 40 46 79 00; www.procope.com; 13 rue de l'Ancienne Comédie, 6e; 2-/3-course menu lunch €22/29, dinner €31.50/38.50; ⊙noon-11pm; MOdéon) If you ever wondered what Voltaire, Molière and Balzac dined on in the heady days of 17th-century Paris, reserve a table at this chandelier-posh restaurant where very little has changed since the day it first opened its doors in 1686. Coq au vin or calf's-head casserole in veal stock are tasty blasts from the past.

interior, the food – inspired by age-old recipes – is no afterthought and is superbly executed (stuffed, spit-roasted suckling pig, pork shank in Rodenbach red beer, scallops and shrimps with lobster coulis).

Finish off your foray into gastronomic history with an old-fashioned sherbet. Two-course children's *menus* (€14.50) mean kids don't miss out.

QUINSOU
FRENCH €€
Map p406 (☑01 42 22 66 09; www.quinsou.fr; 33 rue de l'Abbé Grégoire, 6e; menus €38-54; ⊙7.30-9.30pm Tue, 12.30-1.30pm & 7.30-9.30pm Wed-Sat; MSaint-Placide) The motto here is 'Work Hard & Be Nice to People' – yes, it's in English and written in capital letters near the entrance. And yes, Antonin Bonnet and his team work hard to please our tastebuds with robustly flavoured dishes with a contemporary twist. Enticing decor, with blonde wood furniture and a subtly industrial-chic tone.

RESTAURANT CINQ-MARS
BISTRO €€
Map p402 (☑01 45 44 69 13; www.cinq-mars-restaurant.com; 51 rue de Verneuil, 7e; mains €19-29; ⊙noon-2.30pm & 7.30-10.30pm Mon-Fri, 12.30-3pm & 7.30-10.30pm Sat & Sun; MSolférino, RER Musée d'Orsay) A huge dining room partition with blackboard paint chalks up Cinq-Mars' vast array of wines, while the seasonal menu is scrawled on one side. Traditional bistro dishes are given a contemporary spin (seared fennel with lemon-marinated squid, or veal liver with homemade puree). Desserts include deliciously rich chocolate mousse.

ANICIA
FRENCH €€
Map p406 (☑01 43 35 41 50; www.anicia-bistrot.com; 97 rue du Cherche Midi, 6e; 2-/3-course weekday lunch menu €28/37, 4-/6-course dinner menu €58/74, mains €23-34; ⊙noon-10.30pm Tue-Sat; MDuroc, Vaneau) An advance online booking is essential at this glorious 'bistro nature', showcase for the earthy but refined cuisine of chef François Gagnaire, who ran a Michelin-starred restaurant in the Auvergne before uprooting to the French capital. He still sources dozens of regional products – Puy lentils, meat from Haute-Loire, St-Nectaire cheese – from small-time producers in central France, to stunning effect.

SEMILLA
BISTRO €€
Map p402 (☑01 43 54 34 50; www.semillaparis.com; 54 rue de Seine, 6e; mains €23-39; ⊙12.30-2pm & 7-10.30pm Mon-Sat, to 10pm Sun; MMabillon) Stark concrete floor, beams and an open kitchen (in front of which you can book front-row 'chef seats') set the factory-style scene for edgy, modern, daily changing dishes such as grilled octopus scallops or hake fillet with mashed salsifis. Desserts are equally irresistible. Be sure to book.

If you haven't made a reservation, head to its adjoining walk-in wine bar, **Freddy's** (Map p402; small plates €8-15; ⊙kitchen 12.30-3pm & 6-11pm, bar noon-midnight), serving small tapas-style plates.

LE TIMBRE
BISTRO €€
Map p402 (☑01 45 49 10 40; www.facebook.com/restaurantletimbre; 3 rue Ste-Beuve, 6e; lunch menus €28-34, dinner menus €38-59; ⊙7.30-9.30pm Tue, noon-1.30pm & 7.30-9.30pm

RUE CLER

Pick up fresh bread, sandwich fillings, pastries and wine for a picnic along the typically Parisian commercial street rue Cler, 7e, which buzzes with local shoppers, especially on weekends.

Interspersed between the *boulangeries* (bakeries), *fromageries* (cheese shops), grocers, butchers, delis and other food shops (many with pavement stalls), lively cafe terraces overflow with locals.

Thu-Sat; M Vavin) As tiny as the postage stamp for which it's named, Le Timbre is run by husband-and-wife team Charles Danet (in the kitchen) and Agnès Peyre (front of house) and has a local following for its daily changing, original dishes with a sharp contemporary twist (veal with endives and hazelnuts; hake with saffron and fennel). Dazzling desserts and tempting wine list, too.

HUÎTRERIE REGIS   SEAFOOD €€

Map p402 (☑ 01 44 41 10 07; www.huitrerie-regis.com; 3 rue de Montfaucon, 6e; dozen oysters €19-49; ⊙ noon-2.30pm & 6.30-10.30pm Mon-Fri, noon-10.15pm Sat, noon-10pm Sun; M Mabillon) Hip, trendy, tiny and white, this is the spot for slurping oysters on crisp winter days – inside or on the tiny pavement terrace sporting sage-green Fermob chairs. Oysters arrive live from the Bassin de Marennes-Oléron and come only by the dozen. Wash them down with a glass of chilled Muscadet. No reservations, so arrive early.

A twinset of tables are set on the pavement; otherwise, it's all inside.

CHEZ DUMONET   BISTRO €€

Map p406 (Joséphine; ☑ 01 45 48 52 40; www.facebook.com/chezdumonetjosephine; 117 rue du Cherche Midi, 6e; mains €26-42; ⊙ noon-2pm & 7.30-9.30pm Tue-Sat; M Duroc) Fondly known by its former name, Joséphine, this lace-curtained, mosaic-tiled place with white-cloth tables inside and out is the Parisian bistro of many people's dreams, serving timeless standards such as beef tartare and grilled chateaubriand steak with Béarnaise sauce. Order its enormous signature Grand Marnier soufflé at the end of your meal. Mains, unusually, come in full or half-portion sizes.

During truffle season (November to March), look out for its truffle menus.

UN DIMANCHE À PARIS   FUSION €€

Map p402 (☑ 01 56 81 18 18; www.un-dimanche-a-paris.com; 4-8 Cour du Commerce St-André, 6e; menus lunch/dinner/brunch from €19/28/38; ⊙ restaurant noon-6pm Mon, 7-10pm Tue-Sat, 11am-6pm Sun; M Odéon) Inside covered passageway Cour du Commerce St-André, this glamorous 'chocolate concept store' incorporates a boutique (where you can buy cakes, chocolates and absolutely divine chocolate-coated herbs and spices), patisserie and chocolate classes (€50 to €80), a tearoom serving decadently rich hot chocolate (open noon to 6pm) and a restaurant cooking up chocoholic dishes like zander fillet with white chocolate.

Hours can vary.

AUX PRÉS   BISTRO €€

Map p402 (☑ 01 45 48 29 68; www.restaurantauxpres.com; 27 rue du Dragon, 6e; mains €25-42; ⊙ noon-2.30pm & 7-11pm Mon-Sat, 11.30am-3pm & 7-11pm Sun; M St-Sulpice) This cult filled 1950s bistro with original bar, leather banquette seating and floral wallpaper sizzles with contemporary glamour thanks to celebrity French chef Cyril Lignac, who lures a gourmet crowd here with his modern bistro cuisine: veal sweetbreads, *côte de boeuf* for two or scallops with a chorizo cream. End on a sweet high with a vanilla *millefeuille*.

★ CLOVER GREEN   BISTRO €€€

Map p402 (☑ 01 75 50 00 05; www.clover-paris.com; 5 rue Perronet, 7e; lunch menus €37-47, dinner menus €58-68; ⊙ 12.30-2pm & 7-10pm Tue-Fri, 12.30-2.30pm & 7-10pm Sat; M St-Germain des Prés) Dining at hot-shot chef Jean-François Piège's casual bistro is like attending a private party: the galley-style open kitchen adjoining the 20 seats is part of the dining-room decor, putting customers at the front and centre of the culinary action. Expect a *cuisine du jour*, inspired by the chef's mood and what's available at the market.

★ RESTAURANT
GUY SAVOY   GASTRONOMY €€€

Map p402 (☑ 01 43 80 40 61; www.guysavoy.com; 11 quai de Conti, 6e; lunch menu via online booking €250, 13-course tasting menu €490; ⊙ noon-2pm & 7-10.30pm Tue-Fri, 7-10.30pm Sat; M Pont Neuf) If you're considering visiting a three-Michelin-star temple to gastronomy, this should certainly be on your list. The world-famous chef needs no introduction (he trained Gordon Ramsay, among others); his flagship, entered via a red-carpeted staircase, is ensconced in the neoclassical Monnaie de Paris. Monumental cuisine to match includes Savoy icons such as artichoke and black-truffle soup with layered brioche.

✗ Les Invalides

LE BAC À GLACES   ICE CREAM €
Map p406 (📞01 45 48 87 65; www.bacaglaces.com; 109 rue du Bac, 7e; ice cream 1/2/3 scoops €3.50/5/6.50; ⊘10.30am-7pm Mon-Fri, from 11.30am Sat; Ⓜ Sèvres-Babylone) Apricot and ginger, lemon and basil, cinnamon, pistacchio and flambéed banana are among the 60 flavours of all-natural ice creams at this luscious *glacier* (ice-cream maker). Some are lactose- and gluten-free.

KARAMEL   PASTRIES €
Map p406 (📞01 71 93 02 94; https://karamel paris.com; 67 rue St-Dominique, 7e; ⊘8.30am-7.30pm Tue-Sat, 10am-7pm Sun; Ⓜ Invalides, Tour Maubourg) Sweet-toothed gourmets won't do much better than a pit stop at the specialist boutique and *salon de thé* (tearoom) of *chef-pâtissier* Nicolas Haelewy. Exquisite rows of fresh, caramel-spiked cakes jostle for the limelight with caramel-laced chocolate bars, jars of caramel spread, and chewy bite-sized caramels flavoured with vanilla and *fleur de sel* (rock salt), passion fruit or rose and raspberry.

TOMY & CO   GASTRONOMY €€
Map p406 (📞01 45 51 46 93; www.tomygousset.com; 22 rue Surcouf, 7e; 3-course/tasting menu €58/60, mains €33; ⊘noon-2pm & 7.30-9.45pm Mon-Fri; Ⓜ Invalides) Tomy Gousset's restaurant near the Eiffel Tower has been a sensation since day one. The French-Cambodian chef works his magic on inspired seasonal dishes using produce from his organic garden. The spectacular desserts are equally seasonal. Reservations essential.

CAFÉ CONSTANT   BISTRO €€
Map p406 (📞01 47 53 73 34; www.maisoncon stant.com; 139 rue St-Dominique, 7e; menus €21-37, mains €18-29; ⊘7am-11pm Mon-Sat, 8am-11pm Sun; Ⓜ École Militaire) Run by Michelin-starred chef Christian Constant, this traditional neighbourhood cafe with original bar and mosaic floor cooks up some fantastic staples: poached cod with garlic mayonnaise, herb-roasted chicken or beef stew followed by vanilla rice pudding. Breakfast is served

until 11am, more substantial food continuously from noon until closing time.

No reservations: enjoy a drink at the bar or on the pavement terrace outside while you wait. More upmarket **Les Cocottes** (Map p406; 📞01 45 50 10 28; 135 rue St-Dominique, 7e; menus €25-35, mains €20-31; ⊘noon-11pm; 📶), a couple of doors down on the same street, is another Constant hit.

LE FONTAINE DE MARS   BISTRO €€
Map p406 (📞01 47 05 46 44; www.fontainede mars.com; 129 rue St-Dominique, 7e; mains €18-45; ⊘noon-2pm & 7.30-11pm; Ⓜ École Militaire) For traditional French cooking look no further than this 1930s-styled neighbourhood bistro with signature lace curtains, checked tablecloths and – best of all – a fishmonger in front shucking oysters at his stall beneath the bistro arches. Snails, *boudin* (black pudding), *andouillette* (Lyonnais tripe sausage) and veal cutlet are among the traditional mainstays, alongside sensational seafood platters.

EPOCA   ITALIAN €€
Map p406 (📞01 43 06 88 88; www.epoca.paris; 17 rue Oudinot, 7e; mains €18-23; ⊘noon-2pm & 7.30-10.30pm Tue-Sat, noon-2.30pm Sun; Ⓜ Sèvres-Babylone) Star of the French TV show *Top Chef*, Italian chef Denny Imbroisi is the creative talent behind this A-lister-chic Italian bistro with a sharp, black-and-white interior evocative of 1930s

---

STARS OF THE FUTURE

Founded in 1920, **Restaurants d'Application de Ferrandi** (Map p406; www.ferrandi-paris.fr; 28 rue de l'Abbé Grégoire, 6e; Le Premier lunch/dinner menus €30/45, Le 28 lunch/dinner menus €35/45; ⊘by online reservation, closed school holidays; Ⓜ St-Placide) is arguably France's most prestigious culinary school, turning out a who's who of industry professionals. You can taste these future Michelin-starred chefs' creations at bargain prices at the school's two training restaurants, **Le Premier** (focusing on classical French cookery) and **Le 28** (high-level gastronomy), overseen by Ferrandi's esteemed professors. Hours vary; online bookings (with a minimum of 20 days before the desired date) are obligatory.

art deco. The short, stylish menu features the best of Italian regional cooking, including roasted veal, saffron-laced Milanese risotto or *gnocchi al pesto*.

AU PETIT TONNEAU   BISTRO €€

Map p406 (☑01 47 05 09 01; www.aupetittonneau.fr; 20 rue Surcouf, 7e; mains €16-35, menus €25-42; Ⓜ Invalides) A step away from the Invalides, this archetypal Parisian bistro, complete with red-chequered tablecloths and old tiles, is a joy. The kitchen specialises in French provincial favourites that warm stomachs and satisfy tastebuds. A few examples include veal cutlet and roasted lamb, all accompanied with superb homemade sauces. For dessert, try the textbook-perfect chocolate mousse.

RESTAURANT
DAVID TOUTAIN   GASTRONOMY €€€

Map p406 (☑01 45 50 11 10; www.davidtoutain.com; 29 rue Surcouf, 7e; menus €70-250; ⊙12.30-2pm & 8-10pm Mon, noon-2pm & 8-10pm Tue-Fri; Ⓜ Invalides) Prepare to be wowed: David Toutain pushes the envelope at his eponymous Michelin-starred restaurant with some of the most creative high-end cooking in Paris. All ingredients, from chestnuts and cauliflower to salsify and porcini mushrooms, are sourced from the best purveyors around the country. A meal here is a culinary voyage. Stunning wine pairings are available.

LES CLIMATS   FRENCH €€€

Map p402 (☑01 58 62 10 08; www.lesclimats.fr; 41 rue de Lille, 7e; lunch/dinner menus €49/130, mains €56-65; ⊙12.15-2pm & 7-9pm Tue-Sat; Ⓜ Solférino) Like the neighbouring Musée d'Orsay, this is a magnificent art nouveau treasure. Once a 1905-built former home for female telephone, telegram and postal workers, it features soaring vaulted ceilings and original stained glass, along with a lunchtime summer garden and glassed-in winter garden. Exquisite Michelin-starred dishes complement its 150-page list of wines, sparkling wines and whiskies purely from the Burgundy region.

PLUME   BISTRO €€€

Map p406 (☑01 43 06 79 85; www.restaurant-plume.com; 24 rue Pierre Leroux, 7e; lunch menus €27-37, dinner menus €45-65; ⊙noon-2.15pm & 7.30-10.15pm Tue-Sat; Ⓜ Vaneau, Duroc) A minimalist, 1950s ambience cocoons discerning diners at Plume ('Feather'), the stylish

neobistro of talented young Tunisian chef Youssef Gastli. His modern French cuisine is considered as a *cuisine d'instinct* ('instinctive cuisine'), based on seasonal, top-quality produce. It's complemented by a fantastic wine list featuring wholly organic, biodynamic or natural wines.

🍷 DRINKING & NIGHTLIFE

St-Germain's Carrefour de l'Odéon has a cluster of lively bars and cafes. Rues de Buci, St-André des Arts and de l'Odéon enjoy a fair slice of night action with arty cafes and busy pubs, while place St-Germain des Prés buzzes with the pavement terraces of fabled literary cafes. Rue Princesse and rue Guisarde attract a student crowd with their bevy of pubs, microbreweries and cocktail bars.

Les Invalides is a daytime rather than a night-time venue, with government ministries and embassies outweighing drinking venues. Particularly in summer, however, look out for bars along the Seine's river banks in the Parc Rives de Seine (p233).

🍷 St-Germain

⭐ LES DEUX MAGOTS   CAFE

Map p402 (☑01 45 48 55 25; www.lesdeuxmagots.cafe; 6 place St-Germain des Prés, 6e; ⊙7.30am-1am; Ⓜ St-Germain des Prés) If ever there was a cafe that summed up St-Germain des Prés' early-20th-century literary scene, it's this former hang-out of anyone who was anyone. You'll spend substantially more here to sip *un café* (€4.80) in a wicker chair on the pavement terrace shaded by dark-green awnings, but it's an undeniable piece of Parisian history.

⭐ AU SAUVIGNON   WINE BAR

Map p402 (☑01 45 48 49 02; www.ausauvignon.com; 80 rue des Sts-Pères, 7e; ⊙8am-11pm Mon-Sat, 9am-10pm Sun; Ⓜ Sèvres-Babylone) Grab a table in the evening light at this wonderfully authentic wine bar or head to the quintessential bistro interior, with original zinc bar, tightly packed tables and hand-painted ceiling celebrating French viticultural tradition. A *casse-croûtes au pain*

Poilâne (gourmet sandwich) is the perfect accompaniment.

★ LE BAR DES PRÉS COCKTAIL BAR

Map p402 (☎01 43 25 87 67; www.lebardespres.com; 25 rue du Dragon, 6e; ⏱noon-2.30pm & 7-11pm; ⓂSt-Sulpice) Sake-based craft cocktails and tantalising shared plates (from €20) by a Japanese chef create buzz at the chic cocktail-bar arm of Cyril Lignac's foodie empire on rue du Dragon – his glam, 1950s-styled bistro (p238) is right next door.

COD HOUSE COCKTAIL BAR

Map p402 (☎01 42 49 35 59; www.thecodhouse.fr; 1 rue de Condé, 6e; ⏱noon-2.30pm & 7.30-11pm; ⓂOdéon) 'Oh my cod!' screams the turquoise-neon 'tag' on the wall, and indeed, this Japanese-inspired cocktail and tapas bar with eggshell-blue and exposed-stone interior does excite. Sake-based cocktails play around with matcha-infused cachaça, ginger-infused pisco, homemade lemongrass syrup and fresh yuzu. Creative small plates (from €5) might include salmon in ponzu sauce and fried octopus in tonkatsu sauce.

TIGER COCKTAIL BAR

Map p402 (www.tiger-paris.com; 13 rue Princesse, 6e; ⏱6.30pm-2am; 🛜; ⓂMabillon) Suspended bare-bulb lights and fretted timber make this split-level space a stylish spot for specialist gins (100 varieties), including a devilish Opposite Attraction (gin, chocolate, almonds and orange). Dedicated G&T aficionados can work their way through a staggering 1040 combinations. Gin aside, Tiger serves Japanese sake, wine and craft beer. DJs play some evenings.

CAFÉ DE FLORE CAFE

Map p402 (☎01 45 48 55 26; www.cafedeflore.fr; 172 bd St-Germain, 6e; ⏱7.30am-1.30am; ⓂSt-Germain des Prés) The red upholstered benches, mirrors and marble walls at this art deco landmark haven't changed much since the days when Jean-Paul Sartre and Simone de Beauvoir essentially set up office here, writing in its warmth during the Nazi occupation.

BAR DU MARCHÉ BAR

Map p402 (☎01 43 26 55 15; 75 rue de Seine, 6e; ⏱8am-2am; ⓂMabillon) Yes, the waiters are dressed like *titis parisiens* (hat and overalls) in this busy place in the heart of the 6e. Far from being a tourist trap, this popular bar with a vintage feel attracts a mixed crowd and is a perfect spot to tipple happily on a beer or a glass of wine, which can be accompanied by bistro food if you like.

CASTOR CLUB COCKTAIL BAR

Map p402 (☎09 50 64 99 38; 14 rue Hautefeuille, 6e; ⏱7pm-2am Tue & Wed, to 4am Thu-Sat; ⓂOdéon) Discreetly signed, this superb underground cocktail bar has an intimate English gentleman's club–style upstairs bar with vintage wall lamps and slinky, red velour stools. But it's downstairs, in the 18th-century stone cellar with hole-in-the-wall booths, that the real cocktail-sipping action happens. Blues tracks add to the already cool vibe.

LA PALETTE CAFE

Map p402 (☎01 43 26 68 15; www.lapalette-paris.com; 43 rue de Seine, 6e; ⏱8am-2am Mon-Sat, from 10am Sun; 🛜; ⓂMabillon) In the heart of gallery land, this timeless *fin-de-siècle* cafe and erstwhile stomping ground of Paul Cézanne and Georges Braque attracts a grown-up set of fashion-industry professionals and local art dealers. Its summer terrace is beautiful but overcrowded.

FRAPPÉ PAR BLOOM CAFE

Map p402 (☎07 89 83 79 58; http://frappe.bloom-restaurant.fr; 2 rue Guénégaud, 6e; ⏱11am-7pm Tue-Sun; ⓂPont Neuf) In keeping with Paris' penchant for stylish museum eateries, its 18th-century mint sports a super-stylish cafe–cocktail bar with a designer interior and one of the city's loveliest summertime terraces – in the Cour de la Méridienne, one of the Monnaie de Paris' elegant neoclassical courtyards. It's also a great restaurant, serving tasty dishes made with seasonal produce.

PRESCRIPTION COCKTAIL CLUB COCKTAIL BAR

Map p402 (☎09 50 35 72 87; www.experimentalgroup.com; 23 rue Mazarine, 6e; ⏱7pm-2am Mon-Thu, 7pm-4am Fri & Sat, 8pm-2am Sun; ⓂOdéon) With bowler and flat-top hats as lampshades and a 1930s speakeasy New York air to the place, this cocktail club – run by the same mega-successful team as Experimental Cocktail Club (p127) – is very Parisian-cool.

Getting past the door attendants can be tough, but once in, it's friendliness and old-fashioned cocktails all round.

LA CAVE DES CLIMATS   WINE BAR

Map p402 (☎01 42 33 87 94; www.lacavedes
climats.fr; 35 rue de Verneuil, 7e; ⏱3-10.45pm
Tue-Fri, from noon Sat; Ⓜ Rue du Bac) A wine-
taster's fantasy, this upmarket and convivial *cave à manger* (wine shop where you can
drink and dine) features a great variety of
references, with an emphasis on Burgundy
wines (by the bottle or full glass to suit all
budgets). It also serves up inventive platters
(from €12) in a warm atmosphere. Check
the website for tasting sessions (€50).

LE GATSBY   LOUNGE

Map p406 (☎01 45 55 02 79; www.legatsby.fr;
64 av Bosquet, 7e; ⏱6.30pm-1.30am; Ⓜ Ecole
Militaire) This elegant cocktail bar has an
intimate vibe upstairs with wood panels,
vintage wall lamps and comfy armchairs.
It's even more inviting downstairs in the
vaulted cellar, where it's easy to be a little
overwhelmed by the discreet charm of another era. Enjoy expertly crafted cocktails
(from €12).

AUGUSTIN MARCHAND D'VINS   WINE BAR

Map p402 (☎09 81 21 76 21; www.facebook.
com/augustinmarchanddvins; 26 rue des Grands
Augustins, 6e; ⏱6-11pm Tue-Fri, from 11am Sat
& Sun; Ⓜ Odéon) At a prime address in the
6e, Augustin is a trendy lair for chilled-out
drinking. Enjoy the decor – dim lighting,
stone walls and beamed ceilings – and the
superb wines on offer, some of which are
available by the glass (from €7). If you have
the munchies, order a delicious platter of
charcuterie or cheese (from €10).

🍷 Les Invalides

★COUTUME CAFÉ   COFFEE

Map p406 (☎09 88 40 47 99; www.coutumecafe.
com; 47 rue de Babylone, 7e; ⏱8.30am-5.30pm
Mon-Fri, 9am-6pm Sat & Sun; 📶; Ⓜ St-François
Xavier) 🌱 The Parisian coffee revolution is
thanks in no small part to Coutume, artisanal roaster of premium beans for scores
of establishments around town. Its flagship
cafe – a light-filled, post-industrial space –
is ground zero for innovative preparation
methods, including cold extraction and si-
phon brews.

THE CLUB   COCKTAIL BAR

Map p406 (☎01 45 50 31 54; www.the-club.fr; 24
rue Surcouf, 7e; ⏱4pm-1.30am Mon-Sat; Ⓜ La
Tour-Maubourg) At street level The Club has

New York–warehouse brickwork and big
timber cabinets, but the lounge-like basement, strewn with red and black sofas, is
even cooler. Cocktails include the house-
speciality Club (lime, fresh ginger and
Jack Daniels honey liqueur) and seasonally
changing creations (from €12). Finger food
is available too.

☆ ENTERTAINMENT

St-Germain and especially Les Invalides
aren't major nightlife destinations –
eating, drinking and, above all, shopping
are the main entertainments here. For
live music, check for events in bars
along Les Berges de Seine (p233) or
head to the Latin Quarter or the floating
nightclubs in the 13e.

CHEZ PAPA   JAZZ

Map p402 (☎01 42 86 99 63; www.papajazzclub-
paris.fr; 3 rue St-Benoît, 6e; ⏱concerts 8.30pm-
1.30am Tue-Sat; Ⓜ St-Germain des Prés) The
doors of this snug New York–style jazz club
regularly stay open until dawn. Piano du-
ets, blues, sax solos and singers feature on
the bill from 8.30pm or 9pm. Its restaurant
serves traditional French dishes (snails, tartare, veal stew).

🛍 SHOPPING

The northern wedge of the 6e between
Église St-Germain des Prés and the
Seine is a dream to mooch around with
its bijou art galleries, antique shops,
stylish vintage clothes shops and
designer boutiques (Vanessa Bruno,
Isabel Marant et al). St-Germain's style
continues along the western half of
bd St-Germain and rue du Bac with a
striking collection of contemporary
furniture, kitchen and design shops.
Gourmet food and wine shops galore
make it a foodie's paradise.

🛍 St-Germain

GALERIE TEO LEO   ANTIQUES

Map p402 (☎01 42 61 64 01; www.teoleo-galerie.
com; 37 rue de Verneuil, 7e; ⏱11.30am-7pm Tue-
Sat; Ⓜ Rue du Bac) Not your average antique
shop, Galerie Teo Leo is a treasure trove of

lovingly selected pieces from the the the 1940s to the present day. Items are all collected by gallerist Laurent di Benedetto and include groovy lamps, mirrors, furniture, ceramics and plenty of unique decorative objects.

LE SLIP FRANÇAIS CLOTHING
Map p402 (☎01 45 38 90 56; www.leslipfrancais. com; 20 rue du Vieux Colombier, 6e; ☉10am-7.30pm Mon-Sat; MSaint-Sulpice) A great success story, this outlet in the heart of a chic neighbourhood began as a start-up a few years ago. The French Underwear is known for its instantly identifiable colours and patterns. All items – briefs, underwear, pyjamas, shorts, jerseys and accessories, for men and women – sold in this playful boutique are designed and made in France.

BONNE GUEULE CLOTHING
Map p402 (☎01 43 25 39 89; www.bonnegueule. fr; 4 rue Madame, 6e; ☉10.30am-7.30pm Mon-Sat; MSaint-Sulpice) At the beginning, Bonne Gueule was just a men's fashion blog. It's now a one-stop shop for men's fashion that has become something of an institution among Parisian hipsters. Whether you crave cutting-edge or classic, new or established, this is prime territory. The welcome is warm and the staff are genuinely enthusiastic about helping customers put an outfit together.

CIRE TRUDON GIFTS & SOUVENIRS
Map p402 (☎01 43 26 46 50; www.trudon.com; 78 rue de Seine, 6e; ☉11am-7pm Mon, 10.30am-7.30pm Tue-Sat; MOdéon) Claude Trudon began selling candles here in 1643, and the company – which officially supplied Versailles and Napoléon with light – is now the world's oldest candle-maker (look for the plaque to the left of the shop's royal-blue awning). A rainbow of candles and candlesticks fill the shelves inside.

HERMÈS
PARIS SÈVRES FASHION & ACCESSORIES
Map p402 (☎01 42 22 80 83; www.hermes.com; 17 rue de Sèvres, 6e; ☉10.30am-7pm Mon-Sat; MSèvres-Babylone) A stunning art deco swimming pool (originally belonging to neighbouring Hôtel Lutetia) now houses luxury label Hermès' inaugural concept store. Retaining its mosaic tiles and iron balustrades, the vast, tiered space showcases new directions in home furnishings, including fabrics and wallpaper, along with classic lines such as its signature scarves. Its cafe, Le Plongeoir (the Diving Board), is equally chic.

ART & ANTIQUE STREETS

St-Germain's narrow streets are filled with art and antique shops.

Meander along rue Mazarine, rue Jacques Callot, rue des Beaux Arts and rue de Seine for art galleries.

Edgier galleries include **Galerie Loft** (Map p402; ☎01 46 33 18 90; www.galerie loft.com; 3bis rue des Beaux Arts, 6e; ☉10am-1pm & 2.30-6pm Tue-Fri, 10.30am-1pm & 2.30-6pm Sat; MSt-Germain des Prés), with all forms of art (digital video and performance photography included) by contemporary Chinese artists on show at this courtyard gallery.

Art and antique dealers congregate within the **Carré Rive Gauche**. Bounded by quai Voltaire and rues de l'Université, des St-Pères and du Bac, this 'Left Bank Square' is home to more than 120 specialised merchants. Antiques fairs are usually held in spring, while exhibitions take place during the year.

LA DERNIÈRE GOUTTE WINE
Map p402 (☎01 43 29 11 62; www.ldgparis.com; 6 rue du Bourbon le Château, 6e; ☉3.30-8pm Mon, 10.30am-1.30pm & 3-8pm Tue-Fri, 10.30am-8pm Sat, 11am-7pm Sun; MMabillon) 'The Last Drop' is the brainchild of Cuban-American sommelier Juan Sánchez, whose tiny wine shop is packed with exciting, mostly organic French *vins de propriétaires* (estate-bottled wines) made by small independent producers. Wine classes lasting two hours (two white tastings, five red) regularly take place in English (per person €55); it also hosts free tastings with winemakers most Saturdays.

LE BAZAR FRANÇAIS CONCEPT STORE
Map p406 (☎07 56 80 33 90; www.lebazarfran cais.com; 24 rue de l'Abbé Grégoire, 6e; ☉11am-7pm Mon-Sat; MSèvres-Babylone) All pieces – fashion, homewares, jewellery, accessories – are designed and made in France in this charming boutique that started as an e-shop. A great place to stock up on original, quality gifts.

FERMOB HOMEWARES
Map p402 (☎01 45 44 10 28; www.fermob.com; 17 bd Raspail, 7e; ☉10am-7pm Mon-Sat; MRue du Bac) Fermob is famed for manufacturing iconic French garden furniture, including the Jardin du Luxembourg's signature

LOCAL KNOWLEDGE

SECONDHAND CHIC

When St-Germain's well-heeled residents spring-clean their wardrobes, they take their designer and vintage cast-offs to *dépôt-vente* (secondhand) boutiques, where savvy locals snap up serious bargains. Try your luck at the following addresses:

Catherine B (Map p402; ☑01 43 54 74 18; www.les3marchesdecatherineb.com; 1 rue Guisarde, 6e; ☺11am-1.30pm & 2.30-7pm Tue-Sat; ⓂMabillon) Serious fans of Chanel and Hermès should call into this exceptionally curated boutique, which specialises exclusively in items from these two iconic French fashion houses.

Chercheminippes (Map p406; www.chercheminippes.fr; 102 rue du Cherche Midi, 6e; ☺11am-7pm Mon-Sat; ⓂVaneau) Scoop up secondhand designer women's casual wear at this fashion-chic boutique. Sister boutiques scattered along the same street specialise in homewares (No 104), womenswear (No 109), women's accessories (No 110), menswear (No 111) and women's *haute couture* (No 114).

Le Dépôt-Vente de Buci (Map p402; ☑01 46 34 28 28; 4 rue Bourbon le Château, 6e; ☺9am-noon & 2-6pm Tue-Sat; ⓂMabillon) The boutique to hit for stylish 1960s vintage.

sage-green chairs, actually available in a spectacular rainbow of colours for your own garden or terrace. It also sells lovely cushions and lamps. Fermob has another branch across the river near Bastille.

FINGER IN THE NOSE
CHILDREN, FASHION

Map p402 (☑09 83 01 76 75; www.fingerinthe nose.com; 11 rue de l'Échaudé, 6e; ☺11am-7.30pm Tue-Sat; ⓂMabillon) This finger-on-the-pulse Parisian children's-wear label thumbs its nose at convention and offers edgy streetwear for kids, such as graphic T-shirts, fleeces and jackets along with sophisticated twists like its line of LBDs ('little black dresses') for teenage girls.

MARCHÉ RASPAIL
MARKET

Map p406 (bd Raspail, btwn rue de Rennes & rue du Cherche Midi, 6e; ☺7am-2.30pm Tue & Fri, organic market 9am-1.30pm Sun; ⓂRennes) 🌿 A traditional open-air market on Tuesday and Friday, Marché Raspail is especially popular on Sunday, when it's filled with *biologique* (organic) produce.

SABBIA ROSA
FASHION & ACCESSORIES

Map p402 (☑01 45 48 88 37; www.instagram. com/sabbiarosaparis; 73 rue des Sts-Pères, 6e; ☺10am-7pm Mon-Sat; ⓂSt-Germain des Prés) Only French-sourced fabrics (silk from Lyon, lace from Calais) are used by lingerie designer Sabbia Rosa for her ultra-luxe range at this boutique, open since 1976. Every piece is unique; items can be custommade in 48 hours. The list of clients reads like a who's who: Serge Gainsbourg, Madonna, Naomi Campbell, Claudia Schiffer and George Clooney have all shopped here.

CAFÉ PIERRE HERMÉ
FOOD

Map p402 (☑01 82 73 25 15; www.pierreherme. com; 61 rue Bonaparte, 6e; ☺9am-8pm; ⓂOdéon) Leading *pâtissier* and chocolatier Pierre Hermé has several boutiques and cafes in Paris, including this branch in the heart of St-Germain. It's a veritable feast of perfectly presented cakes, chocolates, *millefeuilles*, tarts, nougats, jams and dazzling macarons. Oh, and the hot chocolate is so thick. You can eat in or take away.

SMALLABLE
CONCEPT STORE
CHILDREN'S CLOTHING

Map p406 (☑01 40 46 01 15; www.smallable. com; 81 rue du Cherche Midi, 6e; ☺2-7.30pm Mon, from 10.30am Tue-Sat; ⓂVaneau) 'Dream big' is the inviting strapline of this Parisian-chic space, a one-stop shop for accessories, fashion and homewares for babies, children and teens. It stocks regularly changing premium brands. You can also buy exquisite cushions and linens.

🏛 Les Invalides

★LE BON MARCHÉ
DEPARTMENT STORE

Map p406 (☑01 44 39 81 81; www.24s.com; 24 rue de Sèvres, 7e; ☺10am-7.45pm Mon-Sat, from 11am Sun; ⓂSèvres-Babylone) Built by Gustave Eiffel as Paris' first department store in 1852, this is the epitome of style, with a superb concentration of men's and women's fashions, homewares, stationery, books and toys. Break for a coffee, afternoon tea or a light lunch at the Rose Bakery tearoom on the 2nd floor. The icing on the cake is the glorious food hall.

★LA GRANDE
ÉPICERIE DE PARIS   FOOD & DRINKS
Map p406 (☑01 44 39 81 00; www.lagrandeep-
icerie.com; 38 rue de Sèvres, 7e; ⊘8.30am-9pm
Mon-Sat, 10am-8pm Sun; ⓂSèvres-Babylone)
The magnificent food hall of department
store Le Bon Marché sells 30,000 rare and/
or luxury gourmet products, including 60
different types of bread baked on-site. Its
fantastical displays of chocolates, pastries,
biscuits, cheeses, fresh fruit and vegetables
and deli goods are a sight in themselves.

It also has plenty of organic products.

MAGASIN SENNELIER   ARTS & CRAFTS
Map p402 (☑01 42 60 72 15; www.magasinsennelier.
art; 3 quai Voltaire, 7e; ⊘2-6.30pm Mon, 10am-
12.45pm & 2-6.30pm Tue-Sat; ⓂSt-Germain des
Prés) Cézanne and Picasso were among the
artists who helped develop products for
this venerable 1887-founded art supplier
on the banks of the Seine, and it remains
an exceptional place to pick up canvases,
brushes, watercolours, oils, pastels, charcoals and more. The shop's forest-green
façade with gold lettering, exquisite original timber cabinetry and glass display
cases also fuel artistic inspiration.

CANTIN   CHEESE
Map p406 (☑01 45 50 43 94; www.cantin.fr; 12
rue du Champs de Mars, 7e; ⊘8.30am-5pm Tue-
Sat; ⓂÉcole Militaire) 🍃 Opened in 1950 and
still run by the same family today, this exceptional shop stocks cheeses only made
in limited quantities on small rural farms.
They're then painstakingly ripened in Cantin's own cellars (from two weeks up to two
years) before being displayed for sale.

POILÂNE   FOOD €
Map p402 (☑01 45 48 42 59; www.poilane.com;
8 rue du Cherche Midi, 6e; breads €3.80-12;
⊘7.15am-8pm Mon-Sat; ⓂSèvres-Babylone)
Pierre Poilâne opened his *boulangerie* (bakery) upon arriving from Normandy in 1932.
Today his granddaughter Apollonia runs
the company, which still turns out wood-
fired, rounded sourdough loaves made with
stone-milled flour and Guérande sea salt.

A clutch of other outlets includes one in
the 15e.

ST-GERMAIN & LES INVALIDES SHOPPING

Montparnasse & Southern Paris

MONTPARNASSE | CHINATOWN | PLACE D'ITALIE | 13E | 14E | 15E

Neighbourhood Top Five

❶ Les Catacombes (p248) Prowling the spine-prickling, skull-and-bone-packed subterranean tunnels of Paris' creepy ossuary.

❷ Butte aux Cailles (p251) Soaking up the village-like atmosphere of this compact area off place d'Italie, where cobblestoned streets are lined with quaint houses.

❸ Cimetière du Montparnasse (p249) Visiting the resting places of local luminaries, including Jean-Paul Sartre, Simone de Beauvoir and Serge Gainsbourg.

❹ Île aux Cygnes (p250) Traversing the tiny, tree-lined inner-city island from the Statue of Liberty replica towards the Eiffel Tower.

❺ Petite Ceinture du 15e (p256) Exploring Paris' former steam railway line on a reclaimed parkland stretch.

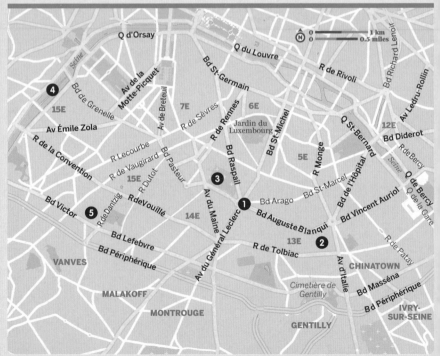

For more detail of this area see Map p412 and p414.

Explore Montparnasse & Southern Paris

Here are the cafes, brasseries and backstreets, now swathed by urban grit, where some of the early-20th-century's most seminal artists and writers hung out. The area's tree-filled cemetery is a peaceful spot to escape to – and to visit the graves of many of those same visionaries.

West in the tranquil 15e, take in more great views by strolling Île aux Cygnes (p250) or boarding a balloon 'flight' in the Parc André-Citroën, one of Paris' most innovative open spaces. Other wonderful local parks in this greenified area include Parc Georges Brassens (p253), with rose gardens and even an apiary, as well as a stretch of the former Petite Ceinture (p256) steam railway line.

To Montparnasse's east, the ever-regenerating 13e is home to the country's national library, Paris' largest Chinatown, some typical village-like areas such as La Butte aux Cailles (p251), some striking street art and even more stunning contemporary (and increasingly sustainable) architecture, including the world's largest start-up incubator, aka the mind-blowing Station F (p252).

The entire area is strewn with exciting neobistros. No matter where you end up for dinner in this sprawling southern sector of Paris, head back to the river to dance until dawn on the floating bars and nightclubs moored on the Seine's quays.

Local Life

Street life Join locals shopping for flowers, cheese, charcuterie and more along traditional commercial street rue Daguerre.

Breton life Take a crêperie crawl through Montparnasse's 'Little Brittany'.

Serene streets Explore the Cité Florale (p251).

Street art Delve in at Galerie Itinerrance (p251).

Getting There & Away

Metro Montparnasse Bienvenüe is the metro hub for Montparnasse and the 15e. Bibliothèque François-Miterrand and Place d'Italie are convenient 13e stops.

Bus Buses fill the gap in areas lacking comprehensive metro coverage. From Gare Montparnasse, bus 91 goes to Bastille. Bus 62 travels from Bibliothèque François-Mitterrand to Javel via the southern *quartiers*. Bus 21 runs from Glacière to Chatelet. Bus 39 links Balard with Gare du Nord via Gare Montparnasse.

Bicycle Handy Vélib' stations include 5-7 rue d'Odessa, 14e; 13 bd Edgar Quinet, 14e; 2 av René Coty, 14e; and two facing place d'Italie, 13e.

Boat The hop-on, hop-off Batobus has a dock at quai St-Bernard, 5e (near quai d'Austerlitz, 13e).

Lonely Planet's Top Tip

The metro is tailor-made for cross-town trips, but to whizz around Paris' perimeter, hop on the T3 tram. From the Pont du Garigliano, 15e, it currently skims the city's edge as far as Porte d'Asnières, 17e. An extension to Porte Dauphine, 16e, is due for completion in 2023, encircling some three-quarters of the city. Passengers use standard t+ tickets. For updates on Paris' trams, visit www.tramway.paris.fr.

MONTPARNASSE & SOUTHERN PARIS

✕ Best Places to Eat

➡ Marso & Co (p257)
➡ Le Beurre Noisette (p254)
➡ Le Cassenoix (p254)
➡ L'Accolade (p255)
➡ Simone Le Resto (p257)
➡ La Tropicale (p256)

For reviews, see p253. ➡

🍷 Best Places to Drink

➡ Poinçon (p258)
➡ Café Oz Rooftop (p253)
➡ La Dame de Canton (p259)

For reviews, see p258. ➡

🔒 Best Shopping

➡ Storie (p260)
➡ Biérocratie (p261)
➡ Adam Montparnasse (p260)
➡ Marché aux Puces de la Porte de Vanves (p260)
➡ La Cave des Papilles (p260)

For reviews, see p259. ➡

TOP EXPERIENCE
SPOOK YOURSELF IN LES CATACOMBES

It is gruesome, ghoulish and downright spooky, but it remains one of Paris' most visited sights. In 1785 subterranean tunnels of an abandoned quarry were upcycled as storage rooms for the exhumed bones of corpses that could no longer fit in the city's overcrowded cemeteries. By 1810 the skull- and bone-lined catacombs – resting place of millions of anonymous Parisians – had been officially born.

The route through Les Catacombes begins at its spacious 2018-opened entrance av du Colonel Henri Rol-Tanguy. Walk down 131 spiral steps to reach the ossuary itself, with a mind-boggling amount of bones and skulls of millions of Parisians neatly packed along the walls. Visits cover about 1.5km of tunnels in all, at a cool 14°C.

The exit is up 112 steps via a minimalist all-white 'transition space' with gift shop at 21bis av René Coty, 14e. Bag searches are carried out to prevent visitors 'souveniring' bones.

Bear in mind that this tour is not suitable for young children or the squeamish; under 14s must be accompanied by an adult.

It's also important to keep in mind that visiting the Catacombes is not for everybody. People with claustrophobia may experience some anxiety in the confined environment. Also note that the Catacombes are not wheelchair accessible – there's no lift and no ramp, only stairs.

DID YOU KNOW?

During WWII the Resistance held meetings in these tunnels. Today, at night, thrill-seeking cataphiles roam the tunnels illegally.

PRACTICALITIES

➜ Map p412, F4

➜ ☎01 43 22 47 63

➜ www.catacombes. paris.fr

➜ 1 av du Colonel Henri Rol-Tanguy, 14e

➜ adult/child €14/free, online booking incl audioguide from €24/5

➜ ⏱9.45am-8.30pm Tue-Sun, last admission 7.30pm

➜ ⓂDenfert-Rochereau

👁 SIGHTS

This vast swath of southern Paris is a perfect place to explore if you're looking for a local experience away from the tourist crowds. There are some big-hitting sights here, too, from the creepy skull-and-bone-packed underground tunnels of Les Catacombes to France's national library, Bibliothèque Nationale de France, and the world's largest campus for start-ups, Station F.

👁 Montparnasse & 15e

LES CATACOMBES CEMETERY
See p248.

MUSÉE DE LA LIBÉRATION DE PARIS – MUSÉE DU GÉNÉRAL LECLERC – MUSÉE JEAN MOULIN MUSEUM
Map p412 (☑01 40 64 39 44; www.museeliberation-leclerc-moulin.paris.fr; 4 av du Colonel Henri Rol-Tanguy, 14e; ◷10am-6pm Tue-Sun; ⓜDenfert-Rochereau) FREE This history museum is devoted to the WWII German occupation of Paris, with its focus on the Resistance and its leader, Jean Moulin

(1899–1943), Free French general Philippe François Marie Leclerc de Hauteclocque, and the Liberation of Paris in August 1944. Chronologically arranged displays include clothing, equipment, personal items and photographs. Opened on 25 August 2019 – the 75th anniversary of the city's liberation – it's housed in the Ledoux pavilions, built in 1787 by architect Claude-Nicolas Ledoux, opposite Les Catacombes.

TOUR MONTPARNASSE VIEWPOINT
Map p412 (www.tourmontparnasse56.com; 33 av du Maine, 15e; adult/child €18/9.50; ◷9.30am-11.30pm Apr-Sep, to 10.30pm Oct-Mar; ⓜMontparnasse Bienvenüe) Spectacular views unfold from this 210m-high smoked-glass-and-steel office block, built in 1973. A 38-second elevator ride whisks visitors up to the indoor observatory on the 56th floor. Finish with a hike up the stairs to the 59th-floor open-air terrace (with a sheltered walkway) and Champagne bar. The building will be closing for a four-year makeover in late 2022.

MUSÉE BOURDELLE MUSEUM
Map p412 (☑01 49 54 73 73; www.bourdelle.paris.fr; 18 rue Antoine Bourdelle, 15e; ◷10am-6pm Tue-Sun; ⓜFalguière) FREE Monumental

---

👁 TOP EXPERIENCE
VISIT THE GRAVES OF LUMINARIES

Opened in 1824, **Cimetière du Montparnasse**, Paris' second-largest cemetery after Père Lachaise, sprawls over 19 hectares shaded by 1200 trees, including maples, ash, limes and conifers. Some of the illustrious 'residents' at Cimetière du Montparnasse include poet **Charles Baudelaire** (No 14, division 6), writer Guy de Maupassant, playwright **Samuel Beckett** (No 66, division 12), painter Chaim Soutine, photographer Man Ray, industrialist André Citroën, sculptor Constantin Brancusi, Captain Alfred Dreyfus of the infamous Dreyfus Affair, and philosophers, writers and life partners **Jean-Paul Sartre** and **Simone de Beauvoir** (No 1, division 20), who are buried together right next to the cemetery entrance on bd Edgar Quinet.

Like Père Lachaise, Cimetière du Montparnasse has its time-honoured tomb traditions. One of the most popular is fans leaving metro tickets atop the grave of crooner **Serge Gainsbourg** (No 60, division 1), in reference to his 1958 song 'Le Poinçonneur des Lilas' (The Ticket Puncher of Lilas), depicting work-a-day monotony through the eyes of a metro ticket-puncher. Gainsbourg enacted the soul-destroying job (since eclipsed by machines) on film when recording the song in the Porte des Lilas station.

DON'T MISS

➡ Serge Gainsbourg
➡ Jean-Paul Sartre and Simone de Beauvoir
➡ Charles Baudelaire
➡ Samuel Beckett

PRACTICALITIES

➡ Map p412, E3
➡ www.paris.fr
➡ 3 bd Edgar Quinet, 14e
➡ admission free
➡ ◷8am-5.30pm Mon-Fri, 8.30am-5.30pm Sat, 9am-5.30pm Sun
➡ ⓜEdgar Quinet

RUE DAGUERRE

Paris' traditional village atmosphere thrives along rue Daguerre, 14e.

Tucked just southwest of the Denfert-Rochereau metro and RER stations, this narrow street – pedestrianised between av du Général-Leclerc and rue Boulard – is lined with florists, *fromageries* (cheese shops), *boulangeries* (bakeries), patisseries, greengrocers, delis (including Greek, Asian and Italian) and classic cafes where you can watch the local goings on.

Shops set up market stalls on the pavement; Sunday mornings are especially lively. It's a great option for lunch before or after visiting Les Catacombes, or packing a picnic to take to one of the area's parks or squares.

bronzes fill the house and workshop where sculptor Antoine Bourdelle (1861–1929), a pupil of Rodin, lived and worked. The three sculpture gardens are particularly lovely, with a flavour of Belle Époque and post-WWI Montparnasse. The museum usually has a temporary exhibition (adult/child from €8/free) going on alongside its free permanent collection. You can rent an audioguide at reception (€5).

INSTITUT GIACOMETTI   MUSEUM

Map p412 (www.fondation-giacometti.fr; 5 rue Victor Schoelcher, 14e; adult/child €8.50/3; 10am-6pm Tue-Sun; Raspail) Opened in 2018, this museum housed in the former studio of artist Paul Follot, in a gold-tiled art deco private mansion (a listed historical monument), is dedicated to Swiss artist Alberto Giacometti (1901–66), who lived and worked in the area. The 350-sq-metre space has a reconstruction of Giacometti's studio, along with 350 of his sculptures, 90 of his paintings and over 2000 of his drawings. Admission is by prior online reservation only; you can't just turn up. Three to four temporary exhibitions take place per year.

FONDATION CARTIER
POUR L'ART CONTEMPORAIN   GALLERY

Map p412 (0142185650; www.fondation.cartier. com; 261 bd Raspail, 14e; adult/child €10.50/7; 11am-10pm Tue, to 8pm Wed-Sun; Raspail) Designed by Jean Nouvel, this stunning glass-and-steel building is a work of art in itself. It hosts temporary exhibits on contemporary art (from the 1980s to today) in a diverse variety of media – from painting and photography to video and fashion, as well as performance art. Artist Lothar Baumgarten created the wonderfully rambling garden.

PARC ANDRÉ CITROËN   PARK

Map p414 (2 rue Cauchy, 15e; 8am-9.30pm Mon-Fri, from 9am Sat & Sun May-Aug, shorter hours rest of year; ; Javel–André Citroën, RER Javel) In 1915 automotive entrepreneur André Citroën built a vast car manufacturing plant here in the 15e. After it closed in the 1970s, the vacated site was eventually turned into this forward-looking 14-hectare urban park. Its central lawn is flanked by greenhouses, dancing fountains, an elevated reflecting pool, and smaller gardens themed around movement and the (six) senses. The helium-filled sightseeing balloon Ballon de Paris is located here. Check seasonal hours signposted at the entrances.

BALLON DE PARIS   VIEWPOINT

Map p414 (01 44 26 20 00; www.ballondeparis. com; 2 rue de la Montagne de la Fage, 15e; adult/child €15/8; 9am-9pm May-Aug, shorter hours Sep-Apr; Balard, Lourmel) Drift up and up but not away – this helium-filled balloon in Parc André Citroën remains tethered to the ground as it lifts you 150m into the air for spectacular panoramas over Paris. The balloon plays an active environmental role, changing colour depending on the air quality and pollution levels. From September to April, the last 'flight' is 30 minutes before the park closes. Confirm ahead any time of year as the balloon doesn't ascend in windy conditions.

ÎLE AUX CYGNES   ISLAND

Map p414 (Isle of Swans; btwn Pont de Grenelle & Pont de Bir Hakeim, 15e; Javel–André Citroën, Bir Hakeim) Paris' little-known third island, the artificially created Île aux Cygnes, was formed in 1827 to protect the river port and measures just 850m by 11m. On the western side of the Pont de Grenelle is a soaring one-quarter scale **Statue of Liberty replica** (Map p414), inaugurated in 1889. Walk east along the Allée des Cygnes – the tree-lined walkway that runs the length of the island – for knockout Eiffel Tower views.

⊙ Place d'Italie, Chinatown & Bibliothèque Nationale de France

LA BUTTE AUX CAILLES   AREA

Map p410 (13e; MPlace d'Italie) Much less touristy and congested than other Parisian villages such as Montmartre or Mouffetard, La Butte aux Cailles extends on a gently sloping hill immediately west of place d'Italie. Wandering its cobblestoned streets bordered by low-rise buildings, you'll feel teletransported to another era in rural France. Its main thoroughfare is rue de la Butte aux Cailles, lined with numerous laid-back bars, shops and restaurants, but all the adjacent streets are well worth a gander, as is the super relaxing Jardin Brassaï.

A few bijou streets to stroll include passage Boiton, rue des Cinq Diamants, rue Samson, rue Alphand, passage Sigaud, passage Barrault and rue Michal, as well as the adorable rue Daviel with the Petite Alsace (Little Alsace) enclave, complete with brick and timbered houses, and Villa Daviel, which is lined with superb houses and gardens.

CITÉ FLORALE   AREA

Map p410 (13e; MPlace d'Italie, RER Cité Universitaire) Is this southern Paris' best-kept secret? This micro-neighbourhood, a stone's throw east of Parc Montsouris, is a gem to wander. Built in the 1920s, the Floral City comprises five streets that were all named after flowers (Iris, Wisteria, Bindweed, Orchid, Volubilis). They are paved and flanked with small houses whose façades are covered with ivy, vines and flowers, which adds to the serene atmosphere. A superb place to explore early in the morning when everything seems to stand still.

GALERIE ITINERRANCE   GALLERY

(📞01 44 06 45 39; www.itinerrance.fr; 24bis bd du Général Jean Simon, 13e; ⊙noon-7pm Tue-Sat; MBibliothèque François-Mitterrand) FREE Testament to the 13e's ongoing creative renaissance, this gallery showcases graffiti and street art, and can advise on self-guided and guided street-art tours of the neighbourhood that take in many landmark works by artists represented by the gallery. Exhibitions and events change regularly.

BIBLIOTHÈQUE NATIONALE DE FRANCE   LIBRARY

Map p410 (📞01 53 79 59 59; www.bnf.fr; 11 quai François Mauriac, 13e; temporary exhibitions €9-11, reference library €3.90; ⊙2-8pm Mon, 9am-8pm Tue-Sat, 1-7pm Sun; MBibliothèque François-Mitterrand) With four glass towers shaped like half-open books, the National

---

MURAL-SPOTTING IN THE 13E

More than 30 giant-sized murals enliven streets and thoroughfares in an area between av de France, rue de Tolbiac and bd Vincent Auriol, with more added every year. Moseying past a few of these cheery murals is a great way to explore less-visited neighbourhoods. Some favourites include a colourful **fresco** (13 rue Lahire) by famous artist Inti, **Bach** (57 rue Clisson), the elaborate **Sun Daze** (167 bd Vincent Auriol) created by the talented twins How & Nosm and, on an adjacent building, a splendid portrait of a geisha-like **woman** (169 bd Vincent Auriol), by British artist Hush, **Le Chat** (corner bd Vincent Auriol and rue Nationale), and monumental **La Marianne** (186 rue Nationale), by Shepard Fairey, which represents the symbol of the French Republic.

Other great works to look for include the strikingly expressive **Turncoat** (190 rue Nationale), by D*Face (who is from London), and the equally stunning **Rise Above Level** (corner bd Auriol and rue Jeanne d'Arc), another massive mural by Shepard Fairey. On the opposite side of bd Vincent Auriol, you can't miss the awesome **Dancer** (98 bd Vincent Auriol), with a strapline ('Et J'ai Retenu Mon Souffle' – And I Hold My Breath), by the collective Faile.

Continue east along bd Auriol until you reach the Chevaleret metro station. Here you can enjoy the poignant **Etreinte et Lutte** (85 bd Vincent Auriol), by Conor Harrington, **Les Oiseaux** (The Birds; 91 bd Vincent Auriol), by Pantonio, and the monochromatic **Le Visage** (The Face; 6 rue Jenner), also by Pantonio. Oh, and there's another masterpiece created by Inti – **La Madone** (81 bd Vincent Auriol).

More information (and a map) can be found on www.boulevardparis13.com.

Library of France, opened in 1995, was one of President Mitterrand's most ambitious and costliest projects. Some 12 million tomes are stored on 420km of shelves and the library can accommodate 2000 readers and 2000 researchers. It also hosts excellent temporary exhibitions (entrance Est), mostly visual arts.

No expense was spared to carry out the library's grand design, which many claimed defied logic. Books and historical documents are shelved in the sunny, 23-storey, 79m-high towers, while patrons sit in artificially lit basement halls built around a 'forest courtyard' of 140 50-year-old pines, trucked in from the countryside.

GALERIE DES GOBELINS GALLERY

Map p410 (☑08 25 05 44 05; www.mobilier national.culture.gouv.fr; 42 av des Gobelins, 13e; adult/child €8/6; ⊙11am-6pm Tue-Sun; Ⓜ Les Gobelins) *Haute lisse* (high relief) tapestries have been woven on specialised looms at the Manufacture des Gobelins since the 18th century along with Beauvais-style *basse lisse* (low relief) tapestries and Savonnerie rugs. Superb examples of carpets and tapestries woven here are showcased in its gallery. It also hosts temporary exhibitions.

LES DOCKS CULTURAL CENTRE

Map p410 (Cité de la Mode et du Design; ☑01 76 77 25 30; www.citemodedesign.fr; 34 quai

---

PARIS RIVE GAUCHE

Paris' largest urban redevelopment since Haussmann's 19th-century reformation continues apace in the 13e *arrondissement* (city district). Centred on a once-nondescript area south of the Latin Quarter spiralling out from big busy traffic hub place d'Italie, the renaissance of the area known as Paris Rive Gauche was heralded in the 1990s by the controversial Bibliothèque Nationale de France (p251) and the arrival of the high-speed Météor metro line (now called line 14). They were followed, among other additions, by the **MK2** (Map p410; www.mk2.com; 128-162 av de France, 13e; adult/child €11.40/4.90; Ⓜ Bibliothèque) and EP7 (p259) entertainment complexes, the Piscine Joséphine Baker (p261) swimming pool and Off Paris Seine (p292) hotel – both afloat the Seine – and the **Passerelle Simone de Beauvoir** (2006), providing a cycle and pedestrian link to the Right Bank. And work isn't slated to stop for several more years.

Pivotal to this 130-hectare redevelopment zone is the **Paris 7** university campus hosting some 30,000 students. Other institutions to have moved in include the **Institut Français de la Mode** (the French fashion institute) in the stylised former warehouse Les Docks.

The area's mainline train station, Gare d'Austerlitz (p331), is undergoing a €600 million makeover by celebrated French architect Jean Nouvel. The station itself will be overhauled (including €200 million alone on the grand hall's glass roof, beneath which hot-air balloons were manufactured during the 1870 siege of Paris), and new shops, cafes and green spaces will open up in the surrounding streets. The renovation was due to wrap up in 2021 but was placed on hold at the time of writing.

Then there is **Station F** (Map p410; www.stationf.co; 5 Parvis Alan Turing, 13e; ⊙English-language tours by reservation 11.30am Tue & Thu; Ⓜ Chevaleret, Bibliothèque François-Mitterrand) **FREE**, the world's largest start-up campus, in business since mid-2017, where 3000 entrepreneurs from all over the globe dream up ground-breaking new projects and businesses, supported by 30 different incubators and accelerators. Guided tours take visitors on a 45-minute waltz through the gargantuan hangar – a railway depot built in 1927–29 to house trains from Gare de Austerlitz. Spaces open to the public include Station F's **Anticafé** co-working space where hipsters pay €5 per hour to eat, drink and hang out; and enormous Italian restaurant **La Felicità** (www.lafelicita.fr; 5 parvis Alan Turing, 13e; mains €7-18; ⊙12.15-2.30pm Mon & Tue, 12.15-2.30pm & 6-10.30pm Wed, 12.15-2.30pm & 6-11pm Thu & Fri, noon-11pm Sat, noon-10.30pm Sun; 🕾☑📶; Ⓜ BibliothèqueFrançois Mitterrand, Chevaleret), with five different kitchens, three bars and a twinset of original, graffiti-covered train wagons.

Track updates on this innovative area at www.parisrivegauche.com.

d'Austerlitz, 13e; ⊙10am-midnight; MGare d'Austerlitz) Framed by a lurid-lime wave-like glass façade, a transformed Seine-side warehouse is home to the French fashion institute, the **Institut Français de la Mode** (hence Les Docks' alternative name, Cité de la Mode et du Design), which mounts fashion and design exhibitions and events throughout the year. Other draws include huge riverside terraces, the odd pop-up shop and popular Australian rooftop bar **Café Oz Rooftop** (Map p410; ☑01 73 71 29 09; www.cafe-oz.com; ⊙5pm-2am Wed-Fri, from 4pm Sat).

PARC MONTSOURIS   PARK

Map p410 (av Reille, 14e; ⊙8am-9.30pm Mon-Fri, from 9am Sat & Sun May-Aug, shorter hours rest of year; MRER Cité-Universitaire) This sprawling lakeside park planted with horse-chestnut, yew, cedar, weeping beech and button-wood trees is a delightful picnic spot and has endearing playground areas. Tip: after your visit, wander the neighbouring 1920s-built Cité Universitaire (student halls of residence), south of the park, as well as rue Georges Braque, impasse Nansouty and rue du Parc de Montsouris, immediately to the west – with their paved roads and stately, ivy-clad houses, they offer a real sense of escape.

An abandoned section of the Petite Ceinture (p256) railway line runs through the park.

PARC GEORGES BRASSENS   PARK

Map p414 (2 place Jacques Marette, 15e; ⊙8am-9.30pm Mon-Fri, from 9am Sat & Sun May-Aug, shorter hours rest of year; MConvention, 🚲Georges Brassens) Covering 7.74 hectares, Parc Georges Brassens (named for the French singer-songwriter and poet, who lived nearby) has a large central pond bordered by lawns, and gardens featuring roses and medicinal and aromatic plants. The sloping hill is home to a wine-producing vineyard and an apiary. Also here is the **Monfort theatre** (look for the building with a conical roof) with dance, circus and theatre performances, and the weekend book market, **Marché Georges Brassens** (Map p414; www.marchedulivre-paris.fr; 104 rue Brancion, 15e; ⊙9am-6pm Sat & Sun; MPorte de Vanves).

🍴 EATING

Since the 1920s bd du Montparnasse has been one of the city's premier avenues for enjoying Parisian pavement life, with legendary brasseries and cafes.

The down-to-earth 15e cooks up fabulous bistro fare – along rues de la Convention, de Vaugirard, St-Charles and du Commerce, and south of bd de Grenelle.

In Chinatown, try av de Choisy, av d'Ivry and rue Baudricourt.

Villagey Butte aux Cailles, 13e, is chock-a-block with interesting addresses: rue de la Butte aux Cailles and rue des Cinq Diamants are the main foodie streets. Vibrant food markets fill the nearby bd Auguste Blanqui every Tuesday and Friday morning.

The up-and-coming area around Bibliothèque Nationale de France (check rue du Chevaleret and rue de Tolbiac) also has great eating options for all budgets.

🍴 Montparnasse & 15e

LE PETIT PAN   FRENCH €

Map p414 (☑01 42 50 04 04; www.lepetitpan.fr; 18 rue Rosenwald, 15e; 2-/3-course lunch menu €16.50/20.50, small plates €3-18; ⊙noon-2.30pm & 7-11pm Tue-Sat; MPorte de Vanves) Parisians working in the 'hood fill this casual bistro to bursting at lunchtime thanks to a fantastic-value lunchtime menu, but it's after dusk that the gourmet action kicks in with small plates of tapas *à la française* designed for sharing: cured ham, mayonnaise eggs or beef tartare, accompanied by superb wines by the glass.

The lunchtime menu includes gourmet sandwiches, quiches and salads. For a meat-oriented feast, nip across the street to big sister restaurant **Le Grand Pan** (Map p414; ☑01 42 50 02 50; www.legrandpan.fr; 20 rue Rosenwald, 15e; mains €14-30; ⊙noon-2pm & 7.30-11pm Mon-Fri; MPorte de Vanves).

LE SAUT DU CRAPAUD   BISTRO €

Map p412 (☑01 40 44 73 09; www.lesautducrapaud.zenchef.com; 16 rue des Plantes, 14e; mains €14-20, lunch menus €16-20, dinner menu €35; ⊙7-10pm Mon-Fri, noon-2pm & 7-10.30pm Sat, 11.30am-3pm Sun; MMouton-Duvernet) Locals pack out this quirky neighbourhood bistro, showcase for the casual Franco-Mexican cuisine of Mexican banker-turned-chef Marco Paz. Cooking pots, a guitar and quirky drawings adorn the stylish vintage interior and the menu features creative dishes like steak coriander and Bolitas de la Abuela (potatoes stuffed with Gouda cheese). Sunday brunch (€22.50) is a fabulously vibrant affair, spilling outside in summer.

LE COMPTOIR DU BO BUN VIETNAMESE €

Map p412 (☎09 86 60 94 50; www.lecomptoirdu bobun.fr; 22 rue Raymond Losserand, 14e; mains €12-15; ⊙noon-2.30pm & 7.30-10pm Mon-Thu, to 10.30pm Fri & Sat; ⓜGaîté) For a Real McCoy, salmon and ginger *bo bun* (cold rice-noodle salad) or *pho* (soup) washed down with a Hanoï or Saigon beer or sassy Vietnamese mojito, make a beeline for this colourful Vietnamese eatery strung with decorative lanterns and bird cages. Kudos for the upcycled plastic crates and train carriage. Takeaway is available.

LA CERISAIE FRENCH €

Map p412 (☎01 43 20 98 98; www.restaurant lacerisaie.com; 70 bd Edgar Quinet, 14e; mains €19-21; ⊙noon-2pm & 7-10pm Mon-Fri; ⓜEdgar Quinet) Chef Cyril Lalanne shows how inventive southwestern French cuisine can be at this snug 22-seat restaurant behind a cherry-coloured façade. Expect rich, often game-based mains (goose with spiced roast pear, for instance) and desserts like *Baba à l'Armagnac*.

L'ATELIER B BURGERS €

Map p412 (☎09 82 41 11 27; www.latelierb.fr; 129 rue du Château, 14e; burgers €12-16; ⊙noon-2pm & 7.30-10.30pm Tue-Sat; ⓜPernety) A brilliant spot for pairing a glass of wine or cocktail with a burger and side of sweet-potato fries, regular fries with melted cheese or homemade coleslaw. Superb burger choices include black Angus with confit onion, rocket and mozzarella cheese, and chunky chicken with aubergine, red onion, *comté* cheese and homemade sauce. Seating is inside or out.

★LE CASSENOIX MODERN FRENCH €€

Map p414 (☎01 45 66 09 01; www.le-cassenoix. fr; 56 rue de la Fédération, 15e; 3-course menu €35; ⊙noon-2.30pm & 7-10.30pm Mon-Fri; ⓜBir Hakeim) The Nutcracker is everything a self-respecting neighbourhood bistro should be. *'Tradition et terroir'* ('tradition and provenance') dictate the menu that inspires owner-chef Pierre Olivier Lenormand to deliver dishes incorporating top-quality ingredients (eg John Dory with potato gratin or beef ribs with fig jus). Vintage ceiling fans add to the wonderful retro vibe. Book ahead.

★LE BEURRE NOISETTE BISTRO €€

Map p414 (☎01 48 56 82 49; www.restaurant beurrenoisette.com; 68 rue Vasco de Gama, 15e; 2-/3-course lunch menu €25/34, 3-/5-/7-course dinner menu €42/50/60, mains €19; ⊙noon-2pm & 7-10.30pm Tue-Sat; ⓜLourmel) *Beurre noisette* (brown butter sauce, named for its hazelnut colour) features in dishes such as beef cheeks braised in red wine and caramelised pork-belly tender with braised radishes, at pedigreed chef Thierry Blanqui's neighbourhood neobistro. Filled with locals, the chocolate-toned dining room is wonderfully convivial – be sure to book. Fantastic value.

'LITTLE BRITTANY'

Trains depart from Gare Montparnasse for the windswept region of Brittany, a couple of hours west, but you don't have to leave the capital for authentic Breton crêpes. Due to the Breton population congregating in this area, the station's surrounding streets – especially rue du Montparnasse, 14e, and rue Odessa, 14e, one block west – are lined with dozens of crêperies. Traditional favourites include the super-atmospheric **Crêperie de Josselin** (Map p412; ☎01 43 20 93 50; 67 rue du Montparnasse, 14e; crêpes & galettes €5-14; ⊙noon-11pm Mon-Sun; ⓜEdgar Quinet), named after a village in eastern Brittany, and **Crêperie Plougastel** (Map p412; ☎01 42 79 90 63; www.leplougastel.fr; 47 rue du Montparnasse, 14e; crêpes €3.20-12; ⊙noon-midnight; 🖼; ⓜEdgar Quinet), named for the Breton commune near Brest.

Breton crêpes are folded envelope-style at the edges, served flat on a plate and eaten using cutlery – and are best washed down with bowls of brut Breton cider. Savoury *galettes* use *blé noir* (buckwheat flour; *sarrasin* in Breton), while both *galettes* and sweet crêpes made from white flour use salted Breton butter. Traditional toppings include *andouille* (Breton sausage) and *caramel au beurre salé* (salted caramel sauce; *salidou* in Breton).

L'ACCOLADE   BISTRO €€

Map p414 (📱01 45 57 73 20; www.laccoladeparis.
fr; 208 rue de la Croix Nivert, 15e; 2-/3-course
lunch menu €19.50/24.50, 3-/6-course dinner
menu €35/60; ⏱noon-2pm & 7-10.30pm Mon-
Fri; MConvention) Seasonal market products
reign supreme at this neighbourhood bistro
where rising star Nicolas Tardivel woos
a local crowd with his creative, modern
French 'bistronomie' – bistro-style gastronomy. The lunchtime *plat du jour* (dish of
the day), at €16 including coffee, is an excellent deal. Should you be open to temptation,
the *compotée de mangue* (mango compote)
is sublime.

L'ASSIETTE   BISTRO €€

Map p412 (📱01 43 22 64 86; www.restaurant-lassi
ette.paris; 181 rue du Château, 14e; lunch menu
€23, mains €25-32; ⏱noon-2pm & 7.30-10.30pm
Wed-Fri, 12.30-2.30pm & 7-10.30pm Sat & Sun;
MPernety, Gaîté) Consistently hailed as one
of Paris' best (and most atmospheric) bistros, 'the Plate' is the culinary powerhouse
of chef David Rathgeber, from Auvergne. He
focuses on age-old traditional French dishes
like *cassoulet maison* (Toulouse sausage
and white bean stew) and *joue de bœuf brai-
sée* (braised beef cheek). Superb decor, too,
with drawings, marble, mirrors, wood and
ornate ceilings. Reservations are essential.

LA CLOSERIE DES LILAS   BRASSERIE €€

Map p412 (📱01 40 51 34 50; www.closeriedeslilas.
fr; 171 bd du Montparnasse, 6e; mains restaurant
€28-55, brasserie €19-27, lunch menu from €52;
⏱restaurant noon-2.30pm & 7-11.30pm, brasserie
noon-12.30am, piano bar 11am-1.30am; MVavin,
RER Port Royal) Brass plaques tell you exactly
where Hemingway (who wrote much of *The
Sun Also Rises* here) and luminaries like Picasso, Apollinaire, Man Ray, Jean-Paul Sartre and Samuel Beckett stood, sat or fell at
the 'Lilac Enclosure' (opened 1847). It's split
into a late-night piano bar, an upmarket restaurant and the more loveable (and cheaper)
brasserie with a hedged-in pavement terrace.

LA ROTONDE   BRASSERIE €€

Map p412 (📱01 43 26 48 26; 105 bd du Montparnasse, 6e; mains €17-48, seafood platters
€29.50-118.50, menu €48; ⏱6am-2am, kitchen
noon-3pm & 7-11pm; MVavin) Around since
1911 and as glamorous as the day it opened,
elegant La Rotonde stands out from the Les
Montparnos 'historic brasserie' crowd for
its superior food. Meat comes from Parisian butcher extraordinaire Hugo Desnoyer,

'LITTLE TEHRAN'

Anyone craving authentic Middle Eastern cuisine should make a beeline for
rue des Entrepreneurs, 15e. This street
has a number of great Iranian restaurants and food stores that should meet
your expectations. *Ghormeh Sabzi*
(herb stew with rice), anyone?

salmon and chicken are organic, and brasserie classics are cooked to perfection. Extravagant seafood platters are piled high
with prawns, lobsters, crabs and shellfish.

LE SÉVÉRO   BISTRO €€

Map p412 (📱01 45 40 40 91; www.lesevero.fr; 8
rue des Plantes, 14e; mains €14-46; ⏱noon-2pm
& 7.30-10pm Mon-Fri; MMouton Duvernet) Steaks
served with sensational *frites* (fries) are the
mainstay of this upmarket bistro (it's run
by ex-butcher William Bernet); other meat
specialities include black pudding and pigs
trotters. Wash them down with any number
of excellent wines, which are chalked on an
entire wall. With just 30 seats, reconfirming
advance reservations by noon is essential.

LE DÔME   BRASSERIE €€€

Map p412 (📱01 43 35 25 81; www.restaurant-
ledome.com; 108 bd du Montparnasse, 14e;
2-/3-course menu €39/45, mains €28-69, seafood
platters €85-159; ⏱noon-3pm & 7-11pm Mon-Sat,
noon-3pm Sun; MVavin) A 1930s art deco ex-
travaganza of the formal white-tablecloth
and bow-tied waiter variety, monumental Le
Dôme is one of the swishest places around
for shellfish platters laden with fresh oysters, king prawns, crab claws and much
more, followed by homemade *millefeuille*
flavoured with rum and vanilla for dessert.

✖ Place d'Italie, Chinatown & Bibliothèque Nationale de France

POPULUS   BISTRO €

Map p410 (📱09 54 96 79 10; www.facebook.
com/PopulusBistrot; 40 rue du Tage, 13e; lunch
menu €14.50, menu €29.50, mains €14.50-
16.50; ⏱noon-2pm Mon-Wed, noon-2pm &
7-9.45pm Thu-Sat; MMaison Blanche) Opened
in late 2019, Populus is that easy-to-miss
'secret spot' that locals like to recommend.
It's somewhat off the beaten track, in a

surprisingly quiet neighbourhood just west of busy av d'Italie, but its combination of excellent cooking, smiling service and terrific value makes it well worth seeking out. The concise menu focuses on French classics.

CAMLY – BO-BUN 2 GO
VIETNAMESE €

Map p410 (☎09 83 29 39 98; www.bobun2go.fr; 83 rue du Château des Rentiers, 13e; mains €7-12, menus €10-17; ◷11.30am-3pm & 6-10pm Mon-Sat, 6-10pm Sun; MOlympiades) Approximately halfway between place d'Italie and Bibliothèque Nationale de France, this great little restaurant serves up some of the 13e's best Vietnamese cuisine (and that's saying a lot) in a sleek interior. Order some spring rolls and don't miss out on the *bo bun* as a main course. Also does takeaway.

LA TROPICALE
ICE CREAM €

Map p410 (☎01 42 16 87 27; www.latropicale glacier.com; 180 bd Vincent Auriol, 13e; 1/2/3 scoops ice cream €3/5/7, lunch menus €8-16; ◷noon-8pm Mon-Fri, 3-8pm Sat & Sun summer, noon-3.30pm Mon, Tue & Thu, noon-7pm Wed & Sat winter; ♿; MPlace d'Italie) 🌿 Pistachio, chestnut from Cévennes and vanilla with rum are among the exciting favours at this exceptional ice-creamery near place d'Italie. Ice cream is made on-site in the tiny space, and seasonal flavours incorporate gorgeous tropical spices sourced by the creative Cambodian owner and ice-cream maker, Thai-Thanh, on her many travels. Also has some great salads, healthy soups and appetising daily specials.

JOHN JOHN JOHN
INTERNATIONAL €

Map p410 (☎09 54 59 08 99; 59 rue de Tolbiac, 13e; mains €11-15; MOlympiades) Food is delicious, innovative and mostly organic, with great bowls, healthy *plats chauds* (hot dishes), zesty salads and tasty buns – not to mention tempting detox juices. There's live music on Thursday evening.

LA PETITE CUISINE DE SANDRINE
FRENCH €

Map p410 (☎06 45 25 68 61; www.lapetitecuisine desandrine.paris; 89bis rue du Dessous des Berges, 13e; menus €9-13; ◷noon-2pm Mon-Fri; MBibliothèque François-Mitterrand) No typo – it's *that* cheap. This pocket-sized den feels like you've been let in on a secret. Sandrine prepares excellent food that anyone can appreciate – soups and French classics that change on a weekly basis. There are only a couple of tables but takeaway is available.

PHO BÀNH CÚON 14
VIETNAMESE €

Map p410 (☎01 45 83 61 15; 129 av de Choisy, 13e; mains €7.80-9.70; ◷9am-11pm; MTolbiac) Factor in a wait at this small, buzzy restaurant (also known as Pho 14) – it doesn't take bookings and is wildly popular with in-the-know locals for its super-fresh and astonishingly cheap *pho;* this steaming Vietnamese broth is richly flavoured with cinnamon and incorporates noodles and traditional beef or chicken. Cash only.

PETITE CEINTURE

Long before the tramway or even the metro, the 35km Petite Ceinture (Little Belt) steam railway encircled the city of Paris. Constructed during the reign of Napoléon III between 1852 and 1869 as a way to move troops and goods around the city's fortifications, it became a thriving passenger service until the metro arrived in 1900. Most passenger services ceased in 1934 and goods services in 1993, and the line became an overgrown wilderness. Until recently, access was forbidden (although that didn't stop maverick urban explorers scrambling along its tracks and tunnels). Of the line's original 29 stations, 17 survive (in various states of disrepair).

Plans for regenerating the Petite Ceinture railway corridor have seen the opening of three sections with walkways alongside the tracks. Other areas remain off limits.

In southern Paris, the **Petite Ceinture du 15e** (PC 15; Map p414; www.paris.fr; opposite 99 rue Olivier de Serres, 15e; ◷9am-8.30pm Mon-Fri, from 9.30am Sat & Sun May-Aug, shorter hours rest of year; MBalard, Porte de Versailles) FREE stretches for 1.3km, with biodiverse habitats including forest, grassland and prairies supporting 220 species of flora and fauna. In addition to the end points, there are three elevator-enabled access points along its route: 397ter rue de Vaugirard; opposite 82 rue Desnouettes; and place Robert Guillemard.

On the eastern side of Parc Georges Brassens, a *promenade plantée* (planted walkway) travels atop a stretch of the Petite Ceinture's tracks by Porte de Vanves.

Old tracks along the Petite Ceinture

YUMAN
HEALTH FOOD €

Map p410 (☎01 73 74 44 79; www.yuman-restaurant.com; 70 rue du Chevaleret, 13e; menus €17-24, mains €16-18; ☉noon-2pm Mon, noon-2pm & 7.30-10.30pm Tue-Sat; ☑; Ⓜ Bibliothèque François Mitterrand) ☙ 'Simple, natural cuisine' is the strapline of this tasty address with scrubbed wood tables and a decent-sized pavement terrace, a short walk away from Station F (p252) and the National Library. Tucked beneath the railway tracks, chef Gilles Tessier cooks up most of his dishes using products sourced within a 200km radius of Paris. Several are vegetarian, gluten-free, dairy-free or vegan. Check its Facebook page for the week's menu.

★ MARSO & CO
FRENCH €€

Map p410 (☎01 45 87 37 00; www.tomygousset.com; 16 rue Vulpian, 13e; lunch menus €20, menus €38, mains €20-29; ☉noon-2pm & 7.15-9.45pm Mon-Fri; Ⓜ Glacière) The menu is devised by Tomy Gousset, one of Paris' top chefs, so it's impossible to go wrong in this modern bistro. Food follows the season, with starters running from cauliflower doughnuts with cumin to chorizo flambéed in brandy. Mains include gorgeous pasta and meat dishes. The poached pear with ginger and chocolate is a dessert delight.

LA BUTTE AUX PIAFS
BISTRO €€

Map p410 (☎09 83 51 07 50; www.labutteauxpiafs-paris.fr; 31 bd Auguste Blanqui, 13e; mains €18-24; ☉noon-3.30pm & 5-10pm Tue-Sat, bar to midnight; Ⓜ Place d'Italie) A cluster of cherry-red chairs flag the pavement terrace of this neighbourhood bistro on the edge of La Butte aux Cailles. Large windows giving plenty of natural light, and an eclectic jumble of vintage (but slightly uncomfortable) seating, creates an inviting setting to dine on appetising dishes such as grilled cod with carrot mousseline and charred pink grapefruit.

SIMONE LE RESTO
BISTRO €€

Map p410 (☎01 43 37 82 70; www.simoneparis.com; 33 bd Arago, 13e; 2-/4-course lunch menu €22/32, 5-course tasting menu €55, mains €28-32; ☉noon-2pm & 7.30-10pm Tue-Fri, 7.30-10pm Sat; Ⓜ Les Gobelins) A generous smattering of pavement-terrace tables flags this vibrant neobistro where inventive *menus* are created in the open kitchen from high-quality products. An exceptional selection of all-natural and biodynamic wines that pair perfectly with each course are also available at Simone's nearby wine shop and bar, Simone La Cave (p258).

MILORD
FRENCH €€

Map p410 (☑01 43 46 80 44; 12 rue de Tolbiac; mains €17-22, lunch menus €18-22, special menu €50; ☻noon-2pm & 7.30-10pm Tue-Sat; Ⓜ Bibliothèque François-Mitterrand) Opened in 2019, this upmarket, industrial-styled eatery features a limited menu that caters for carnivores as well as vegetarians. The three dynamic lads who run the place are of Tuscan descent, so you can expect dishes with an Italian twist, such as tagliatelle with octopus. A great snapshot of the new energy in this neighbourhood.

🍷 DRINKING & NIGHTLIFE

The comings and goings of the Gare Montparnasse and its historic brasseries keep things lively. Southwest of place d'Italie, rue de la Butte aux Cailles and the surrounding Butte aux Cailles molehill have a plethora of fabulous options popular with students and locals; places here have a loyal clientele and lack the pretension of more trendsetting neighbourhoods. You can also head to rue du Chevaleret and av de France, a burgeoning area with great options.

Especially in summer, you can't beat the floating bars and clubs on the Seine.

🍷 Montparnasse & Southern Paris

★ POINÇON
BAR

(☑01 56 08 16 69; www.poinconparis.com; 124 av du Général Leclerc, 14e; ☻8.30am-11.45pm Wed & Thu, to 2am Fri & Sat, 11.30am-5pm Sun; Ⓜ Porte d'Orléans) Bars in the 14e don't come much more atmospheric than this one. Poinçon occupies a delightfully restored 1867-built railway station that was part of the Petite Ceinture. Half trendy bar and half slick bistro bathing in a warm atmosphere, it's much loved by Parisians living in the *arrondissement,* not least for its cocktails, wines, fantastic-value food and Sunday jazz brunches.

ARTHUR & JULIETTE
CAFE

Map p414 (☑01 48 28 15 55; www.arthuretjuliette. fr; 51 rue des Morillons, 15e; ☻8am-11.30pm; Ⓜ Porte de Vanves) Sunny Sunday mornings are the best time to lap up the unpretentious Parisian vibe at this staunchly local neighbourhood bistro, named after the owners' two children. Grab a seat on the terrace, across the street from the bulls guarding Parc Georges Brassens, and kick back over a coffee or something stronger. Tasty bistro fare, too.

LE PETIT GORILLE
CAFE

Map p414 (☑01 48 28 17 57; www.facebook.com/ lepetitgorille; 46 rue de Cronstadt, 15e; ☻10am-1am; ☎; Ⓜ Convention) A collection of miniature cuddly gorillas is the clue to the kitschy-cool vibe at this fun cafe-bar, one notch up from your regular neighbourhood hang-out with its eye-catching marine-blue façade, stylish pavement seating and neo-retro interior. Great cocktails, beers and wines, plus decent bistro food (mains from €13) that draws a regular weekend crowd.

FÉLICIE
BAR

Map p412 (☑01 45 41 05 75; www.felicie.info; 174 av du Maine, 14e; ☻7.30am-2am Mon-Fri, from 8am Sat & Sun; ☎; Ⓜ Mouton Duvernet) Chances are your first visit won't be your last at this unpretentious neighbourhood cafe with a big heated pavement terrace, fun-loving staff and a laid-back vibe. It's a quintessentially Parisian spot to hang out any time of day, but especially during Sunday brunch and late at night.

LE SELECT
CAFE

Map p412 (www.leselectmontparnasse.fr; 99 bd du Montparnasse, 6e; ☻7am-2am Sun-Thu, to 3am Fri & Sat; ☎; Ⓜ Vavin) Dating from 1923, this Montparnasse brasserie, restaurant and *bar américain* was the first of the area's grand cafes to stay open late into the night, and it still draws everyone from beer-swigging students to whisky-swilling politicians and smartly dressed Parisians who've been coming here for years.

🍷 Place d'Italie, Chinatown & Bibliothèque Nationale de France

SIMONE LA CAVE
WINE BAR

Map p410 (☑01 43 37 82 70; www.simoneparis. com; 48 rue Pascal, 13e; ☻5pm-midnight Tue-Sat; Ⓜ Les Gobelins) Tucked away in the 13e, Simone La Cave lures a loyal wine-loving set keen to try its latest outstanding natural and biodynamic wine selection. *Planch-*

es (platters; €12 to €18) stacked high with cured meats and boutique cheeses, oysters and succulent homemade terrines, provide the perfect accompaniment.

LA DAME DE CANTON   CLUB
Map p410 (www.damedecanton.com; ⏰noon-midnight Tue-Sat; MBibliothèque François-Mitterrand) This floating *boîte* (club) aboard a three-masted Chinese junk with a couple of world voyages under its belt bobs beneath the Bibliothèque Nationale de France. Concerts cover pop and indie to electro, hip-hop, reggae and rock; afterwards, DJs keep the crowd hyped. From May to September, its popular bar and restaurant serves wood-fired pizzas on the terrace.

LE MERLE MOQUEUR   BAR
Map p410 (11 rue de la Butte aux Cailles, 13e; ⏰5pm-2am; MCorvisart) The tiny, retro Mocking Magpie serves a huge selection of flavoured rums (more than 20 at last count) and unearths long-forgotten 1980s tracks from the musical vaults.

BATEAU EL ALAMEIN   CLUB
Map p410 (www.bateauelalamein.com; ⏰5.30pm-2am mid-May–mid-Oct, 7pm-2am mid-Oct–mid-May; MBibliothèque François-Mitterrand) Strung with terracotta pots of flowers, this deep-purple boat has a Seine-side terrace for sitting amid tulips and enjoying live bands (flyers are stuck on the lamppost at the front). Concerts starting at 9pm (no reservations) span jazz, world and Piaf-style *chansons*. Hours can vary.

☆ ENTERTAINMENT

Many of the 13e's floating nightclubs have live music. Events regularly take place at Les Docks (p253) and the cutting-edge EP7.

★EP7   ARTS CENTRE
Map p410 (01 43 45 68 07; www.ep7.paris; 133 av de France, 13e; ⏰9.30am-midnight Mon-Wed, 9.30am-2am Thu-Sat, 10am-9pm Sun; 🛜; MBibliothèque François-Mitterrand) Paris' first piece of 'interactive architecture', this cultural cafe and concert venue was unveiled in 2018. Contemporary works of pixel art prance across 12 giant screens covering the façade, creating a dazzling digital gallery. Inside the complex, named after the vintage vinyl format 'extended play',

WORTH A DETOUR
CULTURAL ISLAND: ÎLE SEGUIN

La Seine Musicale (01 74 34 54 00; www.laseinemusicale.com; Île Seguin; MPont de Sèvres) A landmark addition to Paris' cultural offerings, La Seine Musicale opened on the Seine island of Île Seguin in 2017. Constructed of steel and glass, the egg-shaped auditorium has a capacity of 1150, while the larger, modular concrete hall accommodates 6000. Ballets, musicals and concerts from classical to rock are all staged here, alongside exhibitions.

Outside are amphitheatres, while up above is a panoramic rooftop garden with landscaped lawns. There's also a restaurant, a brasserie, a cafe and a bar on the premises.

It's the first of several arts venues, including a contemporary art museum, planned as part of the Île Seguin's transformation from a Renault factory to a cultural island.

you'll find art exhibitions and happenings, DJ sets (Fridays and Saturdays), a bistro and a bar.

L'ENTREPÔT   CULTURAL CENTRE
Map p412 (01 45 40 07 50; www.lentrepot.fr; 7-9 rue Francis de Pressensé, 14e; MPernety) Everything from film screenings to jazz and world music concerts, poetry slams, photography, painting and sculpture exhibitions, art installations and much more take place at this dynamic cultural space. It's a fantastic place to eat, too, with a glassed-in conservatory and dozens of tables beneath the trees in its leafy back garden; Sunday brunch (€28, from 11.30am) is hugely popular.

🛍 SHOPPING

Savvy fashion shoppers head to the southern 14e to shop for discount designer wear, while the 15e is filled with specialist addresses. In the 13e you'll find Asian grocery stores and supermarkets in Chinatown, and an enormous state-of-the-art shopping mall at place d'Italie.

🏠 Montparnasse & Southern Paris

★ STORIE
HOMEWARES

Map p412 (📞 01 83 56 01 98; www.storieshop.com; 20 rue Delambre, 14e; ⏰ 11am-2pm & 3-8pm Mon-Sat; Ⓜ Montparnasse) Beautiful objects with *une histoire* (a story) is what this backstreet boutique is all about. Hand-woven items from West Africa pile next to silk and cashmere from Afghanistan and cushions from Laos. Items are artisan, handmade and personally sourced by the well-travelled, British co-owner Fiona Cameron, a former TV journalist.

ADAM MONTPARNASSE
ARTS & CRAFTS

Map p412 (📞 01 43 20 68 53; www.adamparis. com; 11 bd Edgar Quinet, 14e; ⏰ 9.30am-7pm Mon-Sat; Ⓜ Edgar Quinet) If Paris' art galleries have inspired you, pick up paintbrushes, charcoals, pastels, sketchpads, watercolours, oils, acrylics, canvases and more at this historic shop. Picasso, Brancusi and Giacometti were among Édouard Adam's clients. Another seminal client was Yves Klein, with whom Adam developed the ultramarine 'Klein blue' – the VLB25 'Klein Blue' varnish is sold exclusively here.

BEILLEVAIRE
CHEESE

Map p412 (📞 01 45 42 90 68; www.fromagerie-beillevaire.com; 86 rue Raymond Losserand, 14e; ⏰ 9am-8pm Tue-Sat; Ⓜ Plaisance) For the finest French butter, not to mention a swath of unusual seasonal French cheeses and other top-quality dairy products, make a pit stop at this outstanding place. Cheese can be vacuum-packed to take home.

DISCOUNT DESIGNER OUTLETS

Save up to 70% off men's, women's and kids' fashions from previous seasons' collections, surpluses, prototypes and seconds by name-brand designers at the discounted outlet stores along rue d'Alésia, 14e, west of the Alésia metro station (particularly between av de Maine and rue Raymond-Losserand).

Shops pop up regularly and close just as often, so you can never be sure what you'll find.

DES GÂTEAUX ET DU PAIN
FOOD

Map p412 (📞 06 98 95 33 18; www.desgateaux etdupain.com; 63 bd Pasteur, 15e; ⏰ 9am-8pm Mon & Wed-Sat, to 6pm Sun; Ⓜ Pasteur) Looking more like an exclusive boutique, this ultra-contemporary bakery and patisserie has dramatic black walls that showcase the jewel-like cakes, tarts and artisan breads created by David Granger and Claire Damon – one of France's leading female pastry chefs.

MARCHÉ AUX PUCES DE LA PORTE DE VANVES
MARKET

(www.pucesdevanves.fr; av Georges Lafenestre & av Marc Sangnier, 14e; ⏰ 7am-2pm Sat & Sun; Ⓜ Porte de Vanves) One of the friendliest in Paris, the Porte de Vanves flea market has over 380 stalls. Av Georges Lafenestre has lots of 'curios' that don't quite qualify as antiques. Av Marc Sangnier is lined with stalls of new clothes, shoes, handbags and household items for sale.

LA CAVE DES PAPILLES
WINE

Map p412 (📞 01 43 20 05 74; www.lacavedes papilles.com; 35 rue Daguerre, 14e; ⏰ 3.30-8.30pm Mon, 10am-1.30pm & 3.30-8.30pm Tue-Fri, 10am-8.30pm Sat, 10am-1.30pm Sun; Ⓜ Denfert Rochereau) All of the 1200-plus varieties of wine at this dazzling rue Daguerre wine shop are organic or additive free. There's also a wonderfully chosen selection of rare sakes, armagnacs and brandies.

COMPTOIR CORRÉZIEN
FOOD

Map p414 (📞 01 47 83 52 97; www.comptoir-correzien.fr; 8 rue des Volontaires, 15e; ⏰ 9am-1.30pm & 3-7.30pm Tue-Sat; Ⓜ Volontaires) Caviar, smoked salmon, Corsican honey, wild duck and geese, fresh and dried mushrooms, Berthillon ice cream and truffles in season are among the mouth-watering luxury food products stocked at this head-spinning deli, which supplies some of the city's premier restaurants. If you're staying in a kitchen-equipped apartment, consider picking up pre-made meals (soups, pastas) from here, too.

MARIE-LOUISE ORLACH
JEWELLERY

(📞 06 70 58 82 53; www.marielouiseorlach. net; various outlets) Parisian jeweller Marie-Louise, who works from her home in the 14e *arrondissement,* is renowned for her pieces (earrings and necklaces) made from original clock needles from the early 1900s. Her creations are on sale at various outlets (see the website). Also check www.instagram. com/marielouiseorlach.

MARCHÉ EDGAR QUINET FOOD

Map p412 (www.paris.fr/equipements/marche-edgar-quinet-5497; bd Edgar Quinet, 14e; ⏱7am-2.30pm Wed, to 3pm Sat; Ⓜ Edgar Quinet, Montparnasse Bienvenüe) Opposite Tour Montparnasse, this open-air street market teems with neighbourhood shoppers. There's always a great range of cheeses, as well as stalls sizzling up snacks to eat on the run, from crêpes to spicy felafels.

MARCHÉ DE LA CRÉATION MARKET

Map p412 (www.marchecreation.com; bd Edgar Quinet, 14e; ⏱10am-7pm Sun; Ⓜ Edgar Quinet) Stalls overflowing with handmade arts and crafts fill the western end of bd Edgar Quinet on Sunday, drawing a mixed crowd of locals and travellers in transit from nearby Gare Montparnasse.

MARCHÉ BIOLOGIQUE BRANCUSI FOOD

Map p412 (www.paris.fr/equipements/marche-biologique-brancusi-4516; place Constantin Brancusi, 14e; ⏱9am-3pm Sat; Ⓜ Gaîté) 🕊 Huge selection of *biologique* (organic) produce at this weekly open-air market.

🔓 Place d'Italie, Chinatown & Bibliothèque Nationale de France

BIÉROCRATIE DRINKS

Map p410 (📞01 53 80 16 10; www.bierocratie.com; 32 rue de l'Espérance, 13e; ⏱11am-8pm Tue & Thu-Sat, from 4pm Wed; Ⓜ Corvisart) Craft beers from around the world but especially France (including Paris-brewed Goutte d'Or and Bonjour and Île-de-France brewed Parisis) fill this bottle-lined specialist shop. It's run by fun-loving young husband-and-wife team Jaclyn and Pierre. Check the website for evening tastings (usually once or twice a month).

LAURENT DUCHÊNE FOOD

Map p410 (📞01 45 65 00 77; www.laurent-duchene.com; 2 rue Wurtz, 13e; ⏱7.30am-8pm Mon-Sat; Ⓜ Glacière) Prize-winning croissants made with *beurre Charentes-Poitou* AOC butter are the speciality of this lauded bakery. Plenty of other goodies, too, including macarons and cakes.

🏃 SPORTS & ACTIVITIES

⭐ PISCINE DE LA BUTTE AUX CAILLES SWIMMING

Map p410 (📞01 45 89 60 05; www.paris.fr/equipements/piscine-de-la-butte-aux-cailles-2927; 5 place Paul Verlaine, 13e; adult/child €3.50/2; ⏱hours vary; Ⓜ Place d'Italie) Built in 1924, this art deco swimming complex – a historical monument – takes advantage of the lovely warm artesian well water nearby. It has a spectacular vaulted indoor pool and, since 2017, Paris' only Nordic pool. In the depths of winter, Parisians head here to swim 25m laps in a five-lane outdoor pool, heated to a toasty 27°C. Check schedules online.

PISCINE JOSÉPHINE BAKER SWIMMING

Map p410 (📞01 56 61 96 50; www.piscine-baker.fr; quai François Mauriac, 13e; adult/child from €4/2.20; ⏱hours vary; Ⓜ Quai de la Gare) Floating on the Seine, this striking swimming pool is named after the 1920s American singer. The 25m-by-10m, four-lane pool and large sun deck are especially popular in summer when the roof slides back. Also here is a children's paddling pool. In July and August, plus weekends from late May to September, admission is limited to two hours.

Day Trips from Paris

Disneyland Resort Paris p263

The party never stops at Europe's Disneyland theme park and Walt Disney Studios Park, bringing film, animation and TV production to life.

Château de Versailles p264

When it comes to over-the-top opulence, the colossal Château de Versailles is in a class of its own, even for France.

Fontainebleau p270

A lavish château graces the elegant town of Fontainebleau, but it's the rambling boulder-strewn forest that makes this such a fabulous escape.

Chartres p273

Rising from fertile farmland, Chartres' Cathédrale Notre Dame, famed for its beautiful stained glass, dominates the charming medieval town.

Giverny p276

Art and garden lovers shouldn't miss Giverny's Maison et Jardins de Claude Monet, the former home and flower-filled gardens of the impressionist master.

TOP EXPERIENCE
RELEASE YOUR INNER CHILD AT DISNEYLAND

It took almost €4.6 billion to turn the beet fields 32km east of Paris into Europe's first Disney theme park. What started out as Euro-Disney in 1992 today comprises the traditional Disneyland Park theme park, the film-oriented Walt Disney Studios Park, and the hotel-, shop- and restaurant-filled Disney Village. And kids – and kids-at-heart – can't seem to get enough.

Basic one-day admission fees at Disneyland Resort Paris include unlimited access to attractions in either Disneyland Park or Walt Disney Studios Park. A multitude of multiday passes, special offers and packages are always available.

No picnic hampers or coolers are allowed but you can bring snacks, sandwiches and water bottles (refillable at water fountains). The resort also has over 50 themed restaurants of varying quality and value; look out for regional European food stands at the Rendez-Vous Gourmand between July and October.

Disneyland is easily reached by RER A (€7.60, 40 minutes to one hour, frequent), which runs from central Paris to Marne-la-Vallée/Chessy, Disneyland's RER station.

PRACTICALITIES

➡ ☑08 25 30 05 00, booking 01 60 30 60 53, restaurant reservations 01 60 30 40 50
➡ www.disneyland paris.com
➡ adult/child 1 day single park €89/82, 1 day both parks €109/102, 2 days both parks €179/165
➡ ⊙hours vary

Disneyland Park

Disneyland Park (⊙check website for current opening hours) has five themed *pays* (lands): the 1900s-styled **Main Street USA**; **Frontierland**, home of the legendary Big Thunder Mountain ride; **Adventureland**, which evokes exotic lands in rides including the Pirates of the Caribbean and Indiana Jones and the Temple of Peril; **Fantasyland**, crowned by Sleeping Beauty's castle; and the high-tech **Discoveryland**, with massive-queue rides such as Star Wars Hyperspace Mountain and Buzz Lightyear Laser Blast.

Three new lands – Star Wars, Marvel and Frozen – will begin opening features as early as 2022, with an estimated completion date of 2024.

Walt Disney Studios Park

At **Walt Disney Studios Park** (⊙check website for current opening hours), a sound stage, production backlot and animation studios provide an up-close insight into the production of films, TV programs and cartoons. There are behind-the-scenes tours, larger-than-life characters and spine-tingling rides like the Twilight Zone Tower of Terror, as well as the outsized Ratatouille ride (based on the winsome 2007 film about a rat who dreams of becoming a top Parisian chef), which offers a multisensory rat's perspective of Paris' rooftops and restaurant kitchens aboard a trackless 'ratmobile'.

Top Disney Tips

➡ Crowds peak during European school holidays; visit www.schoolholidayseurope.eu and avoid them if possible.
➡ Pre-plan your day on Disney's website or the excellent www.dlpguide.com, working out which rides and shows you really want to see.
➡ Buy tickets in advance to avoid the ticket queue.
➡ The free Disneyland Paris app provides real-time waiting times for attractions, but note that free wi-fi is only available in limited areas within the park.
➡ Once in, sometimes it is possible to reserve your time slot on the busiest rides using FastPass (€45 to €150), the park's ride reservation system. Check online in advance.
➡ Disney hotel guests are entitled to 'Magic Hours' in Disneyland Park (usually from 8am, May to October) before it opens to the public, although not all rides run during these hours.
➡ Visitors with disabilities should check the website for details on accommodation.

TOP EXPERIENCE
REVEL IN THE SPLENDOUR OF VERSAILLES

Louis XIV transformed his father's hunting lodge into the monumental Château de Versailles in the mid-17th century and it remains France's most famous, grandest palace. Situated 22km southwest of Paris, the baroque château was the kingdom's political capital and the seat of the royal court from 1682 until the French Revolution in 1789.

Intending the château to house his court of 6000 people, Louis XIV hired four talented men to take on the gargantuan task: architect Louis Le Vau; Jules Hardouin-Mansart, who took over from Le Vau in the mid-1670s; painter and interior designer Charles Le Brun; and landscape designer André Le Nôtre, under whom entire hills were flattened, marshes drained and forests moved to create the seemingly endless gardens, ponds and fountains for which Versailles is so well known. It has been on Unesco's World Heritage list since 1979.

Sprawling over 900 hectares, the estate is divided into three main sections: the 580m-long palace; the gardens, canals and pools to the west of the palace; and the Trianon Estate to the northwest, which includes two smaller palaces, the Grand Trianon and the Petit Trianon, and the Hameau de la Reine (Queen's Hamlet) north of the Petit Trianon. Tickets include an English-language audioguide; free apps can be downloaded from the website.

Versailles is easy to reach from Paris. The most convenient option is to take RER C5 (return €7.30, 40 minutes, frequent) from Paris' Left Bank RER stations to Versailles-Château–Rive Gauche station. Be careful which train you board and verify the terminus first – you don't want to go to Versailles-Chantiers station or take the Saint-Ouen line. There are also other rail connections, buses and organised tours.

DON'T MISS

➡ Château de Versailles

➡ Gardens

➡ Trianon Estate

PRACTICALITIES

➡ ☏ 01 30 83 78 00

➡ www.chateau versailles.fr

➡ place d'Armes

➡ adult/child passport ticket incl estate-wide access €20/free, with musical events €27/free, palace €18/free except during musical events

➡ ⏰ 9am-6.30pm Tue-Sun Apr-Oct, to 5.30pm Tue-Sun Nov-Mar

➡ Ⓜ RER Versailles-Château–Rive Gauche

The Palace

Few alterations have been made to the château since its construction, apart from most of the interior furnishings disappearing during the Revolution and many of the rooms being rebuilt by Louis-Philippe (r 1830–48), who opened part of the château to the public in 1837. On our last visit, the château was putting the finishing touches on a thorough €400 million restoration, although you may still see some scaffolding while here.

To access areas that are otherwise off limits and to learn more about Versailles' history, pre-book one of three 90-minute **guided tours** (☑01 30 83 77 88; tours €10, plus palace entry), which cover the most famous parts of the palace.

Prams/buggies, metal-frame baby carriers and luggage aren't allowed inside the palace.

Hall of Mirrors

The palace's opulence peaks in its shimmering Galerie des Glaces (Hall of Mirrors). This 75m-long ballroom has 17 sparkling mirrors on one side and an equal number of windows on the other.

King's & Queen's State Apartments

Luxurious, ostentatious appointments – frescoes, marble, gilt and woodcarvings, with themes and symbols drawn from Greek and Roman mythology – adorn every moulding, cornice, ceiling and door in the palace's Grands Appartements du Roi et de la Reine (King's and Queen's State Apartments).

Gardens

Don't miss a stroll through the château's magnificent **gardens** (place d'Armes; free except during musical events; ⊙gardens 8am-8.30pm Apr-Oct, to 6pm Nov-Mar, park 7am-8.30pm Apr-Oct, 8am-6pm Nov-Mar). The best view over the rectangular pools is from the Hall of Mirrors. Pathways include the Royal Walk's verdant 'green carpet', with smaller paths leading to leafy groves. The gardens' largest fountains are the 17th-century **Bassin de Neptune** (Neptune's Fountain), a dazzling mirage of 99 spouting fountains 300m north of the palace, and the **Bassin d'Apollon** (Apollo's Fountain), built in 1668 at the eastern end of the Grand Canal.

Canals

The **Grand Canal**, 1.6km long and 62m wide, is oriented to reflect the setting sun. It's traversed by the 1km-long **Petit Canal**, forming a cross-shaped body of water with a perimeter of more than 5.5km.

PLANNING FOR VERSAILLES

By noon, queues for tickets and entering the château spiral out of control: arrive early morning and avoid Tuesday, Saturday and Sunday, its busiest days. Pre-purchase tickets on the château's website or at Fnac (www.fnactickets.com) branches and head straight to Entrance A. If you can't get enough of the palace, consider the two-day passport (€25 to €30).

EXPLORING THE ESTATE

The estate is so vast that the only way to see it all is to hire a four-person **electric cart** (☑01 39 66 97 66; www.astel-versailles. com; car hire per hr €34; ⊙10am-6.45pm Apr-Oct, to 5.30pm Feb & Mar, to 5pm Nov & Dec) or hop aboard the **shuttle train** (☑01 39 54 22 00; www.train-versailles. com; adult/child €8/6.10; ⊙every 20min 10.10am-6.50pm Apr-Oct, shorter hours Nov-Mar); you can also rent a **bike** (☑01 39 66 97 66; www.astel-versailles.com; bike hire per hr/day €8.50/20; ⊙10am-6.45pm Apr-Oct, shorter hours Nov-Mar) or a **rowboat** (☑01 39 66 97 66; boat hire per 30min/hr €14/18; ⊙10am-6.45pm Jul & Aug, shorter hours Mar-Jun & Sep–mid-Nov).

DAY TRIPS FROM PARIS CHÂTEAU DE VERSAILLES

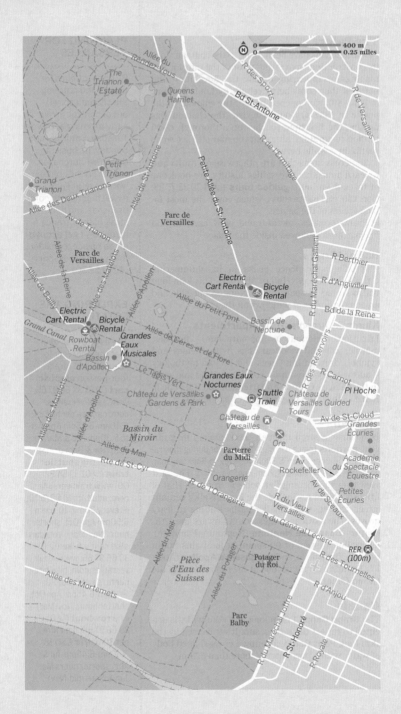

Domaine de Trianon

Trianon Estate

Northwest of Versailles' main palace is the **Domaine de Trianon** (Trianon Estate; adult/child €12/free, with passport ticket free; ⊙noon-6.30pm Tue-Sun Apr-Oct, to 5.30pm Tue-Sat Nov-Mar). Admission includes the Grand Trianon and Petit Trianon palaces, and the 1784-completed Hameau de la Reine (Queen's Hamlet), a mock village of thatched cottages where Marie Antoinette played milkmaid.

The pink-colonnaded Grand Trianon was built in 1687 for Louis XIV and his family to escape the rigid etiquette of the court and was renovated under Napoléon I in the Empire style. The ochre-coloured, 1760s Petit Trianon was redecorated in 1867 by the consort of Napoléon III, Empress Eugénie, who added Louis XVI–style furnishings.

Musical Fountain Shows

Try to time your visit for the **Grandes Eaux Musicales** (www.chateauversailles-spectacles.fr; adult/child €11/9.50; ⊙9am-7pm Sat & Sun Apr-Oct, also 9am-7pm Tue mid-May–mid-Jun) or the after-dark **Grandes Eaux Nocturnes** (adult/child €24/20; ⊙8.30-11.30pm Sat mid-Jun–mid-Sep), truly magical 'dancing water' displays – set to music composed by Baroque- and classical-era composers – throughout the grounds in summer.

DINING AT VERSAILLES

On-site restaurants include Alain Ducasse's Ore. Just across the passageway is the casual Grand Café d'Orléans, which sells snacks to go.

For more maps and advice, download the free Versailles app from the website (www.chateau versailles.fr) before you visit.

THE STABLES

The **Grandes Écuries** (Great Stables; av Rockefeller) are the stage for the prestigious **Académie du Spectacle Équestre** (Academy of Equestrian Arts; ☑01 39 02 62 70; 1 av Rockefeller; stable tour adult/child €7/free, show adult/child from €22/16; ⊙stable hours vary throughout the year, shows 6pm Sat & 3pm Sun Feb-Dec). It presents spectacular Reprises Musicales equestrian shows, for which tickets sell out weeks in advance; book ahead online. In the stables' main courtyard is a *manège* where horses and their riders train. Show tickets and training sessions (reserve) include a stable visit. The Petites Écuries (Lesser Stables) are today used by Versailles' School of Architecture.

Versailles

A DAY IN COURT

Visiting Versailles – even just the State Apartments – may seem overwhelming at first, but think of it as a house where people ate, drank, worked, slept and conspired and you'll be on the right path.

Some two decades into his long reign, Louis XIV began turning his father's hunting lodge into a palace large enough to house his entire court (to keep closer tabs on the 6000-strong army of courtiers). Sparing no expense, the Sun King employed the greatest artists and craftspeople of the day and by 1682 he'd created the most extravagant dormitory in history.

The royal schedule was as accurate and predictable as a Swiss watch. Although it's impossible to recreate the king's day on a visit, the following itinerary does allow you to pass all of the rooms of interest. You'll start with the ❶ Royal Chapel, where morning Mass was held, followed by the ❷ Hercules Drawing Room and ❸ Diana Drawing Room, both sites of evening entertainment, while the ❹ King's Library was visited after lunch. The ❺ Hall of Mirrors was for the royal procession, and the ❻ Council Chamber for late-morning meetings with ministers. The day would have begun in the ❼ King's Bedchamber and the ❽ Queen's Bedchamber, where the royal couple was roused at about the same time.

VERSAILLES BY NUMBERS

Rooms 700 (11 hectares of roof)

Windows 2153

Staircases 67

Gardens and parks 800 hectares

Trees 200,000

Fountains 50 (with 620 nozzles)

Paintings 6300 (measuring 11km laid end to end)

Statues and sculptures 2100

Objets d'art and furnishings 5000

Visitors 8.1 million per year

VICHIE81 / SHUTTERSTOCK ©

Queen's Bedchamber
Chambre de la Reine
The queen's life was on constant public display and even the births of her children were watched by crowds of spectators in her own bedchamber. DETOUR » The Guardroom, with a dozen armed men at the ready.

Guardroom

Gallery of Battles

LUNCH BREAK

Contemporary French cuisine at Alain Ducasse's restaurant Ore, or a picnic in the park.

Hercules Drawing Room
Salon d'Hercule
This salon, with its stunning ceiling fresco of the strong man, gave way to the State Apartments, which were open to courtiers three nights a week. DETOUR » Apollo Drawing Room, used for formal audiences and as a throne room.

TAWWAN URK / SHUTTERSTOCK ©

Hall of Mirrors
Galerie des Glaces
The solid-silver candelabra and furnishings in this extravagant hall, devoted to Louis XIV's successes in war, were melted down in 1689 to pay for yet another conflict. **DETOUR»** The antithetical Peace Drawing Room, adjacent.

WALTER G / SHUTTERSTOCK ©

King's Bedchamber
Chambre du Roi
The king's daily life was anything but private and even his *lever* (rising) at 8am and *coucher* (retiring) at 11.30pm would be witnessed by up to 150 sycophantic courtiers.

Council Chamber
Cabinet du Conseil
This chamber, with carved medallions evoking the king's work, is where the monarch met his various ministers (state, finance, religion etc), depending on the days of the week.

King's Library
Bibliothèque du Roi
The last resident, bibliophile Louis XVI, loved geography and his copy of *The Travels of James Cook* is still on the shelf here. You can only visit this room on a private tour.

Diana Drawing Room
Salon de Diane
With walls and ceiling covered in frescoes devoted to the mythical huntress, this room contained a large billiard table reserved for Louis XIV, a keen player.

Peace Drawing Room

Hall of Mirrors

Marble Courtyard

Entrance

Apollo Drawing Room

North Wing

Souvenirs

Royal Chapel
Chapelle Royale
This two-storey chapel (with gallery for the royals and important courtiers, and the ground floor for the B-list) was dedicated to St Louis, patron of French monarchs. **DETOUR»** The sumptuous Royal Opera.

COJATO / BUDGET TRAVEL ®

SAVVY SIGHTSEEING

Avoid Versailles on Monday (closed), Tuesday (Paris' museums close, so visitors flock here) and Sunday, the busiest day. Also, book tickets online so you don't have to queue.

Fontainebleau

Explore

Fresh air fills your lungs on arriving in the classy town of Fontainebleau, arguably the best springboard for outdoorsy pursuits in the Paris area. The surrounding Forêt de Fontainebleau, a rejuvenating expanse of pine forest and oak trees, lazy sandy clearings and curiously shaped boulders, is a haven for walkers, cyclists and, above all, rock climbers of all nationalities. The town itself grew up around its magnificent château, one of the most beautifully decorated and furnished in France, but consider saving the palace for a rainy day – a trip to the forest is best savoured *en plein air*.

The Best...

→ **Sight** Château de Fontainebleau (p272)
→ **Place to Eat** La Petite Ardoise (p271)
→ **Outdoor Gear** S'Cape Shop

Top Tip

Importantly, train tickets to Fontainebleau/Avon are sold at Paris' Gare de Lyon's SNCF Transilien counter/Billet Ile-de-France machines, *not* SNCF mainline counters/machines. On returning to Paris, tickets include travel to any metro station.

Getting There & Around

Car The forest covers over 280 sq km – hiring a car is the best way to get around.

Train Up to 40 daily SNCF Transilien (www.transilien.com) commuter trains link Paris' Gare de Lyon with Fontainebleau-Avon station (€8.85, 40 minutes).

Bus Local bus line 1 links the **train station** (Gare de Fontainebleau-Avon; place de la Gare) with Château de Fontainebleau (€2), 2km southwest, every 10 minutes; the **stop** is opposite the palace's main entrance.

Need to Know

Location 69km southeast of Paris

Tourist Office (☏01 60 74 99 99; www.fontainebleau-tourisme.com; 4 place de la République; ☺10am-6pm Mon-Sat, 10am-1pm & 2-5.30pm Sun Apr-Oct, shorter hours winter; ☎)

◉ SIGHTS & ACTIVITIES

The **Forêt de Fontainebleau** (Fontainebleau Forest) stretches for 50km from Fontainebleau in the east to Étampes in the west, taking in many small communities along the way, such as Milly-la Forêt and Noisy-sur-École. The many trails here include parts of the **GR1** and **GR11**. Purchase a topo map or walking guide at the tourist office, or try out the **Promenade des Points de Vue**, which leaves from behind the train station. This mellow 12km loop usually takes around four hours, but you can cut it short by walking to the first overlook (30 minutes) and then turning back. Pick up a free map from the tourist office.

But more than any other activity, Fontainebleau is known for its **bouldering** (unroped climbing; *bloc* in French): this is the premier destination in Europe and its thousands of sandstone boulders attract climbers from around the world. It's so big that you can spend a lifetime here and never exhaust the possibilities; a guidebook is essential. The good news is that unlike most bouldering areas, Font has scores of problems that even beginners and children can try – all you need are a pair of shoes and a crashpad (a landing pad that protects you if you fall). Rent them at **S'Cape Shop** (☏01 75 43 19 60; www.scape-shop.com; 21 rue Paul Séramy; crashpads €10-12, climbing shoes €6; ☺10am-7pm Tue-Sat, to 1pm Sun) or sign up for a trip with **Globe Climber** (☏01 64 70 77 69; www.globeclimber.com; from €160). More experienced climbers, note: if you don't want to bring your own crashpad with you, many accommodation options will loan or rent you one.

For more detailed info on bouldering at Font and its iconic colour-coded circuits, check out www.boulderfont.info and www.bleau.info.

✕ EATING & DRINKING

DARDONVILLE BAKERY €
(24 rue des Sablons; sandwiches €2.40-3.50; ☺7am-1.30pm & 3.30-7.30pm Tue-Sat, 7am-1.30pm Sun) Melt-in-your-mouth macarons, in flavours including poppy seed and gingerbread, are refreshingly inexpensive at this beloved patisserie-*boulangerie* (bakery). Queues also form out the door for its amazing breads and great picnic treats like sandwiches and mini quiches.

Fontainebleau

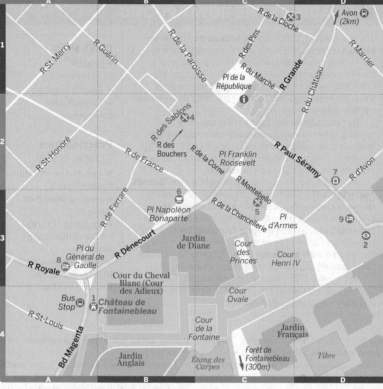

Fontainebleau

CRÊPERIE TY KOZ   CRÊPES €
(📞01 64 22 00 55; www.creperiety-koz.com; 18
rue de la Cloche; crêpes & galettes €3-14; ⊙noon-
2pm & 7-10pm Tue-Sat) Tucked away in a cobbled courtyard, this Breton hidey-hole cooks
up authentic sweet crêpes and *simple* (single thickness) and *pourleth* (double thickness) *galettes* (savoury buckwheat crêpes).

LA PETITE ARDOISE   BISTRO €€
(📞01 64 24 08 66; www.restaurantlapetiteardo
ise.fr; 16 rue Montebello; weekday lunch menu €19,
dinner menu €33; ⊙noon-2pm & 7-10pm Tue-Sat)
Framed by an awning-shaded terrace, the
'little blackboard' has a beamed-ceilinged
interior, stone walls and a scrumptious
variety of daily changing dishes (snail

TOP EXPERIENCE
ADMIRE THE ROYAL ROOMS

The resplendent, 1900-room **Château de Fontainebleau** once housed tenants and guests who were the *crème de la crème* of French royalty and aristocracy. Every square centimetre of wall and ceiling space is richly adorned with wood panelling, gilded carvings, frescoes, tapestries and paintings, with furniture including Renaissance originals.

The first château was built here in the early 12th century, but only a single medieval tower survived the reconstruction undertaken by François I (r 1515–47). It was further enlarged and reworked by successive heads of state, including Napoléon Bonaparte.

Among the château's many highlights are the **Grands Appartements**, which embrace several outstanding rooms, including the Second Empire salon and Musée Chinois de l'Impératrice Eugénie (Chinese Museum of Empress Eugénie). The **Galerie François 1er** (François I Gallery) is a jewel of Renaissance architecture. The château's stately **gardens** (⊙9am-7pm May-Sep, shorter hours Oct-Apr) FREE and courtyards include André Le Nôtre's formal, 17th-century Jardin Français (French Garden), also known as the Grand Parterre, and informal Jardin Anglais (English Garden).

Don't Miss
➜ Grands Appartements
➜ Galerie François 1er
➜ Gardens and courtyards

Practicalities
➜ ☎01 60 71 50 70
➜ www.musee-chateau-fontainebleau.fr
➜ place du Général de Gaulle
➜ adult/child €12/free, 1st Sun of month Sep-Jun free
➜ ⊙9.30am-6pm Wed-Mon Apr-Sep, to 5pm Wed-Mon Oct-Mar

---

cassolette, duck with apricots, honey-roasted pear with salted caramel sauce...). Its kids' menu consists of a smaller portion of an adult dish and a dessert. The wine list is superb.

LE GRAND CAFÉ — CAFE
(www.legrandcafe-fontainebleau.fr; 33 place Napoléon Bonaparte; ⊙8am-1am; 🛜) In a dress-circle position on place Napoléon Bonaparte, this true-to-its-name cafe has a huge terrace; inside it spreads over two chandeliered levels.

🛌 SLEEPING

FONTAINEBLHOSTEL — HOSTEL €
(☎01 78 90 12 90; www.fontainebhostel.com; 14 place de la République, La Chapelle La Reine; dm €32, camping per person €16; 🛜) Housed in an erstwhile Catholic girl's school (1854), this is an invaluable hideaway for climbers and campers, especially if you don't have a car. The six-bunk dorms may be simple, but there are crashpads and mountain bikes for rent, a kitchen, guidebooks for sale, and camping in the garden. Several good boul-

dering areas are a mere 30-minute walk from the hostel.

Located in a small village 15km southwest of Fontainebleau, the hostel can be reached by bus direct from the train station (20 minutes) on the Avon–Malesherbes route.

LA DEMEURE DU PARC — BOUTIQUE HOTEL €€€
(☎01 60 70 20 00; www.lademeureduparc.fr; 36 rue Paul Séramy; d/ste from €286/514; 🅿🛜) A wisteria-draped courtyard garden with chestnut and apple trees is the centrepiece of this charming 27-room hotel. Deluxe-category rooms have their own terraces; ground-floor suites open onto small private gardens. The pick are the suites such as the literary-themed Bibliothèque and travel-themed Voyage (with its own telescope). Its contemporary French restaurant, **La Table du Parc** (mains €25-44; ⊙noon-2.15pm & 7-10.15pm Wed-Sat, noon-2.15pm Sun; 🛜), is one of Fontainebleau's finest.

HÔTEL DE LONDRES — HOTEL €€
(☎01 64 22 20 21; www.hoteldelondres.com; 1 place du Général de Gaulle; d €138-228; 🅿@🛜) Classy, cosy and beautifully kept, the 'Ho-

tel London' faces the château. Its 16 rooms are furnished in warm reds and royal blues. Most have air-conditioning and the priciest rooms (such as room 5) have balconies overlooking the palace. Breakfast is €16.

Chartres

Explore

Step off the train in Chartres and the two very different steeples – one Gothic, the other Romanesque – of its glorious 13th-century cathedral loom above. Follow them to check out the cathedral's dazzling blue stained-glass windows and its collection of relics, including the Sainte Voile (Holy Veil) said to have been worn by the Virgin Mary when she gave birth to Jesus, which have lured pilgrims since the Middle Ages.

After visiting the town's museums, don't miss a stroll around Chartres' carefully preserved old city. Adjacent to the cathedral, staircases and steep streets lined with half-timbered medieval houses lead downhill to the narrow western channel of the Eure River, romantically spanned by footbridges.

The Best...
➡ **Sight** Cathédrale Notre Dame (p274)
➡ **Place to Eat** Le Tripot
➡ **Place to Drink** La Chocolaterie

Top Tip

Allow 1½ to two hours to walk the signposted *circuit touristique* (tourist circuit), taking in Chartres' key sights. Free town maps from the tourist office also mark the route.

Getting There & Away

Train Frequent SNCF trains link Paris' Gare Montparnasse (€14.40, 60 to 75 minutes) with Chartres' **train station** (place Pierre Semard).

Need to Know
➡ **Location** 91km southwest of Paris
➡ **Tourist Office** (☎02 37 18 26 26; www.chartres-tourisme.com; 8 rue de la Poissonnerie; ☺10am-6pm Mon-Sat, to 5pm Sun)

◉ SIGHTS

Chartres' beautiful medieval old city is northeast and east of the cathedral. Highlights include the 12th-century **Collégiale St-André** (place St-André), a Romanesque church that's now an exhibition centre; **rue de la Tannerie** and its extension **rue de la Foulerie**, lined with flower gardens, mill-races and the restored remnants of riverside trades; and **rue des Écuyers**, with many structures dating from around the 16th century.

CENTRE INTERNATIONAL DU VITRAIL
MUSEUM

(International Stained-Glass Centre; ☎02 37 21 65 72; www.centre-vitrail.org; 5 rue du Cardinal Pie; adult/child €7/5.50; ☺2-5.45pm) After viewing the stained glass in Chartres' cathedral, nip into the town's International Stained-Glass Centre, in a half-timbered former granary, to see superb examples close up.

MUSÉE DES BEAUX-ARTS
MUSEUM

(☎02 37 90 45 80; www.chartres.fr/culture/musee-des-beaux-arts; 29 Cloître Notre Dame; ☺10am-12.30pm & 2-8pm Thu, 10am-12.30pm & 2-6pm Fri & Sat, 2-6pm Sun May-Oct, shorter hours Nov-Apr) **FREE** Chartres' fine-arts museum, accessed via the gate next to Cathédrale Notre Dame's north portal, is in the former Palais Épiscopal (Bishop's Palace), built in the 17th and 18th centuries. Its collections include 16th-century enamels of the Apostles made for François I, a collection of paintings by Chaïm Soutine and polychromatic wooden sculptures from the Middle Ages.

✖ EATING & DRINKING

LA CHOCOLATERIE
PASTRIES €

(☎02 37 21 86 92; www.lachocolaterie-chartres.fr; 14 place Marceau; dishes €2.50-4.20; ☺8am-7.30pm Tue-Sat, from 10am Sun & Mon) Soak up local life overlooking the open-air **flower market** (place du Cygne; ☺8am-7.30pm Tue, Thu & Sat). This tearoom-patisserie's hot chocolate and macarons (flavoured with orange, apricot, peanut, pineapple and so on) are sublime, as are its sweet homemade crêpes and miniature madeleine cakes.

LE TRIPOT
BISTRO €€

(☎02 37 36 60 11; www.letripot.wixsite.com/chartres; 11 place Jean Moulin; 2-/3-course lunch menus €16/19, dinner menus €28-38, mains €22; ⊘noon-1.45pm & 7.30-9.15pm Wed-Sat, noon-1.45pm Sun) Tucked off the tourist trail and easy to miss even if you do chance down its narrow street, this atmospheric space with low beamed ceilings is a treat for authentic and adventurous French fare like saddle of rabbit stuffed with snails or grilled turbot in truffled hollandaise sauce. Locals are on to it, so booking ahead is advised.

LE PETIT BISTROT BISTRO €€
(⌨02 37 36 44 52; 12 place Billard; mains €14-21; ⊘11am-2pm Tue & Thu-Sat, plus 7-10pm Tue-Sat) Dishes chalked on the blackboard are all made from the fresh produce at Chartres' iron-canopied market, which the bistro overlooks (terrace seats give you front-row views of the action). Offerings change daily but expect the likes of turbot with black lentils and smoked-garlic aioli or raspberry-marinated veal.

GEORGES GASTRONOMY €€€
(⌨02 37 18 15 15; www.bw-grand-monarque.com; 22 place des Épars; menus €59-103; ⊘noon-1pm & 7.30-9.30pm Tue-Sat) Even if you're not staying at lavish hotel Le Grand Monarque, its refined Georges restaurant is worth seeking out for its Michelin-starred multi-course *menus* and mains such as ginger-marinated salmon with pickled veggies and crustacean bouillon, or blackberry-marinated roast lamb with chestnut puree and green beans. Desserts (confit of grapefruit with Campari gelato, for instance) are inspired.

🛏 SLEEPING

LE GRAND MONARQUE HOTEL €€
(⌨02 37 18 15 15; www.bw-grand-monarque.com; 22 place des Épars; d from €120; ❄🐕📶) With teal-blue shutters gracing its 1779 façade, a lovely stained-glass ceiling and a treasure trove of period furnishings, old B&W photos and knick-knacks, the epicentral Grand Monarque is a historical gem. Some rooms have air-conditioning; staff are charming. A host of hydrotherapy treatments are available at its spa.

◉ TOP EXPERIENCE
VISIT THE MEDIEVAL NOTRE DAME

France's best-preserved medieval cathedral, **Cathédrale Notre Dame**, was built in Gothic style during the early 13th century to replace a Romanesque cathedral devastated by fire in 1194. Construction took just 30 years, resulting in a high degree of architectural unity.

Covering 2.6 sq km, the cathedral's 176 stained-glass windows are mostly 13th-century originals. Three over the west entrance, dating from 1150, are renowned for their brilliant 'Chartres blue' tones.

The 105m-high **Clocher Vieux** (Old Bell Tower) is the tallest Romanesque steeple still standing. The 112m-high **Tour Nord** (North Tower; adult/child €6/free; ⊘10am-12.30pm & 2-6pm Mon-Sat, 2-6pm Sun May-Aug, shorter hours Sep-Apr) or Clocher Neuf justifies the 350-step climb.

Look out for the **Sainte Voile** (Holy Veil), in Chartres since 876, and the enormous medieval labyrinth on the floor (often partially covered by chairs).

Half-hour tours of the 110m-long **crypt** (adult/child €5/4; ⊘up to 5 tours daily) – France's largest – are in French with a written English translation. There are also **English-language guided tours of the cathedral** (⌨Anne Marie Woods 02 37 21 75 02, Malcolm Miller 02 37 28 15 58; visitecathedrale@diocesechartres.com; tours €10; ⊘noon Mon-Sat Easter-Oct & 2.45pm Mon-Sat May-Sep, noon by request Nov-Mar).

Don't Miss
➡ Stained glass
➡ Tour Nord
➡ Sainte Voile
➡ Crypt

Practicalities
➡ www.cathedrale-chartres.org
➡ place de la Cathédrale
➡ ⊘8.30am-7.30pm daily year-round, also to 10pm Tue, Fri & Sun Jul & Aug

Chartres

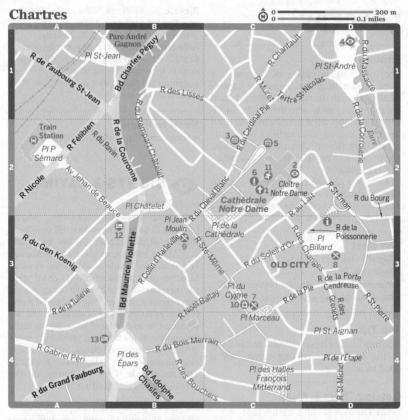

Chartres

HÔTEL DU BŒUF COURONNÉ HOTEL €€
(☎ 02 37 18 06 06; www.leboeufcouronne.com; 15 place Châtelet; d €95-120; 🛜) The red-curtained entrance lends a theatrical air to this two-star Logis guesthouse in the centre of everything. Its summertime terrace restaurant has cathedral-view dining and the bar mixes great cocktails. Cathedral views also extend from some of its 17 modern rooms.

Giverny

Explore

The tiny country village of Giverny is a place of pilgrimage for devotees of impressionism, though the summer months herald the tour-bus crowds, who shatter the bucolic peace. Monet lived here from 1883 until his death in 1926, in a rambling house surrounded by flower-filled gardens; it's now the immensely popular Maison et Jardins de Claude Monet.

Note that the principal sights are closed from November to Easter, along with most accommodation and restaurants, so there's little point visiting out of season.

The Best

➡ **Sight** Maison et Jardins de Claude Monet (p277)

➡ **Place to Eat** Le Jardin des Plumes (p277)

➡ **Place to Sleep** La Musardière (p277)

Top Tip

Advance dining reservations, particularly at the higher end of the market, are a good idea.

Getting There & Away

Train The closest train station is at Vernon, from where shuttle buses, taxis and cycle/walking tracks run to Giverny. From Paris' Gare St-Lazare there are up to 15 daily trains to Vernon (from €14.70, 50 minutes), 7km to the west of Giverny.

Bus Shuttle buses (single/return €5/10, 20 minutes, four daily Monday to Friday Easter to October, five daily Saturday and Sunday Easter to October) meet most trains from Paris at Vernon. There are limited seats, so arrive early for the return trip from Giverny. Tickets are sold on board, cash or credit card accepted. Check the live shuttle schedule on www.sngo-giverny.fr; there is free wi-fi on board.

Taxi Taxis (🕿02 32 51 10 24) usually wait outside the train station in Vernon and charge around €15 for the one-way trip to Giverny. There's no taxi rank in Giverny, however, so you'll need to phone for one for the return trip to Vernon. It is preferable to take the shuttle bus back to Vernon.

Bicycle Rent electric bikes at the **Giver-non Rental Station** (🕿07 66 44 82 22; www.rental-station.givernon.fr; 39-41 rue Emile Steiner, Vernon; half-/full-day bike rental €15/20; ⊗8.30am-7pm), opposite the train station in Vernon, from where Giverny is a signposted 5km along a direct (and flat) cycle/walking track.

Need to Know

➡ **Location** 74km northwest of Paris

⊙ SIGHTS & EATING

MUSÉE DES IMPRESSIONNISMES GIVERNY   GALLERY

(🕿02 32 51 94 65; www.mdig.fr; 99 rue Claude Monet; adult/child €7.50/5; ⊗10am-6pm Easter-Oct) About 100m northwest of the Maison et Jardins de Claude Monet is the Giverny Museum of Impressionisms. It was set up in partnership with the Musée d'Orsay, among other institutions, and the pluralised name reinforces its coverage of all aspects of impressionism and related movements in its permanent collection and temporary exhibitions. Lectures, readings, concerts and documentaries also take place regularly. The audioguide is €4. Admission on the first Sunday of the month is free.

L'ÉGLISE STE-RADEGONDE   CHURCH

Dedicated to St Radegund, this church was originally built in the 11th and 12th centuries, expanded in the 15th century and then greatly restored between 2008 and 2010. The church is most noteworthy for being the **resting place of Claude Monet**, whose tomb can be found to your right as you follow the path around the east side of the house of worship, before you reach the graveyard proper at the rear of the church.

LA CAPUCINE GIVERNY   CAFE €

(🕿02 32 51 76 67; www.lacapucinegiverny.fr; 80 rue Claude Monet; mains €5.50-13.90; ⊗10am-6pm Easter-Oct; 🛜) 🍴 This colourful cafe-restaurant at the heart of Giverny is an excellent pit stop for refreshment and a bite to eat or a beer, either inside or in the garden. The menu runs to reasonably simple fare: sandwiches, quiches, soups and salads, with breakfast served between 9am and 11am. There's live nightly jazz once a month from June through September.

TOP EXPERIENCE
EXPLORE MONET'S GARDENS

Monet's home for the last 43 years of his life is now **Maison et Jardins de Claude Monet**, a delightful house-museum. His pastel-pink house and Water Lily studio stand on the periphery of the **Clos Normand**, with its symmetrically laid-out gardens bursting with flowers. Monet bought the **Jardin d'Eau** (Water Garden) in 1895 and set about creating his trademark lily pond, as well as the famous **Japanese bridge** (since rebuilt).

The charmingly preserved house and beautiful bloom-filled gardens, rather than Monet's works, are the draws here.

Draped with purple wisteria, the Japanese bridge blends into the asymmetrical foreground and background, creating the intimate atmosphere for which the 'painter of light' was renowned.

Seasons have an enormous effect on Giverny. From early to late spring, daffodils, tulips, rhododendrons, wisteria and irises appear, followed by poppies and lilies. By June, nasturtiums, roses and sweet peas are in flower. Around September, there are dahlias, sunflowers and hollyhocks.

Don't Miss
➡ Clos Normand
➡ Jardin d'Eau

Practicalities
➡ 🖉 02 32 51 28 21
➡ www.fondation-monet.com
➡ 84 rue Claude Monet
➡ adult/child €10.50/6.50; combined tickets with Paris' Musée Marmottan Monet (p86) and Musée de l'Orangerie (p118) are also available.
➡ ⊘9.30am-6pm Apr-Oct

★ **LE JARDIN DES PLUMES**　　MODERN FRENCH €€€

(🖉02 32 54 26 35; www.jardindesplumes.fr; 1 rue du Milieu; lunch menu €55, 3-/5-/7-course dinner menus €90/102/115, mains €35-47; ⊘12.15-1.30pm & 7.30-9pm Wed-Sun, hotel closed Jan; 🅿🛜) This gorgeous sky-blue-trimmed property's airy white dining room is a handsome stage for chef Eric Guerin's exquisite and inventive Michelin-starred cuisine, which justifies the trip from Paris alone.

There are also four rooms (€230) and four suites (€330 to €390), combining vintage and contemporary furnishings. It's less than 10 minutes' walk to the Maison et Jardins de Claude Monet. Breakfast is €19.

Little gourmands, aged 12 and under, can enjoy a three-course children's menu for €22.

SLEEPING

HÔTEL LA MUSARDIÈRE　　HOTEL €€

(🖉02 32 21 03 18; www.lamusardiere.fr; 123 rue Claude Monet; d €95-145, f €145-240; 🅿🛜) This two-star 10-room hotel dating back to 1880 and evocatively called the 'Idler' is set amid a lovely garden less than 100m northeast of the Maison et Jardins de Claude Monet. Breakfast costs €14 and savouring a crêpe in the hotel restaurant is a genuine treat. Family rooms sleep three or four people.

LA PLUIE DE ROSES　　B&B €€

(🖉02 32 51 10 67; www.givernylapluiederoses.fr; 14 rue Claude Monet; d/tr from €130/150; 🅿🛜) You'll be won over by this adorable private home cocooned in a dreamy, peaceful garden. Inside, the three rooms (two of which can accommodate families) are so comfy it can be hard to wake up, but the superb breakfast on a verandah awash with sunlight is always further motivation to cast off the duvet. Payment is by cash only.

LE CLOS FLEURI　　B&B €€

(🖉02 32 21 36 51; www.giverny-leclosfleuri.fr; 5 rue de la Dîme; s/d €110/120; ⊘Apr-Oct; 🅿🛜) Big rooms with king-size beds and exposed wood beams overlook the hedged gardens of this delightful B&B within strolling distance of the Maison et Jardins de Claude Monet. Each of its three rooms is named after a different flower; green-thumbed host Danielle speaks fluent English. Cash only.

Sleeping

Paris has plenty of accommodation, spanning all budgets. However, it is often fully booked well in advance, particularly during peak times (April to October, as well as public and school holidays). Reservations are essential at these times, but are also recommended year-round.

While accommodation outside of central Paris might be marginally cheaper, it is invariably a false economy when travel time and costs are considered. Stay in one of Paris' *arrondissements* (city districts) to immerse yourself in Parisian life.

Hotels

Hotels in Paris are inspected by government authorities and classified into six categories, from no stars to five stars. The majority are two- and three-star hotels, which are generally well equipped. All hotels must display their rates, including TVA (*taxe sur la valeur ajoutée;* value-added tax), though you'll often get *much* cheaper prices online, especially on the hotels' own websites.

Parisian hotel rooms tend to be small by international standards. Families may need connecting rooms; if children are too young to stay in their own room, it's often possible to make do with triples, quads or suites.

Cheaper hotels may not have lifts/elevators and/or air-conditioning. Virtually all accept credit cards.

Breakfast is rarely included in hotel rates; heading to a cafe often works out to be better value (and more atmospheric).

Hostels

Paris is awash with hostels, and standards are consistently improving. State-of-the-art properties include Generator's 950-bed 'megahostel' near Canal St-Martin, 10e, and, close by, two by the St Christopher's group.

Some traditional (ie institutional) hostels have daytime lock-outs and curfews; some have a maximum three-night stay. Places that have upper age limits tend not to enforce them except at the busiest of times. Only the official *auberges de jeunesse* (youth hostels) require guests to present Hostelling International (HI) cards or their equivalent.

Not all hostels have self-catering kitchens, but rates generally include a basic breakfast.

B&Bs & Homestays

Bed-and-breakfast (B&B) accommodation (*chambres d'hôte* in French) offers an immersive way to experience the city. Paris' tourist office maintains a list of B&Bs; visit https://en.parisinfo.com/where-to-sleep-in-paris.

Apartment Rentals

Paris has a number of *résidences de tourisme* (serviced apartments, aka 'aparthotels'), such as the chain Citadines (www.citadines.com).

In an effort to keep housing affordable for Parisians, properties on home-share sites such as Airbnb can only be rented out for 120 days and require a 15-digit registration number; check that your rental apartment complies.

Rental agencies also list furnished residential apartments for short to medium stays. Apartments often include facilities such as wi-fi and washing machines, and can be good value. Beware of direct-rental scams (above all, never send money via an untraceable money transfer).

Lonely Planet's Top Choices

L'Hôtel (p291) The stuff of romance, Parisian myths and urban legends.

Hôtel Ritz Paris (p283) Synonymous with Parisian style.

Le Grand Quartier (p284) Canal St-Martin's hippest new hang-out, lounge, garden and rooftop *inclus*.

Hôtel Particulier Montmartre (p286) Montmartre hideaway with an enchanting garden.

Best By Budget

€

Hôtel du Dragon (p290) Homemade jam is on the breakfast menu at this heart-warming spot.

Cosmos Hôtel (p286) Cheap, brilliant value and footsteps from the nightlife of the 11e's rue JPT.

Generator Hostel (p283) Hang-outs include roof terrace, cafe-bar, and basement club styled like a Paris metro station.

Les Piaules (p286) Belleville hotspot to mingle with locals over Parisian craft beer.

€€

Hôtel Diana (p289) Contemporary meets retro in the Latin Quarter.

Hôtel Paris Bastille Boutet (p288) One-time chocolate factory with beautiful art deco tiling and a basement pool.

Terminus Nord (p284) Flamboyant lifestyle hotel opposite Gare du Nord.

Hôtel Providence (p284) Rooms at this luxurious property come with bespoke cocktail bars.

Familia Hôtel (p289) Sepia murals and flower-bedecked balconies in the Latin Quarter.

Hôtel Banke (p281) Spectacularly set in a Belle Époque former bank.

Hôtel Crayon (p282) Line drawings, retro furnishings and coloured-glass shower doors.

€€€

Maison Souquet (p286) Seductive pied-à-terre in Pigalle.

Hôtel Molitor (p281) Stunningly restored art deco swimming pool with gallery-style poolside rooms.

Hidden Hotel (p282) Eco-conscious hideaway near the Champs-Élysée.

Cour des Vosges (p287) Intimate, five-star elegance on Paris' most beautiful square.

Hôtel de Crillon (p282) Palatial hotel on place de la Concorde.

Best Design Hotels

Maison Bréguet (p289) Local artists, writers and musicians worked on this hotel inside a former factory.

Hôtel Georgette (p287) Rooms represent 20th-century art movements displayed at the nearby Centre Pompidou.

Hôtel l'Antoine (p288) Dazzling Christian Lacroix designer creation in Bastille.

Les Bains (p287) Nineteenth-century thermal baths turned nightclub turned rockstar lifestyle hotel.

Off Paris Seine (p292) Paris' first floating hotel is moored on the Seine.

NEED TO KNOW

Prices
The following price ranges refer to a double room with en suite bathroom in high season (breakfast not included).

€	less than €120
€€	€120–€250
€€€	more than €250

Taxe de Séjour
The city levies an accommodation *taxe de séjour* (tourist tax) per person per night:

➜ Palaces (and similar): €5
➜ 5 stars: €3.75
➜ 4 stars: €2.88
➜ 3 stars: €1.68
➜ 2 stars: €1.13
➜ 1 star and B&Bs: €1
➜ Unrated/unclassified: €2.88
➜ 3- to 5-star campgrounds: €0.75
➜ 1- and 2-star campgrounds and marinas: €0.25

Internet Access
Wi-fi (pronounced 'wee-fee' in French) is virtually always free of charge at hotels and hostels. You may find that in some hotels, especially older ones, the higher the floor, the less reliable the wi-fi connection.

SLEEPING

Where to Stay

Neighbourhood	For	Against
Eiffel Tower & Western Paris	Close to Paris' iconic tower and museums. Upmarket area with quiet residential streets.	Short on budget and midrange accommodation. Limited nightlife.
Champs-Élysées & Grands Boulevards	Luxury hotels, famous boutiques and department stores, gastronomic restaurants, great nightlife.	Some areas extremely pricey. Nightlife hotspots can be noisy.
Louvre & Les Halles	Epicentral location, excellent transport links, major museums, shopping galore.	Not many bargains. Noise can be an issue in some areas.
Montmartre & Northern Paris	Village atmosphere and some lively multicultural areas. Many places have views across Paris.	Hilly streets; further out than some areas; some parts very touristy. The red-light district around Pigalle, although well lit and safe, won't appeal to all travellers.
Le Marais, Ménilmontant & Belleville	Buzzing nightlife, hip shopping, fantastic eating options in all price ranges. Excellent museums. Lively gay and lesbian scene. Busier on Sundays than many areas. Very central.	Can be noisy in areas where bars and clubs are concentrated.
Bastille & Eastern Paris	Few tourists, allowing you to see the 'real' Paris up close. Excellent markets, loads of nightlife.	Some areas slightly out of the way.
The Islands	As geographically central as it gets. Accommodation centred on the peaceful, romantic Île St-Louis.	No metro station on the Île St-Louis. Limited self-catering shops, minimal nightlife.
Latin Quarter	Energetic student area, stacks of eating and drinking options, late-opening bookshops.	Popularity with students and visiting academics makes rooms hard to find during conferences and seminars from March to June and in October.
St-Germain & Les Invalides	Stylish, central location, superb shopping, sophisticated dining, proximity to the Jardin du Luxembourg.	Budget accommodation is in seriously short supply.
Montparnasse & Southern Paris	Good value, few tourists, excellent links to both major airports.	Some areas out of the way and/or not well served by metro.

🛏 Eiffel Tower & Western Paris

CAMPING DE PARIS
CAMPGROUND €

(☎01 45 24 30 00; www.campingparis.fr; 2 allée du Bord de l'Eau, 16e; camping/cabin from €28/95; MPont de Neuilly, ☐T2 Suresnes Long-champ) On the Bois de Boulogne's western edge by the banks of the Seine, this year-round campground has 410 sites for tents and campervans, along with kitchen-equipped cabins and static caravans sleeping up to six. Facilities include a cafe, shop, playgrounds and summer bike hire. Some areas have wi-fi. A shuttle bus (return €4) runs to/from the Porte Maillot metro/RER station.

Baby cots, high chairs and barbecues are available for hire.

HÔTEL MOLITOR
HISTORIC HOTEL €€€

Map p366 (☎01 56 07 08 50; www.mltr.fr; 13 rue Nungesser et Coli, 16e; d/ste from €256/581; ❋@🎇❄; MMichel Ange Molitor) Famed as Paris' swishest swimming pool in the 1930s (where the bikini made its first appearance, no less) and a hotspot for graffiti art in the 1990s, the art deco Molitor, built in 1929 and abandoned from 1989, has been restored to stunning effect. All 124 hotel rooms are arranged gallery-style in a U shape overlooking the outdoor pool (heated year-round).

A smaller indoor 'winter' pool is also on the premises. Interconnecting rooms are available for families. The rooftop cocktail bar, brasserie, and original changing cabins transformed into contemporary artworks sign off the dramatic ensemble.

BRACH
DESIGN HOTEL €€€

Map p366 (☎01 44 30 10 00; www.brachparis.com; 1-7 rue Jean Richepin, 16e; d/ste from €450/2600; ❋🎇❄; MRue de la Pompe) A 1970s-built former postal sorting centre was stunningly converted to a hotel by Philippe Starck in 2019. Raw wood, polished concrete, marble, metal, leather and glass feature in the 59 rooms and suites, and public areas including the restaurant and bar (with a street-side terrace) and pool. Top-floor suites have hot tubs and exclusive access to the rooftop kitchen garden. The best have Eiffel Tower views.

Family-friendly amenities include interconnecting rooms and cots.

🛏 Champs-Élysées & Grands Boulevards

HÔTEL CHOPIN
HISTORIC HOTEL €

Map p370 (☎01 47 70 58 10; www.hotelchopin-paris-opera.com; 46 passage Jouffroy, 9e; s/d from €82/103; @🎇; MGrands Boulevards) Dating from 1846, the 36-room Chopin is inside one of Paris' most delightful 19th-century *passages couverts* (covered shopping arcades). Cheaper rooms are small and dark, but the Belle Époque location is beautiful. Baby cots are available.

⭐HÔTEL BANKE
HISTORIC HOTEL €€

Map p370 (☎01 55 33 22 22; www.hotelbanke.com; 20 rue la Fayette, 9e; d/ste from €230/487; ❋@🎇; MChaussée d'Antin–La Fayette) Close to Paris' *grands magasins* (department stores), this spectacular 1908-built former bank, with preserved cash counters, original mosaics and soaring columns topped by a glass dome, is now home to 90 rooms (three wheelchair-accessible) with leather bedheads, designer furniture and marble bathrooms. There are two restaurants, a cocktail bar and a fitness centre.

HÔTEL JOYCE
DESIGN HOTEL €€

Map p370 (☎01 55 07 00 01; www.astotel.com; 29 rue la Bruyère, 9e; s/d from €91/131; ❋@🎇; MSt-Georges) 🌿 Located in a lovely residential area between Montmartre and Opéra, this 44-room hotel has all the modern design touches (individually styled rooms, a skylit breakfast room fitted out with old Range Rover seats) and an ecofriendly policy, including the use of organic products. There are in-room tea and coffee facilities, and free snacks and soft drinks every afternoon.

There are interconnecting rooms for families.

HÔTEL MAISON ATHÉNÉE
BOUTIQUE HOTEL €€

Map p370 (☎01 40 17 99 29; www.maisonathenee.com; 19 rue de Caumartin, 9e; d from €200; ❋🎇; MMadeleine, RER Auber) French interior designer Jacques Garcia used patterned wallpapers, luxury fabrics including heavy velvet and custom-made furniture to create the 20 rooms inspired by operas including *Faust, Aida, La Traviata* and *Don Giovanni* at this sanctum just 300m west of the Palais Garnier. Shimmering mosaic-tiled bathrooms have rain showers and Hermès toiletries.

HÔTEL PRINCESSE CAROLINE HOTEL €€

Map p368 (☑01 58 05 30 00; www.hotelprincesse caroline.fr; 1 rue Troyon, 17e; d from €134; ❋☎; MCharles de Gaulle–Étoile) Footsteps from the Arc de Triomphe, this almost-budget hotel is astonishingly good value. Simple but sweetly decorated rooms with soft lighting and hues of pink, beige and cream are surprisingly spacious for Paris. It's named for Caroline Bonaparte, the younger sister of Napoléon I.

★HIDDEN HOTEL BOUTIQUE HOTEL €€€

Map p368 (☑01 40 55 03 57; www.hidden-hotel. com; 28 rue de l'Arc de Triomphe, 17e; d/ste from €399/559; ❋@☎; MCharles de Gaulle–Étoile) 🖋 The Hidden is one of the Champs-Élysées' best secrets. It's serene, stylish, reasonably spacious, and it even sports green credentials: the earth-coloured tones are the result of natural pigments (no paint), and all rooms feature handmade wooden furniture, stone basins and linen curtains surrounding the beds. The queen-size 'Emotion' rooms are among the most popular.

HÔTEL DE CRILLON HISTORIC HOTEL €€€

Map p368 (☑01 44 71 15 00; www.rosewood hotels.com; 10 place de la Concorde, 8e; d/ste from €970/1750; ❋@☎≋; MConcorde) Built in 1758 by Louis XV–commissioned architect Jacques-Ange Gabriel and transformed into a hotel in 1909, this palatial address at the foot of the Champs-Élysées opposite the Jardin des Tuileries retains its original splendour in its sumptuous rooms and suites, three restaurants and opulent bar.

FAUCHON L'HÔTEL DESIGN HOTEL €€€

Map p370 (☑01 87 86 28 00; www.hotel-fauchon-paris.fr; 4 bd Malesherbes, 8e; d/ste from €423/563; ❋☎; MMadeleine) Luxury caterer Fauchon has opened its own lavish 54-room hotel, with public areas accented in the company's signature fuchsia-pink. Generously sized rooms (25 sq metres to 75 sq metres) all come with herringbone floors, Haussmannian mouldings and a pantry filled with complimentary sweet and savoury treats. There's a fitness centre and spa (in-room treatments available).

HÔTEL EKTA DESIGN HOTEL €€€

Map p368 (☑01 53 76 09 05; www.hotelekta.com; 52 rue Galilée, 8e; d/ste from €290/495; ❋☎; MGeorge V) Psychedelic zebra stripes give this 1970s-style fashionista an unusually playful personality, especially in a neighbourhood where sleeping choices tend more towards the classical. Rooms are smallish but modern – smart TVs, Nespresso coffee makers and universal phone chargers are some of the amenities available. Rooms on the top floor have small, private terraces.

🛏 Louvre & Les Halles

HÔTEL TIQUETONNE HOTEL €

Map p376 (☑01 42 36 94 58; www.hoteltique tonne.fr; 6 rue Tiquetonne, 2e; d from €76, without bathroom from €66; @☎; MÉtienne Marcel) Heart-warmingly good value, this 45-room well-tended address has been in the hotel biz since the 1900s and is much loved by a loyal clientele of all ages. Ranging across seven floors (there's a small lift), rooms are spick and span, and sport an inoffensive mix of vintage decor – roughly 1930s to 1980s, with bathrooms and parquet flooring in some rooms.

Ask for a room in the rooftops with a view of the Sacré-Cœur (701, 702 or 703) or Eiffel Tower (704 and 705)!

★HÔTEL CRAYON BOUTIQUE HOTEL €€

Map p376 (☑01 42 36 54 19; www.hotelcrayon. com; 25 rue du Bouloi, 1er; s/d/ste €140/169/269; ❋☎; MLes Halles, Louvre-Rivoli) Line drawings by French artist Julie Gauthron bedeck walls and doors at this creative hotel. *Le crayon* (the pencil) is the theme, with 26 rooms sporting a different shade of each floor's chosen colour, including coloured-glass shower doors. Guests can swap the books on the bedside table to take home. There's an honesty bar and a lift.

HÔTEL DES GRANDS BOULEVARDS DESIGN HOTEL €€

Map p376 (☑01 85 73 33 33; www.grandsboulev ardshotel.com; 17 bd Poissonnière, 2e; d from €209; ❋☎; MGrands Boulevards) The 50 rooms at this contemporary hotel play with the building's Revolution-era roots, with rustic curtained headboards and vintage wooden stools. Bathrooms come stocked with natural organic soaps. Nonguests should drop by Giovanni Passerini's inner courtyard restaurant, or, even better, for cocktails at the rooftop bar, the Shed.

HÔTEL MANSART HISTORIC HOTEL €€

Map p372 (☑01 42 61 50 28; www.paris-hotel-mansart.com; 5 rue des Capucines, 1er; d/ste from €214/356; ❋@☎; MOpéra) In an 18th-century building based on plans designed by Jules-Hardouin Mansart, Louis XIV's main architect on Château de Versailles, this hotel evokes the era with period furniture, oil paintings and luxury fabrics in its public areas and guest rooms. Mariage Frères teas and Fauchon chocolates are provided in rooms. Fifth-floor rooms have balconies.

HÔTEL ICÔNE
HOTEL €€

Map p372 (✆01 42 97 56 26; www.hotelicone.com; 4 rue d'Amboise, 2e; d from €140; ❄☏; Ⓜ Richelieu–Drouot) From its sleek black lobby to its individually decorated rooms honouring film stars with portraits on the walls, the cinema-themed Icône makes a stylish base close to Palais Garnier, covered arcade Passage des Panoramas and Galeries Lafayette.

HÔTEL RITZ PARIS
HISTORIC HOTEL €€€

Map p372 (✆01 43 16 30 30; www.ritzparis.com; 15 place Vendôme, 1er; d/ste from €1100/1900; Ⓟ❄@☏☀; Ⓜ Opéra) Paris' most rarefied address, the incomparable Ritz retains its original features while incorporating 21st-century technology. Highlights include a manicured French formal garden, a world-first Chanel spa (Coco Chanel lived here), prestigious Ritz Escoffier cookery school and legendary Bar Hemingway (p127).

HOXTON
DESIGN HOTEL €€€

Map p376 (✆0185 65 75 00; www.thehoxton.com; 30-32 rue du Sentier, 2e; d from €299; ❄☏; Ⓜ Bonne Nouvelle) This Parisian outpost of the designer hotel occupies a grand 18th-century former residence. Its 172 striking rooms come in four sizes: Shoebox (from 13 sq metres), Cosy (from 17 sq metres), Roomy (from 21 sq metres) and Biggy (from 32 sq metres). All have intricate cornicing and reclaimed oak floors; some have balconies.

LA CLEF LOUVRE
APARTMENT €€€

Map p372 (✆01 55 35 28 00; www.the-ascott.com/france/paris/la-clef-louvre-paris/index; 8 rue de Richelieu, 1er; studio/1-bedroom apt from €710/850; ❄☏; Ⓜ Palais Royal–Musée du Louvre) The contemporary charm of this *residence* (serviced-apartment hotel) extends from the original sculptures and framed artworks in the lobby to the self-contained apartments. All have nifty compact kitchens fitted with fridges, hotplates, fine bone china, Nespresso machines and all-in-one washing machine/dryers; the pick are the corner apartments (ending with '3') with curvilinear windows overlooking the street. Service is outstanding.

🛏 Montmartre & Northern Paris

★GENERATOR HOSTEL
HOSTEL €

Map p382 (✆01 70 98 84 00; www.staygenerator.com; 9-11 place du Colonel Fabien, 10e; dm/d from €22/77; ❄@☏; Ⓜ Colonel Fabien) From the 9th-floor rooftop bar overlooking Sacré-Cœur and the stylish ground-floor cafe-restaurant to the vaulted basement bar-club styled like a Paris metro station, and supercool bathrooms with 'I love you' tiling, this ultra-contemporary hostel near Canal St-Martin is sharp. Dorms have USB sockets and free lockers, and the best doubles have fabulous terraces with views. Women-only dorms are available.

It's €7.50 for breakfast and €18 for a day's bike rental.

HÔTEL DU NORD – LE PARI VÉLO
HOTEL €

Map p382 (✆01 42 01 66 00; www.hoteldunord-leparivelo.com; 47 rue Albert Thomas, 10e; s/d/q €73/86/125; ☏; Ⓜ Jacques Bonsergent) Offering fantastic value given its prized location near place de la République, this perennial favourite has 23 rooms decorated with flea-market antiques and free bikes for guests to borrow to ride around town. Served in a vaulted stone cellar, breakfast includes locally baked bread and pastries along with homemade jams.

HÔTEL DES BATIGNOLLES
HOTEL €

Map p385 (✆01 43 87 70 40; www.batignolles.com; 26-28 rue des Batignolles, 17e; d €59-119, tr €280; ☏; Ⓜ Rome, Place de Clichy) A twin-set of potted yucca plants herald the entrance to this good-value, three-star hotel in Batignolles. Its 46 rooms come in colour palettes of mellow white, pastel blue and green; smaller attic rooms on the 4th floor particularly appeal to cent-watching travellers. Welcome drinks are served in the stylish lobby-lounge from 3pm until 8pm. No lift. Breakfast is €13.

The hotel also has triple rooms and family-friendly connecting doubles. Some dates require a minimum two-night stay.

DISTRICT RÉPUBLIQUE HÔTEL
DESIGN HOTEL €

Map p382 (✆01 42 08 20 09; www.hoteldistrictrepublique.com; 4 rue Lucien Sampaix, 10e; s/d €112/122; ❄☏; Ⓜ Jacques Bonsergent) Superb-value rates and a clean modern design make this two-star hotel on a quiet backstreet behind place de la République a top sleeping spot in the trendsetting 10e. Its 33 rooms are comfortable (two are equipped for wheelchairs) and come with tea- and coffee-making facilities. Triples and superior doubles with fold-out sofa beds make it a firm family choice. Breakfast is €9.50.

PLUG INN
HOSTEL €

Map p378 (☑01 42 58 42 58; www.plug-inn.fr; 7 rue Aristide Bruant, 18e; dm €25-40, d €90-120, tr €120-150; @🛜; Ⓜ Abbesses, Blanche) Location – a hop and a skip off main street Montmartre – is everything at this bright, clean hostel with bunk-bed dorms and en suite private rooms; doubles come with actual double beds and you can leave the hairdryer at home. Communal areas are small but there's a kitchen, plus staff are superfriendly and rates include breakfast.

Rates can vary considerably depending on when you book and how many beds remain available.

ST CHRISTOPHER'S GARE DU NORD
HOSTEL €

Map p382 (☑01 70 08 52 22; www.st-christophers.co.uk/paris; 5 rue de Dunkerque, 10e; dm/s/d from €10/42/96; @🛜; Ⓜ Gare du Nord) Steps from Gare du Nord, St Christopher's is a modern backpacker hostel with six light-filled floors and 580 beds. Dorms (including women-only dorms) sleep four to 10, but beds are pricey unless you reserve months in advance. Facilities include a laundry and Belushi's bar and restaurant with live music. No kitchen.

HÔTEL MIMOSA
HOTEL €

Map p382 (☑01 42 39 87 10; http://hotel-mimosa.parishotelsweb.com; 16 rue du Faubourg St-Martin, 10e; s/d/q €86/97/174; 🛜; Ⓜ Strasbourg St-Denis) A well-located budget choice for those seeking a bed in the alternative 10e, this two-star budget hotel invariably has a *complet* ('full') sign strung up in its window. Some of its 24 clean, no-frills rooms overlook a quiet interior courtyard; those on the 4th floor require a hike up narrow staircases (leave the jumbo-sized suitcase at home). Breakfast is €7.50.

★ LE GRAND QUARTIER
DESIGN HOTEL €€

Map p382 (☑01 76 21 61 61; www.legrandquartier.com; 15 rue de Nancy, 10e; d from €160; @🛜; Ⓜ Château d'Eau) Hidden on a quiet street near Canal St-Martin, northern Paris' hottest opening doesn't disappoint. A dazzling white façade hides a sharp design interior

with 83 bright hotel rooms (sized 'cocoon' to 'fancy'), a vibrant cafe-bar and lounge (open until 1am), garden with Fermob furniture, pop-up shop and rooftop terrace for occasional yoga classes, after-dark stargazing, romancing...

★ TERMINUS NORD
DESIGN HOTEL €€

Map p382 (☑01 42 80 20 00; www.25hours-hotels.com/en/hotels/paris/terminus-nord; 12 bd de Denain, 10e; s/d from €119/131; ❄@🛜; Ⓜ Gare du Nord) Conveniently located opposite Gare du Nord, this jazzy lifestyle hotel by the 25hours group radically raises the bar in the train-station area with cool interior design and functional but chic Afro-Asian-inspired rooms. Flamboyant street art in public areas is inspired by the 'hood's ethnically diverse make-up, while trendy Israeli-Mediterranean lounge restaurant Neni is a dining address in its own right.

Breakfast is €24.

★ HÔTEL PROVIDENCE
BOUTIQUE HOTEL €€

Map p382 (☑01 46 34 34 04; www.hotelprovidence paris.com; 90 rue René Boulanger, 10e; d from €232; ❄@🛜; Ⓜ Strasbourg–St-Denis) This luxurious hideaway in a 19th-century townhouse in the trendy 10e is exquisite. Its 18 bohemian-chic rooms have rich House of Hackney velvet wallpaper and vintage flea-market finds and some have balconies; the smallest aren't nearly as 'Mini' (by Paris standards) as the name implies. Bespoke cocktail bars in each room come complete with suggested recipes and ingredients.

The downstairs bar-bistro, with a fireplace and delightful summertime pavement terrace, doubles as reception and a rocking 'after work' neighbourhood bar; a pianist plays live jazz and other sounds from 8pm until midnight Tuesday to Saturday.

LE PIGALLE
DESIGN HOTEL €€

Map p378 (☑01 48 78 37 14; www.lepigalle.paris; 9 rue Frochot, 9e; d from €175; ❄@🛜; Ⓜ Pigalle) This offbeat lifestyle hotel's edgy design reflects the neighbourhood's legendary nightlife, while carefully thought-out details like a postcard taped on the bathroom wall and a key ring jangling with Paris souvenirs add personalised touches to the 40 stylish rooms. Each has an iPad loaded with music, and larger rooms have vintage turntables with an eclectic vinyl collection.

The ground-floor bar and restaurant is a happening space, with DJs spinning several nights a week. A restored jukebox with contemporary tunes is set in the basement music room. Kudos for the good-value 'Pigalle 12' rooms – actually tiny twins with bunk beds; some connect, making them ideal for small groups. À la carte breakfast is served until 4pm.

HÔTEL PARADIS
BOUTIQUE HOTEL €€
Map p382 (☑01 45 23 08 22; https://hotelparadis paris.com/; 41 rue des Petites Écuries, 10e; s/d/tr €180/210/310; ❋@☎; MPoissonnière) Soft cream-coloured sofas and design books grace the stylish ground-floor lounge at this three-star hotel in the increasingly fashionable 10e. Stylishly understated rooms mix warm colours and elegant patterned wallpapers, and breakfast (€14) includes housemade yoghurt and croissants baked on-site. A generous sprinkling of on-trend bistros and wine bars are right next door.

GRAND HÔTEL PIGALLE
DESIGN HOTEL €€
Map p378 (☑01 85 73 12 00; www.grandpigalle.com; 29 rue Victor Massé, 9e; d/ste from €209/289; ❋@☎; MPigalle) Created by the cocktail-loving Experimental group, this is a sophisticated lifestyle hotel in south Pigalle (aka 'SoPi') with cocktail 'minibars' in its 37 beautifully crafted rooms and a fabulous no-reservations restaurant, Frenchie Pigalle (p126), the northern outpost of Frenchie by Michelin-starred chef Gregory Marchand.

HÔTEL JOSÉPHINE
BOUTIQUE HOTEL €€
Map p378 (☑01 55 31 90 75; www.hotel-josephine. com; 67 rue Blanche, 9e; s/d €200/220; ❋☎; MBlanche) Life's a cabaret at this novel, four-star boutique address in Pigalle. Named after 1920s cabaret star Josephine Baker, the hotel has 41 rooms with richly patterned wallpapers broken up by solid colours and 1930s period furniture and light fittings. Black-and-white cabaret photos decorate walls, and downstairs in the sociable library-lounge there's an honesty bar, free coffee and board games.

HÔTEL AMOUR
DESIGN HOTEL €€
Map p378 (☑01 48 78 31 80; www.hotelamour paris.fr; 8 rue de Navarin, 9e; d from €165; ☎; MSt-Georges, Pigalle) The inimitable black-clad Amour ('Love') in south Pigalle plays on its long-ago incarnation as a brothel, featuring a soft pink façade and nude artwork (some more explicit than others) in each of its 24 rooms. (No TVs, but that's not the point here.) The beloved ground-floor bistro-bar – open until 2am – has a leafy summer patio garden.

GRAND AMOUR HÔTEL
DESIGN HOTEL €€
Map p382 (☑01 44 16 03 30; www.hotelamour-paris.fr; 18 rue de la Fidélité, 10e; d from €165; ☎; MGare de l'Est) Younger sister to Pigalle's Hôtel Amour, this lifestyle hotel mixes vintage furniture from the flea market with phallic-symbol carpets and the striking B&W nude photography of graffiti artist André Saraiva. The result is an edgy hideaway for lovers in one of Paris' most up-and-coming neighbourhoods. Its bistro is a trendy spot in itself.

R KIPLING HOTEL
BOUTIQUE HOTEL €€
Map p378 (☑01 55 31 91 99; www.kipling-hotel. com; 65 rue Blanche, 9e; d from €148; ❋☎; MBlanche) Part of France's Happy Culture boutique hotel collection, this spellbinding hotel evokes famous works of Nobel Prize–winning writer Rudyard Kipling, such as *The Jungle Book*. Forty rooms, some with balconies and rooftop views, come in soothing pastel blues and greens. Both the lounge and library are beautifully wallpapered.

TERRASS'' HÔTEL
HOTEL €€
Map p378 (☑01 46 06 72 85; www.terrass-hotel. com; 12-14 rue Joseph de Maistre, 18e; d/ste from €153/203; ❋☎; MBlanche) Enjoy one of the finest bird's-eye views of Paris from the rooftop bar of this historic 1911 hotel, which received a stunning designer makeover just over a century later. Darkened corridors lead to 92 rooms with striking black-and-red decor; the vast lobby has a library-lounge and photo booth, and there's a luxurious Nuxe spa, plus running and cycling cabins.

Honey collected from the beehive on the roof is served at breakfast (€25). Weekend brunch (€45) in the panoramic restaurant is worth the advance reservation.

HÔTEL BASSS
BOUTIQUE HOTEL €€
Map p378 (☑01 42 51 50 00; www.hotel-basss. com; 57 rue des Abbesses, 18e; s/d from €109/139; ❋@☎; MAbbesses) In the heart of Montmartre on rue des Abbesses, an original gold-stone doorway marks the entrance to this contemporary hotel inspired by American graphic designer Saul Bass. Soft greys and blues dress its 36 modern rooms, complete with funky chipboard desks and kettle-clad welcome trays. The complimentary coffee and cakes in the lounge-lobby are a welcome touch. Breakfast is €10.

HÔTEL MÔM'ART
BOUTIQUE HOTEL €€
Map p378 (☑01 82 52 26 26; www.hotelmomart. com; 42 rue d'Orsel, 18e; d €185-360; ❋☎; MAnvers) Owned by the Sellam family since 1971,

this up-to-the-minute Montmartre hotel has just 25 generously sized rooms in four different styles – bohemian 'Artistes' rooms sport modern-art motifs while 'Collection Hermès' rooms, clad in beautiful fabrics, scream traditional luxury. There's an interior courtyard, fitness area, spa, fine-dining restaurant and cocktail bar with a tasty tapas menu.

★ **MAISON SOUQUET**   LUXURY HOTEL €€€

Map p378 (📞01 48 78 55 55; www.maisonsouquet. com; 10 rue de Bruxelles, 9e; d from €340; ✳🛜🏊; MBlanche) During the Belle Époque, this mansion sheltered a discreet brothel run by Madame Souquet, which provided the inspiration for its conversion by French interior designer Jacques Garcia into an intimate, five-star boutique hotel. Its 20 ravishing rooms, suites and apartments, with richly patterned wallpapers, silks and embroideries, are named for courtesans, while its lounge areas reflect the bordello's former salons.

Along with a glass-roofed winter garden there's a wood-panelled bar and a library, with a small swimming pool and *hammam* (Turkish bathhouse) in the basement. Look for the art nouveau red lanterns out front.

★ **HÔTEL PARTICULIER MONTMARTRE**   BOUTIQUE HOTEL €€€

Map p378 (📞01 53 41 81 40; www.hotelparticuli er.com; 23 av Junot, 18e; ste from €390; ✳🛜; MLamarck–Caulaincourt) Hidden down a stone-paved alley, this mansion is a magical address. Its five sweeping designer suites are decorated with retro flea-market finds, but it's the garden designed by landscape architect Louis Benech, and the fashionable restaurant and cocktail bar (p148) that really stun. Ring the buzzer outside the unmarked black-gated entrance at No 23.

🛏 Le Marais, Ménilmontant & Belleville

★ **LES PIAULES**   HOSTEL €

Map p390 (📞01 43 55 09 97; www.lespiaules. com; 59 bd de Belleville, 11e; dm/d from €20/72; @🛜; MCouronnes, Belleville) Run by hip, witty staff, this brilliant hostel is the Belleville hotspot to mingle with locals over Parisian craft beer at the stunning ground-floor bar, cosy up in front of the wood-burner, or soak up the sun and panoramic views from the roof terrace. Dorms come with custom bunks and ample bedside plugs; rooftop doubles have sleek all-white decor.

Watch for a second, equally inviting Les Piaules with 192 beds and plant-filled rooftop bar to open on place de la Nation, 11e.

COSMOS HÔTEL   HOTEL €

Map p390 (📞01 43 57 25 88; www.cosmos-hotel-paris.com; 35 rue Jean-Pierre Timbaud, 11e; s/d/tr from €75/92/108; 🛜; MParmentier, Goncourt) Cheap, brilliant value and just footsteps from the nightlife of rue JPT, Cosmos is a shining star with retro style on the budget-hotel scene that, unlike most other hotels in the same price bracket, has been treated to a thoroughly modern makeover this century.

HÔTEL AMERICAIN   HOTEL €

Map p386 (📞01 48 87 58 92; www.hotelamericain. com; 72 rue Charlot, 3e; s/d/tr/q €81/99/140/184; 🛜; MOberkampf, République) It is actually quite astonishing that a no-frills, budget hotel such as this long-standing two-star address still even exists in this impossibly sleek and fashionable part of town. Rooms are plain but functional, and the lobby-lounge with salmon-pink walls and comfy sofas provides a warm welcome. Breakfast is €8.50.

THE LOFT   HOSTEL €

Map p390 (📞01 42 02 42 02; www.theloft-paris. com; 70 rue Julien Lacroix, 20e; dm/d from €32/120; @🛜; MPyrénées, Belleville) This bright, private hostel in Belleville has panache. Dorms sleeping four to eight are decorated with patterned wallpaper, bold colours and contemporary furniture; those on the ground floor open onto an idyllic courtyard patio and one dorm upstairs has its own balcony. All rooms have private bathrooms, breakfast is included, and the well-equipped kitchen, open until 2am, doubles as a bar.

Rooms close between 9.30am and 3pm for cleaning.

MIJE FOURCY   HOSTEL €

Map p386 (📞01 42 74 23 45; www.mije.com; 6 rue de Fourcy, 4e; dm/s/d/tr €34/75/85/111; 🛜; MSt-Paul, Pont Marie) Behind the elegant front door of this *hôtel particulier*, Fourcy welcomes guests with clean rooms and a summer garden to breakfast/hang out in. It's one of three Marais hostels run by the Maison Internationale de la Jeunesse et des Étudiants – the others are **MIJE Le Fauconnier** (Map p386; 11 rue du Fauconnier, 4e; MSt-Paul, Pont Marie) and **MIJE Maubuisson** (Map p386; 12 rue des Barres, 4e; MHôtel de Ville, Pont Marie). Rates include breakfast; evening meals are available in the vaulted cellar.

Rooms (closed noon to 3pm) have a shower but share toilets in the corridor. No alcohol is permitted; there's a curfew from 1am to 7am.

★ HÔTEL GEORGETTE
DESIGN HOTEL €€

Map p386 (☑01 44 61 10 10; www.hotelgeorgette. com; 36 rue du Grenier St-Lazare, 3e; d from €175; ❄🌐; Ⓜ Rambuteau) Taking inspiration from the Centre Pompidou around the corner, this vivacious hotel's 19 rooms reflect major 20th-century artistic movements, including pop art, op art, Dada, new realism and street art, with lots of bold colours and funky touches like Andy Warhol–inspired Campbell's-soup-can lampshades. Art exhibitions regularly take place in the bright lobby. It's gay-friendly and all-welcoming.

HÔTEL CARON DE BEAUMARCHAIS
BOUTIQUE HOTEL €€

Map p386 (☑01 42 72 34 12; www.carondebeaumarchais.com; 12 rue Vieille du Temple, 4e; d from €180; ❄🌐; Ⓜ Hôtel de Ville, St-Paul) The attention to detail at this antique-filled, 19-room hotel is impressive. From the period card table set as if time stopped halfway through a game, to the harp and well-worn sheet music propped on the music stand, along with chandeliers and silk wallpapers, the decor evokes the life and times of the 18th-century playwright after whom the hotel is named.

HÔTEL JACQUES DE MOLAY
BOUTIQUE HOTEL €€

Map p386 (☑01 42 72 68 22; www.hotelmolay.fr; 94 rue des Archives, 3e; d from €180; 🌐; Ⓜ Filles du Calvaire, Arts et Métiers) Muted creams and taupes mix with sassy violet velour at this sleek, three-star boutique hotel footsteps from square du Temple – the Marais location really is five-star. Some rooms, including the stylish bar, feature original beamed ceilings and creamy exposed-stone walls. Extra brownie points for the gym and fitness room, massages on request and tip-top concierge service. Breakfast is €20.

HÔTEL CARON
HOTEL €€

Map p386 (☑01 40 29 02 94; www.hotelcaron. com; 3 rue Caron, 4e; d from €159; ❄❄; Ⓜ St-Paul) Footsteps from delightful place du Marché Ste-Catherine, this is a solid mid-range hotel with comfortable (if smallish) minibar-equipped rooms. Soft natural hues give its 18 double rooms instant appeal and the L'Occitane bathroom products are a sweet-smelling touch. Breakfast (€14) in the cream-stone, vaulted cellar is a highlight.

HÔTEL JEANNE D'ARC
HOTEL €€

Map p386 (☑01 48 87 62 11; www.hoteljeannedarc.com; 3 rue de Jarente, 4e; s/d from €190/212; 🌐; Ⓜ St-Paul) About the only thing wrong with this epicentral Marais address is everyone knows about it; book well in advance. Some of the 34 streamlined, modernised rooms retain timber beams or exposed stone walls, while others have feature walls with patterned wallpaper. The *pièce de résistance:* the 6th-floor attic room (accessible by lift) with a sweeping Paris rooftop view. Breakfast is €12.

HÔTEL DU PETIT MOULIN
BOUTIQUE HOTEL €€€

Map p386 (☑01 42 74 10 10; www.hotelpetitmoulinparis.com; 29-31 rue de Poitou, 3e; d/ste from €255/270; ❄🌐; Ⓜ St-Sébastien–Froissart) A bakery at the time of Henri IV, this 17-room hotel was designed from head to toe by French designer Christian Lacroix. Choose from medieval and rococo Marais rooms sporting exposed beams and dressed in toile de Jouy wallpaper, or more modern surrounds with contemporary murals and heart-shaped mirrors just this side of kitsch.

★ COUR DES VOSGES
BOUTIQUE HOTEL €€€

Map p386 (☑01 42 50 30 30; www.courdesvosges.com; 19 place des Vosges, 4e; d from €490; ❄@🌐; Ⓜ St-Paul) Painted ceiling beams, period terracotta and a mesmerising collection of art, books and curiosities only add to the exceeding charm of this five-star boutique pied-à-terre, hidden in a 17th-century *hôtel particulier* on Paris' most beautiful square. Twelve rooms and suites are a sharp mix of new and old, and all gaze romantically out across place des Vosges.

The vaulted cellar squirrels away a pampering Roman bath with toasty whirlpool, and the hotel's chic *salon de thé* (tearoom) – with a terrace beneath place des Vosges' signature arcades – serves patisserie (cakes) like jewels.

★ LES BAINS
DESIGN HOTEL €€€

Map p386 (☑01 42 77 07 07; www.lesbains-paris.com; 7 rue du Bourg l'Abbé, 3e; d/ste from €292/557; ❄@🌐; Ⓜ Étienne Marcel, Rambuteau) Opened in 1885 as thermal baths (frequented by Marcel Proust, among others), in 1978 this iconic address morphed into the Bains-Douches nightclub, made famous by David

Bowie, Mick Jagger and a galaxy of celebs. Today it's among Paris' most fabulous lifestyle hotels, with 39 bespoke rooms – some with foliage-draped balconies overlooking an interior courtyard – showcasing vintage treasures, luxury fabrics and eclectic design.

LE PAVILLON DE LA REINE
HISTORIC HOTEL €€€

Map p386 (📞01 40 29 19 19; www.pavillon-de-la-reine.com; 28 place des Vosges, 3e; d from €374; ✴@🛜; MChemin Vert) Discreetly set off beautiful place des Vosges, this is a sumptuous address loaded with history – the five-star hotel is named after former guest Anne of Austria, queen to Louis XIII from 1615. Its 56 rooms and suites come in either classical or contemporary decor. A leafy courtyard and revitalising spa render it a real country retreat from the urban hubbub.

There's an on-site gym; free bikes are available for guests.

HÔTEL NATIONAL DES ARTS ET MÉTIERS
HOTEL €€€

Map p386 (📞01 80 97 22 80; www.hotelnational.paris; 243 rue St-Martin, 3e; d from €225; ✴@🛜; MRéaumur–Sébastopol) Behind a classic cream-coloured Haussmannian façade, this contemporary hotel wraps itself seductively around a central atrium. State-of-the-art oak floors, geometric bathrooms with terrazzo bench tops and chic grey-and-blue furnishings dress its 66 rooms, and some interconnect. Tempting public spaces include an Italian trattoria, cocktail bar Herbarium (open until 2am) and a seasonal rooftop bar with swoon-worthy Paris views.

JOBO
BOUTIQUE HOTEL €€€

Map p386 (📞01 48 047 048; www.hoteldejobo.paris; 10 rue d'Ormesson, 4e; s/d from €225/295; ✴@🛜; MSt-Paul) If Joséphine Bonaparte was living in today's celebrity limelight, her nickname would surely be JoBo. That's the philosophy behind the fabulously over-the-top decoration of this 24-room hideaway. Joséphine's favourite motifs adorn sexy, boudoir-style rooms – rose and leopard-skin are used in textured wallpapers – and there's a theatrical canopied courtyard garden.

SINNER
DESIGN HOTEL €€€

Map p386 (📞01 42 72 20 00; www.sinnerparis.com; 116 rue du Temple, 3e; d from €550; 🛜; MRambuteau) The height of luxury and sinful delight, this decadent boutique hotel pushes the boundary of Parisian hospitality: staff sport cheeky black suits with priest-inspired dog collars; erotic reading matter and courtesy products feature in rooms; there's a faux crypt and a candlelit spa with huge bubble pool. Both bar and restaurant buzz with local Marais hipsters.

1K PARIS
DESIGN HOTEL €€€

Map p386 (📞01 42 71 20 00; www.1k-paris.com; 13 bd du Temple, 3e; d €300; ✴🛜; MFilles du Calvaire) Cobalt-blue awnings frame this four-star hotel with colourful Peruvian decor (Inca motifs, photography and two monitor lizards – Macchu and Pichu – in a glass vivarium) in public areas and a funky lounge-bar serving mezcal-based cocktails. By contrast, all-white rooms have a clean, minimalist look. The ultimate indulgence: a penthouse suite with private rooftop terrace and plunge pool.

🛏 Bastille & Eastern Paris

MAMA SHELTER
DESIGN HOTEL €

(📞01 43 48 45 45; www.mamashelter.com; 109 rue de Bagnolet, 20e; s/d/tr/q from €149/159/199/239; ✴@🛜; 🚌76, MGambetta, Alexandre Dumas) This former car park was coaxed into its current zany incarnation by designer Philippe Starck. Its 170 cutting-edge rooms feature catchy colour schemes, polished-concrete walls and free movies on demand. A seasonal rooftop terrace, pizzeria, and restaurant with live music add to its street cred.

★HÔTEL L'ANTOINE
DESIGN HOTEL €€

Map p394 (📞01 55 28 30 11; www.hotelantoine bastilleparis.com; 12 rue de Charonne, 11e; s/d/ste from €171/180/225; ✴@🛜; MBastille, Ledru-Rollin) A showcase for stunning contemporary decor by Christian Lacroix, the 38-room Antoine's five floors reflect a different aspect of the Bastille – the 1950s, nightlife at the Balajo ballroom, romance, technology – where the French designer once lived. Suites have fold-out sofas and can sleep up to four people. Superb amenities include a basement sauna and fitness room, and an honesty bar.

★HÔTEL PARIS BASTILLE BOUTET
HOTEL €€

Map p394 (📞01 40 24 65 65; www.hotel-paris-bastille-boutet.com; 22-24 rue Faidherbe, 11e; d/ste from €225/272; ✴@🛜✴; MFaidherbe-Chaligny) A joinery workshop and later a chocolate factory, the Boutet retains its original 1926 mosaic-tiled façade and art deco canopy, and acknowledges its industrial heritage in its timber-panelled hallways. Ten of its 80 rooms and suites have spectacular terraces. There's a *hammam,* a gym and two beauty treatment rooms, but the biggest bonus is the sky-lit swimming pool with a counter current.

MAISON BRÉGUET   BOUTIQUE HOTEL €€€
Map p394 (✆01 58 30 32 31; www.maisonbreguet. com; 8 rue Bréguet, 11e; d/ste from €228/326; ❄️🛜🏊; Ⓜ️Bréguet–Sabin) Local creatives were involved in the evolution of this former factory turned five-star property: artists' works hang on the walls, writers selected the library's books and films, and musicians put together playlists (performances also often take place here). Some of its 53 art deco–influenced rooms and suites have terraces.

🛏️ The Islands

HÔTEL DES 2 ÎLES   HISTORIC HOTEL €€
Map p396 (✆01 43 26 13 35; www.deuxiles-paris-hotel.com; 59 rue St-Louis en l'Île, 4e; s/d from €179/199; ❄️🛜; Ⓜ️Pont Marie) A venerable 17th-century building shelters this intimate three-star hotel, where 17 classical rooms sport ancient wooden beams and a punchy new decor that evokes the history of the island on which it languishes enchantingly. Top-floor rooms peep out over Parisian rooftops and chimney pots. Breakfast is served in a vaulted stone cellar.

HÔTEL DE LUTÈCE   HOTEL €€
Map p396 (✆01 43 26 23 52; www.paris-hotel-lutece.com; 65 rue St-Louis en l'Île, 4e; s/d/tr from €139/169/209; ❄️🛜; Ⓜ️Pont Marie) An elegant lobby-salon, with ancient fireplace, wood panelling, antique furnishings and traditional board games to borrow, welcomes guests at the lovely Lutèce, a country-style three-star hotel with 23 tastefully decorated rooms across six floors. Those overlooking the village-like street – with *fromagerie* (cheese shop), greengrocer's and chocolate shop – are more atmospheric than those facing the interior courtyard.

⭐**HÔTEL DU JEU DE PAUME**   BOUTIQUE HOTEL €€€
Map p396 (✆01 43 26 14 18; www.jeudepaume hotel.com; 54 rue St-Louis en l'Île, 4e; s/d from €199/268; ❄️🛜; Ⓜ️Pont Marie) Romantically set in a courtyard off Île St-Louis' main street,

this contemporary four-star hotel occupies a 17th-century royal tennis court. Its 30 rooms are each inspired by a different modern artist. Panton chairs add a design edge to the historic beamed and exposed-stone-walled house, and its leafy patio garden is divine. Facilities include a wellness centre.

🛏️ Latin Quarter

⭐**HÔTEL DIANA**   HOTEL €€
Map p398 (✆01 43 54 92 55; www.hotel-diana-paris.com; 73 rue St-Jacques, 5e; s/d/tr from €86/116/165; 🛜; Ⓜ️Maubert-Mutualité) Footsteps from the Sorbonne, two-star Diana is budget-traveller gold. Owner extraordinaire Thérèse Cheval has been at the helm here since the 1970s and the pride and joy she invests in the hotel is boundless. Spacious rooms sport a stylish contemporary decor with geometric-patterned fabrics, the odd retro furniture piece, and courtesy tray with kettle and white-mug twinset.

⭐**FAMILIA HÔTEL**   HOTEL €€
Map p398 (✆01 43 54 55 27; www.familiahotel. com; 11 rue des Écoles, 5e; s €110, d €134-152, tr €175; ❄️🛜; Ⓜ️Cardinal Lemoine) Staff at this friendly, third-generation family-run hotel proudly tell you that nothing ever changes at the Familia. Indeed, the sepia murals of Parisian landmarks, flower-bedecked windows, and exposed rafters and stone walls are clearly from a past era. Some of the 32 rooms have weeny balconies; those on the 6th floor peep at Notre Dame.

HÔTEL ATMOSPHÈRES   DESIGN HOTEL €€
Map p398 (✆01 43 26 56 02; www.hotelatmos pheres.com; 31 rue des Écoles, 5e; s/d/tr/ste from €150/160/240/280; ❄️@🛜; Ⓜ️Maubert-Mutualité) Striking images by award-winning French photographer Thierry des Ouches are permanently exhibited at this design hotel where 56 glam rooms evoke different Parisian 'atmospheres' – nature, monuments, Paris by night, the metro-inspired 'urban' and colourful *salon de thé*–style 'macaron'. A small gym, sauna and water massage bed are tucked away in the basement.

HÔTEL DES GRANDES ÉCOLES   HOTEL €€
Map p400 (✆01 43 26 79 23; www.hotel-grandes-ecoles.com; 75 rue du Cardinal Lemoine, 5e; d €189-219; @🛜; Ⓜ️Cardinal Lemoine) Spanning three two-storey buildings, this welcoming hotel just north of place de la Contrescarpe

has one of the loveliest locations in the Latin Quarter, set around its own private garden courtyard off a medieval street. Rooms are simple but not without charm. Breakfast costs €9; there are 15 on-site car parking spaces costing €30 per night. Rates go up by at least €50 in summer.

HÔTEL ST-JACQUES HOTEL €€

Map p398 (📞01 44 07 45 45; www.paris-hotel-stjacques.com; 35 rue des Écoles, 5e; d €206-290, tr €305; ❄@🛜; MMaubert-Mutualité) Framed reproductions of famous artworks line the walls of this Belle Époque–styled hotel. Original 19th-century details include trompe l'œil ceilings evoking cloud-filled skies, an iron staircase and balconies overlooking the Panthéon. In keeping with its old-world spirit, hotel bar Toulouse Lautrec serves absinthe.

FIVE HOTEL BOUTIQUE HOTEL €€

Map p400 (📞01 43 31 74 21; www.thefivehotel.com; 3 rue Flatters, 5e; d €145-342; ❄@🛜; MLes Gobelins) Fibre-optic lighting enhances the small rooms at this contemporary romantic sanctum. Rooms become more spacious as you move up the price scale; its One By the Five suite has a phenomenal 'levitating' bed. In-room massages and beauty treatments can be arranged. Express/buffet breakfast €9/15.

HÔTEL LA LANTERNE BOUTIQUE HOTEL €€€

Map p398 (📞01 53 19 88 39; www.hotel-la-lanterne.com; 12 rue de la Montagne Ste-Geneviève, 5e; d/ste from €210/380; ❄@🛜🏊; MMaubert-Mutualité) A stunning swimming pool and hammam in a vaulted stone cellar, a topiary-filled courtyard garden, contemporary guest rooms (some with small balconies) with black-and-white photos of Parisian architecture, amenities including Nespresso machines and an honesty bar make this a jewel of a boutique hotel.

HÔTEL MONTE CRISTO DESIGN HOTEL €€€

Map p400 (📞01 40 09 09 09; www.hotelmontecristoparis.com; 20-22 rue Pascal, 5e; d €405-450; ❄🛜🏊; MCensier Daubenton) If you had just escaped from the Château d'If and picked up a shipload of Italian treasure on the way home, perhaps the Monte Cristo is what your Paris pied-à-terre would look like. Sensuous, chic and with the occasional surprise (like the basement pool), this is a fabulous place to lay your head, particularly if you're a Dumas fan.

HÔTEL RÉSIDENCE HENRI IV HOTEL €€€

Map p398 (📞01 44 41 31 81; www.residencehenri4.com; 50 rue des Bernardins, 5e; d €310-410, apt €450-745; ❄🛜; MMaubert-Mutualité) This exquisite late-19th-century cul-de-sac hotel has eight generously sized rooms (minimum 17 sq metres) and five two-room apartments (minimum 25 sq metres), done up with regal touches like draped fabrics and four-poster beds in some rooms. Apartments are equipped with kitchenettes (induction cooktops, fridge, microwave and dishes), making them particularly handy for families and market goers.

🛏 St-Germain & Les Invalides

⭐HÔTEL DU DRAGON HOTEL €

Map p402 (📞01 45 48 51 05; www.hoteldudragon.com; 36 rue du Dragon, 6e; d from €105; 🛜; MSt-Sulpice) It's hard to believe that such a gem of a budget hotel still exists in this ultrachic part of St-Germain. A family affair for the last five generations, today the ever-charming Roy runs the 28-room Dragon with his children, Sébastien and Marie-Hélène. Spotlessly clean rooms are decidedly large by Paris standards, often with exposed wooden beams and lovely vintage furnishings.

HÔTEL LE CLÉMENT HOTEL €€

Map p402 (📞01 43 26 53 60; www.hotelclementparis.com; 6 rue Clément, 6e; s/d/ste from €85/110/160; ❄🛜; MSt-Germain des Prés) Excellent value for the style and tranquillity it offers, the Clément has 28 stylish rooms (with beautiful printed wallpapers and fabrics), some overlooking the Marché St-Germain. Rooms on the top floor have sloping ceilings. The proprietors know what they're doing – this place has been in the same family for over a century.

⭐HÔTEL LE COMTESSE BOUTIQUE HOTEL €€

Map p406 (📞01 45 51 29 29; www.comtesse-hotel.com; 29 av de Tourville, 7e; d from €173; ❄🛜; MÉcole Militaire) A five-star view of Mademoiselle Eiffel seduces guests in every single room at the Countess, an utterly charming boutique hotel at home in a 19th-century building with alluring wrought-iron balconies. Colour palettes are playful, and the feathered quill pen adorning the desk in each room is one of many cute touches. The glamorous, boudoir-styled cafe has a pavement terrace.

SLEEPING ST-GERMAIN & LES INVALIDES

★ **HÔTEL & SPA**
LA BELLE JULIETTE   BOUTIQUE HOTEL €€

Map p406 (☎01 42 22 97 40; www.hotel-belle-juliette-paris.com; 92 rue du Cherche Midi, 6e; d from €200; ✳🛜; MVaneau) The four-star Belle Juliette exudes an air of elegance and class and its atmosphere can be defined as 'modern romantic'. The individually designed rooms and suites and public areas strike a perfect balance between glamour, design and functionality. Amenities include an ultracool spa, a bar, a restaurant and a lovely terrace at the back.

LE BELLECHASSE   DESIGN HOTEL €€

Map p406 (☎01 45 50 22 31; www.lebellechasse.com; 8 rue de Bellechasse, 7e; s/d from €179/189; ✳🛜; MSolférino) Handily placed near the Seine and Musée d'Orsay, 33-room Le Bellechasse is an enticing, sensorial feast. Entrancing room themes by fashion designer Christian Lacroix – including St-Germain, with brocades, zebra striping and faux-gold leafing; Tuileries, with trompe l'œil and palms; and Jeu de Paume, with giant playing-card motifs – create the impression you've stepped into a larger-than-life oil painting.

HÔTEL PRINCE DE CONTI   BOUTIQUE HOTEL €€

Map p402 (☎01 44 07 30 40; www.prince-de-conti.com; 8 rue Guénégaud, 6e; d from €138; 🛜; MPont Neuf) Tucked around the corner from the neoclassical Monnaie de Paris, three-star Prince de Conti lives up to its regal name. Toile de Jouy fabrics, impeccably curated vintage furniture and Fragonard bathroom amenities lend rooms a soothing bourgeois elegance; the downstairs salon – with complimentary coffee, honesty bar and books to browse – is a delightful place to lounge. Breakfast €16.

★ **L'HÔTEL**   BOUTIQUE HOTEL €€€

Map p402 (☎01 44 41 99 00; www.l-hotel.com; 13 rue des Beaux Arts, 6e; d/ste from €332/739; ✳@🛜⌘; MSt-Germain des Prés) In a quiet quayside street, this 20-room establishment is the stuff of romance, Parisian myths and urban legends. Rock- and film-star patrons fight to sleep in the Oscar Wilde Suite, decorated with a peacock motif, where the Irish playwright died in 1900. A stunning, modern swimming pool occupies the ancient cellar.

Guests and nonguests can soak up the atmosphere of the fantastic bar (either for Champagne-fuelled afternoon tea or after dark over live music by up-and-coming new talent) and Michelin-starred restaurant (called, what else, Le Restaurant) under a glass canopy.

HÔTEL D'ANGLETERRE   HISTORIC HOTEL €€€

Map p402 (☎01 42 60 34 72; www.hotel-danglet erre.com; 44 rue Jacob, 6e; d from €222; @🛜; MSt-Germain des Prés) If the walls could talk... This former garden of the British Embassy is where the Treaty of Paris ending the American Revolution was prepared in 1783. Hemingway lodged here in 1921 (in room 14), as did Charles Lindbergh in 1927 after completing the world's first solo nonstop flight from New York to Paris. Its 27 exquisite rooms are individually decorated. Rates include breakfast.

HÔTEL JULIANA   BOUTIQUE HOTEL €€€

Map p406 (☎01 44 05 70 00; www.hoteljuliana.paris; 10 rue Cognacq Jay, 7e; d from €260; ✳🛜; MAlma–Marceau, RER Pont de d'Alma) 🌿 Geometric designs and shimmering mosaics give an updated '70s aesthetic to many of the 40 spacious rooms and suites at five-star Juliana; others have art deco or baroque influences. There's a rooftop sun terrace and the health club has a fitness room and steam room.

LE SAINT   HOTEL €€€

Map p402 (☎01 42 61 01 51; www.lesainthotel paris.com; 3 rue du Pré aux Clercs, 7e; d from €225; ✳🛜; MSt-Germain des Prés) Live the St-Germain des Prés life at this hotel on a peaceful side street strolling distance from the area's churches, markets, literary cafes and the Seine. Some of its 54 rooms and suites have balconies or terraces; all have shimmering fabrics. An open fireplace blazes in the lounge; there's an in-house restaurant, Kult, and a bar.

🛏 Montparnasse & Southern Paris

3 DUCKS HOSTEL   HOSTEL €

Map p414 (☎01 48 42 04 05; www.3ducks.fr; 6 place Étienne Pernet, 15e; dm/d/q from €28.95/89/144; ✳🛜; MFélix Faure) A lively bar (open day and night to guests and nonguests), courtyard BBQ and no curfew or lockout give this reinvigorated hostel, a 10-minute walk from the Eiffel Tower, a good-time vibe. Facilities are excellent (self-catering kitchen, small lockers, plus a luggage room and multiple USB outlets and a lamp per bed), there's a women-only dorm and freebies include breakfast.

OOPS
HOSTEL €

Map p410 (☑01 47 07 47 00; www.oops-paris. com; 50 av des Gobelins, 13e; dm €27-45, d €70-115; ❄️🛜; MGobelins) Two gigantic pot plants herald the entrance to this colourful design hostel above a pizza restaurant on busy av des Gobelins. Four- to six-bed dorms and doubles have en suites and are accessible all day. Some peek at the Eiffel Tower. Rates include breakfast, sheets, use of the kitchen and luggage room. No credit cards; no alcohol allowed.

HÔTEL CARLADEZ CAMBRONNE
HOTEL €

Map p414 (☑01 47 34 07 12; www.hotelcarladez. com; 3 place du Général Beuret, 15e; d from €129; 🛜; MVaugirard) On a quintessentially Parisian cafe-clad square, this very good-value hotel has 27 comfortable rooms with attractive wallpapers and fabrics. Higher-priced superior rooms come with bathtubs, more space and tend to be quieter. Communal coffee- and tea-making facilities let you make yourself at home. Check its website for last-minute deals.

URBAN BIVOUAC HOTEL
HOTEL €

Map p410 (☑01 83 75 69 83; www.ubparis.com; 1 rue Sthrau, 13e; s/d from €82/92; ❄️🛜) Entirely renovated in 2018, the UB is a great base if you want to explore the Bibliothèque Nationale de France area and the Butte aux Cailles neighbourhood. It has sleek modern styling, with blonde wood furniture in the 32 smart, restful rooms. Fantastic deals can be had online.

★HÔTEL HENRIETTE
DESIGN HOTEL €€

Map p410 (☑01 47 07 26 90; www.hotelhenriette. com; 9 rue des Gobelins, 13e; s/d/tr from €109/119/189; ❄️🛜; MLes Gobelins) Interior designer Vanessa Scoffier scoured Paris' flea markets to source Platner chairs, 1950s lighting and other unique vintage pieces for the 32 rooms at bohemian Henriette – one of the Left Bank's most stunning boutique addresses. Guests can mingle in the light-flooded glass atrium and adjoining plant-filled patio with wrought-iron furniture. Prices vary a lot depending on demand and season – check the website.

OFF PARIS SEINE
HOTEL €€

Map p410 (☑01 44 06 62 66; www.offparis seine.com; 86 quai d'Austerlitz, 13e; d/ste from €139/259; 🛜✉️; MGare d'Austerlitz) Should the idea of being gently rocked to sleep take your fancy, check into Paris' first floating hotel. The sleek, 80m-long catamaran-design structure moored by Pont Charles de Gaulle sports sun terraces overlooking the Seine, a chic bar by a 15m-long dipping pool, a lounge and 58 stunning rooms and suites, some of which have Seine views.

There's live music on weekends.

HÔTEL VIC EIFFEL
BOUTIQUE HOTEL €€

Map p412 (☑01 53 86 83 83; www.hotelvic eiffel.com; 92 bd Garibaldi, 15e; d from €130; 🛜; MSèvres-Lecourbe) A short walk from the Eiffel Tower, with the metro on the doorstep, this pristine hotel has chic orange and oyster-grey rooms. Classic doubles are small but perfectly functional and sport a coffee machine, Kusmi tea and sweet-scented L'Occitane bathroom products. Rates plummet outside high season. Breakfast, served in an atrium-style courtyard, costs €14.

HÔTEL MAX
BOUTIQUE HOTEL €€

Map p412 (☑01 43 27 60 80; www.hotel-max.fr; 34 rue d'Alésia, 14e; d from €138; ❄️🛜; MAlésia) Some of the 19 rooms at this contemporary boutique hotel in the heart of the 14e have balconies and all have in-room coffee machines, muted colour palettes, modern art on the walls, timber floors and Italian bathrooms. The stylish lounge and twinset of small gardens beg relaxation. Low season, snag a double for €85 (check the website for deals). Breakfast €12.

★LES RÉSIDENCES LAVAUD
APARTMENT €€€

(☑06 86 48 26 52; www.lrl-guesthouse-paris. com; 13 rue Beaunier, 14e; d/q incl breakfast €308/990; P🛜; MAlésia) This gem feels like a home away from home, in a very quiet street close to Parc Montsouris. The two suites – one for a couple and one for a family – are fully equipped, well designed and very comfortable. Bonus: Claire, the owner (who lives on the premises), is a great source of information and speaks perfect English (she was a former English teacher).

Both units have a private terrace with Jacuzzi. There's a gym and a sauna, and massage can be organised.

Understand Paris

Above: Art nouveau building near place de la Madeleine (p101)

History

With its cobbled streets, terraced cafes and iconic landmarks, Paris evokes a sense of timelessness, yet the city has changed and evolved dramatically over the centuries. Paris' history is a saga of battles, bloodshed, grand-scale excesses, revolution, reformation, resistance, renaissance and constant reinvention. This epic is not just consigned to museums and archives: reminders of the capital's and the country's history are evident all over the city.

Early Settlers: The Celts & Romans

Gallo-Roman Paris (Lutetia) features in several classic Asterix adventures, including *Asterix and the Golden Sickle*.

The early history of Paris is murky, but the consensus is that a Celtic tribe known as the Parisii established a fishing village in the area in the 3rd century BCE. Years of conflict between the Gauls and Romans ended in 52 BCE, when the latter took control of the territory after a decisive victory during Julius Caesar's eight-year Gallic Wars campaign. The Romans promptly established a new town – Lutetia (Lutèce in French) – with the main public buildings (forum, bathhouse, theatre and amphitheatre) all located on the Left Bank, near today's Panthéon. Remnants of both the bathhouse and amphitheatre are still visible.

Though Lutetia was not the capital of its province, it was a prosperous town, with a population of around 8000. However, raids by the Franks and other Germanic tribes during the 3rd century CE left the settlement on the Left Bank scorched and pillaged, and its inhabitants fled to the Île de la Cité, subsequently fortified with stone walls. Christianity was introduced by St Denis – decapitated on Montmartre in 250 CE for his efforts – and the first church was built on the western part of the island.

The Roman town held out until the late 5th century – mythically saved from Attila the Hun by the piety of Geneviève, who became the city's patron saint – only to fall when a second wave of Franks overran the area for good.

TIMELINE	3rd century BCE	52 BCE	250 CE
	Celtic Gauls called Parisii arrive in the Paris area and set up wattle-and-daub huts on the Seine, possibly in the Nanterre area.	Roman legions under Titus Labienus crush a Celtic revolt on Mons Lutetius (site of today's Panthéon) and establish the town of Lutetia (Lutèce in French).	St Denis, who brought Christianity to Lutetia, is executed on Montmartre. According to legend, he then carries his head 10km north, to the site of the future royal necropolis of St-Denis.

The Middle Ages: Paris as Capital

One of the key figures in early Parisian history was the Frankish king Clovis I (c 466–511). Clovis was the first ruler to unite what would later become France, to convert to Christianity and to declare Paris the capital. Under the Frankish kings the city once again began to expand, and important edifices such as the abbey of St-Germain des Prés and the abbey at St-Denis were erected.

However, the militaristic rulers of the succeeding Carolingian dynasty, beginning with Charles 'the Hammer' Martel (688–741), were almost permanently away fighting in the east, and Paris languished, controlled mostly by its counts. When Charles Martel's grandson, Charlemagne (768–814), moved his capital to Aix-la-Chapelle (today's Aachen in Germany), Paris' fate was sealed. Basically a group of separate villages centring on the Île de la Cité, Paris was badly defended throughout the second half of the 9th century and was raided incessantly by Vikings, who eventually established control over northern and northwestern France.

The Paris counts, whose powers had grown as the Carolingians feuded among themselves, elected one of their own, Hugh Capet, as king at Senlis in 987. He made Paris the royal seat and lived in the renovated palace of the Roman governor on the Île de la Cité (site of the present Palais de Justice). Under the 800 years of Capetian rule that followed, Paris prospered as a centre of politics, commerce, trade, religion and culture.

The city's strategic riverside position ensured its importance throughout the Middle Ages. The first guilds were created in the 11th century, and in the mid-12th century the ship merchants' guild bought the principal river port, by today's Hôtel de Ville (City Hall), from the crown. Frenetic building marked the 12th and 13th centuries. The Basilique de St-Denis was commissioned in 1136 and less than three decades later work started on Notre Dame. During the reign of Philippe-Auguste (r 1180–1223), the city wall was expanded and fortified with 25 gates and hundreds of protective towers.

The swampy Marais was drained for agricultural use and settlement, prompting the eventual need for the food markets at Les Halles in 1183 and the Louvre as a riverside fortress in the 13th century. In a bid to resolve ghastly traffic congestion and stinking excrement (by 1200 the city had a population of 200,000), Philippe-Auguste paved four of Paris' main streets with metre-square sandstone blocks. Meanwhile, the Left Bank – particularly in the Latin Quarter – developed as a centre of European learning and erudition. Ill-fated lovers Pierre Abélard and Héloïse penned the finest poetry of the age and treatises on philosophy, Thomas Aquinas taught at the new university, and the Sorbonne opened its scholarly doors.

In the early Middle Ages, most of today's Paris was either a carpet of fields and vineyards or a boggy, water-logged marsh.

HISTORY THE MIDDLE AGES: PARIS AS CAPITAL

In 1292 the medieval city of Paris counted 352 streets, 10 squares and 11 crossroads.

451	509	845–86	987
Attila the Hun unexpectedly turns away from Paris to march south; credit is given to the prayers of Geneviève, who later becomes the city's patron saint.	Clovis I becomes the first king of the Franks and the first Frankish ruler to convert to Christianity. He declares Paris the seat of his new kingdom.	Paris is repeatedly raided by Vikings for over four decades, including the siege of 885–86 by Siegfried the Saxon, which lasts 10 months but ends in victory for the French.	Five centuries of Merovingian and Carolingian rule ends with the crowning of Hugh Capet; the Capetian dynasty will rule for the next eight centuries.

Dark Times: War & Death

Political tension and open insurrection were brought to Paris by the Hundred Years' War (1337–1453); the Black Death (1348–49), which killed over a third of Paris' population; and the development of free, independent cities elsewhere in Europe. In 1420 the dukes of Burgundy, allied with the English, occupied the capital and two years later John Plantagenet, duke of Bedford, was installed as regent of France for the English king, Henry VI, then an infant. Henry was crowned king of France at Notre Dame less than 10 years later, but Paris was almost continuously under siege from the French.

Around that time a 17-year-old peasant girl known to history as Jeanne d'Arc (Joan of Arc) persuaded the French pretender to the throne that she'd received a divine mission from God to expel the English from France and bring about his coronation as Charles VII. She rallied French troops and defeated the English north of Orléans, and Charles was crowned at Reims. But Joan of Arc failed to take Paris. In 1430 she was captured, convicted of witchcraft and heresy by a tribunal of French ecclesiastics and burned at the stake. Charles VII returned to Paris in 1436, ending over 16 years of occupation, but the English were not entirely driven from French territory for another 17 years.

The Rise of the Royal Court

Under Louis XI (r 1461–83) the city's first printing press was installed at the Sorbonne and churches were built around the city in the Flamboyant Gothic style. But it was during the reign of François I in the early 16th century that Renaissance ideas of scientific and geographic scholarship and discovery really assumed a new importance, as did the value of secular matters over religious life. Writers such as Rabelais, Marot and Ronsard of La Pléiade were influential, as were artist and architect disciples of Michelangelo and Raphael who worked towards a new architectural style designed to reflect the splendour of the monarchy (which was fast moving towards absolutism) and of Paris as the capital of a powerful centralised state. At François I's château, superb artisans, many brought over from Italy, blended Italian and French styles to create what is known as the First School of Fontainebleau.

But all this grandeur and show of strength was not enough to stem the tide of Protestant Reformation sweeping Europe in the 1530s, strengthened in France by the ideas of John Calvin. Following the Edict of January 1562, which afforded the Protestants certain rights, the Wars of Religion, which lasted three dozen years, broke out between the Huguenots (French Protestants who received help from the English), the Catholic League (led by the House of Guise) and the Catholic

The population of Paris at the start of François' reign in 1515 was 170,000 – still almost 20% less than it had been some three centuries before, when the Black Death had decimated the city population.

1066	1163	1358	1572
The so-called Norman Conquest of England ignites almost 300 years of conflict between the Normans in western and northern France and the Capetians in Paris.	Two centuries of nonstop building reaches its zenith with the commencement of Notre Dame Cathedral under the bishop of Paris; construction will continue for over a century-and-a-half.	The Hundred Years' War (1337–1453) between France and England and the devastation and poverty caused by the plague lead to the ill-fated peasants' revolt led by Étienne Marcel.	Some 3000 Huguenots who are in Paris to celebrate the wedding of the Protestant Henri of Navarre (the future Henri IV) are slaughtered on 23–24 August.

monarchy. On 7 May 1588, on the 'Day of the Barricades', Henri III, who had granted many concessions to the Huguenots, was forced to flee from the Louvre when the Catholic League rose against him. He was assassinated the following year.

Henri IV, founder of the Bourbon dynasty, issued the controversial Edict of Nantes in 1598, guaranteeing the Huguenots many civil and political rights, notably freedom of conscience. Ultra-Catholic Paris refused to allow the new Protestant king to enter the city, and a siege of the capital continued for almost five years. Only when Henri IV embraced Catholicism at the cathedral in St-Denis – *'Paris vaut bien un messe'* (Paris is well worth a Mass), he is reputed to have said during Communion – did the capital submit to him. Henri's rule ended abruptly in 1610 when he was assassinated by a Catholic fanatic when his coach became stuck in traffic along rue de la Ferronnerie, south of Les Halles.

Arguably France's best-known king of this or any other century, Louis XIV (r 1643–1715), aka 'Le Roi Soleil' (the Sun King), ascended the throne at the tender age of five. He involved the kingdom in a series of costly, almost continuous wars with Holland, Austria and England, which gained France territory but nearly bankrupted the treasury. State taxation, imposed to refill the coffers, caused widespread poverty and vagrancy, especially in cities. In Versailles, Louis XIV built an extravagant palace and made his courtiers compete with each other for royal favour, thereby quashing the ambitious, feuding aristocracy and creating the first centralised French state. In 1685 he revoked the Edict of Nantes.

From Revolution to Republic

During the so-called Age of Enlightenment, the royal court moved back to Paris from Versailles and the city effectively became the centre of Europe. Yet as the 18th century progressed, new economic and social circumstances rendered the *ancien régime* dangerously out of step with the needs of the country.

By the late 1780s the indecisive Louis XVI and his domineering Vienna-born queen, Marie Antoinette, had alienated virtually every segment of society. When they tried to neutralise the power of more reform-minded delegates at a meeting of the États-Généraux (States-General) in Versailles from May to June 1789, the masses – spurred by the oratory and inflammatory tracts circulating at places like the Café de Foy at Palais Royal – took to the streets of Paris. On 14 July a mob raided the armoury at the Hôtel des Invalides for rifles, seized 32,000 muskets and stormed the prison at Bastille. Enter the French Revolution.

During Louis XIII's reign (1610–43) two uninhabited islets in the Seine – Île Notre Dame and Île aux Vaches – were joined to form the Île de St-Louis.

Paintings by Jules Hardouin-Mansart in the Chapelle Royal at Versailles evoke the idea that the French king was chosen by God and is thus his lieutenant on earth – a divinity the 'Sun King' believed in devoutly.

HISTORY FROM REVOLUTION TO REPUBLIC

1589	1643	1756–63	14 July 1789
Henry IV, the first Bourbon king, ascends the throne after renouncing Protestantism.	'Sun King' Louis XIV ascends the throne aged five but only assumes absolute power in 1661.	The Seven Years' War sees France lose flourishing colonies in Canada, the West Indies and India.	The French Revolution begins when a mob arms itself with weapons taken from the Hôtel des Invalides and storms the prison at Bastille, freeing a total of just seven prisoners.

At first the Revolution was in the hands of moderate republicans, the Girondins. France was declared a constitutional monarchy and reforms were introduced, including the adoption of the Déclaration des Droits de l'Homme et du Citoyen (Declaration of the Rights of Man and of the Citizen). But as the masses armed themselves against the external threat to the new government – posed by Austria, Prussia and the exiled French nobles – patriotism and nationalism mixed with extreme fervour and then popularised and radicalised the Revolution. It was not long before the Girondins lost out to the extremist Jacobins, who abolished the monarchy and declared the First Republic. The Assemblée Nationale was replaced by an elected Revolutionary Convention.

Louis XVI was convicted of 'conspiring against the liberty of the nation' in January 1793 and guillotined at place de la Révolution, today's place de la Concorde. Two months later the Jacobins set up the notorious Committee of Public Safety to deal with national defence and try 'traitors'. The subsequent Reign of Terror (September 1793 to July 1794) saw religious freedoms revoked, churches closed and desecrated, cathedrals turned into 'Temples of Reason' and thousands incarcerated in dungeons in La Conciergerie before being beheaded.

After the Reign of Terror faded, a five-man delegation of moderate republicans set itself up to rule the republic as the Directory.

In 1774 a 30m section of the rue d'Enfer (today's av Denfert-Rochereau) disappeared into a sinkhole, revealing an inconceivably precarious network of mining tunnels upon which southern Paris had been built.

Napoléon & Empire

The post-Revolutionary government was far from stable and when Napoléon Bonaparte returned to Paris in 1799, he found a chaotic republic. In November, when it appeared that the Jacobins were again on the ascendancy in the legislature, Napoléon tricked the delegates into leaving Paris for St-Cloud to the southwest ('for their own protection'), overthrew the discredited Directory and assumed power.

At first, Napoléon took the post of First Consul. In a referendum three years later he was named 'Consul for Life' and his birthday became a national holiday. By December 1804, when he crowned himself 'Emperor of the French' in the presence of Pope Pius VII at Notre Dame, the scope and nature of Napoléon's ambitions were obvious to all. But to consolidate and legitimise his authority, Napoléon needed more victories on the battlefield. So began a seemingly endless series of wars and victories by which France would come to control most of Europe.

In 1812 Napoléon invaded Russia and captured Moscow, only for his army to be quickly wiped out by the brutal Russian winter. Two years later Allied armies entered Paris, exiled Napoléon to Elba and restored the House of Bourbon to the French throne at the Congress of Vienna (1814–15).

From 1784 to 1836 the duke of Chartres turned the now-dignified Palais Royal into one of Europe's foremost pleasure gardens – 'the capital of Paris' – home to theatres, casinos, shops, cafes and an estimated 2000 prostitutes.

1793	1799	1815	1830
Louis XVI is tried and convicted as citizen 'Louis Capet' (as all kings since Hugh Capet were declared to have ruled illegally) and executed.	Napoléon Bonaparte overthrows the Directory and seizes control of the government in a coup d'état, opening the doors to 16 years of despotic rule, victory and then defeat.	British and Prussian forces under the Duke of Wellington defeat Napoléon at Waterloo; he is sent into exile for the second time, this time to a remote island in the South Atlantic.	During the July Revolution, revolutionaries seize the Hôtel de Ville and overthrow Charles X (r 1824–30). Place de la Bastille's Colonne de Juillet honours those killed.

But in early 1815 Napoléon escaped the Mediterranean island, landed in southern France and gathered a large army as he marched towards Paris. On 1 June he reclaimed the throne at celebrations held at the Champs de Mars. But his reign came to an end just three weeks later when his forces were defeated at Waterloo in Belgium. Napoléon was exiled again, this time to St Helena in the South Atlantic, where he died in 1821. In 1840 his remains were moved to Paris' Église du Dôme.

The Second Republic was established and elections in 1848 brought in Napoléon's inept nephew, the German-reared (and -accented) Louis Napoléon Bonaparte, as president. In 1851 he staged a coup d'état and proclaimed himself Emperor Napoléon III of the Second Empire, which lasted until 1870.

France enjoyed significant economic growth at this time, and Paris was transformed by town planner Baron Haussmann (1809–91) into the modern city it is today. Huge swaths of the city were completely rebuilt (demolishing much of medieval Paris in the process), and its chaotic narrow streets replaced with the handsome, arrow-straight and wide thoroughfares for which the city is now celebrated.

The Belle Époque

Though it would usher in the glittering Belle Époque (beautiful age), there was nothing particularly attractive about the start of the Third Republic. Born as a provisional government of national defence in September 1870, it was quickly attacked by the Prussians, who laid siege to Paris and demanded National Assembly elections be held. Unfortunately, the first move made by the resultant monarchist-controlled assembly was to ratify the Treaty of Frankfurt, the harsh terms of which – a huge war indemnity and surrender of the provinces of Alsace and Lorraine – helped instigate a civil war between radical Parisians (known as Communards) and the national government. The Communards took control of the city, establishing the Paris Commune, but the French Army eventually regained the capital several months later. It was a chaotic period, with mass executions on both sides, exiles and rampant destruction (both the Palais des Tuileries and the Hôtel de Ville were burnt down). The Wall of the Federalists in Cimetière du Père Lachaise is a sombre reminder of the bloodshed.

The Belle Époque launched art nouveau architecture, a whole field of artistic 'isms' from impressionism onwards, and advances in science and engineering, including the construction of the first metro line (1900). World Fairs were held in the capital in 1889 (showcasing the Eiffel Tower) and 1901 (in the purpose-built Petit Palais). The Paris of nightclubs and artistic cafes made its first appearance around this

Haussmann revolutionised Paris' water-supply and sewerage systems, and created some of the city's loveliest parks. The city's first department stores were built, as were several of Paris' delightful shop-strewn *passages couverts* (covered passages).

The Extraordinary Adventures of Adèle Blanc-Sec features the swashbuckling adventures of Adèle in early 20th-century Paris. Originally a graphic-novel series created by Jacques Tardi, it was released as a film in 2010.

1848	1852–70	1871	1880s
After more than three decades of monarchy, King Louis-Philippe is ousted and the short-lived Second Republic is established with Napoléon's incompetent nephew at the helm.	Paris enjoys significant economic growth during the Second Empire of Napoléon III and much of the city is redesigned or rebuilt by Baron Haussmann as the Paris we know today.	Harsh terms inflicted on France by victor Prussia in the Franco-Prussian War lead to open revolt and anarchy during the Paris Commune.	The Third Republic ushers in the bloody-then-beautiful Belle Époque, a madly creative era that conceives bohemian Paris, with its decadent nightclubs and artistic cafes.

time, and Montmartre became a magnet for artists, writers, pimps and prostitutes.

But all was not well in the republic. France was consumed with a desire for revenge after its defeat by Germany, and was looking for scapegoats. The so-called Dreyfus Affair began in 1894 when a Jewish army captain named Alfred Dreyfus was accused of betraying military secrets to Germany; he was then court-martialled and sentenced to life imprisonment on Devil's Island in French Guiana. Liberal politicians and writers succeeded in having the case reopened despite bitter opposition from the army command, right-wing politicians and many Catholic groups – and Dreyfus was vindicated in 1900. This resulted in more rigorous civilian control of the military and, in 1905, the legal separation of the church and the state. When he died in 1935 Dreyfus was laid to rest in the Cimetière de Montparnasse.

In 1923 French women obtained the right to – wait for it – open their own mail. The right to vote didn't come until 1945, and a woman still needed her husband's permission to open a bank account or get a passport until 1964.

WWII & Occupation

Two days after the German invasion of Poland on 1 September 1939, Britain and France declared war on Germany. For the first nine months Parisians joked about *le drôle de guerre* – what Britons called 'the phoney war' – in which nothing happened. But the battle for France began in earnest in May 1940 and by 14 June France had capitulated. Paris was occupied, and almost half the population fled the city by car or bicycle or on foot. The British expeditionary force sent to help the French barely managed to avoid capture by retreating to Dunkirk, described so vividly in Ian McEwan's *Atonement* (2001), and crossing the English Channel in small boats. The Maginot Line, a supposedly impregnable wall of fortifications along the Franco-German border, had proved useless – the German armoured divisions simply outflanked it by going through Belgium.

The Germans divided France into two: a zone under direct German rule (along the western coast and the north, including Paris); and a puppet state based in the spa town of Vichy and led by General Philippe Pétain, the ageing WWI hero of the Battle of Verdun. Pétain's collaborationist government and French police forces in German-occupied areas (including Paris) helped the Nazis round up 160,000 French Jews and others for deportation to concentration and extermination camps in Germany and Poland.

Historians debate the overall military effectiveness of the Resistance. But it served as an enormous boost to French morale and continues to inspire French literature and cinema.

After the fall of Paris, General Charles de Gaulle, France's undersecretary of war, fled to London. He set up a French government-in-exile and established the Forces Françaises Libres (Free French Forces), a military force dedicated to fighting the Germans alongside the Allies.

1889	1914	1918	1920s
The Eiffel Tower is completed in time for the opening of the Exposition Universelle (World Fair) but is vilified in the press and on the street as the 'metal asparagus' – or worse.	Germany and Austria-Hungary declare war on Russia and France. German troops reach the River Marne 15km east of Paris and the government moves to Bordeaux.	An armistice ending WWI, signed 82km northeast of Paris, returns Alsace and Lorraine; of the eight million French called to arms, 1.3 million die and another million are crippled.	Paris sparkles as centre of the avant-garde with its newfound liberalism, cutting-edge nightlife and painters pushing into new fields of art like cubism and surrealism.

The liberation of France started with the Allied landings in Normandy on D-Day (Jour-J in French): 6 June 1944. On 15 August that same year, Allied forces also landed in southern France. After a brief insurrection by the Resistance and general strikes by the metro and police, Paris was liberated on 25 August by an Allied force spearheaded by Free French units – these units were sent in ahead of the Americans so that the French would have the honour of liberating the capital the following day. Hitler, who had visited Paris in June 1940 and loved it, demanded that the city be burnt towards the end of the war. It was an order that, thankfully, was not obeyed.

Postwar Instability

De Gaulle returned to Paris and established a provisional government. But in January 1946 he resigned as president, wrongly believing the move would provoke a popular outcry for his return. A few months later a new constitution was approved by referendum. De Gaulle formed his own party (Rassemblement du Peuple Français) and spent the next 13 years in opposition.

The Fourth Republic saw a series of unstable coalition cabinets following one after another with bewildering speed (on average, one every six months), and economic recovery, helped immeasurably by massive American aid. France's disastrous defeat in Vietnam in 1954 ended its colonial supremacy in Southeast Asia. France also tried to suppress an uprising by Arab nationalists in Algeria, where more than a million French settlers lived.

The Fourth Republic came to an end in 1958, when extreme right-wingers, furious at what they saw as defeatism instead of tough action in dealing with the uprising in Algeria, began conspiring in an effort to overthrow the government. De Gaulle was brought back to power to prevent a military coup and possible civil war. He drafted a new constitution that handed considerable powers to the president, at the expense of the National Assembly.

Charles de Gaulle & the Fifth Republic

The Fifth Republic was rocked in 1961 by an attempted coup staged in Algiers by a group of right-wing military officers. When it failed, the Organisation de l'Armée Secrète (OAS) – a group of French *colons* (colonists) and sympathisers opposed to Algerian independence – turned to terrorism, trying several times to assassinate de Gaulle and nearly succeeding in August 1962 in the town of Clamart just southwest of Paris.

In 1962, after more than 12,000 had died as a result of this 'civil war', de Gaulle negotiated an end to the war in Algeria. Some 750,000

After Paris fell to German WWII forces on 14 June 1940, the French Resistance cut the Eiffel Tower's lift cables to prevent Hitler from ascending. Faced with the prospect of climbing the stairs, he opted out of visiting altogether.

HISTORY POSTWAR INSTABILITY

Essential Historical Encounters

Arènes de Lutèce (Latin Quarter)

Conciergerie (The Islands)

Hôtel des Invalides (St-Germain & Les Invalides)

Les Catacombes (Montparnasse & Southern Paris)

1940	25 August 1944	1949	1958
After over 10 months of *le drôle de guerre* (phoney war), Germany launches the battle for France, and the four-year occupation of Paris under direct German rule begins.	Spearheaded by Free French units, Allied forces liberate Paris and the city escapes destruction, despite Hitler's orders that it be torched; the war in Europe will end nine months later.	Simone de Beauvoir publishes her ground-breaking and very influential study *Le Deuxième Sexe* (The Second Sex) just four years after French women win the right to vote.	Charles de Gaulle returns to power after more than a dozen years in opposition, to form the Fifth Republic.

On 15 October 1959, then senator and future president François Mitterrand was involved in a staged assassination attempt on his own life, now known as the infamous Observatory Affair.

pieds noirs (black feet), as Algerian-born French people are known in France, came to France and the capital. Meanwhile, almost all of the other French colonies and protectorates in Africa had demanded and achieved independence. Shrewdly, the French government began a program of economic and military aid to its former colonies to bolster France's waning importance internationally and to create a bloc of French-speaking nations – *la francophonie* – in the developing world.

Paris retained its position as a creative and intellectual centre, particularly in philosophy and film-making, and the 1960s saw large parts of the Marais beautifully restored.

A Pivotal Year: 1968

The year 1968 was a watershed. In March a large demonstration in Paris against the war in Vietnam gave impetus to the student movement, and protests ensued. In May police broke up yet another demonstration, prompting angry students to occupy the Sorbonne and erect barricades in the Latin Quarter. Workers joined in very quickly, with six million people across France participating in a general strike that virtually paralysed the country. It was a period of creativity and new ideas with slogans like *'L'Imagination au Pouvoir'* (Put Imagination in Power) and *'Sous les Pavés, la Plage'* (Under the Cobblestones, the Beach) – a reference to Parisians' favoured material for building barricades and what they could expect to find beneath them – popping up everywhere.

But such an alliance between workers and students couldn't last long. While the former wanted to reap greater benefits from the consumer market, the latter supposedly wanted to destroy it. De Gaulle took advantage of this division and appealed to people's fear of anarchy. And just as Paris and the rest of France seemed on the verge of revolution, a mighty 100,000-strong crowd of Gaullists came out on the streets of Paris to show their support for the government, quashing any such possibility. Stability was restored.

The book (1971) and film (1973) *The Day of the Jackal* portray a fictional account of the attempts by the OAS (a renegade paramilitary group who fought against Algerian independence) to take de Gaulle's life.

Modern Society

Once things were stable, the government immediately decentralised the higher-education system and implemented a series of reforms (including lowering the voting age to 18 and enacting an abortion law) throughout the 1970s to create the modern society France is today.

President Charles de Gaulle resigned in 1969 and was succeeded by the Gaullist leader Georges Pompidou and later Valéry Giscard d'Estaing. Socialist François Mitterrand became president in 1981 and immediately nationalised privately owned banks, large industrial groups and other parts of the economy. A more moderate economic

1962	1968	1978	1989
War in Algeria is brought to an end after claiming the lives of more than 12,000 people; three-quarters of a million Algerian-born French citizens arrive in France.	Paris is rocked by student-led riots that bring the nation and the city to the brink of civil war; as a result de Gaulle is forced to resign the following year.	The Centre Pompidou, the first of a string of *grands projets* – huge public edifices through which French leaders seek to immortalise themselves – opens to great controversy.	President Mitterrand's *grand projet*, the Opéra de Paris Bastille, opens to mark the bicentennial of the French Revolution; IM Pei's Grande Pyramide is unveiled at the Louvre.

policy in the mid-1980s ensured a second term in office for the then 69-year-old Mitterrand.

Jacques Chirac (1932–2019), mayor of Paris since 1977, took over the presidential baton in 1995. His decision to resume nuclear testing on the French Polynesian island of Mururoa and a nearby atoll was met with outrage in France and abroad, and when, in 1997, Chirac gambled with an early parliamentary election for June, the move backfired. Chirac remained president, but his party, the Rassemblement Pour la République (RPR; Rally for the Republic), lost support, and a coalition of Socialists, Communists and Greens came to power – under which France's infamous 35-hour working week was introduced.

Chirac's second term, starting in 2002, was marred by violence in autumn 2005, following the death of two teenage boys of North African origin hiding in an electrical substation while on the run from the police. Riots broke out in Paris' *cités,* the enormous housing estates encircling the capital where a dispossessed population lives. The violence quickly spread to other French cities. Only 9000 burnt cars and buildings later was peace in Paris restored.

Paris is run from the Hôtel de Ville (City Hall) by the *maire* (mayor) with help from 27 *adjoints* (deputy mayors), elected by 163 members of the Conseil de Paris (Council of Paris) and serving terms of six years.

The Political Pendulum

Presidential elections in 2007 ushered old-school Jacques Chirac out and the dynamic, ambitious and media-savvy Nicolas Sarkozy in. Contrary to the rigorous economic-reform platform on which he'd been elected and against the backdrop of the global recession, however, Sarkozy struggled to keep the French economy buoyant. Attempts to introduce reforms – such as the scaling back of the extremely generous French pension system – provoked a series of national strikes and protests. Sarkozy's popularity plummeted, paving the way for socialist François Hollande's victory in the 2012 presidential elections.

With France still struggling to restart the economy, Hollande pledged to end austerity measures and reduce unemployment. His failure to deliver on campaign promises saw his popularity plunge even faster and further than Sarkozy's and resulted in a near-total wipeout for French socialists in the 2014 municipal elections. The 2014 election of socialist Anne Hidalgo, Paris' first female mayor, meant the capital was one of the few cities to remain on the political left. Hidalgo quickly set about greening the city and minimising car traffic and pollution, while ramping up pedestrian and cycling infrastructure.

Historical Reads

....

Seven Ages of Paris (Alistair Horne, 2002)

....

Suite Française (Irène Némirovsky, 2006)

....

The Paris Wife (Paula McLain, 2011)

Turbulent Times

The year 2015 was a harrowing one for the French capital. On 7 January the offices of magazine *Charlie Hebdo* were attacked in response to

1998	2001	2002	2004
France beats Brazil to win the World Cup at the spanking-new Stade de France (Stadium of France) in St-Denis, north of central Paris.	Socialist Bertrand Delanoë becomes the first openly gay mayor of Paris (and of any European capital); he is wounded in a knife attack by a homophobic assailant the following year.	The French franc is thrown onto the scrap heap of history as the country adopts the euro as its official currency, along with 14 other EU member states.	France bans the wearing of crucifixes, the Islamic headscarf and other overtly religious symbols in state schools.

satirical images it had published of the Prophet Muhammad. Eleven staff and one police officer were killed and a further 22 people were injured.

Worse still, on the night of 13 November 2015 a series of coordinated terrorist attacks occurred in Paris and St-Denis – the deadliest on French soil since WWII. Three explosions shook the Stade de France stadium during a football friendly match between Germany and France. A series of neighbourhood restaurants and their outdoor terraces in the 10e and 11e were attacked by suicide bombers and gunmen. Three gunmen fired into the audience of Le Bataclan, where American band Eagles of Death Metal were performing. Over the course of the evening 130 people lost their lives (89 in Le Bataclan alone) and 368 were injured, 99 seriously. Paris went into lockdown, the army was mobilised and a state of emergency was declared.

In the aftermath, place de la République became the focal point for the city's outpouring of grief, and defiant Parisians took to cafe terraces and other public spaces to symbolise a refusal to live in fear.

The city of Paris also refused to allow daily life to be disrupted. The long-planned United Nations Climate Change Conference (COP21) went ahead from 30 November to 12 December 2015. During the conference leaders from around the world reached an agreement to limit global warming to less than 2°C by the end of the century.

Changing Directions

During 2017's presidential elections, the traditional parties were eliminated in the first round, with Emmanuel Macron, who launched centrist, pro-EU movement En Marche! in 2016 – now the party La République en Marche – defeating far-right Front National candidate Marine Le Pen 66.1% to 33.9% in the second-round run-off. At age 39, Macron became France's youngest-ever president. La République en Marche went on to field candidates in 2017's legislative elections and secure an absolute majority (308 seats) in the Assemblée Nationale, allowing Macron to forge ahead with reforming the country's economy.

From late 2018, Macron encountered the first serious challenge to his reforms, when *gilets jaunes* ('yellow vests', named for the hi-vis vests French drivers are required to keep in their cars in the event of breakdowns) protested against his government's eco fuel tax, which quickly spread to encompass a broader dissatisfaction felt by citizens affected by high living costs. Rioting, vandalism and looting by extremists caused the worst damage seen in central Paris since 1968. The government abolished the eco tax, and launched a nationwide consultative *grand débat* (great debate).

Bertrand Delanoë, a socialist backed by the Green Party, became the first openly gay mayor of Paris (and any European capital) in 2001. He was re-elected for a second term in 2008.

The French have the right to free education and health care, state-subsidised child care, travel concessions for families, ample leisure time and a 35-hour working week.

2005	2010	2011	2012
The French electorate overwhelmingly rejects the EU Constitution; the suburbs surrounding Paris are wracked by rioting youths.	Countrywide strikes and protests briefly paralyse the country after the government announces plans to raise the retirement age from 60 to 62 years.	The controversial French parliamentary ban on burkas in public comes into effect in April; Muslim women wearing the Islamic face-covering veil risk a fine.	Socialist candidate François Hollande beats Nicolas Sarkozy to become France's new president, but his popularity is short-lived.

A key plank of Macron's ambitious economic reforms is simplifying France's pensions, by streamlining the complex system of 42 different pensions with varying retirement ages and benefits to a single, unified scheme. Incensed workers responded by staging widespread strikes from December 2019 into 2020, shutting down Paris' metro, the national rail network and numerous other services including Paris' national opera and ballet, accompanied by mass street protests, with *gilets jaunes* swelling the ranks. While most such strikes had abated at the time of writing, the situation remained in flux. Protests against the *passe sanitaire* (health pass) introduced to combat the COVID-19 pandemic, as well as against rising fuel prices, were prevalent in 2021, again including *gilets jaunes*.

In Parisian politics, 2020 saw the city's four central *arrondissements* (city districts), the 1er, 2e, 3e and 4e (collectively rebranded 'Paris Centre') governed by a single mayor to better balance services such as childcare based on the number of residents (though the *arrondissements'* postcodes and identities remain the same). The gargantuan Grand Paris (Greater Paris) redevelopment project – which will ultimately connect the outer suburbs beyond the bd Périphérique ring road with the city proper, to be governed by the Hôtel de Ville – also continues apace, with a massive decentralised metro expansion due to be completed by 2030.

After delays due to the COVID-19 pandemic, the 2020 municipal elections saw incumbent Socialist Anne Hidalgo elected for a second term as mayor of Paris. Since re-election, she has continued to implement an eco agenda including further reducing car traffic.

Looking Ahead

The next French presidential election takes place in April 2022. Hidalgo announced her candidacy for the presidency in 2021. Polls at the time of writing, however, anticipate another second-round run off between Emmanuel Macron and Marine Le Pen, with Macron predicted to win.

Looking ahead, all eyes are on the reconstruction of Paris' beloved cathedral, Notre Dame, the city's spiritual and geographic heart on the Île de la Cité, which caught fire during renovation works on 15 April 2019. Now stabilised, it is set to reopen in 2024.

Another Parisian landmark, the Centre Pompidou, will also undergo major renovations. It will close in late 2023 for an estimated four years.

Meanwhile, Paris is busy preparing to host fixtures for the 2023 Rugby World Cup, and to stage the 2024 Summer Olympics and Summer Paralympics.

The Latin motto *'fluctuat nec mergitur'* ('tossed but not sunk') was adopted by Paris around 1358. Officialised by Baron Haussmann in 1853, it still appears on the city's coat of arms. It became emblematic of the city's spirit following the 2015 terrorist attacks, when Parisians' resilience came to the fore.

2015	2018	2019	2020
The year is bookended by deadly terrorist attacks at the offices of magazine *Charlie Hebdo* on 7 January, and at multiple locations, including concert hall Le Bataclan, on 13 November.	Protests by *gilets jaunes* ('yellow vests') against economic reforms and inequality. From late 2019 there are also widespread protests and strikes against pension reform.	Paris' landmark cathedral, Notre Dame, is ravaged by fire on 15 April, causing extensive damage. Rebuilding is expected to take at least several years.	COVID-19 brings widespread restrictions. Anne Hidalgo is re-elected for a second mayoral term in 2020, and in 2021 announces her candidacy for the French presidency.

Fashion as a Way of Life

Yves Saint Laurent once declared that fashion is a way of life, and Parisians invariably agree. Dressing well is part of the Parisian DNA, the world's eyes are on the city during the biannual fashion weeks, and new labels spring up in the French capital every year. But less well known is that Parisian *haute couture* (literally 'high sewing') as it exists today was created by an Englishman.

Revolution & Drama

Above:Chanel
handbag, Paris
Fashion Week

Nicknamed 'the Napoléon of costumers', 20-year-old Englishman Charles Frederick Worth (1825–95) arrived in Paris and revolutionised fashion by banishing the crinoline (stiffened petticoat), lifting hemlines to ankle length and presenting his creations on live models. The House of Worth stayed in the family for four generations, until the 1950s.

Pioneering French designers included Coco Chanel (1883–1971), Christian Dior (1905–57), Yves Saint Laurent (1936–2008) and Sonia Rykiel (1930–2016), who revolutionised garments with inverted seams, 'no hems' and 'no lining'.

In the 1990s highly creative, rebel-yell British designers such as Alexander McQueen (1969–2010) and John Galliano (b 1960) dominated Paris' fashion scene. One of the industry's biggest influencers, Gibraltar-born and London-raised Galliano moved to Paris in 1991 and became chief designer at Givenchy in 1995. A year later he moved to Dior, the legendary French fashion house responsible for re-establishing Paris as world fashion capital after WWII. Galliano's first women's collection for Dior was spectacular – models waltzed down a catwalk framed by 500 gold chairs and 4000 roses arranged to recreate the postwar glamour of Christian Dior's 1946 showroom on av Montaigne, 8e, in Paris' legendary Triangle d'Or (Golden Triangle). Galliano's downfall was dramatic: in 2011 he was caught on camera casting public insults at punters at his neighbourhood cafe-bar La Perle in Le Marais. He was dismissed by the House of Dior and later found guilty in court of anti-Semitic abuse.

During the same era, French designers who made their mark included 'wild child' French couturier Jean-Paul Gaultier (b 1952), who founded his eponymous fashion label in 1982 and remains known for putting men in punky skirts and Madonna in her signature conical bra. In 2020 he announced that year's couture show, marking the 50th anniversary of his career, would be his last.

Ready to Wear

Céline, prized for its stylish and clever minimalism since 1945, is a luxury label so popular it's practically mainstream in its ready-to-wear, 'fashion for everyone' approach. Chloé is the other big ready-to-wear house, created in 1952 and the first *haute couture* label to introduce (in 1956) a designer ready-to-wear collection. Paris' prêt-à-porter (ready-to-wear) industry was born.

Contemporary Fashion

Outlandish designs by rising stars or world-famous couturiers might strut down the Paris catwalk during fashion week. But you'll encounter few women in the metro wearing their creations: Parisian style is generally too conservative for that.

A good place to take Paris' fashion pulse is the Haut Marais neighbourhood in the 3e *arrondissement,* which is known for its emerging-designer boutiques.

BCBG & Intello

In upper-crust circles, the BCBG *(bon chic bon genre)* woman shops at department store Le Bon Marché or Chanel and rarely ventures outside her preferred districts: the 7e, 8e and 16e. Fast-growing brands like Kooples, Maje, Sandro, Comptoir des Cotonniers and Zadig & Voltaire are huge among BCBG.

The chic Left Bank *intello* (intellectual) shops for trendy but highly wearable fashion at upmarket high-street boutiques such as Agnès b (created in Paris in 1975 by Versailles designer Agnès Troublé – the 'b' gives a nod to her husband) and APC (Atelier de Production et de Création).

Bobo

Bastille, Le Marais and the 10e around Canal St-Martin are stomping grounds of the *bobo* (bourgeois bohemian) – modern bohemians with wealthy bourgeois backgrounds, whose style roots itself in nostalgia for

Fashion Museums & Exhibitions

....

Musée Yves Saint Laurent Paris (Eiffel Tower & Western Paris)

....

Palais Galliera (Eiffel Tower & Western Paris)

....

Les Docks Cité de la Mode et du Design (Montparnasse & Southern Paris)

Two films about fashion icon Yves Saint Laurent were released in 2014: the more innocous 'official' film, *Yves Saint Laurent*, directed by Jalil Lespert (using original costumes), and the edgier but much longer unauthorised film, *Saint Laurent*, directed by Bertrand Bonello.

that last voyage to India, Tibet or Senegal and that avowed commitment to free trade and beads. The wildest *bobos* wear Kate Mack and dress their kids in romantic rockesque designs by Liza Korn, at home in 10e.

Younger professional *bobos* frequent concept store Merci or smaller concept stores with carefully curated collections like L'Éclaireur in Le Marais. Isabel Marant enjoys cult worship among Parisian *bobos* thanks to her chic but easy style that teams wearable-year-round floral dresses or denim mini skirts with loose knits and lush scarves. Another favourite is Vanessa Bruno, a Parisian brand again known for its wearable, if slightly edgy, fashion, such as crocheted bra tops, and cotton skirts with metallic thread to maintain shape. On the jewellery front, designs by Marion Vidal are bold, funky and heavily architecture-influenced.

Paris' Brooklyn-styled hipster is similar to a *bobo* but often without the money. Parisian hipsters reject big-name or known fashion labels for a 'purist', often vintage, look.

Streetwear

Streetwear jumps off the shelves in trendy shops around rue Étienne Marcel forming the border of the 1er and 2e, and Le Marais, 4e.

Streetwise menswear brand Pigalle is based in the 9e and 18e neighbourhood of the same name; it was established by local designer and basketball player Stéphane Ashpool.

Nostalgia & Recycling

Parisians' appreciation of quality means that the desire in less-ultra-trendy circles to have an original Hermès scarf or Chanel black dress never tires.

Vintage

Parisian women play safe with classic designs and monotones, jazzed up by a scarf (those by Hermès, founded by a saddle-maker in 1837, are the most famous) or other simple accessory, hence the fervent nostalgia for the practical designs and modern simplicity of interwar designer Coco Chanel (1883–1971), celebrated creator of the 1920s' 'little black dress'. Equal enthusiasm for pieces by Givenchy, Féraud and other designers from the 1950s heyday of Paris fashion contribute to the overwhelming demand today for vintage clothing.

Twice a year Parisian auction house Hôtel Drouot hosts *haute couture* auctions. Collector Didier Ludot has sold the city's finest couture creations of yesteryear in his exclusive boutique at Palais Royal since 1975. In St-Germain, Catherine B specialises in vintage fashion and accessories exclusively from fashion houses Chanel and Hermès, with a collection at any one time of some 1500 pieces.

THE SHOW OF SHOWS

The Paris fashion *haute couture* shows fall in late January for the spring/summer collections and early July for autumn/winter ones. But most established couturiers present a more affordable prêt-à-porter line, and many have abandoned *haute couture* altogether. Prêt-à-porter shows (aka Paris Fashion Week) are in late February/early March and late September/early October. Shows are exclusive affairs not open to the general public.

For some accessible catwalk action, reserve a spot (p104) at the Friday-afternoon fashion show (mid-February to mid-December) at Galeries Lafayette's flagship Grands Boulevards department store in the 9e.

Haute couture show at Paris Fashion Week

Post-Vintage

Sustainably minded post-vintage fashion is about recycling. Art and fashion studio Andrea Crews, originally based in Pigalle and now at home in Le Marais, was among the first to reinvent grandpa's discarded shirts and daughter's has-beens into new hip garments.

Trends of Tomorrow

Whereas once young designers were snapped up by the big fashion houses, industry prizes and government grants have smoothed the way for a new wave of independent labels.

Each year the city of Paris' Grand Prix Création de la Ville de Paris is awarded to the 'Best New Designer' (working in the trade for under three years) and 'Best Confirmed Designer' (at least three years in the fashion biz). The list of prize laureates is tantamount to a who's who of tomorrow's fashion scene.

Names to watch on the Parisian fashion scene include Marine Serre (winner of the LVMH prize in 2017), who launched her eponymous label in 2018, mixing classic women's couture with sportswear fabrics. Also look out for Ilan Delouis and Jenny Mannerheim of Each X Other (enlisting artists to help design unique fabrics, prints and cuts); menswear designer Boramy Viguier, who draws on traditional military styles; brothers Guram and Demna Gvasalia of Vetements (recycled oversized off-kilter but elegant designs), and Julie de Libran, whose finely crafted, customisable couture encompasses sustainable, ethical production – part of a growing commitment in Paris to make it the world's first sustainable fashion capital by 2024 as part of the initiative Paris Good Fashion (p66).

Paris coined the expression *lèche-vitrine* (literally 'window-licker') for window shopping. 'Tasting' without buying is an art like any other, so don't be shy. The fancy couture houses on av Montaigne may seem daunting but, in most, no appointment is necessary and you can simply walk in.

Architectural Splendour

It took disease, clogged streets, an antiquated sewerage system and Baron Georges-Eugène Haussmann to drag architectural Paris out of the Middle Ages and into the modern world. Yet ever since Haussmann's radical transformation of the city in the 19th century, which saw entire sections razed and thousands of people displaced, Paris has never looked back. Today the skyline shimmers with the whole gamut of architectural styles, from Roman arenas and Gothic cathedrals to postmodernist cubes and futuristic skyscrapers.

Gallo-Roman

Above: View of the 7e from the Eiffel Tower (p82)

Traces of Roman Paris can be seen in the residential foundations in the Arènes de Lutèce, and in the *frigidarium* (cooling room) and other remains of Roman baths dating from around 200 CE at the Musée National du Moyen Âge.

The Musée National du Moyen Âge also contains the *Pillier des Nautes* (Boatsmen's Pillar), one of the most valuable legacies of the Gallo-Roman period. It is a 2.5m-high monument dedicated to Jupiter and was erected by the boatmen's guild during the reign of Tiberius (14–37 CE) on the Île de la Cité. The boat has become the symbol of Paris, and the city's Latin motto is *'fluctuat nec mergitur'* ('tossed but not sunk').

Merovingian & Carolingian

Although quite a few churches were built in Paris during the Merovingian and Carolingian periods (6th to 10th centuries), very little of them remains.

When the Merovingian ruler Clovis I made Paris his seat in the early 6th century, he established an abbey on the south bank of the Seine. All that remains is the Tour Clovis, a heavily restored Romanesque tower within the grounds of the prestigious Lycée Henri IV just east of the Panthéon.

Archaeological excavations in the crypt of the 12th-century Basilique de St-Denis have uncovered extensive tombs from the Merovingian and Carolingian periods; the oldest dates from around 570 CE.

Romanesque

A religious revival in the 11th century led to the construction of many *roman* (Romanesque) churches, typically with round arches, heavy walls, few (and small) windows and a lack of ornamentation that bordered on the austere.

No remaining building in Paris is entirely Romanesque, but several have important representative elements. Église St-Germain des Prés, built in the 11th century on the site of the Merovingian ruler Childeric's 6th-century abbey, has been altered many times over the centuries, but the Romanesque bell tower above the west entrance has changed little since 1000 CE. The choir, apse and truncated bell tower of Église St-Nicolas des Champs, now part of the Musée des Arts et Métiers, are Romanesque.

Gothic

The world's first Gothic building was Basilique de St-Denis, which combined various late-Romanesque elements to create a new kind of structural support in which each arch counteracted and complemented the next. The basilica served as a model for many 12th-century French cathedrals, including Notre Dame de Paris (ravaged by fire in April 2019) and Chartres.

In the 14th century the Rayonnant – or Radiant – Gothic style, named after the radiating tracery of the rose windows, developed. Interiors became even lighter thanks to broader windows and more translucent stained glass. One of the most influential Rayonnant buildings was Sainte-Chapelle, whose stained glass forms a curtain of glazing on the 1st floor. The vaulted Salle des Gens d'Armes (Cavalrymen's Hall) in the Conciergerie, the largest surviving medieval hall in Europe, is another fine example of Rayonnant Gothic style.

By the 15th century decorative extravagance led to Flamboyant Gothic, so named because the wavy stone carving made the towers appear to be blazing or flaming *(flamboyant)*. Beautifully lacy examples of Flamboyant architecture include the Clocher Neuf (New Bell Tower) at Chartres' cathedral; Église St-Séverin; and Tour St-Jacques, a 52m tower that is all that remains of an early-16th-century church. Inside Église St-Eustache there's some outstanding Flamboyant Gothic arch work holding up the ceiling of the chancel. Several *hôtels particuliers*

Interesting and frightening were Le Corbusier's plans for Paris that never left the drawing board. Plan Voisin (Neighbour Project; 1925) envisaged wide boulevards linking the Gare Montparnasse with the Seine and lined with skyscrapers. The project would have required bulldozing much of the Latin Quarter.

Architecture Museums

Cité de l'Architecture et du Patrimoine (Eiffel Tower & Western Paris)

Musée des Plans-Reliefs, Hôtel des Invalides (St-Germain & Les Invalides)

Pavillon de l'Arsenal (Le Marais, Ménilmontant & Belleville) (private mansions) were also built in this style, including Hôtel de Cluny, now the Musée National du Moyen Âge.

Renaissance

The Renaissance set out to realise a 'rebirth' of classical Greek and Roman culture and first affected France at the end of the 15th century, when Charles VIII began a series of invasions of Italy, returning with new ideas.

The Early Renaissance style, in which a variety of classical components and decorative motifs (columns, tunnel vaults, round arches, domes etc) were blended with the rich decoration of Flamboyant Gothic, is best exemplified in Paris by Église St-Eustache on the Right Bank and Église St-Étienne du Mont on the Left Bank.

Mannerism was introduced by Italian architects and artists brought to France around 1530 by François I. In 1546 Pierre Lescot designed the richly decorated southwestern corner of the Cour Carrée at the Musée du Louvre.

The Right Bank district of Le Marais remains the best area for Renaissance reminders in Paris proper, with some fine *hôtels particuliers*, such as Hôtel Carnavalet, housing part of the Musée Carnavalet.

Architectural Icons

Eiffel Tower (Eiffel Tower & Western Paris)

Louvre Grande Pyramide (Louvre & Les Halles)

Centre Pompidou (Louvre & Les Halles)

Baroque

During the Baroque period (tail end of the 16th to late 18th centuries), painting, sculpture and classical architecture were integrated to create structures and interiors of great subtlety, refinement and elegance. With the advent of the Baroque, architecture became more pictorial, with painted church ceilings illustrating the Passion of Christ to the faithful, and palaces invoking the power and order of the state.

Salomon de Brosse, who designed the Palais du Luxembourg in the Jardin du Luxembourg in 1615, set the stage for two of France's most prominent early-Baroque architects: François Mansart, designer of Église Notre Dame du Val-de-Grâce, and his young rival Louis Le Vau, architect of Château de Vaux-le-Vicomte, which served as a model for Louis XIV's palace at Versailles.

Other fine French-Baroque examples include Église St-Louis en l'Île, Chapelle de la Sorbonne, Palais Royal and Hôtel de Sully, with its inner courtyard decorated with allegorical figures.

ART DECO RENAISSANCE

Recent years have seen a renaissance of some of Paris' loveliest art deco buildings. Neo-Egyptian cinema Le Louxor reopened in 2013. The following year, the luxury McGallery arm of the Accor hotel group opened a five-star hotel and spa in the celebrated Molitor swimming-pool complex in western Paris, where the bikini made its first appearance in the 1930s. In Le Marais, thermal-baths-turned-1980s-nightclub Les Bain Douches – another legendary address – opened as luxury hotel Les Bains after years of being abandoned.

Restored art deco swimming complexes also include Piscine de la Butte aux Cailles in the 13e, and Piscine des Amiraux, built in 1930 by La Samaritaine architect Henri Sauvage, its pool ringed by two levels of changing cabins.

Founded in 1870 by Ernest Cognacq and Louise Jaÿ, La Samaritaine was, up until its closure in 2005, one of Paris' four big department stores. Bought by the LVMH group at the turn of the millennium and the subject of a bitter preservationist battle in the years that followed, its 2020 reopening includes a luxury hotel, social housing and office space as well as a new department store. The project, awarded to the Pritzker Prize–winning Japanese firm Sanaa, preserves some 75% of the original art nouveau and art deco exterior.

Neoclassical architecture, Assemblée Nationale

Neoclassicism

Neoclassical architecture emerged around 1740, and had its roots in the renewed interest in classical forms – a search for order, reason and serenity through the adoption of conventions of Graeco-Roman antiquity: columns, geometric styles and traditional ornamentation.

Among the earliest examples of this style are the Italianate façade of Église St-Sulpice, and the Petit Trianon at Versailles, designed by Jacques-Ange Gabriel for Louis XV in 1761. The domed building in Paris housing the Institut de France is a masterpiece of early French neoclassical architecture, but France's greatest neoclassical architect of the 18th century was Jacques-Germain Soufflot, creator of the Panthéon in the Latin Quarter.

Neoclassicism came into its own under Napoléon, who used it extensively for monumental architecture intended to embody the grandeur of imperial France and its capital: the Arc de Triomphe, the Arc de Triomphe du Carrousel, Église de Ste-Marie Madeleine, the Bourse de Commerce, and the Assemblée Nationale in the Palais Bourbon. The peak of this great 19th-century movement was Palais Garnier, the city's opera house designed by Charles Garnier.

The iconic apartment buildings that line the boulevards of central Paris, with their cream-coloured stone, wrought-iron balconies and grey metal mansard roofs, are the work of Baron Haussmann (1809–91), prefect of the Seine *département* between 1853 and 1870.

Art Nouveau

Art nouveau, which appeared in Europe and the USA in the second half of the 19th century under various names (Jugendstil, Sezessionstil, Stile Liberty, Modernisme), caught on quickly in Paris during La Belle Époque, and its influence lasted until WWI. The style is characterised by sinuous curves and flowing, asymmetrical forms reminiscent of creeping vines, water lilies, the patterns on insect wings and the flowering boughs of trees. Influenced by the arrival of exotic *objets d'art* from Japan, art nouveau's French name came from a Paris gallery that featured works in the 'new art' style.

A lush and photogenic architectural style, art nouveau is expressed to perfection in Paris by Hector Guimard's graceful metro entrances and Le Marais synagogue, the former train station housing the Musée d'Orsay, and department stores including Le Bon Marché, Galeries Lafayette and La Samaritaine.

20th Century

France's best-known 20th-century architect, Charles-Édouard Jeanneret (aka Le Corbusier), was born in Switzerland but settled in Paris in 1917 at the age of 30. A radical modernist, he tried to adapt buildings to their functions in industrialised society without ignoring the human element. Most of Le Corbusier's work was done outside Paris, though he did design several private residences and the Pavillon Suisse, a dormitory for Swiss students at the Cité Internationale Universitaire in the 14e.

Until 1968, however, French architects were still being trained almost exclusively at the conformist École des Beaux-Arts, reflected in most of the early impersonal and forgettable 'lipstick tubes' and 'upended shoebox' structures erected in the skyscraper district of La Défense, the Unesco building (1958) in the 7e, and the 210m-tall Tour Montparnasse (1973).

For centuries France's leaders have sought to immortalise themselves by erecting huge public edifices ('grands projets') in Paris. Georges Pompidou commissioned the once reviled, now much-loved Centre Pompidou. His successor, Valéry Giscard d'Estaing, was instrumental in transforming the derelict Gare d'Orsay train station into the glorious Musée d'Orsay (1986).

François Mitterrand surpassed all of the postwar presidents with monumental projects costing taxpayers €4.6 billion: Jean Nouvel's Institut du Monde Arabe (1987), built during this time, mixes modern Arab and Western elements and is arguably one of the city's most beautiful late-20th-century buildings. Mitterrand also oversaw the city's second opera house, tile-clad Opéra de Paris Bastille, designed by Uruguayan architect Carlos Ott in 1989 (with expansion including a new 800-seat auditorium due for completion in 2023); the monumental Grande Arche de la Défense by Danish architect Johan-Otto von Sprekelsen (1989); IM Pei's glass-pyramid entrance at the hitherto sacrosanct and untouchable Musée du Louvre (1989); and the four open-book-shaped glass towers of the €2-billion Bibliothèque Nationale de France (Dominique Perrault, 1995).

Jacques Chirac orchestrated the magnificent Musée du Quai Branly – Jacques Chirac, a glass, wood and sod structure with 3-hectare experimental garden, also by Jean Nouvel.

Contemporary

Architectural change doesn't come easy in Paris, given the need to balance the city's heritage with demands on space. But new projects continue to emerge. IM Pei's Louvre pyramid paved the way for Mario Bellini and Rudy Ricciotti's magnificent 'flying carpet' roof atop the museum's Cour Visconti in 2012.

Drawing on the city's long-standing tradition of metalwork and glass in its architecture, Canadian architect Frank Gehry used 12 enormous glass 'sails' to design the Fondation Louis Vuitton, which opened in the Bois de Boulogne in late 2014. Jean Nouvel's Philharmonie de Paris, a state-of-the-art creation with a dazzling metallic façade that took three years to build and cost €381 million, opened in 2015.

Glass is a big feature of the '70s-eyesore-turned-contemporary-stunner Forum des Halles shopping centre in the 1er – a curvaceous, curvilinear

A zany structure if ever there was one is auction house Hôtel Drouat. After a late-1970s surrealist facelift by architects Jean-Jacques Fernier and André Biro, the 19th-century Haussmann building was instantly hailed as a modern architectural gem.

Designer Rooftops

Galeries Lafayette (Champs-Élysées & Grands Boulevards)

Institut du Monde Arabe (Latin Quarter)

Fondation Louis Vuitton (Eiffel Tower & Western Paris)

OLYMPIC INFRASTRUCTURE

As Paris gears up to host the 2024 Summer Olympic Games and Summer Paralympic Games, renovations, redevelopments and a flurry of construction projects are taking place around the city.

A cornerstone of the Games is that 95% of the venues will be pre-existing or temporary, in an effort to minimise not only costs but also the impact on the environment.

Landmark buildings being overhauled and redeployed for the Olympics include the Grand Palais, just off the av des Champs-Élysées in the 8e. Originally built for the 1900 Exposition Universelle (World's Fair) and topped by a 8.5-tonne art nouveau glass roof, it will host Olympic fencing and taekwondo, and Paralympic wheelchair fencing.

Paris' 80,000-seat Stade de France, in St-Denis, which was built for the 1998 FIFA World Cup, will be the Games' main stadium. The year prior to the Olympics, it will also be the site of fixtures of the 2023 Rugby World Cup being hosted by France.

Adjacent to the Eiffel Tower, the Parc du Champ de Mars will have a temporary arena where Olympic wrestling and judo competitions will take place. The Champ de Mars will also be the site of beach volleyball and Paralympic boccia (a precision ball sport similar to bowls and *pétanque*) competitions.

Only three Olympic venues are being built from scratch: the Aquatics Centre, next to the Stade de France; the 51-hectare Olympic and Paralympic Village, 7km north of central Paris and less than 2km from the Stade de France; and the 9-hectare Media Village at Le Bourget, some 10km northeast of central Paris, which forms part of a larger 'garden city' being developed to link the Dugny and Le Bourget communes and the Georges-Valbon parkland. After the Games, all three newly built venues will be repurposed for public use.

Also being constructed at the Olympic village is a transport hub with five metro lines and two RER lines. It will form part of the mammoth Grand Paris (Greater Paris) redevelopment project that will ultimately connect the outer suburbs beyond the bd Périphérique ring road with the city proper. Grand Paris' principal goal is to connect the suburbs with one another, instead of relying on a central inner-city hub from which all lines radiate outwards, with a target completion date of 2030.

and glass-topped construction by architects Patrick Berger and Jacques Anziutti, completed in 2016. Another eyesore undergoing renewal is 1970s skyscraper, the Tour Montparnasse, due for completion in 2023.

Clad in a pixelated matrix of glass embedded with LED lights, the headquarters of national media group Le Monde in the 13e, designed by Norwegian architectural firm Snøhetta, was unveiled in 2020, while the four-year renovations of Paris' history museum, the Musée Carnavalet, was unveiled in 2021 by the same firm in collaboration with François Chatillon Architecte. Duo, two Jean Nouvel–designed towers (180m and 122m) in the 13e, has a 2022 completion date.

Jean Nouvel is heading the ongoing massive, multimillion-euro Gare d'Austerlitz renovation with hotels and a 20,000-sq-metre shopping area. One-third of the budget was allocated to repairing the glass roof. Nouvel is also among the architects working on the 74-hectare Île Seguin-Rives de Seine development of the former Renault plant on a Seine island in Boulogne-Billancourt, which is becoming a Grand Paris cultural hub; concert venue La Seine Musicale was the first to arrive, in 2017.

Porte Maillot will be transformed by Mille Arbres (Thousand Trees), a spectacular tree-topped glass structure by Japanese architect Sou Fujimoto and French architect Manal Rachdi. It will provide a pivotal link between central Paris and Grand Paris when it opens in 2022.

At Porte de Versailles, the Tour Triangle, a glittering triangular glass tower designed by Jacques Herzog and Pierre de Meuron, will be the first skyscraper in Paris since 1973's Tour Montparnasse when it opens in 2024.

A signature architectural feature of Paris is the vertical garden, or *mur végétal* (vegetation wall). Seeming to defy gravity, these gardens cover walls in chic boutique interiors, outside museums, within spas and elsewhere. The Seine-facing garden at the Musée du Quai Branly, by Patrick Blanc, is Paris' most famous.

Literary Paris

Parisians have a deep appreciation of the written word, and literature has long been essential to the French sense of identity. Couple this with the vast amount of writing by both French and foreign authors who continue to be inspired by the City of Light and you can be sure that Paris will never leave you short of a good read.

Medieval

Paris does not figure largely in early-medieval French literature, although the misadventures of Pierre Abélard and Héloïse took place in the capital, as did their mutual correspondence, which ended only with Abélard's death.

François Villon, the finest poet of the Middle Ages, received the equivalent of a Master of Arts degree from the Sorbonne before he turned 20. Involved in a series of brawls, robberies and illicit escapades, 'Master Villon' (as he became known) was sentenced to be hanged in 1462, supposedly for stabbing a lawyer. However, the sentence was commuted to banishment from Paris for 10 years, and he disappeared forever. Villon left behind a body of poems charged with a highly personal lyricism, among them *Ballade des Pendus* (Ballad of the Hanged Men), in which he writes his own epitaph, and *Ballade des Dames du Temps Jadis,* translated by the English poet and painter Dante Gabriel Rossetti as the 'Ballad of Dead Ladies'.

Renaissance

The great landmarks of French Renaissance literature are the works of François Rabelais, Pierre de Ronsard (and other poets of the Renaissance group of poets known as La Pléiade) and Michel de Montaigne. The exuberant narratives of erstwhile monk Rabelais blend coarse humour with erudition in a vast oeuvre that seems to include every kind of person, occupation and jargon to be found in the France of the early 16th century. Rabelais' publisher, Étienne Dolet, was convicted of heresy and blasphemy in 1546, hanged and burned on place Maubert, 5e.

17th & 18th Centuries

During the 17th century François de Malherbe, court poet under Henri IV, brought a new rigour to rhythm in literature. One of his better-known works is his *Ode* (1600) to Marie de Médici. Transported by the perfection of Malherbe's verses, Jean de la Fontaine went on to write his *Fables* (1668) in the manner of Aesop – though he fell afoul of the Académie Française (French Academy) in the process. A mood of classical tragedy permeates *La Princesse de Clèves* (1678), by Marie de la Fayette, widely regarded as the precursor to the modern character novel.

The literature of the 18th century is dominated by philosophers, among them Voltaire (François-Marie Arouet) and Jean-Jacques Rousseau. Voltaire's political writings, arguing that society is fundamentally opposed to nature, had a profound and lasting influence, and he is buried in the Panthéon. Rousseau's sensitivity to landscape and its moods anticipated romanticism, and the insistence on his own singularity in *Les Confessions* (1782) made it the first modern autobiography. He, too, lies in the Panthéon.

French Romanticism

The 19th century produced poet and novelist Victor Hugo, who lived on place des Vosges before fleeing to the Channel Islands during the Second Empire. *Les Misérables* (1862) describes life among the poor of Paris in the early 19th century. *Notre Dame de Paris* (The Hunchback of Notre Dame; 1831), a medieval romance and tragedy revolving around the life of Paris' cathedral, made Hugo the key figure of French romanticism.

Other influential 19th-century novelists include Stendhal (Marie-Henri Beyle), Honoré de Balzac, Amandine Aurore Lucile Dupin (aka George Sand) and, of course, Alexandre Dumas, who wrote the swashbuckling adventures *Le Comte de Monte Cristo* (The Count of Monte Cristo; 1844) and *Les Trois Mousquetaires* (The Three Musketeers; 1844).

Two landmarks of French literature were published in 1857: *Madame Bovary,* by Gustave Flaubert, and *Les Fleurs du Mal*, by Charles Baudelaire. Both writers were tried for the supposed immorality of their works. Flaubert won his case, and his novel was distributed without censorship. Baudelaire was obliged to cut half a dozen poems from his work and fined 300 francs.

The aim of Émile Zola, who came to Paris with his close friend, the artist Paul Cézanne, in 1858, was to transform novel-writing from an art to a science by the application of experimentation. His work influenced most significant French writers of the late 19th century and is reflected in much later fiction as well. His novel *Nana* (1880) tells the decadent tale of a young woman who resorts to prostitution to survive the Paris of the Second Empire.

Symbolism & Surrealism

Paul Verlaine and Stéphane Mallarmé created the symbolist movement, which strove to express states of mind rather than simply detail daily reality. Arthur Rimbaud, in addition to crowding an extraordinary amount of exotic travel into his 37 years and having a tempestuous sexual relationship with Verlaine, produced two enduring pieces of work: *Une Saison en Enfer* (A Season in Hell; 1873) and *Illuminations* (1874). Verlaine died at 39 rue Descartes, 5e, in 1896.

Marcel Proust dominated the early 20th century with his seven-volume novel *À la Recherche du Temps Perdu* (In Search of Lost Time; 1913–27), which explores the true meaning of past experience recovered from the unconscious by 'involuntary memory'. In 1907 Proust moved from the family home near the av des Champs-Élysées to an apartment on bd Haussmann famous for its cork-lined bedroom (now in the Musée Carnavalet). André Gide found his voice in the celebration of gay sensuality and, later, left-wing politics. *Les Faux-Monnayeurs* (The Counterfeiters; 1925) exposes the hypocrisy to which people resort in order to fit in with others or deceive themselves.

André Breton wrote French surrealism's three manifestos, although the first use of the word 'surrealist' is attributed to the poet Guillaume Apollinaire, a fellow traveller of surrealism killed in action in WWI. Colette (Sidonie-Gabrielle Colette) enjoyed ruffling the feathers of conventionally moral readers. Her best-known work is *Gigi* (1945), but more interesting is *Paris de Ma Fenêtre* (Paris from My Window; 1944), dealing with the German occupation of Paris. Her view was from 9 rue de Beaujolais in the 1er, overlooking Jardin du Palais Royal.

In France the *bande dessinée* (comic strip) has a cult following. The genre was originally for children, but comic strips for adults gained popularity in 1959 with René Goscinny and Albert Uderzo's now-iconic *Astérix* series.

FOREIGN LITERATURE: INTERWAR HEYDAY

Foreigners have found inspiration in Paris since Charles Dickens used the city along-side London as the backdrop to *A Tale of Two Cities* in 1859. The heyday of Paris as a literary setting, however, was the interwar period.

Ernest Hemingway's *The Sun Also Rises* (1926) and the posthumous *A Moveable Feast* (1964) portray bohemian life in Paris between the wars. So many vignettes in the latter – dissing Ford Madox Ford in a cafe, 'sizing up' F Scott Fitzgerald in a toilet in the Latin Quarter, and overhearing Gertrude Stein and her lover, Alice B Toklas, bitchin' at one another from the sitting room of their salon near the Jardin du Luxem-bourg – are classic and *très parisien*.

Gertrude Stein let her hair down by assuming her lover's identity in *The Autobiography of Alice B Toklas*, a fascinating account of the author's many years in Paris, her salon on rue de Fleurus, 6e, and her friendships with Matisse, Picasso, Braque, Hemingway and others.

Down and Out in Paris and London (1933) is George Orwell's account of the time he spent working as a *plongeur* (dishwasher) in Paris and living with tramps in the city in the 1930s. Henry Miller's *Tropic of Cancer* (1934) and *Quiet Days in Clichy* (1956) are steamy novels set partly in the French capital. Then there's Anaïs Nin's voluminous diaries and fiction; her published correspondence with Miller is particularly evocative of 1930s Paris.

Existentialism

After WWII, existentialism developed as a significant literary movement around Jean-Paul Sartre, Simone de Beauvoir and Albert Camus, who worked and conversed in the cafes of bd St-Germain in St-German des Prés. All three stressed the importance of the writer's political engagement. De Beauvoir, author of *Le Deuxième Sexe* (The Second Sex; 1949), had a profound influence on feminist thinking. Camus' novel *L'Étranger* (The Stranger; 1942) reveals that the absurd is the condition of modern man, who feels himself an outsider in his world.

L'Âge de Raison (The Age of Reason; 1945), the first volume of Jean-Paul Sartre's trilogy *Les Chemins de la Liberté* (The Roads to Freedom), is a superb Parisian novel. His subsequent volumes recall Paris immediately before and during WWII.

Modern Literature

In the late 1950s certain novelists began to look for new ways of organising narrative. The so-called *nouveau roman* (new novel) refers to the works of Nathalie Sarraute, Alain Robbe-Grillet, Boris Vian, Julien Gracq, Michel Butor and others. But these writers never formed a close-knit group, and their experiments took them in divergent directions.

In 1980 Marguerite Yourcenar, best known for her memorable historical novels including *Mémoires d'Hadrien* (Hadrian's Memoirs; 1951), became the first woman elected to the Académie Française. Marguerite Duras came to the notice of a larger public in 1984 when she won the Prix Goncourt for *L'Amant* (The Lover).

Philippe Sollers, an editor at *Tel Quel*, a highbrow, left-wing, Paris-based review, was very influential in the 1960s and early '70s. His 1960s novels were highly experimental, but with *Femmes* (Women; 1983) he returned to a conventional narrative style. Another *Tel Quel* editor, Julia Kristeva, became known for her theoretical writings on literature and psychoanalysis but subsequently turned her hand to fiction: *Les Samuraï* (The Samurai; 1990), a fictionalised account of the heady days of *Tel Quel*, is an interesting document on Paris intelligentsia life. Roland Barthes and Michel Foucault are other seminal 1960s and '70s authors and philosophers.

In the 1990s French writing focused in a nihilistic way on what France had lost as a nation (identity, international prestige etc), and never more so than in the work of controversial writer Michel Houelle-becq, who rose to national prominence in 1998 with *Les Particules Élémentaires* (Atomised). Houellebecq's most recent works are *Soumission* (Submission; 2015), a contentious political satire featuring some of France's real-life politicians in a fictionalized near-future setting, and equally controversial *Sérotonine* (Serotonin; 2019), about an agricultural expert's self-degrading attempt to relive the past while struggling with the impotency of the future as he travels back and forth between Normandy and Paris.

Contemporary Literature

Some of the best-known contemporary French writers include Marc Levy, autofiction specialist Christine Angot and comedian-dramatist Nelly Alard. Alard was acclaimed for the novel *Moment d'un Couple* (Moment of a Couple; 2013), which was translated into English as *Couple Mechanics* in 2016. Her most recent work is *La Vie que Tu t'Étais Imaginée* (The Life You Imagined; 2020).

Author Yasmina Khadra is actually a man, Mohammed Moulessehoul – a former colonel in the Algerian army who adopted his wife's name as a nom de plume to prevent military censorship. He has won many prizes, including for his 2018 novel, *Khalil*, about the 2015 terrorist attacks in Paris.

Faïza Guène is a French literary sensation who uses an 'urban slang' style. A cramped suburban Paris housing estate where thousands of immigrants live in five-storey blocks stretching for 1.5km is the setting for *Kiffe Kiffe Demain* and for Guène's second (semi-autobiographical) novel, *Du Rêve pour les Oufs* (2006), published in English as *Dreams from the Endz* (2008). Her third novel, *Les Gens du Balto* (2008), published in English as *Bar Balto* (2011), is a series of colloquial first-person monologues by various characters who live on a street in a Parisian suburb. Guène's next work, *Un Homme, ça ne pleure pas* (2014), shifted to Nice in southern France. Her 2018 novel *Millénium Blues* (Millennium Blues) retraces 20 years in the life of Zouzou, a young woman with a French mother and Kabyle father.

Ex–French border guard turned author Romain Puértolas had an instant bestselling hit with his surreal, partly Paris-set 2013 novel *L'Extraordinaire Voyage du Fakir Qui Était Resté Coincé Dans une Armoire Ikea* (The Extraordinary Journey of the Fakir Who Got Trapped in an Ikea Wardrobe), which won the Grand Prix Jules Verne in 2014. It was followed in 2015 by *La Petite Fille Qui Avait Avalé un Nuage Grand Comme la Tour Eiffel* (The Little Girl Who Swallowed a Cloud as Big as the Eiffel Tower) and the zany farce *Re-vive l'Empereur* (Re-live the Emperor), imagining the contemporary return of Napoléon Bonaparte. In 2017 he published *Tout un Été Sans Facebook* (A Summer Without Facebook), centred on a reading club. His most recent work is *La Police des Fleurs, des Arbres et des Forêts* (The Police of Flowers, Trees and Forests; 2019), a murder mystery set in 1961 rural France that marks a departure in subject matter and style for the author.

French journalist, screenwriter and novelist Tatiana de Rosnay has a prolific output that includes the bestselling *Sarah's Key* (2007), her first work written in English, *A Paris Affair* (2015) and *Sentinelle de la Pluie* (The Rain Watcher; 2018), a story of family secrets and disaster set against a flooding city of Paris.

Throughout the 21st century, Guillaume Musso had success with numerous novels including *Un Appartement à Paris* (An Apartment in Paris; 2017) and *La Vie Secrète des Écrivains* (The Writer's Secret Life; 2019).

One of France's top-selling writers is Parisian Marc Levy. His first novel was filmed as 2005's *Just Like Heaven*. His latest, *Ghost in Love* (2019), sees a piano virtuoso embark on a quest with his father's ghost.

LITERARY PARIS MODERN LITERATURE

Literary Cafes

Café de Flore
(St-Germain & Les Invalides)

Les Deux Magots
(St-Germain & Les Invalides)

Shakespeare & Company Café
(Latin Quarter)

Painting & Visual Arts

While art in Paris today means anything and everything – bold installations in the metro, digital art projections both inside and outside exhibition spaces, mechanical sculptures, monumental wall frescoes, tiled Space Invader tags and other gregarious street art, including in dedicated street-art museums – the city's rich art heritage has its roots firmly embedded in the traditional genres of painting and sculpture.

Baroque to Neoclassicism

According to philosopher Voltaire, French painting proper began with Baroque painter Nicolas Poussin (1594–1665), the greatest representative of 17th-century classicism, who frequently set scenes from ancient Rome, classical mythology and the Bible in ordered landscapes bathed in golden light.

In the field of sculpture, extravagant and monumental tombs had been commissioned by the nobility from the 14th century, and in Renaissance Paris Pierre Bontemps (c 1507–68) decorated the beautiful tomb of François I at Basilique de St-Denis, and Jean Goujon (c 1510–67) created the Fontaine des Innocents near the Forum des Halles. No sculpture better evokes Baroque than the magnificent *Horses of Marly* by Guillaume Coustou (1677–1746), at the entrance to the av des Champs-Élysées.

Modern still life pops up with Jean-Baptiste Chardin (1699–1779), who brought the humbler domesticity of the Dutch masters to French art. In 1785 neoclassical artist Jacques-Louis David (1748–1825) wooed the public with his vast portraits with clear republican messages. A virtual dictator in matters of art, he advocated a precise, severe classicism.

Jean-Auguste-Dominique Ingres (1780–1867), David's most gifted pupil in Paris, continued the neoclassical tradition. His historical pictures (eg *Oedipus and the Sphinx,* the 1808 version of which is in the Louvre) are now regarded as inferior to his portraits.

Romanticism

One of the Louvre's most gripping paintings, *The Raft of the Medusa* by Théodore Géricault (1791–1824), hovers on the threshold of romanticism; if Géricault had not died early (aged 33), he probably would have become a leader of the movement, along with his friend Eugène Delacroix (1798–1863; find him in the Cimetière du Père Lachaise), best known for his masterpiece commemorating the July Revolution of 1830, *Liberty Leading the People.*

While romantics revamped the subject picture, the Barbizon School effected a parallel transformation of landscape painting. The school derived its name from a village near the Forêt de Fontainebleau where Jean-Baptiste Camille Corot (1796–1875) and Jean-François Millet (1814–75) painted in the open air. The son of a Norman peasant farmer, Millet took many of his subjects from peasant life; his *L'Angélus* (The Angelus; 1857) is one of the best-known French paintings from this period. View it in the Musée d'Orsay.

METRO ART

Art adorns many of the stations of the city's metro. Themes often relate to the *quartier* (neighbourhood) or the name of the station. Montparnasse Bienvenüe, for example, evokes the creation of the metro – it was engineer Fulgence Bienvenüe (1852–1936) who oversaw the building of the first 91km from 1886.

The following is a sample of the most interesting stations from an artistic perspective.

Abbesses (line 12 metro entrance) The noodle-like pale-green metalwork and glass canopy of the station entrance is one of the finest examples of the work of Hector Guimard (1867–1942), the celebrated French art nouveau architect whose signature style once graced most metro stations. For a complete list of the metro stations that retain *édicules* (shrine-like entranceways) designed by Guimard, see www.parisinconnu.com.

Assemblée Nationale (line 12 platform) Gigantic posters of silhouettes in red, white and blue by artist Jean-Charles Blais (b 1956) represent the MPs currently sitting in parliament.

Bastille (line 5 platform) A 180-sq-metre ceramic fresco features scenes taken from newspaper engravings published during the Revolution, with illustrations of the destruction of the infamous prison.

Chaussée d'Antin-Lafayette (line 7 platform) Large allegorical painting on the vaulted ceiling recalls the Marquis de Lafayette (1757–1834) and his role as general in the American Revolution.

Cluny–La Sorbonne (line 10 platform) A large ceramic mosaic replicates the signatures of intellectuals, artists and scientists from the Latin Quarter through history, including Molière (1622–73), Rabelais (c 1483–1553) and Robespierre (1758–96).

Concorde (line 12 platform) What looks like children's building blocks in white-and-blue ceramic on the walls of the station are 45,000 tiles that spell out the text of the *Déclaration des Droits de l'Homme et du Citoyen* (Declaration of the Rights of Man and of the Citizen), the document setting forth the principles of the French Revolution.

Palais Royal–Musée du Louvre (line 1 metro entrance) The zany entrance on place du Palais by Jean-Michel Othoniel (b 1964) is composed of two crown-shaped cupolas (representing day and night) consisting of 800 red, blue, amber and violet glass balls threaded on an aluminium structure.

In sculpture, the work of Paris-born Auguste Rodin (1840–1917) overcame the conflict between neoclassicism and romanticism. One of Rodin's most gifted pupils was Camille Claudel (1864–1943), whose work can be seen with Rodin's in the Musée Rodin.

Realism

The realists were all about social commentary: Millet anticipated the realist program of Gustave Courbet (1819–77), a prominent member of the Paris Commune whose paintings depicted the drudgery and dignity of working-class lives. In 1850 he broke new ground with *A Burial at Ornans* (in the Musée d'Orsay), painted on a canvas of monumental size reserved until then exclusively for historical paintings.

Édouard Manet (1832–83) used realism to depict the Parisian middle classes, while incorporating numerous references to the Old Masters. His *Déjeuner sur l'Herbe* and *Olympia* were both scandalous, largely because they broke with the traditional treatment of their subject matter. He was a pivotal figure in the transition from realism to impressionism.

One of the best sculptors of this period was François Rude (1784–1855), creator of the relief on the Arc de Triomphe and several pieces in

Sculpture Studios

Musée Rodin (St-Germain & Les Invalides)

Musée Atelier Zadkine (St-Germain & Les Invalides)

Atelier Brancusi (Louvre & Les Halles)

Musée Bourdelle (Montparnasse & Southern Paris)

the Musée d'Orsay. By the mid-19th century, memorial statues in public places had replaced sculpted tombs, making such statues all the rage.

Sculptor Jean-Baptiste Carpeaux (1827–75) began as a romantic, but his work in Paris – such as *The Dance* on the Palais Garnier and his fountain in the Jardin du Luxembourg – recalls the gaiety and flamboyance of the Baroque era.

Impressionism

Both Georges Braque and Picasso experimented with sculpture and, in the spirit of Dada, Marcel Duchamp exhibited 'found objects', one of which was a urinal, which he mounted, signed and dubbed *Fountain* in 1917.

Paris' Musée d'Orsay is the crown jewel of impressionism. Initially a term of derision, 'impressionism' was taken from the title of an 1874 experimental painting, *Impression: Soleil Levant* (Impression: Sunrise) by Claude Monet (1840–1926). Monet was the leading figure of the school, and a visit to the Musée d'Orsay unveils a host of other members, among them Alfred Sisley (1839–99), Camille Pissarro (1830–1903), Pierre-Auguste Renoir (1841–1919) and Berthe Morisot (1841–95). The impressionists' main aim was to capture the effects of fleeting light, painting almost universally in the open air – and light came to dominate the content of their painting.

Edgar Degas (1834–1917) was a fellow traveller of the impressionists, but he preferred painting indoor cafe life *(Absinthe)* and ballet studios *(The Dance Class)* – several beautiful examples hang in the Musée d'Orsay.

Henri de Toulouse-Lautrec (1864–1901) was a great admirer of Degas but chose less salubrious subjects: people in the bistros, brothels and music halls of Montmartre (eg *Au Moulin Rouge*). He is best known for his posters and lithographs, in which the distortion of the figures is both satirical and decorative.

Paul Cézanne (1839–1906) is celebrated for his still lifes and landscapes depicting southern France, though he spent many years in Paris after breaking with the impressionists. The name of Paul Gauguin (1848–1903) immediately conjures up studies of Tahitian and Breton women. Both Cézanne and Gauguin were postimpressionists, a catchall term for the diverse styles that flowed from impressionism.

Pointillism & Symbolism

César Baldaccini (1921–98), known simply as César, used iron and scrap metal to create imaginary insects and animals, later graduating to pliable plastics. Among his best-known works are the Centaur statue in the 6e and the statuette handed to actors at the Césars (French cinema's equivalent of the Oscars).

Pointillism was a technique developed by Georges Seurat (1859–91), who applied paint in small dots or uniform brush strokes of unmixed colour to produce fine 'mosaics' of warm and cool tones. His tableaux *Une Baignade, Asnières* (Bathers at Asnières) is a perfect example.

Henri Rousseau (1844–1910) was a contemporary of the postimpressionists, but his 'naive' art was unaffected by them. His dreamlike pictures of the Paris suburbs and of jungle and desert scenes (eg *The Snake Charmer*) – in the Musée d'Orsay – have influenced art right up to this century. The eerie treatment of mythological subjects by Gustave Moreau (1826–98) can be seen in the artist's studio, now within the Musée Gustave-Moreau in the 9e.

20th-Century Art

Twentieth-century French painting is characterised by a bewildering diversity of styles, including fauvism, named after the slur of a critic who compared the exhibitors at the 1905 Salon d'Automne (Autumn Salon) in Paris with *fauves* (wild animals) because of their wild brushstrokes and radical use of intensely bright colours. Among these 'beastly' painters was Henri Matisse (1869–1954).

Cubism was launched in 1907 with *Les Demoiselles d'Avignon* by Spanish prodigy Pablo Picasso (1881–1973). Cubism, as developed by Picasso, Georges Braque (1882–1963) and Juan Gris (1887–1927), deconstructed the subject into intersecting planes, presenting various aspects simultaneously.

In the 1920s and '30s the École de Paris (School of Paris) was formed by a group of expressionists, mostly foreign born.

Capturing the rebellious, iconoclastic spirit of Dadaism – a Swiss-born literary and artistic movement of revolt – is *Mona Lisa,* by Marcel Duchamp (1887–1968), complete with moustache and goatee. In 1922 German Dadaist Max Ernst (1891–1976) moved to Paris and worked on surrealism, a Dada offshoot that flourished between the wars. Drawing on the theories of Sigmund Freud, surrealism attempted to reunite the conscious and unconscious realms, to permeate everyday life with fantasies and dreams. The most influential proponent of this style in Paris was Spanish-born artist Salvador Dalí (1904–89), who arrived in the French capital in 1929 and painted some of his most seminal works while residing here. To see his work, visit Dalí Paris.

One of the most influential pre-WWII sculptors to emerge in Paris was Romanian-born Constantin Brancusi (1876–1957); view his work at the Atelier Brancusi. Two other Paris-busy sculptors each have a museum devoted to their work: Ossip Zadkine (1890–1967) and Antoine Bourdelle (1861–1929).

WWII ended Paris' role as the world's artistic capital. Many artists left during the occupation, and though some returned after the war, the city never regained its magnetism.

But art endured. Conceptual artist Daniel Buren (b 1938) reduced his painting to a signature series of vertical 8.7cm-wide stripes applied to every surface imaginable – white-marble columns in the courtyard of Paris' Palais Royal included. Partner-in-crime Michel Parmentier (1938–2000) insisted on monochrome painting – blue in 1966, grey in 1967 and red in 1968.

A bill in 1936 provided for 'the creation of monumental decorations in public buildings' by allotting 1% of building costs to art. The concept mushroomed half a century later (with Daniel Buren) and now there's artwork everywhere: in the Jardin des Tuileries, La Défense, Parc de la Villette, the metro...

Contemporary Art

From the turn of the 21st century, artists increasingly turned to the minutiae of daily urban life to express social and political angst, using new mediums to let rip.

Paris-born conceptual artist Sophie Calle (b 1953) brazenly exposes her private life in public with eye-catching installations, such as 107 women reading and commenting on an email she received from her lover, dumping her.

Gallery Le 104, in a former funeral parlour, encourages emerging artists, as does legalised squat 59 Rivoli.

Street art took off in Paris thanks to Blek le Rat (Xavier Prou; b 1951), whose pioneering stencilled black rats across the city inspired artists such as Banksy, as well as French artist Levalet (Charles Leval; b 1988), who pastes lifelike, site-specific images in India ink on craft paper onto walls. Today, street art remains huge; in addition to tiled Space Invader tags and vast murals covering entire high-rise buildings, particularly in the 13e, graffitied streets like Belleville's rue Dénoyez and art-collective canvases like rue Oberkampf's Le MUR, there's a street-art museum, Art 42, and Street Art Paris' dedicated guided tours.

Digital art is also gaining ground, particularly following the 2018 openings of arts centre EP7, which screens projections onto its façade, and Atelier des Lumières, Paris' first digital-art museum.

Keep abreast of current exhibitions, events and happenings with Paris' contemporary art and design magazine *Slash* (www.slash-paris.com), also on Twitter and Facebook.

French Cinema

Paris is one of the world's most cinematic cities. The world's first paying-public screening took place in the French capital in 1895, and Paris has since produced a bevy of independent and blockbuster film-makers and stars, and is the filming location of countless box-office hits by both home-grown and foreign directors, with some 900 film shoots here per year.

Documentaries

One of the earliest Parisian documentaries is *Rien que les Heures* (Nothing But Time; 1926) directed by Alberto Cavalcanti, an experimental silent film showing a day in the life of the city. Writer-director Pierre Bost's *La Libération de Paris* (The Liberation of Paris; 1944) was filmed in secret by units of the French Resistance during the battle for Paris in WWII. *La Seine a Rencontré Paris* (The Seine Meets Paris; 1957), directed by Joris Ivens, is told from the perspective of a boat trip through the city, showing daily life on its banks. Paris' film archive, the Forum des Images, is an excellent place to discover more.

Movie-Makers & Stars

French cinema hasn't looked back since 2012, when *The Artist* (2011), a silent B&W romantic comedy set in 1920s Hollywood, won seven BAFTAs and five Oscars to become the most awarded film in French cinema history. Best Director went to Parisian Michel Hazanavicius (b 1967) and Best Original Score went to French composer-pianist Ludovic Bource (b 1970). Best Actor was awarded to charismatic Jean Dujardin (b 1972), whose varied roles span surfer Brice in *Brice de Nice* (2005) to a secret agent in *OSS 117: Cairo Nest of Spies* (2006), a WWII French soldier in George Clooney's *The Monuments Men* (2014) and military officer and statesman Georges Picquart in 2019's *An Officer and a Spy,* directed by Roman Polanski. Follow-up OSS 117 roles include 2021's *OSS 117: Red Alert in Black Africa.*

Another French blockbuster packed with Parisian talent is Anne Fontaine's *Coco Avant Chanel* (Coco Before Chanel; 2009). The movie tells the compelling life story of orphan-turned-fashion-designer Coco Chanel, played by Audrey Tautou (b 1976), the waifish French actress who earlier conquered stardom with her role as Montmartre cafe waitress Amélie in Jean-Pierre Jeunet's *Le Fabuleux Destin d'Amélie Poulain* (Amélie; 2001).

One of the most successful French-language films ever is *Intouchables* (Untouchable; 2011). Directed by Parisian Éric Toledano and Olivier Nakache, the comic drama is about a billionaire quadriplegic and his live-in Senegalese carer in Paris. The film scooped Best Foreign Film at both the Golden Globes and the BAFTA Awards in 2013.

French-produced *Taken 2* (2012) was directed by Olivier Megaton (b 1965), a graffiti artist from the Parisian suburbs who turned his creative hand to film-making with great success.

Output continues to be diverse. Directed by Pascale Ferrari (b 1960), *Bird People* (2014) takes place in and around a hotel at Paris' Charles de

Cinematic Trips
....

Forum des Images (Louvre & Les Halles)
....

Cinémathèque Française (Bastille & Eastern Paris)
....

Le Grand Rex (Champs-Élysées & Grands Boulevards)

Gaulle airport. Julia Ducournau (b 1983) is the director of *Raw* (2016), about a vegetarian veterinary student who develops a taste for flesh. Jean-Paul Civeyrac (b 1964) directed the black-and-white *Mes Provinciales* (A Paris Education; 2018), exploring bohemian student life. A popular 2019 release was the time-travelling romantic comedy *La Belle Époque,* written and directed by Parisian Nicolas Bedos (b 1980).

France's Leading Lady: Marion Cotillard

France's leading lady is Parisian Marion Cotillard (b 1975), the first French woman since 1959 to win an Oscar, for her role as Édith Piaf in Olivier Dahan's *La Môme* (La Vie en Rose; 2007).

The versatile actress went on to play an amputee in art film *De Rouille et d'Os* (Rust and Bone; 2012) by Parisian director Jacques Audiard (b 1952). In *Deux Jours, Une Nuit* (Two Days, One Night; 2014), Cotillard plays an employee in a solar-panel factory who learns she will lose her job if her co-workers don't each sacrifice €1000 bonuses offered to them.

In 2017, Cotillard starred in *Rock'n Roll* as the partner of Guillaume Canet (her real-life partner), who plays an actor told by his young co-star that he's no longer 'rock 'n' roll' enough to sell films any more, as well as in *Les Fantômes d'Ismaël* (Ismael's Ghosts) as a wife who returns from a 20-year disappearance. This was followed in 2018 by *Gueule d'Ange* (Angel Face), about a mother who abandons her child, and 2020 musical *Annette,* in which she plays a famous soprano whose life is changed by her uniquely gifted daughter.

She also voiced Tutu, a French fox, in 2020's *The Voyages of Doctor Dolittle* as well as the title character of 2015's *Avril et de Monde Truque.*

On Location

Paris is the perfect cinematic setting and a natural movie star, immortalised in French classics such as *Hôtel du Nord* (1938), set along the Canal St-Martin, and *Les Enfants du Paradis* (1946), set in 1840s Paris, both directed by Parisian film-maker Marcel Carné (1906–96).

New Wave film director Jean-Luc Godard followed his B&W celebration of Paris in *À Bout de Souffle* (Breathless; 1959) with *Bande à Parte* (Band of Outsiders; 1964), an entertaining gangster film with marvellous scenes in the Louvre. The Paris-set, semi-autobiographical *Les 400 Coups* (400 Blows; 1959) is a moving portrayal of the magic and disillusionment of childhood by New Wave director François Truffaut, which is today considered one of the best films in French cinematic history.

For decades 'Most Watched French Film' kudos went to *La Grand Vadrouille* (The Great Ramble; 1966), a French comedy in which five British airmen are shot down over German-occupied France in 1942. One is catapulted into Paris' Bois de Vincennes zoo, another into the orchestra pit of Paris' opera house, and so the comic tale unfurls.

FRENCH CINEMA

1895

The world's first paying-public film screening is held in Paris' Grand Café on bd des Capucines, 9e, in December 1895 by the Lumière brothers, inventors of 'moving pictures'.

1902

Paris magician-turned-film-maker Georges Méliès (1861–1938) creates the first science-fiction film with the silent *Le Voyage dans la Lune* (The Trip to the Moon; 1902).

1920s

French film flourishes. Sound ushers in René Clair's (1898–1981) world of fantasy and satirical surrealism. Abel Gance's antiwar blockbuster *J'Accuse!* (I Accuse!; 1919) was filmed on WWI battlefields.

1930s

WWI inspires a new realism: portraits of ordinary lives dominate film. Watch *La Grande Illusion* (The Great Illusion; 1937), based on the trench-warfare experience of director Jean Renoir.

1940s

Surrealists eschew realism, including Jean Cocteau's *La Belle et la Bête* (Beauty and the Beast; 1946) and *Orphée* (Orpheus; 1950). WWII saps the industry of talent and money.

1950s

Nouvelle Vague (New Wave): small budgets, no stars and real-life subjects produce uniquely personal films. Watch Jean-Luc Godard's carefree, B&W celebration of Paris in *À Bout de Souffle* (Breathless; 1959).

1960s

France – land of romance: take in Claude Lelouch's *Un Homme et une Femme* (A Man and a Woman; 1966) and Jacques Demy's *Les Parapluies de Cherbourg* (The Umbrellas of Cherbourg; 1964).

1980s

Big-name stars, slick production values and nostalgia: generous state subsidies see film-makers switch to costume dramas and comedies in the face of growing US competition.

1990s

Box-office hits starring Gérard Depardieu win over French and international audiences. See *Cyrano de Bergerac* (1990).

2000s

Renaissance: Parisian *philanthrope* Amélie is the subject of Jean-Pierre Jeunet's *Le Fabuleux Destin d'Amélie Poulain* (Amélie; 2001), the first of a string of French-made films to succeed globally.

2010s–

Films such as 2018's *Mes Provinciales* (A Paris Education) evoke French Nouvelle Vague.

La Haine (Hate; 1995) was Mathieu Kassovitz' prescient take on social tensions in modern Paris. Also in the 1990s, Juliette Binoche (b 1964) leapt to fame after diving into the shimmering, bright-turquoise water of Paris' art deco swimming pool the Piscine de Pontoise in the 5e, in *Bleu* (Blue; 1993), the first in Krzysztof Kieślowski's *Trois Couleurs* (Three Colours) trilogy. A decade later Binoche wooed cinema-goers with her role as a grieving mother in *Paris, je t'aime* (Paris, I Love You; 2006), a staggering work comprising 18 short films – each set in a different Parisian *arrondissement*.

Honoured with the Palme d'Or at Cannes in 2008, Laurent Cantet's *Entre Les Murs* (The Class; 2008) portrays a year in the school life of pupils and teachers in a Parisian suburb. Based on the autobiographical novel of teacher François Begaudeau, the documentary-drama is an incisive reflection of a multi-ethnic society.

Animated films have enjoyed huge success; 2015's *Avril et de Monde Truque* (April and the Extraordinary World) depicts a fictitious world in 1941 Paris under the rule of Napoléon V in the steam age, where Avril (and her talking cat) searches for her missing scientist parents.

Delightful 2018 animated film *Dilili à Paris* (Dilili in Paris), directed by Michel Ocelot, sees its young heroine Dilili solve a series of kidnappings in Belle Époque Paris. It features famous Parisians from the era, such as artist Toulouse-Lautrec, and won France's national César Award for Best Feature in 2019.

Also garnering awards is 2019's *Les Misérables,* directed by Ladj Ly, which won the Jury Prize at the Cannes Film Festival the same year.

Foreign Films Set in Paris

Paris has always been popular with foreign film directors, whatever their genre: Bernardo Bertolucci's *Last Tango in Paris* (1972) stars Marlon Brando as a grief-stricken American. Roman Polanski's *Frantic* (1988) is a stylish thriller set in and around the city's seedier quarters that sees Harrison Ford enlist the help of a feisty Emmanuelle Seigner to help him track down his kidnapped wife. Doug Liman's fast-moving action flick *The Bourne Identity* (2002) features Matt Damon as an amnesiac government-agent-turned-target in a gripping story that twists and turns against a fabulous backdrop of Paris. Woody Allen's *Everybody Says I Love You* (1996) unfolded on the Left Bank's quai de la Tournelle, while *Midnight in Paris* (2011) evoked the city, along with Hemingway's 'Lost Generation', of the 1920s.

Martin Scorsese's Oscar-winning children's film *Hugo* (2011) paid tribute to cinema and Parisian film pioneer Georges Méliès through the remarkable adventure of an orphan boy in the 1930s who tends the clocks at a Paris train station.

The crazed antics of Gargamel et al in American movie *Smurfs 2* (2013) were shot on location in Paris at Cathédrale de Notre Dame. Parts of 2018's *Fantastic Beasts: The Crimes of Grindelwald,* written by JK Rowling and directed by David Yates, were set in Paris. The city also featured in 2018's *Mission: Impossible – Fallout,* directed by Christopher McQuarrie, which had its world premiere in Paris.

Paris Soundtrack

From organ recitals amid Gothic architectural splendour to a legendary jazz scene, stirring *chansons*, groundbreaking electronica, award-winning world music and some of the world's best rap, music is embedded deep in the Parisian soul. To understand the capital's musical heritage is to enrich your experience of a city where talented musicians have to audition even to perform in the metro.

Jazz & French Chansons

Paris was introduced to jazz during WWI, when African American soldiers from US troops stationed in France came together to play ragtime and jazz in the city's music halls, and really took off during the 1920s, when it attracted US performers such as Josephine Baker who were fleeing segregation. Many returned during the Great Depression, which gave rise to French jazz: Parisian jazz violinist Stéphane Grappelli (1908–97) and three-fingered Roma guitarist Django Reinhardt (1910–53) jammed together in sessions promoted by the Hot Club of France. Claude Luter and his Dixieland band were big in the 1950s.

The *chanson française* tradition dating from troubadours in the Middle Ages was eclipsed by the music halls of the early 20th century, and revived in the 1930s by Édith Piaf (1915–63), Charles Trenet (1913–2001) and later Charles Aznavour (1924–2018). In the 1950s Left Bank cabarets nurtured singers like Léo Ferré (1916–63), Georges Brassens (1921–81), Claude Nougaro (1929–2004), Jacques Brel (1929–78), Barbara (1930–97) and the very sexy, very Parisian Serge Gainsbourg (1928–91). The genre was reborn in the new millennium as *la nouvelle chanson française* by performers like Vincent Delerm (b 1976), Bénabar (b 1969), Jeanne Cherhal (b 1978), Camille (b 1978) and Zaz (Isabelle Geffroy; b 1980), who mix jazz, soul, acoustic and traditional *chansons*. Paris Combo, with seven albums to date, fuses *chansons* with jazz and world music.

Rock & Pop

French pop has come a long way since the *yéyé* (imitative rock) days of the 1960s as sung by Johnny Hallyday.

Indie rock band Phoenix, from Versailles, headlines international festivals. Lead singer Thomas Mars (b 1976), his schoolmate Chris Mazzalai (guitar), his brother Laurent Brancowitz (guitar and keyboards) and Deck d'Arcy (keyboards and brass) have hugely successful albums including 2017's *Ti Amo*.

French psych-punk rock band La Femme debuted with their award-winning album *Psycho Tropical Berlin* in 2013; their latest offering is *Mystère* (2016).

Nosfell is one of France's most creative and intense musicians, who sings in his own invented language called *'le klokobetz'*. His third album, *Armour Massif* (2014), opens and closes in *'le klokobetz'* but otherwise woos listeners with powerful French love lyrics.

Musical Pilgrimages

....

Musée de la Musique (Montmartre & Northern Paris)

....

Musée de Édith Piaf (Le Marais, Ménilmontant & Belleville)

....

Cimetière du Père Lachaise (Le Marais, Ménilmontant & Belleville)

Sylvie Hoarau and Aurélie Saada formed the indie folk duo Brigitte in 2011; their debut album *Et vous, tu m'aimes?* went platinum in France. Their 2019 album *Toutes Nues* also achieved widespread success.

Surrealist 1993-formed pop band Dionysos filmed their late 2019 single Le Chêne in Paris' magical Musée des Arts Forains (p29).

Modern pop stars include singer-songwriter Chris (previously Christine and the Queens; aka Héloïse Letissier; b 1988), who released her first album, *Chaleur Humaine,* in 2014 and most recently *Chris* in 2018, and Jain (Jeanne Galice; b 1992), whose latest album is 2018's *Souldier.*

Electronica

Paris' dance-music scene is cutting-edge, computer-enhanced Chicago blues and Detroit techno often mixed with 1960s lounge music and vintage tracks from the likes of Gainsbourg and Brassens to create a distinctly urban and highly portable sound.

Daft Punk, originally from Versailles, adapts first-wave acid house and techno to their younger roots in pop and indie rock. Their debut album, *Homework* (1997), fused disco, house funk and techno, while *Random Access Memories* (2013) ditched computer-generated sound for a strong disco beat played by session musicians.

Electronica band Justice (Gaspard Michel Andre Augé and Xavier de Rosnay), known for their rock and indie influences, burst onto the dance scene in 2007 with a debut album that used the band's signature crucifix as its title. Justice's more recent works include *Woman* (2016). Electronica duo from Versailles AIR (an acronym for 'Amour, Imagination, Rêve', meaning 'Love, Imagination, Dream') is another internationally renowned band.

David Guetta, Laurent Garnier, Martin Solveig and Bob Sinclair (aka Christophe Le Friant, originally nicknamed 'Chris the French Kiss') are top Parisian electronica producers and DJs who travel the international circuit.

Breakbot (Thibaut Berland; b 1981) gained a rapid following for his remixes. His 2016-released album *Still Waters* includes the track 'Star Tripper', included in Disney's Star Wars–themed music album *Star Wars Headspace*. Parisian musician, producer and DJ Kavinsky (Vincent Belorgey; b 1975), who has appeared alongside many of French electronica's biggest names, is active on the scene.

World

Paris' world beat is strong, encompassing Algerian raï (artists include Cheb Khaled, Natacha Atlas, Jamel, Cheb Mami), Senegalese *mbalax* (Youssou N'Dour), West Indian zouk (Kassav', Zouk Machine) and more. In the late 1980s bands Mano Negra and Les Négresses Vertes combined many of these elements with brilliant results, as did Manu Chao (b 1961; formerly frontman for Mano Negra), the Paris-born son of Spanish parents.

Magic System from Côte d'Ivoire popularised *zouglou* (a kind of West African rap and dance music) with its album *Premier Gaou,* and Congolese Koffi Olomide (b 1956) still packs the halls. Also try to catch Franco-Algerian DJ-turned-singer Rachid Taha, whose music mixes Arab and Western musical styles with lyrics in English, Berber and French.

Paris-born Franco-Congolese rapper, slam poet and three-time Victoire de la Musique award winner Abd al Malik has helped cement France's reputation in world music. His albums *Gibraltar* (2006), *Dante* (2008), *Château Rouge* (2010) and *Scarifications* (2015) are well worth tracking down.

Top Five Albums

Paris, Zaz

Dante, Abd al Malik

Bankrupt, Phoenix

Paris by Night, Bob Sinclair

La Vie en Rose, Édith Piaf

FREEPRO033/SHUTTERSTOCK ©

Survival Guide

Above: Art nouveau
metro entrance, Île de
la Cité (p195)

Transport

ARRIVING IN PARIS

Few roads *don't* lead to Paris, one of the most visited destinations on earth. Practically every major airline flies through one of its three airports, and most European train and bus routes cross it.

On public transport, children under four years travel free and those aged four to nine years (inclusive) pay half price; exceptions are noted.

Flights, tours and rail tickets can be booked online at www.lonelyplanet.com.

Air

Charles de Gaulle Airport

Most international airlines fly to **Aéroport de Charles de Gaulle** (📞01 70 36 39 50; www.parisaeroport.fr; Roissy), 28km northeast of central Paris. In French the airport is commonly called 'Roissy', after the suburb in which it is located. Inter-terminal shuttle services are free. A high-speed train link between Charles de Gaulle and Gare de l'Est in central Paris is planned; when complete in 2024, the CDG Express will cut the current 50-minute journey to 20 minutes. A fourth terminal is due to open by 2028.

TRAIN

Charles de Gaulle Airport is served by the RER B line (€11.40, children aged four to nine €7.90, approximately 50 minutes, every 10 to 15 minutes), which connects with central Paris stations, including Gare du Nord, Châtelet–Les Halles and St-Michel–Notre Dame. Trains run from 4.50am to 11.50pm (from Gare du Nord 4.53am to 12.15am).

TAXI

A taxi to the city centre takes 40 to 80 minutes. Fares are standardised to a flat rate: €53 to the Right Bank and €58 to the Left Bank. The fare increases by 15% between 7pm and 7am and on Sundays.

Only take taxis at a clearly marked rank. Never follow anyone who approaches you at the airport and claims to be a driver.

BUS

Noctilien buses 140 and 143 (€8 or four metro tickets) Part of the RATP night service, Noctilien has two hourly services that link the airport with **Gare de l'Est** (Map p382; rue du 8 Mai 1945, 10e; Ⓜ Gare de l'Est) in northern Paris via nearby **Gare du Nord** (Map p382; 170 rue La Fayette, 10e; Ⓜ Gare du Nord): bus 140 (1am to 4am; from Gare de l'Est 1am to 3.40am) takes 80 minutes, and bus 143 (12.32am to 4.32am; from Gare de l'Est 12.55am to 5.08am) takes 55 minutes.

RATP bus 350 (€6 or three metro tickets, 80 minutes, every 15 to 30 minutes from 5.30am to 9.30pm) Links the airport with **Gare de l'Est** (Map p382; www.ratp.fr; bd de Strasbourg, 10e; Ⓜ Gare de l'Est).

RATP bus 351 (€6 or three metro tickets, 90 minutes, every 15 to 30 minutes from 5.35am to 9.37pm) Links the airport with **place de la Nation** (2 av du Trône, 12e; Ⓜ Nation) in eastern Paris.

Roissybus (€13.70, 75 minutes, from the airport every 15 to 20 minutes from 6am to 12.30am; from Paris every 15 to 20 minutes from 5.15am to 12.30am) Links the airport with **Opéra** (Map p370; 13-15 rue Scribe, 9e; Ⓜ Opéra).

Orly Airport

Aéroport d'Orly (📞01 70 36 39 50; www.parisaeroport.fr; Orly) is 19km south of central Paris but, despite being closer than Charles de Gaulle, it is not as frequently used by international airlines, and public-transport options aren't quite as straightforward. That will change by 2027, when metro line 14 will be extended to the airport. A TGV station is due to arrive here in 2025.

TRAIN

There is currently no direct train to/from Orly; you'll need to change halfway. Note that while it is possible to take a shuttle to the RER C line, this service is quite long and not recommended.

RER B (€12.10, children aged four to nine €6.05, 35 minutes, every four to 12 minutes) This line connects Orly with the St-Michel–Notre Dame, Châtelet–Les Halles and Gare du Nord stations in the city centre. In order to get from Orly to the RER station (Antony), you must first take the Orlyval automatic train. The service runs every five to seven minutes from 6am to 11.35pm and takes six minutes. You only need one ticket to take the two trains.

TAXI

A taxi to the city centre takes roughly 30 minutes. Standardised flat-rate fares mean a taxi costs €32 to the Left Bank and €37 to the Right Bank. The fare increases by 15% between 7pm and 7am and on Sundays.

TRAM

Tramway T7 (€1.90, 30 minutes, every eight to 15 minutes from 6am to 11.45pm) This tramway links Orly with Villejuif–Louis Aragon metro station in southern Paris; buy tickets from the machine at the tram stop as no tickets are sold on board.

BUS

OrlyBus (€9.50, 30 minutes, every eight to 15 minutes from 6am to 12.30am from Orly, 5.35am to midnight from Paris) Runs to/from **place Denfert-Rochereau** (Map p412; www.ratp.fr; 3 place Denfert-Rochereau, 14e; M Denfert-Rochereau) in southern Paris.

Beauvais Airport

Aéroport de Beauvais (☎08 92 68 20 66; www.aeroport parisbeauvais.com; Beauvais) is 75km north of Paris and is served by a few low-cost flights. Before you snap up that bargain, though, consider whether the post-arrival journey is worth it.

SHUTTLE

The Beauvais *navette* (shuttle bus; €17, 1¼ hours) links the airport with **Parking Pershing** (Gare Routière Pershing; Map p366; 22-24 bd Pershing, 17e; M Porte Maillot) on central Paris' western edge; services are coordinated with flight times. See the airport website for details and tickets.

TAXI

A taxi to central Paris (around 1¾ hours) during the day/night costs around €170/210 (possibly more than the cost of your flight!).

Train

Paris is the central point in the French rail network, Société Nationale des Chemins de Fer Français (SNCF), with six train stations that handle passenger traffic to different parts of France and Europe. Each is well connected to the Paris public-transport system, the Régie Autonome des Transports Parisiens (RATP).

To buy onward tickets from Paris, visit a station or go to Oui.SNCF (www.oui. sncf). Most trains – and all high-speed Trains à Grande Vitesse (TGV) – require advance reservations. The earlier you book, the better your chances of securing a discounted fare. Mainline stations in Paris have left-luggage offices and/or *consignes* (lockers) for a maximum of 72 hours.

Gare d'Austerlitz

Gare d'Austerlitz (bd de l'Hôpital, 13e; M Gare d'Austerlitz) The terminus for a handful of trains from the south, including services from Orléans, Limoges and Toulouse. Current renovations are due to continue until 2025. Located in southeastern Paris.

Gare de l'Est

Gare de l'Est (place du 11 Novembre 1918, 10e; M Gare de l'Est) The terminus for trains from Luxembourg, southern Germany (Frankfurt, Munich, Stuttgart) and points further east (including a weekly Moscow service); there are regular and TGV Est trains to areas of France east of Paris (Champagne, Alsace and Lorraine). Located in northern Paris.

Gare de Lyon

Gare de Lyon (bd Diderot, 12e; M Gare de Lyon) The terminus for trains from Lyon, Provence, the Côte d'Azur, the French Alps, Italy, Spain and Switzerland. Located in eastern Paris.

Gare du Nord

Gare du Nord (rue de Dunkerque, 10e; M Gare du Nord) The terminus for northbound domestic trains as well as several international services. Located in northern Paris.

Eurostar (www.eurostar.com) The London–Paris line runs from St Pancras International to Gare du Nord. Voyages take 2¼ hours.

Thalys (www.thalys.com) Trains pull into Paris' Gare du Nord from Brussels, Amsterdam and Cologne.

Gare Montparnasse

Gare Montparnasse (av du Maine & bd de Vaugirard, 15e; M Montparnasse Bienvenüe) The terminus for trains from the southwest and west, including services from Brittany, the Loire Valley, Bordeaux, Toulouse and Spain. Located in southern Paris.

Gare St-Lazare

Gare St-Lazare (rue Intérieure, 8e; Ⓜ St-Lazare) The terminus for trains from Normandy. Located in Clichy, northwestern Paris.

Bus

In France, bus operators consolidated after major European bus company FlixBus (www.flixbus.com) bought Eurolines in 2019.

FlixBus connects all major European capitals to Paris. Its main terminal is at **Bercy Seine** (210 quai de Bercy, 12e; Ⓜ Bercy, Cour St-Émilion). Some services use other bus stops located in and around Paris.

Car & Motorcycle

Cars are a hassle in Paris, so it's only worth bringing one here if you're travelling further afield. To enter the city within the bd Périphérique (ring road) between 8am and 8pm Monday to Friday, cars registered after 1997 (including foreign-registered cars) need a Crit'Air Vignette (compulsory anti-pollution sticker); older vehicles are banned during these hours.

GETTING AROUND PARIS

Train

Paris' underground network is run by RATP (www.ratp.fr) and consists of two separate but linked systems: the metro and the Réseau Express Régional (RER) suburban train line. The metro has 14 numbered lines; the RER has five main lines (but you'll probably only need to use A, B and C). When buying tickets consider how many zones your journey will cover; there are five concentric transport

zones rippling out from Paris (zone 5 being the furthest); if you travel from Charles de Gaulle Airport to Paris, for instance, you will have to buy a ticket for zones 1 to 5.

Metro maps of various sizes and degrees of detail are available for free at metro ticket windows; several can also be downloaded for free from the RATP website.

Metro

➡ Metro lines are identified by both their number (eg ligne 1 – line 1) and their colour, listed on official metro signs and maps.

➡ Signs in metro and RER stations indicate the way to the correct platform for your line. The *direction* signs on each platform indicate the terminus. On lines that split into several branches (such as lines 7 and 13), the terminus of each train is indicated on the cars and on signs on each platform giving the number of minutes until the next and subsequent train.

➡ Signs marked *correspondance* (transfer) show how to reach connecting trains. At stations with many intersecting lines, like Châtelet and Montparnasse Bienvenüe, walking from one platform to the next can take a very long time.

➡ Different station exits are indicated by white-on-blue *sortie* (exit) signs. You can get your bearings by checking the *plan du quartier* (neighbourhood maps) posted at exits.

➡ Each line has its own schedule, but trains usually start at around 5.30am, with the last train beginning its run between 12.35am and 1.15am (2.15am on Friday and Saturday), with all-night services under consideration.

RER

➡ The RER is faster than the metro, but the stops are much further apart. Some attractions, particularly those on the Left

Bank (eg the Musée d'Orsay, Eiffel Tower and Panthéon), can be reached far more conveniently by the RER than by the metro.

➡ If you're going out to the suburbs (eg Versailles or Disneyland), ask for help on the platform – finding the right train can be confusing. Also make sure your ticket is for the correct zone.

Tickets & Fares

➡ Paris is phasing out paper tickets.

➡ A Navigo Easy contactless card (€2, valid for 10 years) allows infrequent transport users, including visitors, to prepay for journeys (single t+ tickets or banks of 10) by topping the card up; cards can be shared between passengers.

➡ The same RATP 'tickets' (loaded onto contactless cards) are valid on the metro, the RER (for travel within the city limits), buses, trams and the Montmartre funicular.

➡ Individual t+ tickets cost €1.90 (half price for children aged four to nine years) if bought individually; a *carnet* (book, ie a bank) of 10 costs €14.90 for adults.

➡ Navigo cards and top-ups are sold at all metro stations. Ticket windows accept most credit cards; however, machines do not accept credit cards without embedded chips (and even then, not all foreign chip-embedded cards are accepted).

➡ One ticket lets you travel between any two metro stations (no return journeys) for a period of 1½ hours, no matter how many transfers are required. You can also use it on the RER for travel within zone 1, which encompasses all of central Paris.

➡ Transfers from the metro to buses (or trams) or vice versa are not possible.

➡ You will have to pay a fine if you don't have a valid ticket.

➡ Mobilis day tickets and Paris Visite tourist passes cover transport.

TOURIST PASSES

The Mobilis and Paris Visite passes are valid on the metro, the RER, SNCF's suburban lines, buses, night buses, trams and the Montmartre funicular railway.

As Paris is phasing out paper tickets, they will be available in contactless card form. Passes operate by date (rather than 24-hour periods), so activate them early in the day for the best value.

Mobilis Allows unlimited travel for one day and costs €7.50 (for two zones) to €17.80 (five zones).

Paris Visite Allows unlimited travel as well as discounted entry to certain museums and other discounts and bonuses. The 'Paris+ Suburbs+ Airports' pass includes transport to/from the airports and costs €25.25/38.35/53.75/65.80 for one/two/three/five days. The cheaper 'Paris Centre' pass, valid for zones 1 to 3, costs €12/19.50/26.65/38.35 for one/two/three/five days. Children aged four to 11 years pay half price.

Bicycle

Paris is increasingly bike-friendly, with more cycling lanes and efforts from the City of Paris to reduce the number of cars on the roads.

Vélib'

The **Vélib'** (☏01 76 49 12 34; www.velib-metropole.fr; day/week subscription €5/15, standard bike hire up to 30/60min free/€1, electric bike €1/2) bike-share scheme puts tens of thousands of bikes (30% of which are electric) at the disposal of Parisians and visitors at some 1400 stations

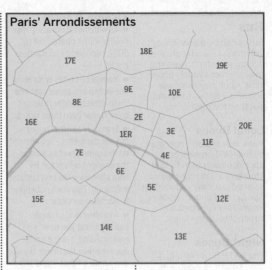

Paris' Arrondissements

throughout Paris, accessible around the clock.

➡ To get a bike, you first need to purchase a one- or seven-day subscription either online (generally EU credit cards only) or at the docking stations.

➡ After you authorise a deposit (€300) to pay for the bike should it go missing, you'll receive an ID number and PIN code and you're ready to go.

➡ Bikes are rented in 30-minute intervals. If you return a bike before a half-hour is up and then take a new one, you will not be charged for a standard bicycle (electric bikes incur charges).

➡ Standard bikes are suitable for cyclists aged 14 and over, and are fitted with gears, an antitheft lock with cable, reflective strips and front/rear lights. Bring your own helmet (they are not required by law).

➡ Electric bikes are also for those aged over 14. They have a top speed of 25km/h and a range of 50km.

Rentals

Most rental places will require a deposit (usually €150 for a standard bike, €300 for electric bikes).

Take ID and your bank or credit card.

Freescoot (☏01 44 07 06 72; www.freescoot.fr; 63 quai de la Tournelle, 5e; 50/125cc scooters per 24hr from €65/75, bicycle/tandem/electric-bike hire per 24hr from €20/40/40; ⏰9am-1pm & 3-7pm Mon-Sat, closed late Jul-late Aug & late Dec-early Jan; Ⓜ Maubert-Mutualité) Rents bicycles (including tandems) and electric bikes.

Gepetto et Vélos (☏01 43 54 19 95; www.gepetto-velos. com; 28 rue des Fossées St-Bernard, 5e; bike rental per hr/day/weekend from €4/16/27; ⏰9am-7pm Tue-Sat, closed Aug; Ⓜ Cardinal Lemoine) Rents city and mountain bikes; you'll need to leave your passport or a deposit (€350 to €500).

Paris à Vélo, C'est Sympa (☏01 48 87 60 01; www. parisavelo.fr; 22 rue Alphonse Baudin, 11e; half-/full day/24hr bike from €13/16/22, electric bike €33/40/50; ⏰9.30am-1pm & 2-6pm Mon-Fri, 9am-7pm Sat & Sun Apr-Oct, shorter hours Nov-Mar; Ⓜ Richard Lenoir) One-stop shop for bicycle hire.

Bus

Buses can be a scenic way to get around – and there are no stairs to climb, meaning they are more widely accessible – but they're slower and less intuitive to figure out than the metro.

Local Buses

Paris' bus system, operated by the RATP, runs from approximately 5am to 1am Monday to Saturday; services are drastically reduced on Sunday and public holidays. Hours vary substantially depending on the line.

Night Buses

The RATP runs night-bus lines known as Noctilien (www.vianavigo.com); buses depart hourly from 12.30am to 5.30am. The services pass through the main *gares* (train stations) and cross the major axes of the city before leading out to the suburbs. Look for navy-blue N or Noctilien signs at bus stops. There are two circular lines within Paris (the N01 and N02) that link four mainline train stations – St-Lazare, Gare de l'Est, Gare de Lyon and Gare Montparnasse – as well as popular nightlife areas (Bastille, Champs-Elysées, Pigalle, St-Germain).

Noctilien services are included on your Mobilis or Paris Visite pass for the zones in which you are travelling. Otherwise you pay a certain number of standard €1.90 metro/bus tickets, depending on the length of your journey.

Tickets & Fares

➺ As with metro tickets, paper tickets will be phased out by 2022, replaced by contactless cards.

➺ Normal bus rides embracing one or two bus zones cost one metro ticket; longer rides require two or even three tickets.

➺ Transfers to other buses – but not the metro – are allowed on the same ticket as long as the change takes place 1½ hours between the first and last validation. This does not apply to Noctilien services.

➺ Whatever kind of single-journey ticket you have, you must validate it in the ticket machine near the driver. If you don't have a ticket, the driver can sell you one for €2 (correct change required).

Boat

Batobus (www.batobus.com; adult/child 1-day pass €17/8, 2-day pass €21/11; ⊙10am-9.30pm late Apr-Aug, shorter hours Sep-late Apr) runs glassed-in trimarans that dock every 20 to 25 minutes at nine small piers along the Seine: Eiffel Tower, Invalides, Musée d'Orsay, St-Germain des Prés, Notre Dame/Latin Quarter, Jardin des Plantes, Hôtel de Ville, Musée du Louvre and place de la Concorde.

Buy tickets online, at ferry stops or at tourist offices. Two-day passes must be used on consecutive days.

You can also buy a Pass+ that includes **L'Open Tour** (☐01 42 66 56 56; www.opentourparis.com; adult/child 1-day pass €35/18, night tour €27/17) buses, to be used on consecutive days. A two-day pass per adult/child costs €47/21; a three day-pass is €51/21.

Taxi

➺ The *prise en charge* (flagfall) is €4 (€7 for advance bookings). Within the city limits, it costs €1.12 per kilometre for travel between 10am and 5pm Monday to Saturday (*Tarif A;* white light on taxi roof and meter).

➺ At night (5pm to 10am), on Sunday from 7am to midnight and during peak travel times (7am to 10am and 5pm to 7pm Monday to Saturday) in the central 20 *arrondissements,* the rate is €1.38 per kilometre (*Tarif B;* orange light).

➺ Travel in inner Paris on Sunday night (midnight to 7am Monday) and in the outer suburbs is at *Tarif C,* €1.61 per kilometre (blue light).

➺ The minimum taxi fare for a short trip is €7.30.

➺ There are flat-fee fares to/from the major airports (Charles de Gaulle from €53, Orly from €32).

➺ A fifth passenger incurs a €4 surcharge.

➺ There's no additional charge for standard-size luggage; larger pieces have a €2 surcharge.

➺ Flagging down a taxi in Paris can be difficult; it's best to find an official taxi stand.

➺ To order a taxi, call or reserve online with **Taxis G7** (☐from a French phone 3607, from an international phone 01 41 27 66 99; www.g7.fr) or **Alpha Taxis** (☐01 45 85 85 85; www.alphataxis.fr).

➺ An alternative is private driver system Uber taxi (www.uber.com/fr/cities/paris); you order and pay via your phone.

SEA BUBBLES

French start-up Sea Bubbles (www.seabubbles.fr) tested its 'flying water taxis' on the Seine in 2019, and plans for them to be operational from 2022. Designed to avoid riverbank erosion, these bubble-shaped electric hydrofoils are set to accommodate 12 to 32 people, and are intended to be booked via an app. Check the company's website for updates.

Car & Motorcycle

Driving in Paris is defined by the triple hassle of navigation, heavy traffic and limited parking. Petrol stations are also difficult to locate and access. A car is unnecessary to get around, but if you're heading out of the city on an excursion, then one can certainly be useful. A Crit'Air Vignette (compulsory anti-pollution sticker) is also required in most instances. If you plan on hiring a car, it's best to do so online and in advance.

Crit'Air Vignette

To enter the city within the bd Périphérique (ring road) between 8am and 8pm Monday to Friday, a Crit'Air Vignette (compulsory anti-pollution sticker) is needed for all cars, motorcycles and trucks registered after 1997, including foreign-registered vehicles. Older vehicles are banned during these hours. The sticker is not necessary for the ring road itself.

There are six colour-coded stickers, ranked according to emissions levels, from Crit'Air 1 to the highest-polluting Crit'Air 6. In instances of elevated pollution levels, vehicles with stickers denoting higher emissions are banned from entering the city. Fines for not displaying a valid sticker start at €68.

For full details and to order stickers online, visit www.certificat-air.gouv.fr, available in multiple languages including English. You'll need to upload a copy of your vehicle's registration certificate. Allow time for it to be mailed to your home. Prices for a Crit'Air Vignette start at €3.62.

Car-Free Streets

Following the success of banishing cars from the av des Champs-Élysées on the first Sunday of each month, Paris' authorities have now also banned cars from Paris Centre (the city's four central *arrondissements*, 1er, 2e, 3e and 4e) on the first Sunday of the month from 10am to 6pm; only emergency vehicles (and some residential traffic) are exempt.

Parking

➡ On-street parking in Paris is severely limited, with more spaces being removed each year in an effort to reduce traffic and pollution.

➡ Parking meters in Paris do not accept coins. You can pay by using a Paris Carte (sold at *tabacs*, ie tobacconists), a European-compatible chip-enabled credit card, or the international 'PayByPhone' app. Tariffs range from €2.40 to €4 per hour. The machine will issue you a ticket for the allotted time (maximum two hours from 9am to 8pm Monday to Saturday), which should be placed on the dashboard behind the windscreen.

➡ Municipal public car parks, of which there are more than 200 in Paris, charge between €2.50 and €8 per hour or €20 to €36 per 24 hours (cash and compatible credit cards accepted). Most are open 24 hours.

Motor Scooters

Cityscoot (www.cityscoot.eu; per 1/100min €0.34/29) Electric mopeds with a top speed of 45km/h are available to rent as part of Paris' scooter-sharing scheme, with all bookings via smartphones. No subscriptions are necessary. Any driver's licence (including a foreign-issued licence) is valid for those born before 1 January 1988; anyone born after that date requires a current EU driver's licence.

Freescoot (☎01 44 07 06 72; www.freescoot.fr; 63 quai de la Tournelle, 5e; 50/125cc scooters per 24hr from €65/75,

bicycle/tandem/electric-bike hire per 24hr from €20/40/40; ⊙9am-1pm & 3-7pm Mon-Sat, closed late Jul-late Aug & late Dec-early Jan; Ⓜ Maubert-Mutualité) Rents 50/125cc scooters in various intervals. Prices include third-party insurance as well as helmets, locks, rain gear and gloves. A motorcycle licence is required for 125cc scooters but not for 50cc scooters, though you must be at least 23 years old and leave a credit-card deposit of €1000.

Left Bank Scooters (☎06 78 12 04 24; www.leftbankscooters.com; 50/125cc scooters per 24hr €70/80) Rents out Vespa XLV scooters including insurance, helmet and wet-weather gear; scooters can be delivered to and collected from anywhere in Paris. You must be at least 20 years old and have had a car or motorcycle licence for two years. Credit-card deposit is €1200.

Trottinettes

Electric *trottinettes* (kick-scooters) have taken off in popularity, with an estimated 20,000 inside central Paris.

These *trottinettes* are hired via an app. There

are numerous operators; Lime (www.li.me) is the most common. Rates per 15/30 minutes are typically €3.25/5.50, with every additional minute costing €0.15.

To increase safety, the city of Paris has introduced laws including a 20km/h speed limit, fines for riding on the pavement and for illegal parking, and a limit of one rider per *trottinette*. Riders must be aged 12 and above.

Tours

As one of the world's most visited cities, Paris is well set up for visitors, offering a host of guided tours, from bike, boat, bus, scooter and walking tours (including some wonderful local-led options in off-the-beaten-track areas) to themed options such as street art.

Bicycle

Bike About Tours (Map p386; ☑06 18 80 84 92; www. bikeabouttours.com; Le Peloton Café, 17 rue du Pont Louis-Philippe, 4e; MHôtel de Ville) This expat-run outfit offers daytime city tours (adult/child €39/34; 3½ hours), trips to Versailles (€95/80), e-bike tours to Champagne (€159/145; minimum four people) and private family tours.

Fat Tire Bike Tours (☑01 82 88 80 96; www.fattiretours. com; tours adult/child from €34/32) Day and night bike tours of the city, both in central Paris and further afield to Versailles and Monet's garden in Giverny.

Paris à Vélo, C'est Sympa! (Map p386; ☑01 48 87 60 01; https://parisavelo.fr; 22 rue Alphonse Baudin, 11e; ⊙3hr tour adult/child €38/32; MRichard Lenoir) Runs three guided bike tours (adult/child €35/29; three hours): a Heart of Paris tour, Unusual Paris (taking in

artist studios and mansions) and the Contrast tour, combining nature and modern architecture. Tours depart from its bike-rental shop.

Boat

A boat cruise down the Seine is the most relaxing way to acquaint or reacquaint yourself with the city's main monuments as you watch Paris glide by. An alternative to a regular tour is the hop-on, hop-off **Batobus** (www. batobus.com; adult/child 1-day pass €17/8, 2-day pass €21/11; ⊙10am-9.30pm late Apr-Aug, shorter hours Sep-late Apr).

Bateaux Parisiens (Map p366; ☑01 76 64 14 45; www. bateauxparisiens.com; Port de la Bourdonnais, 7e; adult/child €15/7; MBir Hakeim or RER Pont de l'Alma) This vast operation runs hour-long river circuits with audioguides in 14 languages (every 30 minutes 10am to 11pm April to September, hourly 10.30am to 10pm October to March), and a host of themed lunch and dinner cruises. It has two locations: one by the Eiffel Tower, the other **south of Notre Dame** (Map p396).

Bateaux-Mouches (Map p368; ☑01 42 25 96 10; www. bateaux-mouches.fr; Port de la Conférence, 8e; adult/child €14/6; ⊙every 30min 10am-10.30pm Apr-Sep, every 40min 11am-9.20pm Oct-Mar; MAlma Marceau) The largest river-cruise company in Paris is a favourite with tour groups. Departing just east of the Pont de l'Alma on the Right Bank, its 70-minute cruises have commentary in French and English.

Vedettes de Paris (Map p366; ☑01 44 18 19 50; www. vedettesdeparis.fr; Port de Suffren, 7e; adult/child €15/7; ⊙10.30am-8.30pm May-Nov, hours vary Dec-Apr; MBir Hakeim or RER Pont de l'Alma) These one-hour sightseeing

cruises on smaller boats are a more intimate experience than those offered by the major companies. It runs themed cruises, too, including imaginative 'Mysteries of Paris' tours for kids (adult/child €15/9).

Vedettes du Pont Neuf (Map p396; ☑01 46 33 98 38; www. vedettesdupontneuf.com; square du Vert Galant, 1er; adult/child €14/7; ⊙10.30am-10.30pm; MPont Neuf) One-hour cruises depart year-round from Vedettes' centrally located dock at the western tip of Île de la Cité; commentary is in French and English. Tickets are cheaper if you buy in advance online (adult/child €10/5). Check the website for details of its one-hour lunch cruises (€42/29), two-hour dinner (€72/35) and two-hour Champagne dinner cruises (€105/35).

Bus

Big Bus Paris (☑01 53 95 39 53; www.bigbustours.com; adult/child 1-day pass €39/19, night tour €27/14) These hop-on, hop-off bus tours operate two different routes around the city, with a total of 13 stops. Commentary is in 11 languages; download free apps for iPhone or Android.

L'Open Tour (☑01 42 66 56 56; www.opentourparis.com; adult/child 1-day pass €35/18, night tour €27/17) Hop-on, hop-off bus tours aboard open-deck buses with four different circuits and 41 stops – good for a whirlwind city tour. Audioguides come in 10 languages.

Walking

Ça Se Visite (☑06 72 20 27 11; www.ca-se-visite.fr; adult/child on foot from €12/10, on kick-scooter from €15/13) Meet local artists and crafts-people on resident-led 'urban discovery tours' of Paris' northeast (Belleville, Ménil-

SPECIALISED TOURS

Meeting the French (☎01 42 51 19 80; www.meetingthefrench.com; tours & courses from €30) Cosmetics workshops, backstage cabaret tours, fashion-designer showroom visits, market tours, baking with a Parisian baker, dinner with a Parisian family – the repertoire of cultural and gourmet tours and behind-the-scenes experiences offered by Meeting the French is truly outstanding. All courses and tours are in English.

THATMuse (www.thatmuse.com; per person excl museum admission Louvre/Musée d'Orsay €29/35) Organises treasure hunts in English and French in the Louvre and Musée d'Orsay. Participants (up to five people, playing alone or against another team) have to photograph themselves in front of 20 to 30 works of art ('treasure'). Hunts typically last 1½ to two hours.

Left Bank Scooters (☎06 78 12 04 24; www.leftbankscooters.com; 3hr tours per 1st/2nd passenger from €200/50) Runs a variety of scooter tours around Paris, both day and evening, as well as trips out to Versailles and sidecar tours. A car or motorcycle licence is required.

Street Art Paris (☎06 52 69 92 40; www.streetartparis.fr; tours €20; ⊙by reservation) Learn about the history of graffiti on fascinating tours taking in Paris' vibrant street art. Tours take place in Belleville and Montmartre and on the Left Bank. If you're inspired to try it yourself, book into a 2½-hour mural workshop (€35).

montant, Canal Saint-Martin, Canal de l'Ourcq, La Goutte d'Or, Oberkampf, La Villette et al) – on foot or *trottinette* (kick-scooter).

Eye Prefer Paris (☎06 31 12 86 20; www.eyepreferparis tours.com; 3-person 3hr tour €225) New Yorker–turned-Parisian Richard Nahem leads offbeat tours of the city. Full-day tours also available.

Localers (☎01 83 64 92 01; www.localers.com; tours from €49) Classic walking tours and behind-the-scenes urban discoveries with local Paris experts: photo shoots, market tours, family tours, themed tours (eg 'history of fashion') and more.

Paris Walks (☎01 48 09 21 40; www.paris-walks.com; 2hr tours adult/child from €15/10) Long established and well respected, Paris Walks offers two-hour thematic walking tours (art, fashion, chocolate, the French Revolution etc).

Parisien d'un Jour – Paris Greeters (www.greeters. paris; by donation) See Paris through local eyes with these two- to three-hour city tours. Volunteers – mainly knowledgeable Parisians passionate about their city – lead groups (maximum six people) to their favourite spots. Minimum two weeks' notice is needed.

Directory A–Z

Accessible Travel

Paris is an ancient city and therefore not particularly well equipped for *visiteurs handicapés* (disabled visitors): kerb ramps are few and far between, older public facilities and budget hotels usually lack lifts, and the metro, dating back more than a century, is mostly inaccessible for those in a wheelchair *(fauteuil roulant)*.

Efforts are being made to improve things, however. The tourist office continues its excellent 'Tourisme & Handicap' initiative, under which museums, cultural attractions, hotels and restaurants that provide access, special assistance or facilities for those with physical, cognitive, visual and/or hearing disabilities display a special logo at their entrances. Online, its FACIL'iti service allows you to create your own profile to personalise the web content of parisinfo.com according to your particular motor, sensory and/or cognitive needs.

The Paris Convention & Visitors Bureau's main office (p343) is equipped with a service called ACCEO, which makes it possible for people who are deaf or hearing impaired to ask for information. With the help of a French sign-language operator, users can communicate via a webcam, microphone and speakers. Instant speech transcription is available, too.

Resources

➡ Visit www.parisinfo.com/accessibility for a wealth of useful information organised by theme – getting there and around, attractions, accommodation and cafes/bars/restaurants – as well as practical information such as where to rent medical equipment or locate automatic public toilets. You can download the up-to-date 26-page Accessible Paris guide, which is also available in hard copy from tourist information centres in the city.

➡ For information about which cultural venues in Paris are accessible to people with disabilities, visit Accès Culture (www.accesculture.org).

➡ J'Accède (www.jaccede.com) maintains a searchable database of accessible venues sourced from the local disabled community and has thousands of entries in Paris alone. It is also available as a smartphone app.

➡ **Mobile en Ville** (Map p412; ☑06 52 76 62 49; www.mobile-enville.org; 8 rue des Mariniers, 14e) works hard to make independent travel within the city easier for people in wheelchairs. Among other things it organises wheelchair *randonnées* (walks) in and around Paris; those in wheelchairs are pushed by 'walkers' on roller skates; contact the association well ahead of your visit to take part.

➡ Sage Traveling (www.sagetraveling.com) is an outstanding resource for Paris and European-wide travel, with accessible travel agent links, planning guides, tips, hotel lists, guided tours and excursions, cruises and more.

➡ Download Lonely Planet's free *Accessible Travel Online Resources* from http://lptravel.to/AccessibleTravel.

Transport

The SNCF has made many of its train carriages more accessible to people with disabilities. For information and advice on planning your journey from station to station, contact the SNCF service **Accès Plus** (☑09 69 32 26 27; www.accessibilite.sncf.com). The SNCF also has an 88-page *Reduced Mobility Guide*, available to view interactively or to download in French; go to www.accessibilite.sncf.com/documents-a-telecharger/guide-des-voyageurs-a-mobilite.

Info Mobi (www.vianavigo.com/accessibilite) has detailed information about public transport in the Île-de-France region, surrounding Paris, filterable by disability type.

Taxis G7 (☑from a French phone 3607, from an international phone 01 41 27 66 99; www.g7.fr) has hundreds of low-base cars and 120 cars equipped with ramps, and drivers trained in helping passengers with disabilities. Guide dogs are accepted in its entire fleet.

Customs Regulations

Residents of non-EU countries must adhere to the following limits:

Alcohol 16L of beer, 4L of wine and 1L of spirits over 22% ABV or 2L not exceeding a total of 22% ABV

Perfume Up to a value of €430 (arriving by air or sea); up to €300 (arriving by land)

Tobacco 200 cigarettes, 50 cigars or 250g of loose tobacco

For visitors from EU countries, limits only apply for excessive amounts; see www.douane.gouv.fr.

Discount Cards

Almost all museums and monuments in Paris have discounted tickets (*tarif réduit*) for students and seniors (generally over 60 years), provided they have valid ID. Children often get in for free; the cut-off age for 'child' is anywhere between six and 18 years. EU citizens under 26 years get in for free at national monuments and museums.

Paris Museum Pass (www. parismuseumpass.fr; two/ four/six days €52/66/78) Gets you into 50-plus venues in and around Paris; a huge advantage is that pass holders usually enter larger sights at a different entrance, meaning you bypass (or substantially reduce) ridiculously long ticket queues.

Paris Passlib' (www.parisinfo. com; two/three/five days €119/139/165) Sold at the Paris Convention & Visitors Bureau (p343) and on its website, this handy city pass covers unlimited public transport in zones 1 to 3, admission to some 50 museums in the Paris

region (aka a Paris Museum Pass), temporary exhibitions at most municipal museums, a one-hour boat cruise along the Seine, and a two-hour bus sightseeing tour around central Paris' key sights. There's an optional €20 supplement for a skip-the-line ticket to levels one and two of the Eiffel Tower.

Electricity

Type E
220V/50Hz

Emergency

Ambulance (SAMU)	15
Fire	18
Police	17
EU-wide emergency	112
France's country code	33

Internet Access

➡ Wi-fi (pronounced '*wee*-fee' in France) is available in most Paris hotels, usually at no extra cost, and in some museums.

➡ Many cafes and bars have free wi-fi for customers; you may need to ask for the code.

➡ Free wi-fi is available in hundreds of public places, including parks, libraries and municipal buildings; look for a purple 'Zone Wi-Fi' sign. To connect, select the 'PARIS_WI-FI_' network. Sessions are limited to two hours (renewable). For complete details and a map of hotspots, see www.paris.fr/wifi.

➡ Hotels will normally print documents (eg tickets and boarding passes) for guests.

➡ Co-working cafes have sprung up across Paris; you typically pay for a set amount of time, with wi-fi, drinks and snacks included.

Legal Matters

If the police stop you for any reason, be polite and remain calm. They have wide powers of search and seizure and can, without any particular reason, decide to examine your passport, visa and so on. (You are expected to have photo ID on you at *all* times.) Do *not* challenge them.

French police are strict about security. Do not leave baggage unattended; they are quite serious when they say that suspicious objects will be summarily blown up.

Medical Services

➡ For minor health concerns and to fill prescriptions, see a local *pharmacie* (chemist).

➡ For more serious problems, go to *urgences* (emergencies) wards at Paris' *hôpitaux* (hospitals).

Hospitals

Paris has some 50 hospitals, including the following with 24-hour emergency rooms:

Hôpital Hôtel Dieu (☏01 42 34 82 34; www.aphp.fr; 7 rue de la Cité, 4e; ⒨Cité) One of the city's main government-run public hospitals; after 8pm use the emergency entrance on rue de la Cité.

L'Institut Hospitalier Franco-Britannique (IHFB; ☎01 46 39 22 08; www.hopitalfrancobritan nique.org; 4 rue Kléber, Levallois-Perret; Ⓜ Anatole France) Private, English-speaking option.

Pharmacies

Pharmacies (chemists) are marked by a large illuminated green cross outside. At least one in each neighbourhood is open for extended hours; find a complete night-owl listing on the Paris Convention & Visitors Bureau website (www.parisinfo.com).

Pharmacie Bader (☎01 43 26 92 66; www.pharmaciebader. com; 10-12 bd St-Michel, 6e; ◷8.30am-9pm Sep-Jul, from 10am Aug; Ⓜ St-Michel)

Pharmacie de la Mairie (☎01 42 78 53 58; www.pharmacie-mairie-paris.com; 9 rue des Archives, 4e; ◷9am-8pm; Ⓜ Hôtel de Ville)

Pharmacie Les Champs (☎01 45 62 02 41; www. boticinal-pharmacie.com; Galerie des Champs-Élysées, 84 av des Champs-Élysées, 8e; ◷8.30am-9pm; Ⓜ George V)

Money

France uses the euro (€), which is divided into 100 centimes. Denominations are €5, €10, €20, €50, €100, €200 and €500 notes, and €0.01, €0.02, €0.05, €0.10, €0.20, €0.50, €1 and €2 coins.

French vendors rarely accept bills larger than €50.

Check the latest exchange rates on websites such as www.xe.com.

ATMs

ATMs (*distributeur automatique de billets* in French) are widespread. Unless you have particularly high transaction fees, ATMs are usually the best and easiest way to deal with currency exchange. Check with your bank before you travel to know if/how much they charge for international cash withdrawals.

Avoid the option to lock in a currency conversion rate in your home currency (known as DCC; dynamic currency conversion) at ATMs that offer it, as exchange rates are inevitably poor. Choosing the local currency (euros in Paris) is always cheaper.

Changing Money

➡ Cash is not a good way to carry money; it can be stolen and in France you often won't get the best exchange rates.

➡ In Paris, *bureaux de change* are usually more efficient, are open longer hours and give better rates than banks – many banks don't even offer exchange services.

Credit Cards

➡ Visa/Carte Bleue is the most widely accepted credit card in Paris, followed by MasterCard (Eurocard). Amex cards are only accepted at more upmarket establishments.

➡ Note that France uses a smartcard with an embedded microchip and PIN. Some foreign chip-and-PIN-enabled cards require a signature, and some chip-embedded foreign cards can't be used at automated machines (such as at a metro station or museum) – ask your bank for advice before you leave.

➡ Many merchants and hotels offer the option of paying in your home currency (DCC; dynamic currency conversion), based on their bank's (invariably poor) exchange rate, in addition to which, your home bank may still charge a foreign-transaction fee. When given the choice, it's always cheaper to pay in the local currency (ie euros in Paris).

Opening Hours

The following list covers *approximate* standard opening hours. Many businesses close in August for summer holidays.

Banks 9am to 1pm and 2pm to 5pm Monday to Friday; some open on Saturday morning

Bars and cafes 7am to 2am

Museums 10am to 6pm; closed Monday or Tuesday

Post offices 8am to 7pm Monday to Friday, and until noon Saturday

Restaurants noon to 2pm and 7.30pm to 10.30pm

Shops 10am to 7pm Monday to Saturday; they occasionally close in the early afternoon for lunch and sometimes all day Monday; hours are longer for shops in defined ZTIs (international tourist zones)

Post

➡ Most post offices (*bureaux de poste*) are open Monday to Saturday.

➡ *Tabacs* (tobacconists) usually sell postage stamps.

➡ The main **post office** (Map p376; www.laposte.fr; 52 rue du Louvre, 1er; ◷8am-midnight Mon, midnight-6am & 8am-midnight Tue-Sat, 10am-midnight Sun; Ⓜ Étienne Marcel, Les Halles, or RER Châtelet–Les Halles), five blocks north of the eastern end of the Musée du Louvre, will reopen in 2022 following major renovations, which include the addition of a restaurant, cafe and rooftop garden with 360-degree views across Paris. Prior to its reopening, postal services are available at a temporary office at 16 rue Étienne Marcel, 2e.

➡ Each *arrondissement* has its own five-digit postcode, formed by prefixing the number of the *arrondissement* with '750' or '7500' (eg 75001 for the 1er *arrondissement*, 75019 for the 19e). The only exception is the 16e, which has two postcodes: 75016 and 75116. Postcodes that don't start with '750' or '7500' are outside the bd Périphérique (ring road). All mail to addresses in France must include the postcode.

Public Holidays

In France a *jour férié* (public holiday) is celebrated strictly on the day on which it falls. Thus if May Day falls on a Saturday or Sunday, no provision is made for an extra day off.

The following holidays are observed in Paris:

New Year's Day (Jour de l'An) 1 January

Easter Sunday & Monday (Pâques & Lundi de Pâques) Late March/April

May Day (Fête du Travail) 1 May

Victory in Europe Day (Victoire 1945) 8 May

Ascension Thursday (L'Ascension) May (celebrated on the 40th day after Easter)

Whit Monday (Lundi de Pentecôte) Mid-May to mid-June (seventh Monday after Easter)

Bastille Day/National Day (Fête Nationale) 14 July

Assumption Day (L'Assomption) 15 August

All Saints' Day (La Toussaint) 1 November

Armistice Day/Remembrance Day (Le Onze Novembre) 11 November

Christmas (Noël) 25 December

Responsible Travel

Travelling responsibly in Paris is increasingly easy. Successful measures implemented by the city span drastically reducing cars, removing street parking,

rolling out cycle lanes, and reclaiming areas for pedestrians to vegetating areas such as rooftops. Paris now aims to become Europe's greenest city by 2030, creating 'urban forests', greenifying landmark areas such as the Champs-Élysées, and ensuring key services are readily accessible on foot as a '15-minute city'.

Tips for a sustainable Paris visit:

Minimise your carbon footprint Consider walking or utilising Paris' shared-bike scheme, **Vélib'** (☑01 76 49 12 34; www.velib-metropole.fr; day/week subscription €5/15, standard bike hire up to 30/60min free/€1, electric bike €1/2), or electric moped scheme, **Cityscoot** (www.cityscoot.eu; per 1/100min €0.34/29).

Sleep green Search for establishments that have signed the tourist office's Charter for Sustainable Accommodation in Paris. Other credentials are Green Key and European Ecolabels, Green Globe, EarthCheck and ISO 14001 certification.

Eat sustainably Grab bargain-priced unsold items at merchants such as bakeries via the app Too Good to Go (www.toogoodtogo.fr); pick up fresh produce at Paris' *biologique* (organic) markets like **Mar-**

ché Raspail (Map p406; bd Raspail, btwn rue de Rennes & rue du Cherche Midi, 6e; ☺7am-2.30pm Tue & Fri, organic market 9am-1.30pm Sun; ⓂRennes) ✔, **Marché Biologique des Batignolles** (34 bd des Batignolles, 17e; ☺9am-3pm Sat; ⓂPlace de Clichy, Rome) ✔, **Marché Biologique Brancusi** (Map p412; www.paris.fr/equipements/marche-biologique-brancusi-4516; place Constantin Brancusi, 14e; ☺9am-3pm Sat; ⓂGaîté) ✔ and **Marché Biologique Place du Père Chaillet** (Map p394; place du Père Chaillet, 11e; ☺10am-8pm Wed, 7am-2.30pm Sat; ⓂVoltaire) ✔; or dine urban-farm-to-fork at **Le Perchoir Porte de Versailles** (☑01 83 62 64 21; www.leperchoir.fr; 2 av de la Porte de la Plaine, 15e, Pavilion 6, Paris Expo Porte de Versailles; mains €22-27, 3-course dinner menu €41; ☺kitchen 7.30-11pm Wed-Fri, noon-3pm & 7.30-11pm Sat & Sun, bar 6pm-2am Mon-Fri, noon-2am Sat & Sun; 🛜☑; ⓂPorte de Versailles).

Buy local Look for the labels Fabriqué à Paris/Made in Paris and Fabriqué en France/Made in France, and discover the Paris Good Fashion (p66) initiative.

Get festive Catch zero-waste, renewable-energy-powered eco festival We Love Green (www. welovegreen.fr; June), with an 'ideas lab', artisan producers, and indie, electro and hip-hop concerts.

Explore more Take a tourist-office-run Sustainable Visit (en.parisinfo.com/guided-tours/142576/Sustainable-Visit) guided tour, and track down Paris' under-the-radar attractions.

Safe Travel

Overall, Paris is well lit and safe. Random street assaults are rare.

➡ Stay alert for pickpockets and take precautions: don't carry more cash than you need, and keep credit cards and passports concealed.

➡ Beware scams such as fake petitions.

➡ Metro stations best avoided late at night include Châtelet–Les Halles, Château Rouge, Gare du Nord, Strasbourg St-Denis, Réaumur Sébastopol, Stalingrad and Montparnasse Bienvenüe. Marx Dormoy, Porte de la Chapelle and Marcadet–Poissonniers can be sketchy day and night.

➡ *Bornes d'alarme* (alarm boxes) are located in the centre of metro/RER platforms and some station corridors.

➡ Avoid street protests, which can turn violent.

➡ The COVID-19 health situation in France continues to evolve. At the time of writing, a *pass sanitaire* ('health pass' aka 'Covid certificate') indicating the holder is vaccinated against COVID-19, or recently recovered or tested negative was required for entry to museums, restaurants, bars and numerous other leisure and cultural locations, as well as domestic travel.

➡ For the latest COVID-19 information, restrictions and requirements, visit www.diplomatie. gouv.fr/en/coming-to-france/coronavirus-advice-for-foreign-nationals-in-france.

Pickpockets & Common Scams

Nonviolent crimes, such as pickpocketing and theft from handbags and packs, are a problem wherever there are crowds, especially of tourists. Places to be particularly careful include Montmartre (especially around Sacré Cœur); Pigalle; the areas around Forum des Halles and the Centre Pompidou; the Latin Quarter (especially the rectangle bounded by rue St-Jacques, bd St-Germain, bd St-Michel and quai St-Michel); beneath the Eiffel Tower; and on the metro during rush hour (particularly on line 4 and the western part of line 1).

On cafe and restaurant terraces, avoid leaving your jacket containing your wallet or handbag over the back of your chair, and don't leave your phone unattended on the table.

Common 'distraction' scams employed by pickpockets include the following:

Fake petitions After approaching you to sign a 'petition', scammers will use the document to cover your belongings while they swipe them.

Gold ring Scammers pretend to 'find' a gold ring (after subtly dropping it on the ground) and offer it to you as a diversionary tactic while they surreptitiously reach into your pockets or bags (variations include offering to sell you the ring for an outrageous price, or having the ring's 'owner' arrive and demand compensation).

Dropped items Often occurs on the metro. Someone will drop something or spill a bag; your reaction might be to bend down and help them, while their accomplices riffle through your belongings.

Friendship bracelets Scammers approach you and tie a 'friendship bracelet' onto your wrist, not only insisting that you pay for it but taking the opportunity to fleece you of your valuables.

Taxes & Refunds

France's value-added tax (VAT) is known as TVA (*taxe sur la valeur ajoutée*) and is 20% on most goods with a few exceptions: for food products and books it's 5.5%, and for medicines it's 2.1%. Prices that include TVA are often marked TTC (*toutes taxes comprises;* literally 'all taxes included').

If you're not an EU resident, you can get a TVA refund provided that:

➡ you're aged over 16

➡ you'll be spending less than six months in France

➡ you purchase goods worth at least €175.01 at a single shop on the same day (not more than 15 of the same item)

➡ the goods fit into your luggage

➡ you are taking the goods out of France within three months of purchase

➡ the shop offers *vente en détaxe* (duty-free sales).

Present a passport at the time of purchase and ask for a *bordereau de vente à l'exportation* (export sales invoice) to be signed by the retailer and yourself. Most shops will refund less than the full amount (about 14%) to which you are entitled, in order to cover the time and expense involved in the refund procedure.

Some larger shops offer the refund on the spot (always ask). Alternatively, as you leave France or another EU country, have all three pages of the *bordereau* validated by the country's customs officials at the airport or at the border. Customs officials will take one sheet and hand you two. You must post one copy (the pink one) back to the shop and retain the other (green) sheet for your records in case there is any dispute. Once the shop where you made your purchase receives its stamped copy, it will send you a *virement* (fund transfer) in the form you have requested. Be prepared for a wait of up to three months.

If you're flying out of Orly or Charles de Gaulle, certain shops can arrange for you to receive your refund as you're leaving the country, though you must complete the steps outlined above. You must make such arrangements at the time of purchase.

For more information contact the **customs information centre** (☑08 11 20 44 44; www.douane.gouv. fr/fiche/eligibility-vat-refunds; ☺phone service 8.30am-6pm Mon-Fri).

Telephone

➡ There are no area codes in France – you always dial the 10-digit number.

➡ Telephone numbers in Paris always start with 01, unless the number is provided by an internet service provider (ISP), in which case it begins with 09.

➡ Mobile-phone numbers throughout France commence with either 06 or 07.

➡ France's country code is 33.

➡ To call abroad from Paris, dial France's international access code (00), the country code, the area code (drop the initial '0', if there is one) and the local number.

➡ Note that while numbers beginning with 08 00, 08 04, 08 05 and 08 09 are toll free in France, other numbers beginning with 08 are not.

➡ Customer-service numbers are generally more expensive than local rates.

➡ Most four-digit numbers starting with 10, 30 or 31 are free of charge but can only be dialled by French phones, not international phones.

➡ If you can read basic French, directory enquiries are best done via the *Yellow Pages* (www.pagesjaunes.fr; click on Pages Blanches for the *White Pages*), which will provide more information, including maps, for free.

Mobile Phones

Phone compatibility You can use your mobile/cell phone (*portable*) in France provided it is compatible and allows roaming. Ask your service provider about using it in France, but beware of roaming costs, especially for data.

Networks Rather than staying on your home network, it is usually more convenient to buy a local SIM card from a French provider, such as Orange (www.orange.fr), SFR (www.sfr. fr) or Free Mobile (www.mobile. free.fr), which will give you a local phone number. Ensure your phone is unlocked to use another service provider.

Call credit Count on paying between €3 and €7 for the initial SIM card (with a few minutes of calls included), then purchase a prepaid Mobicarte for phone credit. *Tabacs*, mobile-phone outlets, supermarkets etc sell Mobicartes.

Time

➡ France uses the 24-hour clock in most cases, with the hours usually separated from the minutes by a lower-case 'h'. Thus, 15h30 is 3.30pm, 00h30 is 12.30am and so on.

➡ France is on Central European Time (like Berlin and Rome), which is one hour ahead of GMT/UTC.

➡ Currently, daylight-saving time runs from the last Sunday in March, when the clocks move forward one hour, to the last Sunday in October. In 2019, the European Parliament voted to scrap daylight saving time, although a timeframe was yet to be set at the time of research. A public consultation by the French National Assembly found a majority of French citizens preferred staying on summer time throughout the year.

Toilets

➡ Public toilets in Paris are signposted *toilettes* or *WC*. On main roads, *sanisettes* (self-cleaning cylindrical toilets) are open 24 hours and are free of charge. Look for the words *libre* ('available'; green-coloured) or *occupé* ('occupied'; red-coloured). Locations are mapped at www.parisinfo.com.

➡ Cafe owners do not appreciate you using their facilities if you are not a paying customer (a coffee can be a good investment); however, if you have young children they may make an exception (ask first!). Other good bets are big hotels and major department stores (the latter may incur a charge).

➡ There are free public toilets near the Arc de Triomphe, down the steps at Sacré-Cœur (to the east and west) and at the north-western entrance to the Jardins des Tuileries.

Tourist Information

Paris' main tourist office, the **Paris Convention & Visitors Bureau** (Paris Office de Tourisme; Map p386; ☑01 49 52 42 63; www.paris-info.com; 29 rue de Rivoli, 4e; ☺10am-6pm; ☎; Ⓜ Hôtel de Ville), is located at the Hôtel de Ville. It sells tickets for tours and several attractions, plus museum and transport passes.

Information desks are located at Charles de Gaulle and Orly airports. For tourist information around Paris, see Paris Region (www.visitparisregion.com).

Gare du Nord Welcome Desk (Map p382; www.parisinfo.com; 18 rue de Dunkerque, 10e; ⊙9am-5pm Mon-Sat; MGare du Nord) Inside Gare du Nord station, under the glass roof of the Île-de-France departure and arrival area (eastern end of station).

Réception du Carrousel du Louvre (Map p372; ☑01 43 16 47 10; www.carrouseldulouvre.com; 99 rue de Rivoli, 1er; ⊙10am-8pm Wed-Mon, 11am-7pm Tue; MPalais Royal–Musée du Louvre) Inside the Carrousel du Louvre shopping complex, this partner of Paris' tourist office has tourist information including maps, and can book taxis and accommodation, though it doesn't sell tickets/passes.

Tourism Office of Montmartre (Map p378; ☑01 42 62 21 21; www.montmartreinfo.com; 7 rue Drevet, 18e; ⊙10am-6pm Mon-Fri, 10am-1pm & 2-6pm Sat & Sun; MAbbesses) Locally run tourist office and shop on Montmartre's most picturesque square. It sells maps of Montmartre and organises guided tours.

Galeries Lafayette (Map p370; http://haussmann.galerieslafayette.com; 48 bd Haussmann, 9e; ⊙9.30am-8.30pm Mon-Sat, 11am-8pm Sun; ☏; MChaussée d'Antin, RER Auber) Major Grands Boulevards department store Galeries Lafayette also has a tourist information point, which sells museum passes and tickets for transport, some attractions, excursions and cruises. It's located on the ground floor of the men's store, Galeries Lafayette L'Homme.

Visas

Citizens or residents of EU and Schengen countries have no entry restrictions.

From late 2022, citizens of countries that don't require a visa for entry to the Schengen area (eg nationals of the UK, US, Australia, Canada etc) will need prior authorisation to enter under the European Travel Information and Authorisation System (ETIAS). Travellers will be able to apply online; the cost is €7 for a three-year, multi-entry authorisation. With ETIAS preauthorisation, visitors who require it can stay for 90 days out of 180 days.

Nationals of other countries should check with a French embassy or consulate about applying for a Schengen visa. A visa for any Schengen country should be valid throughout the Schengen area, but it pays to double-check with the embassy or consulate of each country you intend to visit. Note that the UK and Ireland are not Schengen countries.

Check www.diplomatie.gouv.fr for the latest visa regulations and the closest French embassy to your current residence.

Titre de Séjour

If you are issued a long-stay visa valid for six months or longer, you may need to apply for a *titre de séjour* (residence permit; also called a *carte de séjour*) after your arrival in France. If you are only staying for up to 12 months you may not need it, but you will need to register with the French Office of Immigration and Integration (www.ofii.fr). Check the website of the Préfecture de Police (www.prefecturedepolice.interieur.gouv.fr) or call 01 87 27 85 45 first for instructions.

EU passport holders seeking to take up residence in France don't need to acquire a *titre de séjour;* a passport or national ID card is sufficient. Check the Préfecture de Police website to see which countries are included.

Foreigners with non-European passports should check the website of the Préfecture de Police.

Visa Extensions

Tourist visas *cannot* be extended except in emergencies (such as medical problems). If you have an urgent problem, contact the Service Étranger (Foreigner Service) at the Préfecture de Police for guidance. If you entered France as a non-EU citizen who doesn't require a Schengen visa (eg you are an Australian, Canadian or American tourist) and you have stayed for 90 days, you must leave the Schengen area for an additional 90 days before you can re-enter.

Work & Student Visas

If you would like to work, study or stay in France for longer than three months, apply to the French embassy or consulate nearest to you for the appropriate *long séjour* (long-stay) visa. Au pairs are granted student visas: they must be arranged before you leave home (unless you're an EU resident); the same goes for the year-long working-holiday visa *(permis vacances travail)*.

Unless you hold an EU passport or are married to a French national, it's extremely difficult to get a visa that will allow you to work in France. For any sort of long-stay visa, begin the paperwork in your home country several months before you plan to leave. Applications usually cannot be made in a third country, nor can tourist visas be turned into student visas after you arrive in France. People with student visas can apply for permission to work part time; enquire at your place of study.

Language

The sounds used in spoken French can almost all be found in English. If you read our pronunciation guides as if they were English, you'll be understood just fine. There are a couple of sounds to take note of: nasal vowels (represented in our guides by o or u followed by an almost inaudible nasal consonant sound m, n or ng), the 'funny' u (ew in our guides) and the deep-in-the-throat r. Syllables in French words are, for the most part, equally stressed. As English speakers tend to stress the first syllable, try adding a light stress on the final syllable of French words to compensate.

BASICS

Hello.	*Bonjour.*	bon·zhoor
Goodbye.	*Au revoir.*	o·rer·vwa
Excuse me.	*Excusez-moi.*	ek·skew·zay·mwa
Sorry.	*Pardon.*	par·don
Yes./No.	*Oui./Non.*	wee/non
Please.	*S'il vous plaît.*	seel voo play
Thank you.	*Merci.*	mair·see
You're welcome.	*De rien.*	der ree·en

How are you?
Comment allez-vous?   ko·mon ta·lay·voo

Fine, and you?
Bien, merci. Et vous?   byun mair·see ay voo

What's your name?
Comment vous
appelez-vous?   ko·mon voo·
za·play voo

My name is ...
Je m'appelle ...   zher ma·pel ...

WANT MORE?

For in-depth language information and handy phrases, check out Lonely Planet's *French* phrasebook. You'll find it at **shop. lonelyplanet.com**.

Do you speak English?
Parlez-vous anglais?   par·lay·voo ong·glay

I don't understand.
Je ne comprends pas.   zher ner kom·pron pa

ACCOMMODATION

Do you have any rooms available?
Est-ce que vous avez   es·ker voo za·vay
des chambres libres?   day shom·brer lee·brer

How much is it per night/person?
Quel est le prix   kel ay ler pree
par nuit/personne?   par nwee/per·son

Is breakfast included?
Est-ce que le petit   es·ker ler per·tee
déjeuner est inclus?   day·zher·nay ayt en·klew

dorm	*dortoir*	dor·twar
guesthouse	*pension*	pon·syon
hotel	*hôtel*	o·tel
youth hostel	*auberge de jeunesse*	o·berzh der zher·nes

a ... room	*une chambre ...*	ewn shom·brer ...
single	*à un lit*	a un lee
double	*avec un grand lit*	a·vek un gron lee

with (a) ...	*avec ...*	a·vek ...
air-con	*climatiseur*	klee·ma·tee·zer
bathroom	*une salle de bains*	ewn sal der bun
window	*fenêtre*	fer·nay·trer

DIRECTIONS

Where's ...?	*Où est ...?*	oo ay ...
What's the address?	*Quelle est l'adresse?*	kel ay la·dres

SIGNS

Entrée	Entrance
Femmes	Women
Fermé	Closed
Hommes	Men
Interdit	Prohibited
Ouvert	Open
Renseignements	Information
Sortie	Exit
Toilettes/WC	Toilets

Can you write down the address, please?
Est-ce que vous pourriez écrire l'adresse, s'il vous plaît? — es·ker voo poo·ryay ay·kreer la·dres seel voo play

Can you show me (on the map)?
Pouvez-vous m'indiquer (sur la carte)? — poo·vay·voo mun·dee·kay (sewr la kart)

at the corner	au coin	o kwun
at the traffic lights	aux feux	o fer
behind	derrière	dair·ryair
in front of	devant	der·von
far (from ...)	loin (de ...)	lwun (der ...)
left	gauche	gosh
near (to ...)	près (de ...)	pray (der ...)
next to ...	à côté de ...	a ko·tay der ...
opposite ...	en face de ...	on fas der ...
right	droite	drwat
straight ahead	tout droit	too drwa

EATING & DRINKING

What would you recommend?
Qu'est-ce que vous conseillez? — kes·ker voo kon·say·yay

What's in that dish?
Quels sont les ingrédients? — kel son lay zun·gray·dyon

I'm a vegetarian.
Je suis végétarien/ végétarienne. — zher swee vay·zhay·ta·ryun/ vay·zhay·ta·ryen (m/f)

I don't eat ...
Je ne mange pas ... — zher ner monzh pa ...

Cheers!
Santé! — son·tay

That was delicious!
C'était délicieux! — say·tay day·lee·syer

Please bring the bill.
Apportez-moi l'addition, s'il vous plaît. — a·por·tay·mwa la·dee·syon seel voo play

I'd like to reserve a table for ...
Je voudrais réserver une table pour ... — zher voo·dray ray·zair·vay ewn ta·bler poor ...

(eight) o'clock *(vingt) heures* (vungt) er

(two) people *(deux) personnes* (der) pair·son

Key Words

appetiser	entrée	on·tray
bottle	bouteille	boo·tay
breakfast	petit déjeuner	per·tee day·zher·nay
cold	froid	frwa
delicatessen	traiteur	tray·ter
dinner	dîner	dee·nay
fork	fourchette	foor·shet
glass	verre	vair
grocery store	épicerie	ay·pees·ree
hot	chaud	sho
knife	couteau	koo·to
lunch	déjeuner	day·zher·nay
market	marché	mar·shay
menu	carte	kart
plate	assiette	a·syet
spoon	cuillère	kwee·yair
wine list	carte des vins	kart day vun
with/without	avec/sans	a·vek/son

Meat & Fish

beef	bœuf	berf
chicken	poulet	poo·lay
crab	crabe	krab
lamb	agneau	a·nyo
oyster	huître	wee·trer
pork	porc	por
snail	escargot	es·kar·go
squid	calmar	kal·mar
turkey	dinde	dund
veal	veau	vo

Fruit & Vegetables

apple	pomme	pom
apricot	abricot	ab·ree·ko
asparagus	asperge	a·spairzh
beans	haricots	a·ree·ko
beetroot	betterave	be·trav

cabbage	chou	shoo
celery	céleri	sel·ree
cherry	cerise	ser·reez
corn	maïs	ma·ees
cucumber	concombre	kong·kom·brer
gherkin (pickle)	cornichon	kor·nee·shon
grape	raisin	ray·zun
leek	poireau	pwa·ro
lemon	citron	see·tron
lettuce	laitue	lay·tew
mushroom	champignon	shom·pee·nyon
peach	pêche	pesh
peas	petit pois	per·tee pwa
(red/green) pepper	poivron (rouge/vert)	pwa·vron (roozh/vair)
pineapple	ananas	a·na·nas
plum	prune	prewn
potato	pomme de terre	pom der tair
prune	pruneau	prew·no
pumpkin	citrouille	see·troo·yer
shallot	échalote	eh·sha·lot
spinach	épinards	eh·pee·nar
strawberry	fraise	frez
tomato	tomate	to·mat
turnip	navet	na·vay
vegetable	légume	lay·gewm

Other

bread	pain	pun
butter	beurre	ber
cheese	fromage	fro·mazh
egg	œuf	erf
honey	miel	myel
jam	confiture	kon·fee·tewr
oil	huile	weel
pepper	poivre	pwa·vrer
rice	riz	ree
salt	sel	sel
sugar	sucre	sew·krer
vinegar	vinaigre	vee·nay·grer

Drinks

beer	bière	bee·yair
coffee	café	ka·fay
(orange) juice	jus (d'orange)	zhew (do·ronzh)
milk	lait	lay

red wine	vin rouge	vun roozh
tea	thé	tay
(mineral) water	eau (minérale)	o (mee·nay·ral)
white wine	vin blanc	vun blong

EMERGENCIES

Help!
Au secours! — o skoor

Leave me alone!
Fichez-moi la paix! — fee·shay·mwa la pay

I'm lost.
Je suis perdu/perdue. — zhe swee·pair·dew (m/f)

Call a doctor.
Appelez un médecin. — a·play un mayd·sun

Call the police.
Appelez la police. — a·play la po·lees

I'm ill.
Je suis malade. — zher swee ma·lad

It hurts here.
J'ai une douleur ici. — zhay ewn doo·ler ee·see

I'm allergic (to ...).
Je suis allergique (à ...). — zher swee za·lair·zheek (a ...)

SHOPPING & SERVICES

I'd like to buy ...
Je voudrais acheter ... — zher voo·dray ash·tay ...

Can I look at it?
Est-ce que je peux le voir? — es·ker zher per ler vwar

I'm just looking.
Je regarde. — zher rer·gard

I don't like it.
Cela ne me plaît pas. — ser·la ner mer play pa

How much is it?
C'est combien? — say kom·byun

It's too expensive.
C'est trop cher. — say tro shair

There's a mistake in the bill.
Il y a une erreur dans la note. — eel ya ewn ay·rer don la not

bank	banque	bonk
internet cafe	cybercafé	see·bair·ka·fay
tourist office	office de tourisme	o·fees der too·rees·mer

QUESTION WORDS

What?	Quoi?	kwa
When?	Quand?	kon
Where?	Où?	oo
Who?	Qui?	kee
Why?	Pourquoi?	poor·kwa

TIME & DATES

What time is it?
Quelle heure est-il?   kel er ay til

It's (eight) o'clock.
Il est (huit) heures.   il ay (weet) er

Half past (10).
(Dix) heures et demie.   (deez) er ay day·mee

morning	*matin*	ma·tun
afternoon	*après-midi*	a·pray·mee·dee
evening	*soir*	swar
yesterday	*hier*	yair
today	*aujourd'hui*	o·zhoor·dwee
tomorrow	*demain*	der·mun

Monday	*lundi*	lun·dee
Tuesday	*mardi*	mar·dee
Wednesday	*mercredi*	mair·krer·dee
Thursday	*jeudi*	zher·dee
Friday	*vendredi*	von·drer·dee
Saturday	*samedi*	sam·dee
Sunday	*dimanche*	dee·monsh

TRANSPORT

I want to go to ...
Je voudrais aller à ...   zher voo·dray a·lay a ...

NUMBERS

1	*un*	un
2	*deux*	der
3	*trois*	trwa
4	*quatre*	ka·trer
5	*cinq*	sungk
6	*six*	sees
7	*sept*	set
8	*huit*	weet
9	*neuf*	nerf
10	*dix*	dees
20	*vingt*	vung
30	*trente*	tront
40	*quarante*	ka·ront
50	*cinquante*	sung·kont
60	*soixante*	swa·sont
70	*soixante-dix*	swa·son·dees
80	*quatre-vingts*	ka·trer·vung
90	*quatre-vingt-dix*	ka·trer·vung·dees
100	*cent*	son
1000	*mille*	meel

Does it stop at ...?
Est-ce qu'il s'arrête à ...?   es·kil sa·ret a ...

At what time does it leave/arrive?
À quelle heure est-ce qu'il part/arrive?   a kel er es kil par/a·reev

I want to get off here.
Je veux descendre ici.   zher ver day·son·drer ee·see

a ... ticket	*un billet ...*	un bee·yay ...
1st-class	*de première classe*	der prem·yair klas
2nd-class	*de deuxième classe*	der der·zyem klas
one-way	*simple*	sum·pler
return	*aller et retour*	a·lay ay rer·toor

aisle seat	*côté couloir*	ko·tay kool·war
boat	*bateau*	ba·to
bus	*bus*	bews
cancelled	*annulé*	a·new·lay
delayed	*en retard*	on rer·tar
first	*premier*	prer·myay
last	*dernier*	dair·nyay
plane	*avion*	a·vyon
platform	*quai*	kay
ticket office	*guichet*	gee·shay
timetable	*horaire*	o·rair
train	*train*	trun
window seat	*côté fenêtre*	ko·tay fe·ne·trer

I'd like to hire a ...	*Je voudrais louer ...*	zher voo·dray loo·way ...
car	*une voiture*	ewn vwa·tewr
bicycle	*un vélo*	un vay·lo
motorcycle	*une moto*	ewn mo·to

child seat	*siège-enfant*	syezh·on·fon
helmet	*casque*	kask
mechanic	*mécanicien*	may·ka·nee·syun
petrol/gas	*essence*	ay·sons
service station	*station-service*	sta·syon·ser·vees

Can I park here?
Est-ce que je peux stationner ici?   es·ker zher per sta·syo·nay ee·see

I have a flat tyre.
Mon pneu est à plat.   mom pner ay ta pla

I've run out of petrol.
Je suis en panne d'essence.   zher swee zon pan day·sons

GLOSSARY

(m) indicates masculine gender, (f) feminine gender, (pl) plural and (adj) adjective

ancien régime (m) – 'old order'; France under the monarchy before the Revolution

apéritif (m) – a drink taken before dinner

arrondissement (m) – one of 20 administrative divisions in Paris; abbreviated on street signs as 1er (1st arrondissement), 2e or 2ème (2nd) etc

auberge (de jeunesse) (f) – (youth) hostel

avenue (f) – avenue (abbreviated av)

baguette tradition (f) – traditional-style baguette

banlieues (f pl) – suburbs

Belle Époque (f) – 'beautiful age'; era of elegance and gaiety characterising fashionable Parisian life roughly from 1870 to 1914

bière artisanale (f) – craft beer

billet (m) – ticket

billeterie (f) – ticket office or window

biologique or **bio** (adj) – organic

boucherie (f) – butcher

boulangerie (f) – bakery

boules (f pl) – a game played with heavy metal balls on a sandy pitch; also called *pétanque*

brasserie (f) – 'brewery'; a restaurant that usually serves food all day long

brioche (f) – small roll or cake, sometimes made with nuts, currants or candied fruit

bureau de change (m) – currency exchange bureau

café (m) – espresso

carnet (m) – a book of (usually) 10 bus, tram, metro or other tickets sold at a reduced rate

carrefour (m) – crossroads, intersection

carte (f) – card; menu; map

carte de séjour (f) – residence permit

cave (f) – (wine) cellar

chambre (f) – room

chanson française (f) – 'French song'; traditional musical genre where lyrics are paramount

chansonnier (m) – cabaret singer

charcuterie (f) – a variety of meat products that are cured, smoked or processed, including sausages, hams, pâtés and rillettes; shop selling these products

cimetière (m) – cemetery

consigne (f) – left-luggage office

correspondance (f) – linking tunnel or walkway, eg in the metro; rail or bus connection

cour (f) – courtyard

couvert (m) – covered shopping arcade (also called *galerie*)

dégustation (f) – tasting, sampling

demi (m) – half; 330mL glass of beer

département (m) – administrative division of France

dessert (m) – dessert

digicode (m) – entrycode

eau (f) – water

église (f) – church

entrée (f) – entrance; first course or starter

épicerie (f) – small grocery store

espace (f) – space; outlet

Exposition Universelle (f) – World's Fair

fête (f) – festival; holiday

ficelle (f) – string; a thinner, crustier 200g version of the baguette not unlike a very thick breadstick

fin de siècle (adj) – 'end of the century'; characteristic of the last years of the 19th century and generally used to indicate decadence

forêt (f) – forest

formule (f) – similar to a *menu* but allows choice of whichever two of three courses you want (eg starter and main course or main course and dessert)

fromagerie (f) – cheese shop

galerie (f) – gallery; covered shopping arcade (also called passage)

galette (f) – a pancake or flat pastry, with a variety of (usually savoury) fillings

gare (f) – railway station

gare routière (f) – bus station

goûter – afternoon snack

Grand Paris – greater Paris

grand projet (m) – huge, public edifice erected by a government or politician generally in a bid to immortalise themselves

Grands Boulevards (m pl) – 'Great Boulevards'; the eight contiguous broad thoroughfares that stretch from place de la Madeleine eastwards to place de la République

halles (f pl) – covered food market

hameau (m) – hamlet

hammam (m) – steam room, Turkish bath

haute couture (f) – literally 'high sewing'; the creations of leading designers

haute cuisine (f) – 'high cuisine'; classic French cooking style typified by elaborately prepared multicourse meals

hôtel de ville (m) – city or town hall

hôtel particulier (m) – private mansion

jardin (m) – garden

kir (m) – white wine sweetened with a blackcurrant (or other) liqueur

lycée (m) – secondary school

marché (m) – market

marché aux puces (m) – flea market

matériel de cuisine (m) – kitchenware

menu (m) – fixed-price meal with two or more courses; see *formule*

musée (m) – museum

musette (f) – accordion music

nocturne (f) – late night opening at a museum, department store etc

orangerie (f) – conservatory for growing citrus fruit

pain au chocolat (m) – chocolate croissant

palais de justice (m) – law courts

parc (m) – park

parvis (m) – square in front of a church or public building passage

pastis (m) – an aniseed-flavoured apéritif mixed with water

pâté (m) – potted meat; a thickish paste, often of pork, cooked in a ceramic dish and served cold (similar to terrine)

patisserie (f) – cakes and pastries; shop selling these products

pavés (m) – flattened rectangular loaves of bread

pétanque (f) – see *boules*

place (f) – square or plaza

plan (m) – city map

plan du quartier (m) – map of nearby streets (hung on the wall near metro exits)

plat du jour (m) – daily special in a restaurant

pont (m) – bridge

port (m) – harbour, port

porte (f) – door; gate in a city wall

poste (f) – post office

préfecture (f) – prefecture; capital city of a département

quai (m) – quay

quartier (m) – quarter, district, neighbourhood

raï – a type of Algerian popular music

RATP – Régie Autonome des Transports Parisiens; Paris' public transport system

RER – Réseau Express Régional; Paris' suburban train network

résidence (f) – residence; serviced-apartment hotel

rillettes (f pl) – shredded potted meat or fish

rive (f) – bank of a river

rond point (m) – roundabout

rue (f) – street or road

rue végétale – green-focused, low-traffic street

salle (f) – hall; room

salon de thé (m) – tearoom

SNCF – Société Nationale de Chemins de Fer; France's national railway organisation

soldes (m pl) – sale, the sales

sortie (f) – exit

spectacle (m) – performance, play or theatrical show

square (m) – public garden

tabac (m) – tobacconist (which also sells bus tickets, phonecards etc)

tarif réduit (m) – reduced price (for students, seniors, children etc)

tartine (f) – a slice of bread with any topping or garnish

taxe de séjour (f) – municipal tourist tax

TGV – train à grande vitesse; high-speed train

tour (f) – tower

traiteur (m) – caterer, delicatessen

TVA – taxe sur la valeur ajoutée; value-added tax

Vélib' (m) – communal bicycle rental scheme in Paris

vélo (m) – bicycle

version française (m) – literally 'French version': a film dubbed in French

version originale – literally 'original version': a nondubbed film in its original language with French subtitles

viennoiseries (f) – sweet pastries

Behind the Scenes

SEND US YOUR FEEDBACK

We love to hear from travellers – your comments keep us on our toes and help make our books better. Our well-travelled team reads every word on what you loved or loathed about this book. Although we cannot reply individually to your submissions, we always guarantee that your feedback goes straight to the appropriate authors, in time for the next edition. Each person who sends us information is thanked in the next edition – the most useful submissions are rewarded with a selection of digital PDF chapters.

Visit **lonelyplanet.com/contact** to submit your updates and suggestions or to ask for help. Our award-winning website also features inspirational travel stories, news and discussions.

Note: We may edit, reproduce and incorporate your comments in Lonely Planet products such as guidebooks, websites and digital products, so let us know if you don't want your comments reproduced or your name acknowledged. For a copy of our privacy policy visit lonelyplanet.com/privacy.

OUR READERS

Many thanks to the travellers who used the last edition and wrote to us with helpful hints, useful advice and interesting anecdotes: Robyne Hayes and Anne Emison Wishard.

WRITER THANKS

Catherine Le Nevez

Merci mille fois first and foremost to Julian, and to the innumerable Parisians who provided insights, inspiration and great times. Huge thanks too to my Paris co-authors, and to Sandie Kestell, Genna Patterson and everyone at LP. As ever, a heartfelt *merci encore* to my family for sustaining my lifelong love of Paris.

Jean-Bernard Carillet

Heaps of thanks to the commissioning and production team at LP, especially Sandie, for their trust and support, and to the editorial and cartography teams. In Paris, a special mention goes to my friends Didier, Sarah, Elodie, Marie and many more, who happily shared their passion of Paris. And how could I forget my daughter Eva, who is a *Parisienne par excellence*?

Christopher Pitts

Special thanks to my three great co-writers for their advice and input and to all the crew at LP who have put so much hard work into making this book what it is. Bises as always to the Pavillard clan, and my dearest partners in crime: Perrine, Elliot and Céleste.

Nicola Williams

Many thanks as always to the many good friends and savvy Paris professionals who pulled out all the stops to ensure I tracked down the best of Paris, including street-smart local in the 13e Mary Winston-Nicklin, New Yorker-in-Paris Kasia Dietz, adopted-Parisian-in-London Daisy of the Louvre's fabulous ThatMuse, and the ever-dedicated Elodie Berta at the Paris Convention & Visitors Bureau. On the home front, bisou as always to my tireless, trilingual travel and support team Matthias, Niko, Mischa and Kaya.

ACKNOWLEDGEMENTS

Cover photograph: :Palais Garnier, Hemis/AWL Images ©.

Climate map data adapted from Peel C, Finlayson BL & McMahon TA (2007) 'Updated World Map of the Köppen-Geiger Climate Classification', *Hydrology and Earth System Sciences*, 11, pp1633–44..

Illustrations pp112–13, pp158–9, pp198–9 and pp268–9 by Javier Zarracina.

BEHIND THE SCENES

THIS BOOK

This 13th edition of Lonely Planet's *Paris* guidebook was researched and written by Catherine Le Nevez, Jean-Bernard Carillet, Christopher Pitts and Nicola Williams. Catherine, Christopher and Nicola also wrote the previous three editions. This guidebook was produced by the following:

Senior Product Editor Sandie Kestell

Regional Senior Cartographer Mark Griffiths

Cartographer Rachel Imeson

Product Editors Kate Chapman, Angela Tinson

Book Designer Catalina Aragón

Assisting Editors Andrea Dobbin, Ali Lemer, Anne Mulvaney, Gabrielle Stefanos

Cover Researcher Brendan Dempsey-Spencer

Thanks to Imogen Bannister, Daniel Bolger

See also separate subindexes for:

EATING P357

DRINKING & NIGHTLIFE P359

ENTERTAINMENT P360

SHOPPING P361

SPORTS & ACTIVITIES P361

SLEEPING P362

Index

Paris Maps

Sights

- Beach
- Bird Sanctuary
- Buddhist
- Castle/Palace
- Christian
- Confucian
- Hindu
- Islamic
- Jain
- Jewish
- Monument
- Museum/Gallery/Historic Building
- Ruin
- Shinto
- Sikh
- Taoist
- Winery/Vineyard
- Zoo/Wildlife Sanctuary
- Other Sight

Activities, Courses & Tours

- Bodysurfing
- Diving
- Canoeing/Kayaking
- Course/Tour
- Sento Hot Baths/Onsen
- Skiing
- Snorkelling
- Surfing
- Swimming/Pool
- Walking
- Windsurfing
- Other Activity

Sleeping

- Sleeping
- Camping
- Hut/Shelter

Eating

- Eating

Drinking & Nightlife

- Drinking & Nightlife
- Cafe

Entertainment

- Entertainment

Shopping

- Shopping

Information

- Bank
- Embassy/Consulate
- Hospital/Medical
- Internet
- Police
- Post Office
- Telephone
- Toilet
- Tourist Information
- Other Information

Geographic

- Beach
- Gate
- Hut/Shelter
- Lighthouse
- Lookout
- Mountain/Volcano
- Oasis
- Park
- Pass
- Picnic Area
- Waterfall

Population

- Capital (National)
- Capital (State/Province)
- City/Large Town
- Town/Village

Transport

- Airport
- Border crossing
- Bus
- Cable car/Funicular
- Cycling
- Ferry
- Metro station
- Monorail
- Parking
- Petrol station
- S-Bahn/Subway station
- Taxi
- T-bane/Tunnelbana station
- Train station/Railway
- Tram
- U-Bahn/Underground station
- Other Transport

Routes

- Tollway
- Freeway
- Primary
- Secondary
- Tertiary
- Lane
- Unsealed road
- Road under construction
- Plaza/Mall
- Steps
- Tunnel
- Pedestrian overpass
- Walking Tour
- Walking Tour detour
- Path/Walking Trail

Boundaries

- International
- State/Province
- Disputed
- Regional/Suburb
- Marine Park
- Cliff
- Wall

Hydrography

- River, Creek
- Intermittent River
- Canal
- Water
- Dry/Salt/Intermittent Lake
- Reef

Areas

- Airport/Runway
- Beach/Desert
- Cemetery (Christian)
- Cemetery (Other)
- Glacier
- Mudflat
- Park/Forest
- Sight (Building)
- Sportsground
- Swamp/Mangrove

Note: Not all symbols displayed above appear on the maps in this book

364

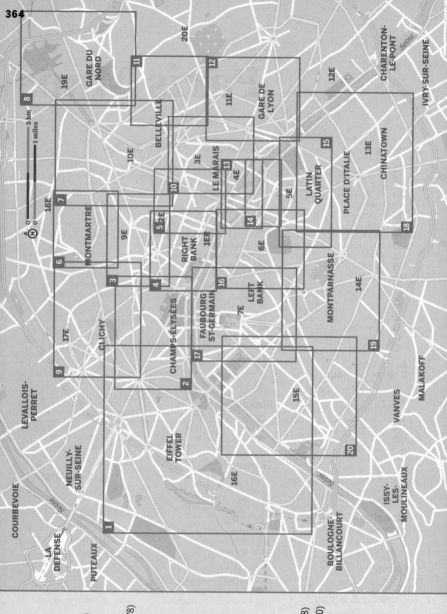

EIFFEL TOWER & WESTERN PARIS

Key on p365

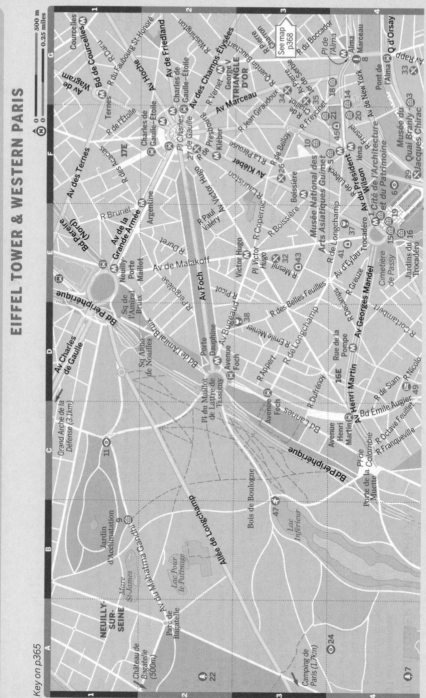

500 m
0.25 miles

NEUILLY-SUR-SEINE

Château de Bagatelle (500m)

Grand Arche de la Défense (3.1km)

Av Charles de Gaulle

Bd Périphérique

Bd de la Famille Brux

Sq Anna de Noailles

Sg de l'Amiral Brux

Av de la Grande Armée

Bd Périphérique (Nord)

Av des Ternes

Bd de Courcelles

Av de Wagram

Courcelles

R Daru

R du Faubourg St-Honoré

Ternes

R de l'Étoile

R des Acacias

R Brunel

R Brunel

Argentine

R Duret

Av de Malakoff

Porte Maillot

Neuilly Porte Maillot

Sq de l'Amiral Bruix

Porte Dauphine

Pl du Maillot de Lattre de Tassigny

Avenue Foch

Av Foch

R Appert

R Picot

Porte

Av Bugeaud

R Émile Menier

R de Longchamp

Av Charles de Gaulle

Charles de Gaulle–Étoile

Pl Charles de Gaulle

27 de Gaulle

Charles de Gaulle–Étoile

Av de Friedland

Av des Champs-Élysées

George V

R Washington

Av Hoche

Charles de Gaulle–Étoile

Av de Wagram

R Vernet

R de Presbourg

R Galilée

R de Tilsitt

R de Bassano

R Quentin Bauchart

TRIANGLE D'OR

R Pierre 1er de Serbie

Av Marceau

R Jean Giraudoux

R de Bellefond

Av Pierre

See map p368

R du Boccador

Pl de l'Alma

Alma Marceau

R de Chaillot

Av de New York

Pont de l'Alma

Av Rapp

Q d'Orsay

R Freycinet

R Jean Goujon

R de Chaillot

Av du Président Wilson

Musée du Quai Branly – Jacques Chirac

Cité de l'Architecture et du Patrimoine

Trocadéro

Iéna

R de Longchamp

Musée National des Arts Asiatiques Guimet

R de Longchamp

R de la Faisanderie

R de Lübeck

R de Belloy

Av Kléber

Av Kléber

R Kléber

R de Presbourg

R La Pérouse

Boissière

Kléber

R Copernic

R Boissière

R Paul Valéry

R Victor Hugo

Av Victor Hugo

Pl Victor Hugo

Victor Hugo

R Mesnil

R Decamps

R Greuze

R d'Eylau

Av Georges Mandel

R de la Pompe

R de la Tour

Rue de la Pompe

R de Longchamp

R des Belles Feuilles

R Lauriston

Av Georges Mandel

Av Henri Martin

Henri Martin

Av Bugeaud

Av Foch

Bd Lannes

Avenue Foch

R Dufrénoy

Avenue Henri Martin

Pl de Colombie

Pl de la Muette

Porte de la Muette

Bd Périphérique

R Octave Feuillet

R Franqueville

R de Siam

R Nicolo

Bd Émile Augier

R Cortambert

Cimetière de Passy

Jardins du Trocadéro

Lac Inférieur

Bois de Boulogne

Allée de Longchamp

Lac Pour le Puthnage

Parc de Bagatelle

Jardin d'Acclimatation

Av du Mahatma Gandhi

Mare St-James

Camping de Paris (1.7km)

16E

17E

1 2 3 4

A B C D E F G H

1 2 3 4

5 9 10 11 14 15 16 18 19 20 21 22 24 26 29 32 33 34 35 37 38 43 45 47 49 7

See map p406

See map p414

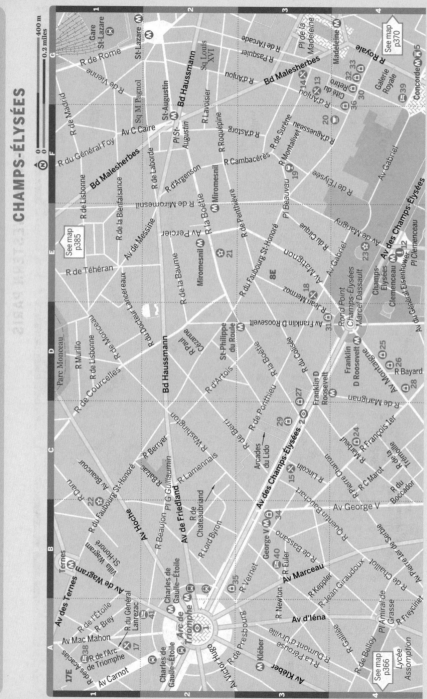

See map p370

See map p385

See map p366

CHAMPS-ÉLYSÉES

See map p372

See map p406

GRANDS BOULEVARDS

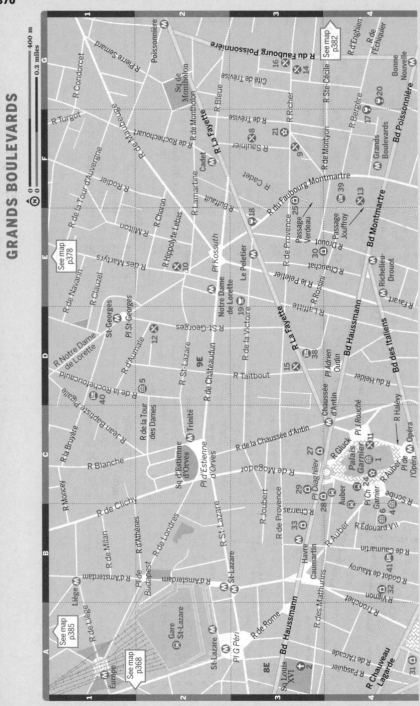

See map p382

See map p378

See map p385

See map p368

See map
p372

Key on p374

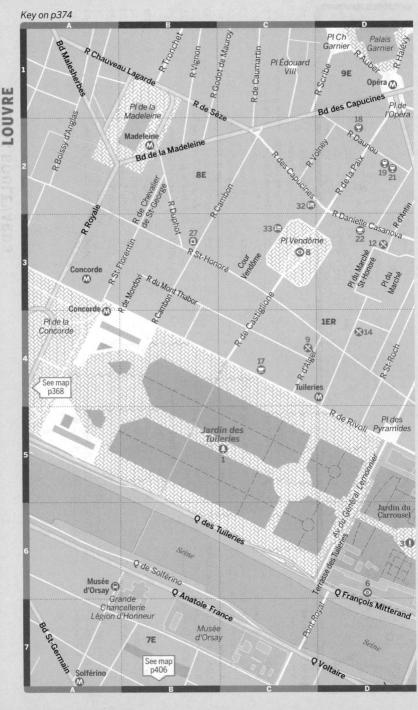

LOUVRE

BOULEVARDS

See map p368

See map p406

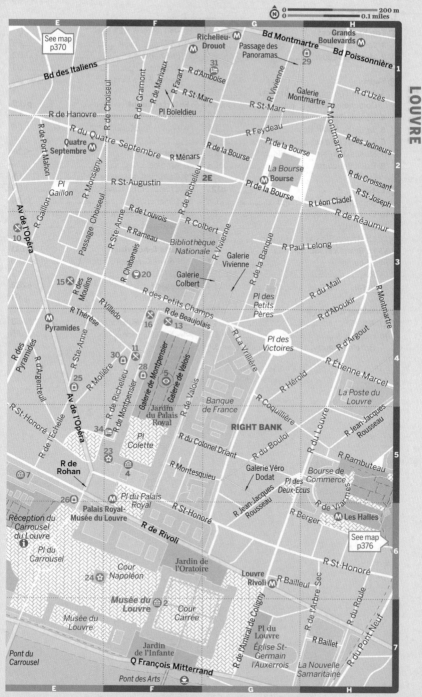

N
0 — 200 m
0 — 0.1 miles

See map p370

Bd des Italiens

Richelieu-Drouot

Bd Montmartre

Grands Boulevards

Bd Poissonnière

Passage des Panoramas 29

R d'Amboise 31

R de Gramont

R de Marivaux

R Favart

R St-Marc

R Vivienne

Galerie Montmartre

R d'Uzès

R de Hanovre

R de Choiseul

Pl Boïeldieu

R St-Marc

R Montmartre

R des Jeûneurs

R de Port Mahon

Quatre Septembre

R du Quatre Septembre

R Ménars

R Feydeau

Pl de la Bourse

R du Croissant

R de Monsigny

R St-Augustin

R de la Bourse

La Bourse
Bourse

R St-Joseph

Pl Gaillon

Passage Choiseul

R Ste-Anne

R de Richelieu

2E

Pl de la Bourse

R Léon Cladel

R de Réaumur

Av de l'Opéra 10

R de Gaillon

R de Louvois

R Colbert

R Vivienne

R Paul Lelong

15

R des Moulins

R Rameau

R Chabanais

Bibliothèque Nationale

Galerie Vivienne

R de la Banque

R du Mail

R Villedo

20

Galerie Colbert

Pl des Petits Pères

R d'Aboukir

Pyramides

R Thérèse

R des Petits Champs

16 13

R de Beaujolais

Pl des Victoires

R Ste-Anne

R Villedo

Galerie de Montpensier

Galerie de Valois

R La Vrillière

R d'Argout

R des Pyramides

R d'Argenteuil

11 30

28

5

R de Valois

R Hérold

R Étienne Marcel

25

Av de l'Opéra

R Molière

R de Richelieu

R de Montpensier

Jardin du Palais Royal

Banque de France

RIGHT BANK

R Coquillière

La Poste du Louvre

R St-Honoré

R de l'Echelle

34

Pl Colette

R du Colonel Driant

R du Bouloi

R du Louvre

R Jean-Jacques Rousseau

R de Rohan

23

4

R Montesquieu

Galerie Véro Dodat

R Rambuteau

7

26

Pl du Palais Royal

Palais Royal-Musée du Louvre

R St-Honoré

R Jean-Jacques Rousseau

Bourse de Commerce

Pl des Deux-Ecus

Bourse de Commerce

R Berger

R de Viarmes

Les Halles

Réception du Carrousel du Louvre

Pl du Carrousel

R de Rivoli

See map p376

24

Cour Napoléon

Jardin de l'Oratoire

Louvre Rivoli

R Bailleul

R St-Honoré

Musée du Louvre 2

Musée du Louvre

Cour Carrée

Pl du Louvre

R de l'Arbre Sec

R du Roule

R du Pont Neuf

Pont du Carrousel

Jardin de l'Infante

Q François Mitterrand

Église St-Germain l'Auxerrois

R d'Amiral de Coligny

R Baillet

La Nouvelle Samaritaine

Pont des Arts

LOUVRE *Map on p372*

LOUVRE

LES HALLES *Map on p376*

See map p370

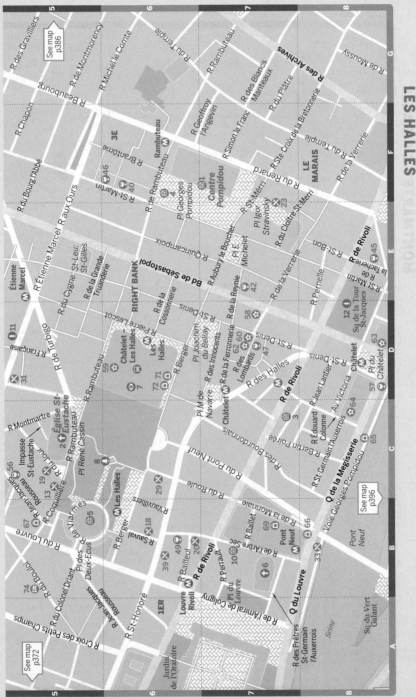

LES HALLES

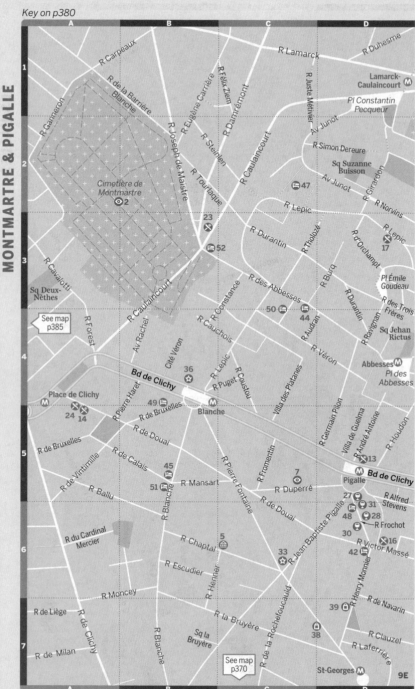

MONTMARTRE & PIGALLE

A | B | C | D

R Carpeaux
R Lamarck
R Duhesme

Lamarck-
Caulaincourt

R de la Barrière
Blanche

Pl Constantin
Pecqueur

R Ganneron

R Eugène Carrière
R Félix Ziem
R Danrémont
R Juste Métivier
Av Junot
R Simon Dereure

R Joseph de Maistre

R Steinlen

R Caulaincourt

Sq Suzanne
Buisson

Cimetière de
Montmartre
⊙ 2

R Tourlaque

☒ 47

Av Junot

Giraudon

R Norvins

R Lepic

R Lepic

☒ 23

R Durantin

R d'Orchampt

☒ 17

R Cavalotti

⊠ 52

Sq Deux-
Nèthes

R des Abbesses

R Tholozé

R Burq

Pl Émile
Goudeau

R Caulaincourt

R Durantin

R des Trois
Frères

See map
p385

R Forest

R Constance

50 ⊟

44 ⊟

R Audran

Sq Jehan
Rictus

Av Rachel

Cité Véron

R Cauchois

R Véron

Abbesses Ⓜ

R Ranignan

Pl des
Abbesses

36 ⊕

R Lepic

R Coustou

Villa des Platanes

Bd de Clichy

R Puget

R Germain Pilon

Villa de Guelma

R Houdon

Place de Clichy Ⓜ

R Pierre Haret

49 ⊟

R André Antoine

24 ☒
14

R de Bruxelles

Blanche Ⓜ

☒ 13

R de Douai

Bd de Clichy

R de Bruxelles

R de Calais

45 ⊟

R Mansart

R Fromentin

7 ⊙

Pigalle

R de Vintimille

51 ⊟

R Pierre Fontaine

R Duperré

27 ⊟ 31

R Ballu

R Blanche

R de Douai

R Alfred
Stevens

48 ⊟ ⊟ 28

R du Cardinal
Mercier

5 ⊞

30

R Frochot

R Chaptal

☒ 16

42 ⊟

R Victor Massé

R Escudier

33 ✪

R Jean Baptiste Pigalle

R Moncey

R Henner

R de Liège

R la Bruyère

39 🔒

R de Navarin

R de Clichy

R Blanche

Sq la
Bruyère

R de la Rochefoucauld

38 🔒

R Clauzel

R de Milan

See map
p370

R Henry Monnier

R Laferrière

St-Georges Ⓜ

9E

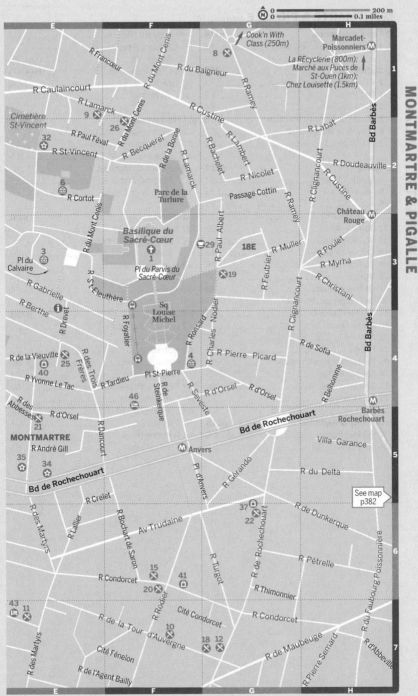

0 — 200 m
0 — 0.1 miles

Marcadet-Poissonniers Ⓜ

Cook'n With Class (250m)

La REcyclerie (800m);
Marché aux Puces de
St-Ouen (1km);
Chez Louisette (1.5km)

R Francœur
R du Mont Cenis
R du Baigneur
R Ramey
Bd Barbès

R Caulaincourt
R Custine
R Lamarck
9
26
R du Mont Cenis
R Labat

Cimetière St-Vincent
R Paul Féval
R Becquerel
R de la Bonne
R Bachelet
R Lambert
R Doudeauville
R Clignancourt
R Custine

32
R St-Vincent
R Nicolet
R Ramey

6
R Cortot
Parc de la Turlure
R Lamarck
Passage Cottin
Château Rouge Ⓜ

Basilique du Sacré-Cœur
29
18E
R Paul Albert
R Muller
R Feutrier
R Poulet
R Myrha

Pl du Calvaire
3
1
Pl du Parvis du Sacré-Cœur
19
R Christiani

R Gabrielle
R Ste-Eleuthère
R Foyatier
Sq Louise Michel
R Ronsard
R Charles Nodier
R Clignancourt

R Berthe
R Drevet
R de Sofia
Bd Barbès

R de la Vieuville
25
4
R Pierre Picard
R Belhomme

40
R des Trois Frères
R Tardieu
Pl St-Pierre
R d'Orsel
R d'Orsel

R Yvonne Le Tac
46
R de Steinkerque
R Séveste
Barbès Rochechouart

R des Abbesses
R d'Orsel
R Dancourt
Bd de Rochechouart

21
MONTMARTRE
R André Gill
Villa Garance

35
34
Ⓜ Anvers
R Gérando
R du Delta

Bd de Rochechouart
Pl d'Anvers
See map p382

R des Martyrs
R Crelet
Av Trudaine
R de Rochechouart
R de Dunkerque

R Lallier
R Bochart de Saron
R Turgot
R Pétrelle
R du Faubourg Poissonnière

15
41
R Thimonnier

R Condorcet
20
Cité Condorcet
R Condorcet

43
11
R Rodier
10
R de Maubeuge

R de la Tour d'Auvergne
18
12
R Pierre Semard
R d'Abbeville

Cité Fénelon
R de l'Agent Bailly

MONTMARTE & PIGALLE *Map on p378*

GARE DU NORD & CANAL ST-MARTIN

Key on p381

0 0.25 miles
0 500 m

19E

9E

See map p384

See map p378

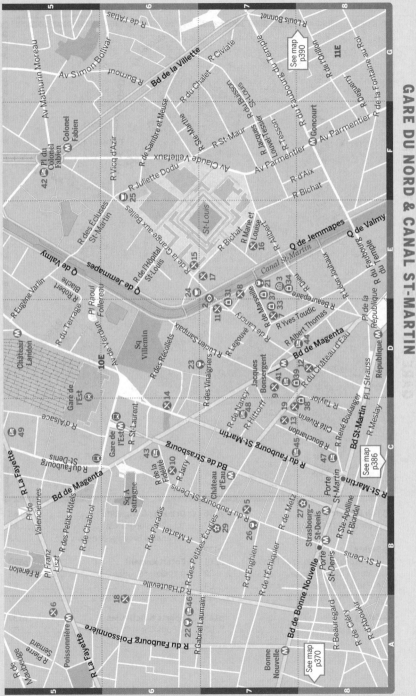

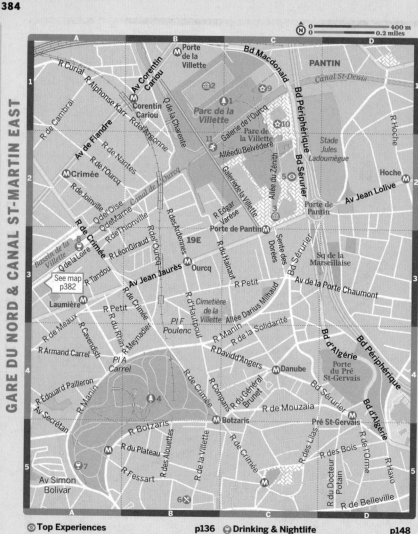

CLICHY & GARE ST-LAZARE

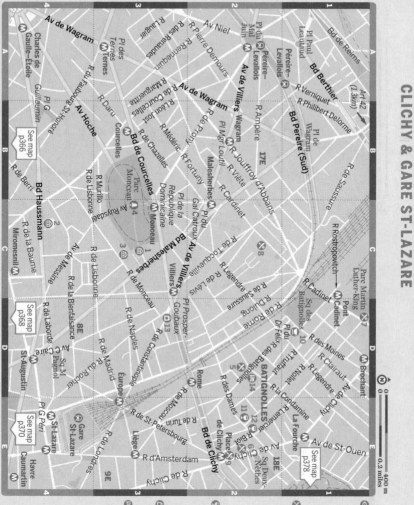

LE MARAIS

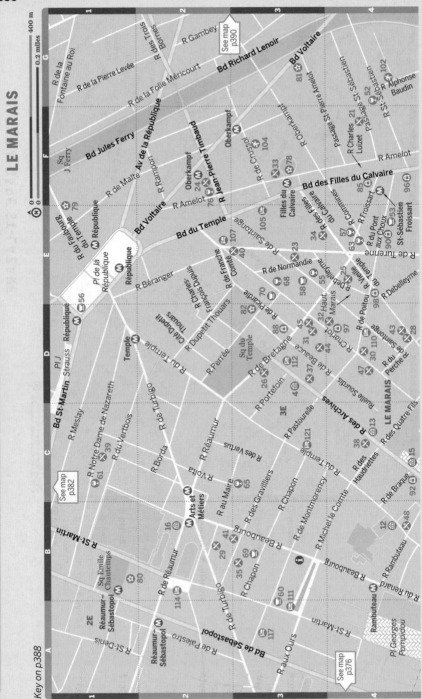

0.2 miles
400 m

See map p390

See map p382

See map p376

Bd Richard Lenoir
Bd Voltaire
R Gambey
R des Trois Bornes
R de la Fontaine au Roi
R de la Pierre Levée
R de la Folie Méricourt
Bd Jules Ferry
Av de la République
R de Malte
R Rampon
Oberkampf
R Jean-Pierre Timbaud
Oberkampf
Bd Voltaire
R Amelot
Bd du Temple
R du Faubourg du Temple
République
Pl de la République
R Béranger
Temple
R Dupetit Thouars
Cité Dupetit Thouars
R du Temple
Sq du Temple
R de Bretagne
R Perrée
R Portefoin
R Pastourelle
R des Archives
LE MARAIS
3E
R des Quatre-Fils
R de Braque
R de Montmorency
R Michel le Comte
R Rambuteau
R Beaubourg
R St-Martin
Bd de Sébastopol
Réaumur – Sébastopol
2E
R St-Denis
Sq Emile Chautemps
Arts et Métiers
R de Réaumur
R du Temple
R au Maire
R des Gravilliers
R Chapon
R des Vertus
R Volta
R Borda
R Beaubourg
R de Turbigo
R Notre Dame de Nazareth
R Meslay
R du Vertbois
Bd St-Martin
Strauss
PIJ
R de Palestro
R aux Ours
Pl Georges Pompidou
R du Renard
R St-Martin
Rambuteau
R de Sébastopol
R de Normandie
R de Saintonge
R de Picardie
R Charlot
R de Beauce
R de Franche Comté
R Charles François Dupuis
R de Poitou
R Debelleyme
R du Perche
R Vieille du Temple
R Debelleyme
R de Turenne
R Froissart
St-Sébastien Froissart
Bd des Filles du Calvaire
Filles du Calvaire
R des Filles du Calvaire
R de Crussol
R d'Oberkampf
Passage St-Pierre Amelot
R Charles Luizet
Passage St-Sébastien
R St-Sébastien
R Alphonse Baudin
R Amelot
R du Pont aux Choux
R Commines
R Debelleyme
Haut Marais
Ruelle Sourdis
R des Haudriettes
R du Temple

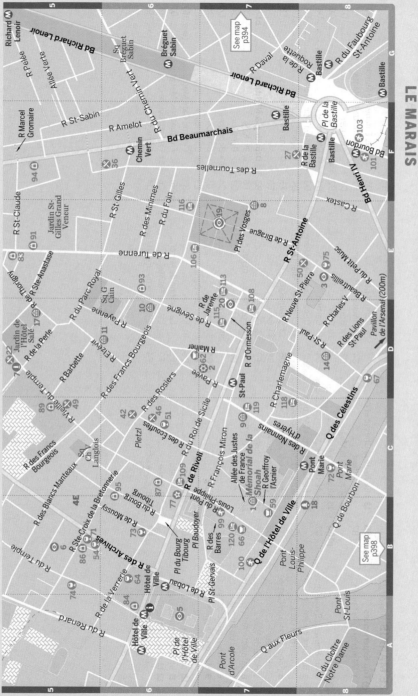

MÉNILMONTANT & BELLEVILLE

Key on p392

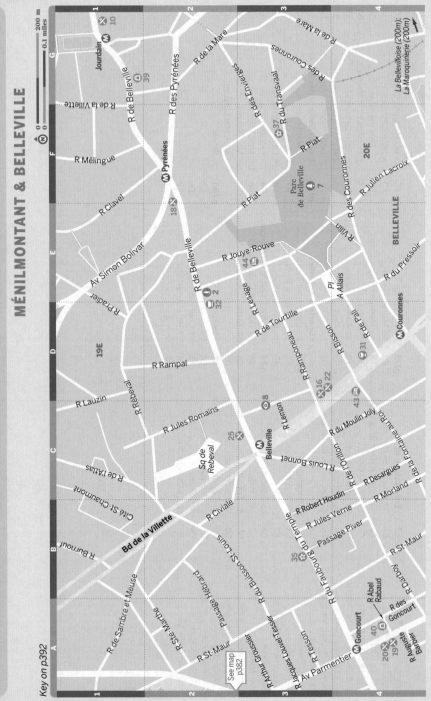

See map p382

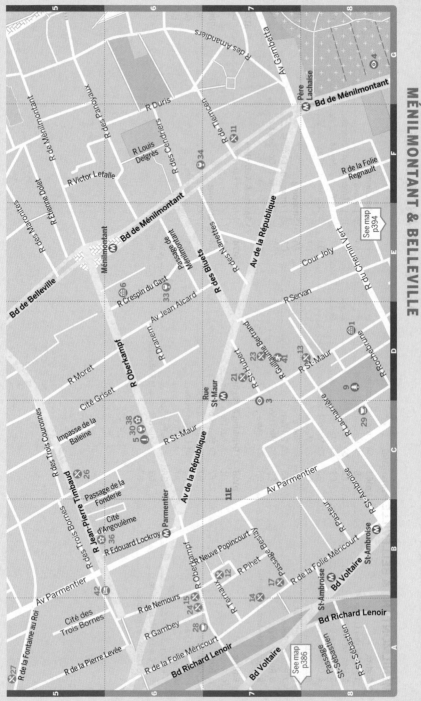

BASTILLE & EASTERN PARIS Map on p394

BASTILLE & EASTERN PARIS

Key on p393

500 m
0.25 miles

See map p390

See map p386

Cimetière du Père Lachaise

Bd de Ménilmontant

Philippe Auguste

Rue des Boulets

Mama Shelter (1km)

Bd Voltaire

11E

4E

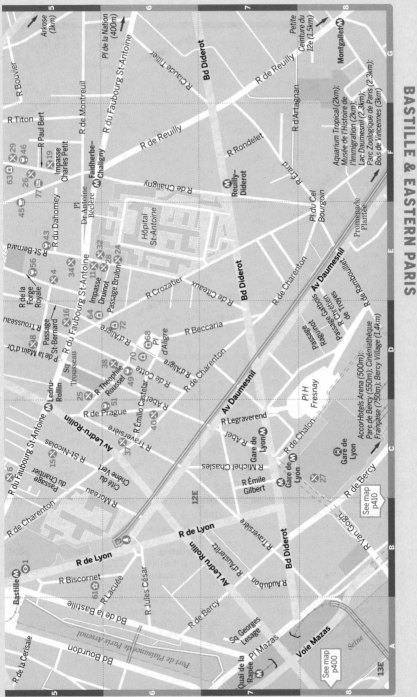

THE ISLANDS

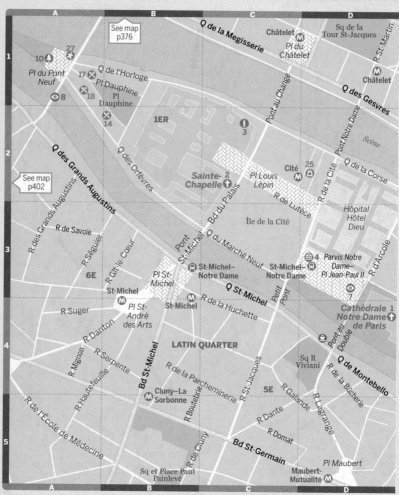

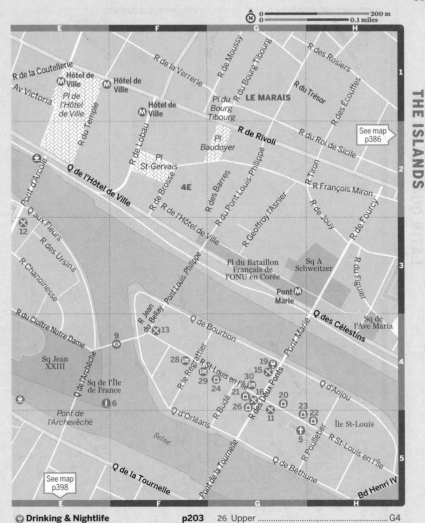

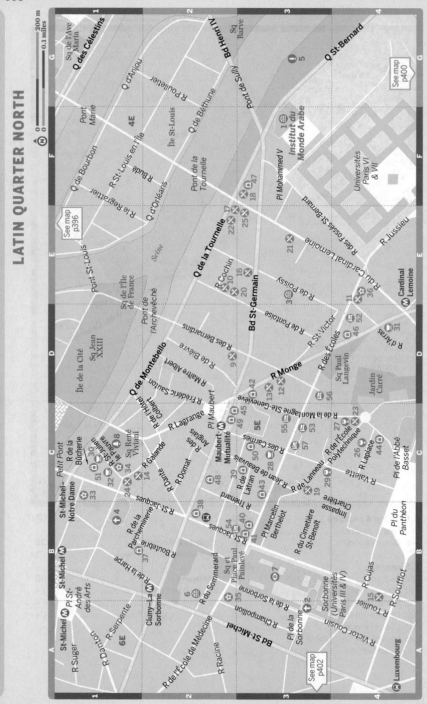

200 m
0.1 miles

G1 Sq de l'Ave Maria
Q des Célestins
Bd Henri IV
Sq Barye
Q St-Bernard

Pont Marie
R Poulletier
Q d'Anjou
Q de Béthune
Pont de Sully
4E
Institut du Monde Arabe 1
Pl Mohammed V

Q de Bourbon
R St-Louis en l'Île
R Budé
Île St-Louis
Q d'Orléans
Pont de la Tournelle
18 47
Universités Paris VI & VII

Q de Béthune
Q de la Tournelle
22 17
25
21
R des Fossés St-Bernard
R Jussieu

See map p396
Pont St-Louis
Seine
Bd St-Germain
R Cochin 16
20
3
R de Pontoise
R du Cardinal Lemoine
R de Poissy
R St-Victor
11
46 52
R d'Arras
31 36
Cardinal Lemoine

Île de la Cité
Sq de l'Île de France
Pont de l'Archevêché
R des Bernardins
R de Bièvre
R Monge
R des Écoles
Sq Paul Langevin
Jardin Carré

Sq Jean XXIII
Q de Montebello
R Maître Albert
R Frédéric Sauton
9
42
12 13
56
R de la Montagne Ste-Geneviève
23 27
R de l'École Polytechnique

R de l'Hôtel Colbert
R Lagrange
Pl Maubert
Maubert-Mutualité
49 45
55
5E
50
26
R Laplace
44
Pl de l'Abbé Basset

R du Sommerard
R René Viriani
8
R des Anglais
R Galande
R Dante
57
R des Carmes
53
R de Lanneau
19 29
R Valette

Petit Pont
R de la Bûcherie
30
St-Julien le Pauvre
51
32
34 24
14
R Domat
39
R de Latran
R Jean de Beauvais
43
28
Impasse Chartière
Pl du Panthéon

St-Michel–Notre Dame
33
4
R St-Jacques
48
R Thénard
Pl Marcelin Berthelot
R du Cimetière St-Benoît
Pl du Panthéon

R de la Parcheminerie
38
R St-Jacques
54 40
41
R Cujas
R Soufflot

St-Michel
Pl St-André des Arts
Cluny–La Sorbonne
R de la Harpe
37
R Boutebrie
6
35 7
R de la Sorbonne
Sq et Place Paul Painlevé
2
Sorbonne (Universités Paris III & IV)
15
R Toullier
R Cujas
R Soufflot

R Suger
R Dauton
R Serpente
6E
Bd St-Michel
R Champollion
Pl de la Sorbonne
R Victor Cousin
Luxembourg

R Racine
R de l'École de Médecine
See map p402
See map p400

Cardinal Lemoine

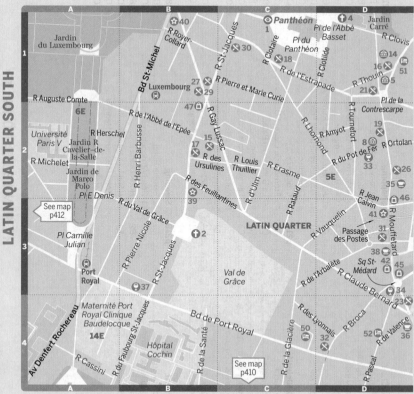

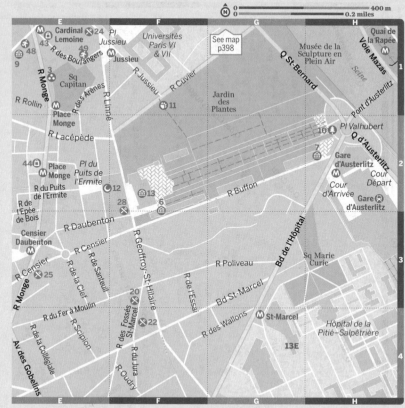

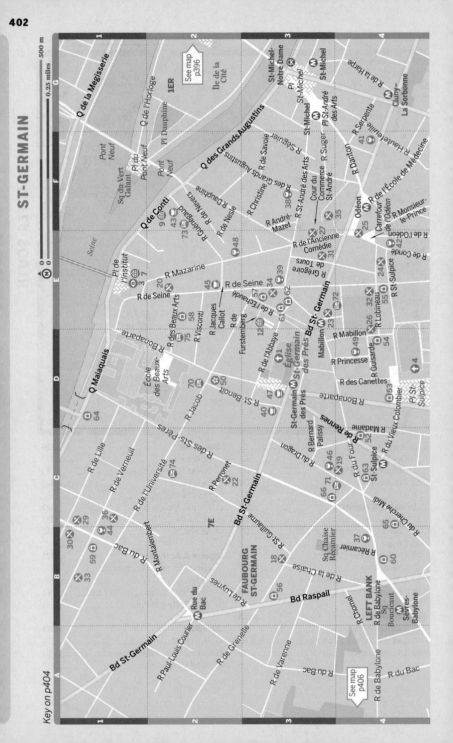

ST-GERMAIN

Key on p404

N
0   0
0   0.25 miles
0   500 m

1ER

7E

FAUBOURG
ST-GERMAIN

LEFT BANK

Q de la Mégisserie
Q de l'Horloge
Q du Pont Neuf
Pont Neuf
Pl Dauphine
Pl de l'Horloge
Île de la Cité
See map p396
St-Michel–
Notre Dame
St-Michel
St-Michel
St-Michel
Pl St-Michel
R de la Harpe
Cluny–
La Sorbonne
R Serpente
R Hautefeuille
R Danton
Pl St-André
des Arts
R St-André des Arts
Cour du
Commerce
St-André
R Suger
R de l'École de Médecine
Carrefour de
l'Odéon
R Monsieur-
le-Prince
Odéon
R de l'Odéon
R de Condé
R St-Sulpice
R St-Sulpice
R Lobineau
R Guisarde
R Princesse
R des Canettes
R du Vieux Colombier
Pl St-
Sulpice
R du Four
R St-Sulpice
R Madame
R de Rennes
R du Dragon
R du Cherche Midi
R Récamier
R Chomel
R de Babylone
Sq
Boucicaut
Sèvres-
Babylone
R de Babylone
R du Bac
See map
p406
R du Bac
R de Varenne
R du Bac
R de Grenelle
Bd St-Germain
R Paul-Louis Courier
Rue du
Bac
R de Luynes
Bd Raspail
R de la Chaise
Sq Chaise
Récamier
R Récamier
R St-Guillaume
Bd St-Germain
R Perronet
R de l'Université
R de Verneuil
R de Lille
R Montalembert
R du Bac
R des Sts-Pères
R St-Benoît
R Jacob
Q Malaquais
Q de Conti
Pl de
l'Institut
Seine
R de Seine
R Mazarine
R Guénégaud
R de Nevers
R Dauphine
Pont Neuf
P du
Pont Neuf
Sq du Vert
Galant
R de Nesle
R Visconti
R des Beaux Arts
R Jacques Callot
R de
Furstemberg
R de l'Abbaye
Église
St-Germain
des Prés
St-Germain
des Prés
Bd St-Germain
Mabillon
Mabillon
R Mabillon
R Gregoire
de Tours
R Dauphine
Q des Grands Augustins
R de Savoie
R Séguier
R Christine
R des Grands Augustins
R André-
Mazet
R de l'Ancienne
Comédie
R de Seine
R de Buci
R de l'Échaudé
R Bernard
Palissy
Bd Raspail
École
des Beaux-
Arts
R Bonaparte
R de Rennes
R de Seine
R Bonaparte

9
43
73
3 7
20
45
57
34
39
62
61
12
61
41
38
35
27
31
25
24
55
32
26
54
49
72
23
53
4
52
63
19
46
66 71
22
74
18
56
37
60
65
70
50
47
40
64
30
33
59
29
36
44
48
75
58

ST-GERMAIN

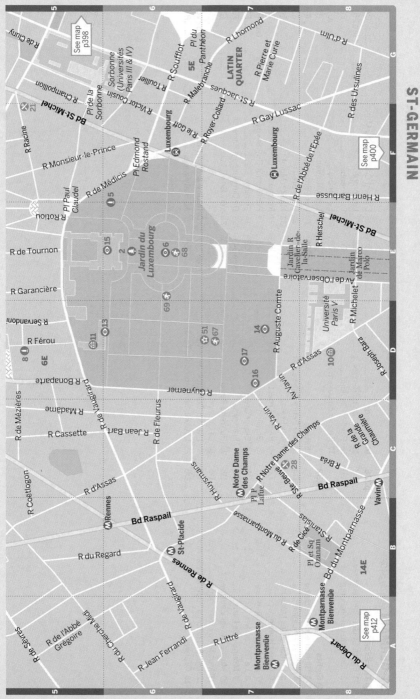

See map p398

LATIN QUARTER

R de Cluny
R de Champollion
Pl de la Sorbonne
Sorbonne (Universités Paris III & IV)
R Victor Cousin
R Toullier
R Soufflot
Pl du Panthéon
5E
R Malebranche
R L'homond
R Pierre et Marie Curie
R d'Ulm

R Racine
Bd St-Michel
21
R St-Jacques
R le Goff
R Royer-Collard
R Gay Lussac
R des Ursulines

R Monsieur-le-Prince
Pl Edmond Rostand
Luxembourg
R de l'Abbé de l'Epée
See map p400

R de Médicis
15
Luxembourg
R Henri Barbusse

R Pl Paul Claudel
R Rotrou
Jardin du Luxembourg
15
2
6
68
Bd St-Michel
R Herschel

R de Tournon
69
Jardin R Cavelier-de-la-Salle
Av de l'Observatoire
Jardin de Marco Polo
R Michelet

R Garancière
R Auguste Comte
Université Paris V

R Servandoni
R Férou
8
9E
13
11
51
67
14
R d'Assas
10
R Joseph Bara

R de Mézières
R Bonaparte
R de Vaugirard
R Guynemer
17
16
Av Vavin
R Vavin

R Madame
R Jean Bart
R de Fleurus

R Cassette
R Huysmans
Notre Dame des Champs
Pl P Lafue
R Notre Dame des Champs
28
R de la Grande Chaumière

R Coëtlogon
R d'Assas
R Ste-Beuve
R Bréa

Rennes
Bd Raspail
R du Montparnasse
Bd Raspail
Vavin

St-Placide
R du Regard
R de Cicé
R Stanislas
Bd du Montparnasse
14E

R de Rennes
R de Vaugirard
Pl et Sq Ozanann

R de Sèvres
R de l'Abbé Grégoire
R du Cherche Midi
R Jean Ferrandi
R Littré
Montparnasse Bienvenüe
Montparnasse Bienvenüe
R du Départ
See map p412

ST-GERMAIN

LES INVALIDES

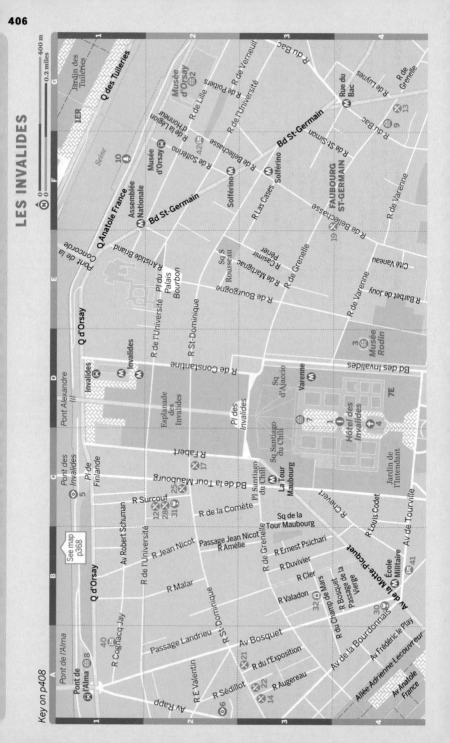

400 m
0.2 miles

Jardin des Tuileries

Q des Tuileries

1ER

Musée d'Orsay 2

R de Lille

R de Poitiers

R de Verneuil

R de l'Université

R du Bac

Rue du Bac

R de Luynes

R de Grenelle

Seine

10

Musée d'Orsay

R de Solférino

R de Bellechasse

Bd St-Germain

9 13

Q Anatole France

Assemblée Nationale

Bd St-Germain

Solférino

Solférino

R Las Cases

FAUBOURG ST-GERMAIN

R de St-Simon

Pont de la Concorde

R Aristide Briand

Pl du Palais Bourbon

R de Bourgogne

Sq Rousseau

R de Martignac

R Casimir Périer

R de Grenelle

19

R de Bellechasse

Cité Vaneau

R de Varenne

Q d'Orsay

R de l'Université

R St-Dominique

R de Varenne

R Barbet de Jouy

Pont Alexandre III

Invalides

Invalides

Invalides

R de Constantine

Musée Rodin 3

7E

Esplanade des Invalides

Pl des Invalides

Bd des Invalides

Varenne

Pont des Invalides

Pl de Finlande

5

R Fabert

17

Bd de la Tour Maubourg

Pl Santiago du Chili

Sq d'Ajaccio

Sq Santiago du Chili

7

Hôtel des Invalides 1

4

Jardin de l'Intendant

See map p368

R Surcouf

12 28 31

R de la Comète

La Tour Maubourg

R Chevert

R Louis Codet

Av de Tourville

Av Robert Schuman

R Jean Nicot

Passage Jean Nicot R Amélie

Sq de la Tour Maubourg

R de Grenelle

R Ernest Psichari

Q d'Orsay

R de l'Université

R Malar

R St-Dominique

R Duvivier

R Cler

École Militaire

41

Av de la Motte-Picquet

Pont de l'Alma

40 8

R Cognacq-Jay

R Valadon

R du Champ de Mars

R Bosquet

Passage de la Vierge

32

30

Av de la Bourdonnais

Av Frédéric le Play

Passage Landrieu

Av Bosquet

R du l'Exposition

21

R E Valentin

R Sédillot

R Augereau

22 14

6

Av Rapp

Allée Adrienne Lecouvreur

Av Anatole France

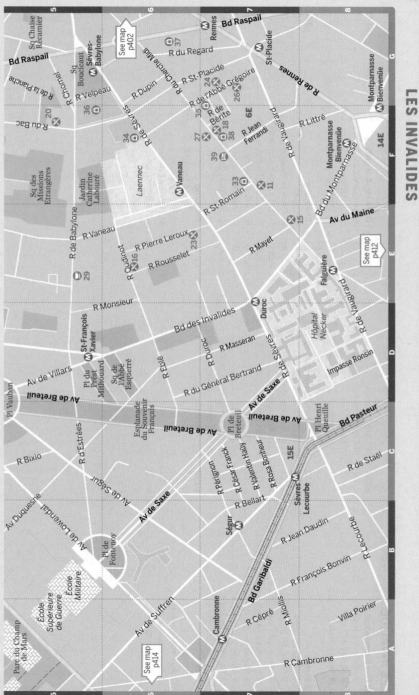

LES INVALIDES

LES INVALIDES *Map on p406*

PLACE D'ITALIE & CHINATOWN *Map on p410*

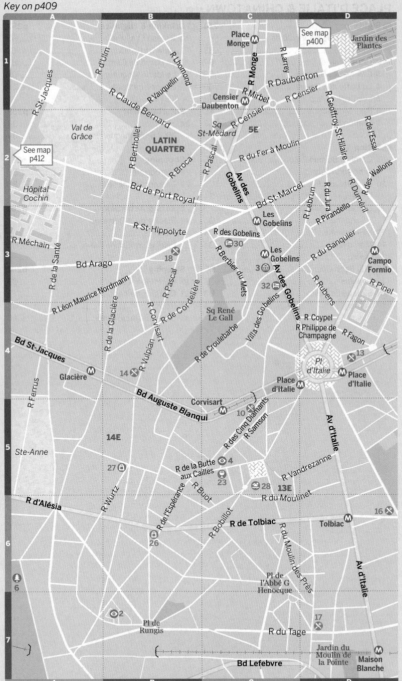

PLACE D'ITALIE & CHINATOWN

See map p400

See map p412

Jardin des Plantes

Place Monge

R St-Jacques

R d'Ulm

R Lhomond

R Vauquelin

R Claude Bernard

R Berthollet

R Monge

R Larrey

R Mirbel

R Daubenton

R Censier

Censier Daubenton

Sq St-Médard

R Censier

R Geoffroy-St-Hilaire

R de l'Essai

5E

LATIN QUARTER

R Broca

R Pascal

Av des Gobelins

R du Fer à Moulin

Val de Grâce

Bd de Port Royal

Bd St-Marcel

R Lebrun

R du Jura

R Duméril

R des Wallons

Hôpital Cochin

R St-Hippolyte

R des Gobelins

Les Gobelins

R Pirandello

R Méchain

R de la Santé

Bd Arago

18

R Berbier du Mets

Les Gobelins

30

3

R du Banquier

R Rubens

Campo Formio

R Pinel

R Léon Maurice Nordmann

R Pascal

R de la Glacière

R Corvisart

R de Cordelière

Sq René Le Gall

Av des Gobelins

32

R Coypel

R Fagon

R Philippe de Champagne

Villa des Gobelins

Bd St-Jacques

R Ferrus

Glacière

R Vulpian

14

R de Croulebarbe

Pl. d'Italie

13

Bd Auguste Blanqui

Corvisart

Place d'Italie

Place d'Italie

10

R des Cinq Diamants

R Samson

14E

27

R de la Butte aux Cailles

4

23

28

R Vandrezanne

Av d'Italie

Ste-Anne

R Wurtz

R de l'Espérance

R Buot

13E

R du Moulinet

R d'Alésia

26

R Bobillot

R de Tolbiac

Tolbiac

16

R du Moulin des Prés

Av d'Italie

6

Pl de l'Abbé G Henocque

2

17

Pl de Rungis

R du Tage

Jardin du Moulin de la Pointe

Maison Blanche

Bd Lefebvre

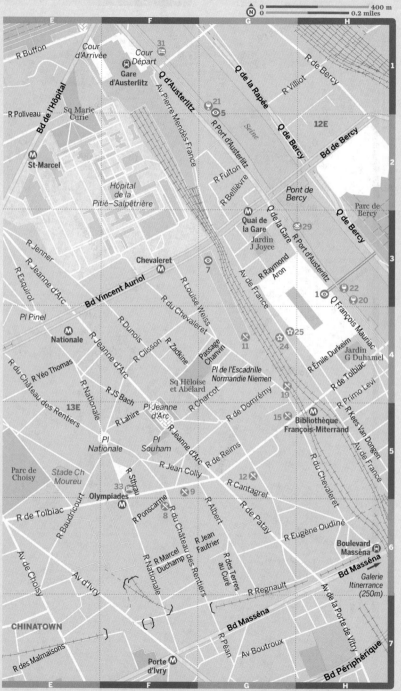

0   400 m
0   0.2 miles

R Buffon

Cour
d'Arrivée

Cour
Départ

Gare
d'Austerlitz

31

Q d'Austerlitz

Av Pierre Mendès France

Q de la Râpée

R de Bercy

R Villiot

R Poliveau

Bd de l'Hôpital

Sq Marie
Curie

21
5

R Port d'Austerlitz

Seine

12E

Q de Bercy

Bd de Bercy

St-Marcel

Hôpital
de la
Pitié–Salpêtrière

R Fulton

R Bellièvre

Pont de
Bercy

Parc de
Bercy

Q de la Gare

Quai de
la Gare

29

Q Port d'Austerlitz

Q de Bercy

R Jenner

R Jeanne d'Arc

R Esquirol

Chevaleret

7

Jardin
J Joyce

R Raymond
Aron

Av de France

Bd Vincent Auriol

R Louise Weiss

R du Chevaleret

1
22
20

Q François Mauriac

Pl Pinel

Nationale

R Dunois

R Clisson

R Zadkine

Passage Chanvin

11

24
25

R Émile Durkeim

Jardin
G Duhamel

R de Tolbiac

R du Château des Rentiers

R Yéo Thomas

R Jeanne d'Arc

13E

R Nationale

R JS Bach

R Lahire

Sq Héloïse
et Abélard

R Charcot

Pl Jeanne
d'Arc

Pl de l'Escadrille
Normandie Niemen

19

R de Domrémy

15

R Primo Levi

R Kees Van Dongen

Av de France

Bibliothèque
François-Miterrand

Parc de
Choisy

Stade Ch
Moureu

Pl
Nationale

R Stibau

Pl
Souham

R Jeanne d'Arc

R de Reims

R Jean Colly

12

R du Chevaleret

R de Tolbiac

R Baudricourt

33

Olympiades

R Ponscarme

8

9

R Cantagrel

R Albert

R de Patay

R Eugène Oudiné

Boulevard
Masséna

Av de Choisy

Av d'Ivry

R Marcel
Duchamp

R du Château des Rentiers

R Nationale

R Jean
Fautrier

R des Terres
au Curé

R Regnault

Bd Masséna

Galerie
Itinerrance
(250m)

CHINATOWN

R des Malmaisons

Porte
d'Ivry

R Péan

Bd Masséna

Av Boutroux

Av de la Porte de Vitry

Bd Périphérique

E   F   G   H

1   2   3   4   5   6   7

MONTPARNASSE

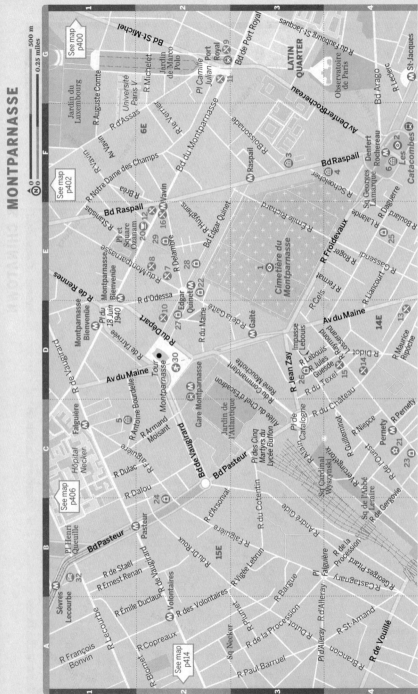

See map p400

See map p402

See map p406

See map p414

500 m
0.25 miles

LATIN QUARTER

Observatoire de Paris

Les Catacombes

Cimetière du Montparnasse

Jardin du Luxembourg

Jardin de l'Atlantique

Gare Montparnasse

Tour Montparnasse

Hôpital Necker

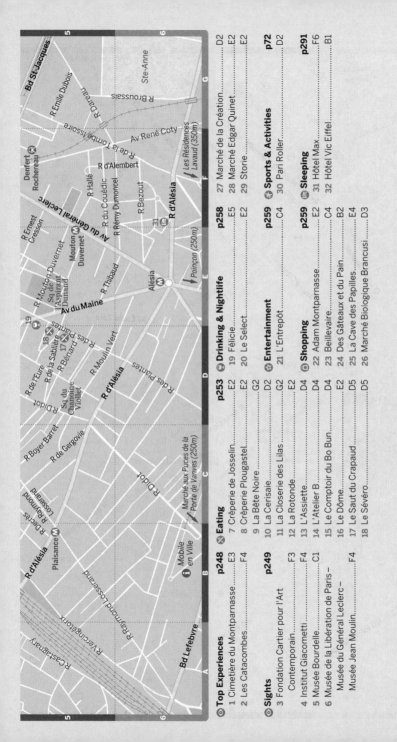

MONTPARNASSE

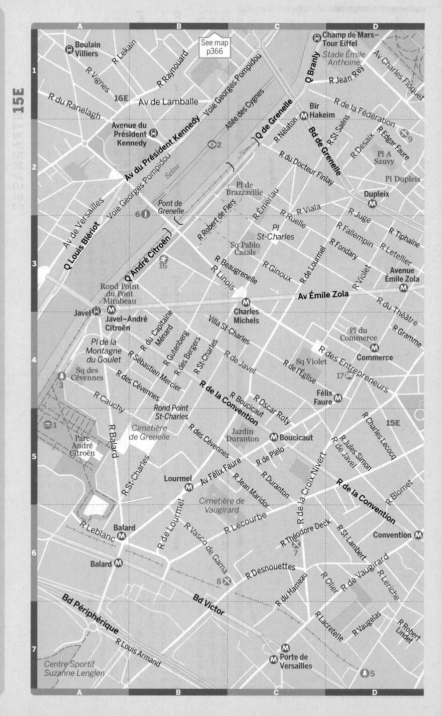

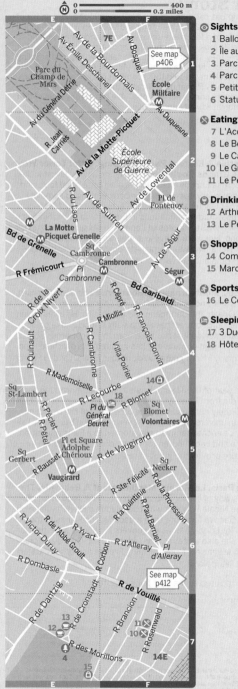

Our Story

A beat-up old car, a few dollars in the pocket and a sense of adventure. In 1972 that's all Tony and Maureen Wheeler needed for the trip of a lifetime – across Europe and Asia overland to Australia. It took several months, and at the end – broke but inspired – they sat at their kitchen table writing and stapling together their first travel guide, *Across Asia on the Cheap*. Within a week they'd sold 1500 copies. Lonely Planet was born. Today, Lonely Planet has offices in the US, Ireland and China, with a network of over 2000 contributors in every corner of the globe." We share Tony's belief that a great guidebook should do three things: inform, educate and amuse.

Our Writers

Catherine Le Nevez

Louvre & Les Halles, Bastille & Eastern Paris, Sleeping, Eiffel Tower West Paris, Champs-Elysees & Grands Boulevards Catherine's wanderlust kicked in when she roadtripped across Europe from her Parisian base aged four, and she's been hitting the road at every opportunity since, travelling to some 60 countries and completing her Doctorate of Creative Arts in Writing, Masters in Professional Writing, and postgrad qualifications in Editing and Publishing along the way. Over the past decade-and-a-half she's written scores of Lonely Planet guides and articles covering Paris, France, Europe and far beyond. Her work has also appeared in numerous online and print publications. To learn more, follow her at www.lonelyplanet.com/authors/catherine-le-nevez. Catherine also wrote the Plan, Understand and Survival Guide sections.

Jean-Bernard Carillet

St-Germain & Les Invalides, Montparnasse & Southern Paris Jean-Bernard is a Paris-based freelance writer and photographer who specialises in Africa, France, Turkey, the Indian Ocean, the Caribbean and the Pacific. He loves adventure, remote places, islands, outdoors, archaeological sites, food and of course Paris, his home. His insatiable wanderlust has taken him to 119 countries across six continents, and it shows no sign of waning. It has inspired lots of articles and photos for travel magazines and some 100 Lonely Planet guidebooks, both in English and in French.

Christopher Pitts

Latin Quarter Born in the year of the Tiger, Chris's first expedition in life ended in failure when he tried to dig from Pennsylvania to China at the age of six. Hardened by reality but still infinitely curious about the other side of the world, he went on to study Chinese in university, living for several years in Kunming, Taiwan and Shanghai. A chance encounter in an elevator led to a Paris relocation, where he lived with his wife and two children for over a decade before the lure of Colorado's sunny skies and outdoor adventure proved too great to resist.

Nicola Williams

Montmartre & Northern Paris, Le Marais, Menilmontant & Belleville, The Islands Border-hopping is way of life for British writer, runner, foodie, art aficionado and mum-of-three Nicola Williams who has lived in a French village on the southern side of Lake Geneva for more than a decade. Nicola has authored more than 50 guidebooks for Lonely Planet and covers France as a destination expert for the Telegraph. She also writes for the Independent, Guardian, lonelyplanet.com, Lonely Planet Magazine, French Magazine, Cool Camping France and others. Catch her on the road on Twitter and Instagram at @tripalong.

Contributing Writer: Alexis Averbuck contributed to the Day Trips chapter.

Published by Lonely Planet Global Limited
CRN 554153
13th edition – April 2022
ISBN 978 1 78868 043 1
© Lonely Planet 2022   Photographs © as indicated 2022
10 9 8 7 6 5 4 3 2 1
Printed in China